Lecture Notes in Computer Science 15749

Founding Editors

Gerhard Goos
Juris Hartmanis

Editorial Board Members

Elisa Bertino, *Purdue University, West Lafayette, IN, USA*
Wen Gao, *Peking University, Beijing, China*
Bernhard Steffen ⓘ, *TU Dortmund University, Dortmund, Germany*
Moti Yung ⓘ, *Columbia University, New York, NY, USA*

The series Lecture Notes in Computer Science (LNCS), including its subseries Lecture Notes in Artificial Intelligence (LNAI) and Lecture Notes in Bioinformatics (LNBI), has established itself as a medium for the publication of new developments in computer science and information technology research, teaching, and education.

LNCS enjoys close cooperation with the computer science R & D community, the series counts many renowned academics among its volume editors and paper authors, and collaborates with prestigious societies. Its mission is to serve this international community by providing an invaluable service, mainly focused on the publication of conference and workshop proceedings and postproceedings. LNCS commenced publication in 1973.

Himanshu Verma · Alessandro Bozzon ·
Andrea Mauri · Jie Yang
Editors

Web Engineering

25th International Conference, ICWE 2025
Delft, The Netherlands, June 30 – July 3, 2025
Proceedings

Editors
Himanshu Verma
Delft University of Technology
Delft, Zuid-Holland, The Netherlands

Alessandro Bozzon
Delft University of Technology
Delft, Zuid-Holland, The Netherlands

Andrea Mauri
Université Claude Bernard Lyon 1
Villeurbanne, France

Jie Yang
Delft University of Technology
Delft, Zuid-Holland, The Netherlands

ISSN 0302-9743   ISSN 1611-3349 (electronic)
Lecture Notes in Computer Science
ISBN 978-3-031-97206-5   ISBN 978-3-031-97207-2 (eBook)
https://doi.org/10.1007/978-3-031-97207-2

© The Editor(s) (if applicable) and The Author(s), under exclusive license
to Springer Nature Switzerland AG 2026

This work is subject to copyright. All rights are solely and exclusively licensed by the Publisher, whether the whole or part of the material is concerned, specifically the rights of translation, reprinting, reuse of illustrations, recitation, broadcasting, reproduction on microfilms or in any other physical way, and transmission or information storage and retrieval, electronic adaptation, computer software, or by similar or dissimilar methodology now known or hereafter developed.
The use of general descriptive names, registered names, trademarks, service marks, etc. in this publication does not imply, even in the absence of a specific statement, that such names are exempt from the relevant protective laws and regulations and therefore free for general use.
The publisher, the authors and the editors are safe to assume that the advice and information in this book are believed to be true and accurate at the date of publication. Neither the publisher nor the authors or the editors give a warranty, expressed or implied, with respect to the material contained herein or for any errors or omissions that may have been made. The publisher remains neutral with regard to jurisdictional claims in published maps and institutional affiliations.

This Springer imprint is published by the registered company Springer Nature Switzerland AG
The registered company address is: Gewerbestrasse 11, 6330 Cham, Switzerland

If disposing of this product, please recycle the paper.

Preface

Welcome to the Proceedings of the 25th INTERNATIONAL CONFERENCE ON WEB ENGINEERING, **ICWE 2025**.

ICWE aims to promote research and scientific exchange related to Web engineering, and to bring together researchers and practitioners from various disciplines in academia and industry to tackle emerging challenges in the engineering of Web applications and associated technologies, as well as to assess the impact of these technologies on society, media, and culture. Supported by the INTERNATIONAL SOCIETY OF WEB ENGINEERING (ISWE), since 2001 ICWE has served as the leading annual conference for the Web Engineering community.

This volume collects the full research papers, short research papers, tool demonstrations, posters, and tutorials presented at the 25th International Conference on Web Engineering (ICWE 2025), held in Delft, the Netherlands, from June 30 to July 3, 2025.

The ICWE 2025 theme, "**The Inclusive Web: Realizing Safe, Accessible, Inclusive, and Sustainable Web Engineering**," invited discussions on creating Web technologies that are not only innovative, but also designed to be fair, ethical, transparent, privacy-preserving, trustworthy, safe, inclusive, and accessible to all. This theme recognized the evolution of the Web engineering landscape, which has been profoundly shaped by significant technological advances in recent years, particularly with the increasing adoption of Large Language Models (LLMs) and Generative Artificial Intelligence (AI). Web systems have become more robust and diverse, enhanced by AI-driven algorithms that personalize user experiences and optimize system performance. Enabled by advances in cloud computing and sophisticated network infrastructures, these developments have enabled a more connected and dynamic online environment. However, as the boundaries of what is possible on the Web continue to expand, critical questions arise: What should our research priorities be? How should we ensure a safe, accessible, inclusive, and sustainable web ecosystem? And how can the Web, powered by cutting-edge AI algorithms, function in an ethical, responsible, and safe way for diverse communities and users?

This year's Call for Papers attracted 72 submissions worldwide, distributed across several tracks. The selection process was rigorous, and facilitated by a Program Committee (PC) of distinguished experts. Each submission was single-blind reviewed by at least three PC members, with final decisions made through thorough discussions. The research track includes 12 full papers, reflecting an acceptance rate of 24.5%. The conference also featured competitive sessions for short papers, industrial contributions, demonstrations, posters, as well as a Ph.D. symposium with five accepted proposals, three leading-edge tutorials, and two workshops. The final program featured innovative approaches, novel findings, and thought-provoking ideas. It covered various topics related to Web infrastructures; the human-centered Web; LLMs, search, and knowledge; security, safety, and privacy; inclusion and the accessible Web; and security, safety, and inclusion on the Web.

We extend our deepest gratitude to everyone who contributed to the organization of the conference, especially the track chairs: MARIOS CONSTANTINIDES & MARCO BRAMBILLA **(Industry Track)**, SIHANG QIU & INES AROUS **(Posters and Demonstrations)**, MARISTELLA MATERA & CESARE PAUTASSO **(Ph.D. Symposium)**, AZZURRA RAGONE & FLAVIUS FRASINCAR **(Tutorials)**, KARI SYSTÄ & YEN-CHIA HSU **(Workshops)**, SOUHAILA SERBOUT & LORENZO CORTI **(Proceedings)**, SHATHA DEGACHI, UĞUR GENÇ, & CARLO VAN DER VALK **(Web and Publicity)**, CATALINA LAGOS ROJAS **(Accessibility)**, and ARIANNE LUCCHINI **(Local and Student Volunteers)**.

Our thanks also go to IRINA SHKLOVSKI *(University of Copenhagen, Denmark)*, LUCIE FLEK *(University of Bonn, Germany)*, and DANIELE QUERCIA *(Nokia Bell Labs Cambridge & King's College London, UK)* who agreed to be our keynote speakers.

We appreciate the invaluable support of the Faculty of Industrial Design Engineering, Delft University of Technology. We are also grateful to *Springer* and *River Publishers* for sponsoring the ICWE 2025 best paper awards, and to *Springer* for publishing these proceedings. Our sincere thanks go to the PC members, additional reviewers, and student volunteers whose dedication ensured the success of ICWE 2025, both academically and practically.

Finally, we thank all the authors and members of the ICWE community for their contributions and participation in making ICWE 2025 a successful event.

June 2025

Himanshu Verma
Alessandro Bozzon
Andrea Mauri
Jie Yang

Organization

General Chairs

Himanshu Verma   Delft University of Technology, Netherlands
Alessandro Bozzon   Delft University of Technology, Netherlands

Program Chairs

Andrea Mauri   Claude Bernard University Lyon 1, France
Jie Yang   Delft University of Technology, Netherlands

Industry Track Chairs

Marios Constantinides   CYENS Center of Excellence, Cyprus
Marco Brambilla   Politecnico di Milano, Italy

Poster and Demo Chairs

Sihang Qiu   State Key Laboratory of Digital-Intelligent Modeling and Simulation, China
Ines Arous   York University, Canada

PhD Symposium Chairs

Maristella Matera   Politecnico di Milano, Italy
Cesare Pautasso   University of Lugano (USI), Switzerland

Tutorial Chairs

Azzurra Ragone   Università degli Studi di Bari, Italy
Flavius Frasincar   Erasmus University Rotterdam, Netherlands

Workshop Chairs

Kari Systä Tampere University, Finland
Yen-Chia Hsu University of Amsterdam, Netherlands

Proceedings Chairs

Souhaila Serbout University of Zurich, Switzerland
Lorenzo Corti Delft University of Technology, Netherlands

Web and Publicity Chairs

Shatha Degachi Delft University of Technology, Netherlands
Uğur Genç Delft University of Technology, Netherlands
Carlo van der Valk Delft University of Technology, Netherlands

Accessibility Chair

Catalina Lagos Rojas Delft University of Technology, Netherlands

Local and SV Chair

Arianne Lucchini Delft University of Technology, Netherlands

Program Committee

Shubhangi Agarwal Claude Bernard University Lyon 1, France
Mouna Ammar University of Leipzig, Germany
Danilo Ardagna Politecnico di Milano, Italy
Lakshit Arora Google, USA
Ines Arous University of Fribourg, Switzerland
Myriam Arrue University of the Basque Country, Spain
Marcos Baez Bielefeld University of Applied Sciences, Germany
Maxim Bakaev Novosibirsk State Technical University, Russia
Agathe Balayn Microsoft Research, USA

Luciano Baresi	Politecnico di Milano, Italy
Antonio Brogi	University of Pisa, Italy
Radek Burget	Brno University of Technology, Czech Republic
Christoph Bussler	Elekta, Sweden
Riccardo Campi	Politecnico di Milano, Italy
Carlos Canal	University of Málaga, Spain
Sven Casteleyn	Universitat Jaume I, Spain
Richard Chbeir	Université de Pau et des Pays de l'Adour, France
Zhijun Chen	Beihang University, China
Pieter Colpaert	Ghent University, Belgium
Linus W. Dietz	King's College London, UK
Schahram Dustdar	Vienna University of Technology, Austria
Hui Fang	Shanghai University of Finance and Economics, China
Kaidong Feng	Yanshan University, China
Pablo Fernandez	University of Seville, Spain
Flavius Frasincar	Erasmus University Rotterdam, Netherlands
Piero Fraternali	Politecnico di Milano, Italy
Martin Gaedke	Chemnitz University of Technology, Germany
Alejandra Garrido	Universidad Nacional de La Plata, Argentina
Irene Garrigos	University of Alicante, Spain
Mathyas Giudici	Politecnico di Milano, Italy
Vijay Govindarajan	Expedia Group, USA
Julián Grigera	Universidad Nacional de La Plata, Argentina
Hao Han	Konica Minolta Japan, Japan
Gaole He	Delft University of Technology, Netherlands
Sebastian Heil	Chemnitz University of Technology, Germany
Radu Tudor Ionescu	University of Bucharest, Romania
Gianpaolo Iuliano	University of Salerno, Italy
Javier Luis Canovas Izquierdo	Universitat Oberta de Catalunya, Spain
Epaminondas Kapetanios	University of Hertfordshire, UK
Alexander Knapp	Universität Augsburg, Germany
In-Young Ko	KAIST, South Korea
István Koren	RWTH Aachen University, Germany
Yu Lei	Yanshan University, China
Maurizio Leotta	Università di Genova, Italy
Chen Li	Yanshan University, China
Mohamed Ragab Moawad	Nahda University in Beni Suef, Egypt
Cesar Gonzalez Mora	University of Alicante, Spain
Nathalie Moreno	Universidad de Málaga, Spain
Michael Mrissa	University of Primorska, Slovenia
Tobias Münch	Münch Ges. für IT-Solutions mbH, Germany

Juan Manuel Murillo	University of Extremadura, Spain
Martin A. Musicante	UFRN, Brazil
Radka Nacheva	University of Economics - Varna, Bulgaria
Elena Navarro	University of Castilla-La Mancha, Spain
Guadalupe Ortiz	University of Cádiz, Spain
Amedeo Pachera	Claude Bernard University Lyon 1, France
Demetris Paschalides	University of Cyprus, Cyprus
Oscar Pastor	Universidad Politécnica de Valencia, Spain
Cesare Pautasso	University of Lugano, Switzerland
Kristo Raun	University of Tartu, Estonia
Werner Retschitzegger	Johannes Kepler University Linz, Austria
Thomas Richter	Rhein-Waal University of Applied Sciences, Germany
Tarmo Robal	Tallinn University of Technology, Estonia
Gustavo Rossi	Universidad Nacional de La Plata, Argentina
Ioannis Petros Samiotis	Delft University of Technology, Netherlands
John Samuel	CPE Lyon, France
Antonio De Santis	Politecnico di Milano, Italy
Sanja Šćepanović	Nokia Bell Labs, UK
Ali Septiandri	Nokia Bell Labs, UK
António Rito Silva	Universidade de Lisboa, Portugal
Thomas Springer	TU Dresden, Germany
Hrishikesh Terdalkar	Claude Bernard University Lyon 1, France
Andrea Tocchetti	Politecnico of Milano, Italy
Riccardo Tommasini	INSA Lyon, France
Markel Vigo	University of Manchester, UK
Antoine Willerval	Claude Bernard University Lyon 1, France
Manuel Wimmer	Johannes Kepler University Linz, Austria
Marco Winckler	Université Côte d'Azur, France
William Van Woensel	University of Ottawa, Canada
Yeliz Yesilada	Middle East Technical University NCC, Cyprus
Gefei Zhang	HTW Berlin, Germany
Peide Zhu	Delft University of Technology, Netherlands
Zhengqiu Zhu	National University of Defense Technology, China

External Reviewers

Istabrak Abbes	University of Montreal, Canada
Bonaventure F. P. Dossou	McGill University, Canada
Juan Luis Herrera	Universidad de Extremadura, Spain

Stefan Klikovits   Johannes Kepler University Linz, Austria
Xiang Li   Yanshan University, China
Michael Luggen   University of Fribourg, Switzerland
Aurora Macías   Universidad de Castilla-La Mancha
Ilir Murturi   TU Wien, Austria

ICWE 2025 Partners

Contents

LLMs, Search and Knowledge Over the Web

Towards Structured Knowledge: Advancing Triple Extraction
from Regional Trade Agreements Using Large Language Models 3
  Durgesh Nandini, Rebekka Koch, and Mirco Schönfeld

Introducing ORKG ASK: An AI-Driven Scholarly Literature Search
and Exploration System Taking a Neuro-Symbolic Approach 11
  Allard Oelen, Mohamad Yaser Jaradeh, and Sören Auer

Leveraging LLMs for Conversational Data Access: A Human-Centred
Perspective 26
  Maristella Matera, Emanuele Pucci, and Vincenzo Manto

A Graph-Based RAG for Energy Efficiency Question Answering 41
  *Riccardo Campi, Nicolò Oreste Pinciroli Vago, Mathyas Giudici,
  Pablo Barrachina Rodriguez-Guisado, Marco Brambilla,
  and Piero Fraternali*

GoRS - A Neuro-Symbolic, User-Centric, and Goal-Oriented
Recommendation System for DIY-Projects 56
  *Jan-David Stütz, Luca Mario Ziegler Felix, Oliver Karras,
  Allard Oelen, and Sören Auer*

AutoS^{2}earch: Unlocking the Reasoning Potential of Large Models
for Web-Based Source Search 71
  *Zhengqiu Zhu, Yatai Ji, Jiaheng Huang, Yong Zhao, Sihang Qiu,
  and Rusheng Ju*

Safe and Inclusive Web Engineering

Enhancing the Aspect Robustness Score of the HAABSA++ Model Using
Adversarial Training 89
  Milad Agha, Flavius Frasincar, Beilly Zhu, and Tarmo Robal

Applying Contrastive Learning to an Attention Neural Model
in a Multilingual Context 104
  Philipp Gottschalk, Flavius Frasincar, and Eyo Herstad

OnToxKG: An Ontology-Based Knowledge Graph of Toxic Symbols
and Their Manifestations 119
   Delfina S. Martinez Pandiani, Erik Tjong Kim Sang, and Davide Ceolin

Evaluating Locally Run Large Language Models on Toxic Meme Analysis 128
   Erik Tjong Kim Sang, Delfina S. Martinez Pandiani, and Davide Ceolin

MoralWeb: Reimagining the Web with Solid, Low-Code Tools, and Moral
Codes for a Democratic and Equitable Future 136
   Tobias Münch, Andreas Schmidt, Sebastian Heil, and Martin Gaedke

A Web Crawling-Based Process and a Graph-Based Database for Mobile
Vulnerability Analysis 145
   Domenico Amalfitano, Andrea Abbate, Damiano Distante,
   Antonio M. Rinaldi, Cristiano Russo, and Cristian Tommasino

MultiWebFacts: A Modular Framework Using Multi-source Fusion
for Fact-Checking 160
   Yung-Ching Yang, Sooji Han, and Rafael Banchs

Semantic Web and SPARQL Querying

SPARQL Query Generation with LLMs: Measuring the Impact of Training
Data Memorization and Knowledge Injection 177
   Aleksandr Gashkov, Aleksandr Perevalov, Maria Eltsova,
   and Andreas Both

Web-SPARQL: Hybrid Querying over Knowledge Graphs, Web,
and Microdata 193
   Aurélien Lamercerie, Peggy Cellier, and Sébastien Ferré

ShEx2SPARQL: Translating Shape Expressions into SPARQL Queries 209
   Christoph Göpfert, Sheeba Samuel, and Martin Gaedke

SciMantify - A Hybrid Approach for the Evolving Semantification
of Scientific Knowledge 217
   Lena John, Kheir Eddine Farfar, Sören Auer, and Oliver Karras

A Knowledge Graph Informing Soil Carbon Modeling 226
   Nasim Shirvani-Mahdavi, Devin Wingfield, Juan Guajardo Gutierrez,
   Mai Tran, Zhengyuan Zhu, Zeyu Zhang, Haiqi Zhang,
   Abhishek Divakar Goudar, Chengkai Li, Virginia Jin,
   Timothy Propst, Dan Roberts, Catherine Stewart, Jianzhong Su,
   and Jennifer Woodward-Greene

User Interface on the Web

HORIZON: A Classification and Comparison Framework
for Pricing-Driven Feature Toggling 245
   *Alejandro García-Fernández, José Antonio Parejo,
and Antonio Ruiz-Cortés*

From Mock-Ups to IFML-Like GUI Models: Using Large Language
Models in Web Engineering 253
   Atefeh Nirumand and Jordi Cabot

UIQLab: Automatic Web User Interface Assessment 269
   Sebastian Heil, Calvin Liusnando, and Martin Gaedke

Web of Things, Services and Decentralized Web

Assessing the Migration from FaaS to IaaS: Cost, Performance,
and Challenges in AWS 287
   Julián Casaburi, Mario Matías Urbieta, and Sergio Firmenich

Link Traversal over Decentralised Environments Using Restart-Based
Query Planning 303
   Jonni Hanski, Simon Van Braeckel, Ruben Taelman, and Ruben Verborgh

Interoperable Cyber-Physical Multi-Agent Systems Through Web
of Things 312
   *Roman Binkert, Fady Salama, Ege Korkan, Sebastian Käbisch,
and Sebastian Steinhorst*

Distributed Detection of Complex Events on Streams of Linked Data 327
   Daniel Schraudner, Sebastian Schmid, and Andreas Harth

LLM-MaGe: A Generative Mashup Planner for the Web of Things 342
   *Fady Salama, Franz J. Ennemoser, Roman Binkert, Ege Korkan,
Sebastian Käbisch, and Sebastian Steinhorst*

Demos and Posters

The Efficiency of Rust and WebAssembly Compared to Plain JavaScript 361
   Kasper Jan Seweryn

KuBench: A Kubernetes-Based Environment for Standardized REST API
Framework Performance Evaluation 366
   Ondrej Olsak, Matej Sauer, Marta Jaros, and Jiri Jaros

Leveraging LLMs for Voice-Based form Filling on the Web: The ConWeb Approach 370
  Ludovica Piro, Giulia Di Fede, Emanuele Pucci, Stefano Tolomeo, and Maristella Matera

Troubleshooting Microservices with Heterogeneous Graph Neural Network 374
  Juyoung Yang, EunChan Park, KyeongDeok Baek, and In-Young Ko

Post-hoc LLM-Supported Debugging of Distributed Processes 379
  Dennis Schiese and Andreas Both

PhD Symposium

Human-AI Collaborative UAV Visual Object Search via Web Platform 385
  Yatai Ji, Sihang Qiu, Zhengqiu Zhu, and Rusheng Ju

Methodological Framework and Digital Environment to Optimize the Treatment of Genetic Markers, Based on Data Science and Artificial Intelligence 391
  Ramon Canelo-Gil, Nicolas Sánchez-Gómez, Julian Alberto García-García, and Maria Jose Escalona

ResearchFlow: An End-User Development Approach to Research Data Management Workflow Composition 397
  Jan Ingo Haas, Martin Gaedke, Sheeba Samuel, and Jeffrey Kelling

You Are What You Click: Web Interaction Analysis for User Profile Detection 404
  Leonardo Germán Loza Bonora, Julián Grigera, and Alejandra Garrido

Designing Hybrid Quantum-Classical Web Applications Across the Computing Continuum 410
  Álvaro M. Aparicio-Morales, Enrique Moguel, and Jose Garcia-Alonso

Tutorials

A Tutorial on Social Media Data Analytics for Disaster Management 419
  Sanjay Madria

Enhancing Reproducibility and Replicability in Information Retrieval: A Path Towards Scientific Integrity and Effective Research 423
  Antonio Ferrara, Claudio Pomo, and Nicola Tonellotto

Creating Accessible Digital Content and Applications 427
  Ombretta Gaggi

Author Index 431

LLMs, Search and Knowledge Over the Web

Towards Structured Knowledge: Advancing Triple Extraction from Regional Trade Agreements Using Large Language Models

Durgesh Nandini[✉], Rebekka Koch, and Mirco Schönfeld

University of Bayreuth, Bayreuth, Germany
durgesh.nandini@uni-bayreuth.de

Abstract. This study investigates the effectiveness of Large Language Models (LLMs) for the extraction of structured knowledge in the form of Subject-Predicate-Object triples. We apply the setup for the domain of Economics application. The findings can be applied to a wide range of scenarios, including the creation of economic trade knowledge graphs from natural language legal trade agreement texts. As a use case, we apply the model to regional trade agreement texts to extract trade-related information triples. In particular, we explore the zero-shot, one-shot and few-shot prompting techniques, incorporating positive and negative examples, and evaluate their performance based on quantitative and qualitative metrics. Specifically, we used the Llama 3.1 model to process the unstructured regional trade agreement texts and extract triples. We discuss key insights, challenges, and potential future directions, emphasizing the significance of language models in economic applications.

Keywords: Large Language Models · Triple Extraction · Knowledge Graph · Regional Trade Agreement

1 Introduction

The evolving landscape of web engineering increasingly demands intelligent systems that can process, structure, and reason over vast, heterogeneous text data published online. Legal, economic, and policy documents are now routinely disseminated through digital platforms, yet remain largely unstructured and inaccessible for automated processing. In response to this challenge, LLMs have emerged as powerful tools for enabling intelligent information extraction at web scale. LLMs have opened avenues for significant techniques of knowledge extraction and processing because of their capabilities to offer pre-trained architectures that have captured vast linguistic and semantic nuances from a wide array of sources. A key technique that enhances their adaptability is prompt engineering [2,5,7] which allows models to be directed toward specific tasks without fine-tuning, making them ideal for dynamic, web-based knowledge systems.

Prompt engineering is a pivotal method that extends the capabilities of large language models (LLMs) [12] towards crafting task-specific inputs as *prompts* that coax outputs from language models. For tasks such as triple generation where subject-predicate-object structures are extracted from unstructured texts, prompt engineering becomes essential because it allows to elicit structured knowledge from LLMs without the need for additional fine-tuning, thus reducing computational resources and expediting experimentation. This approach has become even more valuable in complex domains, where language is ambiguous, and contextual understanding is vital [10]. This study aims to explore the efficiency of language models, in particular the Llama 3.1 [14] model, for subject-predicate-object entity triple extraction from natural language economics legal regional trade agreements. Our work specifically tailors the extraction techniques of economic trade-related triples from regional trade agreements (RTAs) that contain highly formalized, structured yet implicit economic obligations, complex multi-party agreements, and domain-specific terminologies that require nuanced interpretation. Standard information extraction models often struggle with these subtleties, making our adaptation of prompt-based extraction particularly valuable.

Therefore, the **main contribution** of our work is the development of large language model prompt pipeline to extract triples from legal regional trade agreement documents. To the best of our knowledge, triple extraction using large language models (LLMs) is a relatively new field within the domain of economic trade exchange transactions. Our approach contributes to the integration of LLM-based extraction pipelines into web-oriented knowledge infrastructures. To implement this, we adopt the zero-shot [2] and the few-shot [2] prompt engineering methods [2] The extracted triples can serve as foundational building blocks for semantic web applications such as linked data generation, legal knowledge graphs, compliance monitoring tools, and intelligent search engines. These applications lie at the intersection of AI and web engineering, emphasizing the growing role of LLMs in enriching and structuring web-based information.

The rest of the paper is organised as follows: in Sect. 2 we briefly discuss the related works and highlight the significance of this study. In Sect. 3, we describe the dataset used and the methodology that we have used for this study. In Sect. 4 we discuss the experimental setup. We present the results and evaluation in Sect. 5. At last, in Sect. 6, we have the conclusion and the limitations of our work.

2 Related Work

The use of knowledge extraction is a relatively young area of research in the field of Economic trade transactions. However, other related fields such as e-commerce have lightly used knowledge graphs and triples for their studies. The AlimeKG framework [6] is the one focused on the e-commerce domain. The authors introduce a framework for KG construction in the e-commerce domain by integrating NLP components such as named entity recognition (NER) and relation extraction (RE), facilitating a semi-automated process for knowledge acquisition and validation. Similarly, Yu et al. developed FolkScope [16], a framework combining LLMs with human-in-the-loop annotations to build an intention knowledge graph for e-commerce, demonstrating the potential of LLMs in uncovering latent relationships from textual product data. We also identified alternative pipelines, other than LLM based, proposed in other domains. Dessì et al. [4] explored Transformer models to automatically extract entities from scientific texts and generate a KG. Within the economic and trade domain, Nandini et al. proposed KonecoKG [10], a multidimensional economic knowledge graph for international trade, highlighting the need for domain-adaptive models and linked data frameworks to capture the complexities of trade agreements. Liu et al. introduced K-BERT [8], an early attempt to integrate external knowledge into transformer-based models to improve factual consistency and performance on KG-related tasks. More aligned with prompt-based extraction, Yao et al. proposed KG-BERT [15], which treats triples as textual sequences, applying pre-trained transformers to perform relation classification and triple prediction.

Despite these efforts, we see that there is a gap when it comes to utilising knowledge extraction for econometric trade scenarios. Our study builds upon this emerging intersection by evaluating different prompting methods [13].

3 Methodology

In this section we describe the methodology that we have employed for the experimental purposes. To implement and evaluate the zero shot and few shot prompting techniques, we iteratively fine tuned the prompts at different stages. Figure 1 summarises the flowchart of the methodology and we define each step of the methodology in the following subsections.

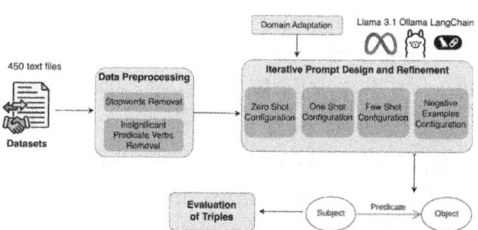

Fig. 1. Overview of the research methodology

Dataset and Data Preprocessing. We use the regional trade agreement dataset by Alschner et al. [1]. Their corpus is based on the WTO Regional Trade Agreements Information System data containing 450 XML files. Each XML file consists of trade agreement between two countries and is composed of multiple Articles and Chapters. The trade agreements texts are categorised into several sectors, such as agriculture, customs, trade in services, and institutions, etc. Since the raw data that we have used is a collection of large natural language texts, we cleaned it to increase the efficiency for the model execution. In particular, we removed stopwords and some commonly occurring trade related terms that appear frequently in the dataset but are not semantically significant when extracting triples from the texts.

Iterative Prompt Design and Refinement. The core of our methodology involved creating and refining four types of prompts, each with increasing task-specific guidance. Starting with a general base prompt, we instructed the model to identify triples within the text. This initial prompt was intentionally broad to gauge the model's baseline performance in a zero-shot setting. In this prompt, the model received minimal guidance on the structure of triples, aiming to determine its capacity to infer task requirements with limited instruction. Each subsequent prompt was progressively refined to include specific instructions that aligned with the nuances of legal text in trade agreements. For example, we added directives for the model to focus on economic trade-related verbs (e.g., "agree," "sign," "ratify," "export," "import") to enhance the relevance of generated triples within the context of trade agreements. Additionally, later prompts emphasized the identification of entities such as contracting parties and economic terms specific to trade, guiding the model to capture legally significant information. By iteratively building upon each prompt, we moved from general language processing toward targeted knowledge extraction that suited the specialized legal domain.

Domain Adaptations and Benchmark Triple Set. Given the specificity of our corpus, legal documents focused on trade agreements, we adapted our prompts to capture the complexity and formality inherent in legal language. To this end, later prompt iterations included instructions to prioritize predicates tied to economic trade-related actions, as these are central to the semantics of trade agreements. Emphasizing such domain-specific verbs helped orient the model toward identifying relationships crucial to understanding trade obligations, rights, and entities within legal texts. Subsequently, we created a benchmark dataset of triples generated manually by a domain expert specializing in economics and trade data. The expert manually curated 100 triples, which serve as the ground truth for evaluation.

Evaluation. The comparison between zero-shot and few-shot prompts enables us to evaluate whether including examples improves the accuracy of extracted triples, particularly in handling domain-specific language. To assess model performance, we employ both quantitative and qualitative evaluation methods. Quantitative metrics, such as precision, recall, F1-score, exact match, partial match, and semantic similarity, provide an objective, reproducible measure of alignment with ground-truth annotations. However, these metrics may not fully capture partial correctness or semantic nuances, especially in complex legal-economic texts. Hence, qualitative evaluation complements this by incorporating human judgment to assess the relevance, interpretability, and domain suitability of the triples. For qualitative evaluation, we propose a curated set of metrics and manually assess 100 randomly sampled triples from each model output. These qualitative metrics are discussed in detail in Sect. 5.

4 Experiments

In our experiments, we utilized the LLaMA 3.1 model containing 70 billion parameters. A Python-based program was developed using Ollama[1] and LangChain[2] to execute the language models for triple extractions, and the outputs were subsequently stored for evaluation purposes. For LLM optimization, parameters such as temperatures and prompt strategies play an essential role.

We have experimented with five types of prompts. We start with a generic prompt. This is the zero shot prompt configuration, wherein we instruct the model to extract subject-predicate-object triples from the texts. We define that the subject and the object must be Named Entities [3,9,11] while the predicates must be English language verbs. Then, for each subsequent prompt we add further instructions and examples. In the second prompt, we add one example and the definition of Named Entity Recognition (NER). This is the one shot prompt configuration. For the third prompt, we enhance the second prompt by adding a few more examples. This is the few shot configuration. In the fourth prompt, we add a few more examples of what the triples should look like. Alongwith that, we also add a few negative examples and negated instructions. This is the negative examples configuration. With negated instructions intend to add examples that suggest the model what would be a wrong outcome. As a feedback from the results generated by prompt 3, we also instruct the model to not include any verbs that we deem are not significant and to refine the results that we deem might require more information. For example, if the model generates triples such as *'Parties'*, *'signed'*, *'contract'* we instruct the model to define what the term *'Parties'* stand for. We also ask the model to deal with coreference resolution and observe the results obtained. An example of each prompt configuration will be provided in the open code access.

Table 1. Comparison of Llama 3.1 performance across different prompts

Metric	Zero Shot Model	One Shot Model	Few Shot Model	Negative Examples Model
Exact Match				
Precision	0.04	0.11	0.25	0.39
Recall	0.22	0.38	0.57	0.66
F1 Score	0.07	0.17	0.35	0.49
Semantic Match (using embeddings)				
Precision	0.06	0.14	0.30	0.46
Recall	0.28	0.44	0.65	0.78
F1 Score	0.10	0.21	0.41	0.57

---

[1] https://ollama.com/library.
[2] https://www.langchain.com/.

The output of each prompt execution is a set of subject-predicate-object triples, where the subject and object are named entities identified by the Named Entity Recognition, while the predicates are English language verbs. We have limited the output to 1000 triples per country pair document. We also observe the results from each prompt and use them to create new prompts, implying an indirect feedback to the model. We then create predicate frequency charts, and heatmaps to evaluate the model output and compare them to the benchmark triple set curated by Economics domain experts. We then evaluate the results generated by the model through various metrics.

5 Results and Evaluation

We evaluate the extracted triples using both quantitative and qualitative metrics. Table 1 presents the accuracy of four models compared to a domain-expert curated dataset. We also analyze predicate frequency, which informs prompt design by highlighting commonly used and foundational predicates like *means* or *includes*. These insights support refining models to better capture both broad and domain-specific concepts. Figure 2 displays bar charts of predicate frequency, illustrating their distribution in economic trade agreements.

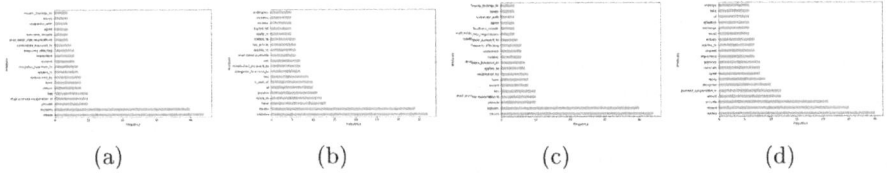

Fig. 2. Predicate frequency charts: (a) Zero Shot, (b) One Shot, (c) Few Shot, (d) Negative Examples

When compared to the benchmark dataset, this distribution suggests that the Llama 3.1 model effectively captures predicates relevant to the domain but may require fine-tuning to enhance the diversity of its outputs. Next, we generated

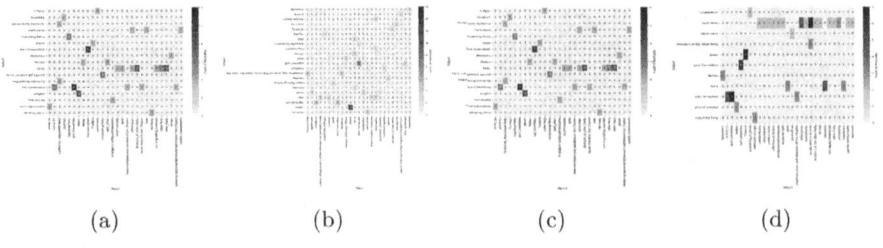

Fig. 3. Heatmap: (a) Zero Shot, (b) One Shot, (c) Few Shot, (d) Negative Examples

heatmaps for each prompt configuration, Fig. 3 shows the heatmaps for each of the prompt configurations.

Lastly, we also evaluate the results through the knowledge of domain experts to qualitatively analyse the triples generated and compare the results to the benchmark triples generated by the economic trade domain experts. We do this by using the metrics defined below.

The first metric, **Relation Validation**, shows that Llama 3.1-generated triples generally have strong contextual and semantic accuracy. Predicates like cooperate_with, expand_trade_with, and invest_in reflect the economic and diplomatic nature of the agreement, though some overly complex predicates reduce usability. The second metric, **Entity-Relation Coherence**, assesses the alignment between entities and predicates. The model typically identifies country-level actors (e.g., Japan, Thailand) correctly and maintains logical relationships, though it occasionally uses general terms like "Parties" instead of specific names. The third metric, **Triple Completeness**, evaluates whether essential information is preserved. While key themes such as trade liberalization and investment protection are captured, some higher-level strategic insights found in manual triples are missed. The fourth metric, **Semantic Correctness**, confirms that most triples are coherent, with logical subject-predicate-object structure, though some would benefit from more standardized predicate forms. The fifth, **Information Gain**, and the sixth metrics **Redundancy**, measures whether the model contributes useful new content and avoids repetition, respectively. It adds detail by breaking down complex clauses but sometimes generates redundant triples with slight predicate variations. The seventh and the eighth metrics, **Predicate Distribution** and **Coverage** respectively, looks at how well the predicates reflect the agreement's scope and balance between countries. Most aspects like trade, cooperation, regulation—are covered, and bilateral relations are reasonably consistent, though bidirectional predicates could better represent reciprocity.

6 Conclusion

In this work, we describe the methodology to extract subject-predicate-object triples from natural language texts using Llama 3.1 and experiment by iteratively improving the prompts for triple extraction and observe that including positive examples and negative examples increases the quality of the triples extracted. Through our experiments, we observed that while the Llama 3.1-generated triples show strong performance in capturing detailed relationships and maintaining semantic coherence. We also observed that in order to generate qualitative results, language models require advance fine tuning and consistent feedback. A major drawback that required a lot of attention was coreference resolution and we observed that the model was insufficient when it comes to resolving conflicts with coreferences.

Acknowledgement. The work has been done as the part of KONECO project, and it has received funding from the Bundesministerium für Bildung und Forschung (BMBF) under grant No 16DKWN095.

References

1. Alschner, W., Seiermann, J., Skougarevskiy, D.: Text-as-data analysis of preferential trade agreements: mapping the PTA landscape (2017)
2. Brown, T., et al.: Language models are few-shot learners. Adv. Neural. Inf. Process. Syst. **33**, 1877–1901 (2020)
3. Chiu, J., Nichols, E.: Named entity recognition with bidirectional LSTM-CNNs. Trans. Assoc. Comput. Linguist. **4**, 357–370 (2016)
4. Dessí, D., Osborne, F., Recupero, D.R., Buscaldi, D., Motta, E.: Scicero: a deep learning and NLP approach for generating scientific knowledge graphs in the computer science domain. Knowl.-Based Syst. **258**, 109945 (2022)
5. Lester, B., Al-Rfou, R., Constant, N.: The power of scale for parameter-efficient prompt tuning. arXiv preprint arXiv:2104.08691 (2021)
6. Li, F.L., et al.: AliMe KG: domain knowledge graph construction and application in e-commerce. In: Proceedings of the 29th ACM International Conference on Information & Knowledge Management, pp. 2581–2588 (2020)
7. Liu, P., Yuan, W., Fu, J., Jiang, Z., Hayashi, H., Neubig, G.: Pre-train, prompt, and predict: a systematic survey of prompting methods in natural language processing. ACM Comput. Surv. **55**(9), 1–35 (2023)
8. Liu, W., et al.: K-BERT: enabling language representation with knowledge graph. In: Proceedings of the AAAI Conference on Artificial Intelligence, vol. 34, pp. 2901–2908 (2020)
9. Nadeau, D., Sekine, S.: A survey of named entity recognition and classification. Lingvisticae Investigationes **30**(1), 3–26 (2007)
10. Nandini, D., Blöthner, S., Schoenfeld, M., Larch, M.: Multidimensional knowledge graph embeddings for international trade flow analysis. arXiv preprint arXiv:2410.19835 (2024)
11. Rau, L.F.: Extracting company names from text. In: Proceedings of the Seventh IEEE Conference on Artificial Intelligence Applications (1991)
12. Sahoo, P., Singh, A.K., Saha, S., Jain, V., Mondal, S., Chadha, A.: A systematic survey of prompt engineering in large language models: techniques and applications (2024). https://arxiv.org/abs/2402.07927
13. Shahi, G., Hummel, O.: On the effectiveness of large language models in automating categorization of scientific texts. In: Proceedings of the 27th International Conference on Enterprise Information Systems - Volume 1: ICEIS, pp. 544–554. INSTICC, SciTePress (2025). https://doi.org/10.5220/0013299100003929
14. Touvron, H., et al.: LLaMA: open and efficient foundation language models. arXiv preprint arXiv:2302.13971 (2023)
15. Yao, L., Mao, C., Luo, Y.: KG-BERT: BERT for knowledge graph completion. arXiv preprint arXiv:1909.03193 (2019)
16. Yu, C., et al.: FolkScope: intention knowledge graph construction for e-commerce commonsense discovery. arXiv preprint arXiv:2211.08316 (2022)

Introducing ORKG ASK: An AI-Driven Scholarly Literature Search and Exploration System Taking a Neuro-Symbolic Approach

Allard Oelen[1](✉)[iD], Mohamad Yaser Jaradeh[2][iD], and Sören Auer[1,2][iD]

[1] TIB – Leibniz Information Centre for Science and Technology, Hannover, Germany
{allard.oelen,auer}@tib.eu
[2] L3S Research Center, Leibniz University of Hannover, Hannover, Germany
jaradeh@l3s.de

Abstract. As the volume of published scholarly literature continues to grow, finding relevant literature becomes increasingly difficult. With the rise of generative Artificial Intelligence (AI), and particularly Large Language Models (LLMs), new possibilities emerge to find and explore literature. We introduce ASK (Assistant for Scientific Knowledge), an AI-driven scholarly literature search and exploration system that follows a neuro-symbolic approach. ASK aims to provide active support to researchers in finding relevant scholarly literature by leveraging vector search, LLMs, and knowledge graphs. The system allows users to input research questions in natural language and retrieve relevant articles. ASK automatically extracts key information and generates answers to research questions using a Retrieval-Augmented Generation (RAG) approach. We present an evaluation of ASK, assessing the system's usability and usefulness. Findings indicate that the system is user-friendly and users are generally satisfied while using the system.

Keywords: AI-Supported Digital Library · Intelligent User Interface · Large Language Models · Scholarly Search System

1 Introduction

Analyzing scholarly literature is a key aspect of research. However, due to the ever-increasing body of scholarly publications, finding scholarly literature becomes increasingly difficult [12]. Consequently, finding literature consumes a substantial portion of researchers' time [15]. Because of the recent developments in generative Artificial Intelligence (AI), and specifically Large Language Models (LLMs), new possibilities arise to extract knowledge from scholarly articles, helping researchers to find relevant literature in the flood of publications.

In this article, we present ORKG ASK (Assistant for Scientific Knowledge), hereafter referred to as ASK, a next-generation scholarly search and exploration system. ASK aims to provide support to researchers in finding relevant scholarly literature. ASK takes a Neuro-Symbolic approach which consists of three key components, namely Vector Search and LLMs for the neural aspect and

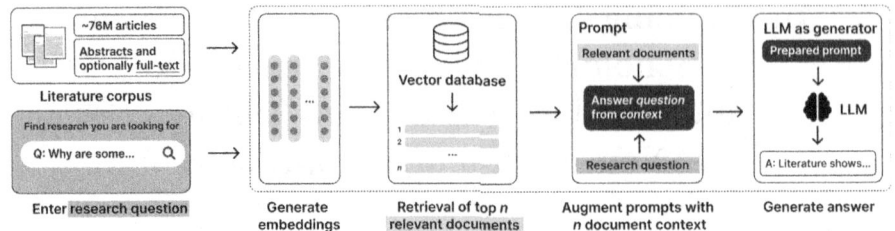

Fig. 1. Explainer depicting our RAG (Retrieval-Augmented Generation) approach for scholarly search. The *Retrieval* step ranks articles by their relevance to the question. The *Augmented* step injects the previously retrieved context in the prompt. The *Generation* step prompts the LLM and displays the answer.

Knowledge Graphs (KGs) for the symbolic part. We build upon our previously presented work where we demonstrated the basic ASK infrastructure [16]. In this paper, we expand on our previous work by providing an in-depth explanation of the approach, technical details of the implementation, and a extensive evaluation. In brief, ASK functions as follows: a user of ASK formulates their information needs as a research question. Afterward, a list of relevant articles is displayed. For each article, an automatically extracted answer for the previously asked question is displayed to the user. Finally, the symbolic aspect ensures users are able to narrow down the search space by providing semantic filters. This provides both the precision of symbolic approach and the flexibility of a neural approach. ASK is running as a publicly available production service online.[1]

The system takes a Retrieval-Augmented Generation (RAG) approach to support the previously described workflow. RAG [14] is commonly used to intertwine LLM extractions with information retrieval systems, as depicted in Fig. 1. Firstly, the Vector Search component ranks documents based on their relevance (Retrieval) for a research question. Secondly, relevant context is collected (i.e., the paper abstract and, if available, full-text) from the previous step (Augmented). Finally, the LLM generates answers and displays this to the user (Generation). A screenshot showing the ranked articles, search query, and generated LLM responses is displayed in Fig. 2. This work introduces the following contributions: i) presents an LLM-supported open-source scholarly literature search and exploration service, ii) describes a scholarly RAG system leveraging LLMs, vector search, and KGs, and iii) provides insights from the design and development process, supported with an evaluation.

2   Related Work

The landscape of scholarly search systems can be categorized into two groups, domain-agnostic and domain-specific systems. Prominent examples of domain-agnostic systems include Google Scholar, Semantic Scholar, and Scopus [6]. Well-known domain-specific systems include PubMed for the medical domain and

---

[1] https://ask.orkg.org.

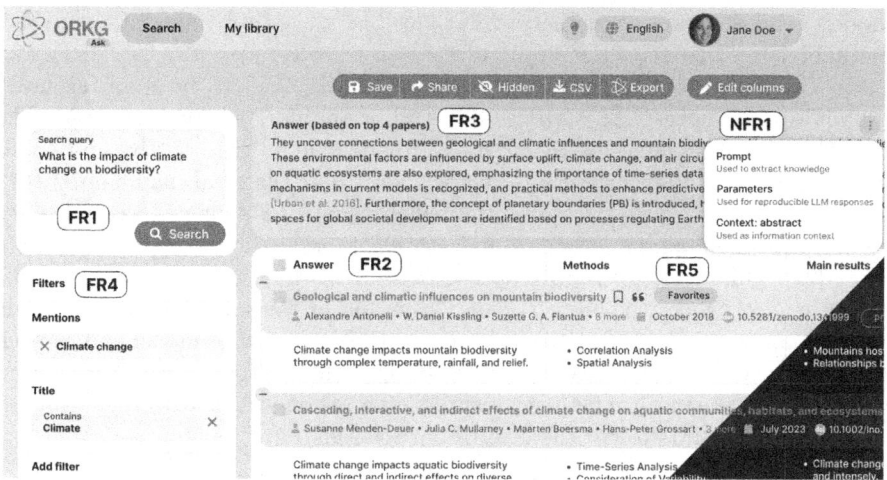

Fig. 2. Screenshot of the ASK search results page. The nodes with (N)FR correspond to the implementation of the (Non-)functional requirements, as listed in Table 1.

ACM Digital Library for the computer science domain. At a high level, these systems function similarly: relevant articles are returned for a set of user-provided keywords. A new generation of scholarly search systems tries to automatically extract relevant information from articles. Among others, those systems include Elicit, Consensus, and Scispace [3]. Those systems are similar in that sense that they are not open source, making it difficult to determine what models are employed and what underlying data corpus is used. This makes the reproducibility of results, for example for a systematic literature review, a challenging task. Additionally, the trustworthiness of generated responses by Large Language Models (LLMs) becomes increasingly problematic when the underlying technologies are not transparent. To the best of our knowledge, the previously mentioned systems typically use a RAG (Retrieval-Augmented Generation) [14] approach, as also mentioned by Bolanos et al. [3]. This roughly resembles the approach of ASK. However, a notable difference between ASK and the other systems is the open nature of ASK. All source code is openly available online, and we clearly communicate which data corpus we use and which models we employ. This makes ASK more suitable for reproducible literature searches.

LLMs gained a lot of traction after the seminal work of Vaswani et al. which paved the way for transformer models like BERT, RoBERTa, and more scientifically-oriented models like SciBERT [2]. Models then quickly started growing in size and capabilities such as GPT3 [4]. From this point on, very large models started to show impressive performance across a vast spectrum of language tasks. Despite their impressive capabilities, LLMs face several key challenges. There are concerns about the use of LLMs in fields requiring high precision, such as healthcare [19] and law, where inaccuracies can have serious consequences. A particular issue is the phenomenon of "hallucinations", where models generate statements that, while plausible, are entirely fabricated and lack factual basis [1].

In the context of the scholarly domain, LLMs need to be more accurate for widespread usage [20]. CORE-GPT [18] is an effort to combine LLMs like ChatGPT with open-access research to provide a more trustworthy and credible scientific question answering. Furthermore, Van Dis et al. highlighted that researchers need to pay extra attention when using LLMs for research purposes specifically when applying them to literature comprehension and summarization tasks [21]. Our work with ASK positions itself in the middle, trying to transparently show where the answers came from and at the same highlight to users that the answers are automatically generated via a language model and as such need to be reviewed by a human. ASK bridges the missing part of search systems which is the natural language expression and connects it with the advanced capabilities of LLMs to get the best of both worlds.

3 Approach

In this section we present our approach for scholarly search and discuss the system requirements, which essentially cultivated in the ASK system.

3.1 RAG for Scholarly Search

For a scholarly search system, parametric knowledge of LLMs should be limited and not used as a main source of information. Parametric knowledge is the knowledge that models encode within their vast number of parameters, and with it, LLMs are able to answer questions. Relying solely on such knowledge can lead to hallucinations and the generation of inaccurate information. For the aforementioned reasons, ASK relies on Retrieval-Augmented Generation (RAG) [14] to combine the parametric knowledge of the models and the non-parametric knowledge stored in vector stores to generate accurate and related text.

Non-parametric Memory. Also referred to as Semantic Search. Non-parametric memory is a part of the procedure that extends the knowledge reservoir of pre-trained language models to the requirements of individual applications. This type of memory provides various benefits to scholarly search: i) Customizability: the knowledge base contains only the items of interest and as such direct the LLM to answer only in relation to documents indexed within the vector store. ii) Updatable knowledge base: since there is no need to retrain the language model with every new document added, new documents can be easily indexed and added to the already-existing knowledge base. iii) Complex filtering capabilities: the vector store also offers the flexibility to further filter or refine search results based on metadata or other available criteria.

In order for the retriever component to work, first a set of documents needs to be processed and indexed inside a vector store. The vector store is populated with a semantic representation of documents, via embeddings. ASK uses the Nomic embedding model[2] which has an embedding size of 768 and a context window sequence length of 8K token. The choice of the embedding model is based on its advanced multilingual capabilities, efficient parameter utilization via MoEs, and its long context handling ability. Finally, the collection of documents retrieved is then passed down to the parametric memory component for further processing.

Parametric Memory. The parametric memory component solely relies on the language model itself. Using both parametric and non-parametric memories side-by-side has multiple benefits for LLM-based applications: i) Tailored responses: rather than posing a general query to the model and expecting an answer, the model now receives the query and the context in which it is supposed to look up the answer. ii) Reduced hallucinations: LLMs are notorious for hallucinating content [17]. With specifying the context, the model is forced to rely on the text that exists within its prompt and not within its own parametric knowledge. iii) Instruction following: the parametric knowledge within the models allows for custom instructions to generate apt responses depending on the use case.

ASK utilizes custom-made prompts containing placeholders that take pieces of information from the non-parametric memory and are then used by the LLM. ASK uses the small variant of Mistral LLM[3] [9]. The usage of a relatively small model reduces the required computational resources and loading times, while still being well capable of following instructions. The Mistral model has a 32K tokens context window which is suitable for passing the full text of articles and getting specific answers. Inferencing with LLMs can be resource-intensive and is usually the bottleneck when it comes to performance in production systems. For this particular reason, a caching mechanism is employed with the parametric memory. Caching is applied on partial hits (i.e., for single cells), making it possible to return single responses partially from the cache and partially from the LLM. The implemented caching mechanism reduces the loading times significantly and prevents calling the LLM, which in turn benefits computational efficiency.

3.2 System Requirements

To provide guidance during development, we formulate a set of system requirements, as listed in Table 1. The requirements are divided into functional and non-functional requirements. For brevity reasons, we list the high-level requirements only. The functional requirements focus on literature search, information extraction, and the ability to filter and organize information. The two most important non-functional requirements are the reproducibility options and the focus on barrier-free access via various accessibility features.

---

[2] In particular "nomic-embed-text-v1.5" which utilizes Matryoshka Representation Learning [11].
[3] ASK uses Mistral 7B Instruct v0.2 with no sliding-window attention.

Table 1. List of functional and non-functional system requirements, outlining the high-level key concepts to guide the system development.

ID	Title	Requirement	Rationale
Functional requirements			
FR1	Literature search	The system shall allow users to find scholarly literature for research questions.	To provide a scholarly search and exploration system.
FR2	Information extraction	The system shall display automatically extracted information from found literature.	To ensure users get a quick overview of the literature so relevancy can be assessed.
FR3	Answer synthesis	The system shall provide a summarized answer to research questions.	To provide a clear answer to the research question based on a set of articles.
FR4	Result filtering	The system shall allow users to set filters for finding related semantic concepts.	To narrow down the search space and provide a more fine-grained search.
FR5	Bibliography manager	The system shall provide a bibliography manager to store related literature.	To ensure collections can be stored and to allow importing existing articles.
Non-functional requirements			
NFR1	Reproducibility	The system shall always produce reproducible responses.	To ensure the system is suitable for scholarly research and is transparent to users.
NFR2	Accessibility	The system shall follow accessibility guidelines to ensure accessibility for all users.	To ensure that users with disabilities can use all features.
NFR3	Usability	The system shall be easy-to-use and can be operated with a minimal learning curve.	To provide an alternative to existing scholarly search systems.
NFR4	Maintainability	The system shall follow established coding standards to facilitate maintainability.	To ensure the system can be employed as a sustainable service.
NFR5	Interoperability	The system shall be interoperable with existing bibliography managers.	To ensure literature can be imported and exported to existing systems.

4 Implementation

In this section, we present the implementation details to realize the ASK system. We present the functional and non-functional requirements, the LLM setup for various use cases, the dataset used to populate the index of the search component, and technical details about the implementation.

4.1 Requirements Realization

In Fig. 2, a screenshot depicts the ASK interface. We will now discuss how the previously listed system requirements are implemented within this interface.

Functional Requirements. The literature search (FR1) is implemented by providing a large search box on the homepage from where users can get started by entering a research question. The research result page shows the question and a list of results ranked by relevance (Fig. 2 node FR1). The LLM-extracted answer is displayed in node FR2, alongside additional columns that are extracted as well. Users can modify those columns to extract specific information by clicking the *Edit columns* button. For the answer synthesis, a summarized answer is displayed at node FR3. Citations within this summarized answer point to the results listed below. Results can be filtered in the box displayed at node FR4. Finally, items can be added to a bibliography collection by clicking the bookmark icon as displayed in node FR5.

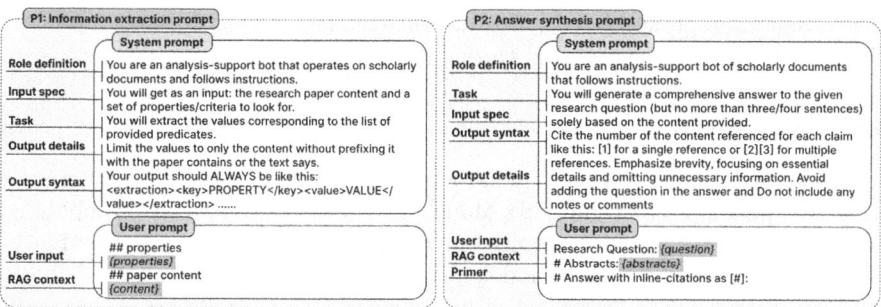

Fig. 3. Sample prompts for different RAG use cases within ASK. The system prompts provide the instructions to the LLM (Prompt P1 trimmed for brevity reasons). The user prompt includes the user input and RAG context. Values highlighted in red are placeholders used to inject user values into the prompt. Additionally, P2 uses a primer to improve the answer of the LLM. (Color figure online)

Non-Functional Requirements. In addition to being open source, ASK also provides data to ensure results are reproducible (NFR1). We created the reproducibility menu (see Fig. 2, node NFR1) that provides for all LLM-generated content: i) the prompts, i) the model, iii) the parameters (such as temperature, seed, etc.), and iv) the context used for the generation (full text or abstract). The transparency helps users to better assess the results' correctness and enables them to reproduce the same results themselves. Among other features, this sets ASK apart from other services, which are often proprietary and lack transparency. Accessibility is another key aspect of ASK. Any user, including those with disabilities, should be able to use the system barrier-free (NFR2). We integrated various features to facilitate accessibility. Firstly, the interface is responsive, making sure that the interface is usable at large zoom levels, benefiting users with visual impairments. As an additional benefit, the service can also be operated on different screen sizes, such as tablets and mobile phones. A dark mode (as displayed on the right bottom of Fig. 2) replaces all light colors with dark ones, and can be enabled to reduce eye strain. Secondly, ARIA attributes are added to facilitate screen reader usage, benefiting users with visual impairments [5]. Finally, the interface is internationalized, meaning that the service can be operated in different languages and different regions. The LLM responses are provided in multiple languages as well, opening up new methods to find related literature in the preferred language of the user, and making literature search more inclusive. In the end, the various accessibility features benefit all users.

The interface is designed to look intuitive and modern benefiting usability (NFR3). To ensure the system is maintainable (NFR4) and can be operated as a production service, it is implemented using the latest technologies and code standards. Details about the implementation are described in Subsect. 4.4. To make the system interoperable with other reference managers (NFR5), we adopted the Citation Style Language (CSL)[4] throughout the system.

4.2 LLM Setup

A construct of an LLM chain is implemented. A chain is the combination of three components: i) Prompt, ii) Model, and a iii) Parser. The prompt is an aggregation of the system and user prompt for a particular task (see Fig. 3). Before the invocation of the model, the relevant information retrieved by the non-parametric memory is injected and formatted into the prompt. Secondly, the model is the LLM and potentially any LoRAs [8] that need to be applied to the language model[5]. Lastly, a parser is a function that gets called on the output (i.e., the response of the LLM) and is then parsed, sanitized, and formatted to be used in other parts of the application. We note that we did not need to employ custom-trained or fine-tuned LLMs for ASK at this stage. As the LLM is mostly used as a means to perform information extraction, and in turn text generation, a fine-tuned model would not necessarily result in higher-quality results.

4.3 Dataset

ASK uses the CORE [10] dataset of open-access research papers as the basis of its indexed corpus. The CORE data is automatically crawled from open-access repositories and publisher websites. This means that there are quality-related issues that require some curation before any ingestion operation takes place. Before indexing the CORE data in the vector store of ASK, a pre-processing phase was implemented to choose, based on a set of heuristics, which items and articles are suitable to be added. This process involves checking if the articles have valid titles and abstracts (i.e., non-empty and have a length greater than a threshold). The abstracts proved to be the most impacting factor within this process. The data import process is a continuous process as the CORE data is growing with time and other sources are also integrated within the ASK system. In total, we imported 76.4M articles from the CORE dataset, excluding items that do not follow the previously mentioned requirements. Of the imported articles, 36.9% have a DOI and 25% have full-text available.

In addition to the CORE data, we imported a subset of BMBF-conform (German Federal Ministry of Education and Research) research reports related to autonomous driving, containing approximately 310 reports.[6] The ASK service is operated by the German National Library of Science and Technology (TIB) and by importing this dataset, we demonstrate how ASK can be leveraged to explore the library's special collections. In the future, we plan to import more of such special collections.

---

[4] https://citationstyles.org.
[5] ASK does not implement any LoRAs at the moment. However, this technique can be integrated to further customize the model for domain-specific use cases.
[6] https://ask.orkg.org/search?query=&filter=AND[0][source][inList][0]=TIB%2520Forschungsberichte%2520Autonomes%2520Fahren.

4.4 Technical Details

The system is developed using a microservices setup[7] and is available as a free online service. The services is divided into the frontend and backend. The frontend is written in TypeScript with React. It uses the Next.js framework, adopting the server components paradigm where suitable. Furthermore, it uses Tailwind for styling and HeroUI as a component library. The use of standardized technologies increases the maintainability, as described in NFR3. The frontend is available as open-source software and is published with a permissive MIT license.[8]

The backend is mainly written in Python leveraging the FastAPI framework. The backend adopts a modular approach where each functionality is in its own module, which improves maintainability and extensibility, as described in NFR4. Other components to serve the language models, vectorized documents, and cache items are part of the backend but are written in different languages and are used as turn-key solutions. The source code of the backend and various components are available publicly under the MIT license.[9] Furthermore, ASK utilizes Qdrant[10] as a vector store and the TGI[11] engine for serving LLMs and inferencing in production. The containers are managed via Podman.

5 Evaluation

We now discuss the system evaluation, which is divided into two parts: subjective user evaluations and objective data analysis.

5.1 Subjective Evaluation

ASK is publicly released as a scholarly information retrieval service and is being actively used by researchers. To gather feedback from real-world system users, we integrated a lightweight feedback collection component into the user interface. The feedback component appears on question pages. The component consists of two different sets of questions. The first set evaluates the helpfulness, correctness, and completeness of the displayed question and its answers. The second set of questions asks users about their general feedback on the ASK system. The questions consist of two standardized and unmodified UMUX-Lite [13] questions and one to assess whether users are satisfied with ASK. User satisfaction is another commonly used method to assess usability. The operational feedback is collected on a running basis, previous results consisting of a small number of responses (approximately 3%) have been published already in a demo article [16].

---

[7] Server configuration: 1 TB of RAM, 15 TBs of SSD storage, 128 CPU cores, and seven GPU cards (Nvidia L4 4 × 24 GB, Nvidia L40S 2 × 46 GB, and Nvidia H100 1 × 80 GB).
[8] https://gitlab.com/TIBHannover/orkg/orkg-ask/frontend.
[9] https://gitlab.com/TIBHannover/orkg/orkg-ask/backend.
[10] https://qdrant.tech.
[11] https://huggingface.co/text-generation-inference.

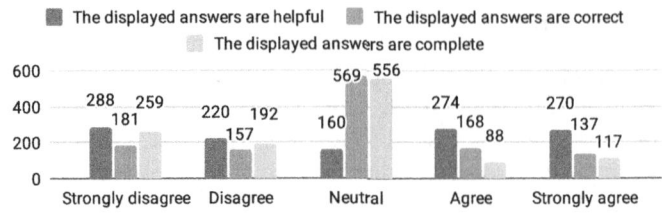

Fig. 4. Question specific results for operational feedback collection.

Participation in the operation feedback questionnaire is on an opt-in basis and users can close the feedback popup if they do not wish to participate.

The question-specific form has been filled out 1,212 times in the period from June 15, 2024, until January 15, 2025. Based on browser fingerprinting, it was completed by 1,032 different users. The results are displayed in Fig. 4. As can be observed, the results of the helpfulness of answers vary among users. This means that participants experience different levels of relevance for the answers, which can be explained by their expectations of the system. The correctness of answers is voted as more neutral. Meaning that users might had difficulty assessing the correctness, or thought answers were neither fully correct nor incorrect. Finally, the results for completeness are similar to correctness, indicating that most users had no strong opinion about the completeness of the answers.

The results of UMUX-lite questions to assess the general usability of the system are displayed in Fig. 5. A total of approximately 443 users filled out this evaluation. As the questions were optional, the number of users differs slightly from the numbers in the figure. The numbers result in a calculated UMUX score of 65.7 on a scale of 0–100, where higher scores indicate better usability. Incomplete partial responses were discarded in the final UMUX calculation, resulting in 409 included responses. As the results show, ASK does not always meet the users' requirements. However, the majority of users do agree that the system itself is easy to use. This indicates the design decisions to make the system easy to use have proven to be effective. Finally, Fig. 6 displays the user satisfaction outcomes. In total, 363 users answered this question. As can be observed, average user satisfaction leans toward more positive than negative opinions.

User Experiment. In addition to the operational feedback, we conducted a small-scale user experiment to compare ASK to an established literature search system, specifically Google Scholar. We were particularly interested in the perceived task load differences between ASK and Google Scholar. For this, we designed a within-subject study where a total of 9 participants had to answer a set of four predefined research questions, two per condition. Most of the participants are engaged in academic research, have either a master or PhD degree, and have used ASK before, but were not involved in the development of ASK. The majority of participants (7 out of 9) searches for academic articles at least on a weekly basis. To counteract sequence bias, the two conditions were evaluated by participants in random order. To answer the questions, the participants had to use at least two references per answer, the references had to be provided

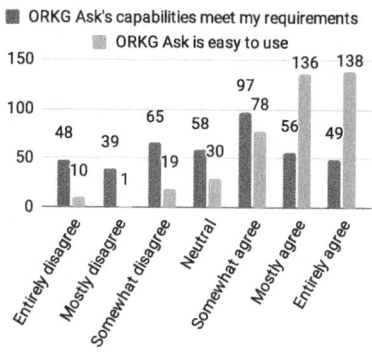

Fig. 5. UMUX-Lite results with a score of 65.7.

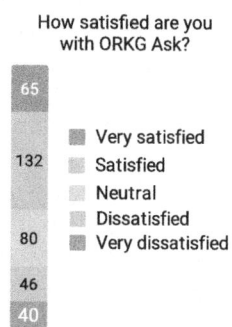

Fig. 6. General user satisfaction of ASK.

by the search system. Additionally, they had to manually verify the correctness of the answer from the source article, consequently, they were not allowed to copy-paste LLM-generated answers. For each condition, they had to indicate their perceived task load, measured with an unweighted NASA Task Load Index (TLX) scale [7]. Additionally, the time to answer a question was recorded.

The results of the comparisons between the ASK and Scholar search condition are displayed in Table 2. As can be observed, the ASK condition has a considerably lower perceived task load compared to the Scholar condition. Regarding the required time, there was an outlier that took more than 113 min to answer the questions via ASK, while only taking 24 min to answer via Scholar. For completeness, the timing results are displayed with and without the outlier. When the outlier is disregarded, the required time to answer questions with ASK is lower than with Scholar. Although ASK and Google Scholar might not be directly comparable, making the conclusions less definitive, the comparison gives insights into the future direction of providing alternatives to established scholarly search systems.

5.2 Objective Evaluation

To gain insights into how to system is used, we collected data using web analytics. We analyzed user interaction data over the period starting from May 15, 2024,

Table 2. Showing a comparison between the ASK and Scholar condition regarding task load and required time. Task load is listed as percentage and time in seconds.

	ASK		Scholar	
	Mean	SD	Mean	SD
Task load (TLX) (%)	26.76	16.65	61.3	16.59
Time (s)	984.41	456.67	1241.39	496.36
Time with outlier (s)	1628.79	1979.78	1267.49	470.86

Table 3. Web analytics data and user interaction statistics of the ASK production service. Measured from May 15, 2024, until February 1, 2025.

Analytics		Events		Device usage	
Visits	74,145	Queries asked	67,949		
Returning visits	26,354	Downloads	7,595	Desktop	76,9%
Pageviews	219,189	Outlinks	19,723	Smartphone	21,2%
Duration visit	4:01m	Custom filters added	723	Other	1,9%
Bounce rate	3%	Custom columns added	415		
		Load more (1 page)	5,067		
		Load more (2 pages)	2,149		
		Load more (>2 pages)	5,010		

until February 1, 2025. Analytics data was recorded via Matomo[12] and used browser fingerprinting to distinguish between users. Additionally, specific events in the interface were logged to determine how frequently they were used. A summarized overview of the analytics and user interaction statistics is presented in Table 3. Visits are defined as users visiting the service who have not visited a page in the last 30 min. The bounce rate of 3% is rather low, indicating that users are actually using the system, and not just visiting a single page and then leaving the service. A considerable amount of users are using ASK on devices other than desktops. This indicates that the service indeed works well for different screen sizes, part of our accessibility requirement NFR2.

The recorded events gain more insights into what features are actually being used. The downloads and out-links relate to the number of articles that are being visited from ASK. This includes following links to the PDF, publisher landing pages, or data repositories. The number of added custom filters is low. Also, the number of columns added is rather low, meaning that most users did not use the functionalities to extract custom data from articles. The low number of custom extractions either means that users were already satisfied with the default extracted properties, or they did not understand how to use the feature. Finally, the load more numbers show the number of times a user clicks the "Load more" button at the bottom of the page, indicating they are interested in finding more related work.

6 Discussion

ASK is meant as a scholarly search system, helping researchers to find and explore scholarly literature. Although ASK indeed also answers research questions while performing a search, first and foremost ASK is a scholarly information retrieval system. Therefore, finding literature is the main objective of ASK. We consider the question-answering feature as a means to find related work, not as an objective by itself. This means that the previously discussed RAG method is a

---

[12] https://matomo.org.

key aspect of our approach and using LLMs in isolation, even when pre-trained or fine-tuned on scholarly articles, would not be sufficient to meet our search goal. Therefore, in the user experiment, we specifically focused on comparing ASK to a scholarly search system and not a question-answering system.

As previously discussed, when employing LLMs, one has to keep in mind that LLMs tend to hallucinate. Hallucinations cannot be completely eliminated, even when using models with a higher number of parameters (i.e., more powerful and capable models). Indeed, for the use case of ASK, hallucinations can also occur, but to a large extent do not pose major challenges. As the question-answering capability is secondary to the main goal of information retrieval, users do not solely rely on the extracted information to find relevant literature. As mentioned, it is only a means to assess the literature's relevance. After potentially relevant articles are discovered, users are expected to perform rigorous analysis of the listed work, as is also expected when using traditional scholarly search systems. To communicate this to users, a warning message is displayed in the interface, informing users that all information needs to be manually checked.

The evaluation presents the results of operational feedback and data collected from a production environment. Consequently, data is collected in an uncontrolled environment, meaning that individual responses and data might be inaccurate or incomplete. For example, the users' intentions of filling out the evaluation forms are unknown, which could be only for testing purposes or without thoroughly reading the questions. Also, for the feedback, no demographics were collected, limiting the possibility of an in-depth analysis of the results. Browser fingerprinting was used to distinguish among different users, which means that unique users cannot be fully accurately determined. Therefore, it should be noted that the evaluation results might contain data from the same users, even though they are reported as different users. However, we do consider the results to be relevant nevertheless, and when aggregated, provide valuable insights.

Finally, we will discuss future work. The usefulness of the approach as a search system heavily depends on the quality and the size of the underlying literature corpus. We plan to extend our literature repository by including more articles from different sources, and by parsing content semantically, for example by performing author name disambiguation, all contributing toward more semantic search. As mentioned in Sect. 2, ASK sets itself apart from similar existing services by providing an open-source service and focusing on literature search reproducibility. A quantitative performance comparison with these services is out of scope for this work, but is an interesting future research direction. ASK's transparency features provide a key advantage over these services, but a comparison regarding the quality of the responses provides helpful insights into other aspects of our approach.

7 Conclusion

In this work, we presented ASK, a scholarly search and exploration system. We examined how AI can be leveraged for literature searches by exploring the direction of using vector search and LLMs to provide active support to users while conducting a literature search. ASK showcases how such a literature search system can operate. Furthermore, we focused on the ability of LLMs to provide value to researchers while performing a literature search. To this end, we leveraged a RAG (Retrieval-Augmented Generation) approach to find and explore scholarly literature. Using a RAG approach, LLMs are used for information extraction and text generation, making a large literature corpus explorable using AI technologies. The RAG approach provides a literature search where source information is more easily traceable while partially mitigating common LLM limitations, such as hallucinations and limited context sizes. Finally, we investigated whether AI-driven tools, such as ASK, are potential alternatives to already established scholarly search tools. By presenting the ASK service and its respective user study, we captured researchers' attitudes toward the new approach and concluded there is indeed potential and interested audience for such new tools.

Acknowledgements. This work was co-funded by NFDI4DataScience (ID: 460234259), and by the TIB Leibniz Information Centre for Science and Technology. We want to thank the entire ORKG team for their contributions to the ORKG platform, including research and development efforts.

References

1. Bang, Y., et al.: A multitask, multilingual, multimodal evaluation of chatGPT on reasoning, hallucination, and interactivity. arXiv preprint arXiv:2302.04023 (2023)
2. Beltagy, I., Lo, K., Cohan, A.: SciBERT: a pretrained language model for scientific text (2019). https://arxiv.org/abs/1903.10676
3. Bolanos, F., Salatino, A., Osborne, F., Motta, E.: Artificial intelligence for literature reviews: opportunities and challenges. arXiv preprint arXiv:2402.08565 (2024)
4. Brown, T.B., et al.: Language models are few-shot learners (2020). https://arxiv.org/abs/2005.14165
5. Craig, J., Cooper, M., Pappas, L., Schwerdtfeger, R., Seeman, L.: Accessible rich internet applications (WAI-ARIA) 1.0. W3C Working Draft (2009)
6. Gusenbauer, M., Haddaway, N.R.: Which academic search systems are suitable for systematic reviews or meta-analyses? Evaluating retrieval qualities of Google Scholar, PubMed, and 26 other resources. Res. Synth. Methods **11**(2), 181–217 (2020). https://doi.org/10.1002/jrsm.1378
7. Hart, S.G.: NASA-task load index (NASA-TLX); 20 years later. In: Proceedings of the Human Factors and Ergonomics Society, pp. 904–908 (2006). https://doi.org/10.1177/154193120605000909
8. Hu, E.J., et al.: LoRA: low-rank adaptation of large language models (2021). https://arxiv.org/abs/2106.09685
9. Jiang, A.Q., et al.: Mistral 7b (2023). https://arxiv.org/abs/2310.06825
10. Knoth, P., et al.: CORE: a global aggregation service for open access papers. Nat. Sci. Data **10**(1), 366 (2023)
11. Kusupati, A., et al.: Matryoshka representation learning (2024). https://arxiv.org/abs/2205.13147
12. Landhuis, E.: Scientific literature: information overload. Nature **535**(7612), 457–458 (2016)

13. Lewis, J.R., Utesch, B.S., Maher, D.E.: UMUX-LITE: when there's no time for the SUS. In: SIGCHI Conference on Human Factors in Computing Systems, pp. 2099–2102 (2013)
14. Lewis, P., et al.: Retrieval-augmented generation for knowledge-intensive NLP tasks. In: Larochelle, H., Ranzato, M., Hadsell, R., Balcan, M., Lin, H. (eds.) Advances in Neural Information Processing Systems, vol. 33, pp. 9459–9474. Curran Associates, Inc. (2020)
15. Niu, X., et al.: National study of information seeking behavior of academic researchers in the United States. J. Am. Soc. Inform. Sci. Technol. **61**(5), 869–890 (2010)
16. Oelen, A., Jaradeh, M.Y., Auer, S.: ORKG ASK: a neuro-symbolic scholarly search and exploration system. Joint Proceedings of Posters, Demos, Workshops, and Tutorials of the 20th International Conference on Semantic Systems (2024). https://ceur-ws.org/Vol-3759/paper7.pdf
17. Perković, G., Drobnjak, A., Botički, I.: Hallucinations in LLMs: understanding and addressing challenges. In: 2024 47th MIPRO ICT and Electronics Convention (MIPRO), pp. 2084–2088. IEEE (2024)
18. Pride, D., Cancellieri, M., Knoth, P.: CORE-GPT: combining open access research and large language models for credible, trustworthy question answering (2023). https://arxiv.org/abs/2307.04683
19. Shen, Y., et al.: ChatGPT and other large language models are double-edged swords (2023)
20. Susnjak, T., Hwang, P., Reyes, N.H., Barczak, A.L.C., McIntosh, T.R., Ranathunga, S.: Automating research synthesis with domain-specific large language model fine-tuning (2024). https://arxiv.org/abs/2404.08680
21. Van Dis, E.A., Bollen, J., Zuidema, W., Van Rooij, R., Bockting, C.L.: ChatGPT: five priorities for research. Nature **614**(7947), 224–226 (2023)

Leveraging LLMs for Conversational Data Access: A Human-Centred Perspective

Maristella Matera[✉], Emanuele Pucci, and Vincenzo Manto

Politecnico di Milano, Milan 20133, Italy
{maristella.matera,emanuele.pucci}@polimi.it,
vincenzo.manto@mail.polimi.it

Abstract. The study reported in this paper advocates the utilization of LLMs to enhance *conversational data exploration*. Our approach harnesses LLMs not only for crafting SQL queries but also for generating visualizations, data summaries and explanations that can enrich the conversational user experience. Building upon user studies involving a total 32 domain experts—middle managers and IT project managers in medium to large IT and manufacturing companies—we approached the problem with a human-centered perspective, and designed a Web platform for querying data using natural language. This paper illustrates the platform's design, emphasizing the integration of LLMs within the data access pipeline, and the user-based evaluation we carried out both from a quantitative and a qualitative perspective. Furthermore, it explores the implications of adopting the conversational interface on the efficiency and satisfaction of users seeking to retrieve and analyze data through self-service platforms catering to situational requirements.

Keywords: Data Exploration · Conversational UIs · LLMs

1 Introduction

In today's data-driven world, effective access to structured data is crucial across industries, yet remains largely dependent on complex technical tools requiring expertise in SQL and other specialized knowledge [28]. This complexity limits accessibility, creating a growing need for intuitive, user-friendly solutions [8]. The emergence of Large Language Models (LLMs) has transformed this landscape, providing enhanced capabilities for query generation, data interpretation, and user interaction [15]. However, designing conversational systems for structured data access requires attention to designing the interaction and the dialogue system to consider the needs of the addressed users [21].

This paper builds on prior research [5,8] and introduces QuerIX (*QUERying through Interactive eXploration*), a web framework that leverages LLMs to facilitate NL-based data access. QuerIX leverages LLMs to enable seamless text-to-SQL conversion, data visualization, and conversational enhancements. The adopted *human-centred approach* is a distinctive aspect of this work. All of the design assumptions were first defined based on user requirements and then validated with users and in real-life scenarios. Through user studies involving 32 domain experts, we demonstrate how integrating LLMs into data access pipelines enhances usability, allowing for more flexible and expressive NL queries while reducing the reliance on rigid chatbot interactions. Our findings highlight the broader implications of generative AI in self-service data environments, offering improved efficiency and user satisfaction.

This paper is organized as follows: Sect. 2 frames the state of the art in NL data exploration, Sect. 3 illustrates the *human-centred process* we followed to design, implement and test QuerIX. Finally, Sect. 7 draws conclusions and distill implications for LLM-based NL querying.

2 Related Work

Using natural language (NL) for querying databases has become a key focus in improving user interfaces, especially with the advent of Large Language Models. Previous studies have proposed chatbots for data exploration [1,3,10], and our past work has examined platforms for automatically generating and executing these chatbots [5,8,20]. This paper builds on those efforts by leveraging the generative capabilities of Large Language Models (LLMs) to enhance the process of transforming NL inputs into actionable data queries. With these recent advances, conversational data access offers a more intuitive way for non-technical users to interact with data [17,32,33]. This approach can greatly enhance productivity and contribute to democratizing data access [11,15].

Extending NL querying capabilities has been a central theme in research, with early work addressing the challenge of translating NL into SQL queries [9,17]. More recent advancements have explored the use of LLMs to facilitate this translation [33], though many systems still face challenges in fully integrating NL processing with database structures. Some works, such as those by Sanyal et al. [29], focus on generating accurate SQL queries from NL inputs, but these methods are often limited by small-scale testing. Song et al. [31] propose SpeechSQLNet, which handles spoken NL queries and translates them into SQL, demonstrating the viability of speech-to-SQL systems. Gassen et al. [12] propose data-aware conversational agents, but these agents still lack robust support for data visualization, which is essential for user understanding. A variety of keyword-based and form-based interfaces have also been explored [18,22], but these often require users to have prior knowledge of database structures. The conversational paradigm has shown promise in addressing these challenges [9], though it is not yet widely adopted for data exploration.

We are now witnessing advancements in LLM-based methods for SQL and data visualization [7]. Recent contributions, such as DIN-SQL [23] and Purple [26], have made significant strides in improving the accuracy and efficiency of text-to-SQL translations using in-context learning and model fine-tuning. Gu et al. [13] explore few-shot learning techniques for SQL translation. In the domain of data visualization, Chen et al. [6] developed a benchmark for evaluating

LLM-based data visualizations, and recent developments emphasize the growing importance of LLMs in enhancing visualization tasks [34,35]. These advancements suggest a promising shift towards more intelligent and user-friendly interfaces, yet, they remain primarily focused on data visualization challenges, often overlooking the querying aspects and the importance of a human-centered approach. Our work brings together the challenges of NL querying and data visualization, and brings a human-centred lense to data analysis by incorporating user needs and perception into the design.

3 Methodology

The design of our paradigm for conversational data access and the enabling architecture engaged relevant stakeholders to identify key requirements and validate design choices. While our previous research examined user attitudes compared to traditional methods like SQL [5,21], with the new study we wanted to focus on domain experts who regularly handle large data volumes but lack technical expertise. To this end, we interviewed 14 managers in IT and manufacturing sectors[1] to gather insights into expectations and preferences, ensuring that the conversational paradigm aligns with actual user needs. Thus, we i) designed a software architecture integrating LLMs for NL request understanding, query generation, and results visualization, ii) developed a prototype to evaluate the technical effectiveness of these choices, iii) conducted user-based evaluation sessions with non-technical domain experts to evaluate the prototype usability in comparison with traditional CSV-based data analysis and visualization tools. The next sections will illustrate each step of the process.

3.1 Requirements for Conversational Data Access

We conducted semi-structured interviews with 14 middle managers from IT and manufacturing sectors (aged between 28 and 68 years, and highly educated) to understand their needs in data analysis. The interview covered their perception of business intelligence, acceptance and concerns regarding an AI-driven tool, confidence with conversational interfaces, and team workflows. Each session lasted about an hour and was video-recorded for analysis[2].

We performed a thematic analysis [30], and identified five primary user needs:
T1 *No need to know data structure*: Users prefer an inferential system that constructs queries automatically.
T2 *Easy configuration*: The system should assist in filtering relevant data while visually conveying database schemas.
T3 *Text-to-query translation*: Queries should be flexible, tolerate errors, and provide quick responses even with large databases.
T4 *Meaningful data presentation*: Extracted data should be visualized through

---
[1] For users' characteristics see: https://tinyurl.com/LLM4NQL-userStudy.
[2] Questions available at: https://tinyurl.com/LLM4NQL-userStudy.

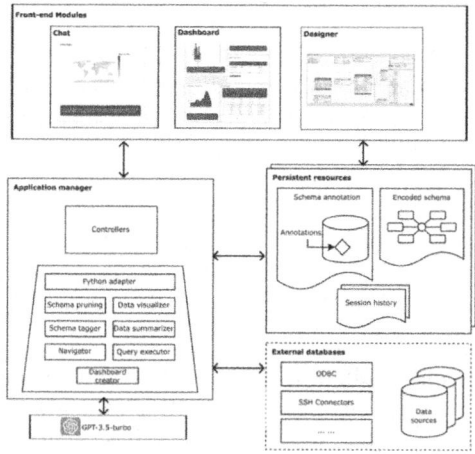

Fig. 1. Platform architecture

intuitive graphics, summaries, and descriptions.

T5 *Flexibility and control*: Users should dynamically refine queries and configure visualizations interactively.

The data analysis also highlighted a "user journey" revolving around three cornerstone activities: a *Configuration* where users select relevant database portions [8,21], *Inquiry* where users retrieve information via NL queries (receiving structured tables, charts, and visual aids), and a *Data Rendering* through a dashboard presenting the extracted data and allowing iterative query refinement for the visualized indicators.

4 Platform Design

Figure 1 illustrates the conceptual architecture resulting from the identified requirements. The system can connect with both local and remote data sources. To address the themes **T1** and **T2** emerged from the user analysis, each new connection can be integrated at runtime, without requiring any recompilation or re-training of the underlying algorithms and models. The current prototype has been evaluated with relational data sources, and its functioning is based on the availability of data schema descriptions. However, the modularity of the designed architecture ensures agnosticism towards the underlying data sources, which prioritizes the definition of data-access pipelines regardless of the underlined technologies. The front-end consists of three interactive environments enabling the three processes outlined above.

Designer. It is the front-end module enabling the *Configuration* process. The back-end logic leverages generative AI to minimize the user's effort, enabling results without manual setup (T1). However, adding annotations enhances text-to-query accuracy and data presentation (T2). Users can then annotate schema

Algorithm 1. Data narrative

1: Attribute types extraction
2: stat ← Statistical analysis on distributions
3: relevantColumns ← Relevant columns based on distribution
4: **for all** column of relevantColumns **do**
5:     text ← text + description(column.data)
6: **end for**
7: text ← rephrase(text)
8: **return** text
---

elements using a visual paradigm [21], refining semantics and prioritization for data extraction, summarization, and visualization. While beneficial, annotations remain optional. Additionally, system-generated schema embeddings leverage semantic similarity and word embedding to enrich data attributes, improving the inquiry process through enhanced semantic analysis.

Chat. This module helps the user explore data through NL request (T3). The front-end module is linked to the back-end *Inquiry* process that translates user requests into executable queries using a GPT 3.5 Turbo-based text-to-code model[3] with upstream and downstream transformations, including few-shot fine-tuning [4,36] for text-to-SQL conversion. The system distinguishes three main intents: Data Visualization (e.g.,"Count the product using a bar chart"), Navigation (e.g., "Get the orders of the product '001'"), and Select query (e.g., "Give me all the orders"). For Select queries, a schema pruning algorithm [19] filters irrelevant tables by balancing semantic similarity and graph-based propagation. The system ensures SQL injection prevention, filters out non-compliant commands, and applies pagination to enhance performance. Error handling includes heuristic typo correction, GPT-based query repair, and detailed error messages, while maintaining request history for robustness.

Dashboard. It supports the user in integrating results gathered through chat (T4, T5)[4], and refers to the *Data Rendering* process. Here, the data summarization logic extracts key attributes from tables to assess their relevance for visualization and narration, using statistical correlation, variance, and semantic relevance within and across columns. A summarization algorithm (Algorithm 1) performs statistical analysis to identify relevant attributes and generates a textual representation refined by NLP techniques, including paraphrasing via LLMs. Data visualization complements this by generating graphical representations, such as bar charts and heatmaps, based on identified attributes and user intent. The *Data Visualizer* module ensures that visual outputs adhere to data storytelling best practices and are integrated into interactive dashboards using JavaScript-based

---
[3] https://platform.openai.com/docs/models.
[4] The interactive modality in which the users execute all the supported steps is shown in the video available at: https://tinyurl.com/LLM4NQL-video.

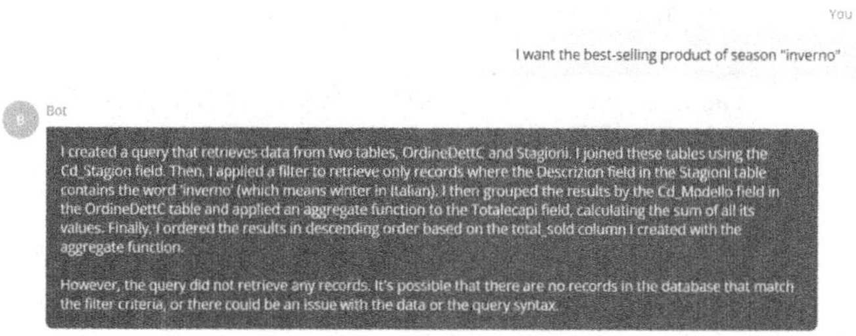

Fig. 2. Example of error explanation.

graphics. Error explanation addresses cases where queries are syntactically correct but yield no meaningful results. In this cases, GPT models with a few-shot prompt generate code-like explanations to help non-technical users understand query misinterpretations, allowing for iterative error correction and enhanced interaction with structured data, as illustrated in Fig. 2.

While the LLM serves as the core of NLP and generative tasks, the processes preceding and following its usage are managed by a library of *Python Modules*, which enable GPT to interface with databases and metadata extracted during the design phase. Each module is specialized in tasks such as the DB-schema pruning prior to query building and data extraction, and data visualization and dashboard creation following data extraction. A *Python Adapter* coordinates the ensemble of functions exposed by both the Python Modules and the LLM, all concurring to interpreting the user request and returning results in the proper format and through a dialog. The adapter choreography supports the polymorphic behavior that might be needed when diverse user requests and varying data sources are managed.

5 Technical Evaluation

We evaluated the performance of our computation strategies based on response time, CPU usage, throughput, and output accuracy. Tests were conducted on a real ERP database (SYS-DAT Group[5]) referring to products and orders data, with 251 tables having between 8 and 139 attributes each, narrowed down to 17 key entities and 196 attributes using the Designer component[6].

Table 1 summarizes efficiency results, showing *Navigation* as the fastest process (1.39 s avg. response time) and *Select query* as the slowest (14.56 s). CPU time differences stem mainly from REST API interactions and SQL execution, which could be optimized through parallelization and caching. Output correctness was assessed via schema pruning and text-to-SQL accuracy, with comparisons against ChatGPT. Our approach achieved 89.31% pruning precision and

---

[5] https://www.sys-datgroup.com/.
[6] The complete schema is available at: https://tinyurl.com/3ewpyr5c.

Table 1. Results for Efficiency measures.

Task	$\bar{r}$(s)	σ_r(s)	X_r	CPU_r(s)
Schema embedding	12.77	2.13	0.07	11.26
Select query	14.56	6.58	0.06	9.78
Navigation	1.39	0.48	0.72	1.21
Data visualization	3.82	1.57	0.26	3.54

superior query dimensionality (+3.79%) and cardinality (+12.3%) over ChatGPT. While ChatGPT had higher recall, our method prioritized precision, reducing query noise and improving result quality.

6 User-Based Evaluation

We conducted a user study to assess the usability of the Inquiry module by comparing the user performances when using our prototype (QerIX) and Excel, which had emerged as the most adopted tool for data analysis by knowledge workers who lack a technological background in Sect. 3.1. The study adopted a *within-subject design*, with the used system as an independent variable and two within-subject factors, i.e., *QerIX* and *Excel*; each participant used the two systems in sequence in a counterbalanced order (Latin-Square design [27]) to reduce learning effects. The working environment (database, tables, and attributes) on which the participants had to operate was the one already described in the previous sections, with data related to products and orders. QerIX was pre-configured to act on the same reduced schema of Sect. 5, and raw data extractions for the same data portion were pre-loaded into an Excel worksheet. We then identified a set of experimental tasks related to navigating the data source and extracting and visualizing data, and we formulated them in NL. The task execution had to be possible using both systems on the reduced data schema. The task adequateness was therefore assessed through pilot sessions that in total involved 6 participants, 3 self-identified as females and 3 as males, with an average age of 26.83 years ($\sigma = 12.02$, min = 18 years, max = 51 years). The pilot participants were asked to use QerIX and Excel to perform 10 different tasks. Observing the completion time allowed us to select a smaller, manageable set of tasks that could be completed within a reasonable time frame, while still maintaining the representativeness of the requests supported by the system and relevant for evaluation.

Participants. We enrolled 12 participants, 3 self-identified as females and 9 as males, who were middle managers or IT project managers in medium/large companies. The mean age of the participants was 48.42 years ($\sigma = 12.52$, min = 28, max = 68)[7]. Before starting the study session, the participants had completed

---

[7] Participants data are available in the additional material at: https://tinyurl.com/LLM4NQL-userStudy.

a demographic questionnaire integrated with a survey in which they rated their experience with technology and data analytics on a 10-point scale. The gathered data revealed a high level of experience in IT in general ($\bar{x} = 7.86$, $\sigma = 1.30$, min = 5, max = 9), in chatbot usage ($\bar{x} = 6.80$, $\sigma = 1.37$, min = 5, max = 9), and a very good confidence with SQL language ($\bar{x} = 7.40$, $\sigma = 1.12$, min = 6, max = 9). In terms of data analysis and visualization, the participants expressed solid level of knowledge for analytical tasks ($\bar{x} = 7.47$, $\sigma = 1.31$, min = 5, max = 9) and a slightly weaker level for building data visualizations ($\bar{x} = 6.93$, $\sigma = 1.58$, min = 3, max = 9). Participants' education was instead heterogeneous, with 5 individuals holding Master's degrees, 4 with Bachelor's degrees, 2 with a Ph.D., and 3 with technical High-School diplomas.

Procedure and Tasks. Sessions were conducted remotely via online calls with remote desktop sharing (RDP) in a controlled virtual environment, blocking outbound internet requests except for OpenAI hosts. Two researchers assisted each participant: one moderated the session, explaining the study's purpose, obtaining consent, and administering a demographic questionnaire, while the other observed and took notes. Participants, familiar with the data domain but not the database schema, received no prior explanation of the QerIX interactive environment. Tasks were assigned sequentially, with each participant using both systems in a counterbalanced order (Latin-Square design [27]) to reduce learning effects. The sessions were recorded, and users' comments were noted. After completing tasks with each system, participants filled out the SUS [2] and NASA-TLX [14] questionnaires. At the end, they ranked the systems based on utility, completeness, ease of use, and satisfaction[8]. Participants completed four tasks (Table 2), selected from pilot studies as representative of two interaction types:

1. Direct data retrieval involving selection, projection, join, and aggregation.
2. Progressive data exploration, encouraging inferential use of system features for query formulation.

Each task had a 3-minute limit. Data collected included execution time, success rate, and qualitative feedback (NASA-TLX, SUS, and final rankings).

Quantitative Analysis. QerIX was compared to Excel in relation to three different quality dimensions: *efficiency, effectiveness* and *satisfaction*.

Efficiency. The system's efficiency is evaluated by considering the time users spent performing tasks, with efficiency defined as the resources used relative to goal achievement Table 2 presents average execution times per task and the results of a paired sample t-test. Task 4, the most complex, shows a statistically significant difference, with Excel requiring more steps compared to QerIX, which uses NL requests transformed into queries. For Tasks 2 and 3, QerIX

---

[8] Questionnaires available at: https://tinyurl.com/LLM4NQL-userStudy.

Table 2. Task descriptions and paired sample single negative tail T-Test results on execution times

Task no.	Task	$\bar{x}_q$ (s)	σ_q (s)	$\bar{x}_e$ (s)	σ_e (s)	T	df	p
1	Extract some sales orders and visualize them	130.50	55.44	127.58	39.03	0.165	12	0.564
2	Extract the total sold per customer	103.92	64.52	134.17	47.41	−1.298	12	0.110
3	Find the best-selling product for sale season *estivo*	125.67	45.48	150.83	35.30	−1.572	12	0.072
4	For each day of the last year, report the daily total sold	138.25	55.57	171.67	17.60	−1.824	12	0.048

shows better performance, though the time difference isn't statistically significant. Excel has an advantage for Task 1 due to task's simplicity and participants' expertise.

Effectiveness. To evaluate the effectiveness of the Inquiry module, we measured the success rate based on task completion. Tasks were categorized as "Success," "Partial Success," or "Failure," with a success index calculated as the percentage of users who fully completed tasks, giving partial successes half the value. QuerIX's success index was 73.95% (30 Success, 11 Partial, 7 Failure) vs. Excel's 64.58% (23 Success, 16 Partial, 9 Failure). Table 3 details the analysis. The difference is not statistically significant (Wilcoxon signed-rank test, $Z = -0.051$, $p = 0.4806$). Longer, more complex tasks benefit from conversational access, enabling more attempts within the same time.

Table 3. Results grouped by success

	QuerIX			Excel		
	Success	Partial	Failure	Success	Partial	Failure
Task 1	6	3	3	7	4	1
Task 2	8	2	2	7	2	3
Task 3	10	1	1	5	5	2
Task 4	6	5	1	4	5	3

Satisfaction. The analysis of satisfaction is crucial to understanding how effective both systems are perceived by users. To this extent, at the end of task execution with each system, participants were asked to fill out the SUS and NASA-TLX questionnaires, leading to the following results.

Perceived Usability. The measures of the perceived usability did not highlighted any significant difference. The average SUS score computed for QuerIX is 70.19 ($\sigma = 8.53$). This corresponds to a good result, as it is aligned with the average assumed score of 69.5 [2]. Excel also received a positive satisfaction evaluation, with an average SUS score of 74.89 ($\sigma = 7.84$). The higher value could be attributed to Excel's status as a well-established and widely recognized tool, frequently utilized within the participants' field. The SUS questionnaire was divided into three sections: *System Learnability* (questions #4, #7, #14,#15), *Results Quality* (#21, #22, #23, #25, #26) and *System Usability* (the remaining questions). QuerIX's learnability was quantified at 65.83 ($\sigma = 16.89$) and was almost in line with the Excel value ($\bar{x} = 67.22$, $\sigma = 13.02$). For the Quality of the results, QuerIX has a higher index than Excel (QuerIX $\bar{x} = 78.70$, $\sigma = 10.96$; Excel $\bar{x} = 70.37$, $\sigma = 10.71$). Finally, the System Usability was evaluated positively for both systems, but with an outperforming result for Excel (QuerIX $\bar{x} = 72.89$, $\sigma = 8.15$; Excel $\bar{x} = 78.40$, $\sigma = 9.09$).

Perceived Workload. To monitor the perceived workload, the final questionnaire embedded the NASA-TLX evaluation. The results (low values represent lower effort, thus higher satisfaction) prove that the conversational approach is slightly more demanding ($\bar{x} = 54.89$, $\sigma = 10.06$) than Excel ($\bar{x} = 48.23$, $\sigma = 10.13$). However, the t-test unveils that the results are not statistically significant ($t = -0.98$, $p = 0.342$). We also analyzed possible differences for each single NASA-TLX dimension. Only the *Temporal Demand*, focusing on the participants' perception of the time pressure, presents a significant difference between the two systems, with an advantage for Excel. The values for the other dimensions are not statistically different, but it is possible to observe a positive QuerIX trend for the *Performance* dimension (the participants' satisfaction with their performance), a positive Excel trend for the perceived *Effort*, and a comparable participants' perception of the *Mental* and *Physical* demand.

Systems Ranking. At the conclusion of each session, participants were asked to complete a questionnaire ranking the two systems—QuerIX and Excel—based on their utility, completeness, ease of use, and overall satisfaction. Of the participants, 5 favored QuerIX over Excel for its utility; however, only 1 participant rated QuerIX higher for completeness. QuerIX was preferred by 8 participants for ease of use and by 5 for overall satisfaction. These results align with the findings discussed for the previous usability measures: they highlight a good level of perceived utility and satisfaction with QuerIX, with a particular appreciation of its ease of use. However, Excel is considered a more comprehensive tool, and this might be attributed to the participants' familiarity.

Qualitative Analysis. All the study sessions were recorded. In addition, the researchers moderating and observing the participants' activities individually took notes on significant participants' behaviors and aloud comments. They individually transcribed their notes and post-experience considerations and extended them by integrating the video analyses. Individually, the researchers first reduced the complexity of data through a *Latent Semantic Analysis* (LSA) [16]; then, they performed an inductive thematic analysis. After a discussion aimed to reduce possible disagreements on the identified topics, they came out with the following themes.

Ease of Use. Users reported that QuerIX is flexible and easy to use. Participant **P4** observed that *"it is easy and simple to interact with, but also extremely satisfying in achieving what's requested"*. Usability issues were reported (**P8**: *"Sometimes QuerIX gets stuck while computing some requests, but this can be easily solved by cleaning the chat"*, **P9** also asked *"Make the areas where one can write more visible to the user"*). Yet the participants stressed how those issues can be easily solved and expressed their appreciation for the new paradigm.

Results' Unpredictability and Control over the Querying Process. Participants noted that responses can seem unpredictable and unforeseeable, leading to a feeling of losing control. This feedback suggests that there may be room for improvement in the system's NLP capabilities to create a dialog with the user and explain, if needed, the computational steps. (**P1**: *"I see great use of the app integrated with virtual assistants"*).

Interactive and Progressive Exploration. Participants appreciated the system's summarization and chart creation but struggled with communication, preferring fewer details in queries and more accurate responses. They wanted the system to infer missing information from context (**P12**: *"requests must be detailed and too accurate, also recalling details already given"*), and a more conversational approach, even for small tasks (**P8**: *"making it even more conversational, even for small tasks"*).

Transparency. Users expressed concern about the opacity of AI-based tools. While they appreciated QuerIX ability to infer information, they also wanted insight into its processes. Providing a clear view of data retrieval and system operations can build trust and enhance understanding.

Autonomy versus Job Damage. During the discussion, a significant theme emerged: the contrast between automation enhancing user autonomy and the potential harm it could pose to developers and domain experts, who would need to acquire additional specialized skills to stay competitive in the face of increasing automation. While there was enthusiasm for automation and conversational support for rapid data exploration (**P1**: *"I like the idea of Conversational BI for fast data exploration"*), there were also concerns about their future roles (**P12**: *This could damage developers' jobs*). These contrasting themes highlight the need to strike a balance between empowering users with autonomous capabilities and letting them perceive their centrality for system control.

7 Conclusion

Conversational UIs have gained significant traction in various domains, representing a crucial step forward in human-computer interaction. When applied to data analysis, they could allow users to extract insights from data by simply conversing with a system, simplifying the analysis process and enhancing its accuracy and speed. This work proposes a novel LLM-based architecture and an interaction paradigm capable of exploiting conversational interfaces to access and elaborate structured data, extract insights, and automatically generate interfaces for data analysis. The findings reveal QuerIX's strong technical performance, especially for complex queries, compared to Excel. User studies show QuerIX offers greater efficiency for complex tasks, while Excel excels at simple numerical tasks. QuerIX stands out for operational efficiency, ease of use, and effectiveness in environments dominated by Excel. Participants familiar with Excel's detailed data manipulation found QuerIX a valid alternative, praising its ease of use and result rendering. Starting from the experimental results, we identified design implications that can guide the definition of approaches for NL querying. In the following, we summarize the main insights together with the limitations of our approach and the future work to address current lacks.

7.1 Implications for LLM-Based NL Querying

Role of the Interaction Paradigm. QuerIX's conversational paradigm enhances intuitive interaction, leveraging LLMs to improve *inferential data access* (**T1**) and provide *high-quality results* in an *understandable format* (**T4**). It simplifies *technical complexity* through *natural-language interactions* (**T3**), making knowledge access more *democratic*. Users' ability to *effectively communicate instructions* remains crucial, necessitating human-centered UI design [24].

Role of Prompt Engineering. LLMs' performance depends on well-crafted prompts. Effective guidance ensures satisfactory results, while poor prompting leads to suboptimal outcomes. The need for *self-correction* in NL requests (**T3**) reinforces the importance of robust prompt engineering. Our query-building approach introduces an ad-hoc prompt-generation layer.

NL Intuitiveness vs. Numerical Manipulation. QuerIX excels in handling complex queries due to its *easy configuration* (**T2**) and fully conversational design, eliminating the need for GUI operations. In contrast, Excel, while familiar, requires additional steps, making complex tasks more time-consuming. However, for *numerical analysis and manipulation*, Excel remains preferable due to its structured environment.

Tool Synergy and Task Suitability. A complementary relationship emerges between QuerIX and Excel, with QuerIX excelling in *ambiguous or complex requests* through *flexible query formulation and control mechanisms* (**T5**), while Excel is optimal for structured numerical tasks. ALso, Excel's transparency aids in validating QuerIX's logic, addressing *query unpredictability and control*.

Role of the Interaction Paradigm. QuerIX's interaction paradigm allows for more intuitive and satisfying interaction, which can be attributed to the conversational paradigm and the improvement brought by the integration of LLMs.

According to the qualitative analysis of the usability study, QuerIX enhances the ability to *easily infer* information from the available data *without the need to know their structure*, thus responding to the user needs identified in the initial requirement analysis (theme **T1**). Coherently with the requirement expressed by theme **T4**, it provides *high-quality results* presented in an *understandable format*. It enables a *lower technical complexity* thanks to *natural-language interactions*, thus responding to need discussed in theme **T3**. In general, the participants perceived QuerIX offers a more *democratic access* to knowledge.

These aspects highlight a promising attitude of the users towards employing a conversational paradigm for information access. Engaging in NL conversations with intelligent systems, extracting relevant insights, and providing contextually appropriate responses can significantly enhance decision-making and problem-solving across a wide range of domains. However, the users' ability to *effectively communicate instructions* in a manner easily decipherable by an AI system proves crucial. It becomes, therefore, fundamental to adopt a human-centered process to design UIs and interaction paradigms that can guide the users in the formulation of effective NL requests. This implies a need for frameworks and methods for prompt-based UIs, a gap that our research is addressing [24].

7.2 Limitations and Future Work

During the design of our framework, we encountered several structural and design choices that, however, were not addressed carefully, as our emphasis was especially on the process for query building and result visualization. *Data security and privacy* poses a significant challenge, emphasizing the need for robust protocols to protect sensitive information. The current architecture ensures that the raw data extracted from data sources are not transferred or used outside QuerIX. This means that third-party services like GPT do not have access to data themselves, except for schemas. Our future work will strengthen security by also introducing mechanisms for authentication and access privileges. Another limitation is the handling of *multimedia files*: the system currently has the capability to process images as part of requests, but some limitations still affect the effectiveness of some queries. The prompt-query-result pipeline we implemented may experience higher latency with *larger schemas and data volumes*, leading to delays in receiving responses. As shown in Sect. 6, execution times were not a concern during the evaluation, with *QuerIX* even outperforming *Excel* in some cases. Nevertheless, we believe performance can still be improved, leading to a better user experience. Moreover, our schema pruning approach based on entity semantics may reduce scalability, particularly for large databases with high cardinality. The nature of conversational inquiries also introduces a *trial-and-error approach* that can be time-consuming and frustrating, as interpreting user intents can be challenging. Additional interaction mechanisms could enrich the UI to guide the users in request formulation. *Presenting complex data sets* effectively and clearly proves to be difficult through the current data summarization and chart-building mechanisms. As already outlined in previous studies

[25], it is important to prioritize *transparency and control*, by allowing the users to understand and control the logic governing query building and data extraction and create trust-building mechanisms. Future work will focus on extending the interaction paradigm to enhance these aspects. Finally, the limited size of the user study and their specific profile might impact the generalizability of the findings to a broader population. Broader studies will be needed to validate these findings across a more representative user base.

References

1. Baig, M.S., Imran, A., Yasin, A.U., Butt, A.H., Khan, M.I.: Natural language to SQL queries: a review. Int. J. Innov. Sci. Technol. **4**, 147–162 (2022)
2. Bangor, A., Kortum, P., Miller, J.: Determining what individual SUS scores mean: Adding an adjective rating scale. J. Usability Stud. **4**(3) (2009)
3. Brabra, H., Báez, M., Benatallah, B., et al.: Dialogue management in conversational systems: a review of approaches, challenges, and opportunities. IEEE Trans. on Cogn. Develop. Syst. **14**(3), 783–798 (2021)
4. Brown, T., et al.: Language models are few-shot learners. arXiv preprint arXiv:2302.11054 (2023)
5. Castaldo, N., Daniel, F., Matera, M., Zaccaria, V.: Conversational data exploration. In: Bakaev, M., Frasincar, F., Ko, I.-Y. (eds.) ICWE 2019. LNCS, vol. 11496, pp. 490–497. Springer, Cham (2019). https://doi.org/10.1007/978-3-030-19274-7_34
6. Chen, N., Zhang, Y., Xu, J., Ren, K., Yang, Y.: Viseval: A benchmark for data visualization in the era of large language models (2024)
7. Daniel, G., Cabot, J.: Applying model-driven engineering to the domain of chatbots: The xatkit experience. Sci. Comput. Program. **232**, 103032 (2024)
8. Desolda, G., Lanzilotti, R., Matera, M., Pucci, E.: Rapid prototyping of chatbots for data exploration. In: BCNC@SPLASH, pp. 5–10 (2021)
9. Dhamdhere, K., McCurley, K.S., Nahmias, R., Sundararajan, M., Yan, Q.: Analyza: exploring data with conversation. In: Proceedings of IUI 2017, Limassol, Cyprus, March 13-16, 2017, pp. 493–504. ACM (2017)
10. Følstad, A., et al.: Future directions for chatbot research: an interdisciplinary research agenda. Computing **103**(12), 2915–2942 (2021). https://doi.org/10.1007/s00607-021-01016-7
11. Galitsky, B.: Developing Conversational Natural Language Interface to a Database, pp. 85–120. Springer International Publishing, Cham (2019)
12. Gassen, M., Hättasch, B., Hilprecht, B., Geisler, N., Fraser, A., Binnig, C.: Demonstrating cat: synthesizing data-aware conversational agents for transactional databases. Proc. VLDB Endow. **15**(12), 3586–3589 (8 2022)
13. Gu, Z., et al.: Few-shot text-to-SQL translation using structure and content prompt learning. Proc. ACM Manag. Data **1**(2) (Jun 2023)
14. Hart, S.G., Staveland, L.E.: Nasa-task load index (nasa-tlx); 20 years later. Human Factors (1988)
15. Hassani, H., Silva, E.S.: The role of ChatGPT in data science: how AI-assisted conversational interfaces are revolutionizing the field. Big Data Cogn. Comput. **7**(2), 62 (2023)
16. Landauer, T.K., McNamara, D.S., Dennis, S., Kintsch, W. (eds.): Handbook of Latent Semantic Analysis. Lawrence Erlbaum Associates (2007)

17. Li, F., Jagadish, H.V.: Constructing an interactive natural language interface for relational databases. Proc. VLDB Endow. **8**(1), 73–84 (2014)
18. Li, Y., Yang, T.: Word Embedding for Understanding Natural Language: A Survey, pp. 83–104. Springer International Publishing, Cham (2018)
19. Manto, V.: Conversational access to structured knowledge exploiting large models. Master's thesis, Politecnico di Milano (7 2023)
20. Pereira, J., Díaz, O.: Chatbot dimensions that matter: Lessons from the trenches, pp. 129–135. Springer-Verlag, Berlin, Heidelberg (2018)
21. Piro, L., Desolda, G., Matera, M., Lanzilotti, R., Mosca, S., Pucci, E.: An interactive paradigm for the end-user development of chatbots for data exploration. In: Ardito, C., Lanzilotti, R., Malizia, A., Petrie, H., Piccinno, A., Desolda, G., Inkpen, K. (eds.) INTERACT 2021. LNCS, vol. 12935, pp. 177–186. Springer, Cham (2021). https://doi.org/10.1007/978-3-030-85610-6_11
22. Popescu, A., Etzioni, O., Kautz, H.A.: Towards a theory of natural language interfaces to databases. In: Leake, D.B., Johnson, W.L., André, E. (eds.) Proceedings of IUI 2003, Miami, FL, USA, pp. 149–157. ACM (2003)
23. Pourreza, M., Rafiei, D.: Din-SQL: Decomposed in-context learning of text-to-SQL with self-correction (2023). https://arxiv.org/abs/2304.11015
24. Pucci, E., Piro, L., Andolina, S., Matera, M.: From conversational web to inclusive conversations with LLMs. In: Proceedings of AVI 2024, Arenzano, Italy. ACM (2024)
25. Pucci, E., Possaghi, I., Cutrupi, C.M., Baez, M., Cappiello, C., Matera, M.: Defining patterns for a conversational web. In: Proceedings of CHI 2023 pp. 1–17 (2023)
26. Ren, T., Fan, Y., He, Z.e.a.: Purple: Making a large language model a better SQL writer. arXiv preprint (2024)
27. Rogers, Y., Sharp, H., Preece, J.: Interaction design: Beyond human-computer interaction. Wiley (2023)
28. Sako, M.: How generative AI fits into knowledge work. Commun. ACM **67**(4), 20–22 (2024)
29. Sanyal, H., Shukla, S., Agrawal, R.: Natural language processing technique for generation of SQL queries dynamically. In: Proceedings of I2CT 2021, pp. 1–6. IEEE (2021)
30. Shakeri Hossein Abad, Z., Gervasi, V., Zowghi, D., Barker, K.: ELICA: An automated tool for dynamic extraction of requirements relevant information. In: 2018 5th International AIRE Workshop, pp. 8–14 (2018)
31. Song, Y., Wong, R.C.W., Zhao, X.: Speech-to-SQL: toward speech-driven SQL query generation from natural language question. VLDB J. 1–23 (2024)
32. Taipalus, T.: The effects of database complexity on SQL query formulation. J. Syst. Softw. **165**, 110576 (2020)
33. Trummer, I.: Codexdb: Synthesizing code for query processing from natural language instructions using GPT-3 Codex. In: Proceedings of VLDB 2022 (2022)
34. Vazquez, P.: Are LLMs ready for visualization? In: IEEE Pacific Visualization Conference, p. 343. IEEE (04 2024)
35. Yang, Z., Zhou, Z., Wang, S., et al: Matplotagent: Method and evaluation for LLM-based agentic scientific data visualization (2024)
36. Zhang, H., et al.: Fine-tuning pre-trained language models for few-shot intent detection: Supervised pre-training and isotropization. In: Proceedings of NAACL, pp. 532–542. ACL (2022)

A Graph-Based RAG for Energy Efficiency Question Answering

Riccardo Campi[1]([✉]), Nicolò Oreste Pinciroli Vago[1], Mathyas Giudici[1], Pablo Barrachina Rodriguez-Guisado[2], Marco Brambilla[1], and Piero Fraternali[1]

[1] Politecnico di Milano, DEIB Department, Milan, Italy
{riccardo.campi,nicolooreste.pinciroli,mathyas.giudici,
marco.brambilla,piero.fraternali}@polimi.it
[2] MIWenergía, Parque Científico de Murcia, Murcia, Spain
pablo.barrachina@miwenergia.com

Abstract. In this work, we investigate the use of Large Language Models (LLMs) within a Graph-based Retrieval Augmented Generation (RAG) architecture for Energy Efficiency (EE) Question Answering. First, the system automatically extracts a Knowledge Graph (KG) from guidance and regulatory documents in the energy field. Then, the generated graph is navigated and reasoned upon to provide users with accurate answers in multiple languages. We implement a human-based validation using the RAGAs framework properties, a validation dataset composed of 101 question-answer pairs, and some domain experts. Results confirm the potential of this architecture and identify its strengths and weaknesses. Validation results show how the system correctly answers in about three out of four of the cases ($75.2 \pm 2.7\%$), with higher results on questions related to more general EE answers (up to $81.0 \pm 4.1\%$), and featuring promising multilingual abilities (4.4% accuracy loss due to translation).

Keywords: Retrieval Augmented Generation (RAG) · Knowledge Graph (KG) · Large Language Model (LLM) · Energy Efficiency · Question Answering · Multilingualism · Sustainability

1 Introduction

The focus on Energy Efficiency (EE) is gaining importance in the energy sector, especially with the aim of reaching net zero emissions [16], as recently outlined by European Institutions [8]. Energy users are identified as key actors, especially when renewable energy sources are used [9]. The implementation by these key actors of the latest guidelines on energy savings [7,11], with the adoption of eco-friendly behaviors, is required to meet EE. Furthermore, EE is improved by matching energy consumption with the availability and production cycles of renewable energy sources [9].

During the last few years, the increasing adoption of Large Language Models (LLMs) offers opportunities to enhance understanding and optimization of energy consumption to meet EE [13]. However, since these models may not fulfill the expectations when asked to provide factual answers, or when local regulations and socioeconomic context must be taken into account [5,12], Retrieval-Augmented Generation (RAG) systems address the matter by coupling the LLM with a knowledge base that formally describes domain-specific information [1].

Considering the above scenario, we propose a Graph-based RAG architecture designed to offer users recommendations to help them achieve EE. Our solution automatically extracts knowledge from the source documents, containing domain-specific information about energy consumption, EE, regulations, and incentives. Then, it answers user queries by implementing a reasoning process that navigates the extracted knowledge. It should also be able to handle multiple languages and extract the semantics of the documents independently from their language. We assess the validity of the architecture with a human-based validation experiment using the properties proposed by the Retrieval Augmented Generation Assessment (RAGAs) framework [6], some domain experts, and a validation dataset composed of 101 question-answers pairs.

2 Background and Related Works

This section contains the relevant literature from both a technical point of view, mainly presenting Large Language Models (LLMs) and Retrieval Augmented Generation (RAG) systems, and an energy sustainability perspective.

LLM. In recent years, there has been significant growth in research on Large Language Models (LLMs), which are AI-based Natural Language Processing (NLP) models built on top of the Transformer architecture. These models exhibit proficiency in comprehending language and generating new content, with robust multilingual and summarization capabilities [1]. However, LLMs often provide nonsensical or entirely made-up answers when asked questions they do not know, such as domain-specific or vague ones [13,17]. These are known as hallucinations and are mainly caused by lack of domain-specific knowledge or context understanding. Hallucinations can have significant negative effects because they are hard to tell apart from accurate information, potentially spreading misinformation and reducing user trust [14].

RAG. To overcome these limitations, Retrieval-Augmented Generation (RAG) systems emerge as a powerful solution by combining the strengths of information retrieval with the generative capabilities of LLMs. This allows RAG systems to solve knowledge-intensive tasks such as handling domain-specific questions or citing the sources of the retrieved information, resulting in more accurate and contextually relevant outputs [1]. While the simplest architectures leverage vector embeddings to store and retrieve their data [15], new graph-based architectures are emerging, allowing RAG to provide more accurate and relevant answers by relying on Knowledge Graphs (KGs) [4], especially for complex questions that require synthesizing information from multiple sources.

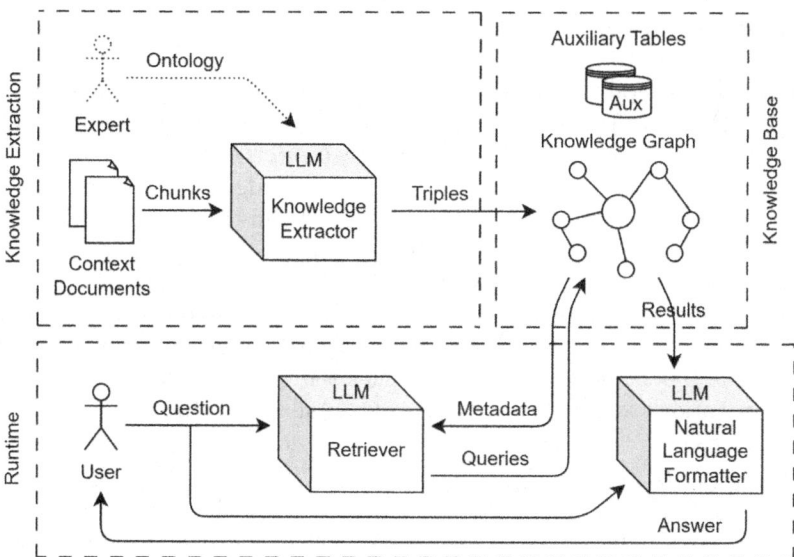

Fig. 1. General architecture of the proposed system. The system relies on 3 main parts: the *Knowledge Extraction*, the *Knowledge Base*, and the *Runtime*.

Related Work. Arslan et al. [2] proposed the use of Energy Chatbot, a vector-based multi-source RAG with the aim of enhancing decision-making for Small and Medium-sized Enterprises by providing comprehensive Energy Sector insights through a Question Answering system. Key findings emphasize how the integration of a RAG significantly enhances the system's ability to deliver accurate, relevant, and consistent information, especially with Llama3.1:8B model. However, a graph-based version of this prototype is still lacking. Similarly, Bruzzone et al. [3] coupled a RAG system to a GPT4-based chatbot to enhance urban planning simulations. The system dynamically simulates different urban scenarios, giving urban planners accurate information and fostering sustainability actions. Another work [10] investigated Graph-based RAG approaches to answer complex questions on electricity with the use of some publicly available electricity consumption KGs. Key findings show promising results in the integration of RAG and LLMs using KGs for electricity-related topics. However, this approach does not include knowledge extraction from domain-specific documents nor its integration into KGs. Lastly, in 2023, Giudici et al. [13] explored ways to enhance understanding and optimize energy consumption to meet EE using LLMs. Their chatbots responded fluently and coherently to general inquiries but fell short in accuracy when addressing domain-specific questions. However, no relevant literature exists at the moment of writing on improving EE for users and households using a Graph-based RAG approach.

3 Methodology

The proposed general architecture can be divided into 3 distinct parts, as shown in Fig. 1. First, a *Knowledge Extractor* takes out triples containing entities and relationships from some domain-specific *Context Documents*. To guide the extraction, a domain expert may inject their knowledge into the Extractor. The extracted triples are then analyzed and used to build the *Knowledge Base*, containing a *KG* and some auxiliary tables. Once the KG is populated, there is no need to run the extraction again, unless it is necessary to add or remove domain-specific information. Finally, a *Runtime* part receives user's questions and uses a *Retriever* to query the Knowledge Base to find relevant information. Then, a *Natural Language Formatter* takes the question and the results from the interrogations and use them to provide an answer to the user.

3.1 Knowledge Extraction

First, Context Documents (e.g., domain-specific documents, encompassing engineering and energy sector notions, available technologies, laws and regulations, and socioeconomic events) are provided to the system in the form of PDFs or web pages. These are cleaned from unnecessary parts such as page numbers or HTML tags and chunked into smaller chunks. The chunking algorithm splits text corpora using a chunk size and an overlapping size. When possible, the algorithm takes into consideration word boundaries, such as full points or commas, to avoid words within the same sentence being split between chunks.

The extraction phase then follows, consisting of the use of an LLM-based algorithm to parse the chunks with the aim of automatically extracting entities and relationships using a prompt-based approach. These are represented as entity-relationship-entity triples, where entities are usually objects and relationships are actions. When relevant, the algorithm adds properties to the nodes, to enrich their semantics. Here, a domain expert may inject his knowledge to guide the system focusing on specific aspects when extracting, eventually forcing it to adhere to a provided ontology or structure with a filtering algorithm.

Finally, entity and relationship names are passed through a text-processing function that unifies their syntax. Similar names (e.g., "Energy Efficiency" and "energy_efficiency") are unified using the same syntax (e.g., "Energy efficiency").

3.2 Knowledge Base

It is designed to hold the KG with nodes and edges derived from the extraction, along with auxiliary tables to manage user metadata, such as their locations and preferences. It is necessary to populate the KG only once, before the system becomes fully operational or when it is time to update the information contained in it. The auxiliary tables can be filled instead at runtime based on user inputs.

First, the KG is initialized with a simple ontology, that defines, under a new namespace ONTO, some objects of type *OWL.Class* such as *Entity*, *Relationship*, *Property*, *Document*, *Chunk*, etc. It also defines, under the same namespace, two new *OWL.ObjectProperties* and *OWL.DatatypeProperties* objects. Some examples of object properties are *hasSource*, *hasTarget*, *hasRelationship*, and *hasChunk*, while examples of datatype properties are *hasName*, *hasContent*, *hasValue*, and *hasValueEmbedding*.

The automatically extracted triples are then iteratively added to the KG as Entity and Relationship objects, as well as the source documents and their chunks, becoming Document and Chunk objects, respectively. The nodes in the graph are identified by hashing the names of the objects. This allows the system to merge extracted entities into a single Entity if they represent the same thing, and the same is true for relationships and other objects. Edges between Entity and Relationship objects (e.g., *hasRelationship*, *hasSource*, *hasTarget*, *isSourceOf*, *isTargetOf*, *relatesTarget*, *relatesSource*) are stored in such a way that allows for the precise reconstruction of the original extracted triple (i.e., the Entity-Relationship-Entity chain). To allow similarity-based local search and reasoning on the graph nodes, embedding vectors are computed starting from Entity and Relationship names with a text embedding model, as well as chunked text contents.

3.3 Runtime

Once the Knowledge Base is ready, the system allows users to ask questions and receive domain-specific answers. The retrieval paradigm relies on a local, entity-based reasoning process. It first identifies relevant Entity objects in the KG by comparing them with the user question using a similarity measure, then it begins a local reasoning process starting from the just identified objects. Finally, it uses the information retrieved to provide an answer, augmenting it with citations to the original source documents. Answers are tailored for each specific user by using personalization metadata from the auxiliary tables.

When the Retriever receives a question, it extracts some triples using the same LLM-based algorithm of the extraction part. Then, it computes the embedding vectors of both the whole question and the extracted entity names, using the same text embedding model employed during graph construction. The just mentioned vectors are then used in a similarity function (i.e., cosine similarity), which identifies the most similar Entity objects among the ones in the KG. The top-k most similar ones are kept, with $3 \leq k \leq 15$ empirically selected.

If no entity exceeds the similarity threshold of t (with $0.5 \leq t \leq 0.75$), the process moves to the Natural Language Formatter, which responds that no results exist for the current question. Otherwise, the process continues by identifying the top-o outgoing and top-i incoming Relationship objects to and from the Entity objects (with $5 \leq o, i \leq 10$ empirically selected). Also, the top-c Chunk objects are retrieved ($5 \leq c \leq 10$). All these objects are then serialized as strings and used, along with other information such as the original question and the user metadata, to construct a prompt for the Natural Language Formatter, which in turn answers to the user.

4 Validation Experiment

We set up a validation experiment to test the ability of the Graph-based RAG architecture to provide correct, accurate, complete, and satisfactory answers in the EE domain. Tests are conducted with a dataset encompassing EE question-answer pairs in different contexts and languages, based on guidance and regulatory documents from the EE field.

Implementation, deployment, and validation of our approach have been performed by incorporating our architecture into the *ENERGENIUS Guru*, a Decision Support System (DSS) in the domain of *EE* with a focus on the transparency and accountability of the knowledge sources, a contribution of the *ENERGENIUS* European project[1]. Since the project is currently in its early stages, real usage data are still being collected. However, as a preliminary investigation, we created a dataset with question-answer pairs simulating real user questions.

4.1 Validation Dataset

The dataset comprises a collection of source websites in Italian and a collection of 101 questions and answers pairs about energy consumption, EE, regulations, and incentives extracted from the websites. The questions are divided as follows:

- 25 questions & answers focusing on Italian regulation and incentives on EE;
- 25 questions & answers addressing Swiss regulations and incentives on EE;
- 51 questions & answers providing recommendations and suggestions on EE, applicable to both Italy and Switzerland.

Questions and answers are made available both in Italian and English to assess the proposed system's ability to answer in a multi-lingual context. A complete list of source websites, in addition to some examples of question-answer pairs, is provided in Appendix A.2.

4.2 Experimental Setup

This section outlines the experimental setup utilized for conducting our tests. Once downloaded the *Context Documents* from the just described source websites, we run the *Knowledge Extraction* by cleaning text corpora from page numbers or HTML tags[2], and then chunking them with $chunk\_size = 1000$, $chunk\_overlap = 200$[3]. Subsequently, we extract entities and relationships in the form of node-relationship-node triples using an LLM-based algorithm[4] using *gpt-4o-mini* by OpenAI. We do not use domain-specific knowledge coming from

---

[1] https://energenius-project.eu/.
[2] Html2TextTransformer by LangChain (langchain_community.document_transformers).
[3] RecursiveCharacterTextSplitter by LangChain (langchain_text_splitters).
[4] LLMGraphTransformer by LangChain (langchain_experimental.graph_transformers).

a domain expert. Once extracted, we standardize the syntax of entity and relationship names by replacing all occurrences of "_" with a space, converting the entire string to lowercase, and then capitalizing the first character only. Below is provided a prompt example used to extract triples from text corpora:

```
You are a top-tier algorithm designed for extracting information
in structured formats to build a knowledge graph. Your task is to
identify the entities and relations requested with the user prompt
from a given text. You must generate the output in a JSON format
containing a list with JSON objects. Each object should have the
keys: ''head'', ''head_type'', ''relation'', ''tail'', and ''tail_type''.
[..]
The ''relation'' key must contain the type of relation between the
''head'' and the ''tail''.
[..]
Attempt to extract as many entities and relations as you can.
Maintain Entity Consistency: When extracting entities, it's vital
to ensure consistency.
[..]
```

We initialize a *KG* in the *Knowledge Base* using the simple ontology described in the Sect. 3.2. We then fill it by iteratively adding the just extracted Entity and Relationship objects. Objects in the KG are identified by hashing their names with MD5. We also compute their name embeddings using the *text-embedding-3-small* model from OpenAI, as well as the chunked text corpora.

Once the Knowledge Base is ready, we simulate user interactions in *Runtime* part by posing the previously mentioned questions from document sources to the system. We pose questions both in Italian and English languages, and we ask the system to answer in the default user's language. This setting simulates the injection of user metadata from the *Auxiliary Tables* to the Knowledge Base. We used the same LLM model and embedding model as those used to populate the KG, *gpt-4o-mini* and *text-embedding-3-small* by OpenAI, respectively. For each question, once obtained the most similar $k = 12$ Entity objects (with $t = 0.5$), their $c = 5$ Chunk objects, and their $i = 10$ ingoing and $o = 10$ outgoing Relationship objects, the system provides these information to an LLM (in this case *gpt-4o-mini* by OpenAI) that produces the final answer using this prompt (derived from a previous study [4]):

```
---Role---
You are a helpful assistant responding to questions about data
in the tables provided.

---Goal---
Generate a response of the target length and format that responds
to the user's question, summarizing all information in the input
data tables appropriate for the response length and format, and
incorporating any relevant general knowledge.
If you don't know the answer, just say so. Do not make anything up.
Points supported by data should list their references as follows:
''This is an example sentence supported by multiple document
references [References: <page link>; <page link>].''

Do not list more than 5 record ids in a single reference. Instead,
list the top 5 most relevant record ids and add ''+more'' to
indicate that there are more.
[..]

Do not include information where the supporting evidence for it
```

is not provided.

```
---Target response length and format---
{"Single paragraph"}
Answer in {language}

---Data tables---
{context_data}

[..]
```

Add sections and commentary to the response as appropriate for
the length and format. Style the response in markdown.

5 Results

The validation experiment takes the 101 questions in both Italian and English and produces as output a list of answers. As an example, Appendix A.3 contains some of these answers. To assess whether our system is effective in answering EE-related questions, we adopt the human-based evaluation paradigm. In our case, this involves engaging domain experts, who are equipped with ground-truth answers, to assess and classify the responses as either valid or not by using the RAGAs framework guidelines [6]. In particular, an answer is valid if it respects all the three RAGAs properties: *faithfullness* (i.e., "the answer should be grounded in the given context"), *answer relevance* (i.e., "the generated answer should address the actual question that was provided"), and *context relevance* (i.e., "the retrieved context should be focused, containing as little irrelevant information as possible"). Experts must proportionally decrease an answer's score when it fails to meet one or more of the required properties until it reaches zero.

Based on our human-based evaluation conducted with $n = 4$ domain experts, we achieve an overall answer validity score of $75.2 \pm 2.7\%$, with an average score of $77.4 \pm 2.9\%$ for responses in Italian language and $73.0 \pm 2.5\%$ for responses in English. A complete report, categorized by both the question-answer language and the context country, can be found in Table 1.

Table 1. Validation experiment results categorized by both language and context country. The experiment is conducted by asking domain experts to assess the answers using the RAGAs properties.

		Context country:			
		IT (25)	CH (25)	Both (51)	All (101)
Language:	IT (101)	$73.3 \pm 0.8\%$	$74.4 \pm 1.9\%$	$81.0 \pm 4.1\%$	$77.4 \pm 2.9\%$
	EN (101)	$73.6 \pm 1.0\%$	$67.7 \pm 2.4\%$	$75.2 \pm 2.9\%$	$73.0 \pm 2.5\%$
	All (202)	$73.4 \pm 0.9\%$	$71.2 \pm 2.1\%$	$78.1 \pm 3.0\%$	$75.2 \pm 2.7\%$

Each question is answered in 19.08 ± 4.48 seconds on average, and involves a fixed number of 2 LLM calls and a variable number of embedding calls depending on the question's complexity, averaging at 3.55 ± 1.01 calls per question.

Ablation Experiment. We performed an ablation experiment in which the RAG answered the 101 questions without any component representing persistent memory or retrieval. In this configuration, the system operates as an LLM-only architecture. The obtained results show that retrieval technology is needed to answer domain-specific questions effectively. The system correctly answers basic or general questions on EE, but in most cases, answers are excessively long and sometimes contain inaccuracies. For instance, when asked why consumption is higher in winter, it reply that "winter causes more frequent baths or showers for hygiene reasons". On the other hand, answers to specific questions, like those about Italian or Swiss regulations, are mostly incorrect and often contain hallucinations or random information. Sometimes, instead of providing a direct answer, they suggest the user search online for the information. For instance, this is the answer to the maximum deductible spending limit in Italy in 2025, which is set to 5,000 euros: "maximum deductible spending limit [..] in Italy for 2025 is set at 8,000 euros [..] please verify this information with the official sources".

6 Discussion

According to domain experts, the validation experiment results in Table 1 indicate that the system produces valid responses in approximately three out of four of the cases. When results are grouped by language, English responses perform almost as well as Italian ones, though slightly lower. This finding demonstrates how the multilingual capabilities of LLMs allow for valid semantic comprehension when information is provided or requested in different languages. The results show a 4.4% reduction in answer accuracy due to translation errors. Finally, the ablation experiment demonstrated the need for systems tasked to answer domain-specific questions of having a retrieval component.

Categorizing results by context country shows how the system scores near the same for country-specific answers (i.e., answers for Italy and Switzerland), while it works slightly better for country-agnostic ones (i.e., answers marked as "both"). In our source documents, country-agnostic questions often allude to general and discursive information, whereas country-specific ones refer more to laws and articles. The slight decrease in performance for this class of questions could be due to laws or articles containing complex information linked by temporal or spatial constraints, which are harder to extract and manage compared to simpler information or general recommendations.

By categorizing the results both by context country and language, we confirm the findings highlighted above. In particular, performance are above average for country-agnostic concepts and in Italian language, but slightly lower for country-specific concepts in a different language from the original documents.

7 Conclusion

Our research highlights the potential of an LLM-based system coupled with a KG-enhanced RAG architecture for EE. This approach enables the system to offer tailored recommendations by integrating domain-specific knowledge such as regulations and incentives on EE.

The LLM-based parsing process of documents allows for automated extraction of entity-relationship-entity triples, which does not require human intervention in most cases. If requested, a domain expert could impose the use of specific terminology or information to the extraction system.

The local reasoning process begins with the most relevant Entity objects in the KG and extends to their neighboring entities, ensuring that the answers are both accurate and contextually enriched. Additionally, results show that performance in Italian and English is similar, proving that LLMs can answer in different languages than the original sources. This allows for a clear separation between the content and the language. Our validation experiment using 101 question-answer pairs in two different languages with domain experts following the RAGAs framework guidelines achieves an overall score of $75.2\pm2.7\%$, demonstrating the validity of our architecture in the field of EE. The best performance is achieved in country-agnostic questions in Italian, with $81.0 \pm 4.1\%$.

Limitations. While this preliminary study highlights our architecture's potential in aiding users with EE, as the *ENERGENIUS* project advances, we will continuously gather and analyze data to enhance it and confirm these initial findings. Moreover, testing the architecture should involve a variety of different LLMs and text embedding systems. To better validate multilingualism, it will be necessary to conduct tests in a broader range of languages beyond those already evaluated with source documents and question-answer pairs in this study.

Acknowledgments. This research was funded by the European Union's Horizon Europe Research and Innovation Framework, under Grant Agreement No 101160720. We acknowledge the use of AI-based tools for grammar corrections. The architecture is inspired by "Knowledge Graph & Graph Retrieval-Augmented Generation (RAG)", an ISWC 2024 Tutorial[7] (https://github.com/kellm-fit/ISWC_tutorial). We extend our gratitude to the domain experts, whose assistance was fundamental in conducting the validation experiment.

A Appendix

This section includes additional information about the validation experiment, specifically listing the source documents used to extract domain-specific knowledge and some of the question-answer pairs used to test the system.

A.1 Source Documents

The source websites used to extract questions and answers to test the system are the following.

- Italian State Revenue Agency:
  - https://www.agenziaentrate.gov.it/portale/web/guest/aree-tematiche/casa/agevolazioni/bonus-mobili-ed-elettrodomestici

- AEG Cooperative:
  - https://www.aegcoop.it/lavatrice-risparmiare/
  - https://www.aegcoop.it/migliori-lampadine/
  - https://www.aegcoop.it/risparmiare-con-gli-elettrodomestici/
  - https://www.aegcoop.it/consumi-standby-elettrodomestici/
  - https://www.aegcoop.it/risparmiare-acqua-calda/
  - https://www.aegcoop.it/riscaldamento-elettrico/
- Luce-gas.it:
  - https://luce-gas.it/guida/risparmio-energetico
- SvizzeraEnergia:
  - https://www.svizzeraenergia.ch/casa/
  - https://www.svizzeraenergia.ch/casa/riscaldamento/
  - https://www.svizzeraenergia.ch/energie-rinnovabili/teleriscaldamento/
- TicinoEnergia:
  - https://ticinoenergia.ch/it/domande-frequenti.html
- Federal Department of the Environment, Transport, Energy and Communications:
  - https://www.uvek.admin.ch/uvek/it/home/datec/votazioni/votazione-sulla-legge-sull-energia/efficienza-energetica.html.

A.2 Question-Answer Pairs Dataset

Here are some question-answer pairs from the dataset in both Italian and English. The system's responses, obtained from the validation experiment, are recorded in Appendix A.3.

IT Qual è il tetto massimo di spesa detraibile nel 2025 per il bonus mobili ed elettrodomestici in Italia?—5.000 euro.
EN What is the maximum deductible spending limit in 2025 for the furniture and household appliances bonus in Italy?—5.000 euros.

IT Quante ore di riscaldamento giornaliere nella zona climatica F in Italia?—Nessuna limitazione.
EN How many hours of heating per day in climate zone F in Italy?—No limitations.

IT Quali sono i vantaggi delle lampadine LED?—Minore consumo energetico, durata maggiore, eco-sostenibilità, illuminazione di elevata qualità e migliore tecnologia.
EN What are the advantages of LED bulbs?—Lower energy consumption, longer life, eco-sustainability, high-quality lighting and better technology.

IT Quanto consuma una lampadina LED?—Tra 1 e 11 W all'ora.
EN How much does an LED bulb consume?—Between 1 and 11 W per hour.

IT Perché si consuma più acqua calda in inverno?—A causa delle basse temperature.
EN Why do we consume more hot water in winter?—Due to the low temperatures.

IT Cosa è l'EtichettaEnergia in Svizzera?—Un'etichetta che fornisce informazioni sugli apparecchi elettrici.
EN What is the Energy label in Switzerland?—A label providing information about electrical appliances.

IT Qual è la legge che definisce la superficie determinante nel Canton Ticino?—La Legge edilizia cantonale (LE), art. 38, cpv. 3.
EN What is the law that defines the determining surface area in the Canton of Ticino?—The Cantonal Building Law (LE), art. 38, paragraph 3.

A.3 Results

This section presents the results of our validation experiment, including example answers to the questions from Appendix A.2.

IT Nel 2025, il tetto massimo di spesa detraibile per il bonus mobili ed elettrodomestici in Italia è fissato a 5.000 euro. Questa detrazione Irpef si applica per l'acquisto di mobili e grandi elettrodomestici destinati ad arredare un immobile oggetto di ristrutturazione. È importante notare che l'importo deve essere ripartito in dieci quote annuali di pari importo e il pagamento deve essere effettuato tramite bonifico o carta di debito/credito, escludendo altri mezzi di pagamento come assegni o contante [Ref: https://www.agenziaentrate.gov.it/portale/web/guest/aree-tematiche/casa/agevolazioni/bonus-mobili-ed-elettrodomestici].

EN In 2025, the maximum deductible spending limit for the furniture and household appliances bonus in Italy is set at 5,000 euros. This amount includes any associated transportation and assembly costs, and the deduction must be divided into ten equal annual installments [Ref: https://www.agenziaentrate.gov.it/portale/web/guest/aree-tematiche/casa/agevolazioni/bonus-mobili-ed-elettrodomestici].

IT Nella zona climatica F, che è caratterizzata da gradi-giorno superiori a 3000, non è prevista alcuna limitazione per l'accensione degli impianti di riscaldamento. Ciò significa che il riscaldamento può essere attivato in qualsiasi momento dell'anno, senza restrizioni di giorni o orari [Ref: https://luce-gas.it/guida/risparmio-energetico].

EN In climate zone F, there are no limitations on the heating period, meaning that heating can be utilized without specific restrictions on days or hours [Ref: https://luce-gas.it/guida/risparmio-energetico].

IT Le lampadine LED offrono numerosi vantaggi rispetto alle lampadine tradizionali. Innanzitutto, presentano un'efficienza energetica superiore, consentendo un risparmio di energia fino al 90% rispetto alle lampadine alogene e a incandescenza, e fino all'80% rispetto alle lampadine fluorescenti. Inoltre, la loro durata media è significativamente più lunga, variando tra 35.000 e 50.000 ore, rispetto alle sole 1.000 ore delle lampadine a incandescenza, riducendo così i costi di sostituzione. Infine, le lampadine LED non contengono sostanze chimiche tossiche, rendendole più ecologiche rispetto alle lampadine a risparmio energetico che possono contenere mercurio [Ref: https://www.aegcoop.it/migliori-lampadine/]. Questi fattori rendono le lampadine LED una scelta vantaggiosa sia dal punto di vista economico che ambientale.

EN LED bulbs offer several significant advantages over traditional lighting options. Firstly, they are highly energy-efficient, consuming much less power; for instance, an LED bulb uses only 5 W compared to 60 W for an incandescent bulb, resulting in substantial energy savings. Additionally, LED bulbs have a longer lifespan, which reduces the frequency of replacements and contributes to lower overall costs. They also support advanced features such as dimmability and smart technology, allowing users to control brightness and color remotely. Furthermore, LED technology is more sustainable, making it a better choice for environmentally conscious consumers [Ref: https://www.aegcoop.it/migliori-lampadine/]. Overall, the combination of energy efficiency, longevity, versatility, and sustainability makes LED bulbs a superior lighting option.

IT Le lampadine LED hanno un consumo che varia generalmente tra i 3 e gli 11 W all'ora, con alcune tipologie che possono consumare solo 1 W all'ora. Questo è notevolmente ridotto rispetto alle lampadine tradizionali, poiché una lampadina LED da 11 W può emettere la stessa quantità di luce di una lampadina a incandescenza da 110–120 Watt. Ad esempio, una lampadina LED da 3 W consuma circa 0,003 kWh in un'ora di funzionamento, permettendo di illuminare un'intera casa con un consumo equivalente a quello di una singola lampadina a incandescenza [Ref: https://www.aegcoop.it/migliori-lampadine/].

EN LED bulbs are known for their energy efficiency, typically consuming between **3 to 11 W per hour**, with some models using as little as **1 W per hour**. For instance, a **3-watt LED bulb** can produce the same amount of light as a traditional **110–120 watt incandescent bulb**. This significant reduction in power consumption translates to substantial savings on electricity bills, allowing an entire home to be illuminated with LED lights while consuming the same energy as a single incandescent bulb [Ref: https://www.aegcoop.it/migliori-lampadine/].

IT In inverno, il consumo di acqua calda tende ad aumentare a causa delle basse temperature esterne, che spingono le persone a cercare comfort attraverso l'uso di docce calde e bagni. Durante i mesi invernali, è comune consumare una quantità di acqua calda superiore rispetto al resto dell'anno, poiché le persone desiderano riscaldarsi e rilassarsi dopo una giornata fredda. Ad esempio, un bagno può richiedere fino a quattro volte più acqua rispetto a una doccia, contribuendo così a un aumento significativo della bolletta del gas o dell'elettricità, a seconda del tipo di riscaldamento utilizzato [Ref: https://www.aegcoop.it/risparmiare-acqua-calda/; https://www.svizzeraenergia.ch/energie-rinnovabili/teleriscaldamento/].

EN In winter, the demand for hot water increases primarily due to the colder temperatures, which lead to higher usage for heating and personal hygiene. During this season, people tend to take longer showers and use more hot water for heating purposes, such as in radiators or underfloor heating systems. Additionally, appliances like dishwashers and washing machines often require hot water, further contributing to increased consumption. The relationship between winter months and hot water consumption is evident as colder weather necessitates more heating and comfort measures [Ref: https://ticinoenergia.ch/it/domande-frequenti.html; https://www.svizzeraenergia.ch/casa/riscaldamento/].

IT L'**etichettaEnergia** in Svizzera è un sistema di etichettatura che fornisce informazioni chiare e uniformi sui consumi energetici degli apparecchi elettrici, aiutando i consumatori a fare scelte più informate. Essa include dettagli come la classe di efficienza energetica, il consumo di energia, e altre caratteristiche importanti come il livello di rumore e il consumo d'acqua. Le etichette possono presentare un codice QR che consente l'accesso a ulteriori informazioni nella banca dati europea dei prodotti. L'etichettaEnergia si applica a vari gruppi di prodotti, tra cui frigoriferi e congelatori, e mira a proteggere sia l'ambiente che il portafoglio dei consumatori [Ref: https://www.svizzeraenergia.ch/casa/; https://www.svizzeraenergia.ch/casa/riscaldamento/; https://www.svizzeraenergia.ch/energie-rinnovabili/teleriscaldamento/].

EN The Energy label in Switzerland, known as "Etichettaenergia," provides clear information about the energy consumption and efficiency of electrical appliances. It categorizes products on a scale from A to G, indicating their energy efficiency, and includes additional details such as noise levels and water consumption. The label is designed to help consumers make informed choices when purchasing appliances, promoting energy efficiency and environmental protection. In Switzerland, both QR-coded and non-QR-coded labels are accepted, ensuring that consumers can access further product information through a European database [Ref: https://www.svizzeraenergia.ch/casa/riscaldamento/; https://www.svizzeraenergia.ch/casa/].

IT La legge che definisce la superficie determinante nel Canton Ticino è l'articolo 38, comma 3 della Legge edilizia cantonale (LE). Secondo questa legge, la superficie determinante è parificata alla superficie edificata e si riferisce alla proiezione sul piano orizzontale dell'ingombro dell'edificio. Inoltre, è importante notare che l'impianto solare deve coprire una superficie pari al 50% della superficie determinante [Ref: https://ticinoenergia.ch/it/domande-frequenti.html].

EN The law that defines the determining surface area in the Canton of Ticino is outlined in the "Regolamento sull'utilizzazione dell'energia" (RUEn). This regulation specifies that the roofs and/or facades of new buildings with a determining surface area greater than 300 m^2 must be equipped with solar systems (both photovoltaic and thermal) until December 31, 2025 [Ref: https://ticinoenergia.ch/it/domande-frequenti.html].

References

1. Arslan, M., Ghanem, H., Munawar, S., Cruz, C.: A Survey on RAG with LLMs. Proc. Comput. Sci. **246**, 3781–3790 (2024), 28th International Conference on Knowledge Based and Intelligent Information and Engineering Systems (KES 2024)
2. Arslan, M., Mahdjoubi, L., Munawar, S.: Driving sustainable energy transitions with a multi-source RAG-LLM system. Energy Build. **324**, 114827 (2024)
3. Bruzzone, A., Giovannetti, A., Genta, G., Cefaliello, D.: Generative AI and Retrieval-Augmented Generation (RAG) in an agent-based simulation framework for urban planning. In: International Conference on Modelling and Applied Simulation (2023)
4. Edge, D., Trinh, H., Cheng, N., Bradley, J., Chao, A., Mody, A., Truitt, S., Larson, J.: From Local to Global: A Graph RAG Approach to Query-Focused Summarization (2024)
5. Eichman, J., Torrecillas Castelló, M., Corchero, C.: Reviewing and exploring the qualitative impacts that different market and regulatory measures can have on encouraging energy communities based on their organizational structure. Energies **15**(6), 2016 (2022)
6. Es, S., James, J., Espinosa Anke, L., Schockaert, S.: RAGAs: automated evaluation of retrieval augmented generation. In: Aletras, N., De Clercq, O. (eds.) 18th Conference of the European Chapter of the ACL: System Demonstrations, pp. 150–158. Association for Computational Linguistics, St. Julians, Malta (Mar 2024)
7. European Parliament and Council of European Union: Directive (EU) 2023/1791 of the European Parliament and of the Council of 13 September 2023 on energy efficiency and amending Regulation (EU) 2023/955 (recast) (2021)
8. European Parliament and Council of European Union: Regulation (EU) 2021/1119 of the European Parliament and of the Council of 30 June 2021 establishing the framework for achieving climate neutrality and amending Regulations (EC) No 401/2009 and (EU) 2018/1999 ("European Climate Law") (2021)

9. European Parliament and Council of European Union: Regulation (EU) 2021/1119 of the European Parliament and of the Council of 10 May 2023 establishing a Social Climate Fund and amending Regulation (EU) 2021/1060 (2023)
10. Fortuna, C., Hanžel, V., Bertalanič, B.: Natural Language Interaction with a Household Electricity Knowledge-based Digital Twin (2024)
11. Fouiteh, I., Cabrera Santelices, J.D., Patel, M.K.: How committed are swiss utilities to energy saving without being obligated to do so? Utilities Policy **82**, 101582 (2023). https://doi.org/10.1016/j.jup.2023.101582
12. Frieden, D., Tuerk, A., Neumann, C., d'Herbemont, S., Roberts, J.: Collective Self-consumption and Energy Communities: Trends and Challenges n the Transposition of the EU Framework. COMPILE, Graz, Austria (2020)
13. Giudici, M., et al.: Assessing LLMs responses in the field of domestic sustainability: an exploratory study. In: 2023 Third International Conference on Digital Data Processing (DDP), pp. 42–48. IEEE (2023)
14. Huang, L., et al.: A survey on hallucination in large language models: principles, taxonomy, challenges, and open questions. ACM Trans. Inf. Syst. **43**(2) (Jan 2025). https://doi.org/10.1145/3703155
15. Lewis, P., et al.: Retrieval-augmented generation for knowledge-intensive NLP Tasks. In: Larochelle, H., Ranzato, M., Hadsell, R., Balcan, M., Lin, H. (eds.) Advances in Neural Information Processing Systems, vol. 33, pp. 9459–9474. Curran Associates, Inc. (2020)
16. Lowitzsch, J., Hoicka, C.E., van Tulder, F.J.: Renewable energy communities under the 2019 European Clean Energy Package – Governance model for the energy clusters of the future? Renew. Sustain. Energy Rev. **122** (2020)
17. Sanguinetti, M., Pani, A., Perniciano, A., Zedda, L., Loddo, A., Atzori, M.: Assessing Italian large language models on energy feedback generation: a human evaluation Study. In: 10th International Conference on Computational Linguistics (CLiC-it) (2024)

GoRS - A Neuro-Symbolic, User-Centric, and Goal-Oriented Recommendation System for DIY-Projects

Jan-David Stütz[1,2]( ), Luca Mario Ziegler Felix[1], Oliver Karras[3], Allard Oelen[3], and Sören Auer[2,3]

[1] Robert Bosch GmbH, Gerlingen, Germany
{jan-david.stuetz,lucamario.zieglerfelix}@de.bosch.com
[2] Leibniz University Hannover, Hanover, Germany
[3] Leibniz Information Centre for Science and Technology (TIB), Hanover, Germany
{oliver.karras,allard.oelen,soeren.auer}@tib.eu

Abstract. In the context of e-commerce, reliable and fitting recommendations are of paramount importance. They help users make faster and more informed purchasing decisions while enhancing satisfaction, engagement, and loyalty. However, delivering such personalized and effective recommendations presents several challenges. Most recommendation systems (RS) rely on sentiment analysis, user goal guessing, and predictions, each of which comes with its own difficulties. We introduce GoRS (Goal-oriented RS), a neuro-symbolic, user-centric, and goal-oriented RS in the Do-it-Yourself (DIY) context. GoRS generates a step-by-step guide tailored to the user's previously entered goal and recommends fitting products like saws, drills, and sanding machines according to each step and the specific restrictions of a user's goal. Therefore, GoRS utilizes the flexible structure of Knowledge Graphs (KGs) and the reasoning capabilities of Large Language Models (LLMs), which makes it a novel neuro-symbolic RS. We evaluated our approach through a between-subject study. Users were asked to create and review their step-by-step guide and recommended products based on a predefined DIY goal and complete a questionnaire investigating, among other things, user satisfaction, workload, and efficiency. The results indicate a significant correlation between mental workload, efficiency, user satisfaction, and user experience—as mental workload decreases, efficiency improves, and user satisfaction and experience increase. Based on our findings, we suggest adopting our novel approach and encouraging the integration of goal-oriented RSs to enhance user satisfaction and experience, efficiency, and trust while providing more intuitive, personalized, and effective recommendations.

Keywords: Recommendation System · Neuro-Symbolic · User-Centric

1 Introduction

Recommendation Systems (RS) are omnipresent in many modern e-commerce and are required to overcome the vast amount of information users are exposed to [1]. Besides providing personalized recommendations leading to more satisfied users, RS also increases sales and benefits sellers [1,33]. However, recent studies have shown that as users purchase recommended products more frequently, the relevance of future recommendations declines, leading to a mismatch with user preferences and, consequently, a decrease in user satisfaction [14,33].

Many RS rely on purchase history, user reviews, and product description and leverage machine learning, Natural Language Processing (NLP), or deep learning to recommend products to users [15,17,28]. Even though they use the latest technology advancements, they still suffer from problems like cold start, unpredictability about new products, miscalculation of a user sentiment or goal, and flooding unnecessary products because of changes in user interest [3,9,17,28].

To overcome those challenges, we present a novel neuro-symbolic, user-centric, and goal-oriented RS dubbed GoRS. By leveraging the reasoning capabilities of Large Language Models (LLMs) and the flexible structure of Knowledge Graphs (KGs), GoRS dynamically generates personalized step-by-step guides based on user-defined goals and provides highly relevant product recommendations for each step.

We evaluated GoRS through a between-subject study, where participants were divided into an experimental group, using GoRS to generate a step-by-step guide and select relevant products, and a baseline group, which manually created a guide and selected products through the Bosch Do-it-Yourself (DIY) shop[1]. Participants were tasked with completing one of two predefined DIY projects. After completing the task, participants completed a questionnaire, including the NASA Task Load Index (TLX), the User Experience Questionnaire (UEQ), and additional questions investigating user satisfaction and efficiency.

The results of our experimental evaluation show that this work provides a novel approach that improves RS through the integration of neuro-symbolic methods, enhancing personalization and goal alignment. This approach tackles issues such as cognitive overload and accuracy in recommendations. As a result, it not only improves the accuracy of recommendations but also makes it easier for users to process information, leading to higher satisfaction and a better overall experience. Additionally, it helps resolve typical problems like cold starts and information overload.

The following work is structured as follows: Sect. 2 provides an overview of related work relevant to our approach, which is detailed in Sect. 3. Section 4 outlines the methodology and experimental design, while Sect. 5 presents the results. In Sect. 6, we discuss the findings and their limitations, followed by Sect. 7, which concludes the paper and suggests directions for future research.

2 Related Work

In the context of e-commerce, RS leverages various approaches that can be grouped into distinct categories. These include popularity-based, content-based,

---

[1] https://www.bosch-diy.com/de/de.

knowledge-based, AI-based, and hybrid RS, which are prominent in current scientific research [1,25,32]. All of them have their own advantages and disadvantages; thus, their use depends on the unique desired characteristic and, consequently, the goal of the RS.

In general, RS in e-commerce is often designed to enhance user satisfaction and to increase a company's profit [19,20]. Ghanew et al. even suggest following a hybrid recommendation strategy, putting more weight on users but without ignoring profitability [9]. As a consequence of a more customer-centric approach, Khatter et al. state that effective RS enhances user experience and engagement while simultaneously driving increased sales for companies [19]. He et al. and Aslaity and Tran highlight the importance of aligning recommendations with user goals to enhance satisfaction [3,11]. While He et al. argue that user satisfaction increases when the recommendation results align with a user's shopping goal [11], Aslaity and Tran [3] propose goal modeling as a method to support the selection of appropriate recommendation algorithms to achieve the same [3,11].

2.1 Artificial Intelligence in Recommendation Systems

There are many different areas where RS are used. Consequently, those RS use techniques that differ in their focus. The work of Bawack et al. aims to uncover current research trends in the existing literature on AI in e-commerce [4]. Their bibliometric study revealed that current research on AI in e-commerce focuses primarily on RS [4]. The work of Valencia-Arias et al. even shows a growth of 97.16% in the AI literature in RS [32]. The authors further revealed that data mining is crucial for extracting relevant data needed to recommend products, that sentiment analysis is vital in RS, and that recurrent neural networks are of significant interest in current research [32].

While Valencia-Arias et al. examine RS in e-commerce broadly, Landim and Bazaki focus their literature review specifically on RS in fashion-related e-commerce, with an emphasis on chatbot design approaches [21]. Almahmood and Tekerek provide a literature review in the specific area of deep learning [2]. Their study demonstrated that deep learning algorithms, including convolutional and recurrent neural networks and sentiment analysis techniques, are particularly effective in addressing recommendation challenges [2]. These approaches are especially beneficial for tackling common issues such as the cold start problem and data sparsity [2,21].

While the aforementioned works focus on reviewing existing literature to identify trends, highlight successful approaches, and propose future research directions, other studies contribute by introducing novel methods for recommending products. So does the work of Islek and Oguducu, which presents a hierarchical RS, called DeepIDRS, which leverages user reviews and deep learning techniques [15]. This approach demonstrates superior performance on a real-world dataset when compared to competing RS [15].

Shankar et al. focus on user reviews, too [28]. The authors argue that NLP sentiment is often done in content-based filtering of user reviews and present an intelligent RS using ensemble learning and NLP sentiment analysis [28]. In addition, Cabrera-Sánchez et al. investigate the factors influencing consumer adoption and usage of AI-driven online purchase RS [5]. Their study employs an adapted version of the Unified Theory of Acceptance and Use of Technology (UTAUT) 2 model to analyze these factors [5].

Based on the presented related work in this subsection, we examine AI-driven techniques such as sentiment analysis, deep learning, and neural networks and underscore the necessity of innovative approaches like neuro-symbolic reasoning in addressing challenges like goal alignment and data sparsity. This relevance reinforces GoRS's novel contribution as a user-centric, goal-oriented recommendation system that improves personalization and efficiency in DIY project planning.

2.2 Knowledge Graphs in Recommendation Systems

While many RS rely on traditional AI approaches, symbolic techniques such as KGs and ontologies are increasingly being employed to enhance performance and interpretability.

For instance, Deng et al. propose a graph-based RS, UNICORN, which is a conversational RS [6]. Unlike traditional conversational systems that infer user intent or goals through dialogue, our approach allows users to specify their goals directly, eliminating the need for conversational inference [6].

The integration of ontologies in RS has also shown promise, as explored in the work of Karthik and Ganapathy [18]. Ontologies facilitate the structuring of domain-specific knowledge, enabling more effective reasoning and personalized recommendations by explicitly representing the relationships between concepts within a domain [18]. Therefore, Karthik and Ganapathy presented an algorithm for computing the sentimental score for products to recommend them more accurately and dynamically based on ontology alignment [18].

Kartheek and Sajeev also propose a semantic-based RS [17]. The authors argue that RS still suffers from the problem of a cold-start [17]. They argue that these problems could be resolved by using KGs since they provide semantic explanations of recommendations through link prediction and graph embedding techniques for extracting the semantics [17].

An RS that also utilizes neuro-symbolic techniques is presented by Zao et al. Concretely, they use LLMs for industrial RS through an inferential KG by capturing user intent transitions [34]. Their results already demonstrate a significant performance improvement compared to existing approaches [34].

Based on the presented approaches and their semantic-based techniques, such as knowledge graphs, it highlights the relevance of a neuro-symbolic foundation, where knowledge graphs provide precise product information, consequently reinforcing a system's ability to provide structured, user-centric, and context-aware suggestions.

3 Approach

RS that utilize neuro-symbolic techniques, such as incorporating KGs or leveraging LLMs, are already well-documented in the current literature. However, to the best of our knowledge, a neuro-symbolic approach that is further user-centric and goal-oriented for product recommendation has not been introduced yet.

In this section, we present such an approach, dubbed GoRS and displayed in Fig. 1, outlining its requirements and highlighting the unique characteristics that set it apart from existing methods.

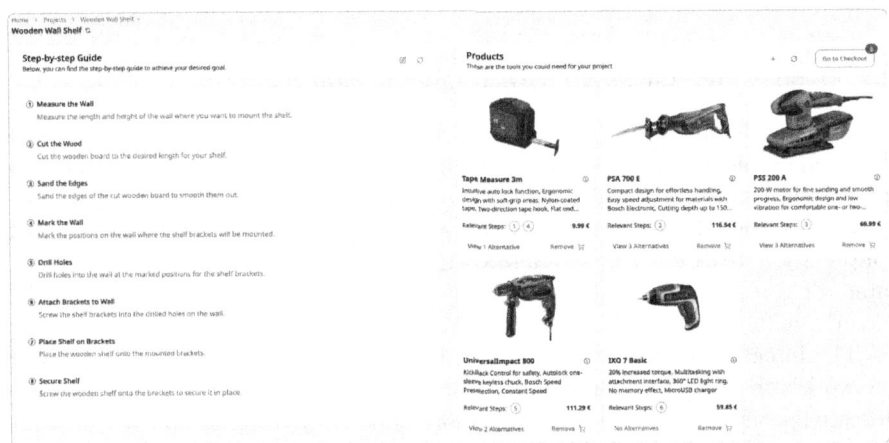

Fig. 1. Step-by-step guide and the recommended products side by side.

3.1 Application Requirements

To ensure the application's functionality aligns with user needs and provides an intuitive and efficient experience, we designed the system to minimize task load, maximize user satisfaction, reduce the time required for achieving goals, and ensure the recommendation of highly relevant and fitting products. These considerations are central to delivering an effective and user-friendly solution (as measured in the work of Fang and Zhan, Ziegfeld et al. [8,35]). To achieve this, we require the application to meet the following requirements:
The application shall be able to...

$R1$: allow users to enter their DIY goal.
$R2$: generate a guide defined by the user's goal.
$R3$: recommend relevant products based on the generated step-by-step guide.
$R4$: show alternatives to the recommended products that still fit a single step of the guide.
$R5$: indicate to which step(s) a recommended product belongs.

R6: allow editing of the guide.
R7: show differences between the suggested product and the found alternatives.
R8: allow users to replace recommended products.
R9: allow users to add new products from the product catalog.

3.2 Neuro-Symbolic, User-Centric, and Goal-Oriented Recommendation System

Sentiment analysis and user goal analysis are considered a challenging task in modern RS [7,13,27]. GoRS bypasses guessing a user's goal and intention by simply asking for the goal and offering a service around that goal. Therefore, a user enters the goal and receives a step-by-step guide and, based on that, product recommendations. This process is further presented in technical detail in Fig. 2.

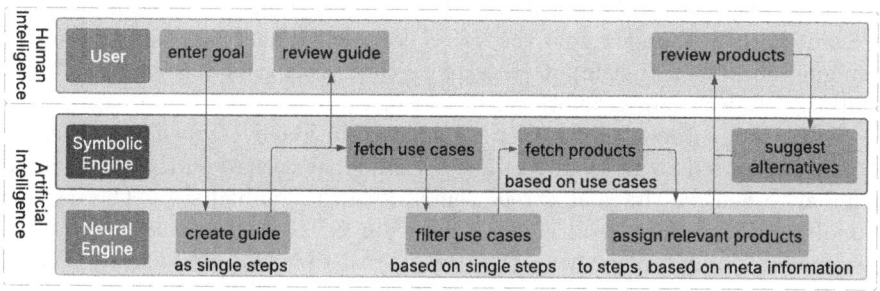

Fig. 2. Process of Generating the Guide and Recommending Products.

Knowledge Graph Preparation. Many RS leverage KGs to store relevant information for product recommendations or to take advantage of a KG's reasoning capabilities [12,29]. In our approach, we capitalize on the dynamic structuring possibilities KGs offer. Unlike conventional databases, where columns must be predefined, KGs allow the usage of flexible properties and semantic relationships. This enables us to link products not only based on their similarities but also by explicitly highlighting their differences.

To create the initial draft of our KG, we scraped product information from the Bosch shop, extracting relevant details such as titles, descriptions, prices, images, and more. This comprehensive dataset served as the foundation for our KG.

We processed the scraped data through a pipeline integrated with an LLM to enrich the KG with more specific product characteristics, such as the cutting depth of saws or the materials suitable for a drill. This process involved using a predefined template that specified the required properties, such as *use-case*, which reflects the intended purpose of a product (e.g., sawing, drilling, or sanding). By passing this structured template to the LLM, we ensured that the extracted information aligned with our desired schema, resulting in a well-organized and semantically rich KG. Subsequently, we refined the KG by clustering products based on their use cases and leveraging the LLM to establish connections between products by highlighting their differences. Consequently, each product in the KG holds at least one property that links to an alternative and indicates their differences. This process was not performed continuously but rather triggered only when a new product was added to the catalog. By clustering products, identifying their differences, and dynamically linking alternatives, the KG became a powerful resource for providing detailed and contextually relevant recommendations.

Step-by-Step Guide Generation. Before GoRS can recommend products, it is essential to first understand the user's goal and generate a tailored step-by-step guide based on that input. To achieve this, users must describe their goals in clear, detailed, and straightforward terms.

GoRS then processes the user's goal description by embedding it into a prompt optimized to generate the desired guide structured so that each action required to achieve the goal is represented as an individual step. The backend of GoRS utilizes the neural engine (based on GPT-4o) to create and stream the generated guide directly to the user in real-time. We decided on GPT-4o since we assume an appropriate tradeoff between reasoning capabilities, content generation, and costs.

Recommend Products Based on the Step-by-Step Guide. Once the guide is finalized, GoRS's recommendation engine is ready to generate tailored product recommendations. Figure 3 outlines the steps involved in this process.

First, GoRS identifies relevant use cases for each step by extracting all use cases from the KG and passing them to the neural engine, which assigns the best-fitting use case (e.g., sawing, drilling, sanding) to the steps. Next, the symbolic engine retrieves all products based on the identified use case of each step individually. Next, each individual step and all found products that belong to one use case, and thus one step, are passed to the neural engine. The neural engine then selects the most suitable product for each step based on the detailed product information (descriptions, materials, and all the custom properties). The final product recommendations are then returned to the user for review, ensuring alignment with the user's guide and, thus, goal.

Review Guide and Recommendations. Users have full control to review and refine the guide, as well as replace recommended products with alternatives. Feedback to the guide can be provided in natural language, enabling users to adjust the guide intuitively. This feedback is processed by the neural engine,

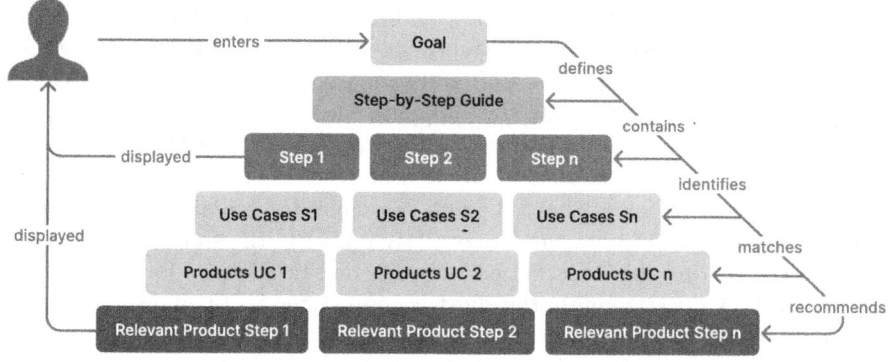

Fig. 3. GoRS recommendation workflow mapping user goals to step-by-step guides and product recommendations.

which regenerates the guide and reruns the recommendation engine to produce updated recommendations based on the revised guide.

If users are dissatisfied with any recommended product, they can also replace it with alternatives. GoRS facilitates this process by suggesting alternatives and indicating the differences between the original recommendation and the alternatives. Those differences have been initially generated, stored, and linked in the KG. Additionally, users have the option to manually browse the product catalog and select a desired product if none of the suggested alternatives meet their needs.

4 Methodology

Ghanem et al. state that repeated bad UX while interacting with an RS might ultimately drive consumers away from the service in the long run [9]. Therefore, we consider it crucial to measure the UX of GoRS. Additionally, Jin et al. investigated a connection between mental load, user controls, and RS's performance [16]. Building on the findings of Longo and Dondio and Schmutz et al., which demonstrate a connection between usability and mental workload, we consider evaluating mental workload alongside UX as a critical factor to gain new insights [23,24,26].

Even though Ghanem et al. argue that consumers might accept non-optimal, more profit-driven recommendations, they may lose their trust in the long run [9]. Nevertheless, we also want to investigate the willingness of GoRS's users to buy the selected products and to gather opinions on the price-performance ratio of the recommended products.

Study Design. To evaluate GoRS, we conducted a between-subject study focusing on the UX, mental workload, and price-performance ratio. We chose a between-subject study to ensure unbiased mental workload measurement, avoiding learning effects and carryover bias from a within-subject design. All study participants, regardless of whether they belonged to the experimental or control group, received the task to create a step-by-step guide for building a *stone table* or a *wooden shelf mounted to the wall* and to place all needed products that are required to realize the guide into the shopping cart.

While the experimental group used GoRS to achieve that task, the control group had to create the guide manually and use the Bosch shop for the product selection. It must be noted that the guide is required to validate if all products required to meet the initial goal are correctly added to the shopping cart.

After completing that task, all participants had to fill out a form containing the NASA TLX questionnaire, the short version of the UEQ, and some custom questions aiming to uncover the experience of a participant, the willingness to buy the products, as well as the perceived price-performance ratio, and the time needed to complete the task[2].

Sample. We published a call for participation in various mailing lists at Bosch to participate in one of the two groups. Participation was voluntary and anonymous; therefore, no personal information was collected. In total, we gathered the data from 19 participants for the experimental group and 11 for the baseline group. One experimental group participant submitted only one product, which did not meet his guide and was consequently removed from further evaluation.

Data Analysis. We analyzed the NASA TLX [10] questionnaire and the UEQ [22] according to the authors. A group of four people who claimed to be experienced in DIY projects (later called DIY experts) validated whether the submission out of the selected products matched the guides created for both groups. As a result, we ended up with 18 participants in the experimental group and 11 in the control group. Based on the restrictions of our dataset, we used Spearman to investigate potential correlations in the questionnaire [30]. All further evaluations were done using common statistical methods.

5 Results

Of the 19 participants in the experimental group, DIY experts rated 16 submissions as valid. Two participants provided incomplete product lists, while one submission was deemed invalid. The submissions of the baseline group were all deemed valid. The experimental evaluation revealed that GoRS users required significantly less time to complete the task than baseline group participants. This time efficiency was accompanied by a notable reduction in mental workload (GoRS: 34.56 weighted; Baseline: 58.97 weighted).

Additionally, further analysis indicated that participants using GoRS reported higher average satisfaction levels with the generated guide, the products in their shopping cart, and the price-performance ratio. Table 1 provides a detailed comparison of all relevant calculated metrics between GoRS and the baseline group. One of the findings is the superior price-performance ratio of

---

[2] The entire questionnaires and all collected datasets are available online [31].

Table 1. Comparison of experimental and baseline averages.

Metric (Average Values)	GoRS	Baseline
Time (minutes)	3.71	11.05
Experience (rating)	3.21	3.45
Guide Satisfaction (rating)	3.68	3.55
Product Satisfaction (rating)	3.63	3.45
Price-Performance Satisfaction (rating)	3.84	3.64
Number of Products (count)	3.84	3.82
Total Price (€)	274.30	355.47

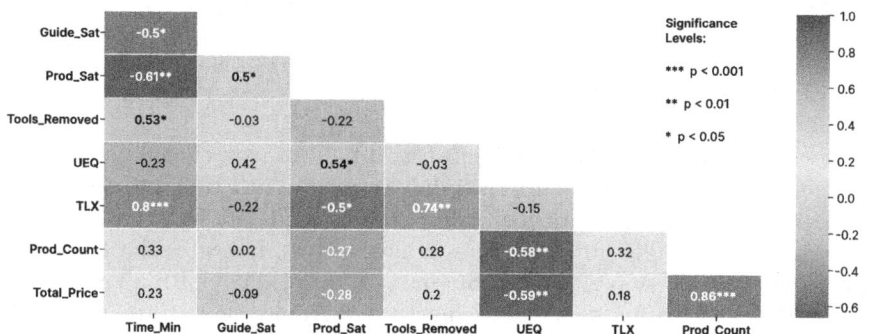

Fig. 4. Correlation Matrix of User Satisfaction, Experience, Productivity, Workload, and Pricing Factors. Note: Non-significant correlations are omitted for clarity.

GoRS-recommended products, as reflected in the table. This is further supported by the fact that 14 out of 19 experimental group participants (compared to 6 in the baseline group) stated they would purchase the recommended products regardless of budget constraints. In contrast, five (three in the baseline) responded with "I don't know." Notably, none (two in the baseline) of the participants indicated that they would choose not to buy the recommended products.

On average, participants in the experimental group removed 0.67 tools from their shopping cart and added 0.73. We found a strong correlation between the number of tools removed and the time needed to complete the task using GoRS.

Additionally, we found several significant correlations, which we present in Fig. 4, like moderate correlations between the time spent and satisfaction levels. We will discuss those findings in detail in the next section. The baseline group only revealed two significant correlations: participants who spent more time completing the task, submitted more products, and were more satisfied with their created guide.

Lastly, GoRS was rated as "excellent" across all categories in the short version of the UEQ, as shown in Fig. 5.

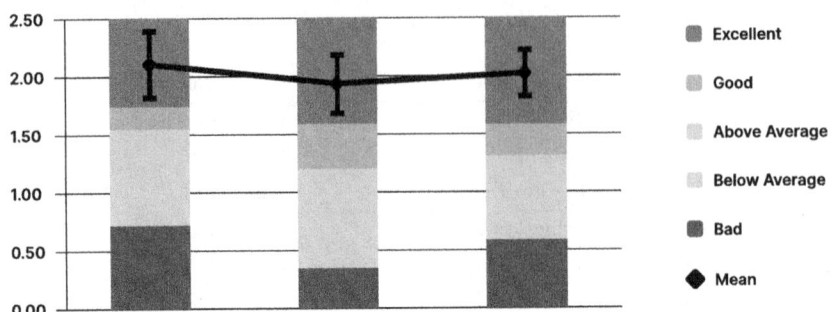

Fig. 5. GoRS's UEQ Scores (the range from −1 to 0 is omitted due to space constraints).

6 Discussion

Reviewing the requirements from Subsect. 3.1, it is clear that all set requirements are met. The application successfully provides a UI that lets users generate a guide based on a user's goal, which recommends products based on that generated guide. GoRS further suggests alternatives, indicates the differences, and displays which step a product fits into. Additionally, GoRS allows manual interactions and editing. Since we defined these requirements to reduce mental workload, enhance user experience, and provide accurate product recommendations efficiently, we conclude that GoRS successfully meets its objective as a user-centric recommendation engine for DIY products.

6.1 General Findings

Some of the various correlations in our dataset we already mentioned in Sect. 5 and displayed in Fig. 4 are between GoRS's usage time, mental workload, and satisfaction levels for the generated guide and the recommended products. The data reveals that mental workload decreases when usage time decreases as well. In addition, similar effects apply to guide and product satisfaction—when satisfaction with the guide and the recommended products is higher, the usage time is shorter, and the mental workload is lower.

Therefore, we can derive that the application successfully handles guide generation and product recommendation. Thus, users spend less time on the platform, leading to fewer interactions with the system, which reduces their mental workload and increases their satisfaction with the guide and recommendations. This observation is reinforced by the correlation between the guide and the recommended products, suggesting that a guide that satisfies users is more likely to serve as a strong foundation for effective product recommendations. This also makes sense since the product recommendation is based on the generated guide.

The data further reveals that mental workload and time increase when more products have to be removed by the users. Interestingly, the same correlation could not be measured when users manually add products. This indicates that GoRS either recommends too many products, and the user's main task is to review them carefully and, depending on the outcome, remove the unwanted ones, or that the user interactions or the process for removing products are unclear. The last assumption is weakened by GoRS scoring high in the UEQ across all categories. The UEQ further correlates with product satisfaction, the product count, and the total price of all recommended products. Concretely, higher product satisfaction increases the UEQ score, while fewer products and a lower total price also improve it.

Beyond these findings, we identified straightforward and logical correlations, such as a significant correlation between the number of products in the shopping cart and the cart's total price. However, no other mentionable correlations were observed with respect to experience levels.

6.2 Generalizability Beyond DIY Projects

While GoRS was initially designed for DIY projects, its underlying neuro-symbolic architecture can also be applied to other domains, such as healthcare and education. When a goal is clear but needs to be broken down into smaller sub-goals, our approach can be particularly effective. In healthcare, doctors could receive a detailed step-by-step treatment plan tailored to each patient's unique background and medical history. Based on this plan, the RS could suggest appropriate medications. In education, learners could enter their learning goals and receive a structured guide on achieving them, along with relevant learning materials such as videos, tutorials, and literature. Also in other typical information system areas, like supply chain management, RS can play a crucial role. Sourcing suppliers is often considered a cumbersome, manually done task. Goal-oriented RS can improve the sourcing of new suppliers and so improve efficiency drastically.

6.3 Limitations

In our experimental evaluation, we compared the performance of GoRS to a baseline scenario in which study participants were required to create a guide on their own and search for suitable tools afterward. Many of the RSs introduced in Sect. 2 evaluated their performance using publicly available datasets, comparing their results against other RS and established benchmarks. We did not compare our results to other RSs, as our approach heavily relies on the KG structure, focusing specifically on restricting products and relationships to alternatives. Even when transforming existing datasets into a KG structure, we would need to adjust the KG to explicitly represent differences and alternatives among related items within each category. This approach would significantly interfere with the structure of existing datasets and their benchmarks, making the results incomparable. Furthermore, our approach is strictly bound to the generation of the guide and so offers an additional service whose outcome influences the recommendation proven significantly.

Nevertheless, qualitative interviews that investigate the strengths and weaknesses would have been helpful. This way, we could have asked for feedback and improvements. One possible improvement could be the indication of why a product was recommended. This would further highlight the benefit of our approach since the neural engine could provide arguments on why it selected one product over another. Another benefit of interviews could have been to investigate potential purchasing intentions. Since GoRS recommended slightly cheaper products, it would be interesting to know why the participants of the baseline group chose the products they have chosen. It has to be noted that we did not design GoRS to recommend certain products over others based on their pricing strategy.

7 Conclusion and Future Work

This paper introduced GoRS, a novel neuro-symbolic, user-centric, and goal-oriented RS that leverages KGs and LLMs to create tailored step-by-step guides and provide precise product recommendations. By explicitly aligning recommendations with user-defined goals, GoRS addresses key challenges in RSs, such as cold starts and information overload. Our evaluation revealed that GoRS significantly reduces mental workload and task completion time while enhancing user satisfaction with the recommendations and the overall experience.

While this work focused on DIY applications, the underlying approach of GoRS is highly adaptable. Future work should focus on expanding GoRS's applicability across diverse domains, such as healthcare, education, and enterprise tools, where task alignment and goal-driven recommendations are equally critical. Additionally, enhancing explainability by providing justifications for recommendations could further elevate user trust and satisfaction. We also suggest benchmarking GoRS against other RSs to quantify its comparative advantages.

In the context of RS, we further recommend that companies develop services around their RS. This eliminates the need to guess a user's goal while providing unique benefits that distinguish them from their competitors.

In conclusion, GoRS demonstrates that designing services around user goals is a powerful way to differentiate RSs, offering meaningful value to both users and businesses. This approach marks a step forward in creating AI systems that are more aligned with human needs, setting the stage for future innovations in personalized, goal-driven technologies.

References

1. Alamdari, P.M., Navimipour, N.J., Hosseinzadeh, M., Safaei, A.A., Darwesh, A.: A systematic study on the recommender systems in the e-commerce. IEEE Access **8**, 115694–115716 (2020)
2. Almahmood, R.J.K., Tekerek, A.: Issues and solutions in deep learning-enabled recommendation systems within the e-commerce field. Appl. Sci. **12**(21) (2022)

3. Alslaity, A., Tran, T.: Goal modeling-based evaluation for personalized recommendation systems. In: Adjunct Proceedings of the 29th ACM Conference on User Modeling, Adaptation and Personalization, UMAP 2021, pp. 276–283. Association for Computing Machinery, New York (2021)
4. Bawack, R.E., Wamba, S.F., Carillo, K., Akter, S.: Artificial intelligence in e-commerce: a bibliometric study and literature review. Electron. Mark. **32**(1), 297–338 (2022)
5. Cabrera-Sánchez, J.P., Ramos-de Luna, I., Carvajal-Trujillo, E., Villarejo-Ramos, íF.: Online recommendation systems: factors influencing use in e-commerce. Sustainability **12**(21) (2020)
6. Deng, Y., Li, Y., Sun, F., Ding, B., Lam, W.: Unified conversational recommendation policy learning via graph-based reinforcement learning. In: Proceedings of the 44th International ACM SIGIR Conference on Research and Development in Information Retrieval, SIGIR 2021, pp. 1431–1441. Association for Computing Machinery, New York (2021)
7. Drachsler, H., Hummel, H., Koper, R.: Identifying the goal, user model and conditions of recommender systems for formal and informal learning. J. Digit. Inf. **10**(2), 4–24 (2009)
8. Fang, X., Zhan, J.: Sentiment analysis using product review data. J. Big Data **2**(1), 5 (2015)
9. Ghanem, N., Leitner, S., Jannach, D.: Balancing consumer and business value of recommender systems: a simulation-based analysis. Electron. Commer. Res. Appl. **55**, 101195 (2022)
10. Hart, S.G., Staveland, L.E.: Development of NASA-TLX (task load index): results of empirical and theoretical research. In: Hancock, P.A., Meshkati, N. (eds.) Human Mental Workload. Advances in Psychology, vol. 52, pp. 139–183. North-Holland (1988)
11. He, X., Liu, Q., Jung, S.: The impact of recommendation system on user satisfaction: a moderated mediation approach. J. Theor. Appl. Electron. Commer. Res. **19**(1), 448–466 (2024)
12. Huang, N., Zhao, W., Nie, Y., Li, C.: The study of ceramic product recommendation system based on knowledge graph. In: 2024 5th International Conference on Computer Engineering and Application (ICCEA), pp. 311–316 (2024)
13. Hussein, D.M.E.D.M.: A survey on sentiment analysis challenges. J. King Saud Univ. Eng. Sci. **30**(4), 330–338 (2018)
14. Hussien, A., Tawfiq, F., Rahma, S., A.M., Abdulwahab, B.H.: An e-commerce recommendation system based on dynamic analysis of customer behavior. Sustainability **13**(19) (2021)
15. Islek, I., Oguducu, S.G.: A hierarchical recommendation system for e-commerce using online user reviews. Electron. Commer. Res. Appl. **52**, 101131 (2022)
16. Jin, Y., Cardoso, B.D.L.R.P., Verbert, K.: How do different levels of user control affect cognitive load and acceptance of recommendations? In: IntRS@ RecSys, pp. 35–42 (2017)
17. Kartheek, M., Sajeev, G.P.: Building semantic based recommender system using knowledge graph embedding. In: 2021 Sixth International Conference on Image Information Processing (ICIIP), vol. 6, pp. 25–29 (2021)
18. Karthik, R., Ganapathy, S.: A fuzzy recommendation system for predicting the customers interests using sentiment analysis and ontology in e-commerce. Appl. Soft Comput. **108**, 107396 (2021)

19. Khatter, H., Arif, S., Singh, U., Mathur, S., Jain, S.: Product recommendation system for e-commerce using collaborative filtering and textual clustering, pp. 612–618 (2021)
20. Kim, J., Choi, I., Li, Q.: Customer satisfaction of recommender system: examining accuracy and diversity in several types of recommendation approaches. Sustainability **13**(11) (2021)
21. Landim, A., et al.: Chatbot design approaches for fashion e-commerce: an interdisciplinary review. Int. J. Fashion Des. Technol. Educ. **15**(2), 200–210 (2022)
22. Laugwitz, B., Held, T., Schrepp, M.: Construction and evaluation of a user experience questionnaire. In: Holzinger, A. (ed.) USAB 2008. LNCS, vol. 5298, pp. 63–76. Springer, Heidelberg (2008). https://doi.org/10.1007/978-3-540-89350-9_6
23. Longo, L.: Experienced mental workload, perception of usability, their interaction and impact on task performance. PLOS ONE **13**(8), 1–36 (2018)
24. Longo, L., Dondio, P.: On the relationship between perception of usability and subjective mental workload of web interfaces. In: 2015 IEEE/WIC/ACM International Conference on Web Intelligence and Intelligent Agent Technology (WI-IAT), vol. 1, pp. 345–352 (2015)
25. Necula, S.C., Păvăloaia, V.D.: AI-driven recommendations: a systematic review of the state of the art in e-commerce. Appl. Sci. **13**(9) (2023)
26. Schmutz, P., Heinz, S., Métrailler, Y., Opwis, K., et al.: Cognitive load in ecommerce applications-measurement and effects on user satisfaction. Adv. Hum. Comput. Interact. **2009**, 121494–1 (2009)
27. van Setten, M., Veenstra, M., Nijholt, A., van Dijk, B.: Goal-based structuring in recommender systems. Interact. Comput. **18**(3), 432–456 (2006)
28. Shankar, A., et al.: An intelligent recommendation system in e-commerce using ensemble learning. Multimedia Tools Appl. **83**(16), 48521–48537 (2024)
29. Singh, M.K., Rishi, O.P.: Event driven recommendation system for e-commerce using knowledge based collaborative filtering technique. Scalable Comput. Pract. Exp. **21**(3), 369–378 (2020)
30. Spearman, C.: The proof and measurement of association between two things. Int. J. Epidemiol. **39**(5), 1137–1150 (2010)
31. Stütz, J.D.: Apendix to Gors's evaluation (2025). https://doi.org/10.5281/zenodo.14770336
32. Valencia-Arias, A., Uribe-Bedoya, H., González-Ruiz, J.D., Santos, G.S., Ramírez, E.C., Rojas, E.M.: Artificial intelligence and recommender systems in e-commerce. Trends and research agenda. Intell. Syst. Appl. **24**, 200435 (2024)
33. Yeung, C.H.: Do recommender systems benefit users? A modeling approach. J. Stat. Mech. Theory Exp. **2016**(4), 043401 (2016)
34. Zhao, Q., Qian, H., Liu, Z., Zhang, G.D., Gu, L.: Breaking the barrier: utilizing large language models for industrial recommendation systems through an inferential knowledge graph. In: Proceedings of the 33rd ACM International Conference on Information and Knowledge Management, CIKM 2024, pp. 5086–5093. Association for Computing Machinery, New York (2024)
35. Ziegfeld, L., Scala, D.D., Cremers, A.H.: The effect of preference elicitation methods on the user experience in conversational recommender systems. Comput. Speech Lang. **89**, 101696 (2025)

AutoS²earch: Unlocking the Reasoning Potential of Large Models for Web-Based Source Search

Zhengqiu Zhu, Yatai Ji, Jiaheng Huang, Yong Zhao(✉), Sihang Qiu, and Rusheng Ju

National University of Defense Technology, Changsha, China
{zhuzhengqiu,jiyatai_1209,zhaoyong15}@nudt.edu.cn, 12254745966@qq.com,
sihangq@acm.org, jrscy@sina.com

Abstract. Web-based management systems have been widely used in risk control and industrial safety. However, effectively integrating source search capabilities into these systems, to enable decision-makers to locate and address the hazard (e.g., gas leak detection) remains a challenge. While prior efforts have explored using web crowdsourcing and AI algorithms for source search decision support, these approaches suffer from overheads in recruiting human participants and slow response times in time-sensitive situations. To address this, we introduce AutoS²earch, a novel framework leveraging large models for zero-shot source search in web applications. AutoS²earch operates on a simplified visual environment projected through a web-based display, utilizing a chain-of-thought prompt designed to emulate human reasoning. The multi-modal large language model (MLLM) dynamically converts visual observations into language descriptions, enabling the LLM to perform linguistic reasoning on four directional choices. Extensive experiments demonstrate that AutoS²earch achieves performance nearly equivalent to human-AI collaborative source search while eliminating dependency on crowdsourced labor. Our work offers valuable insights in using web engineering to design such autonomous systems in other industrial applications.

Keywords: Web Crowdsourcing · Source Search · Multi-modal Large Language Model · Human-AI Collaboration

1 Introduction

In today's rapidly evolving digital landscape, the transformative power of web technologies has redefined not only how services are delivered but also how complex tasks are approached. Web-based systems have become increasingly prevalent in risk control across various domains. This widespread adoption is due their accessibility, scalability, and ability to remotely connect various types of users. For example, these systems are used for process safety management in industry [14], safety risk early warning in urban construction [6], and safe monitoring of infrastructural systems [20]. Within these web-based risk management systems, the source search problem presents a huge challenge. Source search refers to the task of identifying the origin of a risky event, such as a gas leak and the emission point of toxic substances. This source search capability is crucial for effective risk management and decision-making.

Traditional approaches to implementing source search capabilities into the web systems often rely on solely algorithmic solutions [21]. These methods, while relatively straightforward to implement, often struggle to achieve acceptable performances due to algorithmic local optima and complex unknown environments [25]. More recently, web crowdsourcing has emerged as a promising alternative for tackling the source search problem by incorporating human efforts in these web systems on-the-fly [26]. This approach outsources the task of addressing issues encountered during the source search process to human workers, leveraging their capabilities to enhance system performance.

These solutions often employ a human-AI collaborative way [28] where algorithms handle exploration-exploitation and report the encountered problems while human workers resolve complex decision-making bottlenecks to help the algorithms getting rid of local deadlocks [27]. Although effective, this paradigm suffers from two inherent limitations: increased operational costs from continuous human intervention, and slow response times of human workers due to sequential decision-making. These challenges motivate our investigation into developing autonomous systems that preserve human-like reasoning capabilities while reducing dependency on massive crowdsourced labor.

Furthermore, recent advancements in large language models (LLMs) [4] and multi-modal LLMs (MLLMs) [9] have unveiled promising avenues for addressing these challenges. One clear opportunity involves the seamless integration of visual understanding and linguistic reasoning for robust decision-making in search tasks. However, whether large models-assisted source search is really effective and efficient for improving the current source search algorithms [11] remains unknown. *To address the research gap, we are particularly interested in answering the following two research questions in this work:*

RQ1: How can source search capabilities be integrated into web-based systems to support decision-making in time-sensitive risk management scenarios?

RQ2: How can MLLMs and LLMs enhance the effectiveness and efficiency of existing source search algorithms?

To answer the research questions, we propose a novel framework called AutoS^{2}earch (**Auto**nomous **S**ource **Search**) and implement a prototype system that leverages advanced web technologies to simulate real-world conditions for zero-shot source search. Unlike traditional methods that rely on pre-defined heuristics or extensive human intervention, AutoS^{2}earch employs a carefully designed prompt that encapsulates human rationales, thereby guiding the MLLM to generate coherent and accurate scene descriptions from visual inputs about four directional choices. Based on these language-based descriptions, the LLM is enabled to determine the optimal directional choice through chain-of-thought (CoT) reasoning. Comprehensive empirical validation across 20 simplified benchmark scenarios demonstrates that AutoS²earch achieves a success rate of 95–98%, closely approaching the performance of human-AI collaborative search [28].

2 Related Work

2.1 Web Crowdsourcing and Human-AI Collaboration Empowerment

With the advancement of web technologies, crowdsourcing activities have increasingly migrated to web and mobile internet platforms, namely web crowdsourcing [7]. An exponential rise in its applications has witnessed, such as ride-hailing and software development. To tackle complex web-based tasks, scientists at Microsoft introduced human-AI interaction guidelines to assist researchers and practitioners in designing studies utilizing AI technologies [2]. Following this, numerous studies have integrated human intelligence with AI methods to address challenges such as conversational agent learning for intent detection and text classification [3,24]. A recent study, for example, engaged online users from crowdsourcing platforms and implemented advanced computer vision techniques to generate city maps [19]. Given the growing significance of AI-in-the-loop systems in human-intervened tasks, the concept and principles of human-AI decision-making within the context of web crowdsourcing were provided [8].

2.2 Source Search and Crowd-Powered Practices

Source search is a critical problem for both nature and mankind [13] focusing on determining the location of a source (of gas or signal) in the shortest possible time. Existing source search approaches can generally be classified into three categories: information-theoretic [10], biologically-inspired [1], and gradient-based methods [12]. Among these, information-theoretic algorithms, especially those grounded in the Bayesian framework [17], stand out for their distinct advantages. To further enhance the performance (i.e., success rate and efficiency) of a searching algorithm, multi-robot collaboration mechanisms [22] have been designed and adopted. However, when source search takes place in complex environments, the search process always encounters fatal problems, resulting in wrong outcomes. Thus, researchers started to explore effective ways leveraging human intelligence to improve AI-based search algorithms through web platforms [26]. However, this approach also entails substantial costs and imposes considerable burdens on human workers.

2.3 Large Models for Scene Understanding and Reasoning

MLLMs integrate multimodal encoders/decoders with traditional LLMs, enabling cross-modal understanding that overcomes text-only limitations. While these models demonstrate remarkable capabilities across diverse tasks including image-text understanding [16], video-text understanding [15], and even multimodal generation [18], their effectiveness in handling complex tasks remains constrained by predominant single-step reasoning approaches. To this end, CoT prompts are utilized to enhance problem-solving abilities by guiding LLMs through structured multi-step reasoning. Recent work explores CoT adaptations for multimodal problems, for instance, Shikra [5] pioneers CoT application in visual grounding tasks, while SoM [23] introduces structural image annotations like segmentation maps and spatial grids to provide spatial reasoning anchors. However, CoT has not been comprehensively explored for fine-grain reasoning in source search tasks.

3 System Design

To answer **RQ1**, we designed the AutoS^{2}earch framework based on web platforms. This involved migrating our previously developed crowd-powered source search prototype system [27] from a desktop application to a web platform. The primary goals of this implementation were to achieve cross-platform accessibility, real-time interaction, and dynamic visualization.

(1) **Back-End Implementation:** we selected the lightweight and scalable Flask framework, and initialized the application using Flask and Socket.IO. The functions are handled by defining routes and Socket.IO events.
(2) **Real-Time Communication:** Socket.IO was used to support WebSocket and polling to ensure low-latency communication. Data is sent to the front-end using 'socketio.emit', and on the front-end, events sent by the back-end are received using 'socket.on'.
(3) **Map Drawing and Updating:** we first determined the map drawing logic (initializing the map and updating it based on changes), and then converted the map data into a format recognizable by the front-end.
(4) **Front-End Rendering:** we utilized HTML5's Canvas – an ideal choice for dynamic map displays—to achieve efficient graphic rendering. We defined the Canvas element and implemented the drawing logic using JavaScript. To facilitate user interaction, we added control buttons on the interface and bound click events to them. Additionally, a click event is bound to the Canvas to send the user's click coordinates to the back-end.

The user interface of this system, shown in Fig. 1, utilizes graphical elements to illustrate the source search task and the problem. The interface comprises two main sections: a parameter configuration panel and a visual area for source search execution. The parameter configuration panel is primarily used to set source diffusion parameters, particle filter parameters, and to upload scene maps. While visual area of source search displays the robotic searcher, search environment, current state, posterior probability distribution of the source location, and four directional choices. When a problem is detected, the system automatically generates a task for large models, and then large models analyze the scene and reason step by step to plan a path for the robot. Once a deadlock is resolved, the system resumes automatic search, continuing until the source is found. This user interface allows decision-makers to observe the source search process in real-time. It provides the capability to: 1) enable decision-makers to interrupt the search process as needed, 2) facilitate crowdsourcing during the search, and 3) integrate large models for handling the detected problems.

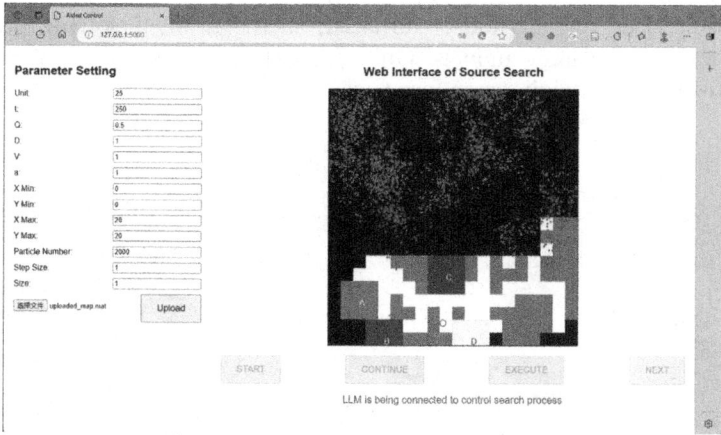

Fig. 1. A screenshot of the web-based source search prototype system. (Color figure online)

4 Method

Previous studies have demonstrated the feasibility and effectiveness of human-AI collaborative source search in addressing fatal problems encountered in search problems (e.g., local optimum, dead end, infinite loop) [27,28]. However, this approach comes with significant costs and imposes considerable burdens on human workers. Therefore, to answer $RQ2$, we elaborate on the design of a large models-assisted source search method and explain how could it achieve human-like scene understanding and multi-step reasoning.

4.1 Method Overview

In this section, we show the design of AutoS²earch, and introduce how MLLM and LLM can be used during the search process to improve the effectiveness and efficiency of search algorithms. There are various ways to achieve this goal in search. Here, we designed a straightforward workflow where the MLLM dynamically interprets visual data from a web-based display interface, converting it into detailed language descriptions for the LLM's CoT reasoning. Notably, no changes are made inside the search algorithm. The overview of the method is shown in as Fig. 2. Similar to the workflow of human-AI collaborative search (Fig. 2(a)), AutoS²earch follows three main steps: initialization, execution, and end. *The* main distinction lies in the execution phase, where $AutoS^2earch$ incorporates four core components: machine-driven problem detection, machine-generated prompt explanations, problem description by the MLLM, and reasoning and acting by the LLM. Except for the problem detection mechanism, the subsequent steps are totally different with those in our previous work [28]. In this work, we leverage human rationale to carefully design prompts, eliminating the need for human intervention after the method is initiated, as the problem-solving process is entirely handled by large models. Our approach helps reduce labor costs and accelerates problem-solving response time.

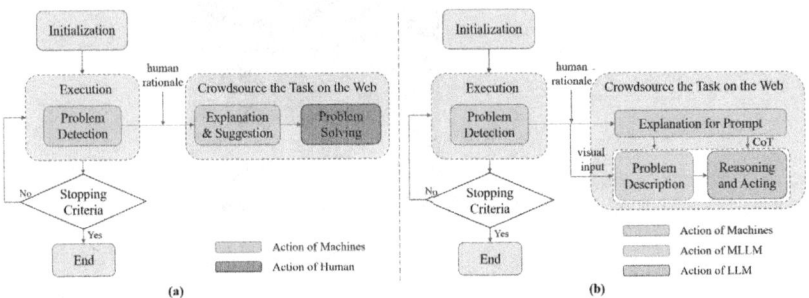

Fig. 2. The schematic diagram of the $AutoS^2earch$ method.

4.2 The Workflow Design of $AutoS^2earch$

The prototype system was designed following the method outlined in Fig. 2(b), employing Infotaxis as the source searching algorithm. Infotaxis is one of the most popular cognitive search strategies, known for its effectiveness in solving source searching problems [21].

(1) Problem Detection and Task Generation. Through discussions with experts on the question, "*what fatal problems could be happened during the search process*", we have already identified common problems found in source search algorithms, such as local optima and deadlocks. Details can be found in [28]. These issues can be detected in various ways, with one simple solution being a rule-based mechanism that automatically identifies the problematic search states and pauses the search process. A task is then generated and pushed to the web, seeking assistance from MLLMs and LLMs to facilitate effective problem-solving. A screenshot of the crowdsourcing task is shown in Fig. 1.

(2) Task Explanation for Prompt Design. AI explanations hold great promise in the field of deep learning. However, explaining problems and search algorithms differs significantly from this domain. To help human workers or large models understand more intuitively, language and visuals are two highly effective means. While search algorithms are clear, the search process (e.g., search states) often remains hidden, making it hard to explain using language alone. Thus, we present key graphic elements to MLLMs or human workers by combining human rationale and AI algorithms, as shown in Fig. 3. These elements are identified through discussions with human experts and are specifically designed for providing explanations and suggestions. To understand the current situation, the robotic searcher's current position, occupied areas, passable areas, and unexplored areas should be prioritized for display. Additionally, to help large models better understand and make decisions, the task could provide a solution suggestion or some directional choices. The solution suggestion features a source estimation method that uses Bayesian inference and sequential Monte Carlo methods to show the distribution of the posterior probability of the source location (see green particles in Fig. 1). Moreover, We also defined four regions—A, B, C, and D—around the robot's current position, representing the top-left, bottom-left, top-right, and bottom-right passable areas nearest to the unexplored areas. The potential goal and four directional choices are critical for large models to understand the problem and to reason better decisions.

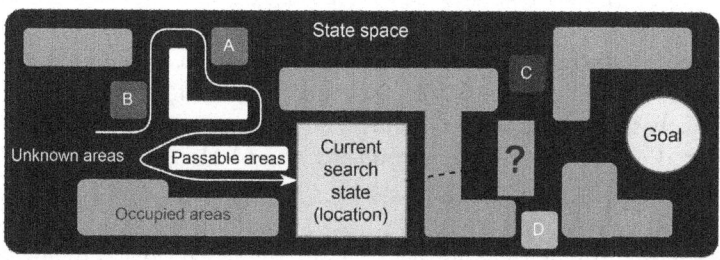

Fig. 3. Elements needed to be presented while explaining the search algorithm and the problem.

Prompt for MLLM
Task Description: Based on the graphic elements, identify the candidate target areas marked with letters in the image. Area A is marked in red; Area B in purple; Area C in blue; and Area D in yellow. Then provide a sequential description of each existing area, focusing on two main aspects for each: 1. Distance to the dense green dot regions (classified as: Far, Medium, or Close) 2. Density of surrounding unexplored black areas (classified as: High, Medium, or Low)
Output Format Example (assuming Area B does not exist):
Area A: Distance to dense green dot region: Far; Density of surrounding unexplored areas: Low
Area C: Distance to dense green dot region: Medium; Density of surrounding unexplored areas: Medium
Area D: Distance to dense green dot region: Close; Density of surrounding unexplored areas: High
Please describe the information for all existing areas in the image following this output format.

(3) **Visual-Language Conversion by MLLM.** When the task is explained through graphic elements, it comes to large models' turn to address the problem that a search algorithm cannot handle on its own. Using graphic elements as visual input, we specifically designed prompts for MLLMs. The main purpose of the prompt is to provide a hierarchical description of the situation around the four directional choices. The description is closely related to the search environment, current location of the searcher, and posterior probability distribution of the source location. We directly leverage the MLLM for visual reasoning, analyzing the given image to determine whether a distance is far, close, or medium. The specific prompt for the MLLM is given.

(4) **Reasoning and Acting by LLM.** Based on the structured descriptions generated by the MLLM, we defined prioritized decision-making rules to enable the LLM to perform optimal strategy selection through chain-of-thought reasoning. These rules include: (1) Ignore non-existent areas (to prevent hallucinations of MLLMs); (2) Prioritize areas with the shortest distance to the dense green dot region; (3) Prioritize areas with the highest density of surrounding unexplored areas. The rationale behind this design is as follows: first, it eliminates potential hallucinated outputs from the MLLM; second, areas with higher particle density are more likely to contain a release source; and finally, a release source may exist in unexplored areas. The specific prompt for the LLM is given.

CoT Prompt for LLM
Task Description: Based on the structured descriptions provided by the MLLM, identify and output the single highest-priority area by following the rules below:
Core Rules (in descending order of priority):
1. Exclude non-existent regions.
2. Prioritize the region closest to the dense green dot cluster.
3. Prioritize the region with the highest density of surrounding unexplored black areas.
Output Requirements:
- Provide a single region letter (e.g., "C") as the result.
- Include a detailed reasoning process leading to the selection of the region.

5 Experiments

In this section, we introduce experimental setup, baseline algorithms, and evaluation metrics. The project code can be found here[1].

5.1 Experimental Setup

The source search activities are performed by a virtual robot within a simulated 2D environment measuring 20 m × 20 m. The search area is divided into a 20 × 20

---
[1] https://gitee.com/parallelsimlab/autos2earch.

grid of cells. Each cell has a probability P_o of containing an obstacle, with P_o set to 0.75 to introduce a relatively high difficulty (more obstacles). This higher complexity is chosen because simpler environments (with fewer obstacles) do not require external assistance. In this study, we did not consider the specific types or shapes of obstacles. If a cell contains an obstacle, it is considered completely obstructed, meaning the robot cannot enter or traverse it.

5.2 Baseline Algorithms

As detailed in the published work [28] on human-collaborative source search, the baselines adopted in this study naturally follow from that setup. Baseline 1 employs the Infotaxis algorithm directly, while Baseline 2 incorporates our proposed automatic problem detection method, navigating the robot to a random location to escape problematic scenarios. For consistency, we adopt an aided control interaction model of human-AI collaboration in this comparative analysis. Furthermore, we introduce Baseline 3, where the robot navigates to a randomly chosen direction from four possible options (mentioned in Sect. 4.2) upon detecting a problem. It is worth noting that both Baseline 2 and Baseline 3 represent state-of-the-art improvements over traditional source search algorithms.

5.3 Evaluation Metrics

In this study, we evaluate the effectiveness and efficiency of the source search process and its outcomes. Effectiveness is measured by the success rate, defined as the robot successfully locating the source within 400 steps (where a step represents one iteration of updating search states). If the robot fails to find the source within 400 steps, regardless of whether large models are involved, the task is considered unsuccessful. Efficiency is assessed by the number of steps the robot takes to find the source, with failed attempts excluded from the calculation. Additionally, we measure the execution time of large models per task to see whether they hold an advantage over human workers in time-sensitive tasks.

6 Results

In this section, we present the results of (1) an illustrative run, (2) the comparison study, and (3) the ablation study. Due to the space limitations of the paper, only the key results and analyses are presented, and the results of the statistical significance tests are not included.

6.1 Illustrative Run

We conducted an experiment using one scenario from a set of 20 benchmark scenarios to illustrate a successful search process. The illustrative run of AutoS^{2}earch is shown in Fig. 4. The process includes the initiation of the search, the progression of the algorithm-driven search, the involvement of large models when a

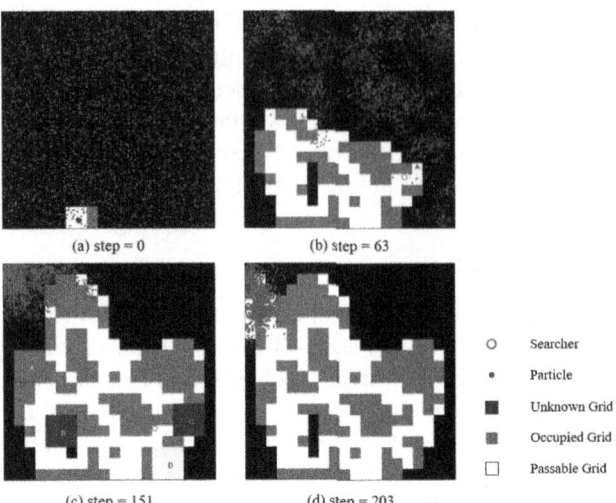

Fig. 4. An illustrative run of the proposed framework at different time steps. (a) step = 0; (b) step = 63; (c) step = 151 (A, B, C, and D are four directional choices); (d) step = 203.

problem is detected, and ultimately resolving the issue to successfully locate the source. As we can see in Fig. 4(c), large models (both GPT-4o[2]) are activated at search step = 151. Based on the current visual inputs and the provided prompt for MLLMs, the language description of this scene is presented as follows.

Using the language descriptions of the four directional choices, the LLM initiates CoT reasoning, guided by the prompt for LLMs. The LLM's final choice is **A**, and its explanation for this selection is also provided. The decision-making process closely mirrors that of humans.

Output of the MLLM
Region A: Distance to dense area of small green dots: close; Density of surrounding black exploration area: medium
Region B: Distance to dense area of small green dots: medium; Density of surrounding black exploration area: medium
Region C: Distance to dense area of small green dots: medium; Density of surrounding black exploration area: medium
Region D: Distance to dense area of small green dots: far; Density of surrounding black exploration area: low

To explore this further, we recruited three human raters to independently evaluate the LLM's reasoning process and compare the rationale behind the optimal choices made by the LLM and human intelligence. Our findings reveal

---

[2] https://github.com/topics/gpt-4o

that the LLM generally adheres strictly to a predefined priority order, whereas humans display an ability to flexibly adjust priorities based on the relative magnitudes of differences between the choices. For instance, when two regions are similarly distant from a dense cluster of green dots (indicating minimal differences in second-level priority), but the surrounding black area densities differ significantly (indicating greater differences in third-level priority), humans tend to prioritize the third-level criteria over the second. In contrast, the LLM struggle with such adaptive decision-making, even when additional rules are introduced.

Reasoning Process of the LLM
Based on the description and priority rules, the analysis is conducted to identify the highest-priority region that meets the criteria:
1.First, check if any regions are missing: Regions A, B, C, and D all exist.
2.Next, consider the closest distance to the dense area of green dots: Region A is "close", regions B and C are "medium", and region D is "far"; thus, region A has the highest priority.
3.Then, consider the density of unexplored black areas surrounding each region: Regions A, B, and C have "medium" density, Region D has "low" density.
According to the priority rules, the region with the highest priority is A. Therefore, my selection is: A.

6.2 Comparative Study

In this subsection, we evaluated the effectiveness of large models-assisted source search over 20 benchmark scenarios (each scenario was run ten times) by measuring the effectiveness (success rate), the efficiency (the number of steps taken to find the source), the execution time of large models. The experimental results, averaged over Monte Carlo simulations across 20 scenarios, are presented in Table 1. Clearly, large models-assisted source search has proved to be effective, achieving a success rate of 97% in most cases. This represents an improvement of approximately 18.5% over Baseline 1, 9% over Baseline 2, and 7% over Baseline 3, while being only 3% lower than the success rate of human-AI collaborative search. Note that Baseline 2 and 3 are improvements based on the original algorithm (Baseline 1) since automatic problem detection and rule-based problem-solving strategies are used. Furthermore, we observe that the efficiency of AutoS^{2}earch (in terms of steps taken) is comparable to that of human-AI collaborative search, while the average execution time of large models is even shorter. For details on how human workers complete the crowdsourcing task, interested readers can refer to the previous work [27].

To further explore whether the impressive performance is solely due to GPT-4o's strong capabilities, we evaluated various combinations of MLLMs and LLMs from different companies. The results, presented in Table 2, reveal that our proposed framework is highly robust, consistently achieving success rates above

Table 1. Results of the comparisons over various baselines.

Methods	Expertise	Effectiveness (% success rate)	Efficiency (# steps per task)	Human/MLLM+LLM execution time (seconds per task)
Human Aided	Expert	100	175.10 ± 67.67	33.58 ± 27.87
	Non-expert	100	165.67 ± 80.60	29.01 ± 29.51
Baseline 1	-	78.5	154.04 ± 91.32	-
Baseline 2	-	88	179.64 ± 96.45	-
Baseline 3	-	90	179.76 ± 97.40	-
Ours	-	97	170.97 ± 89.57	25.95 ± 38.20

95%. Notably, the Qwen model[3] from the Chinese company Alibaba achieves the highest success rate at 98%.

Table 2. Results of the comparisons over various large models.

LLMs	Effectiveness (% success rate)	Efficiency (# steps per task)	MLLM+LLM execution time (seconds per task)
GLM-4v-plus + GLM-4-plus	95	171.13 ± 92.64	26.39 ± 32.75
Qwen-VL-plus + Qwen-max	98	172.85 ± 91.08	26.74 ± 36.39
GPT-4o + GPT-4o	97	170.97 ± 89.57	25.95 ± 38.20

6.3 Ablation Study

We further conducted ablation studies to validate the importance of main elements designed in our framework: the Chain-of-Thought prompt for the LLM and the size of directional choices A, B, C, and D (which determine the number of candidate cells for each option). We designated the model without CoT reasoning as Our-A and the model with reduced block sizes as Our-B. The average results across 20 scenarios are presented in Table 3. As we can see, both the removal of CoT reasoning and the reduction in block sizes significantly decrease the success rate by approximately 6% and 7%, respectively. Notably, while removing CoT reasoning compromises the effectiveness performance, it does lead to improved efficiency and shorter execution time due to fewer reasoning steps.

Table 3. Results of the ablation study.

Methods	Effectiveness (% success rate)	Efficiency (# steps per task)	MLLM+LLM execution time (seconds per task)
Ours-A	91	157.74 ± 85.33	23.82 ± 36.45
Ours-B	90	170.28 ± 93.35	24.49 ± 34.19
Ours	97	170.97 ± 89.57	25.95 ± 38.20

---

[3] https://github.com/JMaiGC/ComfyUI-Qwen-VL-API.

7 Discussions

By applying human rationale to web design, prompt creation, and problem detection mechanisms, and harnessing the visual and textual reasoning of large models, this paper solves the autonomous source search problem. The results convey three main messages: (1) By incorporating carefully-designed prompts and Self-reflection mechanisms that enable large models with scene comprehension and multi-step reasoning capabilities, autonomous source search capabilities can be integrated into web-based systems to support decision-making in time-sensitive scenarios. (2) The large models-assisted method is effective and efficient for improving source search, approaching the performance of human-AI collaborative approaches while reducing execution time by approximately 25%. (3) Whether in scene element presentation, problem detection mechanisms, or CoT prompt design, each component reflects human intelligence, highlighting that complex task solving fundamentally relies on human-AI hybrid intelligence.

Drawbacks. Despite the strengths, this work has several limitations. (1) *Environmental Complexity Gap:* The simplified 20×20 grid with static obstacles fail to capture real-world dynamics (e.g., moving obstructions, multi-source scenarios). The visual environment used here is insufficient to test whether large models truly possess robust scene understanding and multi-step reasoning capabilities in complex settings. (2) *Limited Task Understanding:* While simple scene elements were designed to help the large model understand tasks, the lack of domain-specific knowledge makes it difficult for the model to balance exploration and exploitation during the search, sometimes leading to hallucinations by selecting irrelevant areas. (3) *Underutilization of MLLM Potential*: In this work, MLLMs were mainly used to convert visual observations into textual descriptions, with large language models handling subsequent reasoning. This separation of visual understanding and language reasoning may limit the integrated capabilities MLLMs are designed to offer.

Potential Avenues. To address these limitations, we propose to explore: (1) *Dynamic Environment Adaptation:* Design LLM-empowered search agent and develop online prompt tuning mechanisms where LLMs could adjust decision rules according to the environment variations. (2) *Visual Thinking Augmentation:* Integrate graph-based scene representations and reflection mechanisms to help MLLMs directly reason on the visual inputs without hallucinations. (3) *Human-AI Value Alignment:* Implement human-in-the-loop feedback mechanisms in complex and high-risk scenarios and ensure alignment of decision objectives between humans and AI. (4) *Real-World Implementation:* we would further extend this research by exploring different parameter settings and evaluating on more complex real-world scenarios.

Implications. The implications of AutoS^{2}earch extend far beyond the technical achievements in web-based autonomous systems. Its design reflects a broader trend in human-AI collaborative systems, where the goal is to harness the cognitive strengths of both entities in tandem. Moreover, it may redefine the role of humans in web crowdsourcing systems—from task executors to validators of AI rationality in the future.

8 Conclusions

In this work, we present AutoS^{2}earch to address the issue of human dependency in web-based crowdsourcing systems for source search tasks. Through AutoS^{2}earch, we demonstrate that large models can effectively improve the performance of human-designed search algorithms in complex environments through visual-language translation and CoT reasoning. Our experimental validation shows AutoS^{2}earch achieves 95–98% of human-AI collaborative source search algorithm effectiveness while eliminating labor costs and response time. *This implies that modern large models can sufficiently replicate human scene reasoning for critical tasks like source search in complex environments.* As global industries increasingly lean on such systems for effective management, our work establishes a solid foundation for web engineering in other industrial applications.

Acknowledgement. This study is supported by Youth Independent Innovation Foundation of NUDT (ZK-2023-21) and National Natural Science Foundation of China 62202477.

References

1. Al-Abri, S., Zhang, F.: A distributed active perception strategy for source seeking and level curve tracking. IEEE Trans. Autom. Control **67**(5), 2459–2465 (2021)
2. Amershi, S., et al.: Guidelines for human-AI interaction. In: Proceedings of the 2019 CHI Conference on Human Factors in Computing Systems, pp. 1–13 (2019)
3. Arous, I., Dolamic, L., Yang, J., Bhardwaj, A., Cuccu, G., Cudré-Mauroux, P.: MARTA: leveraging human rationales for explainable text classification. In: Proceedings of the AAAI Conference on Artificial Intelligence, vol. 35, pp. 5868–5876 (2021)
4. Chang, Y., et al.: .A survey on evaluation of large language models. ACM Trans. Intell. Syst. Technol. **15**(3), 1–45 (2024)
5. Chen, K., Zhang, Z., Zeng, W., Zhang, R., Zhu, F., Zhao, R.: Shikra: unleashing multimodal LLM's referential dialogue magic (2023)
6. Ding, L., Zhou, C.: Development of web-based system for safety risk early warning in urban metro construction. Autom. Constr. **34**, 45–55 (2013)
7. Doan, A., Ramakrishnan, R., Halevy, A.Y.: Crowdsourcing systems on the worldwide web. Commun. ACM **54**(4), 86–96 (2011)
8. Green, B., Chen, Y.: The principles and limits of algorithm-in-the-loop decision making. Proc. ACM Hum.-Comput. Interacti. **3**(CSCW), 1–24 (2019)
9. Huang, H., et al.: ChatGPT for shaping the future of dentistry: the potential of multi-modal large language model. Int. J. Oral Sci. **15**(1), 29 (2023)
10. Jang, H., Park, M., Oh, H.: Improved socialtaxis for information-theoretic source search using cooperative multiple agents in turbulent environments. Expert Syst. Appl. **225**, 120033 (2023)

11. Ji, Y., et al.: Source searching in unknown obstructed environments through source estimation, target determination, and path planning. Build. Environ. **221**, 109266 (2022)
12. Jiang, X., Li, S., Luo, B., Meng, Q.: Source exploration for an under-actuated system: a control-theoretic paradigm. IEEE Trans. Control Syst. Technol. **28**(3), 1100–1107 (2019)
13. Jing, T., Meng, Q.H., Ishida, H.: Recent progress and trend of robot odor source localization. IEEJ Trans. Electr. Electron. Eng. **16**(7), 938–953 (2021)
14. Kannan, P., et al.: A web-based collection and analysis of process safety incidents. J. Loss Prev. Process Ind. **44**, 171–192 (2016)
15. Li, K., et al.: VideoChat: Chat-centric video understanding (2023). https://arxiv.org/pdf/2305.06355
16. Liu, H., Li, C., Wu, Q., Lee, Y.J.: Visual instruction tuning. In: Advances in Neural Information Processing Systems, vol. 36, pp. 34892–34916 (2024)
17. Ojeda, P., Monroy, J., Gonzalez-Jimenez, J.: Robotic gas source localization with probabilistic mapping and online dispersion simulation. IEEE Trans. Rob. **40**, 3551–3564 (2024)
18. Peng, Z., et al.: Kosmos-2: grounding multimodal large language models to the world (2023). https://arxiv.org/pdf/2306.14824
19. Qiu, S., Psyllidis, A., Bozzon, A., Houben, G.J.: Crowd-mapping urban objects from street-level imagery. In: The World Wide Web Conference, pp. 1521–1531 (2019)
20. Repetto, M.P., Burlando, M., Solari, G., De Gaetano, P., Pizzo, M., Tizzi, M.: A web-based GIS platform for the safe management and risk assessment of complex structural and infrastructural systems exposed to wind. Adv. Eng. Softw. **117**, 29–45 (2018)
21. Ristic, B., Skvortsov, A., Gunatilaka, A.: A study of cognitive strategies for an autonomous search. Inf. Fusion **28**, 1–9 (2016)
22. Tang, H., Sun, W., Yu, H., Lin, A., Xue, M.: A multirobot target searching method based on bat algorithm in unknown environments. Expert Syst. Appl. **141**, 112945 (2020)
23. Yang, J., Zhang, H., Li, F., Zou, X., Li, C., Gao, J.: Set-of-mark prompting unleashes extraordinary visual grounding in GPT-4V (2023). https://arxiv.org/pdf/2310.11441
24. Yang, J., Drake, T., Damianou, A., Maarek, Y.: Leveraging crowdsourcing data for deep active learning an application: learning intents in Alexa. In: The World Wide Web Conference, pp. 23–32 (2018)
25. Zhao, Y., Chen, B., Zhu, Z., Chen, F., Wang, Y., Ji, Y.: Searching the diffusive source in an unknown obstructed environment by cognitive strategies with forbidden areas. Build. Environ. **186**, 107349 (2020)
26. Zhao, Y., Ji, Y., Qiu, S., Zhu, Z., Ju, R.: A user interface design for collaborations between humans and intelligent vehicles. In: International Conference on Web Engineering, pp. 397–400. Springer (2024)
27. Zhao, Y., Zhu, Z., Chen, B., Qiu, S.: Crowd-powered source searching in complex environments. In: CCF Conference on Computer Supported Cooperative Work and Social Computing, pp. 201–215. Springer (2022)
28. Zhao, Y., Zhu, Z., Chen, B., Qiu, S.: Leveraging human-AI collaboration in crowd-powered source search: a preliminary study. J. Soc. Comput. **4**(2), 95–111 (2023)

Safe and Inclusive Web Engineering

Enhancing the Aspect Robustness Score of the HAABSA++ Model Using Adversarial Training

Milad Agha[1], Flavius Frasincar[1], Beilly Zhu[1], and Tarmo Robal[2]

[1] Erasmus University Rotterdam, Burgemeester Oudlaan 50,
3062 PA Rotterdam, The Netherlands
532622ma@student.eur.nl, frasincar@ese.eur.nl, 611700bz@eur.nl
[2] Tallinn University of Technology, Ehitajate tee 5, 19086 Tallinn, Estonia
tarmo.robal@taltech.ee

Abstract. Sentiment analysis is an important tool in understanding users of the Web through the cues they leave while communicating and providing feedback. Sentiment classification models may have lower robustness because they detect irrelevant patterns instead of sentiment-bearing words related to the target aspects. We evaluated the robustness of the Hybrid Approach for the Aspect-Based Sentiment Analysis++ (HAABSA++) model. We first generated an Aspect Robustness Test Set (ARTS) through the augmentation of the original test set with different augmentation techniques: REVTGT, REVNON, and ADDDIFF. These techniques modify the target and non-target aspects to test whether the model still makes correct predictions. Aspect robustness is evaluated using the Aspect Robustness Score (ARS). In addition, we investigated the improvement of ARS through adversarial training by applying the three data augmentation methods to the training set. We find that the robustness of the HAABSA++ model as measured by ARS is average when we compare the HAABSA++ model with other models found in the literature. We also find that performing adversarial training improves the robustness of the model as measured by ARS. However, this improvement comes at the cost of a lower accuracy of the HAABSA++ model for the original test set instances.

Keywords: Aspect-based sentiment analysis · Aspect robustness · Attention-based model · Neural network

1 Introduction

The field of sentiment analysis has increased in importance with the growth of various Web platforms, including for social media and online reviews. On these Web platforms, vast amount of information is generated daily. Sentiment analysis enables the extraction of opinions and emotions from content, providing valuable insights for businesses, academics, and consumers from brand reputation and customer sentiment to social insights, trend identification, and interdisciplinary studies. This in turn can be utilised for Web Engineering (WE), for instance to enhance user experience, develop better user-centred interfaces, optimize search, and automate processes on Web platforms (e.g., virtual assistants). However, manual analysis of this data is exhaustive and inefficient. As a result, sentiment analysis has become an essential tool [9]. In particular Aspect Based Sentiment Analysis (ABSA) is noteworthy for its approach to evaluate individual aspects or characteristics, rather than assigning an overall sentiment score to each sentence or to the entire text [17].

ABSA can be broken down into three sub-tasks: aspect identification, sentiment classification, and sentiment aggregation [17]. The identification process is about pinpointing the specific aspects mentioned, while the classification process involves labeling these aspects with a sentiment value. Lastly, aggregation is about compiling these sentiment values to reflect the collective sentiment. This work aims to optimize solutions for the sentiment classification task, also known as Aspect-Based Sentiment Classification (ABSC).

ABSC techniques are typically grouped into three main types: knowledge-based approaches, machine learning models, and hybrid models [1]. Studies indicate that the hybrid approach yields superior results to the individual methods [18]. However, it is still an open question which specific mix of these techniques achieves the optimal balance of accuracy and operational effectiveness.

Recent research by [20] has developed the Hybrid Approach for Aspect-Based Sentiment Analysis (HAABSA), which achieves state-of-the-art results in sentiment classification. This approach uses a lexicalized domain-specific ontology to assess the sentiment towards the target. When the results of the ontology are ambiguous, the sentences are processed by a specialized Neural Network (NN) with a Left-Center-Right structure and Rotatory attention (LCR-Rot) [23] mechanism serving as a secondary model.

Two additional extensions to the HAABSA model to improve the accuracy of sentiment classification results were introduced in [19], resulting a model called HAABSA++. These extensions involve the use of deep contextual word embeddings (i.e., ELMO [13] and BERT [2] designed to grasp the semantic information of text by considering the surrounding context) to better account for the semantics of words, and the introduction of hierarchical attention to distinguish the importance of high-level input sentence representations.

Although HAABSA++ achieves cutting-edge results in the sentiment classification task, recent studies have shown that the apparent high performance of most models is due to their ability to detect spurious patterns [10]. As a result, the robustness of these models remains uncertain. Models must respond only to the sentiment-related words associated with the target, without being influenced by the sentiment expressed about unrelated aspects. [21] explored the robustness problem by developing a framework designed to generate a comprehensive Aspect Robustness Test Set (ARTS). Combined with a new measure, the Aspect Robustness Score (ARS), ARTS can be used to assess whether a model can reliably detect the intended sentiment in the presence of spurious patterns. [21] also proposes to improve the ARS with adversarial training by using the automatic generation framework on the training set.

In this paper, we evaluate the robustness of the HAABSA++ model, and investigate the improvement of the ARS through adversarial training. The main novelty of this paper is the generation of ARTS for the SemEval-2015 [14] and SemEval-2016 [15] datasets. The generated ARTS are used to compute the ARS for the HAABSA++ model. We also evaluate whether adversarial training improves the ARS of the HAABSA++ model and how well HAABSA++ compares to other models found in the literature in terms of robustness measured by ARS.

The remaining sections of this paper are organized as follows. Section 2 reviews relevant studies related to ABSC. Section 3 outlines the data used in this study. Section 4 explains the research methodology, with the results reported in detail in Sect. 5. The final section, Sect. 6, summarizes the conclusions and suggests directions for future research. Access to the source code is freely available at https://github.com/MiladAgha/rHAABSA-pp.

2 Related Work

Most approaches to ABSC can be grouped into three types [1]. Knowledge-based methods rely on part-of-speech tags and lexicons. This type of method was the first to tackle the ABSC [8]. Later, machine learning methods emerged as a convenient alternative with high performance rates [16]. These methods offer more flexibility, while knowledge-based solutions are better for sentiment classification within a specific domain because they are based on human labour. These two strategies are complementary [22], giving birth to hybrid approaches.

Recently, a growing number of studies have explored the hybrid models. [3] proposes a hybrid model called BBLSTM, which includes a bitmask layer to focus attention on specific aspects within the text and incorporates sentiment lexicons into the domain-specific word embeddings. [5] enhances conventional attention-based LSTM models by introducing a method that better captures the meaning of the opinion target and by integrating syntactic information into the attention mechanism. [11] proposes a hybrid model called ALDONAr, which merges a lexicalized domain ontology with a regularized neural attention model. [20] introduced a hybrid model called HAABSA, which also uses a lexicalized domain ontology as [11] but combines it with a neural attention model with a rotatory attention mechanism. [19] presented a hybrid model called HAABSA++ that extends the HAABSA model with deep contextual word embeddings and hierarchical attention. These sentiment classification models produce impressive results. However, the robustness of these models must yet be tested [10].

[6] shows that the majority of sentences in existing ABSA datasets contain either a single aspect or multiple aspects of the same polarity, simplifying the ABSC task to sentence-level sentiment classification, thereby causing low robustness. [6] presented a new large-scale dataset called Multi-Aspect Multi-Sentiment (MAMS). Unlike existing ABSA datasets, MAMS sentences contain at least two

different aspects with different sentiment polarities. This protects ABSC models from collapsing into sentence-level sentiment analysis, thereby increasing the robustness of the ABSC model. However, it can be very expensive to annotate the robustly driven MAMS data, as it is fully obtained through human labor.

[21] explored the robustness problem by developing an automatic generation framework designed to generate a comprehensive ARTS used to evaluate aspect robustness. It employs three strategies (REVTGT, REVNON, and ADDDIFF) for generating variations that preserve the original content and aspect terms while separating the sentiment polarity of non-target aspects from the intended target. Combined with the new measure ARS, ARTS can be used to assess whether a model can reliably detect the intended sentiment in the presence of spurious patterns.

3 Specification of Used Datasets

To train and test our model for aspect-based sentiment classification, we use the datasets from SemEval-2015 Task 12 [14] and SemEval-2016 Task 5 Subtask 1 [15]. SemEval is a series of workshops that are commonly used for this type of evaluation task. This is an advantage as our results can be easily compared to other methods using the same datasets.

The SemEval datasets contain restaurant reviews, with each review holding at least one sentence. Each sentence has zero or more opinions, where an opinion is made up of the target aspect, the category of the aspect being evaluated, and a polarity that expresses whether the reviewer is positive, negative, or neutral about the specific aspect. An illustration of a sentence from the SemEval-2016 dataset in XML format is shown in Listing 1.1.

```
<sentence id="404464:2">
  <text>The entree was bland and small, dessert was not inspired</text>
  <Opinions>
    <Opinion target="entree" category="FOOD#QUALITY" polarity="negative" from="4" to="10"/>
    <Opinion target="entree" category="FOOD#STYLE_OPTION" polarity="negative" from="4" to="10"/>
    <Opinion target="dessert" category="FOOD#QUALITY" polarity="negative" from="32" to="39"/>
  </Opinions>
</sentence>
```

Listing 1.1. Example sentence of the SemEval-2016 dataset in XML format.

We clean the data of implicit aspects because our model requires explicit aspects for the aspect-based sentiment classification task. This step removes 25% of the data. We also eliminate repeated annotation of the same target aspects in the data. This happens because aspects belong to more than one aspect category. An example of this is shown in Listing 1.1. This step removes another 5% of the data. After cleaning, the SemEval-2015 data has a training set of 254 reviews with 1210 aspects and a test set of 96 reviews with 559 aspects. The SemEval-2016 data has a training set of 350 reviews with 1769 aspects and a test set of 90 reviews with 623 aspects. For the training set and the test set of the SemEval 2015 and SemEval 2016 data sets, some statistics are shown. Figure 1 shows the division of the aspects according to the sentiments they convey, indicating that positive polarity is the most common among the aspects and that the datasets have comparable proportions of polarity. Figure 2 shows the frequency of the number of aspects per sentence. We can see that sentences with a single aspect are the most common.

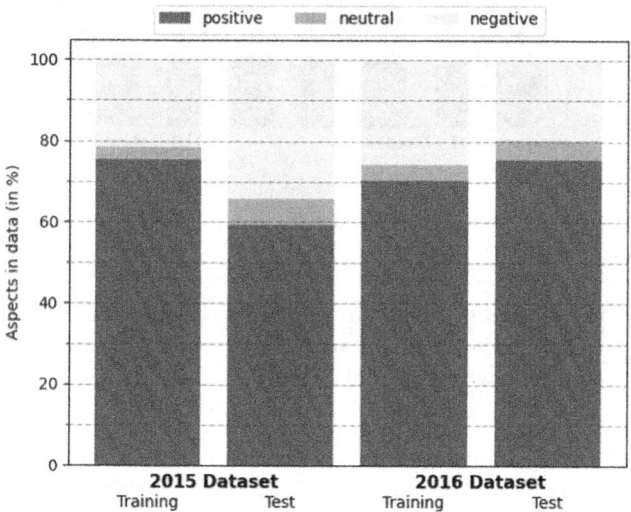

Fig. 1. Relative frequencies of sentiment labels.

4 Methodology

This section outlines the approach to check HAABSA++ robustness. First, the sentiment of the inputs is assessed using a domain sentiment ontology. If this method fails, a neural network is used as a fallback option. The neural network receives augmented data through a proposed data generation method to determine the Aspect Robustness Score (ARS). Furthermore, the study investigates the improvement of the ARS through adversarial training, which involves augmenting the training data.

In this study, we focus on the aspect robustness of the HAABSA++ model. To evaluate the aspect robustness of ABSA models, [21] introduced a novel metric called ARS and developed ARTS to augment the test set with three types of data augmentation techniques: REVTGT, which introduces tokens that invert the sentiment associated with the target aspect, REVNON, which inserts tokens

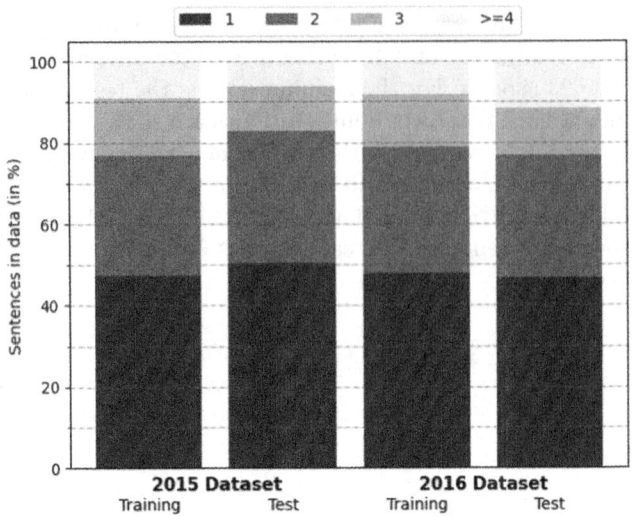

Fig. 2. Relative frequencies of aspects per sentence.

that maintain the sentiment of the target aspect while changing the sentiments of other aspects, and ADDDIFF, which appends new segments containing different aspects than the target with different sentiment from the target. The heuristics of these augmentation techniques are explained in more detail below.

REVTGT. The first augmentation technique aims to generate sentences that reverse the sentiment of the target aspect. This is achieved by two primary methods: opinion reversal and negation addition. When reversing opinion words, the approach starts with antonym replacement using WordNet, a lexical database [12]. However, to ensure context compatibility, only antonyms with the same Part-of-Speech tag as the original word are considered. When multiple options are available, random selection is applied, giving priority to antonyms already in the vocabulary. For target-oriented extraction of opinion words, manually annotated data provided by [4] is used. An example of the flip opinion strategy is shown in Table 1. In this example, the opinion word "best" for the target aspect "meal" in the sentence "It is simply the best meal in NYC" is flipped to the opinion word "worst" to produce the new sentence "It is simply the worst meal in NYC". In cases where no suitable antonyms can be found, or for longer phrases, negation is introduced based on linguistic features. Typically, this involves adding "not" in front of adjectives or verbs that express sentiment. If the sentiment term is not in the form of an adjective or verb, negation is applied to the closest verb.

Table 1 also provides an example of the add negation strategy, where the opinion word "authentic" for the target aspect "food" in the sentence "The food was authentic" is negated to produce the new sentence "The food was not authentic". Adjustments are also made to conjunctions to ensure fluency. Reversing the sentiment of one aspect can result in conflicting sentiments between aspects.

Table 1. Strategies and examples of REVTGT. The target aspects are underlined and all of the relevant opinion words and conjunctions are in bold type.

Strategy	Example
Flip Opinion	It's simply the **best** meal in NYC.
	→ It's simply the **worst** meal in NYC.
Add Negation	The food was **authentic**.
	→ The food was **not authentic**.
Adjust Conjunctions	The food is so **cheap and** the waiters are nice.
	→ The food is so **expensive but** the waiters are nice.

Conjunctions are adjusted accordingly. Cumulative conjunctions such as "and" are used when adjacent sentiments have the same polarity, while adversative conjunctions such as "but" are used when sentiments differ. Also, an example of the adjust conjunctions strategy is shown in Table 1. In this example, because the opinion word "cheap" for the target aspect "food" in the sentence "The food is so cheap and the waiters are nice" is flipped to the opinion word "expensive", the conjunction word "and" is changed to the conjunction word "but" to produce the new sentence "The food is so expensive, but the waiters are nice".

REVNON. The second augmentation technique reverses sentiments for non-target aspects that have the same sentiment as the target aspect, using the REVTGT method. An example of the flip same-sentiment non-target aspects strategy is shown in Table 2. In this example the opinion word "clean" for the non-target aspect "restaurant" in the sentence "The service is good and the restaurant is clean" is flipped to the opinion word "dirty" and the conjunction word "and" is changed to the conjunction word "but" to produce the new sentence "The service is good but the restaurant is dirty". In addition, for non-target aspects that already exhibit sentiments opposite to the target sentiment, the approach amplifies that opposition. This is achieved by randomly selecting adverbs from a specialized dictionary of degree adverbs compiled from the training data. This deliberate exaggeration serves to emphasize the existing contrast. Also, an example of the exaggerated opposite-sentiment non-target aspects strategy is shown in Table 2. In this example the opinion word "amazing" for the non-target aspect "food" in the sentence "Decor needs to be upgraded but the food is amazing!" is exaggerated to "greatly amazing" to produce the new sentence "Decor needs to be upgraded but the food is greatly amazing!".

ADDDIFF. The last augmentation technique explores the impact of appending additional non-target aspects on model performance. The first step of this technique is the creation of the AspectSet, where all aspect expressions from the dataset are extracted. This is achieved by identifying sentiment terms in each instance (e.g., "bad" in "Plain and simple it's bad thai food.") and then retrieving their linguistic branches (e.g., "bad thai food") using pretrained con-

Table 2. Strategies and examples of RevNon. The target aspects are underlined, the non-target aspects are in italics, and all of the relevant opinion words and conjunctions are in bold type.

Strategy	Example
Flip same-sentiment non-target aspects	The service is good **and** the *restaurant* is **clean**.
	→ The service is good **but** the *restaurant* is **dirty**.
Exaggerate opposite-sentiment non-target aspects	Decor needs to be upgraded but the *food* is **amazing**!
	→ Decor needs to be upgraded but the *food* is **greatly amazing**!

stituency parsing [7]. Some examples of found aspect expressions contained in the AspectSet are shown in Table 3.

Table 3. Examples of aspect expressions in the AspectSet.

Sentiment	Aspect Expression
Positive	decor is nice and minimalist
	the service is always outstanding
	every pie is ultra fresh
Negative	the atmosphere is noisy
	lobster ravioli was very salty
	their deliveries take for ever

Then, one to three aspects not mentioned in the original sample and with sentiments different from the target aspect are randomly selected from AspectSet and added to the original instance. For example, the aspect expressions "a lot of food" and "a nice pizza place" are added to the sentence "The kitchen however, is almost always slow" to obtain the new sentence "The kitchen however, is almost always slow, *but* a lot of food *and* a nice pizza place." This augmentation technique allows us to assess whether the introduction of more unrelated aspects with opposite sentiments confuses the model.

The trio of data augmentation techniques are applied to extend the test sets for the SemEval 2015 and 2016 restaurant domain datasets, as [21] did for the SemEval 2014 restaurant domain dataset. Aspect robustness is then evaluated using ARS [21], a measure that considers the accurate classification of the original example and its modified versions (RevTgt, RevNon, and AddDiff) as a single correct instance. Additionally, improving ARS through adversarial training is explored by applying these three data augmentation methods to the training set.

Figure 3 provides a high-level overview of how our method is structured to help to visualise where the augmented data is fed into our method.

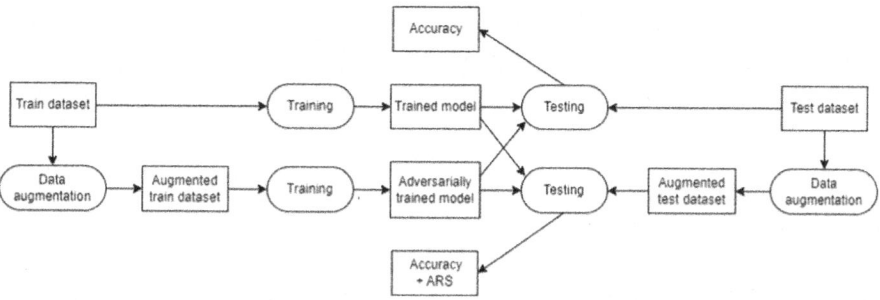

Fig. 3. A high-level overview of the structure of the proposed method, showing where the augmented data is fed into the method.

5 Results

In this section, we present the obtained results. In Sect. 5.1, some statistics for the generated ARTS of SemEval 2015 and SemEval 2016 are discussed. In Sect. 5.2, the results for the adversarial training are presented. Last, in Sect. 5.3, we compare the HAABSA++ model with other models in the literature to see how it performs in terms of robustness as measured by ARS.

5.1 Data Augmentation

In Table 4 the number of instances in the tests and trains set for the original and augmented SemEval 2015 and SemEval 2016 data sets are presented. We see that for the test sets the original data is enriched from 559 and 623 instances to 1725 and 1868 instances of the augmented data for the SemEval 2015 and SemEval 2016 datasets, respectively. This is an increase in size of 209% and 200%, respectively. For the train sets the original data is enriched from 1210 and 1769 instances to 3938 and 5640 instances of the augmented data for the SemEval 2015 and SemEval 2016 datasets, respectively. An increase in size of 225% and 219%, respectively. Ideally, the desired increase in size is 300%, reflecting the three augmentation techniques. However, not all original instances qualify for each strategy, leading to this gap. ADDDIFF is applicable in all cases, but REVTGT and REVNON require explicit opinion words. The main obstacle for REVTGT is the lack of opinion words. Consequently, the number of new test instances generated by REVTGT matches the number of available opinion word instances. REVNON imposes additional constraints. First instances with only one aspect are filtered out. These instances have no non-target aspect and therefore REVNON cannot be applied. Furthermore, instances with overlapping opinion words between target and non-target aspects are also filtered out. This is because in these cases REVNON cannot be used to reverse the sentiment of the non-target aspect without also changing the sentiment of the target aspect. Last, instances with neutral sentiments for all non-target aspects are excluded. There is no point in reversing or exaggerating the neutral sentiment of non-target aspects. Therefore, no new instance is created with REVNON if all non-target aspects have neutral sentiment. The instance counts for each used augmentation technique are also shown in Table 4.

Table 4. The number of instances in the test set and train set for the original and augmented SemEval 2015 and SemEval 2016 datasets. Also, the instance count for each augmentation technique is shown.

Dataset	Original		Augmented		REVTGT		REVNON		ADDDIFF	
	Train	Test	Train	Test	Train	Test	Train	Test	Train	Test
SemEval 2015	1210	559	3938	1725	1068	442	450	165	1210	559
SemEval 2016	1769	623	5640	1868	1498	454	604	168	1769	623

5.2 Model Performance

Because the ontology model is not trainable, we do not use the augmented test data on the ontology model and the ontology part of the HAABSA++ model. To evaluate the robustness of the neural network part of the HAABSA++ model, we feed the original test data into the ontology reasoner and augment the inconclusive instances of the original test data.

In Table 5, we see that the accuracy of the HAABSA++ model with regular training for the original test set of the SemEval 2015 and SemEval 2016 datasets is 74.6% and 83.0%, respectively. After adversarial training, we see that the accuracy for the original test set of the SemEval 2015 and SemEval 2016 datasets drops to 73.2% and 81.5%, respectively. A possible reason for this drop is that by adding the new instances to the training set, the distribution of the training set is changed in a way that makes it more difficult for the HAABSA++ model to correctly predict the sentiment of the original test set. The HAABSA++ model performs better when compared to the stand-alone ontology model, which has an accuracy of 65.7% and 79.0% for the original test set of the SemEval 2015 and SemEval 2016 datasets, respectively. Surprisingly, however, and in contrast to the results found in the paper of [19], the HAABSA++ model performs worse than the standalone neural network model, which has an accuracy of 77.1% and 86.7% with regular training, and 76.6% and 83.3% with adversarial training for the original test set of the SemEval 2015 and SemEval 2016 datasets, respectively. We see again that after adversarial training the accuracy of the original test sets drop.

To better understand the performance of the HAABSA++ model, we look at the performance of the individual parts of the hybrid model. We see that the accuracy of the ontology part of the HAABSA++ model is quite high, with values of 80.1% and 86.2% for the original test set of the SemEval 2015 and SemEval 2016 datasets, respectively. However, we see that the accuracy of the

Table 5. Accuracy of the regularly and adversarially trained HAABSA++ model for the original and augmented test sets of the SemEval 2015 and SemEval 2016 datasets. The accuracy of the ontology and the neural network within the HAABSA++ model as well as stand-alone models are also shown. For the augmented test sets ARS is given in parentheses.

	SemEval 2015		SemEval 2016	
	Original	Augmented	Original	Augmented
HAABSA++				
Regular training	74.6%	-	83.0%	-
Adversarial training	73.2%	-	81.5%	-
Ontology part	80.1%	-	86.2%	-
(If done by Neural Network)	(85.1%)		(92.2%)	
Neural Network part				
Regular training	69.3%	56.7% (24.7%)	77.8%	61.0% (30.1%)
Adversarial training	66.4%	68.5% (47.3%)	74.1%	77.7% (60.7%)
Ontology	65.7%	-	79.0%	-
Neural Network				
Regular training	77.1%	62.0% (24.2%)	86.7%	67.3% (30.5%)
Adversarial training	76.6%	76.9% (57.6%)	83.3%	84.9% (70.9%)

ontology part of the HAABSA++ model is even higher when done by the neural network, with values of 85.1% and 92.2% for the original test set of the SemEval 2015 and SemEval 2016 datasets, respectively. This explains why the HAABSA++ model performs worse than the standalone neural network model. The neural network part of the HAABSA++ model performs rather poorly with an accuracy of 69.3% and 77.8% with regular training and 66.4% and 74.1% with adversarial training for the original test set of the SemEval 2015 and SemEval 2016 datasets, respectively. A possible explanation for this is that the ontology reasoner picks out all of the easy instances of the test set and leaves the neural network with all the difficult instances.

To find the benefits of the adversarial training we have to look at the accuracy and ARS of the models for the augmented test sets. The stand-alone neural network model has an accuracy (ARS) of 62.0% (24.2) and 67.3% (30.5) with regular training but an accuracy (ARS) of 76.9% (57.6) and 84.9% (70.9) with adversarial training for the augmented test set of the SemEval 2015 and SemEval 2016 datasets, respectively. We see a big increase in accuracy and ARS for the adversarially trained model compared to the regularly trained model. This increase in accuracy and ARS is a direct result of the adversarial training. The adversarial training changes the distribution of the training set in a way that allows the model to better recognize the new instances of the augmented test set, increasing accuracy and ARS. We observe a similar but smaller increase in both the accuracy and ARS when we look at the outcomes of the neural network part of the

HAABSA++ model. The neural network part of the HAABSA++ model has an accuracy (ARS) of 56.6% (24.7%) and 61.0% (30.1%) with regular training but an accuracy (ARS) of 68.5% (47.3%) and 77.7% (60.7%) with adversarial training for the augmented test set of the SemEval 2015 and SemEval 2016 datasets, respectively. A possible reason why the increase for both accuracy and ARS is smaller is again that the neural network part of HAABSA++ is initially left with all the difficult instances because the ontology reasoner has picked out all the easy instances of the test set. The augmentation of these difficult instances creates even more difficult new instances, which causes the difference in the increase of both accuracy and ARS.

In all results of the augmented test sets, we see that the ARS is lower than the accuracy when we compare the ARS with the corresponding accuracy of the augmented test sets. This is expected due to the strict definition of ARS. ARS considers the correct classification of the original example and its modified versions as a single correct instance. Thus, if only one is incorrectly classified, ARS will be incorrect for this instance.

If we compare the results of the original test sets with the augmented test sets (Table 5), we see a decrease in accuracy for regular training. This decrease can be explained by the fact that the new instances of the augmented test set are in some way different from the instances on which the model is trained with regular training. When we compare the results of the original test sets with the augmented test sets for adversarial training, this decrease in accuracy turns into a slight increase in accuracy. This is because adversarial training causes the model to better recognize the new instances of the augmented test set.

5.3 Robustness Comparison

Table 6 lists for several models the accuracy for the original test set of the SemEval 2014 Restaurant dataset and the ARS after regular training and after adversarial training for the augmented test set of the SemEval 2014 Restaurant dataset. Except for the HAABSA++ model, all models, accuracies, and ARS values in Table 6 are taken over from the paper of [21]. The accuracy for the augmented test set is not shown because they are not reported in the paper of [21]. To conclude how well the HAABSA++ models compare to these other models in terms of robustness as measured by ARS, we also evaluated our models on the SemEval 2014 Restaurant dataset. From Table 6, we conclude that ARS increases after adversarial training for all models and that the HAABSA++ model without ontology reasoner performs averagely in terms of accuracy and robustness as measured by ARS. The best results for ARS are obtained by the BERT models. It appears that capturing the semantic information of text by considering the surrounding context in addition to the words themselves, as BERT contextual word embeddings do, increases the robustness of these models as measured by ARS. Although the HAABSA++ model also makes use of BERT word embeddings, the performance of the HAABSA++ model without ontology reasoner is more similar to the TD-LSTM model. A possible explanation for this is that the HAABSA++ model uses pre-trained BERT word embeddings, rather than training the word embeddings on the data, as is the case with the other BERT models.

Table 6. The table reports the accuracy for the original test set of the SemEval 2014 Restaurant dataset, and the ARS after regular training and after adversarial training for the augmented test set of the SemEval 2014 Restaurant dataset for several models.

	Accuracy	ARS	
		Regular training	Adversarial training
BERT-PT	86.7%	59.3%	74.6%
CapsBERT	83.5%	55.4%	75.8%
BERT	83.0%	54.8%	74.8%
HAABSA++ (w/o ont)	77.8%	31.5%	66.2%
TD-LSTM	78.1%	30.2%	62.8%
HAABSA++	72.2%	29.6%	55.1%
GCN	77.9%	24.7%	61.5%
MemNet	75.2%	21.5%	38.0%
attLSTM	76.0%	14.6%	48.7%
GatedCNNN	77.0%	13.1%	37.5%
Average	**78.4%**	**31.5%**	**58.4%**

6 Conclusion

In this paper, we inspected the robustness of the HAABSA++ model. This model uses a domain-specific ontology with a specialized neural network as a fail-safe to evaluate the sentiment toward aspect targets. To evaluate the aspect robustness of the HAABSA++ model, we augmented the test set with three types of data augmentation techniques: REVTGT, which inverts the sentiment associated with the target aspect, REVNON, which maintains the sentiment of the target aspect while changing the sentiments of other aspects, and ADDDIFF, which appends new segments containing different aspects than the target with different sentiment from the target. Aspect robustness is evaluated using ARS. Additionally, we explored improving ARS through adversarial training by applying the three data augmentation methods to the training set.

Surprisingly, we find that the HAABSA++ model performs better without using the ontology part of the model. Furthermore, we find that performing adversarial training indeed improves the robustness of the model as measured by ARS. However, this improvement comes at the cost of a lower accuracy of the HAABSA++ model for the original test set instances. When comparing the robustness as measured by ARS of the HAABSA++ model with other models found in the literature, we find that the HAABSA++ score is average.

A suggestion for future work is to improve the data augmentation method. In particular, the need for annotation of opinion words is a major drawback. This limits the use of this method for other datasets where this annotation is not present. Furthermore, the data augmentation techniques could be modified to apply to the entire dataset. When an instance of the original data set has fewer newly created instances in the augmented data set, the ARS is less stringent. A more uniform ARTS prevents this. Also, it would be interesting to test how the change of order of model components in the classification pipeline from ontology first to neural network first, would affect the outcome.

Disclosure of Interests. The authors have no competing interests to declare that are relevant to the content of this article.

References

1. Brauwers, G., Frasincar, F.: A survey on aspect-based sentiment classification. ACM Comput. Surv. **55**(4), 1–37 (2023)
2. Devlin, J., Chang, M.W., Lee, K., Toutanova, K.: Pre-training of deep bidirectional transformers for language understanding. In: 2019 Annual Conference of the North American Chapter of the Association for Computational Linguistics: Human Language Technologies (NAACL-HCL 2019), pp. 4171–4186. ACL (2019)
3. Do, B.T.: Aspect-based sentiment analysis using bitmask bidirectional long short term memory networks. In: 31st International Florida Artificial Intelligence Research Society Conference (FLAIRS 2018), pp. 259–264. AAAI Press (2018)
4. Fan, Z., Wu, Z., Dai, X., Huang, S., Chen, J.: Target-oriented opinion words extraction with target-fused neural sequence labeling. In: 2019 Annual Conference of the North American Chapter of the Association for Computational Linguistics: Human Language Technologies (NAACL-HCL 2019), pp. 2509–2518. ACL (2019)
5. He, R., Lee, W.S., Ng, H.T., Dahlmeier, D.: Effective attention modeling for aspect-level sentiment classification. In: 27th International Conference on Computational Linguistics (COLING 2018), pp. 1121–1131. ACL (2018)
6. Jiang, Q., Chen, L., Xu, R., Ao, X., Yang, M.: A challenge dataset and effective models for aspect-based sentiment analysis. In: 2019 Conference on Empirical Methods in Natural Language Processing and 9th International Joint Conference on Natural Language Processing (EMNLP-IJCNLP 2019), pp. 6280–6285. ACL (2019)
7. Joshi, V., Peters, M., Hopkins, M.: Extending a parser to distant domains using a few dozen partially annotated examples. In: 56th Annual Meeting of the Association for Computational Linguistics (ACL 2018), vol. 1, pp. 1190–1199. ACL (2018)
8. Kiritchenko, S., Zhu, X., Cherry, C., Mohammad, S.: NRC-Canada-2014: detecting aspects and sentiment in customer reviews. In: 8th International Workshop on Semantic Evaluation (SemEval 2014), pp. 437–442. ACL (2014)
9. Liu, B.: Sentiment Analysis: Mining Opinions, Sentiments, and Emotions, 2nd edn. Cambridge University Press (2020)
10. Liu, X., et al.: Towards robust aspect-based sentiment analysis through non-counterfactual augmentations. arXiv preprint arXiv:2306.13971 (2023)

11. Meškelė, D., Frasincar, F.: ALDONAr: a hybrid solution for sentence-level aspect-based sentiment analysis using a lexicalized domain ontology and a regularized neural attention model. Inf. Process. Manag. **57**(3), 102211 (2020)
12. Miller, G.A.: Wordnet: a lexical database for english. Commun. ACM **38**(11), 39–41 (1995)
13. Peters, M.E., et al.: Deep contextualized word representations. In: 2018 Conference of the North American Chapter of the Association for Computational Linguistics: Human Language Technologies, pp. 2227–2237. ACL (2018)
14. Pontiki, M., Galanis, D., Papageorgiou, H., Manandhar, S., Androutsopoulos, I.: SemEval-2015 task 12: aspect based sentiment analysis. In: 9th International Workshop on Semantic Evaluation (SemEval 2015), pp. 486–495. ACL (2015)
15. Pontiki, M., et al.: SemEval-2016 task 5: aspect based sentiment analysis. In: 10th International Workshop on Semantic Evaluation (SemEval 2016), pp. 19–30. ACL (2016)
16. Ren, Y., Zhang, Y., Zhang, M., Ji, D.: Context-sensitive twitter sentiment classification using neural network. In: 13th AAAI Conference on Artificial Intelligence (AAAI 2016), vol. 30, pp. 215–221. AAAI Press (2016)
17. Schouten, K., Frasincar, F.: Survey on aspect-level sentiment analysis. IEEE Trans. Knowl. Data Eng. **28**(3), 813–830 (2016)
18. Schouten, K., Frasincar, F.: Ontology-driven sentiment analysis of product and service aspects. In: Gangemi, A., et al. (eds.) ESWC 2018. LNCS, vol. 10843, pp. 608–623. Springer, Cham (2018). https://doi.org/10.1007/978-3-319-93417-4_39
19. Trușcă, M.M., Wassenberg, D., Frasincar, F., Dekker, R.: A hybrid approach for aspect-based sentiment analysis using deep contextual word embeddings and hierarchical attention. In: Bielikova, M., Mikkonen, T., Pautasso, C. (eds.) ICWE 2020. LNCS, vol. 12128, pp. 365–380. Springer, Cham (2020). https://doi.org/10.1007/978-3-030-50578-3_25
20. Wallaart, O., Frasincar, F.: A hybrid approach for aspect-based sentiment analysis using a lexicalized domain ontology and attentional neural models. In: Hitzler, P., et al. (eds.) ESWC 2019. LNCS, vol. 11503, pp. 363–378. Springer, Cham (2019). https://doi.org/10.1007/978-3-030-21348-0_24
21. Xing, X., Jin, Z., Jin, D., Wang, B., Zhang, Q., Huang, X.: Tasty burgers, soggy fries: probing aspect robustness in aspect-based sentiment analysis. In: 2020 Conference on Empirical Methods in Natural Language Processing (EMNLP 2020), pp. 3594–3605. ACL (2020)
22. Yanase, T., Yanai, K., Sato, M., Miyoshi, T., Niwa, Y.: bunji at SemEval-2016 task 5: neural and syntactic models of entity-attribute relationship for aspect-based sentiment analysis. In: 10th International Workshop on Semantic Evaluation (SemEval 2016), pp. 289–295. ACL (2016)
23. Zheng, S., Xia, R.: Left-center-right separated neural network for aspect-based sentiment analysis with rotatory attention. arXiv preprint arXiv:1802.00892 (2018)

Applying Contrastive Learning to an Attention Neural Model in a Multilingual Context

Philipp Gottschalk, Flavius Frasincar(✉) , and Eyo Herstad

Erasmus University Rotterdam, Burgemeester Oudlaan 50, 3062 PA Rotterdam,
The Netherlands
`595725pg@student.eur.nl`, `{frasincar,herstad}@ese.eur.nl`

Abstract. This research contributes to the field of Aspect-Based Sentiment Classification (ABSC) of Web data by proposing new cross-, multi- and unilingual ASBC models. We do this by improving the state-of-the-art mLCR-Rot-hop++ attention neural model and its variations. We introduce different multilingual XLM-R embedders to replace the multilingual BERT (mBERT) embedder found within the mLCR-Rot-hop++ model. Furthermore, we add two distinct contrastive learning methods to the existing mLCR-Rot-hop++ model. The first approach integrates sentiment-level contrastive learning, adapted to instances rather than individual token embeddings, into the mLCR-Rot-hop++ model. Our second approach considers the high-level opinion representations of the mLCR-Rot-hop++ model within the contrastive loss function. Our findings indicate that replacing the mBERT embedder with an XLM-R_{base} embedder generally improves performance. Furthermore, sentiment-level contrastive learning usually improves the performance of various models, especially compared to representation-level contrastive learning.

Keywords: ABSC · ML-ABSC · XL-ABSC · UL-ABSC · LCR-Rot-hop++

1 Introduction

With the ever-expanding presence of online marketplaces, review platforms, and social media on the Web, opinionated text has become ubiquitous. As a result, there is an escalating interest in being able to aggregate large swaths of opinionated text into useful data, leading to a surge of research in sentiment analysis.

Sentiment analysis concerns itself with the automated classification of opinionated text. In particular, there has been an expanded exploration of Aspect-Based sentiment analysis (ABSA), which focuses on detecting the sentiment of a certain entity, or aspect of an entity, within a given text [17]. ABSA can be subdivided into multiple tasks. Our investigation deals with the subtask of Aspect-Based Sentiment Classification (ABSC), which consists of assigning labels and sentiment scores to previously extracted aspects [2].

A significant challenge when classifying online opinionated texts is the diverse range of languages used. Consequently, there is a vested interest in creating models which can be trained in resource-rich source languages and then applied to resource-poor target languages. This approach is often referred to as Cross-Lingual ABSA (XL-ABSA). As specified by [16], XL-ABSA trains models on a labelled source language and then applies these models to an unlabelled target language. Another possible approach is to train models on a range of different source languages, thereby creating a model which is relatively language-agnostic. This approach is usually referred to as Multilingual ABSA (ML-ABSA). Models trained in the same language later used to evaluate them are referred to as Unilingual ABSA (UL-ABSA) models.

In this paper, we contribute to the ABSC field by proposing new XL-ABSA and ML-ABSA models inspired by those introduced in [5], which use the state-of-the-art ABSC LCR-Rot-hop++ method [13] as a backbone. The improvements that we propose are two-fold. First, we replace the mBERT embedder that the model currently uses with two versions (base and large) of the XLM-RoBERTa (XLM-R) embedder, which have been shown to outperform mBERT on numerous cross-lingual benchmarks [3]. This gives us the $XLMR_{base}$-LCR-Rot-hop++ and XLMR-LCR-Rot-hop++ models.

Moreover, we integrate contrastive learning, proposed for XL-ABSA usage by [6], into the framework of the multilingual LCR-Rot-hop++ models. As mentioned in [6], contrastive learning works by shortening the distance between so-called anchor points and *positive* samples, and increasing the distance between anchor points and *negative* samples. We utilise contrastive learning for the sentiment labels of entire instances, leading to the CLS-$XLMR_{base}$-LCR-Rot-hop++ model. This contrasts [6], which uses contrastive learning for the sentiment labels of tokens. Inspired by the method in [7], we also introduce a novel contrastive learning approach which uses the concatenated high-level representations from LCR-Rot-hop++ model for contrastive learning, giving us the CLR-$XLMR_{base}$-LCR-Rot-hop++ model. The paper's source code is found on GitHub at https://github.com/P-Gottschalk/CL-XLMR_base-LCR-Rot-hop-plus-plus.git.

The rest of the paper is constructed as follows. In Sect. 2, an overview of the current state of the research is provided. Section 3 describes the data utilised throughout this research. Section 4 then details the proposed methodology. The results of the investigation can be found in Sect. 5. In Sect. 6, we provide our research conclusion and suggestions for future work.

2 Related Work

[11], an ABSA survey pre-dating [17], states that research on ABSA falls into three categories: Aspect Detection (AD), Aspect-Based Sentiment Classification (ABSC), and joint AD and ABSC. A summary of AD is provided by [12]. Our investigation focuses on ABSC [2] and its application to a multilingual setting.

As noted by [2], ABSC can generally be categorised into three major categories: knowledge-based, machine learning, and hybrid models. Knowledge-based models classify sentiments using pre-determined rules, relations, and lexicalisations. Machine learning approaches are trained to extract sentiments using a training dataset of feature vectors labelled with sentiments. Hybrid approaches combine knowledge bases and machine learning approaches, aiming to use knowledge bases where a lack of data hinders machine learning approaches.

In our research, we focus on extending a state-of-the-art machine learning approach. [18] introduces a Left-Center-Right separated neural network with Rotary attention (LCR-Rot). [14] utilises this model in a two-stage sentiment analysis algorithm called the Hybrid Approach ABSA (HAABSA) model. A lexicalised domain ontology is used to predict the sentiment, and LCR-Rot-hop, which runs multiple iterations of the rotary attention mechanism of LCR-Rot, is used as a backup model. HAABSA++ is subsequently introduced by [13]. This new model adds hierarchical attention to LCR-Rot-hop and replaces non-contextual word embeddings with deep contextual word embeddings, resulting in LCR-Rot-hop++. [5] then utilises the LCR-Rot-hop++ procedure for cross- and multilingual ABSC, replacing the previously used BERT embedder [4] by mBERT, a multilingual version of BERT trained using 104 languages [4].

We address the issue of low-resource languages by considering cross-lingual sentiment analysis [15] and multilingual sentiment analysis [1]. Both approaches aim to alleviate the issue of low-resource languages as a target language. Here, cross-lingual models are strictly trained on one source language and then applied to different target languages, whilst multilingual models are trained on multiple languages. It should be noted this distinction is often less pronounced in the literature, with multilingual sentiment analysis often serving as an umbrella term for both approaches. We further consider unilingual sentiment analysis for non-English languages, as in [5]. Since ABSA research is generally unilingual, this is rarely isolated as a distinct field of research in a multilingual context.

Numerous approaches to XL-ASBA and XL-ABSC are suggested in the literature. To augment available data, [16] creates an aspect code-switching mechanism, which switches aspect terms between instances in the source language and translated cases in the target language, using a combined dataset to train the model. [6] uses contrastive learning to achieve a convergence of semantic spaces across different languages. As described in Sect. 1, this is done by adjusting the distance between anchor points and corresponding *positive* and *negative* samples. Whilst applying contrastive learning to ABSA is increasing in popularity, to the best of our knowledge, [6] is one of the very few investigations to utilise contrastive learning cross-lingually. Unilingually, [7] presents a token-based approach to contrastive learning in ABSA. Instead of using probability distributions of the predicted sentiment within the contrastive loss function [6,7] uses aspect-oriented sentiment representations. This gives a more fine-grained model, as the aspect-oriented sentiment representations contain more information than the sentiment probability distribution. [10] proposes a multi-layer network with divided attention to perform XL-ABSC. This method extracts Part-of-Speech (POS) information–grammatical properties such as nouns, adjectives, and verbs– and feeds this information to an attention-based convolutional neural network.

[10] further leverages bilingual dictionaries to map converted tokens across languages. As previously stated, [5] adapts the LCR-Rot-hop++ method to both a cross-lingual and a multilingual context.

Multilingual Masking Language Models (MLMs) are also being developed significantly. Improving on the widely utilised baseline model mBERT, [3] proposes XLM-R$_{base}$ and XLM-R, two multilingual versions of Facebook's RoBERTa [8]. Whilst only trained on 100 languages [3], compared to the 104 languages in mBERT's training set, XLM-R$_{base}$ and XLM-R have a larger vocabulary (250k tokens), compared to mBERT's (110k tokens).

3 Data

In this paper we use the SemEval-2016 dataset, developed by [9]. This dataset is widely employed in ABSA research, and is therefore an appropriate benchmark for model evaluation.

We use the Task 5, Subtask 1 (SB1) data of the SemEval-2016 dataset. SB1 is focused on sentence-level ABSA and the identification of opinion tuples from the following three types of information: Aspect Category (AC), Opinion Target Expression (OTE), and Sentiment Polarity (SP). The dataset covers multiple topics, including hotels, consumer electronics, and restaurants. For this investigation, we use the restaurant dataset, as this dataset spans the most languages–English, French, Spanish, Dutch, Turkish, and Russian–out of the available data. Hence, it is therefore most appropriate for investigations into cross- and multilingual sentiment classification.

Firstly, note that Russian uses the Cyrillic alphabet and is consequently ill-suited for investigations into cross- and multi-lingual investigations, as similarities with the other languages are relatively low, so Russian is removed. We also drop Turkish from our dataset due to its comparatively small test sample. As seen in [9], the test set is limited to 39 sentences with 144 sentiments. Comparatively, the second smallest dataset, the English test data, has 90 sentences and 650 expressed sentiments, an almost fivefold increase in sentiments compared to Turkish.

Further, we clean the data according to the methodology set out by [5]. Specifically, we remove any sentiment labels that are related to hidden aspects, as the used LCR-Rot-hop++ method introduced by [13], which serves as the foundation for this research, is not equipped to deal with implicit aspects.

The data files provided are in XML format. An example of a sentence from the dataset is provided in Fig. 1. Here, we see a specific sentence, with attached opinions, is provided. Each includes the target phrase of the opinion, the category of the target phrase, and an attached sentiment polarity.

Summary statistics for the dataset are provided in Table 1, including the frequency of sentiment polarities and their percentage. The data cleaning results in a loss of up to 35.7% for individual datasets.

```
<sentence id="1349391:0">
  <text>sometimes i get good food and ok service.</text>
  <Opinions>
    <Opinion target="food" category="FOOD#QUALITY" polarity="positive" from=
    "21" to="25"/>
    <Opinion target="service" category="SERVICE#GENERAL" polarity="neutral"
    from="33" to="40"/>
  </Opinions>
</sentence>
```

Fig. 1. SemEval-2016 example sentence.

Table 1. Summary statistics for our used data. The parentheses indicate the number of removed polarity labels.

	English		French		Spanish		Dutch	
	Train	Test	Train	Test	Train	Test	Train	Test
# Total	1880 (627)	650 (209)	1770 (706)	718 (236)	1937* (783)	731 (341)	1283 (577)	394 (219)
% Positive	70.2	74.3	50.9	50.7	70.6	71.3	59.1	62.2
% Neutral	3.83	20.8	42.5	39.7	24.7	24.1	31.7	31.7
% Negative	26.0	4.92	6.55	9.61	4.60	4.65	9.20	6.09

*A further opinion was removed during embedding due to an unknown polarity label.

4 Methodology

In this section we present our proposed methodology. We also explain the methodology variations needed to target various tasks: ML-ABSC, XL-ABSC, and UL-ABSC. Last, we discuss the use of contrastive learning for improving results.

4.1 XLMR$_{base}$-LCR-Rot-hop++

The XLMR$_{base}$-LCR-Rot-hop++ model is based on the previously proposed mLCR-Rot-hop++ model introduced by [5]. This model serves as a basis for the remainder of the investigation, consistently achieving strong results when tested against state-of-the-art machine learning ABSC models. The model is trained on English data, embedded using a multilingual embedder. The test set used for the model is the test set for each language.

We use the two pre-trained multilingual configurations first introduced in [3]: XLM-R$_{base}$ and XLM-R, which sets us apart from the works of [5] and of [13], which use mBERT and BERT for the respective embeddings. The XLM-R embedder is the "larger" of the two models, containing approximately twice the number of parameters, double the number of layers, and 30% more hidden states than XLM-R$_{base}$[1]. While XLM-R outperforms the XLM-R$_{base}$ in [3], it is worth testing our model with both embedders, as XLM-R$_{base}$ has similar

---

[1] Model sizes, written as {L, H, A, # param} [3]: mBERT = {12, 768, 12, 172M}; XLM-R$_{base}$ = {12, 768, 12, 270M}; XLM-R = {24, 1024, 16, 550M}.

model parameters to mBERT. Thereby, it could be more suited to the already existent LCR-Rot-hop++ framework, as the larger size of XLM-R embeddings may increase the quantity of data needed to train our model.

The embeddings are subsequently fed into the LCR-Rot-hop++ framework. This model is a neural network with a rotary attention mechanism, which operates at the sentence level. Each instance fed into the model is split into a left context, a target phrase, and a right context. The two-step rotary attention mechanism is then applied: first, the context representations for the left and right contexts are computed using a target representation from a pooling layer. We then introduce hierarchical attention to the model by tuning the context representations with respect to each other. Secondly, we compute target aspect representations using the right and left context representations found previously. Finally, the target representations are tuned using hierarchical attention. This step can be repeated n (here, $n = 3$) times, where the pooling layer target representations are replaced by the computed target representations after these are first computed. Once this attention mechanism has been repeated a sufficient number of times, the four context representations are concatenated to form a representation vector v_i for instance i, and the sentiment polarity is computed using a softmax function. Prediction p_i is evaluated using the cross-entropy loss function:

$$\underset{1\times 1}{L_{CE}} = -\sum_{i=1}^{K} \underset{|C|\times 1}{y_i} \times \log \underset{|C|\times 1}{(p_i)} + \lambda ||\Theta||^2 \qquad (1)$$

where K denotes the size of the batch of training opinions, y_i the sentiment vector of x_i, p_i the prediction vector for instance x_i, $|C|$ the number of different sentiment categories, and λ the L_2 regularisation term for the parameter set Θ. We initialise the weights and bias terms using a uniform distribution and update using stochastic gradient descent with a momentum term. We tune hyperparameters using a Tree-structured Parzan Estimators (TPE) algorithm.

4.2 Variations on XLMR$_{base}$-LCR-Rot-hop++

The base mLCR-Rot-hop++ is trained on the English dataset from SemEval-2016. We use this configuration as a baseline comparison for the XLMR$_{base}$-LCR-Rot-hop++ and XLMR-LCR-Rot-hop++ models, as it is also trained on the English datasets and outperforms most XL-ABSC and ML-ABSC models when tested on the French and Spanish datasets [5]. Moreover, we present further adaptations of the XLMR$_{base}$-LCR-Rot-hop++ model, which are used as comparisons to other well-performing models described in [5]. Table 2 shows the classifications of the variations to the standard XLMR$_{base}$-LCR-Rot-hop++, which we propose in this paper.

Table 2. The classification of the models that are proposed.

	Model Type		
	ML-ABSC	XL-ABSC	UL-ABSC
$XLMR_{base}$-LCR-Rot-hop++	–	x	–
$XLMR_{base}$-LCR-Rot-hop-XX++	–	–	x
$XLMR_{base}$-MLCR-Rot-hop++	x	–	–
$XLMR_{base}$-LCR-Rot-hop-ACS$_{XX}$++	–	x	–

4.2.1 $XLMR_{base}$-LCR-Rot-hop-XX++ $XLMR_{base}$-LCR-Rot-hop-XX++ is a UL-ABSC model. The model is very similar to that of $XLMR_{base}$-LCR-Rot-hop++, with the key distinction being that rather than English, the model is trained on language XX, where XX $\in$ {FR, ES, NL}[2]. We use this model due to the strong performance of the comparable mLCR-Rot-hop-XX++ in [5].

4.2.2 $XLMR_{base}$-MLCR-Rot-hop++ $XLMR_{base}$-MLCR-Rot-hop++ is an ML-ABSA model. For this model, we create one large dataset containing the instances in the training data from all the available languages–English, French, Spanish, and Dutch–and concatenate them into a single dataset. We then train the $XLMR_{base}$-LCR-Rot-hop++ model on this large dataset and test the model's performance separately for each language.

4.2.3 $XLMR_{base}$-LCR-Rot-hop-ACS$_{XX}$++ This model utilises the ACS methodology introduced in [16]. The methodology inflates the size of a dataset both by translation and through code-switched bilingual sentences, thereby increasing the size of the dataset by an approximate factor of four.

We start with a single instance in English. We then translate this instance into a target language. To do so, we utilise Alignment-free Label Projection [16], which aims to obtain pseudo-labeled data in the target language. This involves marking the aspect terms with special symbols before translating the instance. Similar to [5], we utilise Google API, which supports over 130 languages.

After the translation, we extract the aspects from the translated instance, utilising the previously mentioned markings. Note that multiple aspects are not an issue, as different special symbols are used for each subsequent marking. We then assign the sentiment labels to the translated aspect, giving us bilingual data from a singular instance. When running our models, we remove the resulting instances with an empty target.

We subsequently focus on specific Aspect-term Code Switching [16]. This involves taking the two instances obtained from the above steps, one in English and one in the target language, and switching the aspects between the two instances, leaving us with four different instances. These datasets are combined to form a single large dataset, on which we then train our model. Figure 2 shows the structure of the $XLMR_{base}$-LCR-Rot-hop-ACS$_{XX}$++ model.

---

[2] FR stands for French, ES stands for Spanish, and NL stands for Dutch.

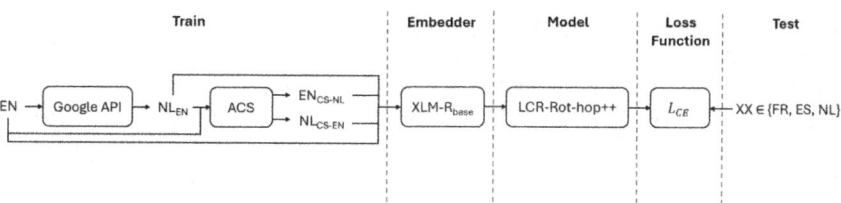

Fig. 2. A diagram of the XLMR$_{base}$-LCR-Rot-hop-ACS$_{XX}$++ model.

4.3 CLS-XLMR$_{base}$-LCR-Rot-hop++

Contrastive Learning Sentiment XLMR$_{base}$-LCR-Rot-hop++ (CLS-XLMR$_{base}$-LCR-Rot-hop++) fuses the previously defined XLMR-LCR-Rot-hop++ model and its variations with a contrastive learning approach, adapted from [6]. The same steps as in XLMR$_{base}$-LCR-Rot-hop++–or for one of its variations–are carried out to obtain a sentiment prediction vector p_i. We combine the cross-entropy function from (1) with a contrastive loss function and take a weighted sum of the two loss functions to evaluate the model.

Our approach is distinct from the work [6], which compares the sentiment labels of tokens, as we instead focus on comparing the sentiment labels of an entire instance. Let us denote our group of sample instances and the matching labels found in a given batch by $\{x_i, y_i\}_{i \in I}$, where set $I = \{1, ..., K\}$ represents the indices of a batch of size K. For all CLS models, we set $K = 32$. We define the positive set of all indices of the instances with the same label as the instance with index i, such that $P_i = \{j : j \in I, y_i = y_j \wedge i \neq j\}$. Here, $y_i \in Y_{sen}$, with Y_{sen} denoting the set of possible sentiments such that $Y_{sen} = \{POS, NEU, NEG\}$.

We then define the contrastive loss function for every $i \in I$ such that:

$$L_{CLS_i} = -\sum_{j \in P_i} \log \frac{\exp(\text{sim}(p_i, p_j)/\tau)}{\sum_{k \in I/i} \exp(\text{sim}(p_i, p_k)/\tau)} \quad (2)$$

where τ is the temperature hyperparameter–set to 0.07, as in [6]–and sim($\cdot$) is the cosine similarity function. The contrastive loss function for the entire batch of size K can then be written as follows:

$$L_{CLS} = \sum_{i=1}^{K} \frac{1}{|P_i|} L_{CLS_i} \quad (3)$$

We combine Eqs. 1 and 3 to obtain our final model loss function:

$$L = (1 - \beta) \cdot L_{CE} + \beta \cdot L_{CLS} \quad (4)$$

where β is a hyperparameter used to weight the cross-entropy and sentiment-level contrastive loss functions.

4.4 CLR-XLMR$_{base}$-LCR-Rot-hop++

As mentioned in Sect. 2, another contrastive learning model is described in [7], using the aspect oriented sentiment representations. This approach is not directly applicable to the LCR-Rot-hop++ model structure, which outputs a concatenated representation vector v to feed into the final MLP layer. To deal with this incompatibility, we propose a contrastive learning methodology which directly utilises the high-level sentiment representation vector v in its contrastive learning function, to decrease the space between representation vectors with the same label. This model exploits the increased information found in the high-level opinion vectors, which may lead to more fine-grained contrastive learning. We call this model Contrastive Learning Representation XLMR$_{base}$-LCR-Rot-hop++ (CLR-XLMR$_{base}$-LCR-Rot-hop++) model.

As in Sect. 4.1, v_i is the concatenated representation vector of the instance x_i in a given batch of size K. Note, however, that due to the significant increase in the input size of the vectors utilised in contrastive learning, we decrease the batch size to $K = 10$ for the sake of computational feasibility, as larger batch sizes failed to run on the T4 GPU used for this project. We then define the individual loss function as follows:

$$L_{CLR_i} = -\sum_{p \in P_i} \log \frac{\exp(\text{sim}(v_i, v_p)/\tau)}{\sum_{k \in I/i} \exp(\text{sim}(v_i, v_k/\tau)} \tag{5}$$

with $\tau = 0.07$. The batch loss function and the final loss function are the same as in (3) and (4), with L_{CLS_i} being replaced by L_{CLR_i}.

5 Results

For each model described in Sect. 4, we run the model using both the XLM-R$_{base}$ and the XLM-R embedder. We compare these to results we obtain from running the models first proposed by [5]. We subsequently also show and explain the results of each model using our two proposed contrastive learning approaches. The models are evaluated using two performance measures: the accuracy score and the (macro-)F_1 score. Whilst the accuracy score is the more interpretable evaluation measure, the macro-F_1 helps account for potentially unbalanced datasets, for example by punishing majority classification.

5.1 XLMR$_{base}$-LCR-Rot-hop++

From Table 3, we notice that, across all languages, the XLMR$_{base}$-LCR-Rot-hop++ tends to outperform the other models, both when evaluated on the accuracy and the F_1 scores. The improvement in accuracy is consistent but small in magnitude. It is striking that the accuracy scores found for the XLMR-LCR-Rot-hop++ model are the same as the percentage of positive instances found in the test data, as shown in Table 1. It is striking that the accuracy scores found for the XLMR-LCR-Rot-hop++ model are the same as the percentage of positive instances found in the test data, as shown in Table 1. Coupled with F_1 scores that are significantly lower than in models with similar accuracy, this strongly indicates that XLMR-LCR-Rot-hop++ cannot distinguish between different sentiments and reverts to classifying all instances as positive opinions. This reduced performance may be due to the model struggling to classify the larger XLM-R embedding vectors. The higher performance of the mLCR-Rot-hop++ and XLMR$_{base}$-LCR-Rot-hop++ on English language data likely stems from the fact that these models are trained on English data, whilst all other models are XL-ABSC.

Table 3. Results for XLMR$_{base}$-LCR-Rot-hop++ and comparable models.

	English		French		Spanish		Dutch	
	Acc. (%)	F_1	Acc. (%)	F_1	Acc. (%)	F_1	Acc. (%)	F_1
mLCR-Rot-hop++	80.6	**0.593**	62.5	0.445	73.6	0.425	68.8	0.445
XLMR$_{base}$-LCR-Rot-hop++	**82.0**	0.504	**63.4**	**0.469**	**76.6**	**0.462**	**71.1**	**0.476**
XLMR-LCR-Rot-hop++	74.3	0.284	50.7	0.224	71.3	0.277	62.2	0.256

We only apply contrastive learning to mLCR-Rot-hop++ and XLMR$_{base}$-LCR-Rot-hop++, as these outperform XLMR-LCR-Rot-hop++.

From Table 4, we observe that sentiment-level contrastive learning outperforms representation-level contrastive learning in terms of accuracy and F_1 score. Adding sentiment-level contrastive learning to a model almost always increases the performance across both measures. In contrast, for the CLR-mLCR-Rot-hop++ model, the performance improves over the mLCR-Rot-hop++ model when classifying Dutch and Spanish data, stays constant for French data, and decreases for English data. Furthermore, CLR-XLMR$_{base}$-LCR-Rot-hop++ only improves relative to XLMR$_{base}$-LCR-Rot-hop++ when tested on the English data, but underperforms for all other languages. This lacklustre performance may be explained by the representation-level vectors containing too much information to effectively decrease the semantic space, instead increasing the noise in the model.

Table 4. Results for the models with contrastive learning.

	English		French		Spanish		Dutch	
	Acc. (%)	F_1	Acc. (%)	F_1	Acc. (%)	F_1	Acc. (%)	F_1
CLS-mLCR-Rot-hop++	81.9	**0.660**	**67.4**	**0.471**	75.8	0.445	71.6	0.476
CLS-XLMR$_{base}$-LCR-Rot-hop++	**84.5**	0.534	62.8	0.453	76.6	**0.473**	**73.1**	**0.497**
CLR-mLCR-Rot-hop++	78.0	0.454	62.5	0.445	**76.9**	0.464	70.1	0.454
CLR-XLMR$_{base}$-LCR-Rot-hop++	83.2	0.521	61.0	0.453	75.7	0.461	67.5	0.449

5.2 XLMR$_{base}$-LCR-Rot-hop-XX++

Table 5 presents the results of the unilingual models. Note that Table 5 also includes the results of the XLMR$_{base}$-LCR-Rot-hop++ model for English, as the XLMR$_{base}$-LCR-Rot-hop++ and XLMR$_{base}$-LCR-Rot-hop-XX++ are identical when trained and tested on an English dataset.

Table 5. Results for XLMR$_{base}$-LCR-Rot-hop-XX++ and comparable models.

	English		French		Spanish		Dutch	
	Acc. (%)	F_1	Acc. (%)	F_1	Acc. (%)	F_1	Acc. (%)	F_1
mLCR-Rot-hop-XX++	80.6	**0.593**	**69.8**	**0.562**	**80.6**	**0.519**	71.1	0.467
XLMR$_{base}$-LCR-Rot-hop-XX++	**82.0**	0.504	66.2	0.486	71.8	0.427	**83.3**	**0.566**
XLMR-LCR-Rot-hop-XX++	74.3	0.284	69.5	0.509	71.3	0.277	62.2	0.256

In contrast to the results found in Table 3, Table 5 gives no obvious indication of a best-performing model. We notice that mLCR-Rot-hop++ performs strongly when applied to French and Spanish data, with this boosted performance being particularly noticeable in the Spanish model's accuracy measures. However, this performance does not carry over to the Dutch dataset, where XLMR$_{base}$-LCR-Rot-hop-XX++ is the best model by a substantial margin. The XLMR-LCR-Rot-hop-XX++ model again seems to classify by majority vote, with an exception for the French model. A possible explanation for this is that the sentiment polarities are more evenly distributed in the French data, with 50.9% of observations being positive. This indicates the model may perform better for the other languages if their training data were more evenly distributed.

Table 6 shows that the CLS-XLMR$_{base}$-LCR-Rot-hop-XX++ model performs best across the board, delivering better results than its counterpart without contrastive learning. The performances of the two contrastive models utilising mBERT embedders are more mixed. Whilst the CLS-mLCR-Rot-hop-XX++ model mostly has better F_1 scores than mLCR-Rot-hop-XX++, its accuracy is relatively worse. From our results, it is unclear whether the CLR-mLCR-Rot-hop-XX++ model improves over mLCR-Rot-hop-XX++. The results in Dutch, French, and Spanish indicate that the CLR-XLMR$_{base}$-LCR-Rot-hop-XX++ model scores poorly, again seeming to revert to majority classification. However, unbalanced data may not cause this phenomenon, as CLR-XLMR$_{base}$-LCR-Rot-hop-XX++ outperforms XLMR$_{base}$-LCR-Rot-hop-XX++ in English, despite 70.2% of the English training data being positive instances.

Table 6. Results for the models with contrastive learning.

	English		French		Spanish		Dutch	
	Acc. (%)	F_1	Acc. (%)	F_1	Acc. (%)	F_1	Acc. (%)	F_1
CLS-mLCR-Rot-hop-XX++	81.9	**0.660**	66.4	**0.569**	73.9	0.437	68.5	0.540
CLS-XLMR$_{base}$-LCR-Rot-hop-XX++	**84.5**	0.534	**68.9**	0.506	**85.1**	**0.554**	**81.2**	**0.708**
CLR-mLCR-Rot-hop-XX++	78.0	0.454	67.3	**0.569**	80.9	0.508	74.6	0.543
CLR-XLMR$_{base}$-LCR-Rot-hop-XX++	83.2	0.521	50.7	0.224	71.3	0.277	62.2	0.256

5.3 XLMR$_{base}$-MLCR-Rot-hop++

Table 7 shows that the models using XLM-R$_{base}$ and XLM-R embedders are consistently more accurate than MLCR-Rot-hop++. This is especially clear in the performance of the XLMR$_{base}$-MLCR-Rot-hop++. However, evaluating by the F_1 measure tells a starkly different story. Here, the MLCR-Rot-hop++ largely outperforms the models using XLM-R type embedders. The accuracy differences between models seem to be more substantive than the F_1 differences. This is most clearly seen in the Dutch results, where XLMR$_{base}$-MLCR-Rot-hop++ increases accuracy over MLCR-Rot-hop++ by 11.4% points, whilst the F_1 score of MLCR-Rot-hop++ is only 0.001 higher. The comparatively higher accuracy when testing on English and Spanish data may be due to the higher fraction of English and Spanish data in the multilingual training set.

Table 7. Results for XLMR$_{base}$-MLCR-Rot-hop++ and comparable models.

	English		French		Spanish		Dutch	
	Acc. (%)	F_1	Acc. (%)	F_1	Acc. (%)	F_1	Acc. (%)	F_1
MLCR-Rot-hop++	69.4	**0.523**	61.4	0.513	76.5	**0.556**	65.5	**0.524**
XLMR$_{base}$-MLCR-Rot-hop++	**80.5**	0.497	**71.5**	**0.519**	**78.8**	0.501	**76.9**	0.523
XLMR-MLCR-Rot-hop++	79.1	0.472	69.6	0.505	75.8	0.456	70.1	0.471

In Table 8, we notice that sentiment-level contrastive learning is extremely effective, regardless of the utilised embedder. The CLS-MLCR-Rot-hop++ outperforms the corresponding MLCR-Rot-hop++ across all languages in both measures. Similarly, the CLS-XLMR$_{base}$-MLCR-Rot-hop++ consistently scores higher than the original XLMR$_{base}$-MLCR-Rot-hop++ model. Representation-level contrastive learning fails to perform to the same degree. The CLR-MLCR-Rot-hop++ outperforms the MLCR-Rot-hop++ model for most measures, albeit to a lesser degree than the CLS-MLCR-Rot-hop++ model. In contrast, CLR-XLMR$_{base}$-MLCR-Rot-hop++ delivers a subpar performance, with the accuracy and F_1 measures suggesting that the model reverts to majority classification when classifying Spanish and Dutch data.

Table 8. Results for the models with contrastive learning.

	English		French		Spanish		Dutch	
	Acc. (%)	F_1	Acc. (%)	F_1	Acc. (%)	F_1	Acc. (%)	F_1
CLS-MLCR-Rot-hop++	**80.0**	**0.583**	73.8	0.621	82.1	0.618	78.2	**0.604**
CLS-XLMR$_{base}$-MLCR-Rot-hop++	74.9	0.507	**77.6**	**0.692**	**84.5**	**0.718**	**83.5**	0.575
CLR-MLCR-Rot-hop++	75.1	0.534	71.0	0.592	78.7	0.544	74.4	0.596
CLR-XLMR$_{base}$-MLCR-Rot-hop++	74.5	0.426	51.3	0.404	71.3	0.277	62.2	0.256

5.4 XLMR$_{base}$-LCR-Rot-hop-ACS$_{XX}$++

For ACS cross-lingual models, we do not include the English test data for our ACS methodology, as English is used to generate our translations.

From Table 9 we find that, generally, the XLMR$_{base}$-LCR-Rot-hop-ACS$_{XX}$++ has the highest accuracy and F_1 scores. The only exception is in the Dutch language test data, where the mLCR-Rot-hop++ model has a substantially higher F_1 and the XLMR-LCR-Rot-hop-ACS$_{XX}$++ model has the highest accuracy. Note that the difference in evaluation measures is relatively lower between the two XLM-R embedding models compared to the other models. This could be attributable to the "artificial" size increase induced by the ACS methodology, which approximately quadruples the size of our dataset. Given that the XLM-R embedder provides larger embeddings than XLM-R$_{base}$ and mBERT, we hypothesize that the subsequent LCR-Rot-hop++ model requires more training data to provide a similar–or potentially superior–level of accuracy.

Table 9. Results for XLMR$_{base}$-LCR-Rot-hop-ACS$_{XX}$++ and comparable models.

	French		Spanish		Dutch	
	Acc. (%)	F_1	Acc. (%)	F_1	Acc. (%)	F_1
mLCR-Rot-hop-ACS$_{XX}$++	66.4	0.526	71.0	0.506	61.4	**0.581**
XLMR$_{base}$-LCR-Rot-hop-ACS$_{XX}$++	**78.7**	**0.550**	**83.5**	**0.535**	68.8	0.467
XLMR-LCR-Rot-hop-ACS$_{XX}$++	75.2	0.525	81.0	0.522	**73.9**	0.492

The results in Table 10 indicate that sentiment-level contrastive learning tends to improve a model's performance. The CLS-mLCR-Rot-hop-ACS$_{XX}$++ improves over the mLCR-Rot-hop-ACS$_{XX}$++ across all languages except for French, whilst the CLS-XLMR$_{base}$-LCR-Rot-hop-ACS$_{XX}$++ has a consistently better F_1 score than the XLMR$_{base}$-LCR-Rot-hop-ACS$_{XX}$++. Representation-level contrastive learning performs less well, although some improvements over the mLCR-Rot-hop-ACS$_{XX}$++ model are noticeable, for example in Spanish. The CLR-XLMR$_{base}$-LCR-Rot-hop-ACS$_{XX}$++ model is not a substantial improvement over the XLMR$_{base}$-LCR-Rot-hop-ACS$_{XX}$++ model.

Table 10. Results for the models with contrastive learning.

	French		Spanish		Dutch	
	Acc. (%)	F_1	Acc. (%)	F_1	Acc. (%)	F_1
CLS-mLCR-Rot-hop-ACS$_{XX}$++	65.7	0.522	76.5	0.513	69.8	0.585
CLS-XLMR$_{base}$-LCR-Rot-hop-ACS$_{XX}$++	**74.9**	**0.664**	74.8	**0.538**	**86.3**	**0.586**
CLR-mLCR-Rot-hop-ACS$_{XX}$++	65.9	0.550	75.7	0.518	66.8	0.425
CLR-XLMR$_{base}$-LCR-Rot-hop-ACS$_{XX}$++	70.2	0.562	**80.4**	0.516	68.8	0.464

6 Conclusion

We contribute to the literature by proposing several extensions to the existing mLCR-Rot-hop++ model. The original mBERT embedder is exchanged for an XLM-R$_{base}$ or an XLM-R embedder. Furthermore, we integrate sentiment-level and representation-level contrastive learning into our proposed models.

Replacing the mBERT embedder with an XLM-R$_{base}$ improves the results for the majority of the proposed models. The XLM-R embedder achieves relatively poor results, only outperforming the other embedders in a single measure across all four proposed model variations. This lacklustre performance by the XLM-R embedder may be caused by the size of the training dataset. As previously mentioned, XLM-R embeddings are larger than mBERT and XLM-R$_{base}$ embeddings. Hence, it can be reasoned that the LCR-Rot-hop++ method could require a larger training dataset when fitted on XLM-R embeddings. Indeed, the performance difference between the XLM-R and XLM-R$_{base}$ embedder decreases for models trained on comparatively larger datasets.

Across all languages, we notice that models which combine sentiment-level contrastive learning with mBERT embedders and XLM-R$_{base}$ embedders tend to outperform the respective base models. In contrast, representation-level contrastive learning only occasionally improves model performance and usually performs worse than sentiment-level contrastive learning. Note here that high-level opinion representations contain significantly more information than the sentiment probability vectors, presumably making it considerably harder to decrease the sentiment space between these vectors, as the likelihood of these vectors displaying any similarity is significantly lower. Additionally, the computational limits to the batch size may also present a hurdle, as larger batches allow more comparisons to occur. Hence, sentiment-level contrastive learning is currently the most compatible with the LCR-Rot-hop++ method in a multilingual context.

A prospective research direction is the introduction of POS tagging into the LCR-Rot-hop++ structure. As explained in [10], POS denotes the grammatical properties of words in an instance, which likely have a strong connection with aspect-based sentiments and could augment model performance.

References

1. Agüero-Torales, M.M., Salas, J.I.A., López-Herrera, A.G.: Deep learning and multilingual sentiment analysis on social media data: an overview. Appl. Soft Comput. **107**, 107373 (2021)

2. Brauwers, G., Frasincar, F.: A survey on aspect-based sentiment classification. ACM Comput. Surv. **55**(4), 65:1–65:37 (2023)
3. Conneau, A., et al.: Unsupervised cross-lingual representation learning at scale. In: 58th Annual Meeting of the Association for Computational Linguistics (ACL 2020), pp. 8440–8451. ACL (2020)
4. Devlin, J., Chang, M., Lee, K., Toutanova, K.: BERT: pre-training of deep bidirectional transformers for language understanding. In: 2019 Conference of the North American Chapter of the Association for Computational Linguistics: Human Language Technologies (NAACL-HLT 2019), pp. 4171–4186. ACL (2019)
5. Horst, S., Frasincar, F.: Multilingual, cross-lingual, and unilingual models for ABSC. In: 25th International Conference on Web Information Systems Engineering (WISE 2024). LNCS, vol. 15436, pp. 89–101. Springer (2024). https://doi.org/10.1007/978-981-96-0579-8_7
6. Lin, N., Fu, Y., Lin, X., Zhou, D., Yang, A., Jiang, S.: CL-XABSA: contrastive learning for cross-lingual aspect-based sentiment analysis. IEEE/ACM Trans. Audio Speech Lang. Process. **31**, 2935–2946 (2023)
7. Lingling, X., Weiming, W.: Improving aspect-based sentiment analysis with contrastive learning. Nat. Lang. Process. J. **3**, 100009 (2023)
8. Liu, Y., et al.: RoBERTa: a robustly optimized BERT pretraining approach. arXiv preprint arXiv:1907.11692 (2019)
9. Pontiki, M., et al.: SemEval-2016 task 5: aspect based sentiment analysis. In: 10th International Workshop on Semantic Evaluation (SemEval 2016), pp. 19–30. ACL (2016)
10. Sattar, K., Umer, Q., Vasbieva, D.G., Chung, S., Latif, Z., Lee, C.: A multi-layer network for aspect-based cross-lingual sentiment classification. IEEE Access **9**, 133961–133973 (2021)
11. Schouten, K., Frasincar, F.: Survey on aspect-level sentiment analysis. IEEE Trans. Knowl. Data Eng. **28**(3), 813–830 (2016)
12. Truşcă, M.M., Frasincar, F.: Survey on aspect detection for aspect-based sentiment analysis. Artif. Intell. Rev. **56**(5), 3797–3846 (2023)
13. Truşcă, M.M., Wassenberg, D., Frasincar, F., Dekker, R.: A hybrid approach for aspect-based sentiment analysis using deep contextual word embeddings and hierarchical attention. In: Bielikova, M., Mikkonen, T., Pautasso, C. (eds.) ICWE 2020. LNCS, vol. 12128, pp. 365–380. Springer, Cham (2020). https://doi.org/10.1007/978-3-030-50578-3_25
14. Wallaart, O., Frasincar, F.: A hybrid approach for aspect-based sentiment analysis using a lexicalized domain ontology and attentional neural models. In: Hitzler, P., et al. (eds.) ESWC 2019. LNCS, vol. 11503, pp. 363–378. Springer, Cham (2019). https://doi.org/10.1007/978-3-030-21348-0_24
15. Xu, Y., Cao, H., Du, W., Wang, W.: A survey of cross-lingual sentiment analysis: methodologies, models and evaluations. Data Sci. Eng. **7**(3), 279–299 (2022)
16. Zhang, W., He, R., Peng, H., Bing, L., Lam, W.: Cross-lingual aspect-based sentiment analysis with aspect term code-switching. In: 2021 Conference on Empirical Methods in Natural Language Processing (EMNLP 2021), pp. 9220–9230. ACL (2021)
17. Zhang, W., Li, X., Deng, Y., Bing, L., Lam, W.: A survey on aspect-based sentiment analysis: tasks, methods, and challenges. IEEE Trans. Knowl. Data Eng. **35**(11), 11019–11038 (2023)
18. Zheng, S., Xia, R.: Left-center-right separated neural network for aspect-based sentiment analysis with rotatory attention. arXiv preprint arXiv:1802.00892 (2018)

OnToxKG: An Ontology-Based Knowledge Graph of Toxic Symbols and Their Manifestations

Delfina S. Martinez Pandiani[1(✉)], Erik Tjong Kim Sang[2], and Davide Ceolin[3]

[1] ILLC, University of Amsterdam, 1098 XG Amsterdam, The Netherlands
d.s.martinezpandiani@uva.nl
[2] Netherlands eScience Center, 1098 XH Amsterdam, The Netherlands
[3] Centrum Wiskunde and Informatica, 1098 XG Amsterdam, The Netherlands

Abstract. Online toxicity, evolving through complex multimodal items like memes, poses a significant challenge. Integrating expert knowledge into moderation systems is increasingly crucial for identifying the nuances of toxic symbology, particularly in memes. Despite the wealth of available expertise, its structured integration into automated systems for online content interpretation remains underdeveloped. This paper introduces the OnTox ontology and OnToxKG Knowledge Graph to address gaps in addressing online toxic symbology. OnTox defines the multimodal semantics of 799 potentially toxic symbols. OnToxKG, a multimodal knowledge graph, integrates these symbols with commonsense sources like Wikidata and WordNet. We demonstrate the practical applications of these resources in automatically analyzing meme toxicity.

Caution: This work includes toxic content that may cause psychological distress and does not represent the views or opinions of the authors.

Keywords: ontology · toxicity · hate speech · symbology · memetics

1 Introduction

Online toxicity encompasses a wide spectrum of harmful behaviors and content. While most research has focused on toxic language in unimodal formats [10], growing attention is now turning to multimodal toxicity [17] as its credibility, memorability, and spreadability make it powerful. Memes are a particularly challenging medium for automatic moderation, as they condense complex, often harmful messages into highly shareable formats using minimal visual and textual cues [16] and relying on implicit cultural references and shared background knowledge [6]. As multimodal content becomes increasingly prevalent online, there is an urgent need for automated tools that can not only detect but also explain toxic material. Recent work has emphasized this need for transparency in content moderation, particularly for memes, where clearer justifications behind labeling decisions are essential [8].

Existing detection methods often struggle with the cultural and symbolic complexity of toxic memes, and have only recently begun integrating background knowledge bases [5,7,19]. While these efforts emphasize commonsense and entity-level knowledge, they often fail to capture the symbolic and intertextual complexity of toxic memes—such as references to popular culture, artifacts, or community-specific symbols—that remain opaque to current systems [16]. Meanwhile, expert-curated resources like the GESD (Global Extremist Symbols Database)[1] offer rich cultural knowledge of online toxic symbology, cataloging a wide range of potentially hateful signs, terms, and images.

Despite their value, existing resources remain largely inaccessible to automated systems due to their lack of machine-readable formats and semantic structure. This paper investigates how structured knowledge representations can enhance the automated understanding of toxicity in multimodal content. Specifically, we study *how ontology-based methods can support the formalization, semantic enrichment, and linking of toxic symbology across modalities*. To address this, we contribute: (1) **OnToX**, an ontology designed to formalize the semantics and online manifestations of toxic terms and multimodal icons; and (2) **OnToXKG**, a knowledge graph incorporating multimodal data from 799 potentially toxic symbols, linked to commonsense knowledge sources.

2 Related Work

Understanding the nuances of online toxicity is crucial for developing effective detection models [14]. Efforts to delineate toxicity-related concepts reveal challenges in classification, often due to contentious definitions [1,3]. Initiatives aim to standardize toxicity labels, ensuring consistency across datasets [4]. Most research has concentrated on textual data, with extensive studies on detecting toxicity, hate speech, and offensive language [18]. Recently, exploring multimodal toxicity from a computational perspective has become increasingly crucial, with studies bridging this gap by offering different perspectives on toxic multimodal content [17]. One study provides a taxonomy covering hate, harassment, self-inflicted harm, ideological harm, and exploitation [2], while another offers a simpler list of harmful categories [9]. The O-Dang! ontology [15] represents annotated data on dangerous speech. Recently, efforts in computational analysis of meme toxicity increased (for surveys on the topic, see [8,13]), In [19], authors enrich semantic representations by integrating conceptual information via their model, MeBERT. In [7], the authors introduce MemeGraphs: a transformer-based method combining scene graphs extracted from the memes, augmented data from Wikidata, and the meme text. Other works utilize ConceptNet as their background knowledge base, e.g., KnowMeme [12] and KERMIT [5].

---

[1] https://globalextremism.org/global-extremist-symbols-database/, developed by the Global Project Against Hate and Extremism (GPAHE).

Pinochet's Helicopters

The Antifa Helicopter Ride meme is an explicit reference to the brutal method of execution that certain Latin American dictators, such as Chilean Augusto Pinochet, used against leftist dissidents in the 1970s. Usage of the meme by the far right is an explicit call for violence against political opponents. The Antifa Helicopter Ride meme is often seen online on sites and forums frequented by far right groups of all kinds. It was particularly popular in the online circles of the white supremacist Proud Boys, who also produced merchandise featuring the meme.

RAHOWA

RAHOWA is shorthand for "Racial Holy War," a popular inside term used by white supremacists and neo-Nazis. RAHOWA refers to a coming race war, often hoped for by these extremists. It is also the name of a now defunct Canadian white supremacist band that was headed by George Burdi, a now- reformed, neo-Nazi skinhead. RAHOWA is a popular tattoo in hate circles and is found throughout neo-Nazi subcultures.

4/20

4/20 is a reference to Adolf Hitler's birthday, April 20, which is celebrated by Nazis around the world. It should be noted that 4/20 is also used in popular culture as a reference to other celebrations, so context is essential to racist usage of the term. The use of 4/20 is usually found on websites and forums frequented by neo-Nazis.

Fig. 1. Motivating examples for OnTox development. Left: symbols and descriptions from GESD. Right: memes referencing these symbols–visually (top), textually (middle), or both visually and textually (bottom).

3 OnTox Ontology and Knowledge Graph

3.1 OnTox: The Ontology of Toxic Symbology

In Fig. 1, we present three symbols sourced from the GESD, each accompanied by a meme that references the symbol. The semantic representation and multimodal expansion of these symbols are categorized into: **(1) Symbol metadata** including information such as the symbol's title, textual description, source database with its original ID, symbol subtype, and metadata regarding its geographical and ideological context of use; **(2) Symbol conceptual semantics** adding a semantic layer on top of the symbol descriptions, using Wikidata nodes for named entities and WordNet concepts. These are linked to the entities extracted from the symbol description and title; and **(3) Symbol manifestations data** capturing how toxic symbols appear in real-world digital content, via visual, textual, or multimodal forms (see Fig. 1).

Ontological Requirements. We derive requirements from the examples above.

OR1: Model the metadata of the symbols. (i) Mandate title and description. (ii) Differentiate symbol types considering database metadata availability. (iii) Assign original and OnTox IDs to each symbol. (iv) Allow symbols to link to multiple manifestations. (v) Discern geographical and ideological tags.

OR2: Model the conceptual semantics of symbol descriptions. (i) Link symbol titles and descriptions to named entities and external resources (e.g., Wikidata). (ii) Associate symbol descriptions with specific concepts using linguistic resources (e.g., WordNet). (iii) Extract LOD entities for ideologies and locations.

OR3: Model the multimodal manifestation of potentially toxic symbology. (i) Link potentially toxic symbols to various manifestations (e.g., tweets). (ii) Share conceptual semantics between symbol description content (e.g., memes). (iii) Specify modal representation type (visual, textual, both).

Ontology Creation and Presentation. We re-use and extend existing models, leveraging DUL [11], O-dang [15], FOAF, Wikidata, and WordNet. OnTox is assigned an IRI[2] and the project has an associated GitHub.[3]

Ontology Presentation. Below we encode the ontological requirements:

OR1: Model the Metadata of the Symbols.

OR1-1: Each `PotentiallyToxicSymbol`'s original title is its `rdfs:label`, and its `:hasSymbolDescription` is linked to a `:SymbolDescription`.
OR1-2: Introduce sub-classes `:HandSign`, `:HateImage`, `:TextualSymbol`, etc., for distinguishing types of toxicity-related symbols.
OR1-3: Assign each symbol an `:originalID` distinct to its OnTox ID, and link to a specific `:Database` via `:hasOriginalDatabase`.
OR1-4: Connect symbols to their depictions using `foaf:depiction`.
OR1-5: Differentiate tags with the properties `:hasGeographicalContext` and `:hasIdeologicalContext`.

OR2: Model the Conceptual Semantics of Symbol Descriptions.

OR2-1: We link symbol descriptions to named entities using `:mentionsConcept` and connect them to Wikidata nodes. Create binary relations between symbols and extracted Wikidata nodes with `:hasRelatedConcept`.
OR2-2: We link symbol descriptions to specific concepts and senses using WordNet properties and `:mentionsConcept`. Create binary relations between symbols and extracted WordNet concepts with `:hasRelatedConcept`.
OR2-3: Ideologies and locations are represented as Wikidata nodes.

---

[2] https://w3id.org/ontox.
[3] https://github.com/EyeofBeholder-NLeSC/onTox/.

OR3: Model the Multimodal Manifestation of Potentially Toxic Symbology.

OR3-1: Connect toxic symbols to manifestations such as `odang:Tweet` and `:Meme`, subclasses of `FRBR:Manifestation`, via `:manifestedIn`.
OR3-2: Link symbol descriptions and manifestations to WordNet and Wikidata using `:hasAutomaticConceptTag`.
OR3-3: Represent modal types (visual, textual, etc.) using `:hasModality`.

3.2 KG Population and Validation

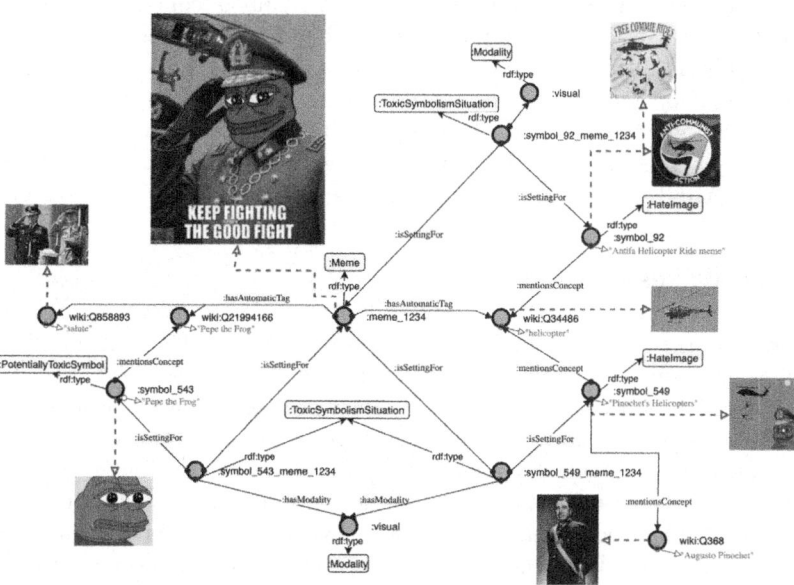

Fig. 2. Subset of OnTox instance data. Red dotted lines denote `foaf:depiction` (Color figure online).

Toxic Symbol Selection and Extraction. We chose the GESD for its global scope and broad ideological coverage. Unlike most databases that focus mainly on antisemitism, GESD includes additional ideologies such as accelerationism, hindu supremacism, fascism, or anti-LGBTQ hate. We collected 799 symbols, including titles, IDs, descriptions, and associated ideologies and locations.

Meaning Extraction and LOD Linking. To enrich the semantic data, we applied a two-step NLP pipeline: NLTK was used for tokenization, part-of-speech tagging, and lemmatization, followed by WordNet synset extraction for key content words. SpaCy was used for named entity recognition, and entities were resolved to Wikidata via API queries. This process yielded 125 unique locations and 27 ideologies; we added Wikidata links for 4 previously unmatched ideologies and corrected 4 mismatches. The results, serialized in Turtle RDF format, are available on GitHub. An example of instance data is shown in Fig. 2.

Validation and Statistics. OnToxKG comprises 110,657 triples and 8,758 unique entities, including 799 Potentially Toxic Symbols, 124 locations, and 27 ideologies. Symbol descriptions are enriched with external knowledge from 2,066 Wikidata and 4,285 WordNet mappings. On average, each symbol is linked to 48.6 external concepts (min 15, max 147). Symbols contain 6.86 Wikidata and 41.64 WordNet concepts on average. Each Wikidata concept is linked to at least one potentially toxic symbol, with *neo-Nazi* as the most connected entity, *United States of America* as the most frequent location, and *white nationalist* as the most common ideology. The integrity of OnTox was validated using automated scripts, Protégé HermiT 1.4.3.456 reasoner, SPARQL queries, and SHACL shapes. SPARQL queries and SHACL shapes are on the GitHub repository.

4 Use Cases

We present five use cases involving symbols in OnToxKG, with all SPARQL queries and results available on GitHub. The first three use cases demonstrate how OnToxKG enriches symbols with finer-grained semantic layers through WordNet synsets and named entity recognition. The final two use cases showcase OnToxKG's support for meme analysis. We processed four memes (three hateful, one benign) using ChatGPT[4] to generate captions for the image, text, and their combination. Named entities were extracted using SpaCy and resolved via Wikidata, while key synsets from the captions were identified with NLTK and added to the knowledge graph for querying.

Q1. Top pairs of symbols grouped by shared concepts Identifies pairs of symbols sharing the most concepts, highlighting semantic proximity. For instance, symbol_565 (Proud Boys of Columbus logo) and symbol_490 (New Hampshire Proud Boys logo) share the most (103) concepts.

Q2. Named Entities linked to a symbol Retrieves named entities extracted from a specific symbol's description. For example, symbol_549 (Pinochet's helicopters) is associated with *Chile, Right Wing Death Squad, Proud Boys, AntiCommunist Action*, and *Augusto Pinochet*.

---

[4] Chatgpt.com (model 4o, July 12, 2024). Prompt: *Here is an image with some text written on it. What is your interpretation of the image and the text? Please provide 1. a separate interpretation of the image; 2. a separate interpretation of the text; and 3. an interpretation of the combination.*

Q3. Symbols described with a named entity Identifies symbols that explicitly mention a given named entity in their descriptions. For example, starting from the Wikidata node for *Pepe the Frog*, symbols such as symbol_182 (Clown World), symbol_529 (Parteiadler/Reichsadler, Nazi Eagle), symbol_381 (Kekistan Flag), symbol_441 (Moon Man), symbol_543 (Pepe the Frog), and symbol_693 (The Groyper) explicitly mention it in their descriptions.

Q4. Top Conceptual Similarity to Potentially Toxic Symbols Counts the concepts that a specific meme shares with toxic symbols. This allows checking which symbols are relevant to each meme. E.g., a 4/20 meme related to Hitler's birthday (Fig. 1) shares more concepts with Nazi symbols than with weed (4/20 is also slang for weed consumption).

Q5. Concept Mention and Modality Detection checks if and how a concept is mentioned in a meme. E.g., results show that the *I Need Rahowa* meme mentions the *Racial Holy War* (Q15994152) concept in text.

5 Discussion

OnTox and OnToxKG offer a comprehensive and structured representation of toxic symbols, providing both ontological depth and extensive knowledge base coverage. While the ontology and knowledge graph are extensible (e.g., by incorporating additional symbols), our validation demonstrates that the current versions already deliver significant utility. The ontology is constructed with strict requirements, ensuring both granularity and accuracy. This granularity enables the capture of key features of online toxic symbols, which are enriched through links to Wikidata and other linked open data (LOD) resources. This enriched representation enhances symbol search, disambiguation, and identification, as demonstrated in our use cases. Although aligned with the GESD, the framework underlying OnToxKG remains independent, offering flexibility for future expansion. Currently, OnToxKG models 799 potentially toxic symbols from the GESD, and while future versions may incorporate symbols from additional datasets, the current scope is already sufficient for key use cases. Looking ahead, we aim to explore the impact of expanding the number of hops in the LOD entities associated with symbols, to better understand when additional information may enhance or degrade performance in downstream tasks. We also recognize the potential for false positives in the toxicity classification, where a meme might be misclassified as toxic based on the current OnTox and OnToxKG representations. Future work will aim to refine the framework to minimize such misclassifications. Additionally, we plan to define a toxicity index for memes, based on the types of toxic symbols they contain (see Q4), which will help address ambiguities in the interpretation of entities derived from various sources and backgrounds, advancing the utility of OnTox in analyzing the toxicity of multimodal content.

6 Conclusion

This paper introduces OnTox and OnToxKG, i.e., an ontology and a knowledge graph to model potentially toxic symbols, their semantics, and their manifestations in digital content. We define OnTox based on a set of rigorously defined requirements based on the features of an expert-curated symbol database. OnToxKG models 799 potentially toxic symbols enriched with links to knowledge sources like Wikidata and Wordnet. We describe our model in detail and showcase how it can be effectively leveraged to search, disambiguate, identify symbols and analyze the potential toxicity of internet memes. We plan to extend the analysis and the coverage of OnToxKG, and to develop meme toxicity indexes leveraging their similarity to the symbols in the database.

Acknowledgements. Supported by the Netherlands eScience Center project "The Eye of the Beholder" (project nr. 027.020.G15), and is part of the AI, Media & Democracy Lab (Dutch Research Council project number: NWA.1332.20.009, https://www.aim4dem.nl/.) We thank The Global Project Against Hate and Extremism who developed the GESD. Generative AI tools were used solely for final copyediting; all edits were reviewed and approved by the authors.

References

1. Alkomah, F., Ma, X.: A literature review of textual hate speech detection methods and datasets. Information **13**(6), 273 (2022)
2. Banko, M., MacKeen, B., Ray, L.: A unified taxonomy of harmful content. In: Proceedings of the Fourth Workshop on Online Abuse and Harms, pp. 125–137 (2020)
3. Chhabra, A., Vishwakarma, D.K.: A literature survey on multimodal and multilingual automatic hate speech identification. Multim. Sys. **29**(3), 1203–1230 (2023)
4. Fortuna, P., Soler, J., Wanner, L.: Toxic, hateful, offensive or abusive? What are we really classifying? An empirical analysis of hate speech datasets. In: Proceedings of LREC, pp. 6786–6794 (2020)
5. Grasso, B., La Gatta, V., Moscato, V., Sperlì, G.: KERMIT: knowledge-empowered model in harmful meme detection. Inf. Fusion **106** (2024)
6. Kostadinovska-Stojchevska, B., Shalevska, E.: Internet memes and their sociolinguistic features. European J. Lit. Lang. Ling. Studies **2**(4) (2018)
7. Kougia, V., et al.: MemeGraphs: linking memes to knowledge graphs. In: Document Analysis and Recognition - ICDAR 2023. vol. 14187, pp. 534–551. Springer (2023)
8. Martinez Pandiani, D.S., Tjong Kim Sang, E., Ceolin, D.: Toxic memes: a survey of computational perspectives on the detection and explanation of meme toxicities. arXiv preprint arXiv:2406.07353 (2024)
9. Nakov, P., et al.: Detecting abusive language on online platforms: A critical analysis. arXiv preprint arXiv:2103.00153 (2021)
10. Piot, P., Martín-Rodilla, P., Parapar, J.: MetaHate: A dataset for unifying efforts on hate speech detection. arXiv preprint arXiv:2401.06526 (2024)
11. Presutti, V., Gangemi, A.: Dolce+ D&S ultralite and its main ontology design patterns. In: Ontology Engineering with Ontology Design Patterns, pp. 81–103. IOS Press (2016)

12. Shang, L., Zhang, Y., Zha, Y.: KnowMeme: a knowledge-enriched graph neural network solution to offensive meme detection. In: eScience, pp. 186–195. IEEE (2021)
13. Sharma, S., et al.: Detecting and understanding harmful memes: a survey. arXiv preprint arXiv:2205.04274 **1**(1), 1–9 (2022)
14. Sheth, A., Shalin, V.L., Kursuncu, U.: Defining and detecting toxicity on social media: context and knowledge are key. Neurocomputing **490**, 312–318 (2022)
15. Stranisci, M.A., et al.: O-dang! the ontology of dangerous speech messages. arXiv preprint arXiv:2207.10652 (2022)
16. Thakur, A., et al.: Explainable classification of internet memes. In: CEUR Workshop Proceedings. vol. 3432, pp. 395–409 (2023)
17. Yankoski, M., Scheirer, W., Weninger, T.: Meme warfare: AI countermeasures to disinformation should focus on popular, not perfect, fakes. Bull. Atomic Sci. **77**(3), 119–123 (2021)
18. Zampieri, M., Malmasi, S., Nakov, P., Rosenthal, S., Farra, N., Kumar, R.: SemEval-2019 task 6: Identifying and categorizing offensive language in social media (offenseval). arXiv preprint arXiv:1903.08983 (2019)
19. Zhong, Q., Wang, Q., Liu, J.: Combining knowledge and multi-modal fusion for meme classification. In: Þór Jónsson, B., et al. (eds.) MMM 2022. LNCS, vol. 13141, pp. 599–611. Springer, Cham (2022). https://doi.org/10.1007/978-3-030-98358-1_47

Evaluating Locally Run Large Language Models on Toxic Meme Analysis

Erik Tjong Kim Sang[1](✉)[iD], Delfina S. Martinez Pandiani[2][iD], and Davide Ceolin[2][iD]

[1] Netherlands eScience Center, 1098 XH Amsterdam, The Netherlands
e.tjongkimsang@esciencecenter.nl
[2] Centrum Wiskunde and Informatica, 1098 XG Amsterdam, The Netherlands
{dsmp,davide.ceolin}@cwi.nl

Abstract. Toxic memes easily spread online, propagating stereotypes, hate, and other stronger or more nuanced types of malicious content. The sheer volume of memes requiring moderation calls for automated methods, but their multiple layers of meaning make them challenging to assess: in some cases, toxicity may stem from subtle wordplay, in others by visual references or evoking hateful symbols, etc. Large language models (LLMs) offer a promising tool for performing toxicity detection, since they can leverage a large amount of contextual information and analyzing content items in depth. In this paper, we investigate the suitability of locally run LLMs to perform such a task. Locally run large language models have several advantages over web-based models like OpenAI's ChatGPT with respect to costs, reproducibility, and data safety. We evaluate the local models on the tasks of automatic meme analysis and toxic symbol identification, and compare the results with analyses of the online model ChatGPT. Our findings reveal that while local models identify only a limited number of toxic memes and symbols, their labels are often accurate (low recall, high precision). Although they do not achieve perfect performance, we believe these models can effectively support human content moderators.

Keywords: locally run large language models · meme analysis · hate speech detection

1 Introduction

Memes are an ideal vehicle for the fast and widespread dissemination of jokes, cultural expressions, and lightweight messages. Their adaptability, shareability, and ability to convey multiple layers of information make them particularly effective in spreading diverse messages that evolve over time and context. These same qualities make memes an ideal vehicle for spreading toxic content: various types and nuances of toxicity can be expressed through memes, combining implicit and explicit layers of meaning. For this reason, meme toxicity analysis and identification are crucial to capturing and, when necessary, filtering hateful information. However, the sheer volume of potentially toxic memes shared online calls for automated approaches. The complexity, subjectivity, and context-dependence of memes, however, make the development of automatic approaches particularly challenging. In this paper, we focus on the task of identifying toxic symbols in memes as a means to reduce the subjectivity of the task. The symbols under consideration are drawn from a database curated by GPAHE[1]

The introduction of the Large Language Model (LLM) ChatGPT by OpenAI[2] in November 2022 has radically changed the field of artificial intelligence (AI). The sheer volume of training data available to the chatbot[3] enables performing AI tasks, and in particular natural language processing (NLP) tasks, which before had seemed hard or impossible to realize in practice. Meme toxicity analysis is one such task: the context information that the LLM can leverage can be used to capture important nuances in memes that imply their toxicity. However, using such systems for science (and for toxic meme analysis specifically) also comes with challenges:

Costs While there is a free version of ChatGPT, usage of the latest version requires a monthly subscription fee. Using the API software interface for larger numbers of requests requires a micropayment per action.

Reproducibility The behavior of the chatbot may change overnight because of updates by OpenAI. Updates are not public, we do not know when something is changed, what is changed, why it is changed, or how it affects the chatbot.

Data safety Any data provided to ChatGPT in requests may be used by OpenAI to improve the system. Thus, ChatGPT should not be used with sensitive data.

Guardrails ChatGPT will refuse tasks that it deems to be inappropriate, and being the content analyzed potentially toxic, guardrails could prevent obtaining useful results [7].

Because of these problems, we are interested in locally run large language models, like Meta's Llama[4]. These models are more sustainable, have a lower CO_2 footprint, and would be embeddable in locally run applications (e.g., browsers), which would help preserve the users' privacy. In this paper, we will compare their performance with that of ChatGPT. Here we foresee several challenges as well:

Processing time Because locally used hardware is smaller than that used by the large online models, we expect the local models to require more time to process requests.

Performance Because the local models are smaller than the large online models, we expect the quality of the local models' output to be lower.

Hardware Some local models may require fast processing hardware (GPUs) which may not be available locally.

---

[1] Global Project Against Hate and Extremism: https://globalextremism.org/.
[2] chtagpt.com.
[3] OpenAI's GPT-3 model was trained on 300 billion words [1]. Most likely, more words were used for training the newer GPT models.
[4] llama.meta.com.

After having discussed related work in Sect. 2, we will present and discuss our experiments on meme toxicity detection (Sect. 3), hateful symbol recognition (Sect. 4) and toxic symbol detection in memes (Sect. 5). We conclude in Sect. 6

2 Related Work

The use of LLMs to identify, evaluate, and assess potentially hateful content has been explored in a significant number of works, but the emphasis is mostly on textual items, while we focus on memes, which are multimodal. Also, the published works test a variety of models, while we focus on locally runnable ones.

Cui et al. [2] propose a benchmark to evaluate the capacity of LLMs to generate harmful content. Their evaluation shows that unfair, inaccurate, or toxic content can actually be used to trigger harmful content generation. This work is complementary to ours but provides an interesting point of view on how to handle toxic content with LLMs.

Zhang et al. [10] propose a method to increase the efficiency of toxic content detection by bootstrapping and distilling LLMs. While their method is inspiring and could be adapted to the multimodal domains, it currently focuses on textual content.

Interesting is also the work of Yang et al. [9] who focus on the possibility of jailbreaking guardrails of LLMs. This is a double-edged sword. On the one hand, guardrails could be forced to produce toxic content, which is undesirable. On the other hand, though, breaking such guardrails could allow LLMs to actually provide useful information about the toxicity of content to be analyzed and moderated.

Sun et al. [3] show how constraining metrics and categories of toxicity can be useful to improve the effectiveness of LLMs in the task of toxic text detection. This suggests that leveraging the taxonomy of toxicity we introduced in a previous work [6] could be an effective solution to boost the analysis of toxic memes as well.

Lastly, De Wynter et al. [8] propose an interesting analysis regarding the identification of toxicity across multiple languages. We will consider this direction in future work.

3 Analyzing Toxic Memes

We test locally run large language models for automatic analysis of memes, which involves image analysis, optical character recognition, and text analysis. Models that cannot perform image analysis and optical character recognition will be provided the textual description of the meme and will only be tested on the text analysis task. We compare the locally run systems with the online models ChatGPT-4 (both ChatGPT-4 and ChatGPT-4o). The tests in this chapter

Fig. 1. Content warning: Includes content that may cause psychological distress and does not represent the views or opinions of the authors. The four main test memes used in this study; one benign meme (dog, left) and three toxic or hateful memes (Hitler, He-Man and Pepe; selected by [5])

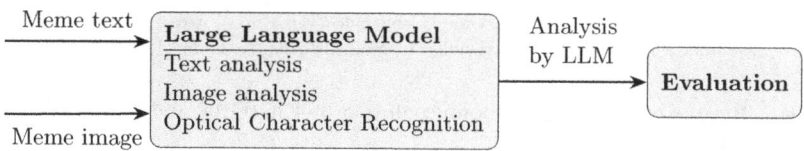

Fig. 2. Setup of the experiments: we provide the text and the image of the meme to the LLM, which performs a text analysis, an image analysis (when available), and optical character recognition (when available). The resulting LLM analysis is evaluated manually (Sect. 3) or automatically (Sects. 4 and 5).

involve four memes, see Fig. 1. A summary of the results of all systems can be found in Table 3.

We used the Ollama[5] interface to test the local LLMs LlaVa 1.6 7b[6] (Large Language and Vision Assistant) [4], LlaVa-Llama 3, Meta's Llama version 3.2, Microsoft's Phi 3 Mini (3.8 billion parameters), Mistral's Mistral (7 billion parameters), and Google DeepMind's Gemma 2 (9 billion parameters). Only the two LlaVa models could process images. LlaVa-Llama 3 has more world knowledge than LlaVa 1.6 but less than Llama 3.2. A summary of the tests can be found in Table 1 while the complete conversations van be found in the appendix of the online version of this paper[7].

4 Evaluating the Recognition of Visual Hate Symbols

In this experiment, we test whether LLMs are capable of identifying ten hate symbols from a curated database, GPAHE. The results of the symbol analysis can be found in Table 2. ChatGPT only recognized three of the ten symbols (one partly). The other seven symbols were not recognized but when provided

---

[5] ollama.com.
[6] github.com/haotian-liu/LLaVA.
[7] https://ifarm.nl/erikt/papers/icwe-2025.pdf.

Table 1. Assessments of the Large Language models tested on the four memes of Fig. 1. The two online multimodal models (top) performed well. The three local multimodal models (center) classified too many memes as benign. The four text-only models (bottom) performed better but their task was easier since they did not have to do the image recognition.

Model	Access	Modality	Dog	Hitler	He-Man	Pepe
ChatGPT-4	online	multi-modal	undecided	toxic	toxic	toxic
ChatGPT-4o	online	multi-modal	benign	toxic	toxic	toxic
Llava 1.6 7b	local	multi-modal	undecided	undecided	benign	benign
Llava 1.6 34b	local	multi-modal	undecided	toxic	undecided	undecided
Llava-Llama 3 8b	local	multi-modal	benign	benign	benign	benign
Lama 3.2 3b	local	text-only	benign	benign	benign	toxic
Phi3 3.8b	local	text-only	undecided	toxic	undecided	undecided
Mistral 7b	local	text-only	undecided	toxic	toxic	toxic
Gemma 2 9b	local	text-only	undecided	toxic	undecided	toxic

Table 2. Results of a hateful symbol recognition by ChatGPT and Llava with a small dataset (n = 10)

Symbol	ChatGPT4	Llava:34b
Pepe in Chili	partly	partly
Confederate flag	recognized	recognized
Oomer Wojak	not recognized	unknown
Russian Z	not recognized	unknown
Proud Boys	not recognized	not recognized
Rasseblement National	not recognized	not recognized
Ku Klux Klan	not recognized	not recognized
Schild & Vrienden	not recognized	unknown
Schutzstaffel (SS)	recognized	not recognized
Happy Merchant	not recognized	unknown

with some extra context the model showed it was aware of the story behind the symbols. Llava did not do better. It recognized two of the ten symbols (one partly) and when provided with extra context, it showed awareness of the stories behind four of the other eight symbols. Llava appeared unaware of the other four symbols. These results indicate that our planned analysis of meme toxicity based on hate symbols, might not work very well in practice. If only a minority of the hate symbols are identified, a process dependent on them could only marginally perform better than other systems. However, we should also make a distinction

Table 3. Comparison of hateful symbol analysis in 542 memes of ChatGPT-4o and Llava:34b. Only a subset of symbols are found and these are mainly textual symbols. The visual symbols found are Pepe the Frog and two flags.

Category	ChatGPT-4o	Llava:34b	Lava:34b (text)
meme images	542	542	542
broken images	15	15	15
memes without metadata	18	18	18
refused memes	96	0	0
target symbols found	145	127	121
textual symbols found	137	119	121
visual symbols found	8	8	0
unique symbols found	30	30	29

between the model's capabilities and the model's knowledge. In fact, in some cases, once the required specific knowledge is provided to the model, the model was capable of making proper use of it. Therefore, it might be worth ensuring the model is capable of leveraging such specific knowledge because ultimately, this would significantly help the accuracy and explainability of the model in performing this task (Fig. 2).

5 Recognizing Hate Symbols in Memes

Next, we tested whether hate symbols could be found when they were part of a meme. This is an important step in the process of toxic meme identification: while the toxicity could be obtained by means of implicit meanings (e.g., juxtaposing otherwise benign content), the explicit use of toxic symbols can be highly correlated with the overall toxicity of the meme. The results of the meme analysis can be found in Table 3. ChatGPT[8] refused to analyze 96 of the images and found hate symbols in 145 memes. For 136 memes this was based on textual information while for nine memes the symbol information was based on visual clues. Llava[9] found fewer symbols than ChatGPT, even in the category of textual symbols, which comes as a surprise because Llava could analyze all memes in the dataset. We tested Llava, requiring only the text in the image[10] but that test performed even worse (see Table 3). A comparison of the analysis differences between ChatGPT and LlaVa revealed that LlaVa made several more OCR errors, possibly because of a limited vocabulary, while ChatGPT would miss texts handled correctly by LlaVa mostly because it (ChatGPT) had refused analyzing the meme, i.e., because of guardrails.

---

[8] ChatGPT prompt: What is in this image?.
[9] Llava:34b prompt: What is in this image? In particular mention all the text you can find in the image.
[10] Llava:34b text prompt: Please give me all the text you can find on this image:.

6 Discussion and Conclusion

In this paper, we discuss the usefulness of locally-run LLMs in analysing the toxicity of memes. We expected local LLMs to have benefits over their online counterparts and these expectations were confirmed:

Costs All tested local LLMs were freely downloadable and could be run on our local machines, requiring no subscriptions or costs for additional software or hardware.

Reproducibility We reported the associated model version numbers in this paper, enabling future researchers to rerun our experiments.

Data safety Data processed by the LLMs did not leave our local machines.

Guardrails LLM guardrails prevented one tested online model to analyze about 20% of the data (see Section ??). However, we found that some locally run LLMs had guardrails as well, so choosing these LLMs does not always safeguard against having to deal with guardrails.

The foreseen challenges of local LLMs were confirmed in our experiments:

Processing time While large online LLMs produced analyses within seconds, local LLMs could take up to ten times as much time, even on fast hardware.

Performance The analyses of the local models were not as good as the ones from the large online models (see Table 1).

Hardware We ran our experiments on hardware with a GPU because otherwise some of the local models would be unmanageably slow.

We ran three experiments and found that the models identified only a small percentage of toxic memes and toxic symbols, although we did not compare them against non-toxic memes. Moreover, our tests indicate that predicted toxicity labels are reliable. Three main reasons can hinder the performance of LLMs in this task: lack of sufficient generic knowledge, lack of specific knowledge about toxic content, and guardrails. While online LLMs can leverage a larger amount of generic contextual information, when running local LLMs, we can easily inject niche and curated information that is useful in performing this kind of analysis and still leverage a sufficient amount of generic knowledge.

While the local LLMs performed worse than the online models, we still see some promising results in these experiments that will inspire future work aimed at relieving humans from the burden of analyzing large amounts of potentially toxic content. In particular, we would like to investigate how to effectively enrich locally-run LLMs with specific knowledge (e.g., via fine-tuning or Retrieval Augmented Generation) and how to safely circumvent guardrails, allowing fast and large-scale automatic analysis of potentially toxic content.

Acknowledgements. This research is supported by the Netherlands eScience Center project "The Eye of the Beholder" (project nr. 027.020.G15), and is part of the AI, Media & Democracy Lab (Dutch Research Council project number: NWA.1332.20.009). For more information about the lab and its further activities, visit https://www.aim4dem.nl/.

References

1. Brown, T.B., et al.: Language models are few-shot learners. In: Proceedings of the 34th International Conference on Neural Information Processing Systems. NIPS '20, Curran Associates Inc., Red Hook, NY, USA (2020)
2. Cui, S., et al.: FFT: Towards harmlessness evaluation and analysis for LLMs with factuality, fairness, toxicity (2024). https://arxiv.org/abs/2311.18580
3. Koh, H., Kim, D., Lee, M., Jung, K.: Can LLMs recognize toxicity? A structured investigation framework and toxicity metric. In: Al-Onaizan, Y., Bansal, M., Chen, Y.N. (eds.) Findings of the Association for Computational Linguistics: EMNLP 2024, pp. 6092–6114. Association for Computational Linguistics, Miami, Florida, USA (2024). https://doi.org/10.18653/v1/2024.findings-emnlp.353, https://aclanthology.org/2024.findings-emnlp.353/
4. Liu, H., Li, C., Wu, Q., Lee, Y.J.: Visual instruction tuning. In: Oh, A., Naumann, T., Globerson, A., Saenko, K., Hardt, M., Levine, S. (eds.) Advances in Neural Information Processing Systems. vol. 36, pp. 34892–34916. Curran Associates, Inc. (2023). https://proceedings.neurips.cc/paper_files/paper/2023/file/6dcf277ea32ce3288914faf369fe6de0-Paper-Conference.pdf
5. Martinez Pandiani, D., Tjong Kim Sang, E., Ceolin, D.: OnToxKG: an ontology-based knowledge graph of toxic symbols and their manifestations. In: 25th International Conference on Web Engineering. Springer (2025)
6. Martinez Pandiani, D.S., Tjong Kim Sang, E., Ceolin, D.: Toxic memes: A survey of computational perspectives on the detection and explanation of meme toxicities (2024). https://arxiv.org/abs/2406.07353
7. Wang, Y., Li, H., Han, X., Nakov, P., Baldwin, T.: Do-not-answer: evaluating safeguards in LLMs. In: Graham, Y., Purver, M. (eds.) Findings of the Association for Computational Linguistics: EACL 2024, pp. 896–911. Association for Computational Linguistics, St. Julian's, Malta (2024). https://aclanthology.org/2024.findings-eacl.61/
8. de Wynter, A., et al.: RTP-LX: Can LLMs evaluate toxicity in multilingual scenarios? (2024). https://arxiv.org/abs/2404.14397
9. Yang, Y., Dan, S., Roth, D., Lee, I.: Benchmarking LLM guardrails in handling multilingual toxicity (2024). https://arxiv.org/abs/2410.22153
10. Zhang, J., Wu, Q., Xu, Y., Cao, C., Du, Z., Psounis, K.: Efficient toxic content detection by bootstrapping and distilling large language models. Proc. AAAI Conf. Artif. Intell. **38**(19), 21779–21787 (2024)

MoralWeb: Reimagining the Web with Solid, Low-Code Tools, and Moral Codes for a Democratic and Equitable Future

Tobias Münch[1,2](✉) , Andreas Schmidt[3,4] , Sebastian Heil[2] , and Martin Gaedke[2]

[1] Münch Ges. für IT-Solutions mbH, Lohne (Oldenburg), Germany
to.muench@muench-its.de
[2] Chemnitz University of Technology, Chemnitz, Germany
{sebastian.heil,gaedke}@informatik.tu-chemnitz.de
[3] Karlsruhe Institute of Technology, Karlsruhe, Germany
andreas.schmidt@kit.edu
[4] Karlsruhe University of Applied Sciences, Karlsruhe, Germany
andreas.schmidt@h-ka.de

Abstract. The World Wide Web (WWW) was created as an open platform where individuals could freely create, share, and interact with information. However, the growing complexity of web engineering and the dominance of proprietary platforms have reduced non-specialist users to passive consumers. Challenges such as surveillance capitalism and disinformation further emphasise the need to restore openness and accessibility for everyday users. Building on our prior low-code web research, we propose a new vision of the web called *MoralWeb* inspired by Blackwell's 'More Open Representations, Access to Learning, and Control Over Digital Expression' (Moral Codes). Therefore, *MoralWeb* combines decentralised ownership, intuitive low-code tools, and educational resources to empower non-specialists with Moral Codes in the WWW. *MoralWeb* provides learning and development environments directly in the browser, enabling users to create web applications with a shared state and identity and access management (IAM). Through a wizard-style interface, users can create, share, and interact with decentralized data sources. We prioritise user agency, data sovereignty, and General Data Protection Regulation (GDPR) compliance, offering a pathway toward an equitable and participatory web.

Keywords: Web Architecture · Moral Codes · Human-centric AI · Web Development · User Participation

1 Introduction

Tim Berners-Lee designed the WWW as an open framework for democratising scientific knowledge and search efforts [1,2]. It changed the way individuals create and share content [1,2]. However, the Web's transformative potential was overshadowed by profit-orientated platforms, which prioritise monetisation over inclusivity [3,5]. Therefore, Zuboff introduced the term *surveillance capitalism* [5]. The comfort of sharing content through social networks has been used to build substantial user bases, but it has been compromised by disinformation and advertising [6]. Simultaneously, the growing complexity of web development makes it difficult for non-specialist users to learn how to create web applications [7]. This development raises questions about the WWW ideals of equality and accessibility [8,9]. In addition, this also brings to light issues about privacy and ethical dilemmas. With the increasing integration of AI and the Web, exchange with Human-Centric AI research becomes more relevant in Web Engineering. Therefore, democratising the WWW is urgent and important.

This situation requires solutions that go beyond proprietary systems and enable users to protect their autonomy while drawing on the school experience with HTML that they usually have [10]. For business developers, this means lowering development expenses [19]. For everyday users, it focuses on regaining control over personal data and digital interactions [5]. Addressing this broad spectrum of needs calls for a concept of a system that bridges the gap between existing technology, security, scalability, transparency and user-friendliness .

This vision paper outlines a vision of a web framework called *MoralWeb* that merges *Solid* principles [8] with low-code web development and ethically grounded design principles. Drawing on Blackwell's Moral Codes [9], we sketch an ecosystem that foregrounds data sovereignty, human-centred interfaces, and educational accessibility. The *MoralWeb* tries to create a more inclusive and sustainable WWW landscape. Therefore, we try to answer our first research questions on this broad topic:

- **RQ1**: What should a web architecture look like that focuses on decentralised data ownership, transparency, and Moral Codes?
- **RQ2**: Which design principles and educational resources empower diverse stakeholders to participate in a future web?

2 Background and Related Work

Evolution of the Web, Centralization and Decentralization: Designed as an open platform, the WWW democratized access, creation and sharing of information [1]. The early versions focused on simple declarative HTML to be accessible to individuals with limited technical expertise [1,7]. However, it became a battleground for commercialization as part of *surveillance capitalism* [5], and only a few influential players dominate this area and its development [7]. Therefore, the Solid project was introduced to restore control over user data even in third-party systems [8]. The goal is to protect user data while maintaining the open ethos of the WWW [8]. Data portability and interoperability are increasingly recognised as vital principles to maintain user autonomy in online ecosystems as part of the GDPR [15]. Also, industry practitioners such as Datev are implementing solutions to this approach [20].

Ethics, Digital Well-Being, and Thoughtful Design: The evolution of the Web is not profoundly ethically driven because of its commercialisation in the 2010s [18]. Currently developed systems include risks such as addictive user interfaces. [17]. As AI-driven algorithms mediate digital platforms, concerns over user attention and mental health have taken centre stage [13]. Moral Codes emphasises the need for tools that help users to shape their digital experiences actively, such as the famous Microsoft Excel [9]. In addition, the ICWE 2024 emphasized this by 'Ethical and Human-Centric Web Engineering: Balancing Innovation and Responsibility in Web Technology' [4].

Table 1. Feature comparison of MoralWeb and selected web platforms (✓= yes, ✗= no, ●= full, ○= partial, ⊙= none)

Feature	MoralWeb	Solid	WordPress	Webflow
Open-source	✓	✓	✓	✗
User data ownership	●	●	○Limited	⊙
Visual development	○Planned	✗	○Partial	✓
Education integration	✓	✗	○Some	✗
Deployment control	✓	✓	○Partial	✗
Privacy by design	✓	✓	✗	✗
Extensibility	★★★★	★★★	★★★★★	★

Bridging Education Gaps with Low-Code Solutions: A challenge in web participation is the unequal distribution of informatics education across regions and demographics [10]. Studies highlight how differences in education limit many students to engage with web technologies [10]. Proprietary low-code platforms such as Bubble or Webflow address these barriers [11]. This is an evolution of the End-User-Development approach to empower individuals with limited expertise to create web applications [11,12]. By abstracting configurations, such platforms open the door for citizen developers to engage in web development [14]. Schmidt and Münch demonstrate how free web components and generic RESTful services enable non-specialists to embed live database content into enterprise systems [19]. While traditional frameworks like htmx, Angular and React focus on experienced developers.

MoralWeb differs from previously approaches, which is shown in Table 1. Unlike these traditional approaches, which focus solely on development tools for experienced users, *MoralWeb* combines a Learning and Development Environment with decentralized data ownership and DevOps systems like GitHub.

3 The Vision of *MoralWeb*

In this section, we describe *MoralWeb*'s vision and core principles, key stakeholders, system architecture, and educational resources.

3.1 Core Principles

Decentralized Data Ownership and RESTful Abstraction: Decentralized Data Ownership and RESTful Abstraction are built on the principle that users maintain complete control over their data [8]. Instead of relying on hand-coded endpoints, our approach provides a streamlined RESTful interface that includes service discovery, standardized schemas (such as OpenAPI), and token-based security. This layer automates IAM, allowing for secure, privacy-focused integrations. There is nearly no manual intervention needed.

Low-Code Development and Educational Accessibility: Based on our prototype [19], our low-code strategy empowers a wide audience to create web solutions. Recognizing that basic HTML is already part of many school curriculums [10], we offer user-friendly web components, visual configuration tools, discoverable RESTful web services with OpenAPI or *Solid* pods, and automated security setups. Therefore, we enable learners to move seamlessly to fully functional, secure, data-driven applications.

Ethical Design and Moral Codes: Based on Moral Codes, we weave privacy, equity, and agency into every layer of our concept [9]. Specifically, we prioritize More Open Representations by making system details transparent to users, Access to Learning by building on school-level HTML skills and low-code tools, and Control Over Digital Expression by enabling self-hosted pods for personal data ownership [8–10]. This approach ensures that novices can join the *MoralWeb*.

Core Vision Contribution: MoralWeb proposes a novel integration of Solid-based decentralized data control, low-code front-end tooling, and educational scaffolding into a unified, user-owned web application stack. Unlike prior systems, MoralWeb explicitly prioritizes ethical design, learner access, and RESTful service discoverability as first-class elements.

3.2 Key Stakeholders

Business developers need tools that reduce development overhead and integration costs, enabling them to build dynamic, data-driven applications without extensive technical expertise. Intuitive visual configuration and discoverable data endpoints allow efficient customization.

Learners need accessible tools to advance from basic HTML to more complex technologies. *MoralWeb* provides educational materials and low-code environments that complement existing curricula.

Platform operators need observable, maintainable and scalable infrastructures that support applications with data privacy and security.

3.3 Key Scenarios

MoralWeb aims to streamline key aspects of modern web development. Below, we outline our primary usage scenarios.

Wizard Mode: Users are familiar with modern Graphical User Interfaces with Drag-and-Drop functionality. Therefore, the framework should allow users to arrange content and components visually, similar to assembling LEGO pieces, with event-based interactions. Therefore, low-code tools should have mechanisms to wire components, forms, data models, and actions to relevant web services. Web browsers should allow direct editing within the browser. This way, changes can be saved to a hosting or local development platform.

Data Connection and Shared State: To integrate data, we must simplify the integration of services, using standardized interfaces like OpenAPI. Based on these data connections, the wizard provides an interface to design web applications for creating, reading, updating, and deleting data using these services. Additionally, IAM offers authentication mechanisms like OAuth2 to offer easy activation and configuration to reduce manual setup overhead.

Learning Mode: The learning mode is for teachers and students. It focuses on business, grammar school, or early university learners. A teacher-led curriculum will support educators in guiding students through hands-on exercises that reinforce fundamental web development principles.

Example Use Case: A student with basic HTML knowledge opens the MoralWeb wizard, selects a "project list" component, links it to a Solid Pod using a visual API selector, and deploys the site to webserver provider—all in the browser, without writing code. This illustrates how MoralWeb enables secure, ethical web creation with minimal technical barriers.

3.4 System Architecture

To answer RQ1, the architecture of *MoralWeb* consists of the core environments Web Data Platform, Client Platform and Web Platform (see Fig. 1). The Web Data and Web Platform could be hosted by providers or on-premise. Essential are the interfaces between these environments. Using existing technologies (see Fig. 1), such as common web servers like NGINX or Apache, enables the solution to be scalable in the WWW environment.

The user interacts with the web browser on the Client Platform extended by a Learning environment and Development environment (DevEnv) (step 1, Fig. 1). Inside the DevEnv, a local Git repository gets created for each project, and a local webserver is running so a preview can be displayed in the Web Browser. The DevEnv is connected to the Web Data Platform Configuration Service to select a specific Data Container like a RESTful web service with OpenAPI or a *Solid* Pod (see Fig. 1). After a project is ready to deploy, it is deployed via Git into the web-based DevOps system (step 2). The used Web Data and Web Platform can be configured in DevEnv.

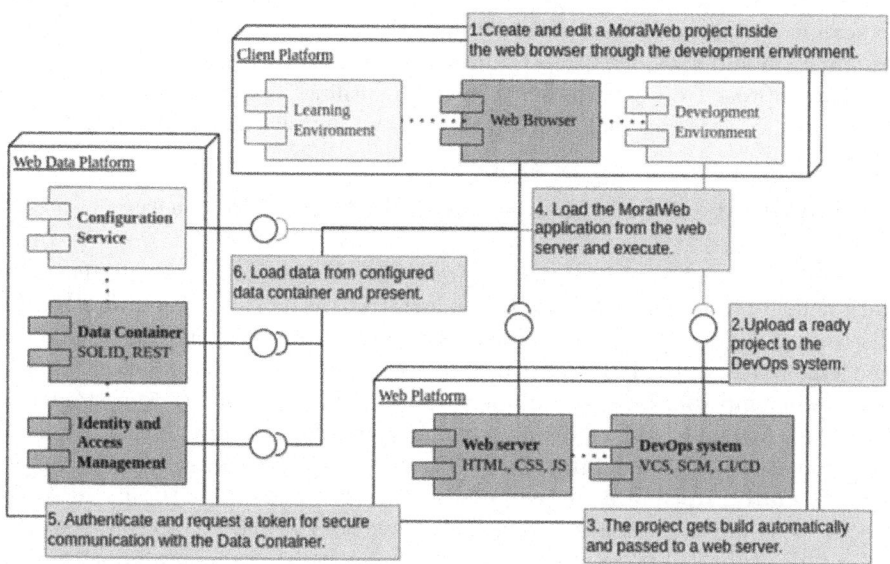

Fig. 1. The architecture of *MoralWeb* consists of a Web Data Platform, a Web Platform, and a Web Browser. The green components already exist, but the grey components have to be created.

The DevOps system is used to host *MoralWeb* projects. The repositories are connected to Deployment Pipelines, which build, test and transfer the projects to a web server (step 3). Afterwards, the user can open the published project in the web browser (step 4). In the runtime phase in the browser, the user can authenticate against the IAM (step 5) and use a generated token to identify after the data containers (step 6). Unlike traditional server-rendered web apps, MoralWeb loads data client-side via authenticated REST or Solid interfaces, enabling user-controlled rendering.

3.5 Educational Resources

Educational materials play a major role in involving our stakeholders (RQ2). These materials should include documentation, tutorials, references, interactive learning, and videos. Each type caters to the distinct learning requirements of various groups, enabling them to successfully adopt and make use of the *MoralWeb*. To ensure broad accessibility and sustainability, MoralWeb's educational content should be aligned with the principles of Open Educational Resources

(OER). The content should be created with partners such as W3C, universities, schools, and private educational institutions.

Beginners benefit from guides, tutorials, and interactive tools, enabling self-paced learning or use in formal courses to master the basics. Practical guidance is for business developers. Tutorials and concise documentation will enable these users to quickly find solutions to their needs without requiring extensive technical expertise. For platform operators, detailed reference materials are crucial. These resources should provide in-depth information about the *MoralWeb*.

This approach aligns with the "Access to Learning" principle from Blackwell's Moral Codes, ensuring that *MoralWeb* remains inclusive and accessible.

4 Challenges, Limitations, and Future Directions

MoralWeb presents our vision of combining Moral Codes, existing web technologies, and areas for improvement to democratise the WWW. **Technically**, the distributed data architecture builds on existing technologies such as Solid Pods and OpenAPI, which have been demonstrated to provide scalable and secure data ownership solutions [8]. In addition, adapting to evolving web standards (e.g., WebAssembly, HTTP/3) are significant hurdles. Security measures, such as automated CORS handling and IAM, are essential to control digital expression. **Socially**, resistance to new models and the need for culturally inclusive resources require collaboration with global stakeholders and targeted educational efforts. **Sustainability** is also challenging because maintaining an open-source system demands innovative funding models and partnerships with browser manufacturers to integrate native editing tools. *MoralWeb* aligns closely with the European Union's strategic emphasis on digital sovereignty [16]. It enables citizens to retain control over their data and reduce dependence on centralised, non-European platforms - data privacy features position *MoralWeb* as a driving force for Europe's digital independence. Therefore, EU funding through programs like Horizon Europe offers an opportunity to support its development and sustainability.

Key open questions include: 1) What funding mechanisms can support *MoralWeb* without introducing conflicts of interest? Can grants from organizations like the EU's Horizon Europe or W3C partnerships provide long-term support?, 2) Should MoralWeb be managed by an open-source community, a nonprofit, or an academic-industry consortium?, 3) How can MoralWeb incentivize adoption by developers and businesses, given the dominance of existing web frameworks and low-code platforms?

Our strategy for future efforts will prioritise 1) partnerships with global stakeholders such as W3C and universities, 2) prototyping of a small-scale *MoralWeb*, 3) creating validation concepts and user studies, and 4) validating and refining through user studies *MoralWeb*'s impact.

5 Conclusion

Inspired by Solid and Moral Codes the *MoralWeb* envisions a WWW grounded in ethical principles, empowering users to reclaim control over their data and shape their digital environments. Aligned with GDPR compliance, *MoralWeb* advances user-centric technologies to create a more equitable and participatory web by using existing technology. In the future, we aim to establish a collaborative group to refine our vision. To ensure sustainability, we will pursue funding opportunities through programs like Horizon Europe and partnerships with industry leaders committed to ethical and decentralized web development.

Acknowledgements. This work is supported by the European Union's HORIZON Research and Innovation Programme under grant agreement No 101120657, project ENFIELD (European Lighthouse to Manifest Trustworthy & Green AI).

References

1. Berners-Lee, T.: Information management. CERN-DD-89-001-OC (1989)
2. Berners-Lee, T., Cailliau, R., Groff, J.F., Pollermann, B.: World-wide web: the information universe. Internet Res. **20**(4), 461–471 (2010)
3. Martínez-López, F.J., Li, Y., Young, S.M.: Social Media Monetization. Future of Business and Finance (2022)
4. Stefanidis, K., Systä, K, Matera, M., Heil, S., Kondylakis, H., Quintarelli, E.: Web Engineering: 24th International Conference, ICWE 2024 (2024)
5. Zuboff, S.: The age of surveillance capitalism. In Social theory re-wired (pp. 203–213) (2023)
6. Tucker, J.A., et al.: Social media, political polarization, and political disinformation: a review of the scientific literature. Political polarization, and political disinformation: a review of the scientific literature (2018)
7. Pemberton, S.: The one hundred year web. In: Companion Proceedings of the ACM Web Conference 2023 (p. 1) (2023)
8. Mansour, E., et al.: A demonstration of the solid platform for social web applications. In: Proceedings of the 25th International Conference Companion on World Wide Web (2016)
9. Blackwell, A.F.: Moral Codes: Designing Alternatives to AI. MIT Press (2024)
10. Vahrenhold, J., Caspersen., Westermeier, M.: Informatics education in Europe: Are we all in the same boat? (2017)
11. Luo, Y., Liang., Zhan, J.: Characteristics and challenges of low-code development: the practitioners' perspective. In Proceedings of the 15th ACM/IEEE ESEM (pp. 1–11) (2021)
12. Chudnovskyy, O., Gaedke, M.: End-user-development and evolution of web applications: the WebComposition EUD approach. In: Grossniklaus, M., Wimmer, M. (eds.) ICWE 2012. LNCS, vol. 7703, pp. 221–226. Springer, Heidelberg (2012). https://doi.org/10.1007/978-3-642-35623-0_23
13. Korte, M.: The impact of the digital revolution on human brain and behavior: where do we stand? Dialogues Clin. Neurosci. **22**(2), 101–111 (2020)

14. Hartmann, B., Wu, L., Collins, K., Klemmer, S.R.: Programming by a sample: rapidly creating web applications with d. mix. In Proceedings of the 20th Annual ACM Symposium on User Interface Software and Technology (pp. 241–250) (2007)
15. De Hert, P., Sanchez, I.: The right to data portability in the GDPR: towards user-centric interoperability of digital services. Comput. Law Secur. Rev. **34**(2), 193–203 (2018)
16. Ivic, S., Troitiño, D.R.: Digital sovereignty and identity in the European union: a challenge for building Europe. Eur. Stud. **9**(2), 80–109 (2022)
17. Ko, A.J., Myers, B.A., Aung, H.H.: Six learning barriers in end-user programming systems. In: 2004 IEEE Symposium on Visual Languages-Human Centric Computing (pp. 199–206) (2004)
18. Bell, J., Loane, S.: 'New-wave' global firms: web 2.0 and SME internationalisation. J. Market. Manag. **26**(3-4), 213–229 (2010)
19. Schmidt, A., Münch, T.: Enable business users to embed dynamic database content in existing web-based systems using web components and generic web services. In: Proceedings of the 20th WEBIST, pp. 296–306 (2024)
20. Both, A., et al.: AuthApp–Portable, reusable solid app for GDPR-compliant access granting. In: International Conference on Web Engineering (pp. 199–214) (2024)

A Web Crawling-Based Process and a Graph-Based Database for Mobile Vulnerability Analysis

Domenico Amalfitano[1]([✉]), Andrea Abbate[1], Damiano Distante[2], Antonio M. Rinaldi[1], Cristiano Russo[1], and Cristian Tommasino[1]

[1] Department of Electrical Engineering and Information Technologies, University of Naples Federico II, Via Claudio 21, 80125 Naples, Italy
{domenico.amalfitano,antoniomaria.rinaldi,
cristiano.russo,cristian.tommasino}@unina.it,
and.abbate@studenti.unina.it
[2] Department of Law and Economics, University of Rome UnitelmaSapienza, Rome, Italy
damiano.distante@unitelmasapienza.it

Abstract. The increasing availability of security-related data on the Web requires efficient and scalable approaches for data integration and analysis. In the context of software security, a holistic methodology that combines multiple data sources is essential to understand evolving threats. This paper presents a novel web crawling-based process designed to systematically retrieve and integrate security-related information from multiple vulnerability data repositories. This process has been leveraged to build G-MAWD, a Graph-based Mobile Application Vulnerability and Weakness Database, that we show to be effective for analyzing web-related security risks in mobile applications, including vulnerabilities in WebView, WKWebView, and authentication mechanisms such as OAuth and JWT. By enabling large-scale security analysis through flexible querying and relationship exploration, this approach highlights the potential of distributed web crawling and graph-based modeling to advance security research and improve software quality.

Keywords: Mobile Security · Vulnerability Database · Graph Databases · Web Architecture · Web Crawlers · Data Integration

1 Introduction

Mobile applications are integral to modern life, facilitating communication, entertainment, shopping, and productivity for billions of users around the world. In 2023, more then 6.92 billion people, or about 86% of the global population, use smartphones, with Android dominating the market at 70.97% and iOS following at 28.3% [25]. These applications extend beyond personal use, playing critical roles in sectors such as healthcare and finance, where security and reliability are paramount [1,20]. Despite their utility, mobile applications significantly expand the threat landscape. The open source nature of Android leads to increased susceptibility to malware and vulnerabilities [28], while iOS, although more controlled, faces advanced attacks [8]. Addressing these security challenges requires robust methodologies, including structured vulnerability datasets, dependency analysis, and predictive modeling [9,10,23]. Furthermore, mobile applications frequently integrate web-based components, such as WebView on Android and WKWebView on iOS, creating additional security concerns that span both mobile and web ecosystems. Our work is inspired by the comprehensive study of Android OS vulnerabilities by Mazuera-Rozo et al. [12], which analyzed 1,235 vulnerabilities reported between 2008 and August 2017. While their work provided key insights into the distribution and persistence of mobile vulnerabilities, our contribution expands this perspective by considering more recent vulnerabilities and a broader, cross-platform scope. In particular, we integrate heterogeneous vulnerability sources into a unified graph-based representation.

The main contributions of this work are twofold. First, we introduce a novel web crawling-based process designed to systematically retrieve and integrate security-related data from multiple vulnerability data repositories. This process orchestrates an automated architecture built on focused web crawlers, which extract structured information from diverse and heterogeneous sources, ensuring a comprehensive and up-to-date view of mobile security threats. Second, we present G-MAWD, a freely available *Graph-based Mobile Application Vulnerability and Weakness Database* [2] built by using the proposed crawling-based process. G-MAWD is a structured knowledge base that integrates curated security data extracted from well-established repositories managed by MITRE [17], including CVE [15], CWE [16], and CAPEC [14], which provide organized information on vulnerabilities, weaknesses, and attack patterns. In addition, it incorporates insights from open source code repositories and bug-tracking systems, offering a broader perspective on how security flaws are introduced and resolved in practice. By organizing this aggregated security intelligence into a structured format, G-MAWD enables researchers to efficiently analyze interconnected threats, attack patterns, and mitigation techniques.

To show the potential of G-MAWD, we employ it to analyze mobile security vulnerabilities, with a specific emphasis on those affecting web-related components and authentication mechanisms. Mobile applications interact extensively with web services and APIs, making them possible vectors for security breaches that impact the broader web ecosystem. By analyzing attack patterns, weaknesses, and mitigation strategies, we identify key trends in mobile web security, quantify the prevalence of authentication-related vulnerabilities, and assess the remediation effort required to address these threats. Our findings provide insights into the security challenges posed by the convergence of mobile and web technologies, offering a foundation for improving protection mechanisms in these environments. By enabling the structured representation of interconnected entities—such as vulnerabilities, weaknesses, attack patterns, and remediation actions—G-MAWD assists web engineers in systematically identifying and reasoning about security flaws that affect web-integrated applications. The querying capabilities of the knowledge base, exemplified through cases involving technologies as WebView, OAuth, and JWT, allow developers to detect misconfigurations, understand attack surfaces, and inform secure design and implementation choices.

The rest of the paper is structured as follows: Sect. 2 discusses related studies, Sect. 3 provides details about the G-MAWD database, including its data sources and the process used to build it. Section 4 presents representative analyses enabled by G-MAWD, while Sect. 5 discusses limitations, possible improvements, and ideas for future research.

2 Related Works

The integration of web crawling techniques for cybersecurity data collection has been widely explored, with various approaches that leverage focused web crawlers, graph-based models, and automated data integration methods. However, our approach uniquely combines rule-based web crawling with dynamic graph-based security data modeling to create a structured and automated system for vulnerability analysis.

Focused web crawlers have been applied in several domains to retrieve structured data from various sources [5,7,18]. Recent studies [3,22] have demonstrated how AI-enhanced crawling improves cybersecurity intelligence collections by extracting real-time data from multiple threat intelligence feeds and generating synthetic data to improve multimedia knowledge base contents [4]. Our work extends these contributions by integrating web crawling with a knowledge graph, allowing a deeper correlation of extracted data points.

The construction of security databases has also been a major research focus, with studies [13,19,24] highlighting the importance of integrating vulnerabilities, weaknesses, and attack patterns into structured representations. Our approach builds upon these efforts by linking extracted data to a graph-based model, ensuring real-time updates and flexible querying.

Graph-based modeling is increasingly used for cybersecurity analysis, enabling relationship discovery and attack path analysis [11,27]. Unlike previous works that focus on temporal threat detection, our method interconnects structured web-crawled data in a persistent, evolving knowledge base.

Automation in security data collection remains critical for up-to-date threat intelligence [6,21]. Our work complements existing reinforcement learning-based crawling techniques by integrating a structured storage model that enhances data representation through interlinked entities in a graph structure. By combining multi-source data collection with structured graph-based representation, our approach improves the efficiency of security intelligence gathering and analysis.

3 The G-MAWD Database

In this section, we describe the data sources used to build G-MAWD (Sect. 3.1), the adopted construction process (Sect. 3.2), and the G-MAWD conceptual schema (Sect. 3.3).

3.1 G-MAWD Data Sources

Different data sources have been used to build G-MAWD, i.e., *Common Vulnerabilities and Exposures (CVE)*, *Common Weakness Enumeration (CWE)*, *Common Attack Pattern Enumeration and Classification (CAPEC)*, and *Open-source Code Repositories and Bug Tracking Systems*, each with a different purpose.

The CVE system [15] provides unique identifiers for security vulnerabilities, i.e., errors in system design, implementation, operation, or management, which are usually exploited by malicious users, a.k.a. attackers, to perform improper actions in the system, e.g., collecting sensible user data [26]. Each CVE entry uniquely identifies a specific software vulnerability, enabling standardized tracking and communication among different stakeholders in the cybersecurity community. Furthermore, for each vulnerability, the CVE provides additional information such as attack vectors, impacts, severity scores, exploitation complexity, and suggested mitigations.

The CWE system [16] focuses on structural software weaknesses rather than specific vulnerabilities. Weaknesses are design or implementation flaws that could lead to exploitable vulnerabilities later in the software lifecycle. Integrating CWE into our database allows us to identify common categories of weaknesses that frequently occur during the development of mobile applications, providing a deeper understanding of the root causes of vulnerabilities. Each CWE entry describes the type of weakness, the context in which it occurs, and countermeasures that can be adopted to prevent its exploitation. This classification helps developers and security experts implement safer coding practices and improve the overall quality of software.

The CAPEC system [14] is designed to catalog and classify known attack patterns. CAPEC is closely linked to both CVE and CWE, as many attacks exploit vulnerabilities cataloged in CVE and weaknesses described in CWE. Including data from CAPEC in our database allows us to better understand how various attacks exploit vulnerabilities and weaknesses in mobile applications. CAPEC offers a detailed taxonomy of attack methods and vectors, enabling a more robust correlation between software weaknesses and common attack patterns. This integration is essential to understanding how technical weaknesses can be exploited in the real world, providing guidance on how to strengthen defenses against known attack vectors.

Open-source code repositories based on Git, SVN, and Mercurial standards, as well as bug tracking systems, such as Bugzilla, provide valuable insights into how vulnerabilities are addressed in real-world applications. For our study, we specifically used these repositories to analyze the code fixes implemented to resolve the identified vulnerabilities. By examining commit histories, pull requests, and code changes, we tracked the nature and implementation of these fixes. This analysis provided insights into common practices for vulnerability remediation and highlighted trends in resolving vulnerabilities within open-source and proprietary projects.

3.2 G-MAWD Construction Process

Figure 1 shows the process we followed to build G-MAWD. The process consists of several steps that focus on querying, collecting, and integrating data from the data sources described in Sect. 3.1.

At this stage of our research, the system is designed for offline analysis. Moreover, data retrieval efficiency is supported by the unified mapping of all considered sources into a single logical graph structure.

The construction of G-MAWD is powered by focused web crawlers designed to automate the extraction and integration of security-related data from multiple sources. Unlike traditional static vulnerability databases, our architecture continuously retrieves, integrates, and organizes security data from multiple sources. Using automated web crawlers and a structured data processing pipeline, we ensure that G-MAWD remains up-to-date and provides a comprehensive view of mobile security threats.

The process begins by querying the REST APIs of the *National Vulnerability Database (NVD)* to retrieve detailed and up-to-date information on mobile application vulnerabilities from CVE.

Following this, a focused web crawler automatically navigates the *CWE* and *CAPEC* repositories to extract information on weaknesses and attack patterns linked to the collected vulnerabilities. These data enrich the dataset by clarifying the root causes of vulnerabilities and documenting common attack techniques used to exploit them.

Once gathered, raw data from CVE, CWE, and CAPEC are integrated into a relational database after automatically resolving inconsistencies and redundancies and establishing structured relationships between vulnerabilities, weaknesses, and attack patterns.

Subsequently, another focused web crawler collects security-related information from *open-source code repositories* and *Bug Tracking Systems*, focusing on identifying *vulnerable source code* and related *fixes*. This step enables a deeper understanding of real-world vulnerability remediation strategies, linking vulnerabilities directly to their corresponding patches and code changes. The *Bugs & Fixes Web Crawler* ensures that software fixes are properly documented, allowing researchers to analyze vulnerability mitigation efforts.

Next, the *Data Integrator* and *Data Organizer* harmonize the extracted data, ensuring that the security information from different sources is properly correlated. This integration phase is crucial for merging heterogeneous datasets and creating a unified view of security threats.

Finally, the enriched dataset is stored in a *Graph Database* using *Neo4j*, where vulnerabilities, weaknesses, attack patterns, and remediation efforts are interconnected. The adoption of a graph-based model allows researchers to efficiently

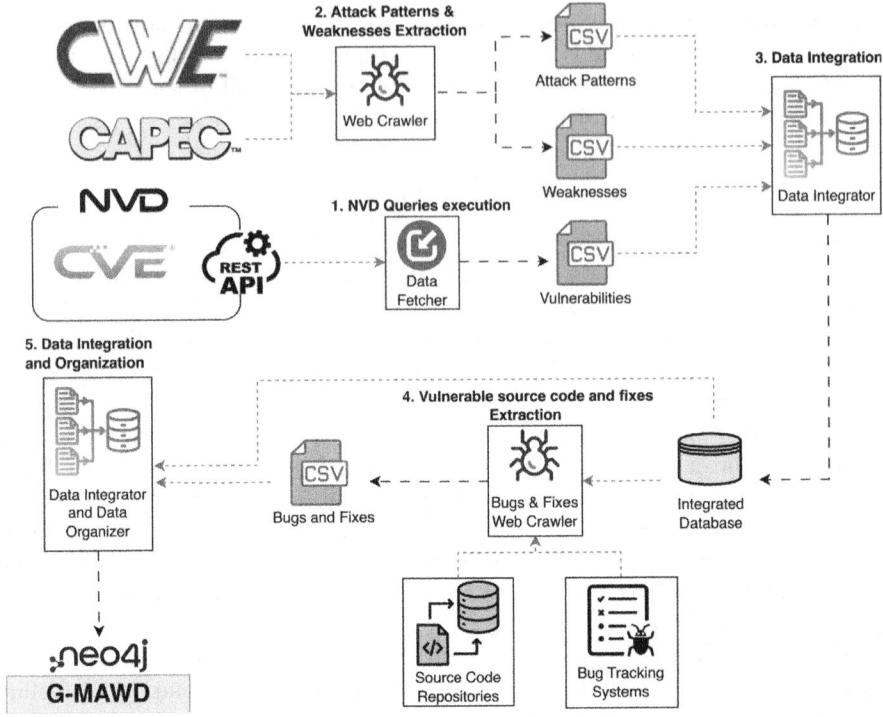

Fig. 1. The G-MAWD Construction Process.

explore security relationships, uncover trends, and perform advanced analytics on mobile vulnerabilities. The structured nature of the graph facilitates semantic querying, enabling security practitioners to trace dependencies and detect systemic weaknesses. The use of NoSQL DBMS and ad hoc focused crawler ensures the scalability of the entire system.

3.3 G-MAWD Conceptual Schema

Figure 2 shows a conceptual schema of G-MAWD. The figure illustrates the interconnected relationships between key entities in the database, including *Vulnerabilities*, *Weaknesses*, *Attack Patterns*, and *Patch Info*. These entities, which are represented as colored nodes in Fig. 2, are the focal points of the subsequent Sect. 4 where we show practical usage examples of the database. The graph leverages a property graph model, enabling a structured and intuitive representation. *Vulnerabilities* are linked to *Weaknesses*, which describe their root causes, and *Weaknesses* are further associated with *Attack Patterns*, which outline the methods used to exploit them in real-world scenarios. Furthermore, *Vulnerabilities* are connected to *Patch Info* nodes, which provide details about patches applied to address these issues, including metrics such as added, removed or modified lines of code. The relationships between these entities, such as *CAUSED_BY* (linking

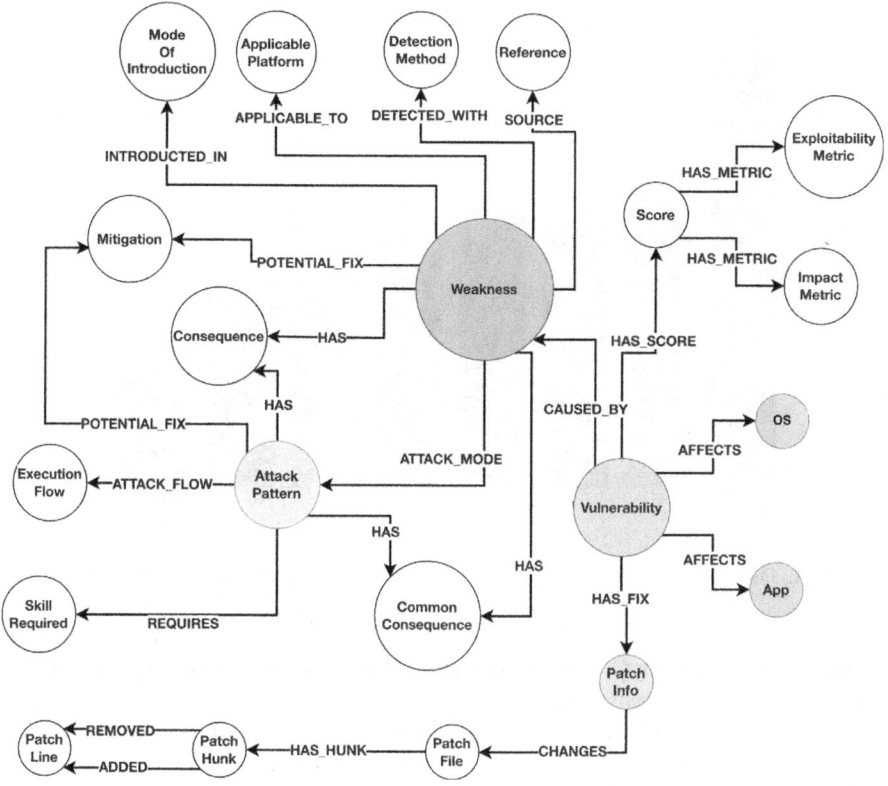

Fig. 2. G-MAWD conceptual schema.

Vulnerabilities to their underlying *Weaknesses*) and *FIXED_BY* (linking *Vulnerabilities* to specific patches), provide a comprehensive view of the life-cycle of security issues.

4 G-MAWD Usage Examples

In this section, we illustrate the potential of G-MAWD by showing how the database can be leveraged through Cypher queries to analyze mobile vulnerabilities, with a specific focus on those related to web technologies and services. This approach allows for a deeper understanding of how mobile vulnerabilities impact web ecosystems, emphasizing their relevance in securing web-integrated mobile applications.

Figure 3 shows the temporal distribution of mobile vulnerabilities in G-MAWD. The number of reported vulnerabilities peaked in 2017 and has gradually decreased in subsequent years. This trend may be influenced by improved security practices, advances in mobile OS protections, and changes in vulnera-

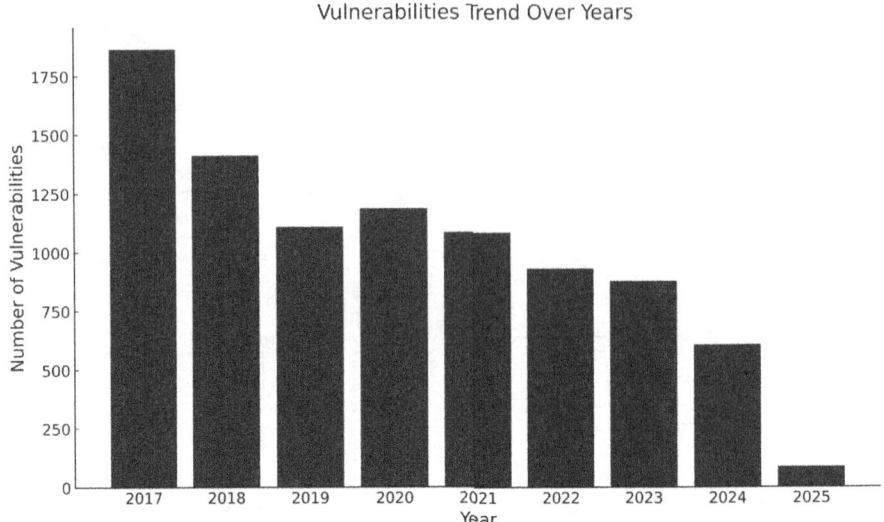

Fig. 3. Distribution of mobile vulnerabilities in G-MAWD over the last 9 years.

bility disclosure policies. The low count for 2025 is probably due to partial data collection for the current year.

These data were obtained by running the Cypher query reported in the Listing 1.1.

```
MATCH (v:Vulnerability)
RETURN substring(v.published_date, 0, 4) AS Year, COUNT(v) AS
    VulnerabilityCount
ORDER BY Year ASC
```

Listing 1.1. Cypher query to obtain the temporal distribution of mobile vulnerabilities in G-MAWD.

G-MAWD enables the analysis of vulnerabilities specifically related to WebView in Android and WKWebView in iOS, two widely used components that allow applications to embed and render web content. Due to their integration with mobile applications, these technologies introduce security risks, including cross-site scripting (XSS), injection attacks, and improper handling of web-based authentication. Additionally, the database allows one to examine the vulnerabilities that impact server-side APIs, identifying whether specific technologies are more affected. This is particularly relevant given the increasing reliance on web services for the functionality of mobile applications.

G-MAWD also facilitates the analysis of authentication mechanisms such as token-based authentication, OAuth (Open Authorization), and JWT (JSON Web Token). These technologies play a crucial role in user authentication and session management, but also introduce potential security flaws, such as token leakage, replay attacks, and improper validation, which can be exploited by attackers. Furthermore, the database provides visibility into vulnerable code and its corresponding fixes, making it possible to assess the patching effort required to address security issues. This enables a broader evaluation of the patching process, providing insights into how vulnerabilities are identified and resolved in real-world scenarios. These components and mechanisms are critical within the security landscape of mobile applications, making them key points of analysis.

Using G-MAWD, it is possible to explore the relationships between vulnerabilities and their exploitation strategies, gaining a more comprehensive understanding of security threats. In addition, the database supports the analysis of detection methods and modes of introduction, providing deeper insights into how these vulnerabilities emerge and spread within mobile ecosystems. In the following of this section, we provide a detailed discussion of these analyses, highlighting key findings and insights derived from G-MAWD.

Table 1. Common attack patterns associated with vulnerabilities in WebView (Android) and WKWebView (iOS) and their corresponding weaknesses.

AttackPattern	Weakness
Manipulating User-Controlled Variables	Improper Control of Generation of Code ('Code Injection')
Code Injection	
Leverage Executable Code in Non-Executable Files	
Reflected XSS	Improper Neutralization of Input During Web Page Generation ('Cross-site Scripting')
XSS Using MIME Type Mismatch	
AJAX Footprinting	
DOM-Based XSS	
Cross-Site Scripting (XSS)	
Stored XSS	
TCP Xmas Scan	Exposure of Sensitive Information to an Unauthorized Actor

Table 1 presents an overview of the most common attack patterns associated with vulnerabilities in WebView (Android) and WKWebView (iOS), highlighting their corresponding weaknesses, as a result of querying G-MAWD. These attack strategies exploit security flaws in mobile applications that render web content, exposing them to various threats such as code injection, cross-site scripting (XSS), and unauthorized data exposure.

Moreover, the analysis conducted using G-MAWD provides key insights into how server-side JavaScript vulnerabilities emerge and are detected, focusing on the three most prevalent weaknesses, as shown in Table 2. The results indicate that these vulnerabilities are introduced primarily during the implementation phase, with some stemming from architectural and design flaws. Detection methods rely on both automated and manual techniques, highlighting the need for a multi-layered security approach in back-end JavaScript applications.

Improper control of code generation and improper neutralization of input during web page generation are frequently introduced due to insecure coding practices, insufficient input validation, and poor security controls. Meanwhile, incorrect input validation often originates at the architectural level, reinforcing the importance of integrating security considerations early in the development life-cycle. Automated static analysis is the most widely used detection method,

Table 2. Most prevalent server-side JavaScript weaknesses, their introduction phases, and detection methods.

Weakness	IntroductionPhase	DetectionType
Improper Neutralization of Input During Web Page Generation ('Cross-site Scripting')	Implementation	Automated Static Analysis
		Black Box
Improper Control of Generation of Code ('Code Injection')	Implementation	Automated Static Analysis
Improper Input Validation	Architecture and Design	Fuzzing
		Manual Static Analysis - Source Code
		Dynamic Analysis with Automated Results Interpretation
		Manual Static Analysis - Binary or Bytecode
		Automated Static Analysis
		Dynamic Analysis with Manual Results Interpretation

particularly effective in identifying injection vulnerabilities before deployment. Fuzzing complements static analysis by testing how applications handle unexpected inputs, while manual code reviews help uncover complex security flaws. Dynamic analysis, both automated and manual, improves detection by identifying vulnerabilities that manifest only during execution.

The findings emphasize the need for secure coding practices, robust static analysis, and early-stage security integration to reduce risk. While static techniques are crucial for early vulnerability detection, dynamic analysis and fuzzing provide additional protection by assessing real-world attack scenarios. Strengthening input validation, adopting secure development frameworks and using multiple detection approaches collectively improve the security of server-side JavaScript applications, reducing their exposure to exploitation.

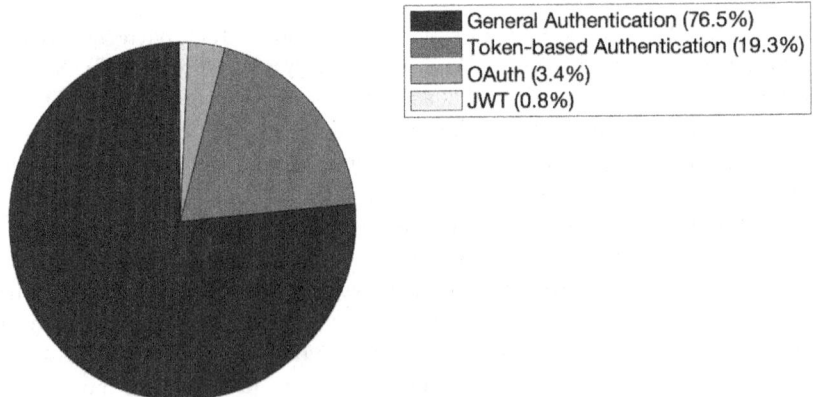

Fig. 4. Distribution of Authentication-Related Vulnerabilities.

The pie chart in Fig. 4 illustrates the distribution of vulnerabilities related to authentication mechanisms. Most vulnerabilities (76%) fall into the category of general authentication issues, indicating widespread weaknesses in the way authentication processes are implemented and managed. Token-based authentication accounts for 19% of the vulnerabilities, suggesting that while token-based mechanisms enhance security, they also introduce specific risks, such as token leakage and improper validation. OAuth-related vulnerabilities represent 3% of the total, highlighting potential misconfigurations or flaws in the implementation of authorization flows. Finally, JWT-related vulnerabilities constitute less than 1%, indicating that while JWT is widely adopted, security issues related to its use are relatively infrequent in the analyzed dataset. This distribution underscores the need for a comprehensive approach to securing authentication mechanisms, ensuring the proper implementation and mitigation strategies across different authentication technologies.

Table 3. Authentication-related vulnerabilities, their descriptions, and the corresponding patching effort measured in code modifications.

Vulnerability ID	Description	Added Lines	Removed Lines	Code Changes
CVE-2020-15679	An OAuth session fixation vulnerability existed in the VPN login flow, where an attacker could craft a custom login URL, convince a VPN user to login via that URL, and obtain authenticated access as that user. This issue is limited to cases where the attacker and victim are sharing the same source IP and could allow the ability to view session states and disconnect VPN sessions. This vulnerability affects Mozilla VPN iOS 1.0.7 <(929), Mozilla VPN Windows <1.2.2, and Mozilla VPN Android 1.1.0 <(1360).	1379	830	2209
CVE-2016-5299	A previously installed malicious Android application with same signature-level permissions as Firefox can intercept AuthTokens meant for Firefox only. Note: This issue only affects Firefox for Android. Other versions and operating systems are unaffected. This vulnerability affects Firefox <50.	79	35	114
CVE-2018-19937	A local, authenticated attacker can bypass the passcode in the VideoLAN VLC media player app before 3.1.5 for iOS by opening a URL and turning the phone.	31	16	47
CVE-2021-29965	A malicious website that causes an HTTP Authentication dialog to be spawned could trick the built-in password manager to suggest passwords for the currently active website instead of the website that triggered the dialog. This bug only affects Firefox for Android. Other operating systems are unaffected. This vulnerability affects Firefox <89.	21	14	35
CVE-2024-41955	Mobile Security Framework (MobSF) is a security research platform for mobile applications in Android, iOS and Windows Mobile. An open redirect vulnerability exist in MobSF authentication view. Update to MobSF v4.0.5.	23	6	29

Table 3 provides an overview of the authentication-related vulnerabilities that required the most significant effort to patch, measured in terms of code lines added and removed. The data reveal substantial variation in the remediation effort across different vulnerabilities, highlighting the complexity involved in addressing authentication security flaws. For example, CVE-2020-15679, an OAuth session fixation vulnerability in Mozilla VPN, required a total of 2209 code changes, making it the most resource-intensive fix among the listed vulnerabilities. This suggests that session management flaws can be particularly challenging to mitigate, likely due to the need for extensive validation and secure state handling. In contrast, other vulnerabilities, such as CVE-2024-41955, an open redirect vulnerability in Mobile Security Framework (MobSF), required significantly fewer modifications, with only 29 code lines changed, indicating that some security issues can be resolved with more localized fixes.

In particular, the presence of authentication vulnerabilities in mobile browsers and VPN applications, as seen with CVE-2016-5299 and CVE-2021-29965, suggests that attackers frequently target weaknesses in session management and credential handling. Furthermore, vulnerabilities affecting mobile security research tools, such as CVE-2024-41955, emphasize the importance of securing security-related applications themselves, as they are often leveraged by researchers and penetration testers. The distribution of remediation efforts further underscores the varying levels of complexity in fixing authentication vulnerabilities, emphasizing the need for proactive security practices in authentication mechanisms across mobile applications and platforms.

The analyses presented in this section illustrate only a subset of the possible investigations that can be conducted using G-MAWD. The database enables a wide range of security analyses, offering researchers the flexibility to tailor their studies according to specific interests and requirements. Given the increasing convergence between mobile and web technologies, G-MAWD is particularly valuable for exploring web-related security issues. As an open and freely accessible resource, G-MAWD provides the foundation for further exploration of mobile and web security vulnerabilities, attack patterns, and mitigation strategies, fostering continued advancements in the field of web engineering.

5 Conclusion and Future Works

In this work, we introduced a novel web crawling-based process to systematically retrieve and integrate security-related data from multiple vulnerability repositories. This process has been leveraged to construct G-MAWD, a Graph-based Mobile Application Vulnerability and Weakness Database, which enables in-depth analyzes of mobile security issues, authentication mechanisms, and web-related threats. By facilitating custom queries, tracking security trends, and linking vulnerabilities with their attack patterns and patches, G-MAWD provides a structured approach to studying mobile security challenges. Beyond its current application in the mobile domain, by adjusting NVD queries and retrieval parameters, the proposed process could be used to generate structured vulnerability databases for other domains, such as embedded systems, computer networks, and IoT systems. This adaptability highlights the scalability of the proposed approach and its ability to support security research in different technological domains. Despite its advantages, some limitations of G-MAWD influence its completeness and usability. One key challenge lies in the vulnerability retrieval method, which relies on domain-specific search queries when extracting data from the CVE database. Although effective, this approach may result in gaps due to variations in vulnerability descriptions.

Future improvements will explore text-mining techniques and ontology-based approaches to refine search criteria and capture a broader range of security issues. Furthermore, the extraction of data from CWE and CAPEC is currently partial, limiting the contextual depth available for each vulnerability. Enhancing the extraction process to integrate more comprehensive data on attack techniques and exploitability will be a priority. In future work, we want to improve both quantitative and qualitative comparisons of G-MAWD with existing vulnerability databases and alternative cybersecurity intelligence frameworks. Another limitation concerns the patch collection process, which relies on heuristics to navigate bug tracking systems and repositories. This method may not always retrieve the complete patch data. To improve this aspect, we plan to develop a knowledge graph that enhances patch identification and retrieval, providing a clearer view of vulnerability remediation efforts. Moreover, reliance on Cypher queries to interact with the Neo4j database may pose challenges for some users. To enhance accessibility, our goal is to develop a web-based interface that simplifies querying while maintaining flexibility for custom analyzes.

Future work will include improvements to the tool's user interface, with the goal of facilitating interaction and usability for security analysts. In addition, we plan to define and execute a set of realistic use cases to assess the practical utility of our graph-based approach. These use cases will be used to compare G-MAWD with traditional solutions such as relational vulnerability databases and public resources such as NVD or CVEdetails, in order to evaluate differences in effectiveness, expressiveness, and ease of use.

Additional future research directions emerge from both G-MAWD and the developed construction process. Mining textual descriptions of vulnerabilities using NLP techniques, such as topic modeling and sentiment analysis, could help uncover trends, refine classifications, and reveal patterns over time and across platforms. Automated categorization based on metadata could facilitate targeted analyses by severity, affected components, or attack vectors. The correlation of vulnerability descriptions with real-world attack data could support early threat detection and prioritization of high-risk vulnerabilities. Another promising avenue involves analyzing patch-related code within the dataset. Techniques like static code analysis and machine learning-based code summarization could reveal common patterns in vulnerability mitigation and enhance patching methodologies. The application of NLP techniques to patch descriptions could provide information on remediation strategies in different projects, ultimately supporting the development of automated vulnerability detection and patch generation tools. These efforts aim to improve the overall security of mobile applications and extend the applicability of the proposed methodology to broader security domains.

References

1. Ahmed, W., et al.: Security in next generation mobile payment systems: a comprehensive survey. IEEE Access **9**, 115932–115950 (2021)
2. Amalfitano, D., Abbate, A.: Replication Package for A Web Crawling-Based Process and a Graph-Based Database for Mobile Vulnerability Analysis (2025). https://doi.org/10.5281/zenodo.14235608
3. Arikkat, D.R., et al.: OSTIS: a novel organization-specific threat intelligence system. Comput. Secur. **145**, 103990 (2024)
4. Benfenati, D., Rinaldi, A.M., Russo, C., Tommasino, C.: GenCrawl: a generative multimedia focused crawler for web pages classification. In: International Joint Conference on Knowledge Discovery, Knowledge Engineering and Knowledge Management, IC3K - Proceedings, 1, pp. 91–101 (2024)
5. Benfenati, D., Montanaro, M., Rinaldi, A.M., Russo, C., Tommasino, C.: Using focused crawlers with obfuscation techniques in the audio retrieval domain. In: Communications in Computer and Information Science, 2022 CCIS, pp. 3–17 (2024)
6. Botelho, J.: How automating data collection can improve cyber-security. Netw. Secur. **2017**(6), 11–13 (2017)
7. Capuano, A., Rinaldi, A.M., Russo, C.: An ontology-driven multimedia focused crawler based on linked open data and deep learning techniques. Multimedia Tools Appl. **79**(11), 7577–7598 (2020)
8. Felt, A.P., Finifter, M., Chin, E., Hanna, S., Wagner, D.: A survey of mobile malware in the wild. In: Proceedings of the 1st ACM Workshop on Security and Privacy in Smartphones and Mobile Devices (SPSM), pp. 3–14 (2011)
9. Guo, W., et al.: MalHAPGNN: an enhanced call graph-based malware detection framework using hierarchical attention pooling graph neural network. Sensors **25**(2), 374 (2025)
10. Guo, Y., Bettaieb, S., Casino, F.: A comprehensive analysis on software vulnerability detection datasets: trends, challenges, and road ahead. Int. J. Inf. Secur. **23**, 3311–3327 (2024)
11. Landauer, M., Skopik, F., Stojanović, B., Flatscher, A., Ullrich, T.: A review of time-series analysis for cyber security analytics: from intrusion detection to attack prediction. Int. J. Inf. Secur. **24**(3) (2025)
12. Mazuera-Rozo, A., Bautista-Mora, J., Linares-Vásquez, M., Rueda, S., Bavota, G.: The Android OS stack and its vulnerabilities: an empirical study. Empir. Softw. Eng. **24**(4), 2056–2101 (2019)
13. Li, X., Moreschini, S., Zhang, Z., Palomba, F., Taibi, D.: The anatomy of a vulnerability database: a systematic mapping study. J. Syst. Softw. **201**, 111679 (2023)
14. MITRE Corporation. CAPEC - Common Attack Pattern Enumeration and Classification. https://capec.mitre.org/. Accessed 1 Dec 2024
15. MITRE Corporation. CVE - Common Vulnerabilities and Exposures. https://cve.mitre.org/. Accessed 1 Dec 2024
16. MITRE Corporation. CWE - Common Weakness Enumeration. https://cwe.mitre.org/. Accessed 1 Dec 2024
17. MITRE Corporation. MITRE - Solving Problems for a Safer World. https://www.mitre.org/. Accessed 1 Dec 2024
18. Montanaro, M., Rinaldi, A.M., Russo, C., Tommasino, C.: A rule-based obfuscating focused crawler in the audio retrieval domain. Multimedia Tools Appl. **83**(9), 25231–25260 (2024)

19. Montanaro, M., Rinaldi, A.M., Russo, C., Tommasino, C.: Using knowledge graphs for audio retrieval: a case study on copyright infringement detection. World Wide Web J. **27**(4), 37 (2024)
20. Newaz, A.I., Sikder, A.K., Rahman, M.A., Uluagac, A.S.: A survey on security and privacy issues in modern healthcare systems: attacks and defenses. ACM Trans. Comput. Healthc. **2**(3), 1–44 (2021)
21. Ren, S., Jin, J., Niu, G., Liu, Y.: ARCS: adaptive reinforcement learning framework for automated cybersecurity incident response strategy optimization. Appl. Sci. **15**(2), 951 (2025)
22. Roshanaei, M., Khan, M.R., Sylvester, N.N.: Enhancing cybersecurity through AI and ML: strategies, challenges, and future directions. J. Inf. Secur. **15**(3), 320–339 (2024)
23. Scarselli, F., Gori, M., Tsoi, A.C., Hagenbuchner, M., Monfardini, G.: The graph neural network model. IEEE Trans. Neural Networks **20**(1), 61–80 (2009)
24. Sikos, L.F.: Cybersecurity knowledge graphs. Knowl. Inf. Syst. **65**, 3511–3531 (2023)
25. Statista. Market share of mobile operating systems worldwide from 2009 to 2025. Statista.com (2024). https://www.statista.com/statistics/272698/global-market-share-held-by-mobile-operating-systems-since-2009/. Accessed 2 Dec 2024
26. Tian-yang, G., Yin-Sheng, S., You-yuan, F.: Research on software security testing. World Acad. Sci. Eng. Technol. **9**(9), 1446–1450 (2010)
27. Zhao, J., Shao, M., Wang, H., Yu, X., Li, B., Liu, X.: Cyber threat prediction using dynamic heterogeneous graph learning. Knowl. Based Syst. **240**, 108086 (2022)
28. Zhou, Y., Jiang, X.: Dissecting android malware: characterization and evolution. In: Proceedings of the 2012 IEEE Symposium on Security and Privacy, pp. 95–109 (2012)

MultiWebFacts: A Modular Framework Using Multi-source Fusion for Fact-Checking

Yung-Ching Yang[1](✉), Sooji Han[1], and Rafael Banchs[2]

[1] Intapp Labs, Berlin, Germany
{yung-ching.yang,sooji.han}@intapp.com
[2] Intapp Labs, Palo Alto, USA
rafael.banchs@intapp.com

Abstract. Fake news, misinformation, and disinformation pose serious threats to society by eroding public trust, deepening divisions, and causing harm across various domains. Several existing deep learning-based fact-checking models are limited by their reliance on static assessments of truthfulness, often evaluating information in isolation or assuming that relevant evidence is readily available. These approaches often overlook the dynamic nature of false information, which spreads rapidly across platforms, making it increasingly difficult to trace its origin and verify its accuracy. In this work, we propose MulitWebFacts, a comprehensive framework for fact-checking that integrates information from multiple online sources. It addresses all essential sub-tasks, including check-worthy claim detection, source collection, sentence relevance classification, veracity estimation, and evidence highlighting. In particular, for veracity estimation, we propose a hybrid model that utilizes a token-level augmented Long Short-Term Memory (sLSTM) network to learn the textual content of a claim and combines sentence-level sLSTMs enhanced with hierarchical attention mechanisms to capture the evolving context of information surrounding the claim. Additionally, attention-based evidence highlighting is incorporated to provide insights into sources and contextual factors that contribute most to the verification process, enhancing transparency and fostering trust in results.

Keywords: Fact-Checking · Information System · Computational Journalism

1 Introduction

False information can destabilize societies and economies, skew political outcomes, undermine public health efforts, and deepen social divisions. It often spreads online across social media and news sites more rapidly than the truth [8], accelerating its harmful impact [27]. This dynamic and multi-platform propagation further hinders the timely tracing of a claim's origin and the accurate assessment of its veracity. Automated fact-checking systems aim to mitigate this issue, but often overlook how narratives, evidence sources, and public discourse evolve as false claims spread. They segment the verification process into discrete sub-tasks and assume that relevant evidence is readily accessible, which is rarely the case in real-world settings.

In this work, we propose *MultiWebFacts*, a modular fact-checking framework covering check-worthy claim detection, source collection, sentence relevance classification, veracity estimation, and evidence highlighting. By integrating multiple online sources, it captures both the static content of claims and their evolving context. For veracity estimation, we adapt RP-DNN [15], a context-aware LSTM [17] neural network for early rumor detection, which leverages textual content and social-temporal contexts. We utilize sLSTM [5], an LSTM variant that incorporates exponential gating and a multi-head memory mixing mechanism. Our hybrid model uses a token-level sLSTM network for semantic structure and sentence-level sLSTMs with Hierarchical Attention Networks (HAN) [36] to effectively analyze claim-source relationships.

Our framework was deployed via FastAPI, Docker, and Kubernetes and released to our journalism partners. Journalists provided feedback highlighting its value in evidence retrieval and veracity assessment. By integrating our system, practitioners can enhance explainable fact-checking and information tracking.

The main contributions of this work can be summarized as follows: (1) We propose a comprehensive framework that addresses all major sub-tasks involved in fact-checking. (2) For veracity estimation, we introduce a hybrid model that incorporates stacked sLSTM networks with HAN to capture the dynamic, multi-source nature of evolving information surrounding a claim. (3) We introduce a benchmark dataset for fact-checking, comprising 6,217 real-world claims and 21,082 associated articles aggregated from multiple non-social media web sources. (4) Our framework empowers media professionals with precise, interpretable veracity assessments and an in-depth analysis of information evolution.

2 Related Work

This section reviews related work in the areas of content-based and explainable fact-checking.

Content-Based Fact-Checking. Content-based methods aim to evaluate the truthfulness of claims or statements by examining quantifiable features [10]. It is often done by analyzing textual or multi-modal content and referencing knowledge bases. A foundational approach is extracting lexical and syntactic features from textual data to identify indicators of misinformation [12,24]. However, this approach focuses on surface-level patterns and often fails to detect more complex forms of misinformation that require deeper contextual understanding and reasoning [19]. As claims grow in complexity and the demand for real-world statement verification increases, research [28] has increasingly focused on multi-step reasoning processes supported by knowledge bases.

Explainable Fact-Checking. Main methods for providing explanations for fact-checking include attention-based techniques [20,34] and supporting text generation, such as justifications [14,38] and summarization [19,26]. Similar to our approach, FaGANet [23] combines encoder-only models with a Graph Attention Network [35] to better capture interrelationships between claims and evidence. Few-shot and zero-shot prompting of LLMs has gained popularity for improving explanation quality. FactISR [39] evaluates several LLMs under few-shot and zero-shot settings to assess their performance in generating explanations. MADR [18] uses multiple LLM agents to iteratively refine explanations to address unreliable explanations generated via zero-shot prompting.

We address limitations of existing methods by covering the full spectrum of linguistic features, platform diversity, and temporal evolution of the information. Although LLM-based methods offer natural language explanations, they lack fine-grained attribution to linguistic cues or individual evidence sentences. Our framework delivers comprehensive content and contextual analysis, multi-platform source assessment, and better support for understanding model output.

3 Methodology

3.1 Problem Statement

To estimate the veracity of check-worthy claims, we analyze articles reporting on these topics over time and across platforms. This approach allows us to track discourse evolution and assess truthfulness based on accumulated evidence and narrative shifts. A check-worthy claim (c_k) is represented as a set **source context (SCxt)** which consists of **informative sentence content** ($\mathbb{S}_k$) and a set of **sentence linguistic features** ($\mathbb{L}_k$) extracted from each sentence. Therefore, a set of check-worthy claims is denoted by $\mathbb{C} = \{c_1, \cdots, c_n\}$, where each claim is denoted by $c_k = [\mathbb{S}_k, \mathbb{L}_k]$. A set of informative sentence content is denoted by $\mathbb{S}_k = \{s_{k,1,1}, \cdots, s_{k,m,i}\}$, which contains i sentences extracted from m articles reporting on the claim. s is a sentence represented as a sequence of words. A set of linguistic features is denoted by $\mathbb{L}_k = \{l_{k,1,1}, \cdots, l_{k,m,i}\}$, which contains linguistic attributes extracted from each informative sentence. Note that $\mathbb{S}_k$ and $\mathbb{L}_k$ are chronologically ordered based on the publication times of associated articles. The task is to predict the most probable label ($\hat{y}_k$) for a claim c_k, where $\hat{y}_k \in \{0, 1\}$. $\hat{y}_k = 1$ if c_k is likely to be fake news, $\hat{y}_k = 0$ otherwise. y_k denotes a ground truth label.

3.2 Overview of Framework

Figure 1 visualizes MultiWebFacts comprising six modules: 1) check-worthy claim detection, 2) source collection, 3) sentence relevance classification, 4) feature extraction, 5) veracity estimation, and 6) evidence highlighting. In this section, we provide a brief introduction to the overall framework. Detailed descriptions of the technical modules can be found in Sects. 3.3–3.5.

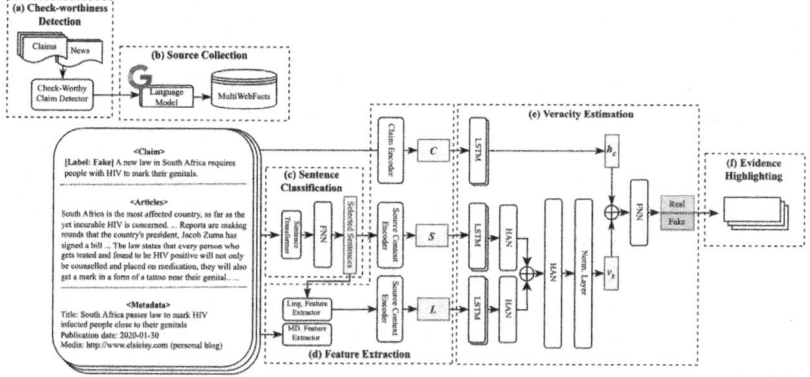

Fig. 1. Visualization of the MultiWebFacts framework.

First, we fine-tune DistilBERT [31] for the **check-worthy claim detection** module, which automatically identifies claims requiring further analysis and verification. Given an identified claim c, we gather and pre-process relevant information from diverse web sources, such as news outlets, blogs, educational and academic websites, and government and company websites, using Google Search Results API. By incorporating data from these diverse sources, the **source collection** module ensures a comprehensive understanding of the claim's origin, dissemination across platforms, and changes in public perception over time.

The third module, **sentence relevance classification** employs a three-layer feed-forward network (FNN) with ReLu activations to select informative sentences from the gathered source articles. This module helps the verification effort focus on the most relevant excerpts of the collected data. Subsequently, the **feature extraction** module computes embeddings of the input claim (c_k) and associated source sentences ($\mathbb{S}_k$) and extracts linguistic features ($\mathbb{L}_k$) from the source sentences. These attributes include various linguistic aspects: emotion [2], polarity [22], subjectivity [21], text formality [13], irony [4], and stance [37]. For example, emotion covers 11 categories (e.g., anger, joy, anticipation, disgust); polarity is a three-class classification (positive, negative, neutral); and stance includes agree, disagree, discuss, and unrelated. Subjectivity is a continuous value between 0 and 1, while formality and irony are binary.

In the **veracity estimation** module, we employ a neural network model that takes the generated input representations (i.e., c_k, $\mathbb{S}_k$, and $\mathbb{L}_k$) as input and outputs a veracity estimate $\hat{y}_k$. The claim representation is fed into a multi-head sLSTM network. To enhance the impact of key contextual elements and filter out noise or irrelevant information in the final representation, we introduce Hierarchical Attention Networks (HAN) [36]. Source context representations (i.e., $\mathbb{S}_k$ and $\mathbb{L}_k$) are arranged in chronological order and fed into source context encoders consisting of multi-head sLSTM networks and HAN, respectively. The contextual representations (hidden states) from the two encoders are then concatenated to form a joint representation (h_s). Another HAN layer is applied to this joint hidden sequential embedding, and its output v_s is fed into layer normalization (v'_s). Finally, the output of the last layer of the claim encoder (h_c) and that of the normalized source context encoder (v'_s) are concatenated. The concatenated representation is fed into a three-layer FNN. The first two layers apply LeakyReLU activations with dropout rates of 0.2 and 0.3, respectively. The final layer is a linear projection to the label space without additional activation. Cross-entropy loss is used to train the model parameters.

Finally, the **evidence highlighting** module identifies the most relevant source sentences, linguistic features, and origin articles for veracity estimation using attention weights. This enables users to evaluate the reliability of evidence and the trustworthiness of sources (see Sect. 4 for details on the datasets used and generated).

3.3 Check-Worthy Claim Detection

To enhance the efficiency of fact-checking, identifying check-worthy claims is a crucial first step. We propose a model designed to identify check-worthy claims across a broad range of online platforms. To this end, we fine-tune a pre-trained language model, distilbert-base-uncased classifier [31], on the ClaimBuster data [3]. We set a binary threshold of 0.4 by optimizing F1 on ClaimBuster to adjust for domain shift between its political focus and our multi-domain data (see Sect. 4.1). Although not derived from exhaustive ground-truth tuning, this pragmatic threshold reflects industry practice of prioritizing performance and efficiency over extensive annotation.

3.4 Sentence Relevance Classification

This component extracts relevant information from source articles to identify sentences that support or refute a claim. Articles are first segmented into sentences using NLTK [7]. To annotate the training data, we prompt GPT-4o [1] with "You are a professional journalist. Given a pair of [claim, sentence], identify if the sentence is helpful evidence to support or oppose the claim following the steps..." A complete prompt is available upon request. We manually examine the GPT-4o annotations and set the relevance threshold to 0.8 in the classifier based on the best F1 score. Since all sentences from the evidence article are inherently relevant, our classifier is designed to tolerate noise and excludes clearly irrelevant and noisy inputs rather than precise tuning. Consequently, the resulting training dataset consists of 33,554 relevant sentences and 84,564 irrelevant sentences associated with 5,891 claims. For classification, claims and sentences are encoded using all-MiniLM-L6-v2 [30]. Input representations are computed by subtracting sentence embeddings from claim embeddings to capture relational dynamics [25]. A feed-forward neural network classifies relevance, normalizing confidence scores via Z-score normalization. We retain all positively classified sentences and low-confidence negatives. Finally, for each source article, up to 10 top-ranked sentences are selected.

3.5 Veracity Estimation

The veracity estimation module takes claims ($\mathbb{C}$) and corresponding contexts ($\mathbb{S}$ and $\mathbb{L}$) as input and outputs estimates $\hat{y}$.

Claim Encoder. Given claims in $\mathbb{C}$, we obtain the claim embedding matrix **C** using an English GTE-base model [40] with 1.5B parameters. Next, the token-level sLSTM network is applied to process the claim embedding:

$$h_c = sLSTM_c(\mathbf{C}),$$

where h_c is the hidden states produced by the sLSTM network.

Source Context Encoder. Each claim is supported by a varying number of evidence sentences, $\mathbb{S}$ (e.g., 20–100). We encode each sentence using the GTE-base model [40]. This produces a d-dimensional embedding s_i for each sentence ($d = 768$). We then construct the source context matrix

$$\mathbf{S} = [s_1, s_2, \ldots, s_l] \in \mathbb{R}^{l \times d}.$$

l denotes the maximum number of evidence sentences associated with the claim. We truncate or zero-pad the sequence of sentence embeddings to l. We evaluate $l \in \{30, 50, 138\}$, where 28 and 138 are the mean and maximum context size, respectively. $l = 138$ has the highest F1 score. We compute a vector matrix of linguistic context extracted from all informative sentences $\mathbb{L}$, denoted by **L**.

Our *Attention-enhanced stacked sLSTM encoder* consists of a multi-head sLSTM network followed by HAN. The encoder is able to capture both short- and long-term dependencies in the input data, providing rich contextual representations. We employ HAN [36] to process input sequences and learn to assign attention weights to different parts of the sequences, highlighting the most relevant elements for generating the final output. The attention mechanism is modeled as a probabilistic distribution over the temporally ordered inputs from the source context. Let h_s be the recurrent hidden states of the source input. The attention block $HAN(\cdot)$ is defined by:

$$\alpha_s^t = softmax(tanh(Wh_s^t + b)), \quad h_{s\_attended}^t = \alpha_s^t h_s^t \quad \forall t \in [0, i]$$

Here, W and b are a learnable weight matrix and a bias term, respectively. Both source sentence content (sc) and linguistic feature (sl) embeddings are fed into multi-head sLSTM networks to generate their respective hidden states:

$$h_{sc} = sLSTM_{sc}(\mathbf{S}), \quad h_{sl} = sLSTM_{sl}(\mathbf{L})$$

Next, $HAN(\cdot)$ is applied to h_{sc} and h_{sl}. The attention mechanisms are used to compute weighted hidden states for source sentence content and linguistic feature representation separately:

$$h_{sc\_attended} = HAN(h_{sc}), \quad h_{sl\_attended} = HAN(h_{sl})$$

Table 1. Statistics of datasets.

Dataset	# of claims	# of articles		# of sentences	
		True	Fake	True	Fake
Fin-Fact [29]	1,355	2,514	2,158	83,584	66,563
AVERITEC [32]	1,621	2,083	3,658	67,056	118,568
UKP Snopes [16]	2,499	2,464	5,341	63,595	150,039
KaggleFN [6]	660	1,033	1,537	29,730	50,220
BuzzFeed News [11]	82	195	99	5,832	3,455
MultiWebFacts	6,217	8,289	12,793	249,797	388,845

The outputs from the attention-enhanced stacked sLSTM encoders for the source sentence content and linguistic features are concatenated to form a richer, more comprehensive representation of the source context. This combined sequence is then passed through the final HAN layer, and the attended representations are summed up over all time steps, resulting in the final source vector v_s.

$$h_s^t = HAN(h_{sc\_attended}^t \oplus h_{sl\_attended}^t), \quad v_s = \sum_{t=0}^{i} h_s^t \quad \forall t \in [0, i]$$

4 Datasets

We leverage the following public datasets selected to capture the diversity of claims across domains and media platforms: ClaimBuster [3], ISOT [9], Fin-Fact [29], AVERITEC [32], UKP Snopes [16], KaggleFN [6], and BuzzFeed News [11]. For brevity, we omit the details of the datasets.

Claim Reformation. Claims collected from the three datasets (i.e., ISOT, KaggleFN, and BuzzFeed News) are often written in a headline-style language. To maintain consistency and reduce bias in the dataset, we convert these headlines into claim-like statements by prompting GPT-4o-mini [1] with "You are an expert in crafting claims. Transform the given news title into a definitive claim that maintains its core message. Discard headlines that are too abstract or lack substantive information..." A complete prompt is available upon request. Manual evaluation shows that GPT-4o-mini extracts each headline's essence and filters out uninformative or irrelevant titles.

Dataset Construction. We utilize ClaimBuster [3] for check-worthy claim detection and ISOT for sentence relevance classification. The remaining five datasets are combined to create the MultiWebFacts Dataset, as detailed in Sect. 4.1. After claim reformation, the ClaimBuster is split into 8,844 training, 1,106 validation, and 1,106 test claims. For sentence relevance classification, we split the ISOT subset into 53,470 training, 6,684 validation, and 6,684 test claims.

4.1 MultiWebFacts Dataset

Existing datasets for fact-checking face several limitations, including insufficient or outdated evidence sources, a lack of detailed annotations, and an over-reliance on artificial claims that are not intended to be checked by journalists. We construct an English multi-source claim dataset, named *MultiWebFacts Dataset*, that addresses these gaps by collecting relevant sources discussing target claims over time and across diverse non-social media platforms. This dataset is constructed using five public datasets. Table 1 summarizes the statistics for these datasets augmented with sources and the MultiWebFacts Dataset.

Data Aggregation. Our dataset comprises 6,217 real-world claims and 21,082 associated articles, including 638,642 sentences in English. It is built by aggregating claims and augmenting evidence sources through a web search tool.

Data Augmentation. We employ the Google Search Results API. Claims are used as queries. To ensure relevance, we use all-MiniLM-L6-v2 to generate sentence embeddings for both the target claim and the titles of retrieved pages. Relevance is assessed using cosine similarity. The optimal threshold is determined through heuristic manual experiments and reviews. For each claim, the system retrieves the top 15 relevant web pages, including page titles, publication dates, and domain names. Claims without sufficiently relevant pages are discarded. Retrieved sources are chronologically ordered by their publication dates to track the evolution of information over time.

Data Filtering and Splitting. We retain only claims with explicit binary labels (i.e., True and False), deduplicate claims, and remove non-English web pages. The cleaned dataset is split into 4,973, 622, and 622 claims with their associated source sentences for training, validation, and testing, respectively.

5 Experiments

5.1 Experimental Settings

Baselines. The proposed model is compared with two models.

- **BERT-FC**: Inspired by a BERT model fine-tuned for claim verification [33], we fine-tune bert-base-uncased on our MultiWebFacts dataset and refer to our version as BERT-FC. We chose a BERT-based baseline as its pretrained representations have set the state of the art on multiple fact-verification benchmarks. And this approach [33] also utilizes evidence sentences as feature inputs to justify the claim, which is directly comparable to our architecture. The original approach [33] prepends Wikipedia page titles to potential evidence sentences as input. Similarly, our adaptation prepends source article titles to their corresponding sentences. Unlike the original, our model classifies claims into two categories: "True" and "Fake".
- **MultiWebFacts(LSTM)**: A MultiWebFacts variant with sLSTMs replaced by LSTMs. Each LSTM network has two forward layers with a 0.3 dropout rate to minimize overfitting.

Ablation Study Setup. A set of exploratory experiments is conducted to study the relative contribution of each component in our model.

- **MultiWebFacts**: This is our full model configuration that uses claim content, source sentence content, and linguistic features.
- **MultiWebFacts-SL**: Claim and source sentence content are used.
- **MultiWebFacts-SC**: Claim and linguistic features are used.
- **MultiWebFacts-SCxt**: Only claim content is used.
- **BERT-FC-SCxt**: A BERT-FC variant using claim content only.

Evaluation Setup. Our evaluation includes two validation methods: K-fold cross-validation (CV) and leave one (dataset) out cross-validation (LOO-CV). We use stratified 5-fold cross-validation to maintain a consistent label distribution across training, validation, and test sets. This approach is implemented for all variants of the MultiWebFacts model and baseline models. To assess our model in more realistic settings, we also utilize LOO-CV. We specifically use three augmented datasets (Fin-Fact, AVERITEC, and UKP Snopes) as alternating test sets. The other datasets, which include two additional sets (KaggleFN and BuzzFeed News) not used for testing, are utilized to construct the training and validation sets. We use four performance metrics focused on the positive class (i.e., fake news): F1 score (F1), accuracy (Acc.), precision (P), and recall (R). The results are reported as averages over five iterations.

6 Results

6.1 Check-Worthy Claim Detection

The check-worthy claim detector achieves an F1 score of 0.906 on the ClaimBuster test set and maintains strong performance with an F1 score of 0.917 on our MultiWebFacts Dataset, which covers varied linguistic styles and topics. This demonstrates the model's robustness in generalizing across domains and content styles, enhancing its adaptability to diverse fact-checking contexts.

6.2 Sentence Relevance Classification

The sentence relevance classifier achieves an F1 score of 0.741, accuracy of 0.833, precision of 0.834, and recall of 0.666. There is a distinct difference in performance between identifying relevant and irrelevant sentences. For irrelevant ones, the model achieves high precision (0.833) and recall (0.979), indicating its effectiveness in accurately filtering out non-relevant content. However, for relevant sentences, while precision remains high at 0.835, recall significantly drops to 0.353. This indicates that the model effectively filters non-relevant sentences but often misses relevant ones, likely due to overly strict relevance criteria.

6.3 Veracity Estimation Performance

Table 2 shows the 5-fold CV results of our proposed model and the baseline. MultiWebFacts achieves an average F1 score of 0.939 and an accuracy of 0.944. It increases the F1-score achieved by MultiWebFacts(LSTM) and BERT-FC by 1.8% and 28.5%, respectively. Table 3 shows LOO-CV results obtained by MultiWebFacts. We observe different patterns in the model's generalization capabilities across different benchmark datasets. Testing on the Fin-Fact [29] yields the best performance among the three datasets, with an F1 score of 0.626 and an accuracy of 0.632. This suggests that the model, trained on multi-domain datasets, generalizes effectively to the financial domain. In contrast, we observe decreases in F1-score for AVERITEC [32] and UKP Snopes [16]. This could be attributed to the increased complexity and diversity of claim styles and topics. Additionally, larger data sizes of AVERITEC and UKP Snopes present broader linguistic and contextual variations, which make veracity estimation more challenging.

Table 2. Veracity estimation 5-fold CV results.

Methods	F1	P	R	Acc.
MultiWebFacts	0.939	0.940	0.938	0.944
MultiWebFacts-SL	**0.945**	0.946	**0.945**	**0.951**
MultiWebFacts-SC	0.929	0.936	0.924	0.937
MultiWebFacts-SCxt	0.917	0.927	0.909	0.925
MultiWebFacts(LSTM)	0.922	0.926	0.919	0.929
MultiWebFacts(LSTM)-SL	0.944	**0.948**	0.940	0.949
MultiWebFacts(LSTM)-SC	0.926	0.927	0.924	0.932
MultiWebFacts(LSTM)-SCxt	0.912	0.917	0.908	0.920
BERT-FC	0.731	0.730	0.732	0.756
BERT-FC-SCxt	0.705	0.706	0.716	0.716

Table 3. Veracity estimation LOO-CV results. LOO dataset refers to a test set.

LOO Dataset	F1	P	R	Acc.
Fin-Fact [29]	**0.626**	**0.654**	**0.638**	0.632
AVERITEC [32]	0.624	0.630	0.621	0.679
UKP Snopes [16]	0.605	0.609	0.604	**0.708**

6.4 Ablation Study

The ablation study results are shown in Table 2. MultiWebFacts outperforms MultiWebFacts-SCxt by 2.4% in terms of F1 score, highlighting the importance of multiple sources for robust fact-checking. MultiWebFacts-SL achieves

Table 4. The top three source sentences for two fake news claims.

Claim 1: Sharonda Banks, 28, of Newark, New Jersey died after a maggot-infested weave was sewn into her scalp.
The story was completely **fabricated**.
News 10 Live is one of a growing number of fake news websites that publish **clickbait** fake news articles to generate ad revenue via the Internet.
Most of these events are truthful in nature while some may content [sic] **satire**.
Claim 2: The CDC have to stop calling COVID-19 an epidemic due to a remarkably low death rate.
But heart disease and cancer deaths rose, and covid-19 **remained remarkably lethal**, killing more than 500 people a day.
Covid has not gone away, William Schaffner, an infectious disease doctor at Vanderbilt University School of Medicine, said in an email after reviewing the report.
Covid drove life expectancy even lower, to the same level as 1996, according to CDC data released last year.

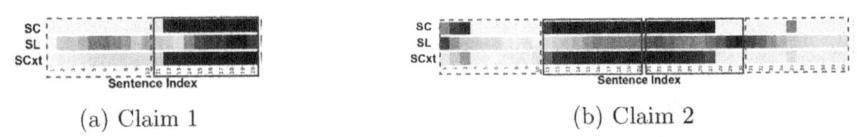

(a) Claim 1   (b) Claim 2

Fig. 2. Visualization of attention weights for two fake news claims. The darker the color of an instance is, the higher its attention weight is.

the highest performance with an F1 score of 0.945 and an accuracy of 0.951, demonstrating the significant influence of textual content on veracity estimation. However, the MultiWebFacts model sees a slight decline with a 0.6% drop in F1 score compared to MultiWebFacts-SL. MultiWebFacts-SC achieves an F1 score of 0.929, outperforming MultiWebFacts-SCxt by 1.3%. These observations suggest that the MultiWebFacts model might encounter interaction effects among different features, introducing noise or redundancy and slightly reducing performance compared to MultiWebFacts-SL. Excluding linguistic features (MultiWebFacts-SL) may help prevent overfitting or misalignment with content-based features, leading to a more optimized model. However, linguistic features remain valuable as their inclusion in MultiWebFacts-SC improves performance over MultiWebFacts-SCxt. This demonstrates their complementary role in veracity estimation, particularly when content-based features are limited.

BERT-FC-SCxt shows a 3.6% drop in F1 score compared to BERT-FC, highlighting a significant performance drop in BERT-based models when source context is removed. In contrast, MultiWebFacts exhibits only a 2.34% decline compared to MultiWebFacts-SCxt, and MultiWebFacts(LSTM) shows an even smaller drop of 1.1% compared to MultiWebFacts(LSTM)-SCxt. This observation suggests that the LSTM-based encoders effectively capture essential information from the claims' textual content. The resilience of LSTM-based architectures indicates robustness that could prove particularly useful in scenarios where feature extraction is limited or computational resources are constrained.

6.5 Evidence Highlighting

Table 4 shows the top three source sentences ranked by joint attention weights for two fake news claims. For Claim 1, the chosen sentences from a fact-checking article directly contradict the claim, using terms like "fabricate" and "clickbait". Linguistic analysis shows that these sentences predominantly convey strong negative sentiments and emotions (e.g., disgust, anger) and high subjectivity. For Claim 2, top-ranked sentences from mainstream news sources take a "discuss" stance, offering counter-evidence rather than outright refutation.

Figure 2 visualizes attention weights for the two claims across different levels of context: source sentence content (SC), linguistic features (SL), and joint representation of source context (SCxt). Sentences from the same article are grouped within a box. We note that the distribution of attention weights showcases distinct patterns across different sources. For Claim 1, the red-boxed article is from a fact-checking site, while the dotted gray-boxed article is from a secondary news source. For Claim 2, red-boxed sentences originate from mainstream news, whereas dotted gray-boxed ones come from an academic or governmental source. Informative sentences from fact-checking and mainstream news sources, which are generally considered more trustworthy, receive higher joint attention weights.

To improve usability for media professionals, we generate a structured report summarizing veracity estimation and key evidence. It includes the predicted label, probability score, and a ranked list of evidence sentences with their sources.

7 Conclusion

We proposed MultiWebFacts, a modular framework for automated fact-checking designed to assist journalists in combating false information by integrating evidence from multiple sources. Additionally, we provided a multi-domain benchmark dataset for fact-checking, which spans various non-social media platforms and temporal dimensions. MultiWebFacts systematically addresses key sub-tasks in fact-checking. They can provide independent yet valuable insights for journalists and fact-checkers at different stages of fact-checking. Extensive experiments and comparative evaluations confirm its effectiveness, and an ablation study highlights the advantage of multi-layer attention and multi-source context. By modeling the evolution of contextual information associated with the claims, MultiWebFacts helps journalists to report complex stories accurately, mitigate the spread of false information, and maintain public trust. In future work, we will extend our linguistic-feature analysis, explore additional contextual attributes, and investigate retrieval methods for real-time evidence. We plan to benchmark MultiWebFacts against graph-attention models (e.g., FaGANet) and few-shot LLM fact-checkers under dynamic evidence conditions. Finally, we aim to do a large-scale deployment study with our media partners to further evaluate the generalizability, timeliness, and practicability of our framework.

Acknowledgments. This research is funded by the Federal Ministry of Education and Research (BMBF, reference: 03RU2U151C) in the scope of the research project news-polygraph (https://news-polygraph.com).

Disclosure of Generative AI Usage. We used GPT-4o and GPT-4o-mini to assist with data annotation to generate annotations for training data, which were reviewed and verified by the authors to ensure accuracy.

References

1. Achiam, J., et al.: GPT-4 technical report. arXiv preprint arXiv:2303.08774 (2023)
2. Antypas, D., et al.: SuperTweetEval: a challenging, unified and heterogeneous benchmark for social media NLP research. In: Findings of the Association for Computational Linguistics: EMNLP 2023, Singapore, pp. 12590–12607. Association for Computational Linguistics (2023). https://doi.org/10.18653/v1/2023.findings-emnlp.838. https://aclanthology.org/2023.findings-emnlp.838
3. Arslan, F., Hassan, N., Li, C., Tremayne, M.: A benchmark dataset of check-worthy factual claims. In: Proceedings of the International AAAI Conference on Web and Social Media, vol. 14, no. 1, pp. 821–829 (2020). https://doi.org/10.1609/icwsm.v14i1.7346. https://ojs.aaai.org/index.php/ICWSM/article/view/7346
4. Barbieri, F., Camacho-Collados, J., Espinosa Anke, L., Neves, L.: TweetEval: unified benchmark and comparative evaluation for tweet classification. In: Findings of the Association for Computational Linguistics: EMNLP 2020, pp. 1644–1650. Association for Computational Linguistics (2020). https://doi.org/10.18653/v1/2020.findings-emnlp.148. https://aclanthology.org/2020.findings-emnlp.148
5. Beck, M., et al.: xLSTM: extended long short-term memory. arXiv preprint arXiv:2405.04517 (2024)
6. Bharadwaj, A., Ashar, B., Barbhaya, P., Bhatia, R., Shaikh, Z.: Source based fake news classification using machine learning. Int. J. Innov. Res. Sci. Eng. Technol. 2320–6710 (2020)
7. Bird, S., Loper, E.: NLTK: The natural language toolkit. In: Proceedings of the ACL Interactive Poster and Demonstration Sessions, Barcelona, Spain, pp. 214–217. Association for Computational Linguistics (2004). https://aclanthology.org/P04-3031
8. Bovet, A., Makse, H.A.: Influence of fake news in twitter during the 2016 us presidential election. Nat. Commun. **10**(1), 7 (2019)
9. Bozkus, E.: ISOT fake news dataset (2022). https://www.kaggle.com/datasets/emineyetm/fake-news-detection-datasets/. Accessed 15 Sept 2024
10. Capuano, N., Fenza, G., Loia, V., Nota, F.D.: Content-based fake news detection with machine and deep learning: a systematic review. Neurocomputing **530**, 91–103 (2023)
11. Chauhan, K.: Buzzfeed news dataset (2018). https://www.kaggle.com/code/kumudchauhan/fake-news-analysis-and-classification/input. Accessed 15 Sept 2024
12. Choudhary, A., Arora, A.: Linguistic feature based learning model for fake news detection and classification. Expert Syst. Appl. **169**, 114171 (2021)

13. Dementieva, D., Babakov, N., Panchenko, A.: Detecting text formality: a study of text classification approaches. In: Proceedings of the 14th International Conference on Recent Advances in Natural Language Processing, Shoumen, Bulgaria, Varna, Bulgaria, pp. 274–284. INCOMA Ltd. (2023). https://aclanthology.org/2023.ranlp-1.31
14. Eldifrawi, I., Wang, S., Trabelsi, A.: Automated justification production for claim veracity in fact checking: a survey on architectures and approaches. In: Proceedings of the 62nd Annual Meeting of the Association for Computational Linguistics (Volume 1: Long Papers), Bangkok, Thailand, pp. 6679–6692. Association for Computational Linguistics (2024). https://doi.org/10.18653/v1/2024.acl-long.361. https://aclanthology.org/2024.acl-long.361
15. Gao, J., Han, S., Song, X., Ciravegna, F.: RP-DNN: a tweet level propagation context based deep neural networks for early rumor detection in social media. In: Proceedings of the Twelfth Language Resources and Evaluation Conference, Marseille, France, pp. 6094–6105. European Language Resources Association (2020). https://aclanthology.org/2020.lrec-1.748
16. Hanselowski, A., Stab, C., Schulz, C., Li, Z., Gurevych, I.: UKP Snopes corpus (2019). https://tudatalib.ulb.tu-darmstadt.de/handle/tudatalib/2081
17. Hochreiter, S., Schmidhuber, J.: Long short-term memory. Neural Comput. **9**(8), 1735–1780 (1997). https://doi.org/10.1162/neco.1997.9.8.1735
18. Kim, K., Lee, S., Huang, K.H., Chan, H.P., Li, M., Ji, H.: Can LLMs produce faithful explanations for fact-checking? Towards faithful explainable fact-checking via multi-agent debate. arXiv preprint arXiv:2402.07401 (2024)
19. Kotonya, N., Toni, F.: Explainable automated fact-checking for public health claims. In: Proceedings of the 2020 Conference on Empirical Methods in Natural Language Processing (EMNLP), pp. 7740–7754. Association for Computational Linguistics (2020). https://doi.org/10.18653/v1/2020.emnlp-main.623. https://aclanthology.org/2020.emnlp-main.623
20. Kruengkrai, C., Yamagishi, J., Wang, X.: A multi-level attention model for evidence-based fact checking. In: Findings of the Association for Computational Linguistics: ACL-IJCNLP 2021, pp. 2447–2460. Association for Computational Linguistics (2021). https://doi.org/10.18653/v1/2021.findings-acl.217. https://aclanthology.org/2021.findings-acl.217
21. Loria, S.: textblob documentation. Release 0.15, 2 (2018)
22. Loureiro, D., Barbieri, F., Neves, L., Anke, L.E., Camacho-Collados, J.: Timelms: diachronic language models from twitter. arXiv preprint arXiv:2202.03829 (2022)
23. Luo, W., Ran, J., Tian, Z., Li, S., Sui, Z.: Faganet: an evidence-based fact-checking model with integrated encoder leveraging contextual information. In: Proceedings of the 2024 Joint International Conference on Computational Linguistics, Language Resources and Evaluation (LREC-COLING 2024), pp. 7082–7088 (2024)
24. Mahyoob, M., Al-Garaady, J., Alrahaili, M.: Linguistic-based detection of fake news in social media. Int. J. English Linguist. **11**(1) (2020)
25. Mikolov, T., Yih, W.t., Zweig, G.: Linguistic regularities in continuous space word representations. In: Proceedings of the 2013 Conference of the North American Chapter of the Association for Computational Linguistics: Human Language Technologies, Atlanta, Georgia, pp. 746–751. Association for Computational Linguistics (2013). https://aclanthology.org/N13-1090
26. Mishra, R., Gupta, D., Leippold, M.: Generating fact checking summaries for web claims. In: Proceedings of the Sixth Workshop on Noisy User-generated Text (W-NUT 2020), pp. 81–90. Association for Computational Linguistics (2020). https://doi.org/10.18653/v1/2020.wnut-1.12. https://aclanthology.org/2020.wnut-1.12

27. Modi, A., Mishra, P.: Exploring the expansion of fake news: investigating its effects on media trust and the credibility of authentic news. J. ReAttach Therapy Dev. Diversities **6**(6s), 855–871 (2023)
28. Pan, L., Lu, X., Kan, M.Y., Nakov, P.: QACheck: a demonstration system for question-guided multi-hop fact-checking. In: Proceedings of the 2023 Conference on Empirical Methods in Natural Language Processing: System Demonstrations, Singapore, pp. 264–273. Association for Computational Linguistics (2023). https://doi.org/10.18653/v1/2023.emnlp-demo.23. https://aclanthology.org/2023.emnlp-demo.23
29. Rangapur, A., Wang, H., Jian, L., Shu, K.: Fin-fact: a benchmark dataset for multimodal financial fact checking and explanation generation (2024). https://arxiv.org/abs/2309.08793
30. Reimers, N., Gurevych, I.: Sentence-BERT: sentence embeddings using Siamese BERT-networks. In: Proceedings of the 2019 Conference on Empirical Methods in Natural Language Processing and the 9th International Joint Conference on Natural Language Processing (EMNLP-IJCNLP), Hong Kong, China, pp. 3982–3992. Association for Computational Linguistics (2019). https://doi.org/10.18653/v1/D19-1410. https://aclanthology.org/D19-1410
31. Sanh, V., Debut, L., Chaumond, J., Wolf, T.: Distilbert, a distilled version of bert: smaller, faster, cheaper and lighter. arXiv abs/1910.01108 (2019). https://api.semanticscholar.org/CorpusID:203626972
32. Schlichtkrull, M., Guo, Z., Vlachos, A.: Averitec: a dataset for real-world claim verification with evidence from the web. In: Proceedings of the 37th International Conference on Neural Information Processing Systems. NIPS 2023. Curran Associates Inc., Red Hook (2024)
33. Soleimani, A., Monz, C., Worring, M.: BERT for evidence retrieval and claim verification. In: Jose, J.M., et al. (eds.) ECIR 2020. LNCS, vol. 12036, pp. 359–366. Springer, Cham (2020). https://doi.org/10.1007/978-3-030-45442-5_45
34. Trueman, T.E., Kumar, A., Narayanasamy, P., Vidya, J.: Attention-based c-bilstm for fake news detection. Appl. Soft Comput. **110**, 107600 (2021)
35. Velickovic, P., Cucurull, G., Casanova, A., Romero, A., Lio, P., Bengio, Y., et al.: Graph attention networks. Stat **1050**(20), 10-48550 (2017)
36. Yang, Z., Yang, D., Dyer, C., He, X., Smola, A., Hovy, E.: Hierarchical attention networks for document classification. In: Proceedings of the 2016 Conference of the North American Chapter of the Association for Computational Linguistics: Human Language Technologies, San Diego, California, pp. 1480–1489. Association for Computational Linguistics (2016). https://doi.org/10.18653/v1/N16-1174. https://aclanthology.org/N16-1174
37. Pan, Y., Sibley, D., Baird, S.: Repository Name (2019). https://github.com/Cisco-Talos/fnc-1. Accessed 01 Sept 2024
38. Zeng, F., Gao, W.: Justilm: few-shot justification generation for explainable fact-checking of real-world claims. Trans. Assoc. Comput. Linguist. **12**, 334–354 (2024)
39. Zhang, X., et al.: Augmenting the veracity and explanations of complex fact checking via iterative self-revision with LLMs. arXiv preprint arXiv:2410.15135 (2024)
40. Zhang, X., et al.: mGTE: generalized long-context text representation and reranking models for multilingual text retrieval (2024). https://arxiv.org/abs/2407.19669

Semantic Web and SPARQL Querying

SPARQL Query Generation with LLMs: Measuring the Impact of Training Data Memorization and Knowledge Injection

Aleksandr Gashkov[1], Aleksandr Perevalov[1], Maria Eltsova[1,2](✉), and Andreas Both[1]

[1] Web & Software Engineering (WSE) Research Group, Leipzig University of Applied Sciences (HTWK Leipzig), Leipzig, Germany
maria.eltsova@gmail.com
[2] CBZ München GmbH, Heilbronn, Germany

Abstract. Nowadays, the importance of software with natural-language user interfaces cannot be underestimated. In particular, in Question Answering (QA) systems, generating a SPARQL query for a given natural-language question (often named Query Building) from the information retrieved from the same question is the central task of QA systems working over Knowledge Graphs (KGQA). Due to the rise of Large Language Models (LLMs), they are considered a well-suited method to increase the quality of the question-answering functionality, as there is still a lot of room for improvement, aiming for enhanced quality and trustworthiness. However, LLMs are trained on web data, where researchers have no control over whether the benchmark or the knowledge graph was already included in the training data. In this paper, we introduce a novel method that evaluates the quality of LLMs by generating a SPARQL query from a natural-language question under various conditions: (1) zero-shot SPARQL generation, (2) with knowledge injection, and (3) with "anonymized" knowledge injection. This enables us, for the first time, to estimate the influence of the training data on the QA quality improved by LLMs. Ultimately, this will help to identify how portable a method is or whether good results might mostly be achieved because a benchmark was already included in the training data (cf. LLM memorization). The developed method is portable, robust, and supports any knowledge graph; therefore, it could be easily applied to any KGQA or LLM, s.t., generating consistent insights into the actual LLM capabilities is possible.

Keywords: Question Answering · SPARQL query generation · Large Language Models · Knowledge Graph · LLM memorization

1 Introduction

Question Answering (QA) is aimed at providing a user with precise answers to questions formulated in a natural language (NL). KGQA systems are filling up the gap between Linked Data and end-users by transforming NL questions into structured queries (e.g., represented as SPARQL[1]) to make the information accessible using NL requests. However, translating NL queries into SPARQL is still a challenge in the field of KGQA (cf. [4,19,29]). This task is supposed to be solved with the advent of Large Language Models (LLMs) that have significantly furthered the field of natural language processing (NLP) lately (e.g., [20,21,32]). The rapidly growing number of research papers over the past two years confirms the fact that the possibility of LLMs to efficiently generate machine-readable queries from the questions written in NL is being actively discussed. However, according to [23], LLMs often perform well on entities and relationships with high frequencies but face challenges in less popular topics (long-tail knowledge problem). Furthermore, the capabilities of LLMs could be questioned as they show anomalies in terms of *memorization* concerning the actual ability to generate correct SPARQL queries obeying a defined context. From this context, we derive the following *research questions*:

RQ1 Assuming a perfect knowledge injection (i.e., in-prompt context definition), how well does the SPARQL query generation perform?

RQ2 What is the impact of memorization on the SPARQL query generation capabilities of LLMs?

In summary, these research questions are intended to shed light on the capabilities of LLMs in generating SPARQL queries so that software engineers can better assess the usefulness of LLMs for non-popular or private knowledge graphs.

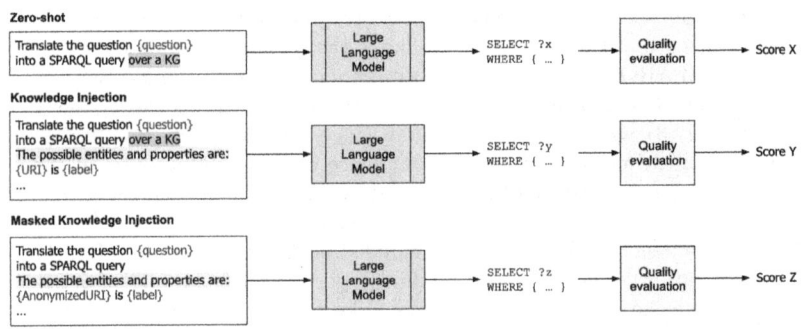

Fig. 1. Overview of the proposed evaluation approach and prompting strategies

In this paper, we present a novel method for evaluating the quality of LLMs by generating SPARQL queries from a NL question under various conditions (see Fig. 1 for the general idea): (1) SPARQL generation without additional information provided to the LLM (*zero-shot*), (2) Providing specific and complete knowledge about the information (*knowledge injection*) required to generate the

---

[1] https://www.w3.org/TR/rdf-sparql-query/.

correct SPARQL query (e.g., URI to label mappings), and (3) Reusing knowledge injection with anonymized URIs (*masked knowledge injection*).

In contrast to prior contributions, our work focuses on estimating the influence of the training data on the QA quality improved by LLMs. Our method is ultimately aimed at recognizing of the fact whether good results are only achieved because an LLM or benchmark was already included in the training data (which might lead to LLM memorization effects). In our investigation, we assessed our method using the different (regarding the question structures) KGQA datasets, QALD-9-plus [18] and MCWQ [3]. In addition, we conducted our experiments on various LLMs of different sizes, ranging from 7B to 123B parameters.

This paper is structured as follows. In Sect. 2, we summarize related work on the integration of LLMs with KGs for improving semantic parsing and generation of SPARQL queries from a NL questions. Thereafter, in Sect. 3, we present an overview of our approach, the used datasets, and LLMs. Section 4 evaluates and analyzes the experimental results and erroneous queries produced by LLMs during the experiments. The obtained results and limitations are discussed in Sect. 5. Finally, we conclude our work in Sect. 6.

Reproducibility Statement: The source code and data for experiments are available on GitHub[2].

2 Related Work

The integration of LLMs with various data sources (in particular, knowledge bases, KGs, and the Web of Data) for solving different QA tasks in the last two years has evidenced the high scientific interest in this topic in the research community. Some of the recent approaches try to exploit LLMs as semantic parsers (e.g., [7,14,16,17]) directly or by fine-tuning the models. Mecharnia and d'Aquin [16] presented experiments in fine-tuning LLMs (Llama-3-8B, Llama-2-7B, Llama-3-70B, and Mixtral-8x7B) for the task of NLQ-to-SPARQL transformation on QALD-9-plus [18] and QALD-10 [26]. Their approach demonstrated promising results (for QALD, the average Macro F1 is near 60% for all LLMs).

Meyer et al. [17] presented a set of automated benchmarking tasks to assess the basic capabilities of LLMs to deal with SPARQL SELECT queries without special architectures or fine-tuning. Completing experiments on different benchmarks like well-known LC-QuAD 2.0 [5], CoyPu-Mini [2], Bestiary [10] and state-of-the-art LLMs families (Claude, Gemini and GPT), the authors conclude that most evaluated LLMs have no significant challenges when perceiving SPARQL SELECT query syntax or its semantics, however, generating the SELECT queries with correct semantics still seems to be a difficult task for the models.

Recent research also tried to integrate LLMs with KG and other solutions (e.g., [1,10,23,30]). Zhang et al. [31] introduced Rule-KBQA, a framework that employs learned rules to guide the generation of logical forms. Initially, rules are extracted from existing data, after that the authors employed the Rule-Following

---

[2] https://github.com/WSE-research/LLM-generated-SPARQL/.

Fine-Tuned (RFFT) LLM to generate additional rules, ultimately constructing a comprehensive rule library. Shen et al. [23] suggested a novel framework – Reasoning with Trees – that reformulates KGQA as a discrete decision-making problem, leveraging Monte Carlo Tree Search to iteratively refine reasoning paths.

Zahera et al. [30] developed an approach to generate SPARQL queries that employs Chain-of-thoughts (CoT) prompting [27] and incorporates entities and relations from the input question. Their approach evaluated on the LC-QuAD 2.0, VQuAnDa [9], QALD-9, and QALD-10 datasets demonstrates an improvement in F1 score for both QALD benchmarks.

Another decision is proposed by Kovriguina et al. [10] who developed SPARQLGEN – a one-shot approach for generating SPARQL queries with prompting LLMs. Their approach reached outstanding results on the well-known QALD-9, but did not generalize well on the recently appeared, structurally equivalent QALD-10 [26] and the BESTIARY benchmark (proposed by the authors) that obviously was not part of the model training. Their results also showed that the model struggled to deal with an unknown KG. The inconsistent performance is explained by the possible memorization of the datasets by the models.

Some studies (e.g., [6, 13, 22]) addressed an investigation of benefits from using LLMs for domain-specific or KG-specific tasks in KGQA by leveraging, fine-tuning LLMs, or prompting with intelligent few-shot selection. Recent papers from Lehmann et al. [11] and Zong et al. [33] leverage the novel LLM agent paradigm, where the model calls are streamlined into a predefined workflow and augmented with available tools – external services that supply LLMs with additional information.

From this brief analysis, we can conclude that, on one hand, combining LLMs with KGs might represent a promising technology for constructing KGQA systems; on the other hand, well-known and often exploited benchmarks like QALD, LC-QuAD 2.0 provide the researchers with much better results.

3 Approach and Materials

3.1 Approach

Our primary research objective is to determine if state-of-the-art LLMs are capable of generating valid SPARQL queries over a KG. Our approach (presented in Fig. 1) is tailored to answer the research questions while evaluating how well the SPARQL query generation process performs with or without knowledge injection (i.e., incorporation of external knowledge into models to improve their performance and/or influence their behavior). To answer RQ1 and RQ2, we carried out experiments for generating SPARQL queries from NL questions with LLMs by using three prompting techniques. For all LLMs, we used the same prompts.

The first type of prompt used in the experiments was ***zero-shot prompting***. This means that a question is sent to a model "as-is" accompanied only by instructions to prevent extra text generation. Figure 2a illustrates the structure of this prompt.

```
Translate the question "Who developed Skype?" into a SPARQL query
using the Wikidata Knowledge Graph.
Have the query return only resources.
Provide only the generated SPARQL query.
```
(a) Example of zero-shot prompting.

```
Translate the question "Who developed Skype?" into a SPARQL query
using the Wikidata Knowledge Graph.
Have the query return only resources.
Provide only the generated SPARQL query.
The possible entities and properties are:
wd:Q40984 is Skype
wdt:P178 is developer.
```
(b) Example of a prompt with knowledge injection.

```
Translate the question "Who developed Skype?" into a SPARQL query
using a Knowledge Graph.
Have the query return only resources.
Provide only the generated SPARQL query.
The possible entities and properties are:
kg:6211 is Skype
kg:1548 is developer.
```
(c) Example of a prompt with "anonymized" knowledge injection. The information regarding linked URIs and masks was stored to be unmasked after a query generation.

Fig. 2. Examples of prompts to generate the SPARQL query for the question "Who developed Skype?" from the QALD-9-plus dataset by exploiting different LLMs.

The second prompt, whose example is presented in Fig. 2b, was defined with the presumption that a Named Entity Recognition component was already executed and provided a perfect set of information about the named entities (including its linking to the KG) within the given NL question. Here, the relevant entities were extracted from the gold standard queries and paired with the labels of each entity or property. Pairs of the Entity Name and corresponding URI (in prefixed form) were injected into the prompt. Therefore, we call this a ***knowledge injection prompt***.

The third type of prompt (see Fig. 2c) was tailored to hide sensitive information from the model, trying to prevent the use of the memorized data. Note, we additionally did not refer to the Wikidata KG in the prompts. To mask the Wikidata URIs, we changed them to random (yet unique) numbers with the SPARQL prefix kg: pointing to some graph that is unknown to the model. Thus, in comparison to the knowledge injection prompt, all relevant information is recognizable from the prompt, however, there is no direct reference to Wikidata. Hence, we name this approach ***masked knowledge injection prompt.***

We therefore infer that all three types of prompts supplement each other, so they are enough to answer the research question of this paper. Using other types of prompts for investigating their influence of the LLMs performance in generating SPARQL queries from a NL could be a subject of future research.

3.2 Materials

Datasets. During the past decade, researchers introduced to the community numerous KGQA benchmarks with logical forms whose quantitative comparison was presented by Liu S. et al. [15] when introducing their own benchmark.

While executing our process, we aim also to find out how much the LLM-generated output is affected by memorized data. Therefore, we suggest that the two benchmarks exploited are quite different in terms of using frequency and, respectively, in training datasets. We suppose that there is a higher tendency of LLMs to memorize popular datasets and this should appear in the resulting metrics. Hence, we require a popular dataset and a dataset that is rarely used where both are defined over data from the same KG.

To evaluate the effectiveness of the proposed method, we carried out our experiments on two public benchmarks executable over the Wikidata knowledge graph: QALD-9-plus [18] and MCWQ [3]. Both datasets are multilingual; however, we used only their English parts for our current research.

QALD-9-plus[3] [18] is an extension of the well-known QALD-9 dataset where extended language support was added, and the translation quality for existing languages was significantly optimized (e.g., via Spanish [24]) though the questions' translations were provided by multiple native speakers. The dataset contains 558 questions incorporating information from the Wikidata knowledge base. In addition to the textual presentation, each question contains the corresponding SPARQL query, the answer entity URI, and the answer type. The datasets of the QALD series are widely used since more than a decade for scientific challenges and publications.

MCWQ[4] [3] is a rarely used dataset transformed from the CFQ (Compositional Freebase Questions) benchmark that was aimed at parsing questions into SPARQL queries executable on the Freebase knowledge base. The dataset has 2,444 question patterns (mod entities, verbs, etc.). There are 1,835 unique SPARQL query patterns in MCWQ, resulting in 16.9% instances covering 100% of unique SPARQL query patterns. According to the authors, the dataset "poses a greater challenge for compositional semantic parsing, and exhibits less redundancy in terms of duplicate patterns." In total, MCWQ contains 124,187 question query pairs, but our experiments were carried out on the gold test set. It should be pointed out that (1) the dataset has a focus on history and cinematography, (2) several questions express multiple restrictions to find the correct answer (sometimes much more restrictions than QALD-9-plus has), and (3) multiple questions address the same topic but work with different restrictions.

---

[3] https://github.com/KGQA/QALD_9_plus.
[4] https://github.com/coastalcph/seq2sparql.

LLMs. We employed 11 LLMs from four developers in our experiments: Qwen 2.5 [28] (7B, 14B, 32B, and 72B), DeepSeek-r1 [8] (7B, 14B, 32B, and 70B), Mistral-Small and Mistral-Large[5], and Llama 3.3 70B[6] presented in Table 1. We chose these latest open-source models because of their significant variability in dimension, which allows us to evaluate different options on the selected benchmarks, as well as the high quality declared by developers.

The models were executed with the Ollama engine[7] on a server with two NVIDIA L40S GPUs (48GB VRAM). All models are quantized in 4-bit with quantization type "Q4_K_M" due to the limited resources.

Table 1. Overview of the LLMs used within our work

Model name	Developed by	Year	Model size
Qwen 2.5 7B	Alibaba Cloud	2024	7B
Qwen 2.5 14B	Alibaba Cloud	2024	14B
Qwen 2.5 32B	Alibaba Cloud	2024	32B
Qwen 2.5 72B	Alibaba Cloud	2024	72B
DeepSeek-r1 7B	DeepSeek	2025	7B
DeepSeek-r1 14B	DeepSeek	2025	14B
DeepSeek-r1 32B	DeepSeek	2025	32B
DeepSeek-r1 70B	DeepSeek	2025	72B
Mistral-Small	Mistral AI	2025	24B
Mistral-Large	Mistral AI	2025	123B
Llama 3.3 70B	Meta	2024	70B

Metrics. For measuring the quality of the experimentally obtained results, we used two metrics: 1) the relative frequency of valid queries (P_{val}) and 2) precision (P) – the relative frequency of correct answers. Only a valid query can produce the correct answer, therefore, $P \leq P_{val}$ applies. In our setting, a correct answer exists for all questions. This means that precision, recall, and F1 score are always equal in one experiment.

4 Evaluation and Analysis

4.1 Results

Table 2 reports the complete set of experiments on all models, covering all the metrics introduced in Sect. 3.2. For the sake of space, we will primarily focus on

---
[5] https://mistral.ai/en/news/mistral-small-3.
[6] https://huggingface.co/meta-llama/Llama-3.3-70B-Instruct.
[7] https://github.com/ollama/ollama.

the top results. Smaller models (7B and in some cases 14B) experienced difficulty in solving the zero-shot task and the masked injection task, especially regarding MCWQ. The best overall quality demonstrated Qwen 2.5 72B, Mistral-Large, Llama 3.3 70B, and DeepSeek-r1 32B, the worst one – Qwen 2.5 32B.

Table 2. Experimental results

Model	Zero-shot					Knowledge injection					Masked injection				
	Total records	Valid queries	Correct	P_{val}	$P = R = F1$	Total records	Valid queries	Correct	P_{val}	$P = R = F1$	Total records	Valid queries	Correct	P_{val}	$P = R = F1$
MCWQ															
Qwen 2.5 7B	155	55	0	0.35	0.00	155	81	11	0.35	0.07	155	90	0	0.35	0.00
Qwen 2.5 14B	155	45	0	0.29	0.00	155	66	6	0.29	0.04	155	78	0	0.29	0.00
Qwen 2.5 32B	155	0	0	0.00	0.00	155	0	0	0.00	0.00	155	1	0	0.00	0.00
Qwen 2.5 72B	155	18	0	0.12	0.00	155	95	24	0.12	**0.15**	155	65	2	0.12	**0.01**
DeepSeek-r1 7B	155	2	0	0.01	0.00	155	11	0	0.01	0.00	155	4	0	0.01	0.00
DeepSeek-r1 14B	155	76	0	0.49	0.00	155	26	2	0.49	0.01	155	45	0	0.49	0.00
DeepSeek-r1 32B	155	59	0	0.38	0.00	155	10	6	0.38	0.04	155	9	0	0.38	0.00
DeepSeek-r1 70B	155	69	0	0.45	0.00	155	12	2	0.45	0.01	155	49	2	0.45	**0.01**
Mistral-Small	155	92	0	0.59	0.00	155	71	11	0.59	0.07	155	38	0	0.59	0.00
Mistral-Large	155	135	1	0.87	**0.01**	155	112	12	0.87	0.08	155	110	0	0.87	0.00
Llama 3.3 70B	155	118	0	0.76	0.00	155	122	16	0.76	0.10	155	112	1	0.76	**0.01**
QALD-9-plus															
Qwen 2.5 7B	471	266	0	0.56	0.00	460	357	109	0.56	0.24	460	347	37	0.56	0.08
qwen2.5 14B	471	268	1	0.57	0.00	460	342	209	0.57	0.45	460	246	126	0.57	0.27
Qwen 2.5 32B	471	10	0	0.02	0.00	460	5	3	0.02	0.01	460	21	8	0.02	0.02
Qwen 2.5 72B	471	247	6	0.52	0.01	460	400	257	0.52	0.56	460	425	229	0.52	**0.50**
DeepSeek-r1 7B	471	31	0	0.07	0.00	460	84	3	0.07	0.01	460	30	0	0.07	0.00
DeepSeek-r1 14B	471	293	0	0.62	0.00	460	198	77	0.62	0.17	460	46	4	0.62	0.01
DeepSeek-r1 32B	471	354	4	0.75	0.01	460	347	212	0.75	0.46	460	335	181	0.75	0.39
DeepSeek-r1 70B	471	370	3	0.79	0.01	460	144	64	0.79	0.14	460	55	14	0.79	0.03
Mistral-Small	471	338	6	0.72	0.01	460	399	241	0.72	0.52	460	347	151	0.72	0.33
Mistral-Large	471	447	30	0.95	**0.06**	460	450	279	0.95	**0.61**	460	426	212	0.95	0.46
Llama 3.3 70B	471	330	14	0.70	0.03	460	371	186	0.70	0.40	460	372	161	0.70	0.35

Comparing on F1 score in the experiments with knowledge injection prompting, both Mistral models (Mistral-Large = 0.61 vs. Mistral-Small = 0.52), and Qwen 2.5 72B (0.52), demonstrated the best results on QALD-9-plus, while only the top result in the same experiment on MCQW only a $F1 = 0.15$ was achieved by Qwen 2.5 72B followed by Llama 3.3 70B (0.1). It is also noteworthy that even much smaller models of Qwen 2.5 demonstrated comparable results in the experiments where knowledge injection prompting was used.

However, the results of experiments with zero-shot prompting on both benchmarks are unsatisfactory: only Qwen 2.5 72B, Mistral-Large, Mistral-Small,

Table 3. Experimental results for optimized MCWQ

Model	Zero-shot					Knowledge injection					Masked injection				
	Total records	Valid queries	Correct	P_{val}	$P=R=F1$	Total records	Valid queries	Correct	P_{val}	$P=R=F1$	Total records	Valid queries	Correct	P_{val}	$P=R=F1$
Qwen 2.5 7B	146	51	0	0.35	0.00	140	77	12	0.35	0.09	140	70	0	0.35	0.00
Qwen 2.5 14B	146	24	0	0.16	0.00	140	44	7	0.16	0.05	140	37	0	0.16	0.00
Qwen 2.5 32B	146	0	0	0.00	0.00	140	0	0	0.00	0.00	140	1	0	0.00	0.00
Qwen 2.5 72B	146	22	0	0.15	0.00	140	107	16	0.15	**0.11**	140	99	0	0.15	0.00
DeepSeek-r1 7B	146	4	0	0.03	0.00	140	7	0	0.03	0.00	140	4	0	0.03	0.00
DeepSeek-r1 14B	146	66	0	0.45	0.00	140	51	7	0.45	0.05	140	6	0	0.45	0.00
DeepSeek-r1 32B	146	66	0	0.45	0.00	140	69	16	0.45	**0.11**	140	40	0	0.45	0.00
DeepSeek-r1 70B	146	67	0	0.46	0.00	140	20	2	0.46	0.01	140	27	0	0.46	0.00
Mistral-Small	146	95	0	0.65	0.00	140	56	8	0.65	0.06	140	53	0	0.65	0.00
Mistral-Large	146	123	2	0.84	0.01	140	101	12	0.84	0.09	140	92	0	0.84	0.00
Llama 3.3 70B	146	103	0	0.71	0.00	140	97	20	0.71	0.14	140	89	0	0.71	0.00

DeepSeek-r1 32B, DeepSeek-r1 70B, and Llama 3.3 70B were able to generate a few correct SPARQL queries from the given NL questions from the QALD-9-plus dataset, while only Mistral-Large – from MCWQ.

The experiment with masked knowledge injection prompting on MCWQ should be a challenge for all LLMs. Only Qwen 2.5 72B, Mistral-Large, and Llama 3.3 70B were able to generate one or two correct SPARQL queries for 155 NL questions. Nevertheless, the same experiment on QALD-9-plus unpredictably did not cause problems for most LLMs besides Qwen 2.5 32B, DeepSeek-r1 7B, DeepSeek-r1 14B, and DeepSeek-r1 70B.

The general observation is that all metrics on the MCWQ benchmark are much worse when compared to QALD-9-plus. Trying to find out the reason for the poor quality of MCWQ results, we selectively analyzed questions from the dataset and ascertained that the fluency, semantic, and grammatical correctness of some questions do not conform to language norms. Therefore, 140 questions were reformulated using OpenAI's well-performing GPT-4o[8], manually validated, and optimized the generated questions, s.t., a smaller, semantically equal, yet (language quality wised) improved dataset was generated[9] to evaluate the impact of the *language quality of the NL questions* in comparison to the memorization effect. The results of the experiment with this improved MCWQ dataset are presented in Table 3. However, they do not provide any noticeable improvement, and, therefore, refute the hypothesis that the MCWQ language quality has heavily impacted the LLM performance. Instead, we can conclude

---

[8] https://platform.openai.com/docs/models#gpt-4o.
[9] The dataset is stored in the online appendix including the generated NL question and the manually optimized queries.

that the (missing) memorization effect was actually the reason for the observed SPARQL query generation quality. It is worth noting that each request was carried out in a new conversation.

4.2 Error Analysis

We performed an analysis of erroneous queries by defining those not correspond to the expected response. Research papers offer different error classifications (e.g., [1,4,12,13,25]), however, we consider the error analysis as an additional result helping us to further evaluate the performance of our method. We identified four error categories, which are presented with some examples in Fig. 3.

1. *Invalid format or query* (cf. Fig. 3a).
    – *Invalid JSON format.* The model's output did not follow the correct JSON format, so the query text cannot be extracted.

```
SELECT ?resource
WHERE { >// Instance of film
```

(a) Error Category 1 – Invalid format/query

```
SELECT ?newSeriesEpisodes ?oldSeriesEpisodes
WHERE {
    wd:Q162594 wdt:P1113 ?newSeriesEpisodes .
    wd:Q180755 wdt:P1113 ?oldSeriesEpisodes .
ORDER BY DESC(?newSeriesEpisodes)
LIMIT 1
}
```

(b) Error Category 2 – Empty answer

```
SELECT ?mountain
WHERE   ?mountain wdt:P31 wd:Q8502 .
SELECT (MAX(?elevation) AS ?maxElevation)
```

(c) Error Category 3 – Incorrect set of entities

```
SELECT ?moon
WHERE { ?moon kg:is_moon_of_Jupiter wd:Q61702557 .
?moon kg:is_mass wdt:P2067
}
```

(d) Error Category 4 – Occurrence of Wikidata URIs although a masked knowledge injection was used.

Fig. 3. Examples from the identified error categories in the generated SPARQL queries.

- *Invalid SPARQL query*. The query did not pass the syntax check (done with the help of RDFlib[10]) or caused an error while being executed on Wikidata.
2. *Empty answer* (cf. Fig. 3b): all questions in the considered datasets would lead to a non-empty result from the Wikidata knowledge graph, hence at least one entity as an answer (or true/false value) is expected; therefore, an empty answer is an error.
3. *Incorrect set of entities* (cf. Fig. 3c): we compared the set of expected entities with the set of produced entities. In a correct answer, the query must produce the same list of entities as the gold standard, without regard to order.
4. *Occurrence of Wikidata URIs* (cf. Fig. 3d): A Wikidata URI occurred in the generated query, while the prompt requires URIs from the sample KG (which is unknown to the LLM).

The error analysis clearly shows that all models are relying on the memorized data while generating SPARQL query. In particular, a model was asked to generate a SPARQL query for an imaginary KG, but it produced the (correct) Wikidata's URI instead (hence, Error Category 4 as presented on Fig. 3d).

Table 4. Categories of errors and their frequencies (note, multiple errors per query are possible).

Model	Benchmarks/Error categories							
	QALD-9-plus				MCWQ			
	1	2	3	4	1	2	3	4
Qwen 2.5 7B	0.30	0.19	**0.59**	0.30	0.48	0.03	0.49	0.00
Qwen 2.5 14B	0.38	0.33	0.37	0.31	0.57	0.06	0.42	0.06
Qwen 2.5 32B	**0.97**	0.01	0.02	0.27	**1.00**	0.00	0.00	0.02
Qwen 2.5 72B	0.23	**0.51**	0.42	**0.32**	0.61	0.13	0.34	0.05
DeepSeek-r1 7B	0.90	0.05	0.10	0.16	0.96	0.01	0.04	0.02
DeepSeek-r1 14B	0.61	0.16	0.33	0.08	0.66	0.05	0.34	0.01
DeepSeek-r1 32B	0.26	0.45	0.46	0.29	0.81	0.02	0.18	0.00
DeepSeek-r1 70B	0.59	0.18	0.35	0.20	0.70	0.04	0.29	**0.16**
Mistral-Small	0.22	0.43	0.49	0.29	0.55	0.06	0.43	0.00
Mistral-Large	0.05	0.59	0.58	**0.32**	0.19	**0.14**	**0.78**	0.02
Llama 3.3 70B	0.23	0.42	0.51	**0.32**	0.21	0.08	0.75	0.02

Table 4 presents the frequency of erroneous queries for all LLMs. Investigating the data, we should point out that Error Category 1 (Invalid format or query) is more usually the case for the MCWQ dataset while Error Category 4 (occurrence of Wikidata URIs) is rather relevant for QALD-9-plus besides the DeepSeek-r1 models which demonstrate (excluding DeepSeek-r1 32B) high rate of Error Category 1 also when experimenting with QALD-9-plus. Error Category 3 (incorrect set of entities) is comparable for both datasets.

---

[10] https://github.com/RDFLib/rdflib.

When analyzing the error categories by models, the noticeable fact is that Qwen 2.5 32B always produced invalid queries or did not follow the correct JSON format, i.e., the query text cannot be extracted, while prompts to Mistral-Large hardly result in such errors. In addition, the DeepSeek-r1 models (besides DeepSeek-r1 32B) return the lowest number of empty answers (Error Category 2) on both datasets. However, Mistral-Large often produces the incorrect set of entities, which is typically for all larger models (the size is 24B and over) on the QALD-9-plus dataset and a small one – Qwen 2.5 7B. Therefore, the error frequency suggests that there is still much to be done to achieve acceptable results.

5 Limitations and Discussion

This paper focuses on the ability of state-of-the-art LLMs to generate SPARQL queries with or without knowledge injection. However, when appraising the findings, it is essential to take into consideration some limitations and factors w.r.t. the general applicability of the proposed method. First, we did not exploit commercial LLMs like GPT, Claude, or other open-source LLMs. The exploited models are the newest ones, vary significantly in their dimensions, and demonstrate better results declared by developers. Second, we carried out our experiments only in English as the majority of research in this field is dominated by this language, and we paid most attention to SPARQL queries here and not to the language capabilities. On the other hand, the approach is portable to non-English languages, hence, we leave the exploration of this direction for future work.

A further limitation is that we conducted our experiments on two datasets. Since the approach has been proven, the experiments could be repeated on other datasets, which might make a further contribution to the study of the memorization phenomenon. However, it is worth noting that finding question-answering datasets that are rarely used is hard. Several questions are raised for the discussion. First, synergistic integration of LLMs with KG (i.e., "knowledge injection" experiments) is still a promising direction for further research. Even smaller models might provide benefits and, therefore, decent results to the users. However, we have to point out the fact that all LLMs demonstrated very poor quality when zero-shot-prompting. Therefore, the exploited LLMs are hardly able to generate SPARQL queries from given NL questions without knowledge injection. So, one might come to the conclusion that the memorization effect needs to be triggered by a significant knowledge injection. Second, the results of all experiments on QALD-9-plus outperform those on MCWQ. All LLMs struggled with this task on this infrequently exploited dataset, although the data provided via the knowledge injection prompting again provided all the needed information to generate a correct SPARQL query. Our final experiment with an improved MCWQ dataset demonstrated that the linguistic quality of NL questions does not impact the LLM's performance significantly and, therefore, the final results. In this regard, our results correlate with the ones from SPARQLGEN paper [10]. Third, the error analysis revealed that during the "masked injection" experiments, Wikidata's URIs occurred in the generated query while the prompt does not give any indicator that the generated query should be generated for the Wikidata KG, instead it would have required URIs from the sample (unknown) KG. Hence, this evidence shows that memorized data significantly influences the output of LLMs. At the moment, there are still additional opportunities for process improvement.

6 Conclusions and Future Work

In this study, we explored the capabilities of Large Language Models (LLMs) in generating SPARQL queries from natural language (NL) questions under three different conditions: zero-shot prompting, knowledge injection, and masked knowledge injection. Our primary goal was to assess the impact of structured knowledge integration on query generation performance, while also examining whether LLMs rely on memorization rather than true reasoning when dealing with knowledge graphs (KGs).

To address RQ1 ("Assuming a perfect knowledge injection, how well does the SPARQL query generation perform?"), our findings demonstrate that knowledge injection significantly enhances LLM performance. Models provided with explicit entity and property mappings consistently outperformed those operating under zero-shot conditions. This suggests that LLMs, despite their vast pre-training, still benefit greatly from additional structured context. Even smaller models showed considerable improvement with knowledge injection, highlighting the importance of integrating external knowledge sources when leveraging LLMs for SPARQL query generation. However, performance varied among different models, with larger architectures generally yielding better results.

Regarding RQ2 ("What is the impact of memorization on the SPARQL query generation capabilities of LLMs"), our experiments revealed strong indications of memorization effects. When using masked knowledge injection, where original Wikidata entity URIs were anonymized to prevent recognition, several models still generated queries containing correct Wikidata URIs. This suggests that LLMs often rely on memorized training data rather than true reasoning capabilities, raising concerns about their generalizability to unseen datasets or novel KGs. Moreover, models performed significantly better on the well-known QALD-9-plus dataset compared to the less frequently used MCWQ dataset, reinforcing the notion that model familiarity with a dataset influences results.

In conclusion, researchers and practitioners need to be cautious when using LLM-based SPARQL generation approaches and always keep in mind that the results of the presented methods are unlikely to be fully reproducible on a private or new dataset because the memorization effect will significantly increase the quality and consequently degrade the results in a dataset without this effect. Further research will be necessary to compensate for this effect.

Future Work. While our study provides valuable insights into SPARQL query generation with LLMs, several limitations should be considered. First, our experiments were conducted using a large but still selected set of open-source models and two benchmark datasets. Further research could expand the scope to involve additional models, including proprietary LLMs such as GPT, Claude, or Gemini, to determine whether similar trends persist. Second, our experiments were performed exclusively on English questions. Given that many knowledge graphs contain multilingual data, assessing LLM performance across different languages remains an important avenue for future exploration. Third, the detailed error analysis and an entire error classification could provide the researchers with ways to improve the performance of LLM-based SPARQL generation approaches.

Additionally, our findings highlight the need for improved strategies to mitigate memorization effects and the new strategies for creating and publishing benchmarking datasets. Future research should investigate fine-tuning methods or hybrid approaches that combine LLMs with rule-based or symbolic reasoning techniques to enhance generalization. Another promising direction is the integration of external knowledge retrieval mechanisms, such as KG-based embeddings or reinforcement learning strategies, to improve query accuracy while minimizing reliance on pre-trained data.

Finally, evaluating LLM performance across a broader range of KGQA tasks (e.g., handling complex queries, reasoning over multiple hops, and supporting federated queries) could provide further insights into their real-world applicability. By addressing these challenges, we can advance the development of more reliable, interpretable, and generalizable LLM-driven approaches for knowledge graph-based question answering.

References

1. Bhandiwad, D., et al.: Bridging language models and knowledge graphs with controlled natural languages. Available at SSRN 5009450
2. Brei, F., Frey, J., Meyer, L.P.: Leveraging small language models for Text2SPARQL tasks to improve the resilience of AI assistance. arXiv:2405.17076 (2024)
3. Cui, R., Aralikatte, R., Lent, H., Hershcovich, D.: Compositional generalization in multilingual semantic parsing over Wikidata. Trans. ACL **10** (2022)
4. Diallo, P.A.K.K., Reyd, S., Zouaq, A.: A comprehensive evaluation of neural SPARQL query generation from natural language questions. IEEE Access (2024)
5. Dubey, M., Banerjee, D., Abdelkawi, A., Lehmann, J.: LC-QuAD 2.0: a large dataset for complex question answering over Wikidata and DBpedia. In: International Semantic Web Conference, pp. 69–78. Springer (2019)
6. Emonet, V., Bolleman, J., Duvaud, S., de Farias, T.M., Sima, A.C.: LLM-based SPARQL query generation from natural language over federated knowledge graphs. arXiv preprint arXiv:2410.06062 (2024)
7. Faria, B., Perdigão, D., Oliveira, H.G.: Question answering over linked data with GPT-3. Open Access Ser. Inform. (OASIcs) **113**, 1–15 (2023)
8. Guo, D., et al.: DeepSeek-r1: incentivizing reasoning capability in LLMs via reinforcement learning. arXiv preprint arXiv:2501.12948 (2025)
9. Kacupaj, E., Zafar, H., Lehmann, J., Maleshkova, M.: VQuAnDa: verbalization question answering dataset. In: The Semantic Web, pp. 531–547. Springer, Cham (2020)
10. Kovriguina, L., et al.: SPARQLGEN: one-shot prompt-based approach for SPARQL query generation. In: SEMANTiCS (Posters & Demos) (2023)

11. Lehmann, J., Bhandiwad, D., Gattogi, P., Vahdati, S.: Beyond boundaries: a human-like approach for question answering over structured and unstructured information sources. Trans. ACL **12**, 786–802 (2024)
12. Lehmann, J., Gattogi, P., Bhandiwad, D., Ferré, S., Vahdati, S.: Language models as controlled natural language semantic parsers for knowledge graph question answering. In: ECAI 2023, pp. 1348–1356. IOS Press (2023)
13. Lehmann, J., et al.: Large language models for scientific question answering: an extensive analysis of the SciQA benchmark. In: European Semantic Web Conference, pp. 199–217. Springer (2024)
14. Liu, J., et al.: How proficient are large language models in formal languages? An in-depth insight for knowledge base question answering. In: Findings of the Association for Computational Linguistics ACL 2024, pp. 792–815 (2024)
15. Liu, S., Semnani, S., Triedman, H., Xu, J., Zhao, I.D., Lam, M.: SPINACH: SPARQL-based information navigation for challenging real-world questions. In: Findings of the Association for Computational Linguistics: EMNLP 2024, pp. 15977–16001. Association for Computational Linguistics (2024)
16. Mecharnia, T., d'Aquin, M.: Performance and limitations of fine-tuned LLMs in SPARQL query generation. In: Proceedings of the Workshop on Generative AI and Knowledge Graphs (GenAIK), pp. 69–77 (2025)
17. Meyer, L.P., Frey, J., Brei, F., Arndt, N.: Assessing SPARQL capabilities of large language models. arXiv preprint arXiv:2409.05925 (2024)
18. Perevalov, A., Diefenbach, D., Usbeck, R., Both, A.: QALD-9-plus: a multilingual dataset for question answering over DBpedia and Wikidata translated by native speakers. In: 2022 IEEE 16th International Conference on Semantic Computing (ICSC), pp. 229–234 (2022)
19. Perevalov, A., Gashkov, A., Eltsova, M., Both, A.: Language models as SPARQL query filtering for improving the quality of multilingual question answering over knowledge graphs. In: International Conference on Web Engineering, pp. 3–18. Springer (2024)
20. Perevalov, A., Gashkov, A., Eltsova, M., Both, A.: Understanding SPARQL queries: are we already there? Multilingual natural language generation based on SPARQL queries and large language models. In: International Semantic Web Conference, pp. 173–191. Springer (2024)
21. Qin, L., et al.: Large language models meet NLP: a survey. arXiv:2405.12819 (2024)
22. Rangel, J.C., de Farias, T.M., Sima, A.C., Kobayashi, N.: SPARQL generation: an analysis on fine-tuning OpenLLaMA for question answering over a life science knowledge graph. In: SWAT4HCLS 2024: The 15th International Conference on Semantic Web Applications and Tools for Health Care and Life Sciences (2024)
23. Shen, T., Wang, J., Zhang, X., Cambria, E.: Reasoning with trees: faithful question answering over knowledge graph. In: Proceedings of the 31st International Conference on Computational Linguistics, pp. 3138–3157 (2025)
24. Soruco, J., Collarana, D., Both, A., Usbeck, R.: QALD-9-ES: A Spanish Dataset for Question Answering Systems, pp. 38–52. Studies on the Semantic Web (2023)
25. Taipalus, T., Siponen, M., Vartiainen, T.: Errors and complications in SQL query formulation. ACM Trans. Comput. Educ. (TOCE) **18**(3), 1–29 (2018)
26. Usbeck, R., et al.: QALD-10-the 10th challenge on question answering over linked data: shifting from DBpedia to Wikidata as a KG for KGQA. Semantic Web **15**(6), 2193–2207 (2024)
27. Wei, J., et al.: Chain-of-thought prompting elicits reasoning in large language models. Adv. Neural. Inf. Process. Syst. **35**, 24824–24837 (2022)

28. Yang, A., et al.: Qwen2.5 technical report. arXiv preprint arXiv:2412.15115 (2024)
29. Yani, M., Krisnadhi, A.A.: Challenges, techniques, and trends of simple knowledge graph question answering: a survey. Information **12**(7), 271 (2021)
30. Zahera, H.M., Ali, M., Sherif, M.A., Moussallem, D., Ngomo, A.C.N.: Generating SPARQL from natural language using chain-of-thoughts prompting. In: SEMANTiCS (2024)
31. Zhang, Z., Wen, L., Zhao, W.: Rule-KBQA: Rule-guided reasoning for complex knowledge base question answering with large language models. In: 31st International Conference on Computational Linguistics, pp. 8399–8417 (2025)
32. Zhuang, Y., Yu, Y., Wang, K., Sun, H., Zhang, C.: ToolQA: a dataset for LLM question answering with external tools. In: Advances in Neural Information Processing Systems, vol. 36 (2024)
33. Zong, C., Yan, Y., Lu, W., Huang, E., Shao, J., Zhuang, Y.: Triad: a framework leveraging a multi-role LLM-based agent to solve knowledge base question answering. In: Conference on Empirical Methods in Natural Language Processing (2024)

Web-SPARQL: Hybrid Querying over Knowledge Graphs, Web, and Microdata

Aurélien Lamercerie[(✉)], Peggy Cellier, and Sébastien Ferré

Univ Rennes, CNRS, Inria, Insa Rennes, IRISA,
263 av. Général Leclerc, 35042 Rennes, France
{aurelien.lamercerie,peggy.cellier,sebastien.ferre}@irisa.fr

Abstract. This paper addresses the problem of querying semantic data from heterogeneous web sources. On one hand, centralized knowledge graphs, such as RDF stores, can be accessed with flexibility and efficiency using SPARQL queries. On the other hand, distributed knowledge graphs, such as microdata, are not directly queryable, and are rather exploited by search engines. RDF stores and microdata provide complementary information: RDF stores typically offer higher-quality data, while microdata delivers fresher content. The research problem considered in this paper is the hybrid querying of a centralized RDF store and distributed microdata on the web. To this aim, we introduce Web-SPARQL, an extension of SPARQL with property functions that link the centralized entities to the distributed entities on the web.

Keywords: Knowledge Graph · RDF Store · Microdata · SPARQL · Decentralized Querying

1 Introduction

Regardless of the domain (e.g., medicine, literature, sales), an increasing amount of semantic data in the form of triples is becoming available, either in RDF stores (e.g., DBpedia, Wikidata), or in web pages as microdata. RDF stores and microdata offer complementary information: general knowledge vs specific knowledge, static knowledge vs dynamic knowledge, consensual vs critical. In addition, those semantic data are generally searched in different ways, strongly influenced by their form and their associated technical constraints. RDF stores are typically searched through SPARQL queries. Although microdata are exploited by search engines to improve their results – this was the motivation for them – it is not easy to search for the microdata themselves. Thus, on one hand, centralized static knowledge graphs, such as RDF stores, can be accessed with flexibility and efficiency using SPARQL queries. On the other hand, distributed specialized knowledge graphs, such as microdata, are not directly queryable.

This research is supported by ANR project MeKaNo (ANR-22-CE23-0021).

The problem we address in this paper is the hybrid querying of a centralized RDF store and distributed microdata on the Web. A key benefit of RDF is to allow for precise question answering through a formal query language, and we want to retain this benefit. In this work we consider a single RDF store, a priori of encyclopedic nature like DBpedia or Wikidata, and we leave the use of a federation of RDF stores to future work. Of course, we want to avoid the centralization of all microdata on the Web in an RDF store, although there has been efforts made in this direction[1], the main difficulty being to keep up to date with rapidly changing information on the web, e.g. e-commerce microdata. The research questions are: How to discover the relevant web pages for microdata? How to establish relationships between store entities and microdata entities? What is a hybrid query, and how to evaluate it?

Another important issue is the production of such hybrid queries by end-users. It is already a difficult task to produce queries over a single RDF store because it requires an acute knowledge not only of the vocabulary but also of how it is actually used. An advantage with microdata is that there is a large agreement on the schema.org vocabulary. However, the risk for empty results is high because the available information varies a lot from a website to another, and also from a page to another on the same website. We think that it is therefore necessary to provide an incremental building process for hybrid queries, supporting the exploration of the available data.

Our main contribution is an extension of SPARQL, named Web-SPARQL, to support the combined querying of an RDF store and the web, with the dynamic integration of microdata. A query evaluation workflow is designed to dynamically retrieve and aggregate data from heterogeneous sources, searching the web in real time, and then exploiting the microdata embedded into the found webpages. Another contribution is an extension of Sparklis, an incremental query builder, to Web-SPARQL.

The paper is organized as follows. Section 2 presents the related work. Section 3 defines Web-SPARQL queries and their building while Sect. 4 explains the evaluation workflow. Finally, experimental results are reported in Sect. 5.

2 Related Work

Microdata, integrated into web pages via standards such as RDFa, Microdata or JSON-LD, have been the subject of several studies looking to quantify their presence and assess their value in various contexts [6]. Some studies have focused on the exhaustiveness and quality of the microdata available, highlighting their potential for improving search engines and enriching knowledge bases [13].

Querying multiple semantic data sources is challenging due to heterogeneous formats and models. Federated queries, such as those using the SPARQL SERVICE construct [2], enable integration across distributed knowledge bases. Various strategies address RDF server limitations by decomposing federated queries [4], integrating heterogeneous Linked Data Fragments (LDF) [7], and optimising LDF query plans [8]. Other work refines Triple Pattern Fragments

---

[1] http://webdatacommons.org/.

(TPFs) to reduce server load [3]. Recent efforts focus on processing SPARQL queries at scale, where source selection – identifying relevant endpoints per triple pattern – is key. FedUP [1] tackles this by ensuring subqueries contribute to final results. Yet, these methods are limited to SPARQL-compliant RDF and overlook other web data forms, notably microdata.

From a different perspective, SPARQL has been extended in several ways to improve its expressiveness and its ability to query heterogeneous sources. SPARQL-Generate [10] is an extension for querying structured and semi-structured data other than RDF, e.g. CSV. Techniques combining information extraction and semantic querying can be used to enrich search results by exploiting both structured knowledge bases and textual documents [16].

An alternative strategy involves hybrid queries that combine fast-access centralised data with more up-to-date distributed sources. One approach splits a query between cached data and live web execution, improving freshness while reducing response time compared to fully live queries [15]. However, existing methods often rely on prior source indexing or enforce a strict divide between SPARQL and web querying. Our approach differs by extending SPARQL to jointly query traditional knowledge bases and microdata embedded in web pages. Rather than relying on implicit hybridisation via optimisation, our method provides a way of explicitly expressing, in the query itself, the requirement to dynamically fetch data from the Web. This is likely to improve control over query execution and ensure results with up-to-date information, by natively including the range of sources available on the web.

Whatever the approach to evaluate queries, it is a challenge for users to understand and exploit large knowledge graphs, and a number of approaches have been proposed to address this issue [12]. Among those we are interested in *query builders*, which are tools that guide users in the formulation of their information needs through a graphical user interface, and query suggestions and refinements at each step. A number of query builders were compared in terms of availability, usability, and expressiveness [9]. In this work, we have chosen to use Sparklis [5] as a basis for our implementation and experiments, because of its availability (most other published query builders are no more available), its expressiveness, and also its extensibility through a client-side Javascript API.

3 Web-SPARQL Queries

In this section we first define the notion of *Web-SPARQL queries*, i.e. SPARQL queries that combine data from heterogeneous sources: RDF stores, web pages, and microdata. Then, we give a concrete and detailed example. Finally we discuss how to build Web-SPARQL queries in an exploratory way.

3.1 Extending SPARQL with Web-Properties

Web-SPARQL extends SPARQL w.r.t. the source of RDF nodes and triples. The primary source remains a centralized RDF store. In this paper we use DBpedia as this primary source but any other RDF store would do. Our extension brings in two additional distributed sources: web pages and microdata. Web pages bring in additional nodes representing the web pages themselves, identified by their URL, and possibly triples representing metadata about those pages (e.g., title, last modification date). Microdata brings in nodes and triples that are already following the RDF model, in general using the JSON-LD notation, but that are scattered across the web.

There are two main difficulties to query over those three sources of nodes and triples. First, there is in general no direct link between store entities, web pages, and microdata entities. Without such links, it is pointless to join the three data sources. Second, how to query the web and microdata without scrapping and centralizing them in a local store upfront? Our approach is to start with store entities, then to retrieve web pages about those entities – typically by using a search engine – and from there to extract the microdata embedded into those web pages. An objective is to make the Web-SPARQL queries as transparent as possible. In particular, it should be possible to have graph patterns in the queries that mix store triples and microdata triples (see example in Sect. 3.2).

Table 1. Three new property functions to link an RDF store, the Web, and microdata.

Property	Domain	Range	Description
wsp:aboutEntity	webpage URL	store entity	links a webpage URL to a store entity that it is about
wsp:describes	webpage URL	microdata entity	links a webpage URL to a microdata entity that it describes
wsp:containsKeyword	webpage URL	keyword	links a webpage URL to a keyword it contains

In order to fill in the missing links between store entities, web pages, and microdata entities in a way that is compatible with the dynamic retrieval of data from the web, we introduce three special Web-properties that characterize our extension of SPARQL. In this section, we only define their syntax and expected semantics; their implementation is detailed in Sect. 4. Table 1 summarizes those three properties with their name, domain, range, and description. Prefix wsp: is an abbreviation for the hypothetical namespace http://web-sparql.org/ in which we define our Web-properties.

The first Web-property is wsp:aboutEntity. It serves to link a web page to any store entity it is about. Its subject is therefore a URL node, and its object is a URI node. Here are two examples of triples using this Web-property, relating both a Wikipedia page and a commercial page to the same DBpedia book entity.

```
https://en.wikipedia.org/wiki/The_Name_of_the_Rose
    wsp:aboutEntity dbr:The_Name_of_the_Rose.
https://www.fnac.com/mp34316346/The-Name-of-the-Rose
    wsp:aboutEntity dbr:The_Name_of_the_Rose.
```

The second Web-property is wsp:describes. It serves to link a web page to any microdata entity it describes. Its subject is therefore a URL node again, and its object can also be a URI node but it is often a blank node. In the commercial page above, there is one microdata description whose root node is a blank node, and whose triples provide useful information: e.g., a cover image, an offer with price, currency, and availability. Like in this example, most microdata on the web use the schema.org vocabulary [14]. This is a key advantage when it comes to write SPARQL queries that are expected to run on microdata dynamically retrieved from different web sites.

We also introduce the Web-property wsp:containsKeyword to express full-text constraints on the retrieved web pages. It is comparable with special properties introduced in store implementations, like bif:contains in Virtuoso or text:query[2] in Apache Jena Fuseki. This property is just one example of many possible properties about the metadata of web pages (e.g., creation date).

Those Web-properties cannot be considered as normal properties because it would require to materialize their triples, which is not practically feasible here. It would amount to create a Web-scale index akin to those used by search engines. We rather choose to specify our Web-properties as *property functions*[3], i.e. where the solution mappings of a triple pattern using this property results from a computation, like for functions. Unlike a BINDING construct using functions, it is possible to have multiple solutions, or none. For instance, in the triple pattern ?webpage wsp:aboutEntity dbr:The_Name_of_the_Rose, there are multiple bindings for the variable ?webpage because there are multiple web pages about the book. Unlike a normal property, there are constraints on the boundedness of variables in the triple pattern, due to tractability issues. We here describe those constraints for each Web-property:

- ?webpage wsp:aboutEntity ?entity. At least one variable should be bound when evaluated because otherwise, it amounts to enumerate a Web-scale index. In this paper, we require ?entity to be bound to a store entity.
- ?webpage wsp:describes ?entity. Variable ?webpage must be bound in order to locate the search for microdata entities, and also because most microdata entities are blank nodes.
- ?webpage wsp:containsKeyword ?kwd. Like for similar property functions, variable ?kwd must be bound to specify the full-text search.

The information retrieval therefore flows from store entities and keywords to web pages, and then from web pages to microdata entities.

3.2 Example

Figure 1 shows an example of a Web-SPARQL query and Fig. 2 its graphical representation. In the query, the user is looking for the price and availability on the web of books written by the same author as book "The Name of the Rose". It refers to a situation where the end-user remembers only the title of a book but has forgotten the author's name. The centralized RDF store is DBpedia [11].

---

[2] https://jena.apache.org/documentation/query/text-query.html.
[3] See a description at https://jena.apache.org/documentation/query/extension.html# property-functions. Property functions are also called magic properties.

```
PREFIX dbo: <http://dbpedia.org/ontology/>
PREFIX dbr: <http://dbpedia.org/resource/>
PREFIX sc: <https://schema.org/>
PREFIX wsp: <http://web-sparql.org/>

SELECT DISTINCT ?book ?webpage ?price ?availability
WHERE {
    # Store part
    ?book a dbo:Book .
    ?book dbo:author ?author .
    dbr:The_Name_of_the_Rose dbo:author ?author .

    # Web part
    ?webpage wsp:aboutEntity ?book .
    ?webpage wsp:containsKeyword "purchase" .
    ?webpage wsp:describes ?book_microdata .

    # Microdata part
    ?book_microdata sc:offers ?offer .
    ?offer sc:price ?price .
    ?offer sc:availability ?availability . }
```

Fig. 1. Web-SPARQL query to find information – webpage, price and availability – for the purchase of books with the same author as "The Name of the Rose".

The query has three parts. The Store part (in the blue box in Fig. 2) identifies books written by the same author as "The Name of the Rose" in the RDF store. Only information from the RDF store is used in this part. The Web part links the RDF store, web pages and microdata thanks to the three Web-properties presented in the previous section. On one hand, the `wsp:aboutEntity` property is used to link the previously identified store entity (books written by the same author as "The Name of the Rose") with the web pages that are about it. On the other hand, the `wsp:describes` property is used to link the web pages (about the identified entity) with the microdata entities described in the web pages. The `wsp:containsKeyword` property is used to restrict the web pages to those that contain the keyword "purchase". Indeed, the user intent is to find a commercial website where to buy books. Finally, the Microdata part extracts the information the user is interested in, namely the price and the availability of offers for books written by the same author as "The Name of the Rose". In this last part, only information from the microdata triples is used.

Note that when linking webpages with microdata from the webpages, there may be some noise, meaning microdata that are unrelated to the purchase of a book (e.g., breadcrumbs). However, the Microdata part in the query helps to select the relevant information. In the example, the last part enables to select only the microdata that are about purchase offers with price and availability.

3.3 A Query Builder for Exploratory Search

In order to support exploratory search over both centralized and decentralized KG we adopt the query builder approach that enables the incremental and

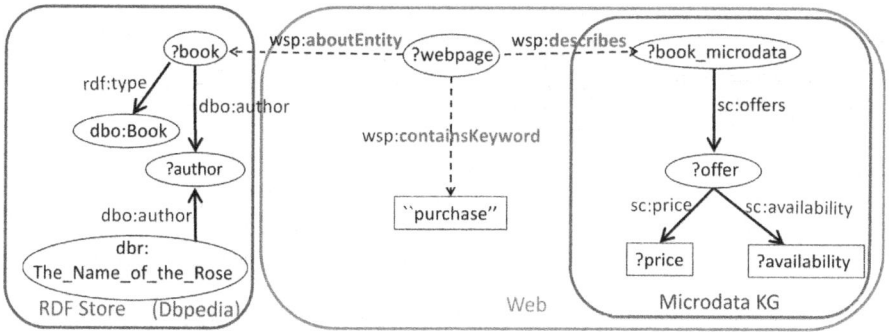

Fig. 2. Graphical representation of the Web-SPARQL query in Fig. 1, showing the split of information between the centralized RDF store, the Web, and Microdata. Web-properties are emphasized with dashed lines and red labels.

exploratory construction of SPARQL queries. As said in Sect. 2, we implement it by extending Sparklis [5] – a generic query builder for SPARQL endpoints – to our Web-properties. Our Web-SPARQL query evaluation engine is implemented as a SPARQL endpoint agreeing to the standard protocol (see Sect. 4), hence abstracting over the different KG sources. Sparklis can therefore connect to it without having to care whether the information comes from the store or from the web. However the suggestion of properties rely on stored triples, and therefore does not work for property functions like our Web-properties.

We exploit the extension mechanisms of Sparklis in order to add our Web-properties as an additional list of suggestions, when this is relevant. For instance, the property wsp:aboutEntity is suggested when the nodes under focus are store entities. Those entities play the role of the object of the property; and a new variable is introduced for the subject, which becomes the new focus about web pages. These suggestions validate the boundedness constraints on the property (see Sect. 3.1). Similarly, properties wsp:containsKeyword and wsp:describes are suggested when the nodes under focus are webpages, to allow for full-text constraints and access to microdata entities respectively. The wsp:containsKeyword suggestions come with a text field where the user can input a keyword. Figure 3 shows a screenshot of our Sparklis extension, emphasizing how the additional suggestions are displayed.

4 Evaluation of Web-SPARQL Queries

The objective is here to extend the evaluation of SPARQL queries to Web-SPARQL so that clients of our Web-SPARQL query engine (end-users or Sparklis) can use it in a transparent way. It should therefore follow the standard SPARQL protocol, taking a Web-SPARQL query as input and returning a sequence of solution mappings as output. To this aim, a number of challenges need to be addressed. A first challenge is that the data is not centralized in

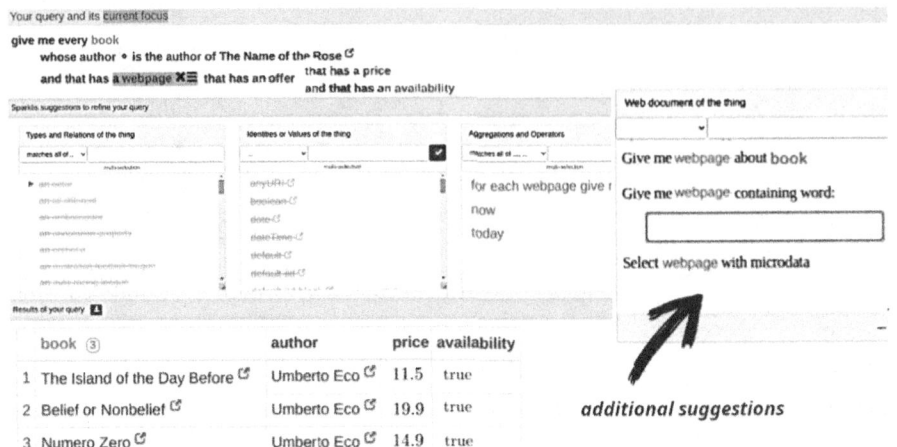

Fig. 3. Screenshot of the Web-SPARQL query builder tool.

a single RDF store, not even in a few RDF stores, but scattered on the web in unpredictable locations. The evaluation of Web-SPARQL queries therefore involves the use of a search engine to locate relevant information on the web, in addition to matching triples in the centralized RDF store as well as in the retrieved microdata. The Web-properties precisely serve to abstract over the call to search engines, and it remains to define how to implement them as property functions.

A second challenge is the latency involved by searching the web, and processing the retrieved webpages and microdata. This is especially the case in the exploratory setting where many similar queries are evaluated in the query building process, and where reasonable response times are needed for usability. We address this challenge by extending the *static* RDF store (e.g., DBpedia) by a *dynamic* store designed to collect as triples all the information retrieved from the web. In this way, we hope that for each query refinement, unnecessary recomputations are avoided.

Figure 4 summarizes our workflow from a Web-SPARQL query to its results. It is composed of five steps that must be run in a strict order. The query is first decomposed into three parts: a *static query*, a *parametrized web query*, and a *dynamic query*. Those three parts are then evaluated in order, each one feeding the next one with the relevant data. The static query results inform about what to search on the web, and the web search results enable to feed the dynamic store. Finally, the results of the static query and the dynamic query are joined to form the results of the Web-SPARQL query. This process is implemented in WeSET[4], a Web-SPARQL evaluation tool. Each step is detailed below.

---

[4] Available at https://gitlab.inria.fr/alamerce/weset.

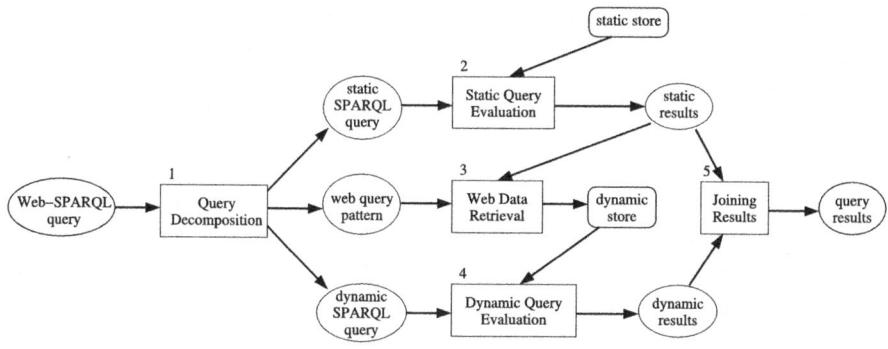

Fig. 4. Web-SPARQL Query Evaluation Workflow.

Step 1: Decomposition of the Web-SPARQL Query. In each basic graph pattern, triple patterns can be partitioned in three sub-patterns: store, web, and microdata. The web sub-pattern P_{web} is easy to identify as it is exactly made of the triple patterns using the three Web-properties. From there, the variable w for the retrieved web pages can be identified as the subject of those triples. The variable x for the store entities can be identified as the object of property wsp:aboutEntity; and the variable y for the microdata entities can be identified as the object of property wsp:describes. Variable x must be present because the web page cannot be introduced without an entity to start with; but variable y can be missing. Considering the pattern resulting from the removal of the web part from the initial basic graph pattern, the sub-pattern P_{store} is the connected component that contains x; and the sub-pattern P_{micro} is the connected component that contains y, if any, or the empty pattern otherwise.

From these three sub-patterns, we define three different queries:

- Q_{static} = SELECT X_{store} WHERE { P_{store} }: a SPARQL query over the static store where X_{store} is the subset of the SELECT variables that occur in P_{store}, which includes x. This query will provide bindings for x.
- $Q_{web}(x)$ = x kwd_1 kwd_2 ...: a web search query (a string), parametrized by the store entity x to search. It is simply the concatenation of (the label of) the store entity and the keywords provided through property wsp:containsKeyword, if any. This query will provide bindings for w, which will help to feed the dynamic store.
- $Q_{dynamic}$ = SELECT x w Y_{micro} WHERE { P_{web} P_{micro} }: a SPARQL query over the dynamic store where Y_{micro} is the subset of the SELECT variables that occur in P_{micro}, which includes y.

Note that the two SPARQL queries have x as a common variable in their results. This will enable to join their results in Step 5.

Step 2: Evaluation of the Static Query. The static query Q_{static} is evaluated on the static store, i.e. the centralized RDF store, in order to obtain a first partial result R_{static}. This is a standard SPARQL evaluation. It provides, among other things, bindings of the variable x to store entities.

Step 3: Retrieval of Data from the Web. Using the static results R_{static} obtained on the static store and the web query pattern $Q_{web}(x)$, a set of web queries is generated by applying this pattern to each store entity x_i bound to x in the static results. In the example, if 10 books are found in the RDF store, then 10 web queries will be generated.

All generated web queries are processed in the same way and independently. Each web query $Q(x_i) = x_i \ldots kwd_l \ldots$ is evaluated using a search engine, resulting in a set of URLs $\{w_{ij}\}$. Then for each URL w_{ij}, the webpage is retrieved, its microdata extracted and parsed, and the set of description root entities $\{y_{ijk}\}$ identified. At this stage, all the required data was retrieved from the web, and it remains to feed the dynamic store. The set of triples to be loaded in the dynamic store is made of:

- all triples from the microdata embedded in all web pages at URLs w_{ij};
- triples (w_{ij} wsp:aboutEntity x_i), for all w_{ij};
- triples (w_{ij} wsp:containsKeyword kwd_l), for all w_{ij}, and keywords kwd_l;
- triples (w_{ij} wsp:describes y_{ijk}), for all microdata entity y_{ijk}.

The last three items are a materialization of the Web-properties. This is useful to allow the evaluation of the dynamic query in the next step, and also for the joining of results in the last step.

Step 4: Evaluation of the Dynamic Query. The dynamic query is evaluated on the dynamic store, after it was fed in the previous step, in order to obtain a second partial result $R_{dynamic}$. This can be conducted like a standard SPARQL evaluation as the relevant triples are materialized and centralized in an RDF store. It provides bindings for variables x, w, y, plus possibly additional variables on the microdata side. Those mappings therefore reflect the virtual links from store entities to web pages, and from web pages to microdata entities.

Step 5: Joining Results. The two partial results obtained in Step 2 (R_{static}) and Step 4 ($R_{dynamic}$) must then be joined to obtain complete results for the Web-SPARQL query. This is possible because variable x about store entities appears in the two partial results, and also because the dynamic results were retrieved from the particular entities found in the static results.

5 Experiments

This section presents the experiments that we conducted about hybrid querying with Web-SPARQL. We aim to answer two questions: (a) How often and how many microdata can be found on the web in typical usage scenarios; (b) What is the execution time of evaluating Web-SPARQL queries, and how it varies under different usage scenarios? Those experiments require a dataset of queries representing usage scenarios mixing data from an RDF store and the web.

```
SELECT DISTINCT ?book ?web ?price
WHERE {                                    ?web md:containsThing ?book .
    ?book a dbo:Book .                     ?web md:containsWord "purchase" .
    ?book dbo:author dbr:Terry_Pratchett . ?web md:hasMicrodata ?microdata .
    ?book foaf:name "Pyramids"@en .        ?microdata schema:offers ?offer .
}                                          ?offer schema:price ?price .
```

?book	?web	?price
dbr:Pyramids_(novel)	https://www.fnc/Terry-Pratchett-Pyramids	22.51
dbr:Pyramids_(novel)	https://www.amzn.com/Pyramids-Discworld	10.11

Fig. 5. Example of query and result corresponding to *"Give me the price of the book whose title is Pyramids and whose author is Terry Pratchett"*.

5.1 Methodology

Query Dataset. We have built a dataset[5] consisting of a collection of Web-SPARQL queries that are about two domains: books and cinema. For instance, book-related queries may look for the price of Tolkien's books, while cinema-related queries may look for streaming platforms for Nolan's movies. As described above, Web-SPARQL queries are made of three parts: store, web, and microdata. The store part selects either books or films based on available information in the KG store (DBpedia), such as authors, directors, actors, literary genres, cover artists, or awards. The web part retrieves webpages related to the selected entity, guided by a web search intent. Each domain has up to ten search intents, expressed by distinct keywords (e.g., "purchase", "official trailer", or "movie reviews"). The microdata part extracts various features defined by schema.org, such as *price*, *review content* or *video object URL*. The features to extract depend on the search intent. As a seed to generate the queries, we used a hand-crafted selection of books by several authors, such as Terry Pratchett and J. R. R. Tolkien, and films by several directors, such as Christopher Nolan and Steven Spielberg. Figure 5 presents an example of a Web-SPARQL query that searches for the price of the book 'Pyramids', along with a table showing two possible results, each consisting of a book entity, a webpage URL, and a price.

We distinguish two kinds of queries: complex and simple. The 1170 *complex queries* (CQ) search for one or several features of a set of entities. They represent realistic use cases of searching for information, such as purchasing books, finding movie streaming platforms, or comparing movie reviews. The 7176 *simple queries* (SQ) search for a single feature of a single entity (book or film). They are derived from complex queries by replacing their store query by one of its entities, and by choosing one feature from the microdata query. They primarily serve to analyze the amount of available microdata per entity.

For the purpose of reproducibility, we include in our dataset *reference web data*, i.e. a snapshot of the information collected from the web when evaluating the dataset queries. It is made of two dictionaries. The first dictionary records for each web query a list of webpage URLs. The second dictionary records for each

---

[5] Available at https://gitlab.inria.fr/alamerce/wesed.

Table 2. Microdata statistics on the two query collections, simple queries and complex queries. *Rate* is the percentage of queries returning at least one result for the variable, among queries having this variable (100% for Entity and Webpage). *Count* is the average number of results for this variable when at least one result is found.

Domain	Query type	number	Entity count	Webpage count	Microdata rate	count	Features (avg) rate	count
cinema	CQ	910	6.4	192	100%	52.74	70%	15.33
cinema	SQ	5824	1	30	83%	9.99	40%	4.24
book	CQ	260	5.2	156	100%	65.72	72%	13.82
book	SQ	1352	1	30	100%	12.64	46%	4.14

webpage URL a list of JSON-LD descriptions. They also record the response times for retrieving data from the web. This reference web data was used in our experiments so that results be comparable between different configurations.

Execution modes (cold, warm, hot). Retrieving data from the web takes time. It is therefore beneficial to cache previous web search results and microdata. In real usage, the content of this cache strongly depends on previous queries, and on the similarity of the current query with previous queries. For this reason, it is important to consider various modes from cold to hot execution. Cold execution assumes that no query was previously executed, so that the cache is empty. Warm execution, on the opposite, assumes that all required web data is already in the cache, so that no web access is needed. Hot execution further assumes that the required microdata is already loaded into the microdata store. Warm and hot modes actually happen in real usage when only the microdata part of a Web-SPARQL query is modified before re-evaluation.

Settings. The RDF store targeted in our experiments is DBpedia, queried through the SPARQL endpoint at https://dbpedia.org/sparql. For web searches, the DuckDuckGo search API is used.[6] The maximum number of URLs per search is set to 30. Microdata extraction is implemented using the Beautiful-Soup and Json python libraries, targeting JSON-LD.

5.2 Microdata Statistics

The first experiment aims to determine whether enough microdata is retrieved to make Web-SPARQL queries useful in practice. Table 2 reports statistics about the amount of microdata found when evaluating the Web-SPARQL queries of both domains: cinema and books. The second column of the table indicates the number of complex (CQ) and simple queries (SQ), the third column shows the average number of entities per query, and the fourth indicates the average number of webpages per query.

The "Microdata" column gives two pieces of information: the *rate*, i.e., the percentage of queries for which at least one microdata is returned; and the *count*,

---

[6] https://github.com/deedy5/duckduckgo_search.

Table 3. Top-10 feature statistics per entity in the *cinema* and *book* domains

Cinema			Book		
Feature	Rate	Count	Feature	Rate	Count
director/name	80%	3.94	rating/value	94%	5.80
movie/url	78%	3.60	rating/review	94%	5.76
image	73%	3.51	rating/count	94%	5.43
review/author	73%	1.57	offer/price	36%	2.86
review/content	73%	1.47	offer/availability	28%	2.34
review/rating	69%	1.07	review/author	23%	1.25
actor/name	64%	13.83	review/content	21%	1.00
logo	64%	2.15	review/rating	21%	1.00
breadcrumblist/item	59%	2.66	publisher	4%	1.00
clip/description	55%	1.57			

i.e., the average number of microdata per query. For complex queries in both datasets, the rate is 100% whereas it is lower for simple queries. It is explained by the fact that contrary to simple queries, complex queries involve several entities which automatically increases the probability of having microdata. On this column we observe the substantial amount of microdata available for both domains. Indeed, on average around 10 microdata are available per entity in the cinema domain, and more than 12 for entities in the book domain.

The "Features" column indicates two elements: the *rate*, i.e., the percentage of queries for which at least one value is returned for each measured feature; and the *count*, i.e., the average number of values per feature per query. On this column we note two facts. First, the number of values per feature per query is very different between complex and simple queries (more than 70% for CQ and 40% for SC). As above the difference is explained by the fact that several entities are selected by complex queries, and only one for simple queries. Second, although there is disparity between complex and simple queries, we observe that on average each feature has a large number of retrieved values (CQ/cinema: 15.33; CQ/book: 13.82; SQ/cinema: 4.24; SQ/book: 4.14).

In order to better measure the disparity between the features themselves, Table 3 provides a more fine-grained analysis by reporting statistics for the top-10 most frequent microdata features per entity in both domains. In this table, only simple queries are considered, meaning that each query is associated with a single entity. For each feature, we give its presence rate (i.e., the percentage of entities for which it was found), and the average number of values when present. In the cinema domain we observe that regardless the feature, the rate is quite high for all of them (from 55% to 80%). In the book domain, it is interesting to note that "dynamic features" such as information about the ratings, the commercial offers or the reviews are frequently present whereas "static features" like

Table 4. Average execution times per query, in seconds

Mode	T_1	T_2	T_3	T_4	T
Cold	0.23	3.96	8.17	2.39	14.75
Warm	0.23	-	-	2.39	2.62
Hot	0.23	-	-	-	0.23

publisher, which can generally be retrieved in the KG store, are less often found in microdata.

In conclusion, those statistics highlight that although microdata is unevenly available, a lot of relevant microdata for the considered tasks (e.g., searching information, book purchase) are available and should be exploited. It confirms the importance of hybrid Web-SPARQL querying as we propose in this paper.

5.3 Execution Times

The execution time for a hybrid query can be decomposed as $T = T_1+T_2+T_3+T_4$, where T_1 is the time taken by workflow steps that run locally (steps 1, 2, 4, 5), hence excluding web data retrieval (step 3); T_2 is the time taken for n web searches, with n the number of store entities; T_3 is the time taken to extract the nk microdata from webpages, with k the number of web pages per entity; and T_4 is the time taken to load all this microdata in the local store.

Table 4 shows the measured execution times in seconds, averaged over cinema queries, for each execution mode. Over all queries, the average number of entities per query is $n = 6.4$, and the number of web pages per query is $nk = 192$ ($k = 30$). The measures show that local computations (T_1) are negligible compared to web data retrieval. It takes only 0.23 s to decompose the query (step 1), evaluate the static query (step 2), evaluate the dynamic query (step 4), and join the results (step 5). Most of the time is spent at retrieving data from the web. It takes about 4 s to perform web search (T_2), and 8 s to retrieve microdata (T_3). As those parts are performed asynchronously, issuing web requests in parallel, those times are strongly impacted by network latency. Loading microdata in the dynamic store (T_4) takes about 2 s, a significant but minor part of the whole. In warm and hot mode, web retrieval disappears but in warm mode it remains to load the cached microdata into the dynamic store (T_4).

Overall, we observe large differences in total time between execution modes, from under a second in hot mode to 14.75 s in cold mode. It should be possible to improve the cold mode but it will remain bounded by network latencies. In practice however, when using Sparklis, the consequence is that the insertion of property functions wsp:aboutEntity and wsp:describes entail important response delays because it triggers the retrieval of new web data, but then the refinement of the microdata query works in hot mode, hence efficiently.

6 Conclusion

Web-SPARQL enables hybrid querying by combining a static RDF store queries and microdata that is dynamically retrieved from the web. The hybrid Sparklis query builder supports users in their exploratory search, smoothly spanning the RDF store and the web. The experimental results confirm the feasibility and appeal of this approach. Future work will focus on the challenge of efficiency in query evaluation, and responsiveness in query building.

Disclosure of Interests. The authors have no competing interests to declare that are relevant to the content of this article.

References

1. Aimonier-Davat, J., Nédelec, B., Dang, M.H., Molli, P., Skaf-Molli, H.: FedUP: querying large-scale federations of SPARQL endpoints. In: ACM Web Conference 2024, pp. 2315–2324. Association for Computing Machinery, New York, USA (2024)
2. Aranda, C.B., Arenas, M., Corcho, Ó., Polleres, A.: Federating queries in SPARQL 1.1: syntax, semantics and evaluation. J. Web Semant. **18**, 1–17 (2013)
3. Azzam, A., Polleres, A., Fernández, J.D., Acosta, M.: smart-KG: partition-based linked data fragments for querying knowledge graphs. Seman. Web **15**, 1791 (2024)
4. Buil-Aranda, C., Polleres, A., Umbrich, J.: Strategies for executing federated queries in SPARQL1.1. In: International Workshop on the Semantic Web (2014)
5. Ferré, S.: SPARKLIS: an expressive query builder for SPARQL endpoints with guidance in natural language. Seman. Web **8**(3), 405–418 (2017)
6. Guha, R.V., Brickley, D., Macbeth, S.: Schema.org: evolution of structured data on the web. Commun. ACM **59**(2), 44–51 (2016)
7. Heling, L., Acosta, M.: Federated SPARQL query processing over heterogeneous linked data fragments. In: ACM Web Conference, pp. 1047–1057. WWW '22, Association for Computing Machinery, New York, USA (2022)
8. Heling, L., Acosta, M.: Robust query processing for linked data fragments. Seman. Web **13**, 623–657 (2022)
9. Kuric, E., Fernández, J.D., Drozd, O.: Knowledge graph exploration: a usability evaluation of query builders for laypeople. In: SEMANTiCS. Springer (2019)
10. Lefrançois, M., Zimmermann, A., Bakerally, N.: A SPARQL extension for generating RDF from heterogeneous formats. In: Semantic Web, pp. 35–50. Springer (2017)
11. Lehmann, J., et al.: DBpedia-a large-scale, multilingual knowledge base extracted from Wikipedia. Seman. web **6**(2), 167–195 (2015)
12. Lissandrini, M., Mottin, D., Hose, K., Pedersen, T.B.: Knowledge graph exploration systems: are we lost? In: Conference on Innovative Data Systems Research (2022)
13. Meusel, R., Petrovski, P., Bizer, C.: The WebDataCommons Microdata, RDFa and Microformat Dataset Series. In: Mika, P., et al. (eds.) ISWC 2014. LNCS, vol. 8796, pp. 277–292. Springer, Cham (2014). https://doi.org/10.1007/978-3-319-11964-9_18

14. Mika, P.: On schema.org and why it matters for the web. IEEE Internet Comput. **19**(4), 52–55 (2015)
15. Umbrich, J., Karnstedt, M., Hogan, A., Parreira, J.X.: Hybrid SPARQL queries: fresh vs. fast results. In: The Semantic Web, pp. 608–624. ISWC'12, Springer (2012)
16. Usbeck, R., Ngomo, A.C.N., Bühmann, L., Unger, C.: Hawk – hybrid question answering using linked data. In: The Semantic Web, pp. 353–368. Springer (2015)

ShEx2SPARQL: Translating Shape Expressions into SPARQL Queries

Christoph Göpfert[(✉)], Sheeba Samuel, and Martin Gaedke

Technische Universität Chemnitz, 09111 Chemnitz, Germany
{christoph.goepfert,sheeba.samuel,
martin.gaedke}@informatik.tu-chemnitz.de

Abstract. The Shape Expressions (ShEx) Language provides a powerful tool for describing and validating structures in RDF knowledge graphs. While Shape Expressions are primarily used for validation, they also describe graph structures, enabling knowledge graph exploration. However, existing ShEx engines focus on validation rather than data exploration. In this paper, we introduce ShEx2SPARQL, an approach to systematically translate shape expressions into corresponding CONSTRUCT, SELECT, or ASK SPARQL queries. This enables knowledge graph exploration based on already available ShEx schemas. Our approach imposes certain restrictions, notably the exclusion of recursive shape references, as SPARQL lacks sufficient support for recursive expressions. To evaluate our approach, we selected 292 Wikidata Entity Schemas, translated them into corresponding SPARQL queries and executed them against the Wikidata SPARQL endpoint. The results confirm the feasibility of our approach, but also reveal performance issues when executing complex SPARQL queries resulting from complex shapes with a multitude of constraints.

Keywords: Shape Expressions · ShEx · SPARQL · Knowledge Graph · Exploration · Linked Data · Semantic Web

1 Introduction

Knowledge graphs (KGs) have become a key technology for the structured organization and integration of information in a machine-readable format. KGs store knowledge as a collection of entities and their relationships using the Resource Description Format (RDF) [1] data model. RDF data can be queried and manipulated using the standardized query language SPARQL [2]. However, constructing effective queries requires knowledge of the graph's structure and its underlying ontologies to construct correct query patterns. This structure is typically described in ontologies such as the Web Ontology Language (OWL) [3] ontologies. If information about the structure of a KG is not available, it can be derived either by analyzing the ontologies used or by using exploratory queries, before being able to construct the desired query.

The Shape Expressions Language (ShEx) [4] offers a schema language for formally describing and validating the structure of RDF data by defining "shapes". Shapes define expected properties of RDF nodes, including required predicates in a triple, permitted datatypes for a specified literal, cardinality constraints, or logical combinations of graph patterns. Although designed as a validation language, ShEx shapes encapsulate rich structural information offering a blueprint for SPARQL query patterns.

We introduce ShEx2SPARQL, a novel approach leveraging ShEx schemas for KG exploration. ShEx provides rich, declarative descriptions of shapes which our approach repurposes to guide data discovery in KGs. ShEx2SPARQL translates Shape Expressions into CONSTRUCT, SELECT, or ASK SPARQL queries. Our approach enables the easy retrieval and inspection of data in a KG that conforms to a respective shape, eliminating the need for extensive, manual query construction. Furthermore, it can be applied for other use cases, such as identifying incomplete or inconsistent data, or revealing latent relationships among entities. However, not all graph structures describable with ShEx can be translated into SPARQL, leading to certain restrictions. We evaluated our approach using Wikidata's [5] knowledge base. Wikidata uses Entity Schemas expressed using ShEx to validate graph structures. We selected 292 of these, translated them into queries which we executed to demonstrate the feasibility of our approach.

2 Related Work

A template-based query generation approach is presented by Cocco et al. [6], using a training set of natural language questions with associated SPARQL queries to answer natural language questions. A tagger is used to identify entities and relations in a question. Then, predefined query templates are selected based on similarity and presented iteratively to the user to select. Light-QAWizard [7] applies an RNN-based multi-label classification to map a natural language question to templates. These are then used for query generation, attempting to exclude irrelevant clauses to reduce query complexity. More recently, Taffa and Usbeck [8] presented a few-shot LLM-based approach using Vicuna-13B to retrieve similar question-query template pairs. However, queries are associated with question embeddings, which are also used for finding similar questions.

Tools such as Sparklis [9] and the Wikidata Query Builder[1] employ an interactive, visual approach to enable users to construct queries by providing a faceted view. Similarly, the tools Protégé [10] and QueryVOWL [11] enable users to visualize and edit ontologies. Protégé allows users to execute SPARQL queries in its user interface but does not provide pre-defined templates. QueryVOWL allows SPARQL query construction, but is limited to SELECT queries.

Linked Data Objects (LDO) [12] represents RDF data as JavaScript objects. Modifications to objects can automatically be translated into SPARQL update queries. SELECT, ASK or CONSTRUCT queries are not supported.

In contrast, ShEx2SPARQL translates formal constraints specified in a ShEx schema directly into executable SPARQL graph patterns. No intermediate steps – such as template completion or mapping of entities and relations – are required. Further, by reusing schemas, ShEx2SPARQL provides an alternative approach to knowledge graph exploration with SELECT, ASK or CONSTRUCT queries, without the need for training data or manual query construction.

---

[1] https://query.wikidata.org/querybuilder/.

3 Mapping ShEx to SPARQL

Shape expressions provide a formal schema language designed to validate RDF data by defining shapes, specifying expected node properties. These may include constraints on predicates, permitted datatypes, cardinality, and logical combinations of graph patterns. There are three types of ShEx syntaxes. In the following, we use the terminology of the JSON-LD-based ShExJ grammar in ShEx version 2. Its building blocks include **Schema**, **Shape Expression** (shapeExpr), **NodeConstraint** and **TripleConstraint**. Below, we provide a shortened (indicated by "(...)") excerpt of the ShExJ syntax [13]:

Schema { start:shapeExpr? shapes:[ShapeDecl+]? (...) }
ShapeDecl { id:shapeExprLabel shapeExpr:shapeExpr (...) }
shapeExpr = ShapeOr | ShapeAnd | ShapeNot | NodeConstraint | Shape | ShapeExprRef ;
ShapeOr { shapeExprs:[shapeExpr{2,}] }
ShapeAnd { shapeExprs:[shapeExpr{2,}] }
ShapeNot { shapeExpr:shapeExpr }
Shape { expression:tripleExpr? (...) }
NodeConstraint { id:shapeExprLabel? nodeKind:(...) datatype:IRIREF? (...) }
tripleExpr = EachOf | OneOf | TripleConstraint | tripleExprRef ;
EachOf { id:tripleExprLabel? expressions:[tripleExpr{2,}] (...) }
OneOf { id:tripleExprLabel? expressions:[tripleExpr{2,}] (...) }
TripleConstraint { id:tripleExprLabel? predicate:IRIREF valueExpr:shapeExpr? (...)}

Schema represents the main building block, optionally specifying a start shape and a collection of shape declarations. A shape declaration (*ShapeDecl*) consists of an identifier and a shape expression (*shapeExpr*), which in turn can take various forms: logical combinations of two or more shapes (*ShapeOr* and *ShapeAnd*), the negation of a shape (*ShapeNot*), define structural constraints in triple expressions (*Shape*), impose constraints on a subject or object of a triple (*NodeConstraint*), and reference another shape expression in the schema (*ShapeExprRef*). A shape element may contain a triple expression (*tripleExpr*), which can be logically combined (*EachOf* and *OneOf*), impose triple constraints (*TripleConstraint*), or reference a triple expression (*tripleExprRef*). The following challenges need to be addressed when mapping ShEx to SPARQL:

Recursion: ShEx allows recursive references of shapes. This enables the definition of nested or hierarchical relationships at arbitrary depth. However, SPARQL does not provide the means to express constrained traversal. Consequently, recursive relationships cannot be expressed in SPARQL and must either be omitted or simplified.

Start Shape: In ShEx, the presence of a start shape is optional. Without a specified start shape, however, a definite entry point when translating the schema may not be determinable. Selecting a start shape at random may result in different queries depending on the selected shape, which we believe to be undesirable for exploration. Instead, a "root shape" would need to be identified, i.e., a shape not referenced by any other shape. Further, a schema may contain isolated clusters of shapes. If a start shape is specified, this may not represent an issue, as other clusters will be disregarded in the generated queries. In the absence of a specified start shape, it would not be possible to identify a definitive root shape, as several options may be available, possibly resulting in differing queries. This can be solved by moving shape clusters into distinct schemas.

Variable Naming: A shape describes the structure of a resource. Consequently, a resource represents the subject of the graph patterns generated to express the constraints of a shape. However, shape ids may contain characters that are not valid in SPARQL variable names. To avoid this, shape ids should not be used in the constructed query. Shape ids may be hashed to create SPARQL syntax compliant variable names.

Cardinality Constraints: A triple expression may impose cardinality constraints, such as the minimum or maximum number of times a triple with a specified predicate may occur. Mapping such constraints requires a mechanism to count the occurrence of certain predicate-object pairs for a given subject. An approach to solving this is described by Prud'hommeaux[2], using a counter function generating a query block to count the matching predicate-object pairs. This block then aggregates using the function *COUNT()* combined with a *GROUP BY* clause. Cardinality constraints are then specified using the *HAVING* clause to enforce the count value to be within the specified minimum and maximum limits. Both GROUP BY and HAVING can be represented in the post-modifier of a block, explained in Sect. 4.

Node Constraints: A Node Constraint imposes restrictions on a node and may specify its datatype, node kind or permitted values. These constraints can be mapped to corresponding SPARQL FILTER operations.

Based on these background considerations and challenges in mapping ShEx schemas to SPARQL queries, we discuss the specifics of our approach in Sect. 4.

4 The ShEx2SPARQL Approach

This section introduces ShEx2SPARQL and describes how it translates key ShEx schema elements into SPARQL query patterns to enable knowledge graph exploration. It supports SELECT, CONSTRUCT and ASK queries and imposes two restrictions on source schemas to ensure executable and valid queries: **1)** A start shape with a provided id must be defined in the source schema. As stated in Sect. 3, several scenarios exist that hinder effective exploration if no start shape is given. For this reason, we consider the definition of a start shape to be mandatory. **2)** schemas containing recursive shape references cannot be translated, as SPARQL lacks support for constrained traversal.

ShEx2SPARQL begins by parsing a given schema, identifying its start shape. The structure of the query is then constructed by traversing the elements of the schema and converting any constraints into a hierarchical representation of **blocks** and **statements**.

A **block** represents a grouping of statements and blocks nested within the current block. A block may include a "pre"- and "post"-modifier and a list of statements and sub-blocks. Pre- and post-modifiers specify optional or excluded graph patterns and group by variables with cardinality constraints. They also specify cardinality ranges. A **statement** corresponds to a triple pattern, filter, or VALUES condition. Sub-blocks handle nested shape expressions or patterns that are optional or need to be excluded.

---
[2] https://www.w3.org/2013/ShEx/toSPARQL.html.

After processing the schema, its root block representing the outermost structure of the query is returned. Then, each schema element is processed using a corresponding "visit" function to map its contents to SPARQL constructs. These are described below:

1) Schema

The start shape specified in the schema is identified and visited using the *visitShape* function, returning a new block. This block element represents the root block, which will also be returned by the *visitSchema* function.

2) Shape

As a shape represents an entity, its expressions describe the expected structure of this entity. The shape id is used in the SPARQL translation process as the subject for the triple patterns generated from its expressions. We use hashed (MD5) shape ids to ensure SPARQL compliant variable names. Each shape's shape expression is visited with the *visitShapeExpr* function. This function takes the hashed shape id as a parameter and recursively processes the shape's constraints. It returns a block with statements representing the structure of the shape as SPARQL graph patterns. The *visitShape* function returns this block without any modifications.

3) Shape Expression

Each type of shape expression needs to be processed differently:

Shape: A shape may contain a triple expression which is visited, returning a new block and statements. The new block is added as a sub-block to the current expression. New statements are then appended to the statements of the current triple expression.

ShapeOr: A *ShapeOr* represents two or more shapes linked by logical OR. This is translated by iterating through each shape, visiting their shape expression. Each visit results in a new block and statements. For each new block, the pre-modifier "UNION" is set to translate the OR relation of the shapes to blocks of triple patterns. For the first block, the "UNION" pre-modifier is not set, as only the blocks from the second onward must be joined via "UNION". New blocks and statements are handled as described for *Shape* elements. Statements consisting of SPARQL FILTERs require special handling. Multiple FILTER statements must be merged by logical OR into a single FILTER.

ShapeAnd: A *ShapeAnd* represents an AND relationship between two or more shapes. Similarly to *ShapeOr*, this relation is translated by iterating through each of the shapes, visiting each shape expression. New blocks and statements are processed as described for the *Shape* element. Unlike *ShapeOr*, FILTER constraints do not require any special handling, as an AND condition requires all FILTER constraints to apply.

ShapeNot: A *ShapeNot* represents a negated shape expression. The shape expression is visited, creating a new block and statements. These are processed as described for the *Shape* element. However, the pre-modifier of the block is set to "MINUS" to force the exclusion of the specified constraints in SPARQL.

NodeConstraint: A NodeConstraint specifies constraints for individual nodes. Node constraints are translated into statements as opposed to blocks. The created statements are appended directly to the list of statements of the current shape expression.

ShapeExternal: A *ShapeExternal* represents a reference to a shape in an external schema. The referenced shape must be retrieved from the imported schema and is then processed according to the procedure described in **2) Shape**. The resulting new block and statements are integrated as described for the *Shape* element.

shapeExprRef: *shapeExprRef* is a reference to another shape within the current schema. The referenced shape is processed in the same way as an external shape, with the only difference being that the shape does not need to be looked up first.

4) Triple Expression

Each type of triple expression is processed differently. For the type *TripleConstraint*, the triple constraint is visited using the function *visitTripleExpression*, returning a new block and statements. A *TripleExpression* of type *EachOf* or *OneOf* contains multiple linked expressions. In these cases, a new block with statements is created to encapsulate the entire triple expression before iterating through each sub-expression using *visitExpression*. In each visit, a new block and statements are returned. Each new block is added as sub-block to the block of the triple expression. Each *EachOf* triple expression needs to be linked by OR, the pre-modifiers of the corresponding blocks are set to "UNION", as described for the *ShapeOr* element. Similarly to *shapeExprRef*, *tripleExprRef* represents a reference to a triple expression within the schema. The referenced triple expression must be visited and subsequently processed as described in this section. Finally, the block and statements of the triple expression are returned.

5) Node Constraint

A *NodeConstraint* may contain constraints on a triple's subject or object. Object constraints also specify the triple's predicate in a *NodeConstraint*. A randomized hash is used to refer to the object, as a schema may contain multiple node constraints on triples with the same subject and predicate, but differing objects. A constraint will either specify a datatype, values, or node kind, all of which can be translated to FILTER operations as described in Sect. 3. The *numericFacets* can be translated with comparison operators, and by using the functions STRLEN() or SUBSTR(), etc. Finally, the *visitNodeConstraint* function returns the created statements.

6) Triple Constraint

Triple constraints define a triple's predicate and may include a value expression with a shape expression. The triple's subject is the variable of the shape associated with the triple constraint through a triple expression. The triple's object is described by an optional value expression. A new block and statements are created if either a value expression is specified, or the triple expression is optional or exclusive. ShEx2SPARQL creates a random variable for the constrained triple's object, unless the shape expression is referencing a shape in the schema, where the referenced shape id's hash is used instead. If a triple constraint does include a value expression, the generated variable is passed to the *visitShapeExpr* function as subject, as its shape descriptions relate to the constrained triple's object. The new blocks and statements returned are appended as sub-blocks to the priorly created block and triple constraint's list of statements.

Value expressions of type node constraint are visited, adding statements it returns to the list of statements. These must be moved as statements of the created block if the constraint is optional or excluding, as this block may contain an "OPTIONAL" or "MINUS" pre-modifier. Finally, the created block and statements are returned.

ShEx2SPARQL supports the query methods CONSTRUCT, SELECT and ASK. For CONSTRUCT queries, the graph patterns within the CONSTRUCT clause are populated with all unique statements, omitting FILTER and VALUES statements. Additionally, ShEx2SPARQL provides the option to specify the URI of the start shape, essentially querying a specific instance of the start shape. This is realized by replacing the variable name of the start shape by a provided URI. An ASK query can be constructed to verify whether a resource identified by a provided URI complies with the shape of the schema. Consequently, the provision of a URI is mandatory for ASK queries. For SELECT queries, no further modifications to the constructed query are necessary.

5 Evaluation

We created a proof-of-concept prototype of the ShEx2SPARQL approach, currently providing limited support for cardinality constraints. For parsing schemas, the tool relies on shexjs/parser[3]. Source code is available via https://purl.org/shex2sparql/code.

To assess feasibility, we obtained 422 Entity Schemas (ShEx schemas) from Wikidata. We removed schemas that were either 1) empty, 2) invalid or obviously incorrect, 3) made use of schema imports, 4) lacked a start shape, or 5) included recursive shape references. The last three criteria are based on the previously mentioned limitations. The selection based on the above criteria was automated with a script to ensure the reproducibility of our evaluation, available via https://purl.org/shex2sparql/evaluation. A total number of 292 schemas remained after filtering.

For each schema, we generated a CONSTRUCT query and executed it against Wikidata's SPARQL endpoint. 187 of 292 queries succeeded (HTTP 200), while 105 timed out. Re-executing them with "LIMIT 1" recovered 47 more results. We found no simple correlation between query complexity (number of triple patterns or FILTERs) and time-outs. Four highly complex queries (>164 graph patterns) all timed out, yet even some seemingly trivial queries (containing one graph pattern and a filter) did so too, suggesting endpoint load and queried data volume also play roles. We provide a digital appendix including a detailed list of executed queries and their results at https://purl.org/shex2sparql/data. Among the 234 successful queries, 56 returned no data (44 of the original 187, and 12 of the 47 limited). Investigation (cf. Digital appendix) showed two causes: 1) some shapes simply had no matching instances in Wikidata, and 2) several schemas contained errors such as invalid IRIs, deprecated or mistyped properties, misused value sets. Thus, the queries were incapable of retrieving data.

6 Conclusion

We presented ShEx2SPARQL, a novel approach leveraging the Shape Expressions Language (ShEx) for knowledge graph exploration. ShEx2SPARQL utilizes a given ShEx schema to systematically translate it into a corresponding SPARQL query. This enables

---
[3] https://www.npmjs.com/package/@shexjs/parser.

users to explore knowledge graphs by re-utilizing available ShEx schemas. We evaluated our approach using real-world ShEx schemas from Wikidata and demonstrated its feasibility by generating SPARQL queries that yielded data conforming to the shapes specified in the schemas. However, we also found limitations, as a subset of queries resulted in timeouts—an issue largely attributable to external endpoint performance and inherent query complexity. Future work will focus on extending the capabilities of ShEx2SPARQL by supporting schema imports and optimizing generated SPARQL queries to better handle complex constraints and to mitigate timeout issues.

Acknowledgements. This work was funded by the Deutsche Forschungsgemeinschaft (DFG, German Research Foundation) – Project-ID 514664767 – TRR 386 and by the European Commission [grant 101120657 "European Lighthouse to Manifest Trustworthy and Green AI" – ENFIELD].

Disclosure of Interests. The authors have no competing interests to declare that are relevant to the content of this article.

References

1. Klyne, G., Carroll, J.J., McBride, B.: RDF 1.1 Concepts and Abstract Syntax (2014)
2. Harris, S., Seaborne, A., Prud'hommeaux, E.: SPARQL 1.1 Query Language (2013)
3. W3C OWL Working Group: OWL 2 Web Ontology Language Document Overview, 2nd edn. (2012)
4. Prud'hommeaux, E., Boneva, I., Emilio, J., Kellog, G.: Shape Expressions Language 2.1 (2019)
5. Vrandečić, D., Krötzsch, M.: Wikidata: a free collaborative knowledgebase. Commun. ACM **57**(10), 78–85 (2014). https://doi.org/10.1145/2629489
6. Cocco, R., Atzori, M., Zaniolo, C.: Machine learning of SPARQL templates for question answering over LinkedSpending. In: 28th International Conference on Enabling Technologies: Infrastructure for Collaborative Enterprises (WETICE), pp. 156–161, June 2019
7. Chen, Y.-H., Lu, E.J.-L., Lin, Y.-Y.: Efficient SPARQL queries generator for question answering systems. IEEE Access **10**, 99850–99860 (2022)
8. Taffa, T.A., Usbeck, R.: Leveraging LLMs in scholarly knowledge graph question answering (2023)
9. Ferré, S.: SPARKLIS: an expressive query builder for SPARQL endpoints with guidance in natural language. Semant. Web **8**(3), 405–418 (2016)
10. Musen, M.A.: The Protégé project: a look back and a look forward. AI Matters **1**(4), 4–12 (2015). https://doi.org/10.1145/2757001.2757003
11. Haag, F., Lohmann, S., Siek, S., Ertl, T.: QueryVOWL: visual composition of SPARQL queries. In: Gandon, F., Guéret, C., Villata, S., Breslin, J., Faron-Zucker, C., Zimmermann, A. (eds) ESWC 2015. LNCS, vol. 9341, pp. 62–66. Springer, Cham (2015). https://doi.org/10.1007/978-3-319-25639-9_12
12. Morgan, J.: Linked data objects (LDO): a TypeScript-enabled RDF devtool. In: Payne, T.R., et al. (eds.) ISWC 2023. LNCS, vol. 14266, pp. 230–246. Springer, Cham (2023). https://doi.org/10.1007/978-3-031-47243-5_13
13. Shape Expressions Language 2.next. https://shex.io/shex-next/. Accessed 19 Feb 2025

SciMantify - A Hybrid Approach for the Evolving Semantification of Scientific Knowledge

Lena John(✉), Kheir Eddine Farfar, Sören Auer, and Oliver Karras

TIB - Leibniz Information Centre for Science and Technology, Hannover, Germany
{lena.john,kheir.farfar,soeren.auer,oliver.karras}@tib.eu

Abstract. Scientific publications, primarily digitized as PDFs, remain static and unstructured, limiting the accessibility and reusability of the contained knowledge. At best, scientific knowledge from publications is provided in tabular formats, which lack semantic context. A more flexible, structured, and semantic representation is needed to make scientific knowledge understandable and processable by both humans and machines. We propose an evolution model of knowledge representation, inspired by the 5-star Linked Open Data (LOD) model, with five stages and defined criteria to guide the stepwise transition from a digital artifact, such as a PDF, to a semantic representation integrated in a knowledge graph (KG). Based on an exemplary workflow implementing the entire model, we developed a hybrid approach, called *SciMantify*, leveraging tabular formats of scientific knowledge, e.g., results from secondary studies, to support its evolving semantification. In the approach, humans and machines collaborate closely by performing semantic annotation tasks (SATs) and refining the results to progressively improve the semantic representation of scientific knowledge. We implemented the approach in the Open Research Knowledge Graph (ORKG), an established platform for improving the findability, accessibility, interoperability, and reusability of scientific knowledge. A preliminary user experiment showed that the approach simplifies the preprocessing of scientific knowledge, reduces the effort for the evolving semantification, and enhances the knowledge representation through better alignment with the KG structures.

Keywords: Evolution model · Semantification · Hybrid approach

1 Introduction

Publications remain the primary medium for scientific communication [8]. Despite efforts to digitize them as PDFs, scientific knowledge largely remains static and unstructured [2]. The next step in digital transformation calls for flexible, structured, and semantic representations to make knowledge more accessible and usable by humans and machines [10,11]. Structured, machine-actionable knowledge is increasingly necessary due to the growing volume of publications and the demand for reusability [18]. While some approaches, such as *SciKG-TeX* [2], enable *FAIR-by-Design* publications [17], most are only published as

PDFs. At best, data is shared in tabular formats, such as results from secondary studies, which offer promising potential for semantification according to the SemTab Challenge [6]. In this paper, we propose an evolution model of knowledge representation inspired by the 5-star Linked Open Data (LOD) model. This model defines five stages with criteria to guide the transformation from static digital artifacts, e.g., PDFs, to semantic representations integrated into a knowledge graph (KG). We illustrate the implementation of the model through an exemplary workflow based on the established services ORKG Ask [1] and ORKG [18] Building on this model, we introduce *SciMantify*, a hybrid approach that leverages tabular formats to support the gradual semantification of scientific knowledge. Hybrid methods, combining human insight and machine automation, emerged as a promising solution to this task [4]. In *SciMantify*, humans and machines collaboratively perform semantic annotation tasks (SATs), refining results and incrementally improving semantic representations. The approach is implemented within ORKG, a core service in Germany's National Research Data Infrastructure for FAIR scientific knowledge [9,18]. We evaluated *SciMantify* in a preliminary user experiment with eight participants. Results show high usability (SUS score: 87.5) [12], and participants agreed it significantly reduces preprocessing and semantification effort, averaging 17 min overall. We provide the following contributions: 1) The evolution model of knowledge representation, 2) The hybrid approach *SciMantify*, 3) A first release of *SciMantify* in the ORKG, and 4) Preliminary results indicating promising support by *SciMantify*.

2 Related Work

Evolution of Knowledge Representation. Liang et al. [14] propose a three-layer network combining citation and content analysis to trace knowledge flow and evolution. Li et al. [13] present the MGraph approach, a semantic data model that transforms unstructured data into structured to track concept evolution over time. In contrast, our approach presents a generic evolution model emphasizing the transition from unstructured scientific knowledge in a digital artifact to a flexible, structured, and semantic representation integrated in a KG.

Semantic Annotation. Semantic table annotation (STA) enriches tabular data by linking it to KGs, enhancing its meaning and interoperability [5]. Recent approaches, with significant contributions by the SemTab challenge [6], include heuristic, feature engineering, and deep learning-based methods [15]. Tools like DAGOBAH UI [7] and TabbyLD2-Client [4] offer user-friendly interfaces: The former focuses on automation, while the latter supports hybrid annotation with manual refinement for broader accessibility.

STA faces key challenges, such as handling context, data heterogeneity, and metadata [3,15], as well as unmatched entities and incomplete KGs, that reduce annotation accuracy [3,7]. Most works focus on tables with single value-cells, limiting real-world application [4,7,15], and often lack intuitive UIs [3,4]. To address these issues, we propose *SciMantify*, a hybrid approach introducing SATs as human-machine collaboration. Unlike fully automated methods that trade off accuracy for efficiency [15], *SciMantify* aims to achieve both through integration with the ORKG's user-friendly UI to better support non-technical users.

3 Evolution Model, Workflow, and Hybrid Approach

3.1 Evolution Model of Knowledge Representation

The starting point of our work is the evolution model of knowledge representation (see Fig. 1), which we developed iteratively by testing, evaluating, and refining it through its application to different digital artifacts.

Inspired by the 5-star LOD model, our five-stage evolution model defines criteria for transitioning from unstructured scientific knowledge in a digital artifact to a semantic representation integrated in a KG. Unlike the LOD model, which focuses on the progressive openness and interoperability of data, our model focuses on the specific challenges to represent scientific knowledge.

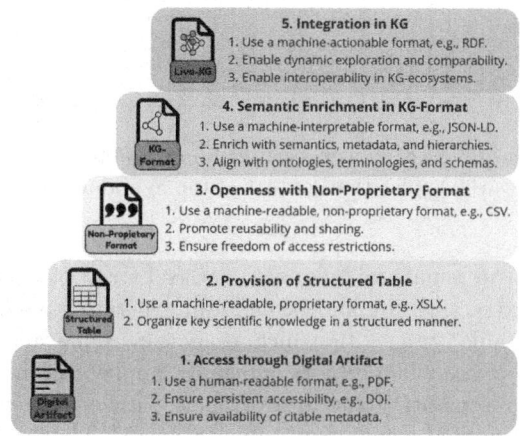

Fig. 1. Evolution model of knowledge representation.

The first stage **Access through Digital Artifact** ensures scientific knowledge is accessible in human-readable digital formats, e.g., PDFs, with stable identifiers like DOIs for long-term availability. It also emphasizes citable metadata to support reliable knowledge integration. The second stage **Provision of Structured Table** structures key scientific knowledge in a tabular format using machine-readable formats, e.g., XLSX, enabling preprocessing, computational analysis, and efficient data management. The third stage **Openness with Non-Proprietary Format** enhances accessibility and reusability by using open, non-proprietary formats, e.g., CSV, promoting interoperability and open science without technical or legal barriers. The fourth stage **Semantic Enrichment in KG-Format** enriches scientific knowledge with semantics, metadata, and hierarchies in machine-interpretable formats, e.g., JSON-LD, improving interpretability, linking, and contextualization for better integration in KGs. The fifth stage **Integration in KG** integrates scientific knowledge into KGs using machine-actionable formats, e.g., RDF or OWL, enabling dynamic exploration, comparability, and interoperability across ecosystems to support advanced data analysis and interdisciplinary collaboration.

3.2 Exemplary Workflow

The workflow combines two established services ORKG Ask [1] and ORKG [18] to demonstrate the transition from unstructured scientific knowledge to semantic representations in a KG. As shown in Fig. 2, the activity diagram maps each step to a model stage, including human or machine involvement and service usage.

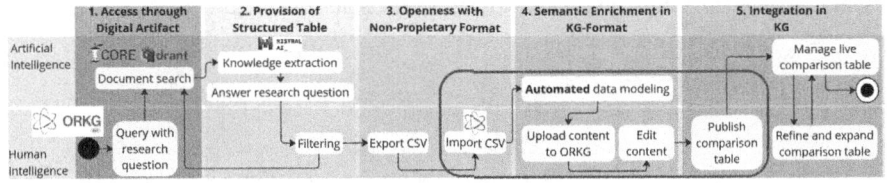

Fig. 2. Exemplary workflow demonstrating the implementation of the evolution model. The red box outlines the application context of the hybrid approach.

ORKG Ask answers natural language queries by retrieving relevant publications (Stage 1), extracting key knowledge, and generating a synthesized answer and comparison table (Stage 2), which users can refine and export as CSV (Stage 3). ORKG allows CSV import (Stage 3), applies automated data modeling to create initial semantic structures (Stage 4), and enables users to manually edit and publish the final comparison table (Stage 5). Though based on ORKG Ask and ORKG, the workflow is service-agnostic, tools like Elicit or Wikidata could be used instead. This workflow does not only show that the evolution model is feasible with current tools but also highlights key limitations, such as the strict separation of human and machine contributions. As Liu et al. [15] emphasize, modern UIs are crucial for enhancing human-machine collaboration. To address this issue, we introduce *SciMantify*, a hybrid approach integrated into ORKG that supports collaborative semantification, particularly in the critical stages three to five (cf. Fig. 2, red box), where current support is lacking.

3.3 Hybrid Approach: SciMantify

The core idea of *SciMantify* is to introduce semantic annotation tasks (SATs) as collaborative efforts between humans and machines. As shown in Fig. 3, we define four SATs that improve the automated assignment of predicates and data types during CSV import, and supporting the evolving semantification of scientific knowledge of the uploaded content in the ORKG. Inspired by the SemTab Challenge tasks [6], we propose four SATs: CTA, CEA, HCS, and PCG, that enable progressive refinement (see Fig. 4):

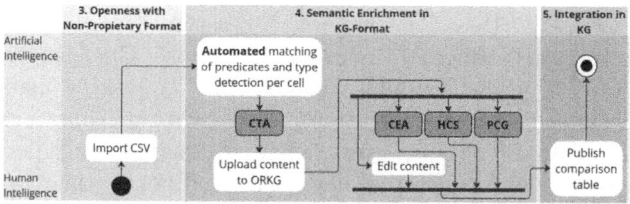

Fig. 3. Hybrid approach in context of the exemplary workflow (cf. Fig. 2).

CTA (Column Type Annotation) assigns data types and semantic properties to columns. The machine suggests types, e.g., boolean or integer, and properties; the human reviews and corrects them for contextual accuracy.

CEA (Cell Entity Annotation) links cell values to KG entities. The machine suggests matches (including handling multi-value cells by splitting), while the human verifies or refines them to improve alignment and linking.

HCS (Hierarchical Content Structuring) organizes rows into hierarchies by identifying sub-properties (rows) of existing concepts in other rows. The human defines structural relationships, and the machine applies them consistently.

PCG (Property Concept Grouping) promotes reuse by grouping related properties under a new concept. The human creates the grouping, and the machine ensures consistent application across the entire table.

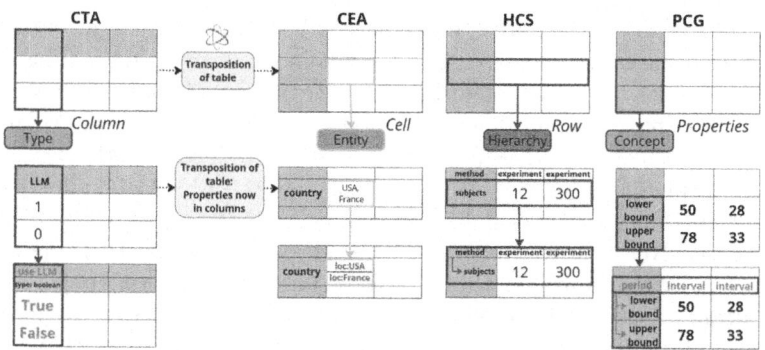

Fig. 4. Semantic annotation tasks: CTA, CEA, HCS and PCG.

4 Implementation

Given the advanced state of the ORKG, we adopted an agile development approach for integrating *SciMantify*. The first release focuses on CTA and CEA tasks by embedding human input into existing automated processes. The remaining tasks will follow in the second release.

CTA. The original ORKG CSV import auto-assigned predicates and treated unmatched content as strings, without editing options. Changes required modifying and re-uploading the CSV file. We enhanced this task by enabling users to edit properties and data types directly in the UI with machine support. Predicates are still auto-assigned, but users can revise them. Data types are inferred via majority voting, and inconsistencies are flagged in real-time for resolution.

CEA. The original contribution editor allowed only basic edits. While users could add new cell values (suggested by the machine), aligning existing values with ORKG entities required manual deletion and re-entry, offering no true CEA support. For this reason, we introduced the "Semantify" function: Users can now align existing values with suggested entities or create new ones. Enumerations in a cell can be split and semantically aligned to enhance data integration.

5 Evaluation

To assess the hybrid approach proposed in this paper, we conducted a preliminary user experiment focusing on the first release of *SciMantify*, which integrates humans into automated processes for CTA and CEA. The aim was to explore the approach's effectiveness, efficiency, and user satisfaction in supporting the evolving semantification of scientific knowledge in the ORKG.

> *Research question:* How does the implementation of the hybrid approach (CTA & CEA) support users with prior knowledge of semantic data modeling in terms of effectiveness, efficiency, and satisfaction in the ORKG?

Participants performed the CTA and CEA tasks using a simplified ORKG comparison table [16], adapted to emphasize data modeling. Eight participants familiar with the ORKG took part, half of whom regularly used the CSV import.

Subjective feedback indicated that most participants found *SciMantify* effective and efficient, particularly for CTA and CEA. However, the predicate selection feature received mixed feedback, with some participants overlooking it. Task completion times (see Fig. 5a) averaged 16:38 $\pm$ 6:04, [9:15–23:44] min, with 3:08 $\pm$ 1:33, [1:10–5:02] for CTA and 13:30 $\pm$ 4:41, [7:45–19:10] for CEA. The number of reused KG entities (see Fig. 5b) varied, with most participants aligning with or exceeding the original table, except one, who was unfamiliar with the contribution editor. The overall usability (see Fig. 5c) was rated high, with a mean SUS score of 87.5 $\pm$ 7.68, [75 - 100], i.e., excellent usability [12].

In summary, the experiment showed encouraging initial results for the hybrid approach. However, future larger studies are need to compare *SciMantify* with a baseline of the original ORKG workflow to quantify improvements.

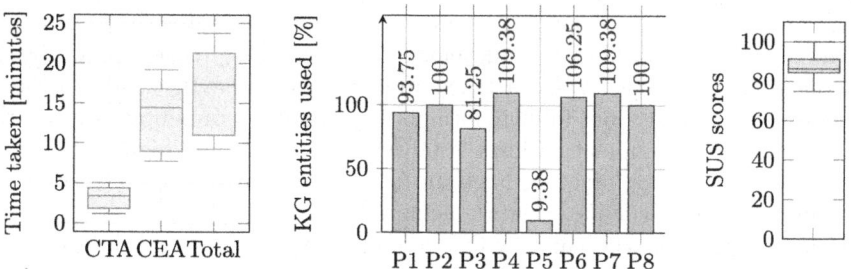

(a) Times for CTA task, (b) Ratio of entities used and 32 enti- (c) SUS scores
CEA task, and in total. ties of the original comparison table. for *SciMantify*.

Fig. 5. Objective assessment of effectiveness, efficiency, and satisfaction.

6 Discussion

A more structured and semantic representation of scientific knowledge is essential to advancing the digital transformation of scientific communication. To address this, we proposed an evolution model of knowledge representation, demonstrated through an exemplary workflow and implemented as *SciMantify*, a hybrid approach supporting human-machine collaboration in the semantification process. Our preliminary user experiment indicates that *SciMantify* effectively supports the transformation of scientific content from tabular formats to semantic representations. With an average completion time of 17 min (3 for CTA, 14 for CEA), results show efficient preprocessing and highlight the need for human input in refining machine-suggested entity alignments. The high usability score (SUS 87.5) confirms the system's user-friendliness and overall satisfaction. The integration of CTA and CEA tasks proved essential, though feedback also pointed to areas for improvement. In particular, predicate selection was often overlooked, suggesting the need for better UI guidance. Additionally, variability in CEA task times indicates that users would benefit from more structured support when aligning entities, especially in complex contexts. Several participants also expressed the need for hierarchical structuring and grouping, aligning with our planned integration of HCS and PCG in the next release of *SciMantify*. While results are promising, the evaluation has limitations. The study included only eight participants, and the scenario was based on a simplified, fictitious example. Broader studies using real-world data and a baseline comparison are needed to validate the findings. Furthermore, only CTA and CEA tasks were implemented so far. The full potential of the hybrid approach will be assessed after integrating HCS and PCG in the upcoming release.

7 Conclusion and Future Work

The proposed evolution model for knowledge representation offers a structured approach to transforming static, unstructured knowledge into flexible, semantic formats. Based on the exemplary workflow that demonstrates the implementation of the evolution model, we developed *SciMantify*, a hybrid approach combining human expertise with machine automation to evolve the representation of scientific knowledge from tabular formats to semantic representations in a KG. A preliminary experiment within the ORKG context showed high usability and positive feedback, highlighting *SciMantify*'s ability to reduce preprocessing and semantification efforts. Future work includes implementing the remaining semantic annotation tasks HCS and PCG, and adding AI-driven suggestions to better support complex content. We plan a broader user study to assess performance across research domains and compare it to a baseline workflow to increase generalizability. Overall, the evolution model and *SciMantify* represent a key step toward more accessible, reusable, and interoperable scientific knowledge.

References

1. Auer, S., et al.: Open research knowledge graph: a large-scale neuro-symbolic knowledge organization system. In: Handbook on Neurosymbolic AI and Knowledge Graphs. IOS Press (2025)
2. Bless, C., Baimuratov, I., Karras, O.: SciKGTeX - a LATEX package to semantically annotate contributions in scientific publications. In: ACM/IEEE Joint Conference on Digital Libraries (2023)
3. Cremaschi, M., et al.: Survey on semantic interpretation of tabular data: challenges and directions. arXiv Preprint arXiv2411.11891 (2024)
4. Dorodnykh, N., Yurin, A.: Knowledge graph engineering based on semantic annotation of tables. Computation **11** (2023)
5. Dorodnykh, N.O., Shigarov, A.O., Yurevich Yurin, A.: Using the semantic annotation of web table data for knowledge base construction. In: 4th Artificial Intelligence and Cloud Computing Conference (2022)
6. Hassanzadeh, O., Abdelmageed, N., Cremaschi, M., Cutrona, V., et al.: Results of SemTab 2024. In: CEUR Workshop Proceedings (2024)
7. Huynh, V.P., Liu, J., Chabot, Y., Deuzé, F., et al.: DAGOBAH: table and graph contexts for efficient semantic annotation of tabular data. In: 20th International Semantic Web Conference (2021)
8. Johnson, R., Watkinson, A., Mabe, M.: The STM Report: An Overview of Scientific and Scholarly Publishing (2018)
9. Karras, O., Budde, L., Merkel, P., Hermsdorf, J., et al.: Organizing scientific knowledge from engineering sciences using the open research knowledge graph: the tailored forming process chain use case. Data Sci. J. (2024)
10. Karras, O., Wernlein, F., Klünder, J., Auer, S.: Divide and conquer the EmpiRE: a community-maintainable knowledge graph of empirical research in requirements engineering. In: ACM/IEEE International Symposium on Empirical Software Engineering and Measurement (2023)
11. Karras, O., et al.: Researcher or crowd member? why not both! the open research knowledge graph for applying and communicating CrowdRE research. In: 29th International Requirements Engineering Conference Workshops. IEEE (2021)
12. Lewis, J.R., Sauro, J.: Item Benchmarks for the System Usability Scale. J. Usability Stud. **13**(3) (2018)
13. Li, X., Liu, L., Wang, X., Li, Y., et al.: Towards evolutionary knowledge representation under the big data circumstance. Electron. Libr. (2021)

14. Liang, Z., Liu, F., Mao, J., Lu, K.: A knowledge representation model for studying knowledge creation, usage, and evolution. Divers. Divergence, Dialogue (2021)
15. Liu, J., et al.: From tabular data to knowledge graphs: a survey of semantic table interpretation tasks and methods. J. Web Semant. (2023)
16. Lozynska, O.: Deep learning methods for fake news detection. Open Res. Knowl. Graph (2024). https://doi.org/10.48366/R739984
17. Stocker, M., et al.: SKG4EOSC - scholarly knowledge graphs for eosc: establishing a backbone of knowledge graphs for FAIR scholarly information in EOSC. Res. Ideas Outcomes **8** (2022)
18. Stocker, M., et al.: FAIR scientific information with the open research knowledge graph. FAIR Connect **1**(1) (2023)

A Knowledge Graph Informing Soil Carbon Modeling

Nasim Shirvani-Mahdavi[1]((✉))[iD], Devin Wingfield[1], Juan Guajardo Gutierrez[1], Mai Tran[1], Zhengyuan Zhu[1], Zeyu Zhang[1], Haiqi Zhang[1], Abhishek Divakar Goudar[1], Chengkai Li[1]((✉))[iD], Virginia Jin[2], Timothy Propst[2], Dan Roberts[2], Catherine Stewart[2], Jianzhong Su[1], and Jennifer Woodward-Greene[2]

[1] University of Texas at Arlington, Arlington, TX 76013, USA
Nasim.shirvanimahdavi2@mavs.uta.edu,cli@uta.edu
[2] United States Department of Agriculture, Washington, USA

Abstract. Soil organic carbon is crucial for climate change mitigation and agricultural sustainability. However, understanding its dynamics requires integrating complex, heterogeneous data from multiple sources. This paper introduces the Soil Organic Carbon Knowledge Graph (SOCKG), a semantic infrastructure designed to transform agricultural research data into a queryable knowledge representation. SOCKG features a robust ontological model of agricultural experimental data, enabling precise mapping of datasets from the Agricultural Collaborative Research Outcomes System. It is semantically aligned with the National Agricultural Library Thesaurus for consistent terminology and improved interoperability. The knowledge graph, constructed in GraphDB and Neo4j, provides advanced querying capabilities and RDF access. A user-friendly dashboard allows easy exploration of the knowledge graph and ontology. SOCKG supports advanced analyses, such as comparing soil organic carbon changes across fields and treatments, advancing soil carbon research, and enabling more effective agricultural strategies to mitigate climate change.

Keywords: Knowledge Graph Construction · Ontology Engineering · Soil Organic Carbon · Carbon Sequestration

1 Introduction

Soil is the largest terrestrial carbon sink and contains more carbon than vegetation and atmosphere combined, positioning it as a key player in global efforts to reduce greenhouse gas (GHG) emissions [15,22]. Soil organic carbon (SOC) is key to soil health, influencing nutrient cycling, water retention, and microbial activity [14]. By enabling the understanding, measurement, and management of SOC dynamics, soil carbon modeling provides the foundation for strategies to sequester carbon, mitigate climate change, and promote sustainable land management [16]. Modeling SOC dynamics helps target agricultural practices that improve soil fertility, enhance productivity, and increase resilience to climate extremes such as droughts and floods [1]. By advancing environmental sustainability, soil carbon modeling supports global food security while reducing the risk of land degradation [8].

Carbon farming practices, such as reduced tillage, crop rotation diversification, cover cropping, and the application of organic amendments, are essential for enhancing SOC levels [12,20]. By sequestering carbon in soils, land managers can earn carbon credits, providing financial incentives for adopting sustainable practices [2]. Effective soil carbon modeling sustains the soil credit markets, ensuring accurate accounting of SOC changes and building trust among stakeholders.

Despite the potential benefits, the complexity of soil carbon modeling presents significant challenges, including complex and dynamic soil processes influenced by biological, chemical, and climatic factors, and uncertainties in measurements. Several notable efforts have been made to develop tools for soil carbon modeling and management. The International Soil Carbon Network (ISCN) has created a global database of soil carbon measurements, facilitating data sharing and analysis across diverse ecosystems [19]. Similarly, the Soil Survey Geographic Database (SSURGO)[1] provides detailed spatial data on soil properties across the United States, supporting site-specific analyses and modeling efforts. The Rapid Carbon Assessment (RaCA) dataset[2] offers a robust inventory of soil organic and inorganic carbon stocks across over 6,000 U.S. locations, providing critical data for carbon modeling and management.

This paper presents the development of the Soil Organic Carbon Knowledge Graph (SOCKG), a semantic infrastructure designed to support robust and user-friendly soil carbon modeling. The primary objective of this knowledge graph is to aid the investigation of factors influencing SOC dynamics and other critical soil measurements. By facilitating carbon sequestration in agricultural soils at large, SOCKG offers support for mitigating climate change and enhancing farm productivity and sustainability. In summary, this work contributes the following:

- **Ontology development:** An ontological model semantically aligned with the National Agricultural Library Thesaurus (NALT)[3], ensuring dataset interoperability and consistent terminology for soil carbon research.
- **Knowledge graph construction:** Integration and mapping of SOC data from Agricultural Collaborative Research Outcomes System (AgCROS)[4], which contains detailed information collected from across 58 experimental fields over a span of 45 years, including soil properties (e.g., bulk density, pH) and management practices (e.g., crop rotation). The knowledge graph organizes this data to support the analysis of SOC dynamics and their relationship with soil properties and management practices.

---

[1] https://websoilsurvey.nrcs.usda.gov/.
[2] https://www.nrcs.usda.gov/resources/data-and-reports/rapid-carbon-assessment-raca.
[3] https://agclass.nal.usda.gov/.
[4] https://doi.org/10.15482/USDA.ADC/1529828.

- **User-friendly tools:** Development of tools and interfaces to improve SOCKG accessibility and usability, including Neo4j and GraphDB hosting of the knowledge graph for advanced querying and visualization, an interactive dashboard and a data cube with simplified analytical capabilities for diverse stakeholders, and ontology documentation generated using LLM.
- **Application insights:** Demonstrations of SOCKG's capabilities in supporting SOC-related use cases.
- **Open-source resources:** We have open-sourced several resources at https://idir.uta.edu/sockg/. These resources include an ontology in the Turtle[5] format, the data graph in formats such as Turtle, N-triples[6] and Neo4j dump, the source code for preprocessing the source AgCROS data file and populating the knowledge graph with the prepocessed data, and the source code of the dashboard. Additionally, we provide detailed documentation on design and implementation of SOCKG and its various tools.

The paper is structured as follows. Section 2 reviews background concepts in soil carbon modeling and data. Section 3 details the development and population of SOCKG, as well as its ontology and data integration. Section 4 describes the developed query endpoints and dashboard. Section 5 presents SOCKG's use cases. Section 6 discusses conclusions and future directions for extending SOCKG's capabilities.

2 Background

2.1 Key Concepts in Soil Carbon Modeling

Carbon cycle is a fundamental Earth system process that governs the movement of carbon among the atmosphere, oceans, terrestrial ecosystems, and geological reservoirs [3,21]. In this cycle, carbon transitions between organic and inorganic forms, playing an important role in maintaining the planet's climate balance [11]. Terrestrial ecosystems, particularly soils, act as significant carbon sinks [22]. This sequestration process helps regulate levels of atmospheric carbon dioxide (CO_2), a major GHG driving global climate change [22]. Human activities such as deforestation, fossil fuel combustion, and unsustainable agricultural practices disrupt this balance, releasing large amounts of carbon into the atmosphere. Soils contribute to the carbon cycle primarily through the accumulation of SOC, derived from decomposed plant and microbial matter [13]. Promoting soil carbon sequestration has emerged as a strategy to mitigate climate change [6].

Voluntary carbon markets provide a mechanism for organizations and individuals to offset their unavoidable GHG emissions by purchasing carbon credits or earn revenue by selling the credits [5]. Each credit typically represents the removal or avoidance of one metric ton of GHG [5]. These markets provide

---
[5] https://www.w3.org/TR/rdf12-turtle/.
[6] https://www.w3.org/TR/rdf12-concepts/.

farmers and land managers with financial incentives, encouraging the adoption of sustainable practices that improve soil carbon levels [4]. By verifying and monetizing the carbon stored in soils, these markets reward sustainable farming practices while fostering broader participation in climate action. The credibility of these markets depend on robust methodologies to quantify, report, and verify SOC changes [24]. However, predicting changes in soil carbon remains a significant challenge due to the inherent heterogeneity of soils and their complex interactions with environmental factors and land use [24]. Addressing these challenges requires comprehensive and integrated soil carbon modeling approaches to better quantify and manage soil carbon dynamics effectively.

Agricultural practices for soil carbon sequestration focus on minimizing carbon losses and increasing organic carbon inputs. Reduced tillage and no-till farming preserve soil structure and limit carbon loss [7,17]. Cover cropping with legumes or grasses protects soil from erosion and adds organic matter, while crop rotation improves soil biodiversity and nutrient cycling [24]. Organic amendments, such as compost or manure, directly increase SOC levels and microbial activity [23]. These practices not only enhance carbon sequestration but also improve soil fertility, productivity, and resilience to climate change.

2.2 Soil Organic Carbon Experimentation Data

The data for this study is derived from the Agricultural Collaborative Research Outcomes System (AgCROS), a repository available by the United States Department of Agriculture (USDA). The AgCROS dataset is provided in an Excel spreadsheet, which contains detailed information about various experimental fields. The spreadsheet contains multiple sheets, with most columns associated with contextual notes (an example contextual note in Fig. 1, with yellow background) which offer additional details, such as measurement scale and range. The dataset is structured around several key elements, as follows.

Experimental Unit (Subplot). It is the basic building block of data collection, organized in a hierarchical structure. Each experimental field is divided into blocks, which are further divided into plots, and then into subplots. The subplots serve as the experimental units where specific treatments are applied and observations are recorded. For example, Fig. 2 illustrates an experimental field in Mead, NE, showing how it is subdivided into these units.

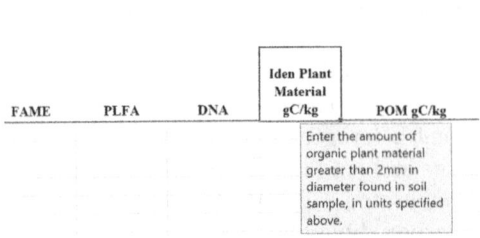
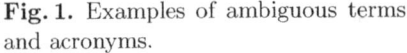
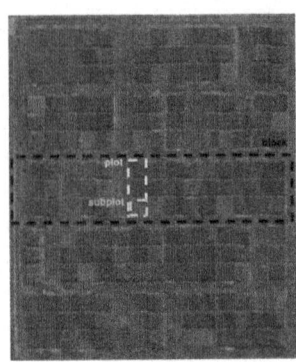

Fig. 1. Examples of ambiguous terms and acronyms.

Fig. 2. An experimental field in NE.

Treatment. It refers to the agricultural practices applied to the experimental units. These practices, designed to assess their effects on soil health and crop performance, include variations in nitrogen levels and crop rotations, accounting for both the crops used and the duration of the rotation cycles. For example, a treatment with the rotation "continuous corn" indicates that corn is the only crop grown in that treatment every year. In contrast, a rotation labeled "corn/soybean (2-yr)" signifies that corn is grown in the first year, followed by soybeans in the second year, and this pattern alternates annually, repeating in subsequent years. Nitrogen levels are categorized into three groups: 0, low, and high. However, the specific values for low and high nitrogen levels vary depending on the crop involved in the treatment. For example, for "corn" or "sorghum," low nitrogen is defined as 33 kg N/ha, and high nitrogen as 67 kg N/ha. For "soybean" or "oat+clover," the corresponding values are 90 kg N/ha and 180 kg N/ha.

Soil Sample. Soil samples were collected from various depths in each experimental unit, with each sample defined by its upper and lower depth boundaries. From a given soil sample, one, two or three types of measurements—physical, chemical, and biological—may be taken. However, the AgCROS dataset does not provide information to reflect whether these measurements were taken from the same sample or not. Therefore, a single soil sample in the real world may exist in SOCKG as one, two, or three samples, as follows. A *soil physical sample* is associated with measurements of structural properties of soil such as bulk density. A *soil chemical sample* includes measurements of attributes critical for understanding soil's chemical balance, such as pH and organic matter content. A *soil biological sample* captures information on microbial activity and other biological indicators that reflect soil health and its capacity for carbon sequestration.

The AgCROS dataset encompasses data collected over a span of up to 45 years from 4,220 experimental units distributed across 58 fields, 33 cities, and 20 states. It includes 37,214 soil physical samples, 77,167 soil chemical samples, and 19,572 soil biological samples collected from these experimental units.

3 Knowledge Graph Construction

This section outlines the creation of SOCKG, starting with data modeling and ontology development. We then describe how SOCKG was populated, integrated with NALT, and enriched with resolvable Uniform Resource Identifiers URIs[7], along with key statistics to highlight its scale and structure.

3.1 Data Modeling and Ontology Development

One of the first and most crucial steps in this work was designing the underlying structure of the knowledge graph, specifically the ontology. The ontology's development was informed by a comprehensive analysis of the dataset and carried out using the ontology editor Protégé [18]. We used fundamental Web Ontology Language (OWL)[8] constructs to define *classes*, *object properties*, and *data properties*. Furthermore, the ontology incorporated a specific RDFS relationship, rdfs:seeAlso, to support semantic mapping, as explained in Sect. 3.3. Figure 3 provides an overview of the SOCKG ontology, excluding data properties, with nodes in the depicted graph representing classes and edges representing object properties. The SOCKG ontology contains 46 classes, 64 object properties, and 590 data properties. Table 1 provides more detailed statistics, including the number of data instances for these concepts.

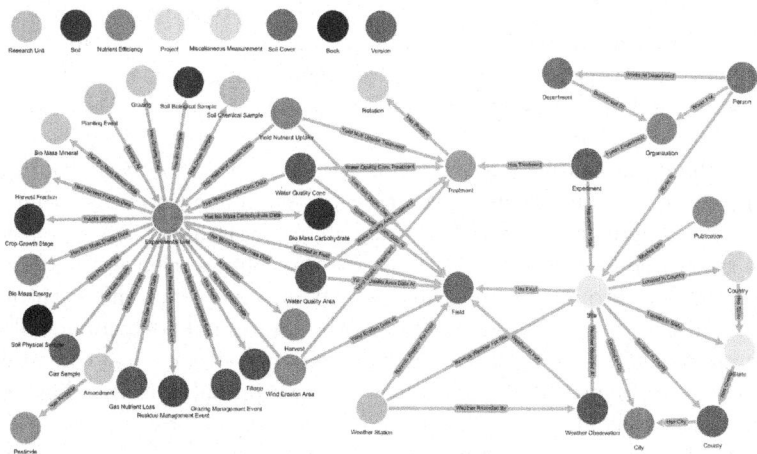

Fig. 3. The SOCKG ontology, depicting classes (nodes) and object properties (edges), excluding data properties. Some nodes (e.g., ResearchUnit) are disconnected due to missing semantic relationships, while synthetic classes (e.g., Version, for tracking dataset history) are inherently unconnected.

---

[7] https://www.rfc-editor.org/rfc/rfc3986.
[8] https://www.w3.org/TR/owl2-overview/.

The initial step was to identify the primary concepts represented in the data, which are incorporated into the ontology as classes. This process involved examining the dataset's structure, such as column names and their contextual notes in the AgCROS spreadsheet. For example, concepts such as "Site," "Field," "Experimental Unit," and "Treatment" emerged as foundational classes.

Table 1. Statistics of SOCKG

	# of types in ontology	# of types in data graph	# of instances
class	46	46	509,745
object property	64	53	738,114
data property	590	489	9,934,733

Once the main classes were established, data properties were derived by examining attributes that describe each class. Identifiers (e.g., "Site ID"), numerical metrics (e.g., "bulk density" and "electrical conductivity"), and descriptive attributes were systematically analyzed and assigned to their respective classes. Each data property has a *domain* and a *range*. The domain refers to the class that owns the data property. For example, bulkDensity_g_per_cm_cubed is a physical attribute of soil, hence its domain is SoilPhysicalSample. Conversely, the range defines the type of the data property. Each data property's range was determined by evaluating dataset values and formats. Text attributes (e.g., crop) were assigned xsd:string, while numerical values (e.g., bulkDensity_g_per_cm_cubed, elevation_m) were modeled as xsd:float or xsd:int, as appropriate.

Throughout the ontology development process, attention was given to accurately representing all aspects of the dataset, including attributes that lacked current data. There are cases where, while a column header defines a data property, no corresponding data records exist for the column. Hence, the data graph contains 489 data properties, compared to 590 data properties in the ontology, as shown in Table 1. In these cases, analysis of the contextual notes found within the dataset and consultation with domain scientists played a critical role in making educated assumptions about the data property's probable range. This ensured that the ontology could accommodate potential future data.

In addition to data properties, relationships between classes were modeled using object properties. The creation of object properties required an in-depth understanding of the dataset's inherent relationships, often necessitating collaboration with domain experts. For example, relationships between monitoring classes such as experimental units and the phenomena they observe (e.g., soil chemical attributes), were explicitly modeled to reflect their interdependence. One such example is the object property hasChemSample, which has a domain of ExperimentalUnit and a range of SoilChemicalSample, reflecting that an experimental unit observes a soil chemical sample. For this relationship,

A Knowledge Graph Informing Soil Carbon Modeling   233

ExperimentalUnit is the subject and SoilChemicalSample is the object. Listing 1.1 shows how SoilPhysicalSample, bulkDensity_g_per_cm_cubed, and hasChemSample are defined in the ontology using Turtle format.

```
@prefix sockg: <https://idir.uta.edu/sockg-ontology/docs/> .

###    https://idir.uta.edu/sockg-ontology/docs/SoilPhysicalSample
sockg:SoilPhysicalSample rdf:type owl:Class ;
    rdfs:comment 'Represents a sample of soil collected from a specific depth range encompassing
        various physical properties essential for agricultural analysis and land management.' ;
    rdfs:seeAlso <https://lod.nal.usda.gov/nalt/5142> .

###    https://idir.uta.edu/sockg-ontology/docs/bulkDensitySd_g_per_cm_cubed
sockg:bulkDensitySd_g_per_cm_cubed rdf:type owl:DatatypeProperty ;
    rdfs:domain sockg:SoilPhysicalSample ;
    rdfs:range xsd:float ;
    rdfs:seeAlso <https://lod.nal.usda.gov/nalt/20349> .

###    https://idir.uta.edu/sockg-ontology/docs/hasChemSample
sockg:hasChemSample rdf:type owl:ObjectProperty ;
    rdfs:domain sockg:ExperimentalUnit ;
    rdfs:range sockg:SoilChemicalSample .
```

Listing 1.1. Definitions of class SoilPhysicalSample, data property bulkDensity_g_per_cm_cubed, and object property hasChemSample.

The dataset's specialized nature necessitated an intricate naming convention. For clarity and consistency, class names were formatted in upper camel case (e.g., ExperimentalUnit), while data properties and object properties followed lower camel case (e.g., hasAmendment). Data properties that include units are formatted with the units separated by underscores (e.g., aboveGroundBiomass_kg_per_ha). To make the ontology accessible to all users, abbreviations and acronyms that are not universally recognized and unambiguous were avoided. For instance, acronyms such as "FAME," "PLFA," and "POM," seen in Fig. 1, were expanded to their full terms fattyAcidMethylEsters, phospholipidFattyAcids and particulateOrganicMatter_gC_per_kg, respectively. Similarly, ambiguous terms were clarified using contextual notes (cf. Section 2.2). For instance, the term "Iden Plant Material gC/kg", also in Fig. 1, was modeled as the data property organicPlantMaterial_gC_per_kg, reflecting the description provided in the contextual note. On the other hand, the term "DNA", as also seen in Fig. 1, is common knowledge; thus, it was simply modeled as the data property soilDna. These choices demonstrate the ontology's focus on clarity and minimizing potential confusion, ensuring that it remains intuitive and precise for all users.

An Example of Design Choices in Ontology Development. As described in Sect. 2.2, soil samples are used to measure various physical, chemical, and biological properties of soil within an experimental unit. These samples have attributes such as sample depth, which includes both upper and lower depth boundaries. Initially, we considered a design that defined the following classes: ExperimentalUnit, SoilSample, SoilPhysicalMeasure, SoilChemicalMeasure, and SoilBiologicalMeasure. Corresponding object properties included hasSample (linking ExperimentalUnit to SoilSample) and hasMeasure (linking SoilSample to one or more of SoilPhysicalMeasure, SoilChemicalMeasure, or SoilBiologicalMeasure). However, as mentioned earlier in Sect. 2.2, further analysis of the data and consultations with domain scientists revealed that the AgCROS dataset does not reflect, for instance, whether the SoilPhysicalMeasure and SoilChemicalMeasure recorded at the same depth and the same time from the same experimental unit were from the same real-world sample or not. To address this, we abandoned the design of the classes SoilSample, SoilPhysicalMeasure, SoilChemicalMeasure, and SoilBiologicalMeasure. Instead, we introduced distinct classes for each type of sample: SoilPhysicalSample, SoilChemicalSample, and SoilBiologicalSample. This approach avoids separate measure definitions by directly associating each sample type with the experimental unit through the object property hasSample.

3.2 Knowledge Graph Population

SOCKG is populated from the AgCROS spreadsheet through an automated two-step process. The first step involves preprocessing the spreadsheet and creating ontology mappings aligned with the data models. The second step focuses on formulating queries to construct SOCKG and storing it in graph databases (GraphDB and Neo4j in this study).

Data Preprocessing. The AgCROS spreadsheet includes domain-specific terminology, including chemical abbreviations and shortened terms that could be misinterpreted and cause confusion. To address this issue, a mappings dictionary was created to standardize the column names by mapping them to their corresponding terms in the ontology. This helps with querying the SOCKG, as described in Sect. 5, and exploring it via the dashboard described in Sect. 4. In addition to the mappings dictionary, we assign unique IDs (UIDs) to each row in *measurement* tabs. These UIDs are necessary because each data instance is inserted into the SOCKG based on a unique identifier. Using existing values from the AgCROS spreadsheet as UIDs is not feasible due to repeated values and inconsistencies across different tabs. To address this, we implemented a new column that concatenates multiple columns based on input from domain scientists. Lastly, we used the value "NaN" to represent missing values in the spreadsheet, distinguishing them from empty values denoted by "None". The distinction between empty and missing values is determined based on notes provided by domain scientists.

Data Loading. The data loading process consists of converting the processed data into a structured RDF file. To begin, the ontology is parsed using RDFlib[9], generating an RDF graph that contains the ontology's *classes*, *data properties*, and *object properties*. This graph provides the structure needed to build an RDF graph of the processed data. Next, entities are added by going through the ontology's classes and assigning their corresponding data properties. After the entities are added, object properties are added using a similar approach. Once the graph is built, it can be serialized into any RDF format, such as Turtle, N-Triples, or JSON-LD/XML, and then exported to a database such as Neo4j or GraphDB for analysis.

---

[9] https://github.com/RDFLib/rdflib.

3.3 NALT Integration and Accessibility

NALT Integration. Following the design of the ontology, we prioritized integrating the terms from our ontology with those in the National Agricultural Library Thesaurus (NALT), a widely recognized controlled vocabulary in agriculture developed and maintained by USDA. This integration is crucial for achieving interoperability, standardizing terminology, and enhancing compatibility with other datasets that reference NALT. The mapping process involved mostly manual curation to verify accuracy. The primary challenges involved addressing terms in the ontology that represented broader or combined concepts, which often did not align directly with individual NALT terms, thus preventing straightforward one-to-one mappings.

Approximately 61% of SOCKG's classes and properties have been aligned with NALT. For integration, we utilize the built-in `rdfs:seeAlso` annotation property in Protégé to provide supplementary links to related or equivalent concepts. For instance, the NALT term corresponding to the class `Treatment` is "experimental treatments", with the URI https://lod.nal.usda.gov/nalt/6148134. For our future work, we plan to utilize additional OWL constructs, such as `owl:equivalentClass` to establish precise equivalences between SOCKG ontology classes and NALT terms and `owl:equivalentProperty` to link equivalent properties between the ontology and NALT. This ongoing integration effort will lead to a strong foundation for improving data consistency across agricultural research platforms.

Resolvable URIs. To improve clarity, accessibility and interoperability, all classes, object properties and data properties in SOCKG ontology are made resolvable through URIs. These URIs enable users to retrieve detailed information about each entity and facilitate integration with external datasets. Designed for human readability, the URI structure follows the format https://idir.uta.edu/sockg-ontology/docs/conceptName, where conceptName can represent the name of a class, an object property, or a data property. These URIs are hosted on a managed publicly accessible server to ensure reliability and long-term availability. Users can access the resolvable pages via a browser, where they can view metadata such as descriptions, equivalent NALT terms, related object properties of each class, and the domain and range of each data property. Currently, only classes and properties have resolvable URIs, but work is in progress to extend this functionality to individual data instances.

4 Query Endpoints, Dashboard, and Data Cube

4.1 Query Endpoint

SOCKG is stored in two widely used graph databases—Neo4j and GraphDB—both with dedicated browsers for user access. GraphDB, a semantic graph database, supports RDF data and enables users to query using SPARQL, making it suitable for applications requiring complex semantic search and reasoning capabilities. Neo4j, on the other hand, is a property graph database optimized for highly connected data, allowing users to query through the Cypher query language, which is well-suited for traversing relationships in large networks.

The inherent complexity of the semantic web and the steep learning curve of SPARQL can limit access to semantic data, especially for users unfamiliar with query languages. To make SOCKG more accessible, we developed an interactive dashboard that simplifies data exploration and analysis.

4.2 Dashboard

The dashboard is built using the Streamlit framework[10], which provides a visual interface that abstracts the underlying complexity and organizes the knowledge graph into multiple pages, each dedicated to a specific data region. The following is an overview of the design and functionality of the dashboard's pages.

Experimental Unit Exploration. This page visualizes SOCKG data across the U.S. using a heat map, where darker colors indicate states with more experimental units. Users can apply filters (State, County, Site, Field) to refine their search. Clicking on an experimental unit shows its location on the map (if available) and a pie chart of soil sample counts (Fig. 4). Users can also view soil samples in a table and plot data from selected columns using customizable chart types (Fig. 5).

Treatment Exploration. This page helps users explore treatments using filters such as crop type and fertilizer type (organic, synthetic, etc.), as shown in Fig. 6. The search interface is designed according to the principles of a faceted interface [10]—whenever a value is chosen in a drop-down box, the available options in other drop-down boxes will be updated accordingly. Once a treatment is selected, all experimental units associated with that treatment are displayed, and the user can jump from current page to an experimental unit page by clicking.

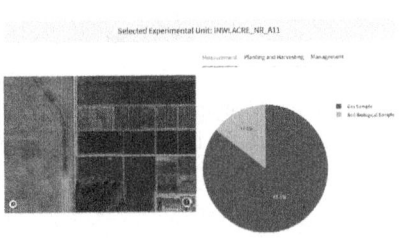

Fig. 4. Satellite image and pie chart displaying soil sample count of experimental unit INWLACRE_NR_A11.

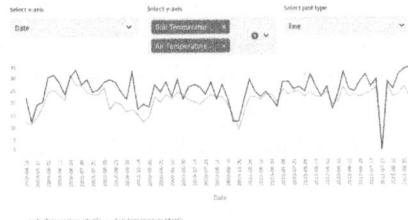

Fig. 5. A 2D line chart with the x-axis representing the dates and the y-axis representing soil temperature and air temperature (in degrees) collected from the experimental unit INWLACRE_NR_A11.

---

[10] https://streamlit.io/.

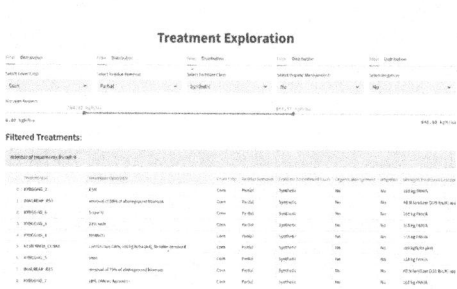
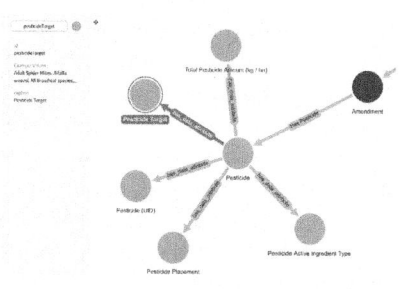

Fig. 6. Filtered treatments meeting criteria such as crop type (Corn), residue removal (Partial), and fertilizer class (Synthetic).

Fig. 7. Expanded Pesticide class with its corresponding data properties (e.g., pesticideTarget) and example property values (e.g., "Adult Spider Mites," "Alfalfa Weevil," and "All Broadleaf Species").

Ontology Exploration. This page (Fig. 3) offers users a visual overview of the SOCKG ontology. A user can click on any node to view the total number of instances in that class (e.g., 3,809 experimental units). By double clicking a class, the user can see its data properties, and by clicking an data property, they can view the corresponding sample values and data types (as shown in Fig. 7). The ontology explorer was also beneficial in validating the ontology in its development process, helping identify missing relationships and verifying the consistency of class relationships.

4.3 Data Cube

Motivation. While representing soil carbon data as a knowledge graph is essential for integrating it with the broader semantic web, addressing analytical questions from end users, such as *what is the influence of certain agricultural practices on soil health?*, is not inherently straightforward using data in RDF format due to several reasons. *First*, RDF stores data in triples, and queries are similar to graph traversal, meaning that execution time often correlates with the number of possible paths (both incoming and outgoing) from the current nodes. Unfortunately, SOCKG has a high degree of centralization on the Experimental Unit node (see Fig. 3). Analytical questions often require examining multiple experimental units and their measurements. This traversal is costly, as many experimental units have lifespans of up to 15 years and take multiple measurement samples at different depths daily, resulting in an enormous number of outgoing degrees. In our experiments, this traversal process took an average of around 15 s for such an analytical question. *Second*, RDF can be queried using standard query languages such as SPARQL. In practice, we found a simple question such as *What is the average SOC stock (kgC/ha) for 0–30* cm? would require around 45 lines of SPARQL code in its most compact form. The primary challenges stem from the need to derive analytical data through the aggregation of raw database records, as well as the reliance on implicit knowledge for calculations.

For instance, computing SOC stock (kgC/ha) requires applying formulas involving organic carbon content, bulk density, soil depth, and unit conversions (e.g., 1 ha = 10,000 m^2). Translating these calculations into SPARQL code involves multiple steps and intermediate results.

Given these challenges, we identified two key objectives: simplifying SPARQL query writing and minimizing response time for analytical questions. To address these, we utilize multidimensional data cubes [9] to model soil carbon questions, incorporating factors such as weather, soil management practices, and soil type, each represented as a dimension in the data cube.

Implementation. While tools like Apache Kylin[11] support both data cube modeling and precomputation, they are not a good fit for our use case. Kylin requires data to be structured in relational tables and, by default, precomputes the entire data cube. This approach is well-suited for industrial applications but is excessive for our needs. Fully precomputing the data cube would demand significant storage space, as the required storage grows exponentially with the number of dimensions. Therefore, our design seeks a balance between full precomputation, which is storage-intensive, and on-the-fly query processing, which requires noticeable CPU computation time. Therefore, we leverage the concept of the data cube to systematically structure such analytical questions. For example, a data cube for SOC treats soil organic carbon as the fact, with influencing factors as dimensions. The same approach applies to harvest yield or greenhouse gas emissions (with slightly adjusted dimensional tables). Once the data cube model is created, we can easily identify various analytical question instances at different granularity levels by examining the dimension tables. This allows us to precompute results for common queries and store them for later retrieval. The entire process is described below.

Dimension Value Selection. For each dimension table (e.g., time, location, management), we define a set of relevant values at a reasonable granularity based on domain scientists' input. For example, in the management dimension, the user might be interested in scenarios with no tillage or with disk tillage. This step involves the most manual work, as it is challenging to determine the optimal granularity and it is impossible to account for all possible values, especially for continuous dimensions such as time. However, it remains a trade-off between performance and completeness, as discussed earlier.

Combination Generation. Using the values identified for each dimension, we write a script to iterate over all possible combinations. This generates a list of all potential combinations of dimension values, with the option to include an empty value for each set. For example, a combination might be *no tillage, synthetic fertilizer, use irrigation*, corresponding to the question: *"What is the average SOC stock on experimental units with no tillage but irrigation?"* In practice, the combinations are more complex, as we have 9 dimension tables, each with about 3 attributes.

---

[11] https://kylin.apache.org/.

Pre-computation and Result Storage. Using the generated list of combinations, we insert them into a pre-defined SPARQL template to fetch the corresponding results. We then store all combination-result pairs in a NoSQL database, allowing for constant-time lookups during query time through our custom API.

Using the above pipeline, we implemented a test version with a simplified data cube design (i.e., using soil carbon stock as the fact) via FAST API. For this version, we limited the data included, and storing pre-computed data in a database showed minimal benefit, so we simplified the process. Currently, we provide a REST API that can be used by both end-users and dashboard developers, with dimensional values flattened into GET request parameters; an example is shown in Fig. 8. In the future, we aim to refine the data cube design and cache results in a NoSQL database.

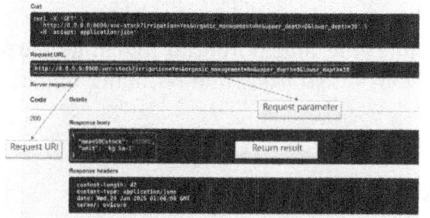

Fig. 8. Example usage of the data cube API to retrieve the average SOC stock for all experimental units where irrigation is applied, measured at a depth of 0–30 cm.

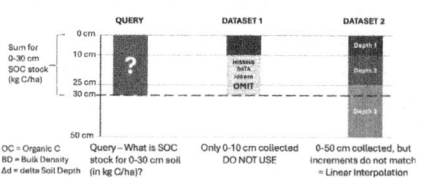

Fig. 9. An example of linear interpolation where the equation $\sum_i (OC_i \cdot BD_i \cdot \Delta SD \cdot 100)$ applies to layers between 0–30 cm.

5 Use Cases and Discussion

This section highlights how SOCKG can support scientists in answering their research questions through an illustrative query provided by the USDA soil scientists. This query was created to address vital SOC stock questions that allow for deeper understanding of how to increase crop productivity and decrease carbon within the atmosphere. The query seeks to determine *the average SOC stock (kgC/ha) for every treatment ID between 0–30* cm where *SOC stock (kgC/ha) = Organic C percentage (gC/kg soil) * Bulk Density(g soil/cm³) * ΔSoil Depth(cm) * 100*. Due to data variability, the query required handling several edge cases which, if unaddressed, could compromise the validity of the results. The most important case is the variability in parameters in data collections, such as depth, which are not always consistent. For example, some samples extend only 10 cm into the soil, or employ depth partitions that differ from other intervals such as 0–10 cm, 10–15 cm, and 15–30 cm. Thus, we must consider a few scenarios that require further calculation or filtering. Samples that do not reach the user-defined lower depth, 30 cm in this case, are filtered out of the results. Furthermore, if a sample's layers do not align with the 30 cm mark, linear interpolation is applied to the layer containing 30 cm to calculate the SOC stock (see Fig. 9 for details). According to the USDA soil scientists, obtaining valid results requires adherence to following standardized calculation procedure. First, the SOC stock for each layer within the 0–30 cm range must be calculated and summed across all layers in the same sample. The summed SOC stock values are then averaged across similar treatment IDs, fields, or other relevant groupings for analysis. Given the aforementioned query, these values will be averaged based on treatment IDs.

Upon completing this query, further analyses can be performed to extract meaningful insights—for example, ranking treatment IDs or methods based on their impact on increasing SOC stock in the soil. Through the integration and standardization of diverse data sources, SOCKG makes it possible to generate these queries and others of a similar nature, providing scientists and decision makers with accurate data and insights on soil carbon stocks, fluxes, and dynamics. SOCKG facilitates large-scale research to enhance carbon sequestration strategies and, through advanced querying and potential machine learning integration, improves predictions of soil carbon stocks while reducing uncertainties.

6 Conclusion and Future Work

We developed SOCKG, a semantic infrastructure designed to integrate and analyze diverse soil organic carbon data. By creating a robust ontological model and aligning it with the NALT, SOCKG ensures interoperability and consistent terminology across datasets. Implemented in GraphDB and Neo4j and complemented by an intuitive dashboard and a data cube, it enables advanced analyses, such as cross-field comparisons of soil carbon dynamics. SOCKG offers a resource for studying carbon sequestration and informing sustainable agricultural practices, with potential relevance for researchers, land managers, and policymakers. Future work includes expanding the dataset, enhancing analytical capabilities, and deepening integration with global agricultural research networks.

Acknowledgments. This material is based upon work supported by the National Science Foundation under Grants TIP-2333834.

References

1. Ahmed, M., Ali, S., Zahid, A., Ahmad, S., Yasin, N.A., Hayat, R.: Climate change and process-based soil modeling. In: Global Agricultural Production: Resilience to Climate Change, pp. 73–106. Springer (2023)
2. Barbato, C.T., Strong, A.L.: Farmer perspectives on carbon markets incentivizing agricultural soil carbon sequestration. Clim. Action **2**(1), 26 (2023)
3. Bralower, T., Bice, D.: Overview of the carbon cycle from a systems perspective (2016). https://www.e-education.psu.edu/earth103/node/1019. Accessed 5 Dec 2024

4. Buck, H.J., Palumbo-Compton, A.: Soil carbon sequestration as a climate strategy: what do farmers think? Biogeochemistry **161**(1), 59–70 (2022)
5. Dawes, A., McGeady, C., Majkut, J.: Voluntary carbon markets: a review of global initiatives and evolving models (2023). https://www.csis.org/analysis/voluntary-carbon-markets-review-global-initiatives-and-evolving-models. Accessed 5 Dec 2024
6. Fawzy, S., Osman, A.I., Doran, J., Rooney, D.W.: Strategies for mitigation of climate change: a review. Environ. Chem. Lett. **18**(6), 2069–2094 (2020). https://doi.org/10.1007/s10311-020-01059-w
7. Fazli, S., et al.: Cultivating climate resilience: hydrological shifts and agricultural strategies in California's central valley. In: AGU Fall Meeting Abstracts, vol. 2023, pp. H33I–1906 (2023)
8. Gomiero, T.: Soil degradation, land scarcity and food security: reviewing a complex challenge. Sustainability **8**(3), 281 (2016)
9. Gray, J., et al.: Data cube: a relational aggregation operator generalizing group-by, cross-tab, and sub-totals. Data Min. Knowl. Disc. **1**, 29–53 (1997)
10. Hearst, M.: Faceted metadata for information architecture and search. In: SIGCHI. New York, NY, USA (2007)
11. Isson, T.T., et al.: Evolution of the global carbon cycle and climate regulation on earth. Global Biogeochem. Cycles **34**(2) (2020)
12. Kane, D., Solutions, L.: Carbon sequestration potential on agricultural lands: a review of current science and available practices. National sustainable agriculture coalition breakthrough strategies and solutions, LLC pp. pp. 1–35 (2015)
13. Keenan, T., Williams, C.: The terrestrial carbon sink. Annu. Rev. Environ. Resour. **43**(1), 219–243 (2018)
14. Kibblewhite, M., Ritz, K., Swift, M.: Soil health in agricultural systems. Philos. Trans. R. Soc. B: Biol. Sci. **363**(1492), 685–701 (2008)
15. Lal, R.: Soil carbon sequestration impacts on global climate change and food security. Science **304**(5677), 1623–1627 (2004)
16. Luo, Z., Wang, E., Sun, O.J., Smith, C.J., Probert, M.E.: Modeling long-term soil carbon dynamics and sequestration potential in semi-arid agro-ecosystems. Agric. For. Meteorol. **151**(12), 1529–1544 (2011)
17. Mehra, P., et al.: A review of tillage practices and their potential to impact the soil carbon dynamics. Adv. Agron. **150**, 185–230 (2018)
18. Musen, M.A.: The protégé project: a look back and a look forward. AI Matters **1**(4), 4–12 (2015)
19. Nave, L., Johnson, K., van Ingen, C., Agarwal, D., Humphrey, M., Beekwilder, N.: International Soil Carbon Network (ISCN) Database v3-1. Technical report ISCN (2016)
20. Paustian, K., Lehmann, J., Ogle, S., Reay, D., Robertson, G.P., Smith, P.: Climate-smart soils. Nature **532**(7597), 49–57 (2016)
21. Riebeek, H.: The carbon cycle (2011). https://earthobservatory.nasa.gov/features/CarbonCycle. Accessed 5 Dec 2024
22. Rodrigues, C., Brito, L.M., Nunes, L.J.: Soil carbon sequestration in the context of climate change mitigation: a review. Soil Syst. **7**(3), 64 (2023)
23. Thangarajan, R., Bolan, N.S., Tian, G., Naidu, R., Kunhikrishnan, A.: Role of organic amendment application on greenhouse gas emission from soil. Sci. Total Environ. **465**, 72–96 (2013)
24. Zhang, K., Liu, Z., McCarl, B.A., Fei, C.J.: Enhancing agricultural soil carbon sequestration: a review with some research needs. Climate **12**(10), 151 (2024)

User Interface on the Web

HORIZON: A Classification and Comparison Framework for Pricing-Driven Feature Toggling

Alejandro García-Fernández[✉], José Antonio Parejo, and Antonio Ruiz-Cortés

SCORE Lab, I3US Institute, Universidad de Sevilla, Seville, Spain
{agarcia29,japarejo,aruiz}@us.es

Abstract. The rise of the Software as a Service (SaaS) paradigm has popularized subscription-based models, enabling user-specific customization but complicating the enforcement of pricing constraints across the codebase. Feature toggles are a common tool for managing dynamic behavior, but applying them to pricing-driven environments introduces new challenges that, among others, the vision of pricing-driven development and operation aims to address. While some studies have pointed out the lack of support in current industrial tools and the limited scope of academic proposals, the specific improvements needed to fully realize this vision remain unclear. To fill this gap, we present HORIZON, a framework for classifying and comparing feature toggling tools in pricing-driven contexts. By applying it to existing literature, the framework was able to highlight key strengths, weaknesses, and research opportunities, guiding the development of more robust solutions for pricing-aware SaaS.

Keywords: Web Engineering · iPricing · Software as a Service · Feature Toggling

1 Introduction

Software as a Service (SaaS) has gained widespread adoption [8], mainly due to its flexibility in meeting diverse user needs through subscription-based models. However, as pricing models evolve from offering a few configurations to thousands –e.g., Salesforce went from 10 in 2019 to over 13,000 in 2025 (source)– the development and operation of SaaS has become error-prone and time-consuming [3].

In this context, the vision of *Pricing-driven DevOps*[1] emerges, which proposes to turn pricings into software artifacts –referred to as iPricings– that can be leveraged to optimize, and even automate, tasks impacted by these structures.

Feature toggles, which allow dynamic behavior changes without modifying code [1], are a promising solution. Yet, due to pricing variability [3], their manual management becomes unwieldy. Although industrial tools exist, they are primarily built for A/B testing or canary releases, and are not well-suited for high-variability environments, such as those driven by pricing. This gap stems from

---
[1] For brevity, we may also refer to this concept as Pricing-driven SaaS DevOps.

the historical absence of standardized pricing metamodels [4], forcing providers to create ad-hoc solutions. Notably, the only approach supporting automated pricing-driven feature toggling –Pricing4SaaS [5]– has been validated exclusively in academic settings and for client-server architectures.

Hence, to guide future research and industrial efforts toward better support for feature toggling in pricing-driven scenarios, this paper introduces HORIZON: a framework for classifying and comparing feature toggling tools in pricing-driven environments. We apply it to extend the analysis in [3], which evaluated the level of support offered by 21 feature toggling tools for managing toggles in pricing-driven scenarios, by identifying the specific capabilities still missing in the most promising ones to achieve effective support.

The remainder of this paper is structured as follows: Sect. 2 presents the core concepts of pricings and feature toggles, and frames our contribution in the literature. Next, Sect. 3 introduces HORIZON and Sect. 4 demonstrates its application in assessing the capabilities of feature toggling tools within the context of pricing-driven DevOps. Finally, Sect. 5 showcases the conclusions.

2 Related Work: SaaS Pricing and Feature Toggles

A pricing is a part of a SaaS customer agreement [2]. It structures the *features* of a service –defined as the distinctive characteristics whose presence/absence may guide a user's decision towards a particular subscription– into *plans* and *add-ons* to control users' access to such features. While users can only subscribe to one of the available plans, they can subscribe to as many add-ons as they want, as long as they are available for the contracted plan.

Figure 1 represents an excerpt of the pricing of Zoom, a cloud-based video conferencing service that enables users to conduct virtual meetings.[2] In this example, nine features are managed through plans, one feature is associated with an add-on ("translated captions"), and one is governed by both ("phone

	BASIC FREE	PRO $15.99 per user/month	BUSINESS $21.99 per user/month	ADD-ONS
Max assistants per meeting	100	100	300	Huge meetings $50 / month
Max time per meeting	40 mins	30 hours	30 hours	
Recordings cloud storage	-	5 GB	5 GB	
Automated subtitles	✓	✓	✓	
Reports		✓	✓	Translated captions $5 / month
Voting in meetings		✓	✓	
Phone Dialing		Add-On	Add-On	
LTI integration			✓	Phone Dialing $100 / month
Administrator portal			✓	
End-to-end encryption	✓	✓	✓	
Chat support		If more than $50 invoiced	✓	

Fig. 1. Excerpt of Zoom's pricing with 11 features, three plans and three add-ons.

---

[2] Pricing entries that impose or extend limits on meetings are considered usage limits rather than individual features –the overarching feature in this case is "meetings".

dialing"). The pricing also enforces usage limits on the "meetings" feature (e.g., maximum assistants per meeting and maximum meeting duration) meaning that although the feature is available in all plans, the extent of their usage differs — higher-priced plans offer higher limits. The Pricing4SaaS metamodel represents one of the first generalized attempts to standardize pricings, defining them as combinations of plans and add-ons that regulate access to features whose usage may be limited by usage limits [4]. Its YAML-based serialization, Pricing2Yaml, laid the groundwork for Pricing-driven DevOps and thus iPricings.[3]

Building on this foundation, a recent large-scale study [3] modeled 162 pricings from 30 SaaS providers across multiple years, revealing that the configuration space –i.e., the number of possible subscriptions derivable from a pricing[4]– tends to grow exponentially over time, mainly due to the proliferation of add-ons. While this growth enhances customization, it also increases the complexity of development and operation tasks impacted by these structures.

Feature toggling —a technique for dynamically enabling or disabling features at runtime without altering the code— is a promising approach for managing such complexity [1]. In a nutshell, this behavior is implemented by using boolean expressions whose values can be assigned, or modified, at runtime, thus providing dynamic evaluations. Building on this concept, a widely recognized classification of feature toggles distinguishes a type known for its high dynamism and extended lifespan —namely, permission toggles [1]. In pricing-driven SaaS environments, permission toggles that are used to provide each user with a different configuration of the service at runtime according to their subscription have been referred to as pricing-driven feature toggles [3]. By mapping iPricings to these toggles, developers can serve multiple configurations within a single deployment, maximizing the benefits of multi-tenancy [7]. However, this flexibility introduces significant challenges, as each toggle increases service variability, thus complicating testing [9], and contributing to long-term technical debt [11].

Modern feature toggle management solutions address toggle complexity by externalizing their logic from application code into configurable systems, enabling dynamic evaluations through simple method calls (e.g., *isFeatureAvailable(featureId)*) based on runtime context. These tools typically redefine a *feature* as a toggleable unit governed by *rules* (the logic dictating whether the feature is enabled or not) that is evaluated against a given *context* (the data used to evaluate the rule, such as a user's plan or subscription) representing a user or *segment* (group of users that share a common context). However, as shown in [3], current solutions struggle to cope with the growing variability introduced by modern pricings, revealing a gap between pricing configurability and tool capabilities. While that study proposed a classification to assess the level of support offered by tools for pricing-driven feature toggling, it lacked actionable insights into the specific areas requiring improvement.

---

[3] You can find the Pricing2Yaml serialization of Zoom's pricing here.

[4] For instance, Zoom's configuration space is 20.

3 HORIZON: Guiding Pricing-Driven Solutions

As discussed in Sect. 2, current industrial tools struggle to manage the variability introduced by evolving SaaS pricings. None has yet reached full support for pricing-driven feature toggling, still relying on manual processes that become unsustainable as pricing complexity increases. To address this gap, we introduce HORIZON: a capability-based framework for classifying and comparing feature toggling tools in pricing-driven environments. It defines the functionalities of an ideal system that is able to provide automatic adaptation to pricing changes, organizing them into five functional areas:

Feature Management is the foundation of any toggling system, enabling external control over feature availability without modifying or redeploying the application. In pricing-driven contexts, however, traditional boolean toggles fall short. Instead, features must be evaluated dynamically through rules based on runtime data –such as subscription constraints or quotas– retrieved from external sources. To meet these requirements, HORIZON defines the following characteristics as required for an ideal pricing-driven feature toggling management system: i) feature CRUD operations, ii) rule CRUD operations, iii) feature dependency management, and iv) centralized feature management.

Evaluation Configuration focuses on defining the logic behind feature activation. Beyond supporting dynamic data, evaluation expressions must be flexible and expressive –handling multiple data types (e.g., boolean, numeric, text) and allowing logical operations to model complex pricing conditions effectively. The features required for achieving such expressiveness are: i) dynamic evaluation of features, ii) boolean, numeric and text values support, iii) dynamic context-aware evaluation, iv) dynamic context-aware evaluation, v) custom attributes for evaluations, and vi) complex logical evaluations.

Feature Evaluation defines the mechanisms for executing feature evaluations –referred to as queries–, enabling applications to determine whether a feature is available to a given user based on their subscription state –i.e., features within the subscription and current quota usage– without needing to manage the underlying evaluation logic. HORIZON defines the following capabilities for an ideal solution in this area: i) single feature evaluation, ii) multi-feature evaluation, iii) default values configuration, iv) standardized boolean results.

Integration concerns how applications interface with the feature toggling system. To ensure seamless adoption, evaluations should be abstracted behind simple calls (e.g., *isFeatureAvailable(featureId)*). To do so, HORIZON identifies two main approaches: SDK-based and API-based integration. SDKs enable in-context evaluations, with server-side implementations handling dynamic requests per user and client-side ones favoring cached results for single-user contexts. API-based integration, by contrast, offers a language-agnostic interface but requires secure handling of user and pricing data to prevent unauthorized access.

Pricing-Driven Automation is the defining capability of a pricing-driven toggling system. While previous areas enable effective manual management in pricing-aware environments, this one focuses on automating the creation and configuration of toggles based on a pricing model –such as Pricing2Yaml [4]. To fully support this approach, the system must: (i) support a formal pricing model; (ii) leverage it to automatically generate the corresponding toggles and evaluation rules; and (iii) enable hot context change management, allowing updates to take effect at runtime without requiring application redeployment –typically through custom event mechanisms.

This section has provided an overview of HORIZON by outlining its five functional areas and the core capabilities required for supporting pricing-driven feature toggling. However, due to space limitations, it does not delve into the specific evaluation criteria or detailed guidelines associated with each capability. Readers interested in a deeper understanding of the framework can refer to the technical report accompanying this article [6].

4 Validation of Feature Toggling Solutions

In this section, we aim to demonstrate the utility of HORIZON by applying it to the set of industrial feature toggling tools identified in [3] as having the potential to reach full support for pricing-driven feature toggling, along with the academic solution which indeed achieves it: Pricing4SaaS. Our objective is twofold. First, we aim to verify that our framework produces similar results to those reported in [3], thereby confirming that HORIZON serves as a refined, i.e. more granular, twin of the classification previously proposed. Second, we seek to point out the specific areas where industrial tools fall short in supporting pricing-driven feature toggling, a topic that was not addressed in the earlier study.

To perform the classification, several considerations were taken into account. First, if a solution includes a pricing, we selected the most comprehensive subscription available for that tool. Second, only features accessible through an SDK or an API were considered supported. The core results of our evaluation are summarized in Table 1, which captures the support provided by each solution across the HORIZON's capabilities.

This evaluation confirms that while existing industrial feature toggling tools are robust in addressing general toggling use cases, they are not inherently equipped to support the variability of pricing-driven environments out of the box. In particular, solutions such as Unleash, DevCycle, LaunchDarkly, and Togglz —originally designed to facilitate canary releases and A/B testing— often include functionalities that exceed the minimal requirements for pricing-driven scenarios, yet they fall short in several critical areas. For instance, many of these tools lack comprehensive support for multi-feature evaluation, or restrict logical evaluations to conjunctive (AND) operations. Although disjunctive logic (OR) can be simulated by applying De Morgan's laws [10], this approach complicates configuration, so it doesn't compensate for the absence of native support.

Focusing on each tool, Unleash is one of the most comprehensive solutions; however, it suffers from a significant drawback: features cannot be deleted via API or SDK —they can only be archived, with full deletion available solely through the UI. This limitation hinders the implementation of automated, pricing-driven generation of the toggling infrastructure, as features cannot be

Table 1. Comparison of feature toggling tools based on HORIZON capabilities.

HORIZON Capabilities	Unleash	DevCycle	LaunchDarkly	Togglz	Pricing4SaaS	HORIZON Capabilities	Unleash	DevCycle	LaunchDarkly	Togglz	Pricing4SaaS
Feature Management						**Feature Evaluation**					
Feature CREATE	✓	✓	✓	✓	✓	Single feature evaluation	✓	✓	✓	✓	✓
Feature READ	✓	✓	✓	✓	✓	Multi-feature evaluation	~	~	✓	✗	~
Feature UPDATE	✓	✓	✓	✓	✓	Default values support	✓	✓	✓	✗	✓
Feature DELETE	✗	✓	✓	✓	✓	Standardized boolean results	✓	✓	✓	✓	✓
Rule CREATE	✓	✗	✓	✓	✓	**Integration**					
Rule READ	✓	✗	✓	~	✓	Server SDK	✓	✓	✓	✓	✓
Rule UPDATE	✓	✗	✓	✓	✓	Client SDK	✓	✓	✓	✗	✓
Rule DELETE	✓	✗	✓	✓	✓	API-based integration	✓	✓	✓	✗	✗
Feature dependency management	✓	✗	✓	✗	~	Secure communication	~	✓	✓	✗	✓
Centralized feature management	✓	✓	✓	✓	✓	**Pricing-Driven Automation**					
Evaluation Configuration						Support of pricing model	✗	✗	✗	✗	✓
Dynamic feature evaluation	✓	✓	✓	✓	✓	Pricing-driven toggle generation	✗	✗	✗	✗	✓
Boolean value support	✗	✓	✗	✓	✓	Hot context change management	✓	✓	~	✗	✓
Numeric value support	✓	✓	✓	✓	✓						
Text value support	✓	✓	✓	✓	✓						
Context-aware evaluation	✓	✓	✓	✓	✓						
Custom attributes for evaluations	✓	✓	~	✓	✓						
Complex logical evaluations	~	~	~	✓	✓						

programmatically removed and re-created. Moreover, Unleash relies on string comparisons for boolean evaluations, which further complicates configuration. Similarly, DevCycle confines rule management to manual operations through its UI, precluding programmatic creation or modification of rules.

LaunchDarkly offers a competitive feature set but presents some limitations. Its boolean evaluations rely on string comparisons (as well as Unleash), and its custom context creation does not allow for defining fixed schemas —potentially leading to unpredictable behavior in dynamic environments (such as pricing-driven ones). Additionally, its hot context change management is indirect, requiring the development of custom analytics that must be tracked to trigger reloads. Even so, this solution meets all the essential requirements for initiating the implementation of pricing-driven support, as these shortcomings do not significantly hinder its overall viability for the task.

Togglz distinguishes itself with high programmability, permitting the implementation of custom activation strategies, i.e. rules. Yet, this flexibility comes at a cost: evaluation rules are embedded within strategy classes and lack centralized visibility, complicating management. Moreover, since features are defined within an enum, any configuration change necessitates a full application redeployment, making hot context change management impossible.

In contrast, the academic solution, Pricing4SaaS, fully satisfies the criteria outlined by HORIZON. It automates the generation of feature toggles from a pricing serialized in Pricing2Yaml (see Sect. 2) and supports hot context change management, because the evaluation engine reads the serialized pricing file on every evaluation —so any update to the file is automatically reflected without redeployment. Although it currently offers a limited set of SDKs (for React, Node, and Java) and does not integrate via API, Pricing4SaaS is purpose-built for pricing-driven feature toggling. Nonetheless, there remains room for improvement, such as enabling bulk evaluation of feature subsets and expanding dependency management between features beyond merely linking usage limits.

In summary, our evaluation validates the results of [3]. Although none of the industrial tools currently support pricing-driven feature toggling, they achieve the basics allowing dynamic and contextual evaluation of toggles –defined by "dynamic feature evaluation", "centralized feature management", "context-aware evaluations", and "single feature evaluations" features in HORIZON. With the exception of LaunchDarkly –which already provides all the essential functionalities to extend pricing-driven support– the remaining tools lack some key features that must be implemented before being adapted to pricing-driven environments. Therefore, our framework has not only identified these gaps but also specified the improvements needed to bridge them, confirming both the utility of HORIZON and its ability to serve as a benchmark for future development.

5 Conclusions and Future Work

In this paper, we introduced HORIZON—a capability-based framework for classifying and comparing the suitability of feature toggling tools for pricing-driven environments. By identifying functional gaps, HORIZON enables more precise assessments than previous approaches. An initial application to industrial tools confirms prior findings [3], highlighting LaunchDarkly as the only tool with the foundational capabilities for pricing-driven feature toggling automation.

Future work will focus on two key directions. First, we plan to apply HORIZON to a broader range of industrial tools and conduct real-world case studies to further leverage its practical applicability. Second, given that Unleash is an open-source solution and ranks as the second most promising tool for pricing-driven feature toggling in our evaluation, we intend to contribute to the project by developing an extension that implements the missing functionalities for pricing-driven automation. This contribution will serve as a stepping stone toward achieving full support for pricing-driven feature toggling in industrial systems.

As a final remark, it is important to recognize that although the concept of pricing traditionally connotes monetary values, the underlying mechanisms of pricing-driven feature toggling extend well beyond cost considerations. The auto-adaptability inherent in these methodologies provides a powerful framework not only for managing dynamic pricings, but also for handling variability in systems that must cater to diverse user segments. For example, the same feature toggling techniques used to adjust feature availability based on subscriptions can be employed to differentiate configurations for various organizational roles or user groups. In such cases, the pricing metaphor is applied without an associated price, leveraging a structured approach to variability and automated adaptation to deliver tailored experiences. This broader applicability underscores the versatility of pricing-driven approaches and highlights their potential to simplify the management of complex, multi-dimensional system configurations.

Acknowledgments. This work has been partially supported by grants PID2021-126227NB-C21, and PID2021-126227NB-C22 funded by MCIN/AEI/10.13039/501100 011033/FEDER and European Union "ERDF a way of making Europe"; and TED 2021-13102 3B-C21 and TED2021-131023B-C22 funded by MCIN/AEI/10.13039/ 501100011033 and European Union "NextGenerationEU"/PRTR.

References

1. Fowler, M.: Feature toggles (aka feature flags) (nd). https://martinfowler.com/articles/feature-toggles.html. Accessed Jan 2025
2. García, J.M., Martín-Díaz, O., Fernandez, P., Müller, C., Ruiz-Cortés, A.: A flexible billing life cycle for cloud services using augmented customer agreements. IEEE Access **9**, 44374–44389 (2021)
3. García-Fernández, A., Parejo, J.A., Cavero, F.J., Ruiz-Cortés, A.: Racing the market: an industry support analysis for pricing-driven devops in saas. In: International Conference on Service-Oriented Computing, pp. 260–275 (2024)
4. García-Fernández, A., Parejo, J.A., Ruiz-Cortés, A.: Pricing4SaaS: towards a pricing model to drive the operation of SaaS. In: Intelligent Information Systems, - CAiSE Forum, Proceedings. Lecture Notes in Business Information Processing, vol. 520, pp. 47–54 (2024)
5. García-Fernández, A., Parejo, J.A., Trinidad, P., Ruiz-Cortés, A.: Towards pricing4saas: a framework for pricing-driven feature toggling in saas. In: International Conference on Web Engineering, pp. 389–392 (2024)
6. García-Fernández, A., Parejo Maestre, J.A., Ruiz-Cortés, A.: Horizon: a classification and comparison framework for pricing-driven feature toggling – technical report (2025). https://doi.org/10.5281/zenodo.15189284
7. Ghaddar, A., Tamzalit, D., Assaf, A., Bitar, A.: Variability as a service: outsourcing variability management in multi-tenant saas applications. In: International Conference of Advanced Information Systems Engineering, pp. 175–189 (2012)
8. Jiang, Z., Sun, W., Tang, K., Snowdon, J., Zhang, X.: A pattern-based design approach for subscription management of software as a service. In: 2009 Congress on Services - I, pp. 678–685 (2009)
9. Rahman, M.T., Querel, L.P., Rigby, P.C., Adams, B.: Feature toggles: practitioner practices and a case study. In: Proceedings - 13th Working Conference on Mining Software Repositories, MSR 2016, pp. 201–211 (2016)
10. Rosen, K.H., Krithivasan, K.: Discrete Mathematics and Its Applications, vol. 6. McGraw-hill New York (1999)
11. Tërnava, X., Lesoil, L., Randrianaina, G.A., Khelladi, D.E., Acher, M.: On the interaction of feature toggles. In: Proceedings of the 16th International Working Conference on Variability Modelling of Software-Intensive Systems (2022)

From Mock-Ups to IFML-Like GUI Models: Using Large Language Models in Web Engineering

Atefeh Nirumand[1(✉)] and Jordi Cabot[1,2]

[1] Luxembourg Institute of Science and Technology, Esch-sur-Alzette, Luxembourg
{atefeh.nirumand,jordi.cabot}@list.lu
[2] University of Luxembourg, Esch-sur-Alzette, Luxembourg

Abstract. The development of web applications often requires the translation of design mock-ups into functional code, a process that is time-consuming and inaccessible to those without technical expertise. This research addresses this challenge by leveraging Large Language Models (LLMs) to automate the derivation of IFML-like Graphical User Interface (GUI) models from mock-up images. These models serve as a foundation for the validation and subsequent generation of web applications using available deterministic code-generators. By enhancing the BESSER low-code framework with this extension, we provide an advanced pipeline that integrates LLMs into model-driven web application development relying on the UML (for the structural models) and IFML (for the GUI ones) standards. Our LLM-based approach achieves high accuracy for both digital and hand-drawn mock-ups, demonstrates efficiency with rapid run-time performance, and delivers web pages that have a high structural similarity to their corresponding mock-ups. The complete infrastructure is available in an open-source repository.

Keywords: Large Language Models (LLMs) · IFML · Graphical User Interface (GUI) · Design-to-Code · Web Engineering

1 Introduction

Front-end development for software systems, including web applications, focuses on creating visually appealing and responsive GUIs. In the early stages, mock-ups are often used to clarify design intentions and validate these designs with stakeholders. Indeed, these mock-ups, ranging from low-fidelity wireframes to high-fidelity visuals, help ensure accurate implementation of UI elements [2, 19]. Tools like Figma allow mock-up creation and front-end code export (e.g., HTML) but lack flexibility for full-stack development, including back-end logic and data management. While technologies such as HTML, CSS, and JavaScript have evolved and become more user-friendly, they still require technical expertise to employ them to code front-ends, which is a challenge for individuals and small businesses lacking technical skills [10,22]. Additionally, the need for a back-end to handle data flow and logic further increases development complexity. Manual coding is error-prone, and template-based methods often lack the flexibility to address unique business needs [10].

Model-Driven Development (MDD) has emerged as a solution to the increasing complexity of software development, including web application development. This is achieved by utilizing standardized modelling languages such as the Interaction Flow Modelling Language (IFML) [16] to abstract UI design and functionality. IFML-based models visually represent UIs along with their navigation flows and interactions with business logic, enabling a structured, reusable framework. This reduces errors, automates repetitive tasks, improves development efficiency, and enhances flexibility. Moreover, low-code development, a style of MDD [4], simplifies the development workflows by combining visual design tools and pre-built generator/interpreter components, reducing the need for manual coding.

The research [10,11,20,22] identifies key areas for enhancing automatic website generation: converting screen captures into code, utilizing LLMs, creating multi-page websites, and enhancing scalability through back-end integration. Addressing these challenges can further democratize web development, enabling users of all skill levels to build complex applications. However, current solutions often prioritize direct sketch to front-end code generation via AI-based coding assistants, neglecting intermediate modeling representations such as IFML.

Neglecting intermediate modeling representations, such as IFML, can lead to several drawbacks, including lack of consistency, difficulty in maintaining and validating the code, and limited flexibility for scaling across different platforms. Using IFML helps address these problems. From the IFML models, deterministic code generators (or model interpreters) could derive the final application. In contrast to non-deterministic direct sketch-to-code approaches, in our approach, the final code does not need to be re-verified.

In this sense, our proposal aims to bring the best of both worlds: AI and MDD. We use AI for the sketch-to-modeling phase and MDD for the models-to-code one. For the AI phase, we rely on the last generation of LLMs and use prompt engineering [5,13] to maximize the accuracy of the results for this specific task. We have evaluated the approach using 100 case studies from the CodePen[1] repository, focusing on accuracy, flexibility, and run-time performance. In addition, we have integrated a Django-based CRUD application generator into the workflow. This generator translates extracted GUI models into functional web applications, adhering to Django best practices and supporting seamless front-end and back-end integration. Thanks to the generator, we can provide a full AI-enhanced model-driven pipeline for the generation of web applications from an initial set of mock-ups.

The rest of the paper is organized as follows: Sect. 2 details the proposed approach. Section 3 describes the tool support, while Sect. 4 presents the evaluation. Section 5 discusses limitations and threats. Section 6 reviews related work, and finally, Sect. 7 concludes the paper and highlights potential areas for future research.

---

[1] https://codepen.io/.

2 Approach Overview

This section presents an LLM-driven, low-code approach to automate the extraction of UML class diagrams and IFML-like GUI models from mock-up images. The versatility of LLMs enables processing diverse data inputs, making our approach adept at efficiently handling various UI mock-up contexts. The work focuses on two key aspects:

1. **Structural Model Extraction.** Utilizing LLM to derive Structural models (also known as domain models or data models) in the form of UML class diagrams from UI mock-ups. A Structural model is needed to derive functional GUIs capable of performing CRUD operations (Create, Read, Update, and Delete) on data (typically stored in a relational database). Instead of asking the designer to provide this model, we aim to infer it from the mock-up itself.
2. **GUI Model Extraction**: Utilizing LLM to produce IFML-like GUI models that: 1) depict the mock-up GUI structure and 2) are aligned with the Structural model obtained in the preceding step.

This is depicted in Fig. 1. As shown in the picture, once the models have been inferred, a Django [6] code generator uses them to create a fully functional CRUD web application. An extension for complex, multi-page applications is discussed in Sect. 2.3.

Note that our approach has been implemented on top of the BESSER low-code platform [1]. BESSER comes with a B-UML (standing for BESSER Universal Modeling Language) language with packages to represent UML class diagrams and IFML-like GUI models. BESSER is python-based and therefore Jinja is chosen as a template-engine for creating and executing the code generators. Technical details are available in Sect. 3.

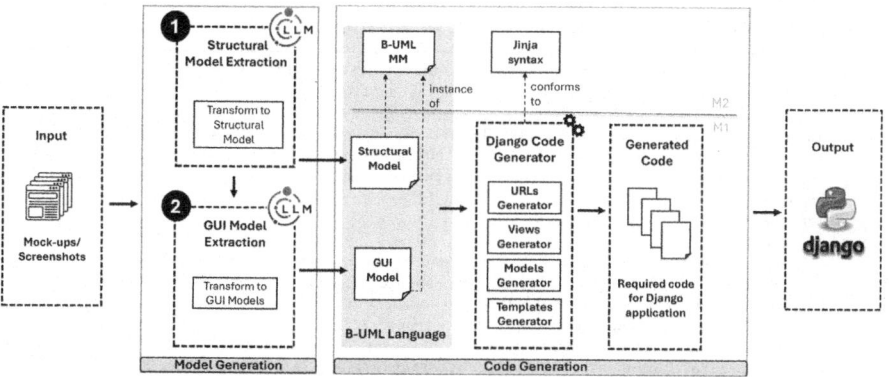

Fig. 1. Proposed Approach: Transforming UI Mock-Ups (Hand-Drawn or Digital) into IFML-like GUI Models with an Integrated Django Code Generation.

2.1 Structural Model Extraction

To extract Structural model, we ask the LLM to generate a PlantUML[2] description from the UI mock-ups passed as images to the LLM. As shown in Fig. 1, this method supports screenshots as input, extending applicability to web page captures. We have chosen PlantUML as it is a textual syntax, which is easier for LLMs to generate. Among the available textual syntaxes, PlantUML is assumed to be one of the most frequently encountered in LLM training data due to its popularity. Additionally, Conrardy and Cabot [7] have demonstrated that LLMs are able to provide correct PlantUML syntax from images.

To generate PlantUML descriptions, a task-specific prompt guides the LLM to ensure an accurate and valid generation of PlantUML text. As demonstrated in Listing 2.1, this prompt specifies how the UI elements identified by the LLM are translated into structured representations, effectively mapping each UI image to a corresponding PlantUML class. Multi-shot prompting was considered, but one-shot prompting proved highly effective and simpler. This process ensures alignment between the generated structural representations and the application design. An alternative is to have the designer provide the Structural model as a separate input, but this way we simplify the development flow.

The prompt outlines valid attribute types (*int, float, str, bool, time, date, datetime, timedelta*) aligned with BESSER's supported data types for mapping PlantUML to the Structural model. These types are assigned based on UI data components. Adherence to PlantUML syntax prevents errors like duplicate associations or invalid methods. Class relationships mirror logical UI connections, ensuring consistency and avoiding redundancy. The approach covers essential components (classes, attributes, relationships), and PlantUML descriptions map directly to BESSER's internal representation, available as an import option. Given a hand-drawn mock-up of a simplified library app with three pages (Fig. 2), the LLM generates a UML class diagram based on key entities like books, libraries, and authors. For brevity, we focus on the *Book* page. The structural model for this page is shown in Listing 2.2.

```
Task: Generate a PlantUML code that represents the Structural model of an application based
      on the provided UI image from one page of the application.

Description: You will receive a UI image that represents one page of a web application. Your
      goal is to analyze the provided UI image and use it to generate a PlantUML model that
      accurately represents the application's structure in a PlantUML file. Please note that
      each UI image corresponds to one class in PlantUML, representing a single page of the
      web app.
Instructions:
      1. You will be given an example UI image and its corresponding PlantUML code,
            demonstrating how each UI component maps to the application's structural model.
      2. Based on the provided UI image (and the example as guidance), generate a PlantUML
            file that represents the web page's structure.
      3. Ensure the generated PlantUML does not have any syntax errors.
      4. Make sure to consider the following attribute types: int, float, str, bool, time,
            date, datetime, and timedelta in resulting PlantUML code.
      5. Ensure that the PlantUML code does not contain methods within the class definition.
      6. Please ensure that buttons are not treated as attributes for any classes in the
            PlantUML code.
```

---

[2] https://plantuml.com/.

> 7. Ensure the generated PlantUML includes all relevant classes, attributes, and relationships between components, accurately reflecting the entire application's design as seen in the UI image.

Listing 2.1. Direct Prompt for Extracting PlantUML code from UI Mock-up.

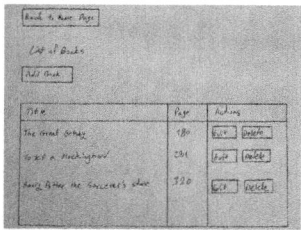

Fig. 2. UI Mock-Up for the *Book* Page in the Library Example.

```
# Classes
Book = Class(name="Book") # Other info omitted for brevity

# Book class attributes and methods
Book_pages: Property = Property(name="pages", type=IntegerType)
Book_title: Property = Property(name="title", type=StringType)
Book.attributes = {Book_pages, Book_title} # Other info omitted for brevity

# Relationships
writes: BinaryAssociation = BinaryAssociation(
    name="writes",
    ends={Property(name="Author", type=Author, multiplicity=Multiplicity(1,
        9999)), Property(name="Book", type=Book,
        multiplicity=Multiplicity(1, 1))
}) # Other info omitted for brevity

# Domain Model
domain_model = DomainModel(
    name="Domain Model",
    types={Library, Author, Book}, # Other info omitted for brevity
)
```

Listing 2.2. Code excerpt of the Structural Model.

2.2 GUI Model Extraction

After extracting the Structural model, the next phase focuses on deriving IFML-like GUI models from the images of UI mock-ups. Each mock-up is analyzed to generate a GUI model instantiating a simplified IFML metamodel.

Figure 3 presents a simplified excerpt of this metamodel, focusing on the GUI elements central to our analysis. The green metaclasses represent the structural metamodel of B-UML. The complete metamodel is available in our repository[3] Due to space limitations, a detailed explanation is omitted; for a comprehensive discussion, refer to our previous work [15].

Note that, as BESSER is in Python, the models follow the syntax of IFML-like GUI metamodel, serving as textual representations of the GUI model. These differ from plain Python code, like the Django code generated later.

---

[3] https://besser.readthedocs.io/en/latest/buml_language/model_types/gui.html

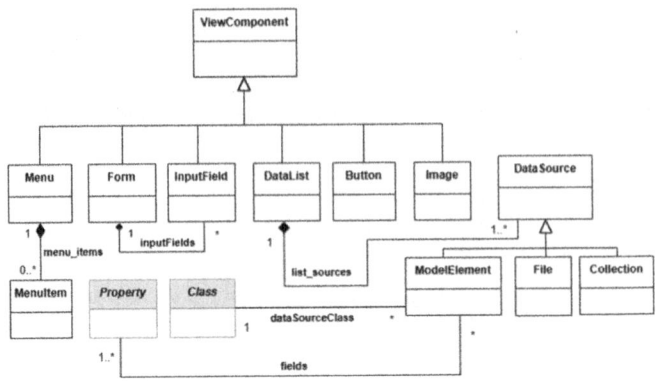

Fig. 3. Subset of the IFML-like GUI Metamodel.

A two-step methodology was employed for the GUI model extraction: Direct Prompting and Self-Improvement Prompting. As shown in Listing 2.3, in **Direct Prompting** step, the LLM generates the GUI model elements corresponding to the mock-up, ensuring alignment with both the Structural model and the IFML-like metamodel.

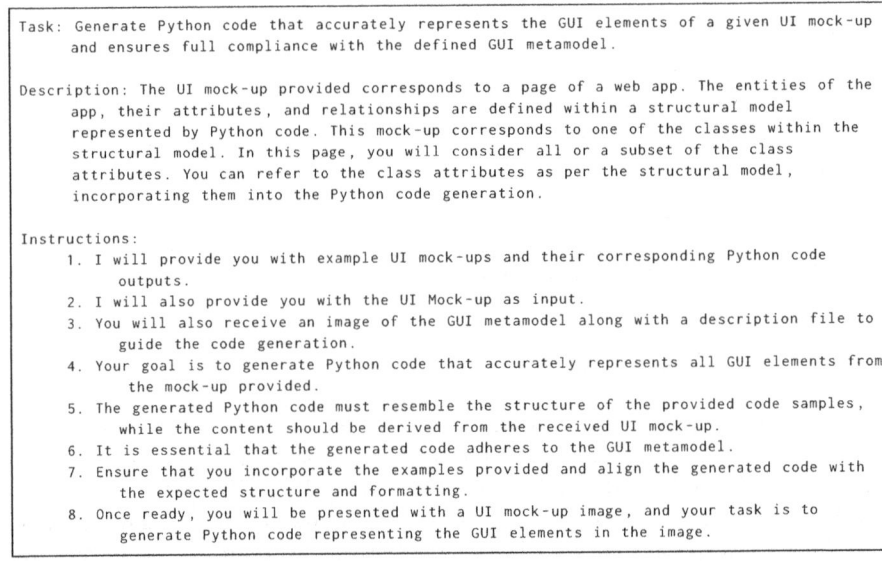

Listing 2.3. Direct Prompt for Extracting GUI Model from UI Mock-up.

The second step, the **Self-improvement Prompting** process is an iterative process, refining the generated code by comparing it to the mock-up and correcting inconsistencies. This process ensures alignment with the Structural model and removes unnecessary metaclasses. The number of iterations is predefined or determined dynamically based on thresholds such as achieving accurate mock-up reflection and eliminating redundant metamodel definitions. A fail-safe mechanism triggers if no improvement is detected for a fixed number of iterations or when the maximum iteration limit is reached. Listing 2.4 shows an excerpt of the GUI model for the *Book* page, including data sources, buttons, lists, and screens. The *BookListScreen* features a back button, an add button, and a book list, while the application *MyApp* organizes these elements within *MyModule*. Detailed instructions are available in our repository[4].

```
1  # DataSource for Book
2  datasource_book: ModelElement = ModelElement(
3      name="Book Data Source",
4      dataSourceClass=Book,
5      fields=[Book_title, Book_pages]
6  )
7
8  # Button for adding a book
9  addBookButton: Button = Button(...)   # Other info omitted for brevity
10
11 # Button for navigating back to the home page
12 backButton: Button = Button(...)   # Other info omitted for brevity
13
14 # List for displaying books with edit and delete actions
15 bookList: DataList = DataList(...)   # Other info omitted for brevity
16
17 # Screen for displaying the list of books
18 BookListScreen: Screen = Screen(
19     view_elements={backButton, addBookButton, bookList}  # Other info omitted
            for brevity
20 )
21
22 # Module definition
23 MyModule: Module = Module(
24     screens={BookListScreen}  # Other info omitted for brevity
25 )
26
27 # Application definition
28 MyApp: Application = Application(
29     name="Library Management",
30     modules={MyModule}  # Other info omitted for brevity
31 )
```

Listing 2.4. Code excerpt of the GUI Model (illustrating the *Book* page).

2.3 Multi-Page Web App Generation

So far, we have dealt with each page individually. This section proposes an extension that, given some additional navigational information in the mock-up, it manages to consolidate individual GUI models in a unified multi-page model representation.

The extension is based on a series of prompts that: 1) create a unified and consistent global model with all GUI models generated before, 2) refine the result, and 3) use additional graphical information from the mock-up to derive a navigation layout among the pages in the unified model.

In what follows, we detail each prompt. As shown in Listing 2.5, the **Direct Prompt** enables integration into a unified structure, ensuring consistent navigation, adherence to the GUI metamodel, and organizing screens within a single Python module for easy access and extensibility.

---

[4] https://github.com/BESSER-PEARL/BESSER.

```
Task: Generate Python code that represents the integration of GUI elements from multiple
      pages of a web application into a single GUI model.

Description: The GUI Python files that you will receive are related to different pages of a
      web application. Each Python file represents a specific page's GUI elements. This
      structure is defined in the structural model by Python code, representing the entities,
      their attributes, and the relationships between them. Your goal is to integrate these
      individual GUI models into a cohesive Python file that represents the entire web
      application's UI design elements. Ensure that the integration maintains consistency in
      design and functionality across the different pages.

Instructions:
      1. You will be provided with example GUI models for each page of the web application
         and its expected Python output for the whole of the application.
      2. You will also provide the GUI Python files that are related to different pages of a
         web application.
      3. Your task is to combine these individual GUI models into a single Python code
         representation that reflects the complete UI design of the application.
      4. The integrated code should ensure smooth navigation between the different pages and
         maintain a coherent user experience.
      5. The Python code should adhere to the GUI metamodel provided for the web application.
      6. Make sure to follow the design principles and layout specifications of each page
         while integrating them into the final GUI model.
      7. Consider one module for the app that has a 'screens' attribute including all screens
         of the app, similar to the style of the provided example.
```

Listing 2.5. Direct Prompt for integrating GUI models into a unified model.

To improve integration, we implemented a **Self-improvement Prompt** to refine the generated Python code. Similar to the process used for individual pages, this prompt ensures alignment between the combined GUI model and individual GUI models by guiding the removal of redundant elements and correcting inconsistencies. Detailed instructions are available in our repository[5]

Finally, to manage the navigation logic between web pages, a **Navigation Logic Prompt** was developed. As shown in Listing 2.6, this prompt guides the LLM to generate navigation flows using two inputs: 1) a plain text navigation order file specifying the screen sequence and 2) a simple image illustrating the navigation flow, where connections between screens are visually defined. This ensures accurate, consistent navigation logic in the generated code.

```
Please review the Python code below. You will receive a text file that specifies the order of
      pages. Please reorder the content based on the order specified in a text file, but in
      the reverse order compared to the provided sequence. You will receive an image
      illustrating the navigation flow between multiple screens of the web application.
      Complete the code by just specifying target screens for buttons with 'actionType=
      ButtonActionType.Navigate'. Focus solely on adding the target screen attribute for
      buttons with 'actionType=ButtonActionType.Navigate'. Once you've made the necessary
      additions, kindly respond with the updated version of the Python code.
```

Listing 2.6. Navigation Logic Prompt.

By combining these three prompts, direct integration, self-improvement, and navigation logic, our approach streamlines the generation of a complete GUI model from individual page representations, ensuring robustness and consistency in the resulting GUI model. The unified GUI model, along with the Structural model, was then used to generate Django code for the entire application, covering

---

[5] https://github.com/BESSER-PEARL/BESSER.

all three pages of the library example. The generated *Book* page, adhering to Django's default styling, is shown in Fig. 4.

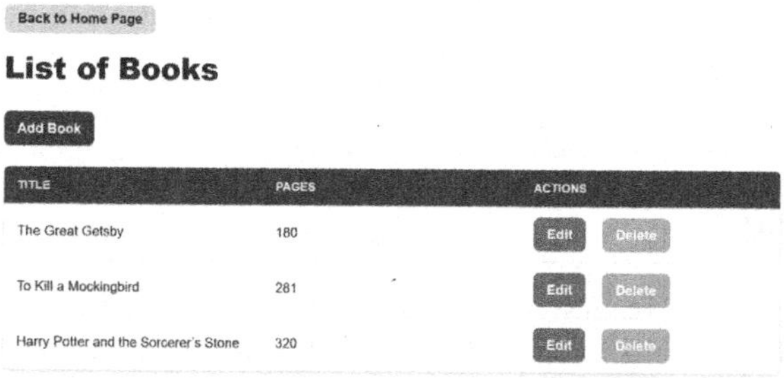

Fig. 4. Generated Web Page for the *Book* Page in the Library Example.

In the process of designing our prompts, we tested multiple styles (e.g., zero-shot, multi-shot, step-by-step) and selected the one that produced the most coherent outputs, strongest alignment with the LLM's training data, and most reliable performance. Our strategy incorporates best practices from OpenAI's prompt engineering guidelines[6] including role-based prompts, assistant-style examples, and structured output formatting.

To evaluate the fidelity of the generated web pages, we used an image similarity algorithm based on OpenAI's CLIP model. Both input and generated UI images were converted to grayscale, binarized to remove styling, and then encoded using CLIP's ViT-B/32 model. Cosine similarity between feature vectors quantified layout alignment. The model prioritizes structural layout over visual details like color, font, or size, aligning evaluation with our goal of generating functional, CRUD-optimized web pages rather than aesthetic replicas. Results showed 86% similarity for the *Library* page, 72% for the *Author* page, and 87% for the *Book* page, demonstrating the effectiveness of our approach. A more systematic evaluation, based on examples from the CodePen repository, is described in Sect. 4.

3 Tool Support

The full approach is implemented on top of the BESSER [1] platform, integrating MDD and AI for automating front-end and back-end generation with an IFML-like metamodel for GUI modeling. We use GPT-4o for prompt execution due to its high accuracy and ability to handle complex tasks like GUI modeling and back-end integration [17]. While other LLMs can be used, GPT-4o has shown the best performance in our tests, providing reliable and precise results.

---

[6] https://platform.openai.com/docs/guides/prompt-engineering/six-strategies-for-getting-better-results#six-strategies-for-getting-better-results.

Moreover, BESSER has also been enhanced with a Django code generator (with additional details available in our repository[7] that converts GUI and Structural models into functional web components, completing the full pipeline presented in this paper. The generator handles both back-end and front-end tasks, creating a database schema using Django's ORM for the back-end and building a responsive, CRUD GUI for the front-end. A similar approach could be adapted to other ecosystems.

4 Evaluation

We evaluate the effectiveness of the proposed approach for UI mock-ups into IFML-like GUI models, by answering the following research questions:

- **RQ1 (Accuracy)**: To what extent does the generated GUI model accurately represent the original mock-up?
- **RQ2 (Flexibility)**: Can the approach handle different UI mock-ups with different styles and complexities?
- **RQ3 (Run-time Performance)**: How efficient is the approach in processing mock-ups and generating GUI model?

To evaluate the approach, the CodePen repository was selected for its diverse real-world web pages. A total of 100 case studies (categorized in Sect. 4.2) were

Table 1. Accuracy Results of the approach applied to Digital UI mock-ups.

Feature (widget(s))	#GT	Approach		
		TP	FN	FP
Items	39	39	0	3
Menu	8	8	0	2
Button	223	213	10	2
Input Field	371	361	10	1
Form	59	59	0	0
Data List	42	41	1	0
Property*	144	144	0	0
Image	10	7	3	0
Total	896	872	24	8
Precision P = TP /(FP + TP)	99%			
Recall R = TP / (FN + TP)	97%			
F-measure = 2pr/(p+r)	98%			

Legend: GT: Ground Truth, TP: True positive, FP: False positive, FN: False negative
* This element pertains to the fields within each Data List.

---

[7] https://besser.readthedocs.io/en/latest/generators.html.

manually selected across 13 UI categories, ensuring a representative sample. Examples with overly simple layouts (e.g., plain text, no interactivity) were excluded, with preference given to pages featuring diverse UI elements (e.g., buttons, inputs) to reflect realistic interface complexity. Our experiments were conducted on a device with Windows 11 Enterprise, an Intel(R) Core(TM) i7-1280P 1.80 GHz CPU, and 32.0 GB RAM.

4.1 Accuracy (RQ1)

The approach supports both digital and hand-drawn mock-ups. Accuracy was assessed through precision, recall, and F-measure metrics, focusing on structural aspects of UI elements rather than layout details (e.g., colors, sizes).

Digital UI Mock-ups. A total of 100 CodePen case studies, each with a corresponding HTML file and UI image, were analyzed, achieving 99% precision, 92% recall, and 98% F-measure (see Table 1). The evaluation process involved manually reviewing each case study and comparing, for each one, the *ground truth* consisting of the UI elements in the original HTML files, with the UI model elements in the UI model extracted from the corresponding image. This analysis identified True Positives (correctly identified elements), False Positives (inaccurately extracted elements), and False Negatives (missed elements).

Hand-Drawn UI Mock-ups. For hand-drawn UI mock-ups, we created equivalent hand-drawn versions for 15 case studies selected from 13 categories (listed in Table 3) on CodePen. The same evaluation approach was applied to these images, and the results, presented in Table 2, demonstrate precision (98 %), recall (99%), and F-measure (98%).

These results demonstrated the efficacy of the approach in accurately extracting GUI models from both digital and hand-drawn mock-ups. To ensure replicability, we provide a package with 100 CodePen examples, their generated GUI models, and data from the hand-drawn evaluation[8].

4.2 Flexibility (RQ2)

The flexibility is assessed indirectly through precision measurement across 13 UI mock-up categories, reflecting various interaction types, complexity levels. These categories, created manually using relevant keywords from the CodePen search engine (since CodePen lacks categorization), encompass both application domains and distinct UI components. See the categories in Table 3. The quality results (see RQ1) were consistent across all categories.

---

[8] https://github.com/AtefehNirumandJazi/MockupsToGUI_Replicability/tree/main.

4.3 Run-Time Performance (RQ3)

The run-time performance of the approach was evaluated by measuring execution times for the two key phases: phase 1, Structural model extraction, which

Table 2. Accuracy results for approach applied to Hand-Drawn UI mock-ups.

Feature (widget(s))	#GT	Approach		
		TP	FN	FP
Menu	0	0	0	1
Button	13	13	0	0
Input Field	75	74	1	0
Form	12	11	1	0
Data List	3	3	0	0
Property*	9	9	0	0
Total	112	110	2	1
Precision P = TP /(FP + TP)	98%			
Recall R = TP / (FN + TP)	99%			
F-measure = 2pr/(p+r)	98%			

Legend: GT: Ground Truth, TP: True positive, FP: False positive, FN: False negative
* This element pertains to the fields within each Data List.

Table 3. Categories of UI Mock-ups

Row	Category	#Apps	Row	Category	#Apps
1	Social	6	8	Pet	7
2	Educational	19	9	Library	1
3	Media	3	10	E-commerce	3
4	Contact Manager	7	11	CRUD	17
5	Registration	9	12	Dashboard	5
6	Productivity	17	13	Authentication	2
7	Inventory	4	**Total Apps**		**100**

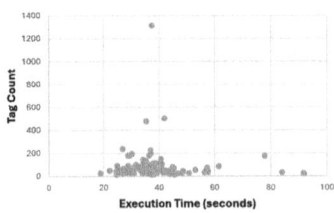

(a) Processing Time vs. Tag Count

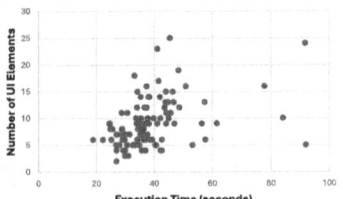

(b) Processing Time vs. Number of UI elements

Fig. 5. Scatter Plots of Processing Time vs. Tag Count and Number of UI elements: Evaluating across 100 Case Studies in the evaluation.

averaged 8.88 s, and phase 2, GUI model extraction, which averaged 27.85 s. The total average run-time was 36.96 s, reflecting the approach's efficiency in extracting GUI models from UI images.

As shown in Fig. 5, we analyzed the relationship between application size (measured by tag and UI elements) and processing time using 100 case studies. While larger models tend to take longer, the relationship is not strictly linear. For all case studies, processing time remains below 100 s, with a median of 36.52 s and an interquartile range of 9.89 s, indicating the method's efficiency and consistency.

5 Limitations and Threats to Validity

Limitations. While the proposed approach exhibits strong accuracy and flexibility in handling diverse UI mock-ups, it has notable limitations. It focuses primarily on identifying UI elements and does not account for design choices such as colors, sizes, text fonts, or other aesthetic features, which are crucial for user experience. Additionally, it does not address precise positional accuracy, spatial alignment, or hierarchical relationships between elements, leaving room for further refinement.

Threats to Validity. The reliability of the evaluation is contingent upon the quality of the dataset and the nuances of the implementation, with the results being influenced by the diversity of the datasets utilized. To address this, we employed CodePen, a well-recognized repository of diverse web mock-ups. A generalization issue persists, as the findings may not be applicable to unconventional designs or novel interaction paradigms. To mitigate this, we evaluated categories like social apps, e-commerce, productivity tools, educational apps, and CRUD applications, reflecting globally common web functionalities[9].

6 Related Work

This section reviews related studies pertinent to our research, grouped into different categories.

Model-Driven Approaches. Rivero et al. [18] pioneered a model-driven framework that translates mock-ups into UI models. Building on this work, Sinha and Karim [21] extended the paradigm by compiling mock-ups into flexible interfaces for various platforms. However, both approaches emphasize adaptability but lack focus on multi-page navigation and offer limited results by not relying on more powerful LLM-driven strategies as we do.

---

[9] https://www.similarweb.com/top-websites/.

Visual-to-Code Translation. Huang et al. [9] use Convolutional Neural Networks (CNNs) for visual-to-code translation, generating static layouts from visual inputs. Pix2code [3] combines CNNs and Long Short-Term Memory (LSTM) networks for visual-to-code translation, handling image processing and code generation. Liu et al. [14] have improved contextual accuracy using bidirectional sequential models. However, these methods do not address back-end integration or multi-page navigation nor use software models as intermediate representations. Kim et al. [12] and Yan et al. [24] employed deep learning algorithms for the identification of components in GUI images. They could serve as alternatives to LLM-driven strategies and be integrated into our model-driven pipeline if the primary LLM-based method fails for niche mock-ups. CNN-based approaches may be effective in specialized domains where training datasets are available.

Leveraging LLMs for Model Extraction. Conrardy and Cabot [7] demonstrate the versatility of LLMs in extracting UML-like models from hand-drawn class diagrams. In contrast, our work derives UML class diagrams and IFML-like GUI models from UI mock-ups for web application design.

Front-End Code Generation. Image2emmet [23] uses template matching and heuristic rules, while Ferreira et al. [8] applies machine learning for front-end code generation. Both lack back-end integration and a model-based approach. Similarly, Wan et al. [22] and Design2Code [20] highlight limitations in end-to-end design-to-code systems. Our work addresses these gaps in full-stack automation.

While existing methods focus on GUI model extraction and front-end code generation, our approach integrates structural models, GUI models, and navigation logic for a deterministic model-to-code generation once the models are automatically created leveragin LLMs. We believe this combination offers a better trade-off towards the semi-automatic development of maintainable web applications. Moreover, by leveraging a model-based approach, we can generate code for multiple platforms.

7 Conclusion and Future Work

This work proposes a novel approach, based on a combination of LLMs and MDD, to speed up the development of web applications. The proposed approach offers a scalable, low-code solution that streamlines workflows, reduces costs, and democratizes web development for users of varying expertise.

Future work includes refining prompt strategies for better alignment with different LLMs, particularly for multi-page applications. We plan to integrate complementary image-to-model techniques (e.g., for deployment models) and add a conversational interface for iterative refinement of prototypes. Additionally, we aim to explore how mock-up characteristics (e.g., clarity, fidelity) affect extraction accuracy and introduce additional evaluation metrics to assess the quality and similarity between mock-ups and generated models.

Acknowledgments. This research is supported by the Luxembourg National Research Fund (FNR) through the PEARL program under grant agreement 16544475.

References

1. Alfonso, I., et al: Building BESSER: an open-source low-code platform. In: International Conference on Business Process Modeling, Development and Support, pp. 203–212. Springer (2024)
2. Bajammal, M., Mazinanian, D., Mesbah, A.: Generating reusable web components from mockups. In: Proceedings of the 33rd ACM/IEEE International Conference on Automated Software Engineering, pp. 601–611. ACM (2018)
3. Beltramelli, T.: pix2code: generating code from a graphical user interface screenshot. In: Proceedings of the ACM SIGCHI Symposium on Engineering Interactive Computing Systems, pp. 1–6 (2018)
4. Cabot, J.: Positioning of the low-code movement within the field of model-driven engineering. In: Proceedings of the 23rd ACM/IEEE International Conference on Model Driven Engineering Languages and Systems: Companion Proceedings, pp. 1–3 (2020)
5. Chang, Y., et al.: A survey on evaluation of large language models. ACM Trans. Intell. Syst. Technol. **15**(3), 1–45 (2024)
6. Chen, S., Ahmmed, S., Lal, K., Deming, C.: Django web development framework: powering the modern web. Am. J. Trade Policy **7**(3), 99–106 (2020)
7. Conrardy, A., Cabot, J.: From image to UML: first results of image based UML diagram generation using LLMs. arXiv preprint arXiv:2404.11376 (2024)
8. Ferreira, J.S., Restivo, A., Ferreira, H.S.: Automatically generating websites from hand-drawn mockups. In: Proceedings of the 16th International Joint Conference on Computer Vision, Imaging and Computer Graphics Theory and Applications (2021)
9. Huang, R., Long, Y., Chen, X.: Automaticly generating web page from a mockup. In: SEKE, pp. 589–594 (2016)
10. Kaluarachchi, T., Wickramasinghe, M.: A systematic literature review on automatic website generation. J. Comput. Lang. **75**, 101202 (2023)
11. Kaluarachchi, T., Wickramasinghe, M.: WebDraw: a machine learning-driven tool for automatic website prototyping. Sci. Comput. Program. **233**, 103056 (2024)
12. Kim, B., Park, S., Won, T., Heo, J., Kim, B.: Deep-learning based web UI automatic programming. In: Proceedings of the 2018 Conference on Research in Adaptive and Convergent Systems, pp. 64–65 (2018)
13. Liu, P., Yuan, W., Fu, J., Jiang, Z., Hayashi, H., Neubig, G.: Pre-train, prompt, and predict: a systematic survey of prompting methods in natural language processing. ACM Comput. Surv. **55**(9), 1–35 (2023)
14. Liu, Y., Hu, Q., Shu, K.: Improving pix2code based bi-directional LSTM. In: 2018 IEEE International Conference on Automation, Electronics and Electrical Engineering (AUTEEE), pp. 220–223. IEEE (2018)
15. Nirumand Jazi, A., Alfonso, I., Cabot, J.: Low-code flutter application development solution. In: Proceedings of the ACM/IEEE 27th International Conference on Model Driven Engineering Languages and Systems, pp. 838–847 (2024)
16. OMG: O.M.G.: About interaction flow modeling language specification (2025). https://www.omg.org/spec/IFML

17. OpenAI: GPT-4O mini: advancing-efficient-intelligence (2025). https://openai.com/index/gpt-4o-mini-advancing-cost-efficient-intelligence/
18. Rivero, J.M., Rossi, G., Grigera, J., Burella, J., Luna, E.R., Gordillo, S.: From mockups to user interface models: an extensible model driven approach. In: Daniel, F., Facca, F.M. (eds.) ICWE 2010. LNCS, vol. 6385, pp. 13–24. Springer, Heidelberg (2010). https://doi.org/10.1007/978-3-642-16985-4_2
19. Samir, M., Elsayed, A., Marie, M.I.: A model for automatic code generation from high fidelity graphical user interface mockups using deep learning techniques. Int. J. Adv. Comput. Sci. Appl. **15**(3) (2024)
20. Si, C., Zhang, Y., Yang, Z., Liu, R., Yang, D.: Design2Code: how far are we from automating front-end engineering?. arXiv preprint arXiv:2403.03163 (2024)
21. Sinha, N., Karim, R.: Compiling mockups to flexible UIS. In: Proceedings of the 2013 9th Joint Meeting on Foundations of Software Engineering, pp. 312–322 (2013)
22. Wan, Y., et al.: Automatically generating UI code from screenshot: a divide-and-conquer-based approach. arXiv preprint arXiv:2406.16386 (2024)
23. Xu, Y., Bo, L., Sun, X., Li, B., Jiang, J., Zhou, W.: image2emmet: automatic code generation from web user interface image. J. Softw. Evol. Process **33**(8), e2369 (2021)
24. Yun, Y.S., Jung, J., Eun, S., So, S.S., Heo, J.: Detection of GUI elements on sketch images using object detector based on deep neural networks. In: Proceedings of the Sixth International Conference on Green and Human Information Technology: ICGHIT 2018, pp. 86–90. Springer (2019)

UIQLab: Automatic Web User Interface Assessment

Sebastian Heil[1](✉)[iD], Calvin Liusnando[2][iD], and Martin Gaedke[1][iD]

[1] Technische Universität Chemnitz, 09111 Chemnitz, Germany
{sebastian.heil,martin.gaedke}@informatik.tu-chemnitz.de
[2] Staffbase SE, 09111 Chemnitz, Germany

Abstract. Assessment of Web User Interfaces is an important activity for engineering usable frontends and guiding design decisions that can be automated to reduce expertise demands, costs and time. However, existing metrics and models are too scattered and prototypical to find wider adoption in industry practice and require consolidation. Even the most advanced assessment platforms are limited in their computational performance, handling of inputs and results, and extensibility. By applying Web Engineering knowledge and principles, we devise a novel web-based platform that provides unified access to state-of-the-art assessments and addresses the identified shortcomings of existing solutions. We address the technical challenges of improving the assessment performance and supporting extensibility to facilitate the integration of new assessment models. Our experiments with 14 assessment models in two different scenarios show that implementing such a platform is feasible and that the assessment performance for multiple assessments can be improved by more than 55% through shared preprocessing and parallel computation.

Keywords: Web User Interfaces · User Interface Quality · Automated Software Engineering · Human-centered AI

1 Introduction

Web User Interface (WUI) assessment is an important activity for engineering usable frontends and guiding design decisions. It serves as a foundation for a systematic approach of iteratively building, evaluating, and improving user interfaces of web applications, allowing to optimize them towards desired target characteristics in terms of aesthetics, complexity, and usability. Automatic approaches for WUI assessment [2,8,9,11,14] reduce the need for expensive and time-consuming empirical evaluations with human users. The automation allows for a high evaluation frequency and therefore for smaller increments being created more often, which is crucial when integrating with agile software development methods widely adopted for the creation of web applications. Various automatic approaches have been proposed to evaluate WUIs and, fueled by advances in Machine/Deep Learning, shown to be able to predict relevant characteristics [3,6–9,12].

Most of these proposed metrics and models, however, remain experimentally validated proofs of concept and automatic assessment of WUIs has yet to make the transfer from academia into industry practice [4]. The effort for practitioners to adopt the proposed automatic WUI assessment approaches in their development processes is high. Information about existing assessment possibilities is scattered in publications setting additional expertise requirements to employ them and the implementations are heterogeneous with regard to their technological platforms and maturity levels. This situation represents an obstacle for a wider adoption in the software industry, which has not received much attention in academia so far

Applying Web Engineering knowledge and principles, existing approaches can be consolidated into a web-based platform to lower the adoption barrier for industry practitioners. The benefits of such a platform lie in an improved guidance for selecting the suitable assessments and interpretation of results as well as in the convenience of a setup-free SaaS access to state-of-the-art WUI assessments. Even the most advanced assessment platform, AIM [17], so far has limitations in the ability to process multiple inputs, persistence of analysis results, computational performance, and extensibility, which impede wider adoption. Reduced costs spent on user evaluations, increased consistency, and a higher evaluation frequency facilitating iterative frontend development cycles are the potential outcomes of lowering the barrier of automatic WUI assessments.

The objective of this paper is to devise a novel web-based assessment platform that provides unified access to existing WUI metrics and models and addresses the identified shortcomings of existing solutions. We address the purpose of increasing the practicality of automatic WUI assessments by improving the performance of metrics computation and by enabling extensibility to facilitate the integration of new assessment models and propose solutions for each of the challenges. The platform architecture was implemented and put to test with existing automatic WUI assessments in two different experimental scenarios. To delimit our paper, our contributions are focused on the creation of the platform described above. Support for non-web user interfaces, definition of new metrics or the aggregation of assessment results into a single holistic value are out-of-scope. The remainder of this paper is structured as follows: in Sect. 2 we review existing automatic WUI assessment approaches and platforms and identify current shortcomings, in Sect. 3 we outline our solution architecture, in Sect. 4 we evaluate its computational performance, and Sect. 5 concludes this paper with an outlook on directions for future work.

2 Related Work

2.1 Automated Evaluation of User Interfaces

There is a wide range of methodologies and software tools based on quantitative metrics for evaluating various aspects of WUIs. They are characterized by their use of specific, measurable, and often empirically validated parameters to objectively evaluate a certain quality such as usability, aesthetics, accessibility, or visual complexity. To systematize the following overview, we structure the field in two orthogonal dimensions: by analysis input and result. *Static code analysis methods* [11,14,16] use the source code of the web user interface to calculate metrics related to layout and page structure, which enables prediction models for classification [11]. *Image-based analysis methods* [3,5,8,9,13,15,18,19] operationalize evaluation parameters based on the visual representation of the WUI – e.g. through screenshot analysis – using symbolic CV-based models or ML models. *Combined analysis methods* [2,14,21] process both code and visual information to compute the assessment. The analysis output and intended use of existing models for automated user interface evaluation is quite diverse. Some aim at providing a basis for classification ("good" vs "bad") [11] based on structural metrics like absolute numbers of words, links, fonts etc. and ratios of text/graphics.

Quantifying aesthetics is a major research focus in which various models [18,23,24] are based on the 14 fundamental measures introduced by Ngo et al. [16], representing the well-established Gestalt principles of design. Similar work [15] has introduced 8 aesthetics metrics taking into account psychological studies on perception. Image-based DNN-based models like Webthetics [8] have been shown to outperform previous models [12,18] in predicting subjective visual appeal ratings. The perceived colorfulness of a WUI [18] can be predicted based on a quantification of image colors in CIELab color space [10].

Predicting Subjective User Perceptions. Even ratings on custom subjective semantic differential scales can be predicted through NN-based models, allowing the application of Kansei Engineering to tailor WUI designs to achieve a set of desired target characteristics [2]. Depending on the availability of training data, both traditional NN-models based on features like compression rate and information entropy as well as DNNs operating directly on the raw image data of user interface screenshots can predict subjective user perceptions [3,5].

Complexity. Visual clutter is analyzed to reduce the cognitive load of users using metrics such as feature congestion, subband entropy [19], or edge density [13]. Similarly, assessment of visual complexity [14,21] aims at facilitating users' cognition of a WUI. The analysis result can be either a scalar value [21], or 3D representation of spatial complexity distribution similar to a heat map [14].

Saliency. Predicting the spatial distribution of saliency [6,7,9] allows to identify areas in the user interface which attract users' attention and models typically produce a heatmap as output.

While the various approaches for automated evaluation of UIs demonstrate a large potential to support UI/UX related Web Engineering activities, they remain isolated and not easily accessible for practicioners. The majority of metrics and models are research prototypes and making use of them in professional settings would require extensive search, understanding and technical setup efforts.

2.2 Multi-metric Approaches and UI Evaluation Platforms

Several assessment tools support a more comprehensive evaluation computing multiple UI metrics. While some focus on metrics from a single assessment scope like accessibility [20], or Aesthetics [23], there are also first attempts to consolidate assessments of usability, accessibility, aesthetics, and visual complexity in a single platform [1,17]. Web accessibility evaluation tools like WAVE [20] assess the accessibility of web user interfaces against guidelines such as WCAG or Sect. 508, typically providing summary reports as well as in-page highlighting of identified issues. QUESTIM (Quality Estimator using Metrics) [23] is a web-based tool allowing designers to define regions of interest in a user interface screenshot for which various aesthetics metrics are computed and represented using color gradients from green to red. Bakaev et al. proposed an integration platform architecture [1] for the assessment of web user interfaces which supports static code-based as well as image-based analysis models and integration of remote evaluation services, and collecting their results and allows designers to choose a subset of the available metrics for the current assessment.

The **Aalto Interface Metrics Service (AIM)**[1] [17] is the most comprehensive web-based UI evaluation platform available. It features 26 empirically validated assessments selectable by the user across 4 categories: 1 metric accessibility, 1 metric for aesthetics, 12 metrics for color perception, and 12 for perceptual fluency. The main assessment focus is on visual characteristics. Results are presented along explanations of the chosen metrics and an indication of the strength of empirical evidence for its predictive power. However, AIM exhibits some limitations with regard to handling multiple inputs, persistence of analysis results, computational performance, and extensibility, which we consider an impediment for wider adoption. It does not support running assessment of a selection of metrics on several inputs at once, which makes analysis of larger web systems and comparative analysis (cf. split testing) tedious. Once computed, assessment results are not persistently saved, requiring repeated execution for later review and causing efforts for sharing of results with other team members, who have to manually provide the same inputs, select the same metrics and wait for the computation again. The assessment performance is limited by sequential execution of the selected metrics. Performance deficits further stem from redundancies in preprocessing (e.g. CIELab color space conversion), except image segmentation, when several selected metrics repeatedly perform the same preprocessing tasks. While AIM supports extension, adding new metrics is not possible without changing the source code and re-deploying the platform.

In the following section, we therefore introduce a novel assessment platform for web user interfaces and apply Web Engineering principles and techniques to address the limitations prevalent in existing solutions, contributing to move the field of automated UI evaluation one step closer to a wider adoption.

---

[1] https://interfacemetrics.aalto.fi.

3 The UIQLab Platform

In this section, we present our solution to empower Web Engineers to automatically assess the quality of user interfaces of the web systems they build. To that end, we propose a novel software architecture – UIQLab– that addresses shortcomings of existing platforms with regard to handling several inputs, persistence of analysis results, performance, and the ability to extend the scope of the available assessment. Note that for brevity, we use the term metrics for WUI metrics and assessment models together.

Figure 1 provides an overview of the main components of the UIQLab platform and their interactions with each other. The Frontend is managed by the Frontend Controller and consists of three main components: Assessment UI, Results Dashboard, and Extension UI. The Assessment UI allows Web Engineers to specify multiple inputs, either by specifying URLs or via upload of their screenshots or source code. Available metrics are listed along with explanatory information and can be selected in arbitrary combinations to create an assessment request. The Web Engineer is then re-directed to the Results Dashboard, which asynchronously displays the analysis results as they are becoming available from the server, so that results of fast computations are displayed first and long-running ones later. The dashboard visualizes the results Employing a community-driven approach, new metrics can be proposed via the Extension UI by specifying their dependencies and metadata and uploading their implementations. These extension requests need to be approved by platform administrators to complete the integration in UIQLab. All frontend components implement a *guided interaction* pattern, leading platform users through the necessary steps.

In the Backend, assessment and extension requests are handled by the Backend Controller via a REST interface. It invokes the Metrics Evaluator to process assessment requests, which invokes the Preprocessor for the selected metrics. To enable the asynchronous display of results in the Results Dashboard, the Backend Controller immediately returns a response containing the identifier and type (URL, PNG, or HTML) of each WUI requested, and a unique URL as persistent identifier for the assessment results. This enables Web Engineers to share results of previously run assessments with other team members. The conceptual details of the Metrics Evaluator and Preprocessor as well as of the metrics programming model are described in Sect. 3.1, 3.2, and 3.3 respectively.

Our proposed approach comprises solutions to three main challenges in the context of a web-based platform for automatic WUI assessment:

1. the asynchronous parallel execution of selected metrics,
2. the specification and resolution of preprocessing dependencies shared across metrics, and
3. the extension of the platform by new metrics.

The following subsections detail our solutions to these three challenges. While the proposed UIQLab architecture is technology-agnostic, our proof-of-concept implementation is based on python due to its wide support for computer vision and machine learning models employed in automated user interface assessment.

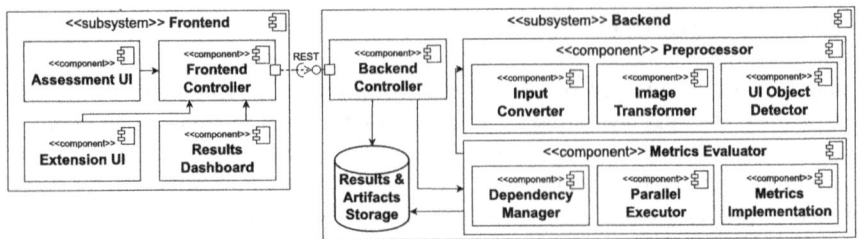

Fig. 1. Main Components and Interactions of the UIQLab platform.

3.1 Parallel Computation of Selected Metrics

Incoming assessment request are handled by the `Metrics Evaluator`. This comprises loading the metrics and executing them in parallel. In the following, we outline these two steps and further detail metrics implementations.

Metrics Loading. First, the Metrics Evaluator invokes the `Dependency Manager`. It has two responsibilities: 1) to dynamically load the implementations of the selected metrics, and 2) to request the necessary preprocessing tasks from the Preprocessor as in Sect. 3.2. Dynamic loading of metrics is implemented as a lookup of the metric identifier in the metrics directory on the file system and supported through python importlib, allowing to import modules at runtime. Software dependencies are available a-priori as their installation is handled via the package manager (pip) when new metrics are accepted, cf. Sect. 3.3.

Metrics Computation. The control flow then is passed to the `Parallel executor`. Process-based parallelism is used, where multiple processes execute the assessment tasks concurrently. This approach leverages multicore CPUs, avoiding the bottlenecks of thread-based parallelism, which shares a single memory space and is constrained by mechanisms like Python's Global Interpreter Lock, making it less suitable for the resource-intensive metrics computations. For each metric, a dedicated runner process is created and executed simultaneously to the others. The implementation uses a process pooling from the Pathos library due to its advanced serialization support for complex python objects such as the Pillow image objects resulting from image transformations. Once a computation completes, the result is stored in the results & artifacts storage, which supports both structured results like single or multiple numerical values as well as binary artifacts such as PNG files containing a heatmap as shown in Fig. 2.

Metrics Implementations. The actual computations are defined through the metrics implementations, which are adhering to the interface specified in 3.3. As a proof of concept, we implemented 14 metrics from literature aiming to cover the range of input types, output types, methods and foci described in Sect. 2. This selection does not claim quality or utility of the models. Table 1 provides an overview of these 14 metrics. **PNG file size** is the numerical value representing the size of a WUI screenshot image in bytes in PNG format with 24 bits per pixel, RGB color space. It is used for the analysis of visual complexity and aesthetics

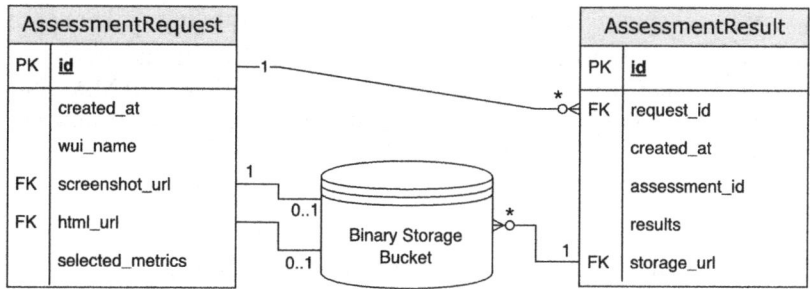

Fig. 2. Assessment Requests and Results Data Model.

[5,15]. **JPEG file size and compression ratio** are derived from converting a WUI screenshot to JPEG (24 bits/pixel, RGB, Quality 0.8) and represented as a two-component vector, typically used for visual complexity and aesthetics [5,15]. **Colorfulness** is computed as scalar used in aesthetics analysis and computed taking into account the standard deviation and average range of colors in the RGB channel [10]. **CIELAB color average & standard deviation** similarly considers the color distribution in CIELAB space and is an example of a metric requiring an image transformation as pre-processing and producing a 6-tuple of 2 values per each of the three space dimensions. **Whitespace ratio** is computed as the share of white space of the overall screen estate of a WUI screenshot, used for aesthetics assessment [15]. It has a complex preprocessing dependency as it requires prior UI Object detection. Our implementation of this metric was adapted from AIM [17]. **UI Interpretation** is an example of a complex DNN-based assessment employing the UIED model [22]. It results in a JSON representing the identified bounding boxes and labels. **UMSI (Unified Model of Saliency and Importance)** is a predictive model of visual importance based on deep learning. It produces an image representing the heatmap of saliency and an overlaid version of the WUI screenshot. [9] **Word count** is a scalar value representing the number of visible words in the WUI, taking the DOM as input and is used as a predictive model for website ratings [11]. **Edge density** is a computer-vision based metric computed as the percentage of edge pixels in the WUI screenshot implemented as a Canny edge detector on grayscale images and used to assess visual complexity [13,19]. **Feature congestion** as measure of visual clutter [19] requires CIELAB conversion as preprocessing and is an example of an assessment producing two different types of result: a scalar representing the feature congestion value and an image visualizing the spattial distribution. Our implementation is adapted from AIM [17]. **Subband entropy** is a similar metric for visual clutter [19] based on computation of entropy in CIELAB color space, but producing only a single scalar value. **Shannon's information entropy** quantifies the amount of information in the WUI agnostic of colors, which requires grayscale conversion as preprocessing and resulting in a single numerical value. It is used for the assessment of subjective orderliness and aesthetics [5]. **Accessibility Analysis** is an assessment based

on the aXe accessibility checking engine operating on HTML input. It produces the number of violations found and a structured JSON output detailing these and was implemented using the selenium-axe-python library. **NIMA (Neural IMage Assessment)** uses a CNN to predict the distribution of human opinion scores of a WUI screenshot. It results in the numerical NIMA mean score, and the NIMA standard deviation score and was adapted from [17].

Table 1. Characteristics of proof-of-concept metrics

ID	Short Name	Input	Output	Preprocessing
01	PNG Size	Image	Numerical	N/A
02	JPEG Size/Compr.	Image	Vector	Format
03	Colorfulness	Image	Numerical	N/A
04	Color AVG/STD	Image	Vector	CIELAB
05	Whitespace	Image	Numerical	Object Detection
06	UI Interpretation	Image	JSON	N/A
07	UMSI	Image	Binary	N/A
08	Word Count	HTML	Numerical	DOM
09	Edges	Image	Numerical, Binary	Grayscale
10	Congestion	Image	Numerical, Binary	CIELAB
11	Subband Entropy	Image	Numerical	CIELAB
12	Shannon Entropy	Image	Numerical	Grayscale
13	Accessibility	HTML	JSON	N/A
14	NIMA	Image	Vector	N/A

3.2 Metrics Preprocessing Dependencies

In this subsection, we outline our concept of handling required preprocessing steps for the computation of selected metrics and improving assessment performance by avoiding redundant computations, and the currently available prepossessing components within the `Preprocessor`.

Resolving Metrics Preprocessing Dependencies. To improve efficiency of assessments, we propose to split computations into preprocessing tasks and the actual metrics. In this way, redundant computations can be reduced when several metrics share the same preprocessing requirements. Thus, the `Dependency Manager` identifies for each metric selected by the user the required preprocessing tasks in the metric's configuration (cf. 3.3). The tasks are added to a shared set of preprocessing for all selected metrics. Each preprocessing task in that set is executed only once, with the results shared to any metric implementation requiring them. UIQLab supports the most common preprocessing tasks used in automated WUI assessment models. Currently, this comprises of screenshot capture, dom analysis, image transformations and UI object detection.

Input Preprocessing Tasks. For user-provided inputs of type URL or HTML and selected metrics based on image analysis, the `Input Converter` supports automatic screenshot capture, following the W3C's recommendation[2] using Selenium WebDriver. After the `document.readyState ==="complete"` signal, it waits for an additional 5 s to balance a high probability of a completely rendered screenshot[3] and preventing excessive delays. In the same way, URL and HTML inputs for metrics requiring DOM access [14] are supported through DOM preprocessing. Screenshots are available as PNG, RGB color space, 2400 × 2400 px (window size = 1200 × 1200 px, device pixel ratio = 2) to accomodate even complex CV methods.

Image Preprocessing Tasks. Image-based analysis methods (cf. 2.1) often require image transformations to be applied before they can be computed. This comprises conversion to grayscale [1, 5, 13, 18, 19], image format conversions (e.g. to JPEG) [1, 3, 5, 15, 19, 21], color space conversion (e.g. to CIELAB) [10, 18, 19] or image segmentation [21]/UI object detection [1, 7, 16]. Basic image transformations are performed by the `Image Transformer` using the CV libraries Pillow, OpenCV and scikit-image. UI object detection is provided by the `UI Object Detector`, implementing a version of UIED [22] adapted for Tesseract OCR and producing a list of bounding boxes and labels.

3.3 Extensible Metrics Interface

As the field of automated assessment of web user interfaces is rapidly evolving, it is important that the platform supports adding new assessment models. The architecture of UIQLab addresses this non-functional extensibility requirement through the specification of a metrics interface, the metrics metadata schema, and the extension process described in the following.

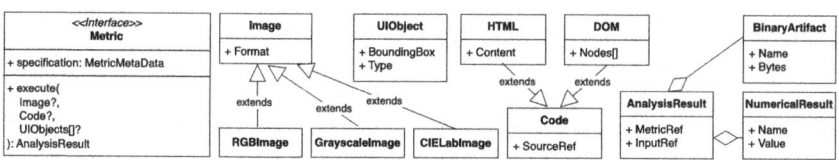

Fig. 3. Extensible Metrics Interface.

Metrics Interface. In order to allow the execution of assessment models, their implementations must implement the UIQLab metrics interface shown in Fig. 3.

---
[2] cf. https://www.w3.org/TR/webdriver1/.
[3] average load time on desktop is 2.5 s, cf. https://www.tooltester.com/en/blog/website-loading-time-statistics/.

It requires the availability of a class method `execute` which is invoked when the assessment is run by the Parallel executor. The input parameters represent the different types of inputs supported by UIQLab: images in different formats and color spaces, the static HTML code, DOM or UI objects.

Metrics Metadata Scheme. All metrics must provide a metadata description containing the information necessary for supporting an informed choice and interpretation of results for the user, and for the technical handling of inputs, preprocessing and outputs. These descriptions are represented as JSON following the UIQLab metadata scheme as in Table 2.

Table 2. Metrics Metadata Scheme Properties

Field	Explanation
Name	Name of the metric
Description	Brief description to display to users
Input	Array of accepted input types, e.g. `url`,`html`,`png`, ...
Preprocessing	Array of required preprocessing identifiers, e.g. `grayscale`,`dom`,`cielab`, ...
References	Array of references to related scientific publications
Results	Array of results descriptions consisting of name, type and explanation for interpretation

Extension Process. To add new metrics to the plattform, the following extension process is defined. 1) The implementation needs to be prepared, adhering to the interface described above and described according to the above metadata scheme. 2) An extension request is created via the extension UI, uploading the required artifacts, namely a) the metrics implementation file, named according to the patter `{metric_id}_{metric_description}.py`, b) the metrics metadata description as JSON file `metric.json`, and c) the deployment dependencies as `requirements.txt` file. 4) Optionally, for required binary computational models (e.g. keras HDF5 files), the URLs can be provided, supporting deployment of implementations relying on corresponding model loaders. 5) The extension request is manually checked by the platform operator. 6) If approved, the new metric is deployed on the platform and available for subsequent assessments. The overall submit-approval process is similar to AIM, which uses GitHub's merge-request mechanism. However, UIQLab focuses on loose coupling via its defined extension interface, thus not requiring contributors to modify the platform's core itself and simplifying the addition of new metrics.

4 Evaluation

In this section, we present the experimental results from our evaluation of UIQLab. To demonstrate the scalability and showcase the impact of shared preprocessing and parallel metrics execution on computation times, we conducted a comparative performance analysis in two different scenarios, available in the replication package in the digital appendix[4] of this paper.

4.1 Method

Study Design and Rationale. The performance analysis employs a factorial design, analyzing the effect of the independent variable execution mode $M \in \{sequential, parallel\}$ on the computation time t in two different scenarios. The hypothesis tested is the difference between computation times of the two modes. This design aims at investigating the impact of the main architectural difference of UIQLab compared to existing approaches on performance. For a more detailed analysis, the two scenarios represent different levels of computational complexity of the metrics, allowing to draw conclusions for different types of metrics.

Material and Procedure. The experimental material comprises the running instance of UIQLab, two scenarios, and the instrumentation of the performance measurements. The measurements were run on a MacBook Pro (M1 Pro CPU with 10 cores (8 Firestorm and 2 Icestorm), 32 GB RAM, macOS 14.4). To enable precise measurements, the codebase was adapted for the performance experiments by disabling the storage of evaluation results, setting screenshot delay time to zero, and awaiting metric computations instead of spawning them as background tasks. cURL was used to measure the assessment request completion time, thus including the screenshot capture and preprocessing steps in our measurements. Our measurements compared sequential and parallel computation of a single WUI input in two scenarios: Scenario I represents assessment with fast to compute metrics (PNG Size, JPEG Size/Compression, Colofulness, Color AVG/STD, Edges, Shannon Entropy, NIMA), Scenario II represents assessment with moderate to slow metrics (Whitespace, UI Interpretation, UMSI, Word Count, Congestion, Subband Entropy, Accessibility).

The assignment of metrics to the two scenarios was based on single-metric requests of the platform's main UI itself for each metric, repeated 500 times, as shown in Table 3. Based on this, metrics below an average of 5 s execution time were classified as fast to compute (Scenario I), others as medium to slow (Scenario II). Then, we ran Scenario I and II on the same input with sequential and with parallel execution and 500/100 repetitions respectively.

4.2 Results

Table 3 shows the measured average times $\bar{t}$ for single metric computation, ordered by increasing time and the separation between Scenario I and Scenario II metrics indicated as a horizontal line. All sample standard deviations s are well below 10% of the sample mean except for metric 04 (11.7%), as seen in the

---

[4] https://vsr.informatik.tu-chemnitz.de/projects/2025/UIQLab.

coefficients of variation $\widehat{c_v} = \frac{s}{\bar{x}}$, indicating overall reliable measurements without large fluctuations. We tested for normality of the measured times using the Shapiro-Wilk test at $alpha = 0.05$ and Tukey Fence $k = 1.5$, which found metrics 03, 02 and 10 to be normal distributed. Additionally, based on the Kolmogorov-Smirnov effect sizes KS-d, the difference between the sample distributions and the normal distribution for all except metric 11 is small or very small, and can practically be assumed to be normal.

Figure 4 shows the results of the accumulated times of the 7 fast to compute metrics for scenario I and of the 7 medium-to-slow to compute metrics for scenario II. For **Scenario I**, surprisingly, the average execution time for sequential execution $\bar{t}_s = 3.66s$ is less than the time for parallel execution $\bar{t}_p = 4.38s$. As the measurements in Scenario I were not normal distributed (Shapiro-Wilk $p < 0.001$), we tested the difference using left-sided Mann-Whitney-U. The difference is found highly significant at $p < 0.001$ with a large effect of $Z/\sqrt{n1+n2} = 0.84$ of the independent factor execution model on the dependent variable time. For **Scenario II**, the average execution times for sequential execution $\bar{t}_s = 151.9s$ is more than 1.5 times larger than the time for parallel execution $\bar{t}_p = 97.5s$. The right-sided Mann-Whitney-U test shows that this difference is highly significant at $p < 0.001$ and corresponds to a large effect size of 0.86 of the independent factor execution model on the dependent variable time.

Table 3. Assessment Times for Individual Metrics (increasing)

ID	Short Name	$\bar{t}$	s	$\widehat{c_v}$	SW-p	KS-d
01	PNG Size	2.41 s	0.168 s	0.07	0.0325	0.0498
03	Colorfulness	2.43 s	0.185 s	0.08	0.0807	
12	Shannon E.	2.44 s	0.118 s	0.05	0.0294	0.0450
02	JPEG Size/Compr.	2.46 s	0.194 s	0.08	0.1365	
09	Edges	2.66 s	0.128 s	0.05	<0.001	0.0579
14	NIMA	2.67 s	0.123 s	0.05	<0.001	0.0677
04	Color AVG/STD	3.05 s	0.358 s	0.12	0.0419	0.0470
05	Whitespace	5.42 s	0.224 s	0.04	0.0208	0.0516
06	UI Interpretation	5.38 s	0.147 s	0.03	<0.001	0.0556
08	Word Count	8.50 s	0.281 s	0.03	0.0072	0.0571
13	Accessibility	8.89 s	0.328 s	0.04	0.0034	0.0576
07	UMSI	11.55 s	0.406 s	0.04	0.0371	0.0380
11	Subband E.	42.34 s	1.175 s	0.03	<0.001	0.1887
10	Congestion	92.54 s	0.781 s	0.01	0.1292	

4.3 Discussion

Scenario I, representing the fast-to-compute metrics, showed a 19.6% better performance for sequential compared to parallel execution. A possible explanation for this observation is the low computation times for these metrics. In relation to the time for loading and rendering the UI from the URL input and taking the screenshot, the fast metrics' computation times are short. Thus, the overhead of parallel execution via process pools outweighed the time savings. This is an important finding, helping to better optimize future execution policies for different metrics. It indicates that the performance can further be improved through an algorithmic strategy that selectively chooses the computation mode based on the complexity of the selected metrics. In contrast, Scenario II showed improvements through shared preprocessing and parallel execution of 55.8%. In particular, the mean time for parallel mode of 97.5 s is only 5% higher than the 92.5 s of the slowest metric, 10 feature congestion. The 5% overhead reflects the necessary process pooling, as the 10 CPU cores were likely sufficient for parallel execution of the other metrics. These observations make a strong case for the advantage of the parallel computation of UIQLab for complex metrics, especially in the light of an increasing use of deep neural networks for UI assessments.

Threats to Validity. *Internal validity* can be threatened by the definition of the metrics for the two scenarios in our experiments. To address this, we decided the assignment of metrics based on the results of individual executions and the threshold shown in Table 3. Another potential bias comes from the code adaptions described in Sect. 4.1. All adaptions, however, are independent of metrics execution and apply to fast and medium-to-slow metrics and sequential and parallel execution mode alike. The reported times resulting from the adapted code are not used to argue about the expected platform performance itself. The reduced repetition count of 100 is due to feasibility for the long-running computations and the distributional statistics and significance tests indicate that this

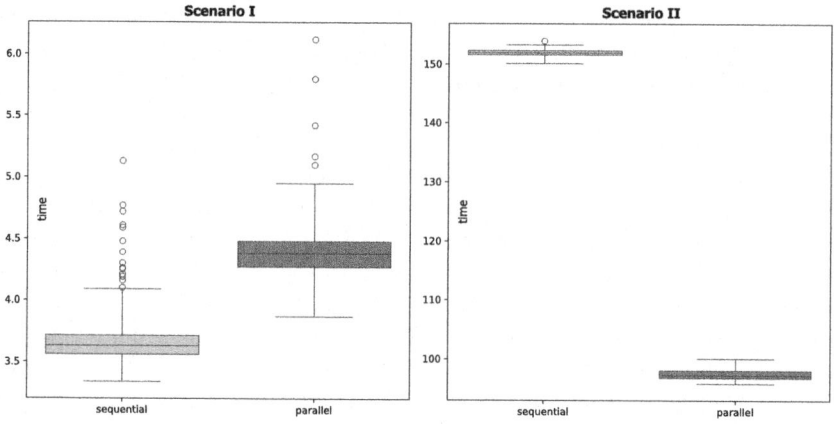

Fig. 4. Scenario Results.

did not compromise the validity. All reported time measurements were automatically measured using curl without the potential for subjective biases. Furthermore, all evaluation materials are available on GitHub for replication. *External validity* of our experiments is limited by the choice of metrics and the hardware platform. The 14 implemented metrics were chosen from existing literature and representing a wide range of inputs, outputs, preprocessing requirements and implementation types as well as computational complexities. The experimental hardware affected the measured times. It represents a dedicated multi-core system to allow analysis of parallel execution. While our findings are valid for the relative comparison of execution modes, we are not making any claims towards the absolute values of the measured times. In particular, we do not claim the times to be representative of the assessment times of the platform in production use. Generalization of our experimental results beyond the presented analysis, e.g. to other metrics, is not intended and would require dedicated experimentation. We are also not claiming that automated assessments could make subjective design choices more objective. *Construct validity* is threatened by our instrumentation of the time measurements. We used curl, a widely-used used tool, to automatically measure the entire round-trip-time for assessment requests. Potential impact of network conditions was mitigated by executing the experiments on localhost. The choice of measuring the entire assessment request time was made as it represents the delays experienced by users in the most direct way. We do not make specific numerical claims for the time measurements beyond.

5 Conclusion and Future Work

In this paper, we proposed a novel web-based WUI assessment platform that provides unified access to existing WUI metrics and models. It enables Web Engineers to automatically assess their user interfaces using 14 state-of-the-art models. Unlike previous existing platforms, it supports parallel computations, can handle multiple inputs, persists analysis results, and can be extended without changing the platform code. Based on extensive experimentation, we provided insights on the impact of the computation mode on performance, showcasing the advantage of parallel execution for medium-to-complex metrics. All implementation and experimental materials are provided to allow the Web Engineering community to replicate our experiments and extend the approach.

Future work can further improve the assessment performance through implementation of an algorithmic strategy for selecting sequential/parallel computation for subsets of selected metrics according to our identified preferences. Likewise, load balancing for the metrics computation could further improve performance in larger-scale deployments. A user study will provide insights on the usability of the UIQLab user interface. Aggregation of the individual assessment results into a holistic assessment for entire web applications as well as automatic remediation suggestions are promising directions for future research to which we plan to contribute first insights from currently ongoing experiments soon.

Acknowledgements. This work is supported by the EU's HORIZON Research and Innovation Programme under grant agreement No 101120657, project ENFIELD (European Lighthouse to Manifest Trustworthy and Green AI).

References

1. Bakaev, M., Heil, S., Khvorostov, V., Gaedke, M.: Auto-extraction and integration of metrics for web user interfaces. J. Web Eng. **17**(6), 561–590 (2019). https://doi.org/10.13052/jwe1540-9589.17676
2. Bakaev, M., Khvorostov, V., Heil, S., Gaedke, M.: Evaluation of user-subjective web interface similarity with kansei engineering-based ANN. In: IEEE RE 2017 Workshops, pp. 125–131. IEEE (2017). https://doi.org/10.1109/REW.2017.13
3. Bakaev, M., Speicher, M., Heil, S., Gaedke, M.: I don't have that much data! reusing user behavior models for websites from different domains. In: Bielikova, M., Mikkonen, T., Pautasso, C. (eds.) ICWE 2020. LNCS, vol. 12128, pp. 146–162. Springer, Cham (2020). https://doi.org/10.1007/978-3-030-50578-3_11
4. Bakaev, M., Speicher, M., Jagow, J., Heil, S., Gaedke, M.: We don't need no real users?! surveying the adoption of user-less automation tools by UI design practitioners. In: ICWE 2022. LNCS, vol. 13362, pp. 406–414. Springer, Cham (2022) .https://doi.org/10.1007/978-3-031-09917-5_28
5. Boychuk, E., Bakaev, M.: Entropy and compression based analysis of web user interfaces. In: Bakaev, M., Frasincar, F., Ko, I.-Y. (eds.) ICWE 2019. LNCS, vol. 11496, pp. 253–261. Springer, Cham (2019). https://doi.org/10.1007/978-3-030-19274-7_19
6. Bylinskii, Z., et al.: Learning visual importance for graphic designs and data visualizations. In: Proceedings of UIST2017, pp. 57–69. ACM (2017). https://doi.org/10.1145/3126594.3126653
7. Cornia, M., Baraldi, L., Serra, G., Cucchiara, R.: Predicting human eye fixations via an LSTM-based saliency attentive model. IEEE Trans. Image Process. **27**(10), 5142–5154 (2018). https://doi.org/10.1109/TIP.2018.2851672
8. Dou, Q., Zheng, X.S., Sun, T., Heng, P.A.: Webthetics: quantifying webpage aesthetics with deep learning. Int. J. Hum. Comput. Stud. **124**, 56–66 (2019). https://doi.org/10.1016/J.IJHCS.2018.11.006
9. Fosco, C., Casser, V., Bedi, A.K., O'Donovan, P., Hertzmann, A., Bylinskii, Z.: Predicting visual importance across graphic design types. In: Proceedings of UIST2020, pp. 249–260. ACM, New York (2020). https://doi.org/10.1145/3379337.3415825
10. Hasler, D., Suesstrunk, S.E.: Measuring colorfulness in natural images. In: Rogowitz, B.E., Pappas, T.N. (eds.) Proceedings of IS&T/SPIE Electronic Imaging 2003: Human Vision and Electronic Imaging VIII, vol. 5007, p. 87 (2003). https://doi.org/10.1117/12.477378
11. Ivory, M.Y., Sinha, R.R., Hearst, M.A.: Empirically validated web page design metrics. In: Proceedings of the SIGCHI Conference on Human Factors in Computing Systems, pp. 53–60. ACM, New York (2001). https://doi.org/10.1145/365024.365035
12. Khani, M.G., Mazinani, M.R., Fayyaz, M., Hoseini, M.: A novel approach for website aesthetic evaluation based on convolutional neural networks. In: 2016 Second International Conference on Web Research (ICWR), pp. 48–53. IEEE (2016). https://doi.org/10.1109/ICWR.2016.7498445

13. Mack, M.L., Oliva, A.: Computational estimation of visual complexity. In: The 12th Annual Object, Perception, Attention, and Memory Conference (2004)
14. Michailidou, E., Eraslan, S., Yesilada, Y., Harper, S.: Automated prediction of visual complexity of web pages: tools and evaluations. Int. J. Hum.-Comput. Stud. **145**, 102523 (2021). https://doi.org/10.1016/j.ijhcs.2020.102523
15. Miniukovich, A., De Angeli, A.: Computation of interface aesthetics. In: Proceedings of the 33rd Annual ACM Conference on Human Factors in Computing Systems, pp. 1163–1172. ACM, New York (2015). https://doi.org/10.1145/2702123.2702575
16. Ngo, D.C.L., Teo, L.S., Byrne, J.G.: Modelling interface aesthetics. Inf. Sci. **152**, 25–46 (2003). https://doi.org/10.1016/S0020-0255(02)00404-8
17. Oulasvirta, A., et al.: Aalto interface metrics (AIM)): a service and codebase for computational GUI evaluation. In: Proceedings of UIST2018 Adjunct, pp. 16–19. ACM Press, New York (2018). https://doi.org/10.1145/3266037.3266087
18. Reinecke, K., et al.: Predicting users' first impressions of website aesthetics with a quantification of perceived visual complexity and colorfulness. In: Proceedings of CHI2013, pp. 2049–2058. ACM, New York (2013). https://doi.org/10.1145/2470654.2481281
19. Rosenholtz, R., Li, Y., Nakano, L.: Measuring visual clutter. J. Vis. **7**(2), 17 (2007). https://doi.org/10.1167/7.2.17
20. WebAIM at Utah State University: WAVE Web Accessibility Evaluation Tools (2001). https://wave.webaim.org/
21. Wu, O., Hu, W., Shi, L.: Measuring the visual complexities of web pages. ACM Trans. Web **7**(1), 1–34 (2013). https://doi.org/10.1145/2435215.2435216
22. Xie, M., Feng, S., Xing, Z., Chen, J., Chen, C.: UIED: a hybrid tool for GUI element detection. In: ACM FSE 2020, pp. 1655–1659. ACM, New York (2020). https://doi.org/10.1145/3368089.3417940
23. Zen, M.: Metric-based evaluation of graphical user interfaces: model, Method, and Software Support. In: ACM EICS 2013, pp. 183–186. ACM, New York (2013). https://doi.org/10.1145/2494603.2480331
24. Zen, M., Vanderdonckt, J.: Assessing user interface aesthetics based on the intersubjectivity of judgment. In: Proceedings of the 30th International BCS Human Computer Interaction Conference, HCI 2016, vol. 2016-July, pp. 1–12 (2016). https://doi.org/10.14236/ewic/HCI2016.25

Web of Things, Services and Decentralized Web

Assessing the Migration from FaaS to IaaS: Cost, Performance, and Challenges in AWS

Julián Casaburi[1], Mario Matías Urbieta[1]([✉]), and Sergio Firmenich[2]

[1] Facultad de Informática - Universidad Nacional de La Plata, Buenos Aires, Argentina
murbieta@lifia.info.unlp.edu.ar
[2] Universidad Loyola Andalucía, Sevilla, Spain
sdfirmenich@uloyola.es

Abstract. In cloud-native environments, service model selection is critical for optimizing both operational and economic outcomes. This study investigates the migration from a serverless Function-as-a-Service (FaaS) model, specifically AWS Lambda, to a monolithic solution deployed on Amazon EC2. We examine this transition to evaluate cost savings, performance improvements, and architectural considerations across various scenarios. Our findings indicate that migrating to Infrastructure-as-a-Service (IaaS) can offer notable cost benefits in specific contexts, though it also introduces infrastructure management requirements. This work provides insights into migration decisions and practical considerations when transitioning from FaaS to IaaS-based models.

Keywords: Cloud Computing · Function as a Service (FaaS) · Infrastructure as a Service (IaaS) · AWS Lambda · Monolithic Architecture · Performance Benchmarking · Cost Optimization

1 Introduction

Function-as-a-Service (FaaS), a serverless computing model, allows developers to execute code fragments without managing the underlying infrastructure. AWS Lambda [9] is a prominent example of FaaS, offering automatic scaling, high availability, and a usage-based pricing model. However, as applications grow in complexity or scale, FaaS can face limitations, making it less suitable or even inadequate for certain use cases.

Real-world migration cases reinforce the limitations of FaaS for high-demand applications. A notable example is Amazon Prime Video's transition from AWS Lambda to a monolithic solution in 2023 [15]. Prime Video initially developed a serverless solution for its video quality monitoring service, orchestrated by AWS Step Functions and powered by Lambda functions. By consolidating operations into a monolithic solution on Amazon EC2, Prime Video achieved an approximately 90% cost reduction.

Given the above, this work explores the migration from AWS Lambda to a monolithic solution through an analysis of key considerations and an empirical evaluation, motivated by the following factors:

- **Cost efficiency:** FaaS can incur higher costs in high-demand scenarios compared to other solutions. This is due to FaaS pricing being based on the number of invocations and execution time, which can lead to escalating costs as traffic increases.
- **Resource utilization:** FaaS can lead to underutilized resources for I/O-intensive tasks or those with high inactivity, such as database queries or API calls. Each function instance handles a single request, regardless of its resource needs. Migrating to IaaS enables multithreaded processing of multiple requests within a single instance, improving resource efficiency.
- **Service model limitations:** AWS Lambda imposes a maximum execution time of 15 min per function instance. In some cases, long-running tasks cannot be split into multiple function instances, making Lambda unsuitable. Even when splitting is feasible, additional costs arise due to AWS Step Functions, which charge per state transition [10].

In this study, we introduce an approach to migrate components and assets from a FaaS architecture to a monolithic one in order to reduce costs. The contribution is manyfold: we discuss current costs related to FaaS solutions. Additionally, we propose steps to refactor FaaS assets to run as a monolithic solution, discuss the practical challenges introduced by the migration, and, finally, we introduce a preliminary cost-saving analysis after the migration to evaluate the financial benefits. To evaluate these aspects, we implemented multiple test scenarios, executing load tests with varying request rates and workload characteristics. These scenarios include high and constant traffic loads, unpredictable spikes, I/O-bound processing, and long-running tasks that exceed Lambda's execution limits. The results provide insights into when and why such migrations may be beneficial or impractical, isolating real features from unexpected variables that could affect the assessment.

This work is structured as follows: Sect. 2 presents related work. Section 3 introduces pricing model concepts. Section 4 discusses key migration considerations, Sect. 5 examines migration challenges and Sect. 6 reports the results of the analyzed scenarios. Finally, Sect. 7 presents the main conclusions and discusses potential areas for future work.

2 Related Work

The migration from monolithic architectures to microservices [1,16], as well as to FaaS [19,21] (a particular case of microservices), has been extensively researched in the literature, detailing challenges and best practices. However, the reverse direction—migrating FaaS solutions to other types—has been less explored. In this regard, a noteworthy study was conducted in 2020 by BBVA, a multinational financial services company, comparing AWS Lambda with Amazon EC2

[2]. Their study challenged the prevailing assumption that FaaS is universally more cost-effective by examining realistic traffic patterns and workload distributions. The findings indicated that the cost advantages of Lambda diminish in high-traffic scenarios characterized by constant or long-running processes. While Lambda proved to be cost-efficient and low-maintenance for sporadic or low-traffic use cases, EC2 was more economical for stable and high-volume traffic. Lambda's invocation-based pricing model quickly led to costs surpassing those of a highly available EC2 setup.

Notably, following BBVA's cost study and Prime Video's migration, AWS introduced a tiered pricing model for Lambda in August 2022 [3]. This new pricing structure offers differentiated rates based on the volume of GB-seconds consumed. For example, a Lambda function running on an x86 architecture with 2048 MB of memory, an average duration of 60 s, and 75 million monthly invocations would experience the following cost changes: USD 150,015.30 without tiered pricing and USD 145,015.29 with tiered pricing. This results in a monthly saving of USD 5,000.01. Therefore, after this update, Lambda costs can become more competitive for large workloads. These modifications may impact the conclusions of previous cost analyses, justifying a reassessment of various scenarios. Thus, this work conducts a cost and performance analysis across different types of scenarios and evaluates the associated challenges, aiming to provide a better understanding of when and why this type of migration may be advantageous.

3 Pricing Models

This section details the key aspects of each service's pricing structure, laying the groundwork for the cost comparisons and analyses presented later in this paper.

3.1 AWS Lambda

The AWS Lambda pricing model [4] is based on requests and duration (in "GB-seconds"). For example, a function using 1 GB of memory for 1 s consumes 1 GB-second. Memory allocation ranges from 128 MB to 10,240 MB, with CPU resources proportional to memory. More memory can potentially reduce execution time and lower costs.

AWS Lambda features a tiered pricing structure [3] that offers discounts based on the total number of GB-seconds consumed, with savings of up to 20% for the highest usage tier. This pricing model is differentiated by architecture (x86 and ARM64) and region.

3.2 Amazon EC2

The comparison with Amazon EC2 in this analysis is particularly relevant because EC2 offers full compatibility with the broader AWS ecosystem, facilitating seamless integration with other AWS services commonly used in conjunction with AWS Lambda.

Amazon EC2 users are billed for the entire capacity of their instances, regardless of actual utilization. Pricing depends on various configuration factors, including instance type, CPU, RAM, network capabilities, and storage options.

AWS offers several payment plans to cater to different needs [5]. In this work, we analyze the following two:

- **On-Demand:** Pay by the second with a minimum charge of 60 s, suitable for unpredictable workloads.
- **Reserved Instances:** Commit to 1- or 3-year terms to receive significant discounts, ideal for stable, long-term usage.

3.3 Conclusion

In summary, the pricing models reveal that AWS Lambda is particularly advantageous for workloads with infrequent access. However, AWS Lambda can incur higher costs for workloads characterized by consistent high volume or significant processing demands. Organizations must acknowledge that while managed services alleviate infrastructure management, they come at a premium. Therefore, assessing usage patterns thoroughly is essential for making informed decisions regarding AWS Lambda's suitability for specific workloads.

4 Migration Key Concepts

Although alternative approaches exist, such as open-source FaaS frameworks and other serverless services like AWS Fargate, this analysis focuses on the monolithic approach.

Transforming a FaaS-based system into a monolithic one involves modifying architectural decisions to consolidate functionalities into a single cohesive application. This process requires a thorough analysis of the application's requirements to ensure equivalent behavior.

Regarding the following concepts, while the monolithic solution can be deployed on various platforms—whether in on-premises environments, cloud services such as Amazon EC2 (virtualized or bare metal IaaS), or AWS Elastic Beanstalk (PaaS)—the focus here will be on EC2 (IaaS).

For a comparative overview, a table summarizing the considerations discussed in this section is available in the project repository [11].

4.1 Functional Requirements

Code. When considering code migration from FaaS to IaaS, the structure of the original Lambda-based solution plays a significant role. Specifically, the number of Lambda functions directly impacts the migration complexity. We can identify two extremes:

- **Lambdalith:** A single Lambda function handles all endpoints, covering multiple aspects. Migrating this type of solution to a monolithic architecture is simpler; however, it is recommended to separate the logic into distinct modules to ensure code maintainability.
- **Single-Purpose Functions:** Functions are decoupled and highly focused on a specific domain aspect. For each endpoint, the solution may consist of a single function. Migrating this type of solution introduces a higher level of complexity, as the interaction flow of the functions must be carefully analyzed.

State. AWS Lambda is stateless, meaning any data that needs to persist between invocations must be stored externally (e.g., AWS DynamoDB, AWS S3). In contrast, monolithic solutions can be either stateful or stateless. In a monolithic solution using horizontal scaling, persistent sessions (sticky sessions) can be used at the load balancer level. Ideally, the application should be stateless, meaning each instance should not rely on locally stored data or the state of other instances to process requests.

Event-Driven Programming. A key pattern in AWS Lambda is event-driven programming, where functions automatically execute in response to events generated by other services, such as uploading a file to S3 or inserting a record into DynamoDB. To replicate an event-driven system in an IaaS environment, message queues can be implemented. For example, to migrate a workflow where uploading a file to an Amazon S3 bucket triggers a Lambda function, to a monolithic application hosted on Amazon EC2 instances, S3 can be configured to publish a message to an Amazon SQS queue. The monolithic application can then consume this message via polling. Alternatively, S3 events can be sent to Amazon EventBridge, which can route them based on rules to various targets, such as an API endpoint in the application itself.

Rate Limiting. Rate limiting sets limits on the number of requests allowed within a specific time interval. Once this limit is reached, additional requests may be rejected, delayed, or processed differently to prevent system overload and performance degradation. When developing solutions with AWS Lambda, rate limiting can be implemented for each function using services like Amazon API Gateway. In contrast, within a monolithic application, rate limiting implementation depends on whether the application runs on a single instance or is horizontally scaled. For single instances, in-memory rate limiting can be used, while for horizontally scaled applications, external databases like Redis can be leveraged. Furthermore, rate limiting can be enforced at the reverse proxy level using solutions like NGINX or managed services like Amazon API Gateway.

Database Transactions. In a Lambda-based solution with multiple functions orchestrated by AWS Step Functions, the SAGA pattern [7] is used to manage distributed transactions and maintain consistency. This pattern breaks a transaction into a series of smaller steps, where each service executes a portion of the transaction and coordinates with others through messages and events. If an error occurs, the pattern ensures that changes up to the failure are undone using compensatory actions. When migrating to a monolithic application, the distributed transaction logic must be consolidated.

Authentication. In AWS Lambda-based solutions, authentication is typically managed through cloud services such as Amazon Cognito or Auth0, providing robust and scalable identity and access management. When migrating to a monolithic architecture, several options are available for handling authentication:

- **Option 1: Retain the Existing Authentication Service.** This approach can be achieved through API calls or SDKs.
- **Option 2: Implement a Single Sign-On (SSO) System.** The SSO mechanism allows users to authenticate once and access multiple applications or services without re-entering credentials. Various open-source solutions, such as Red Hat's Keycloak, can be used to implement SSO.
- **Option 3: Authentication Managed by the Monolithic Solution.** In this case, an authentication policy needs to be implemented, such as using the JSON Web Token (JWT) standard.

4.2 Non-functional Requirements

Logging and Monitoring. Effective logging and monitoring are essential non-functional requirements for diagnosing issues, ensuring system reliability, and gaining insights into application performance. Logging is the process of recording events or actions within a system, providing a crucial audit trail for troubleshooting and analysis.

In AWS Lambda, function logs are automatically captured and centralized in Amazon CloudWatch Logs, simplifying log management. For monolithic applications, especially horizontally scaled ones, a centralized logging solution is equally critical. Logs from each instance should be aggregated in a repository for effective analysis and monitoring. This can be achieved using tools like Logstash, Splunk, or cloud services such as Amazon CloudWatch Logs. Beyond logging, comprehensive monitoring is necessary to track performance metrics, detect anomalies, and ensure the overall health of the application. Solutions like Amazon CloudWatch or Prometheus can be used to monitor key performance indicators (KPIs) and trigger alerts for proactive issue resolution.

Permissions for Accessing AWS Services. In AWS Lambda-based solutions, permissions to access other services (e.g., S3, DynamoDB, or SQS) are managed through AWS Identity and Access Management (IAM) policies directly attached to each Lambda function. This model allows for granular access control, adhering to the principle of least privilege. When migrating to a monolithic solution, if hosted on AWS using EC2, permissions can be managed by attaching an IAM role to the EC2 instance with policies granting the necessary access. For a monolithic solution hosted on another cloud provider or on-premises, integration with AWS services requires securely managing access credentials.

High Availability. Lambda functions are highly available by default, as they are deployed across multiple Availability Zones (AZs). In a monolithic solution deployed on IaaS, high availability can be achieved with the appropriate deployment configuration. It should be noted that not all application use cases require high availability. Scenarios where high availability is unnecessary and cost savings can be achieved include temporary testing, internal use, or limited-use applications that are not critical.

For Amazon EC2, configuring the distribution of instances across multiple Availability Zones (AZs) is essential to achieve availability similar to Lambda. Auto Scaling Groups (ASG) can automatically manage the number of EC2 instances based on defined conditions such as CPU load or scheduling and can span multiple AZs within a region.

5 Migration Challenges

Various operational and organizational issues may arise during the migration and subsequent operation. For each issue identified, we also propose preliminary solutions to mitigate potential negative impacts. A summary can be found in the repository [11]. The challenges are described next.

5.1 Downtime During System Updates

In a monolithic solution, updates tend to be riskier, as they can introduce downtime if errors are detected during development. A failure in one component can compromise the stability of the entire application, potentially causing service disruptions [13]. To minimize this risk, a blue/green deployment strategy is recommended, allowing traffic to be redirected to the stable version in case of issues with the new version.

5.2 Increase in Operational Costs Due to Infrastructure Management and Maintenance

Migrating to IaaS increases operational costs due to the need to manage and maintain the underlying infrastructure. To mitigate these costs, the following preliminary solutions are proposed:

– **Automated Infrastructure Provisioning:** Use Infrastructure as Code (e.g., Terraform) to automate the provisioning and configuration of infrastructure resources, ensuring consistency and reducing the potential for manual errors.

- **Dynamic Scalability:** Configure Auto Scaling Groups to automatically adjust the number of EC2 instances based on demand or use similar mechanisms in other cloud environments to optimize resource allocation.
- **Automated Monitoring and Proactive Management:** Set up automatic alerts and corrective scripts to address issues such as server failures, minimizing the need for manual intervention.

5.3 Resource Underutilization Due to Horizontal Scaling

Horizontal scaling can lead to resource underutilization, as the last instance added to an Auto Scaling Group often remains underutilized. Consequently, costs increase without fully leveraging the instance's capacity. As a preliminary solution, it is recommended to configure Auto Scaling Groups with a larger number of smaller instances rather than fewer larger ones, to achieve more efficient utilization.

5.4 Increased Provisioning Time for Horizontal Scaling

Unlike AWS Lambda, which scales almost instantly, deploying on IaaS requires starting new instances as demand increases. Provisioning delays can impact the application's responsiveness to traffic spikes, affecting availability and performance. The proposed solutions include:

- **Predictive Scaling Combined with Dynamic Scaling:** Implement predictive scaling based on historical load patterns or anticipated events, allowing pre-scaling to handle demand spikes together with dynamic scaling.
- **AMI Optimization:** Minimize initialization time by integrating dependencies and configurations within the Amazon Machine Image (AMI), instead of relying on instance startup scripts.

5.5 Increased Security Risks

AWS Lambda's sandboxed environment significantly reduces the attack surface, whereas deploying on IaaS infrastructure exposes servers to additional security risks. For example, failing to apply regular operating system updates may leave the server vulnerable to known exploits. Specific risk factors include:

- Direct server management via SSH access, in contrast to AWS Lambda, which does not provide such access.
- Potential misconfiguration of firewall rules, which could increase exposure to threats.

To mitigate these risks, the following solutions are proposed:

- **Abstraction and Segmentation via a Reverse Proxy:** Implement a reverse proxy (e.g., NGINX or AWS Elastic Load Balancer) as an intermediary to hide the IP addresses of origin servers, making them more resilient against attacks such as Distributed Denial of Service (DDoS). Attackers would only target the proxy, which can be hardened and scaled to withstand attacks.
- **Automated Operating System Updates:** Use tools like AWS Systems Manager Patch Manager to schedule and automate OS patches and updates.
- **Regular Updates of Languages, Frameworks, and Dependencies:** Frequent updates reduce vulnerability by incorporating the latest security mitigations.
- **Automated Code Security Analysis:** Integrate static code analysis and dependency checks into the CI/CD pipeline to identify vulnerabilities before deployment.
- **SSH Access Security:** Disable password-based SSH access, allowing only public key authentication, or remove SSH access entirely if not required.

6 Results

This section evaluates the feasibility of migration by measuring differences in performance and cost in scenarios with different functional requirements and traffic patterns. For each scenario, the application code, Infrastructure as Code templates, and load testing scripts are available in the repository [11] to ensure the reproducibility of the tests. The following methodology was applied:

- **Application of Migration Patterns:** For each scenario, the applicable migration concepts discussed in Sect. 4 were used. For instance, all scenarios incorporated the approaches for code migration and high availability.
- **Load Testing:** Load tests were conducted using K6 [12] on an EC2 m5.2xlarge instance in a separate VPC within the same region as the applications, collecting metrics such as response times and failure rates. Each test was repeated three times, and results were averaged for consistency.
- **Languages and Runtime Environments:** All applications were developed in JavaScript using the Node.js runtime environment (version 20) [18].
- **Monolithic Applications:** For monolithic applications, the PM2 process manager was used in cluster mode [14] to run multiple instances of the application in parallel. This configuration leverages available hardware resources by distributing the load across multiple CPU cores.
- **Instance Selection:** Instance types were selected based on their ability to handle the required number of requests per second for each scenario while maintaining cost-effectiveness. For scenarios using burstable instance types, the standard credit mode was configured. Tests confirmed that the credits earned consistently exceeded the credits consumed, ensuring sustained CPU performance during the tests.
- **Cost Optimization in Lambda:** Optimal resource configurations for each scenario were identified using the AWS Lambda Power Tuning application [6], as recommended in the Amazon Web Services documentation.

- **Exclusions**: The comparison excludes AWS Lambda's "Always free" tier, API Gateway costs (which are identical for both solutions), and data transfer costs, as they are billed similarly for AWS Lambda and Amazon EC2.
- **Lambda Function Duration**: The cost of the Lambda solution was calculated using the average function execution duration as reported by Amazon CloudWatch.
- **Load Balancer Costs**: For scenarios involving horizontally scaled EC2 instances, the costs include both the fixed and variable fees associated with the AWS Application Load Balancer (ALB).

6.1 Cost-Driven Migration Scenarios

The following section presents detailed results for three scenarios, each representing different load patterns and workloads that could influence the feasibility of migration.

Scenario 1: High and Constant Traffic Pattern. In this scenario, we tested a CPU-intensive workload with sustained traffic. To do so, we implemented a simple single-endpoint application that performs base64 encoding of text data. The following configurations were used: **EC2 Instance Type** t3.small, **Lambda Configuration** 128 MB of RAM, and **Request Rate** 100 RPS, maintained using k6's constant arrival rate executor.

Table 1 lists the performance and cost results for both solutions. Under a constant load of 100 RPS, the monolithic solution outperformed AWS Lambda in terms of average response times. In this configuration, without considering high availability, on-demand EC2 instances resulted in a 73.76% cost saving, while reserved instances provided an 83.48% reduction compared to Lambda. Furthermore, Fig. 1 represents the break-even point for the two solution types, with and without high availability.

If high availability is a mandatory requirement, with a horizontal scaling configuration including at least two active instances running continuously (such as t3.micro, costing USD 54.97 per month) and an AWS Application Load Balancer (USD 39.79 per month), the monthly savings are reduced to 4.38% for on-demand instances and 14.25% for reserved instances. It is important to note that the ALB incurs a fixed base cost of USD 16.43 per month. As the request volume increases, the fixed cost of the ALB becomes a smaller portion of the total, optimizing resource usage and improving cost efficiency. Additionally, to address resource underutilization, we used smaller instances for horizontal scaling, as noted in Sect. 5.

It is also important to highlight that potential savings can be achieved if the API Gateway service is unnecessary in the monolithic solution, depending on the required features such as rate limiting, authentication, payload validation, and transformation. For example, in the tested scenario, the monthly cost of using API Gateway is USD 262.80 for an HTTP API or USD 919.80 for a REST API.

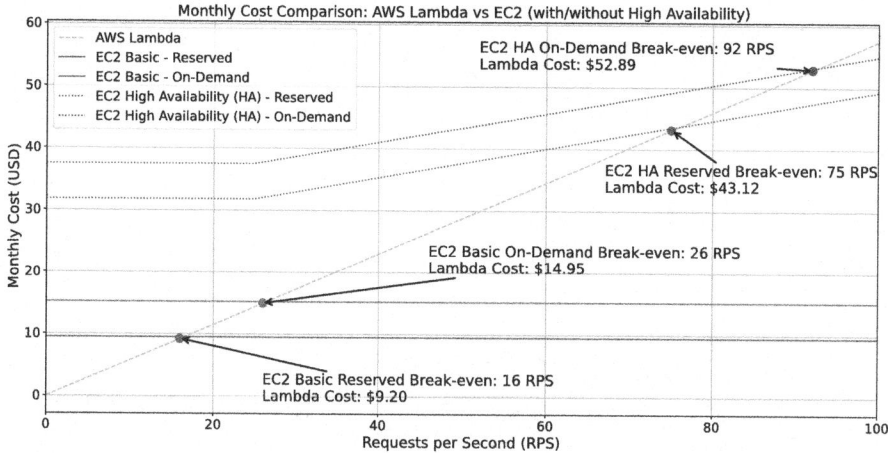

Fig. 1. Break-even point of different solution types for Scenario 1: High and constant traffic pattern (RPS).

Scenario 2: Unpredictable Traffic. In this scenario, an application experiencing sudden traffic spikes was tested to evaluate how well monolithic architectures deployed on IaaS handle abrupt increases in demand. To do so, we implemented a single-endpoint application that calculates the 100,000th Fibonacci number, making it CPU-bound. The following configurations were used: **EC2 Instance Type** t3.small, **Lambda Configuration** 1536 MB of RAM, and **Request Rate** 10 RPS and 20 RPS.

Table 1 lists the performance and cost results for both solutions. The monolithic solution consistently showed lower response times than Lambda for both test rates, while also offering a significant cost advantage. Despite having four instances running at all times, the Lambda solution remains more expensive, resulting in a cost reduction of 43.82% when using EC2 instances with autoscaling and an AWS Application Load Balancer. Additionally, the break-even point is shown in Fig. 2.

Scenario 3: I/O-Bound Workload. In this scenario, an I/O-bound application was tested. As discussed in the introduction (1), Lambda's execution model incurs costs even during idle periods, such as when waiting for responses from third-party APIs, database queries, or other I/O operations. This waiting time can significantly reduce Lambda's cost efficiency in such use cases. This scenario was proposed as a potential area for future testing in the comparative study by Villamizar et al. [20]. To simulate an I/O-bound workload, we implemented an application that simulates fetching data from an external API. Upon receiving a request, it initiates three parallel API calls, each introducing a fixed delay of 50 ms. Once all responses are received, the application processes the data by converting the text to uppercase and appending a status message. This workload

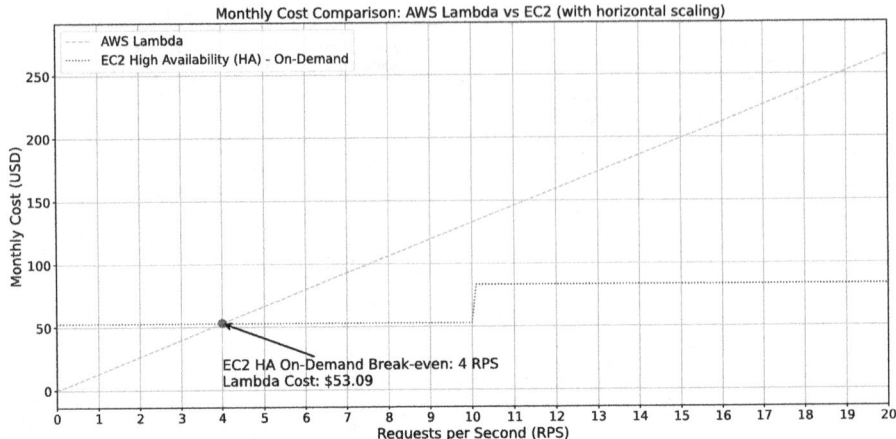

Fig. 2. Break-even point for different solution types in Scenario 2: Unpredictable Traffic.

reflects real-world scenarios in which a significant portion of execution time is spent waiting for I/O operations to complete.

The following configurations were used: **EC2 Instance Type** m5.large, **Lambda Configuration** 128 MB of RAM, and **Request Rate** 4000 RPS.

Table 1 presents the detailed performance and cost results for both solutions. As illustrated there, the monolithic solution demonstrated lower response times compared to Lambda. Furthermore, the Lambda solution incurred significantly higher costs, resulting in substantial monthly savings of 70.69% for on-demand

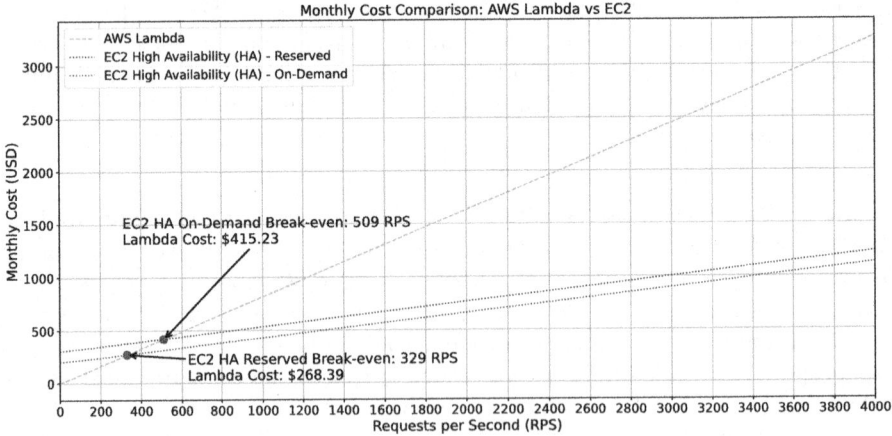

Fig. 3. Break-even point for different solution types in Scenario 3: I/O-Bound Workload.

EC2 instances and 72.10% for reserved instances when adopting the monolithic approach. Additionally, the break-even point is shown in Fig. 3.

6.2 Migration Scenario Driven by Architectural Limitations Scenario 4: Long-Running Application

The proposed example for this scenario involves a function triggered by the upload of video files to an Amazon S3 bucket. The function downloads the file to the ephemeral storage of the instance, re-encodes it using FFmpeg to reduce its bitrate and size, and then uploads the processed file to another S3 bucket for storage.

If a video with a duration of 43 min and 32 s, dimensions of 1280 × 720, a bitrate of 584 kbit/s, and a frame rate of 30 fps is uploaded to the input bucket, the video exceeds the 15-min limit mentioned in the introduction (1). Consequently, the video processing remains incomplete. The original solution was designed for videos with a duration limit but now requires an extension of this limit. As a result, it becomes necessary to migrate to a different solution that supports long-running processing. We tested two alternatives using the following configurations: **EC2 Instance Type** c6a.4xlarge, **Lambda Configuration** 3008 MB of RAM (for all functions, both in the single Lambda solution and the orchestrated solution).

The first alternative is a Lambda-based solution orchestrated by AWS Step Functions. In this approach, the video is split into smaller chunks, each processed individually, and then reassembled. While this method allows for longer processing times compared to a single Lambda function, it incurs additional costs due to state transitions and multiple Lambda invocations.

In contrast, the monolithic EC2 solution involves message handling via SQS and processing through EC2 instances. Horizontal scaling is managed by a target tracking policy [8], which adjusts based on the queue length (measured using the ApproximateNumberOfMessagesVisible metric reported by SQS). To mitigate the challenge of increased provisioning time during horizontal scaling in IaaS, we implemented AMI Optimization, building the Amazon Machine Image with all necessary dependencies, including a pre-installed FFmpeg environment, to reduce instance initialization time.

The results, listed in Table 1, show that the monolithic solution is faster and less expensive.

6.3 Cost and Performance Comparison

Table 1 presents a cost and performance comparison of the solutions discussed in the previous four scenarios. The results highlight that, while AWS Lambda provides a highly scalable and maintenance-free execution environment, it is not always the most cost-effective option.

Table 1. Cost and Response Time Comparison Between AWS Lambda and EC2 On-Demand Instances

Scenario	Lambda Cost	EC2 Cost	Lambda Time	EC2 Time
1 (Single EC2 instance)	$57.49	$15.18	25.79 ms	7.04 ms
1 (Two EC2 instances)	$57.49	$54.97	25.79 ms	7.23 ms
2	$147.90	$83.08	220.36 ms	178.92 ms
3	$3,723.00	$1,090.80	73.01 ms	59.20 ms
4	$0.06483	$0.02856	3 min 34 s	2 min 48 s

7 Conclusions and Future Work

This study analyzed the migration of a FaaS solution deployed on AWS Lambda to a monolithic solution on Infrastructure-as-a-Service (IaaS), highlighting the challenges, benefits, and key considerations.

In the tested scenarios, infrastructure cost savings of up to 80% were achieved when features such as high availability were not required, as seen in Scenario 1. Although savings were lower in other cases, they remained significant. Therefore, it is recommended to use AWS Lambda for internal or low-demand tasks, while for other cases, architects should carefully evaluate requirements and costs before making a decision. Finally, since the tests were conducted in a production-ready AWS setup focusing on costs, the evaluation of other scenarios is suggested for a more comprehensive cost analysis.

We plan a few lines of research as future work. In this work, we focused on a monolithic solution but the feasibility of migrating to self-managed FaaS solutions, such as OpenFaaS [17], could be analyzed to determine whether they offer a better cost-performance ratio compared to AWS Lambda and EC2. On the other hand, a catalog of different scenarios could be developed based on those discussed in this work, to explore a broader range of experimental configurations to further strengthen empirical validation. This could involve testing with more diverse workload types, traffic patterns, and application complexities. Finally, migration is a major concern for any development team, so both manual and automated approaches should be analyzed. This may require developing tools to automate the migration process, thereby reducing manual effort and minimizing associated errors.

Disclosure of Interests. The authors have no competing interests to declare that are relevant to the content of this article.

References

1. Abgaz, Y., McCarren, A., Elger, P., Solan, D., Lapuz, N., Bivol, M.: Decomposition of monolith applications into microservices architectures: a systematic review. IEEE Trans. Softw. Eng. **49**(8), 4213–4242 (2023). https://doi.org/10.1109/TSE.2023.3287297

2. Alda Rodríguez, Á., Álvarez, F., Díaz López, G., Evgeniev, M., Horrillo, P.: Cost comparison of running web applications in the cloud using monolithic, microservice, and AWS lambda architectures (2018). https://www.bbva.com/en/innovation/economics-of-serverless/. Accessed 21 Mar 2024
3. Amazon Web Services: Introducing tiered pricing for aws lambda (2022). https://aws.amazon.com/blogs/compute/introducing-tiered-pricing-for-aws-lambda/. Accessed 19 Feb 2024
4. Amazon Web Services: Aws lambda pricing (nd). https://aws.amazon.com/lambda/pricing/. Accessed 19 Feb 2024
5. Amazon Web Services: How aws pricing works (nd). https://docs.aws.amazon.com/whitepapers/latest/how-aws-pricing-works/amazon-ec2.html. Accessed 11 Apr 2024
6. Amazon Web Services: Profiling functions with aws lambda power tuning (nd). https://docs.aws.amazon.com/lambda/latest/operatorguide/profile-functions.html. Accessed 8 Aug 2024
7. Amazon Web Services: Saga pattern (nd). https://docs.aws.amazon.com/prescriptive-guidance/latest/modernization-data-persistence/saga-pattern.html. Accessed 4 Dec 2024
8. Amazon Web Services: Target tracking scaling policies for amazon ec2 auto scaling - amazon web services (nd). https://docs.aws.amazon.com/autoscaling/ec2/userguide/as-scaling-target-tracking.html. Accessed 19 Oct 2024
9. Amazon Web Services: What is aws lambda? (nd). https://docs.aws.amazon.com/lambda/latest/dg/welcome.html. Accessed 19 Feb 2024
10. Amazon Web Services: What is aws step functions? (nd). https://docs.aws.amazon.com/step-functions/latest/dg/welcome.html. Accessed 19 Mar 2024
11. Casaburi, J., Urbieta, M., Firmenich, S.: Github repository - applications, load testing scripts, and infrastructure as code (2025). https://github.com/juliancasaburi/icwe-faas
12. Grafana: Grafana k6 (2024). https://k6.io/. Accessed 16 July 2024
13. Kaloudis, M.: Evolving software architectures from monolithic systems to resilient microservices: Best practices, challenges, and future trends. Int. J. Adv. Comput. Sci. Appl. (IJACSA) **15**(9) (2024). https://doi.org/10.14569/IJACSA.2024.0150901
14. Keymetrics: Pm2 documentation - cluster mode (2024). https://pm2.keymetrics.io/docs/usage/cluster-mode/. Accessed 16 July 2024
15. Kolny, M.: Scaling up the prime video audio/video monitoring service and reducing costs by 90% (2023). https://www.primevideotech.com/video-streaming/scaling-up-the-prime-video-audio-video-monitoring-service-and-reducing-costs-by-90. Accessed 19 Feb 2024
16. Newman, S.: Monolith to Microservices: Evolutionary Patterns to Transform Your Monolith. O'Reilly Media (2019)
17. OpenFaaS: Openfaas - serverless functions, made simple (2024). https://www.openfaas.com/. Accessed 14 Dec 2024
18. OpenJS Foundation: Node v20.9.0 (lts) (2024). https://nodejs.org/en/blog/release/v20.9.0. Accessed 19 Feb 2024
19. Pedratscher, S., Ristov, S., Fahringer, T.: M2faas: transparent and fault tolerant faasification of node.js monolith code blocks. Future Gener. Comput. Syst. **135**, 57–71 (2022). https://doi.org/10.1016/j.future.2022.04.021

20. Villamizar, M., et al.: Cost comparison of running web applications in the cloud using monolithic, microservice, and AWS Lambda architectures. SOCA **11**(2), 233–247 (2017). https://doi.org/10.1007/s11761-017-0208-y
21. Würz, H., Kramer, M., Kaster, M., Kuijper, A.: Migrating monolithic applications to function as a service. Softw. Pract. Experience **53**(12), 2353–2373 (2023). https://doi.org/10.1002/spe.3263

Link Traversal over Decentralised Environments Using Restart-Based Query Planning

Jonni Hanski[✉], Simon Van Braeckel, Ruben Taelman, and Ruben Verborgh

IDLab, Department of Electronics and Information Systems,
Ghent University – imec, Ghent, Belgium
{jonni.hanski,simon.vanbraeckel,ruben.taelman,ruben.verborgh}@ugent.be

Abstract. With the emergence of decentralisation initiatives to address various issues around regulatory compliance and barriers of entry to data-driven markets, data access abstraction layers in the form of query engines are needed to assist in developing services on top of such environments. Prior work, however, has demonstrated significant network overhead during data retrieval in traversal-based query execution over decentralised Linked Data sources, dwarfing the relative impact of local processing and query optimisations. Certain decentralisation initiatives, however, offer an environment with seemingly sufficient structure to address this, allowing client-side query engines to attain measurable performance improvements through local optimisations. One example is the Solid initiative, offering distributed well-defined user data stores, helping traversal-based query execution approaches in efficiently locating and accessing query-relevant data. Within this work, we demonstrate the impact of client-side adaptive query planning optimisations within structured distributed environments, using the Solid ecosystem as an example, to highlight the potential for tangible improvements in traversal-based execution. Through the implementation of a restart-based query planning technique, we achieve average query execution time *reductions of up to 36%* compared to a baseline of unchanged query plan execution. Conversely, we also demonstrate how such techniques, when applied without robust cost-benefit estimation, can effectively *double* the query execution time. This illustrates the importance and potential of client-side techniques even in such distributed environments, and highlights the importance of further investigation in the direction of these techniques.

1 Introduction

With the emergence of various decentralisation initiatives to address challenges around centralised data storage solutions, ranging from privacy-related legislation to barriers to entry for a given data-driven market, there is also the emerging need for query engine-based abstraction layers to assist developers in creating services on top of such distributed environments, allowing them to write declarative queries to extract the data they need, without having to be aware of the details of its distribution. Thus, the discovery, acquisition and processing of data becomes the responsibility of the query engine, and for interactive user-facing applications, the engine has to perform these tasks with sufficient user-perceived performance to make such solutions viable in practice [16].

The challenges around data discovery can be addressed through Link Traversal Query Processing (LTQP) [11]. However, even with the varous heuristics of *zero-knowledge query planning* [10], the lack of prior knowledge of the data being queried over may result in suboptimal query plans [18]. And even though the relative impact of the query plan, as compared to the cost of data access over network, may be marginal in some environments [13], in more structured ones it has been shown to be significant [18], with potential for theoretically halving the total execution time. Thus, additional *adaptive query processing* [7] techniques should be explored, for the purposes of adapting the initial plan or its execution to runtime conditions based on feedback, to reach more optimal query plans.

Within this work, we have chosen to employ a client-side restart-based query planning technique over a Solid environment [19], to investigate the impact of adaptive techniques on client-side query processing even in distributed environments with data access overhead, such as with link traversal query execution.

The remainder of this paper is structured as follows. Section 2 briefly discusses related work, followed by Sect. 3 introducing our research question and hypotheses, as well as Sect. 4 outlining our approach to tackling them. Section 5 explains our experiments, followed by the results in Sect. 6. The paper is concluded by our conclusions in Sect. 7.

2 Related Work

Through widespread adoption of the Linked Data principles, the World Wide Web enables a globally distributed dataspace in the form of *the Web of Linked Data* [12,13]. The *traversal-based query execution* technique [10,11,13], building upon these principles, allows for evaluation of queries over Linked Data using a *follow-your-nose* approach to traversing URIs. This technique allows a query engine to evaluate a SPARQL query over an increasing number of data sources on the Web of Linked Data by intertwining triple pattern matching with link traversal to discover query-relevant data sources on-the-fly [12]. With such a traversal approach, the cost of data retrieval over the network has been shown to marginalise the cost of locally processing that data [13].

Constrained and well-defined data access environments, however, have been shown to increase the relative impact of query planning [18]. The Solid initiative [19] offers one such environment. The initiative seeks to offer individuals greater control over their own data, by storing it in user-controlled permissioned datastores, referred to as *pods*, encouraging and facilitating the reuse of personal data. Notably, pods expose their contents following a set of specifications such as the Solid protocol [3], to assist query engines in data discovery. For this reason, we have chosen Solid as the basis for our experiments, and the SolidBench benchmark for the evaluation to align with existing work.

To take advantage of information discovered during query execution, to overcome limitations imposed by insufficient or inaccurate information on the planning phase, an *adaptive query processing* technique can be used [7]. Such approaches have been categorised as either *inter-query* adaptivity for changes between executions, or *intra-query* adaptivity for changes during execution. Although inter-query techniques are deemed easier to incorporate into existing *optimise-then-execute* processes, they essentially require executing similar queries over similar data to be able to take advantage of the information acquired [7]. This has been demonstrated through the use of a theoretical oracle in prior work [18], to achieve up to double the query performance of zero-knowledge query planning. Intra-query techniques, on the other hand, aim to take advantage of information as it is discovered *during* the execution of a query plan. Among such approaches are *postponing of plan selection to runtime* [4], as well as various *operator-internal* approaches, for example to allow modifying join operations [6]. Within this work, we demonstrate the potential of intra-query techniques using a restart-based approach detailed in Sect. 4.

The approaches employed within this work rely on selectivity or cardinality estimates of triple patterns to determine the join plan between them, in an effort to minimise the number of intermediate results. Although centralised storage solutions are often capable of pre-computing such information or providing estimates efficiently, such as through the use of *characteristics sets* [14], within decentralised scenarios this may not always be the case. Thus, various purpose-built estimation techniques have to be applied, such as *variable counting* [15] that estimates the relative selectivities of triple patterns using the type and number of unbound components. Other approaches, such as the set of formulae by Hagedorn et al. [9], make use of the statistics offered in dataset descriptions published using the Vocabulary of Interlinked Datasets (VoID) [5]. Within this work, we have chosen to employ a variable counting approach due to its lack of preconditions, as well as the formulae from Hagedorn et al. due to their suitability for decentralised scenarios with VoID metadata available.

3 Research Question

The purpose of this work is to explore the relative impact of applying client-side adaptive query processing techniques in traversal-based query execution within decentralised environments where data access costs do not dwarf the impact of the query plan, such as with Solid. We use a restart-based approach for this purpose, evaluating the current query plan and restarting it if the plan would differ based on information available during the evaluation. The following research question serves as the basis for our work:

Question 1. Can overall query performance be improved through the application of client-side adaptive techniques, compared to heuristics-based zero-knowledge query planning?

We derived the following hypotheses to answer this research question:

Hypothesis 1. Compared to a heuristic zero-knowledge query planning technique, a restart-based planning approach produces the first and last result faster, and achieves lower total execution time.

Hypothesis 2. Performing plan evaluation and optional restart after uniform amount of execution time for all queries will result in lower performance than baseline for at least a third of the queries.

Hypothesis 3. Performing plan evaluation and optional restart only upon cardinality estimate updates will result in better performance for all queries.

This research question and hypotheses are addressed through a practical implementation and experiments described below.

4 Approach to Client-Side Adaptive Optimisation

We employ an operator-internal technique to restart query plans from the beginning during *pipelined* query execution, where bindings pass through the query plan one by one as they are produced and consumed by the operators, with our wrapper operator encapsulating the query plan by acting as the topmost join in the *tree of joins* of any kind realised by their corresponding *physical operators* that forms the body of the query plan. This wrapper, illustrated in Fig. 1, is responsible for *i)* evaluating at the chosen intervals whether the current query plan is still optimal or not, and *ii)* restarting the encapsulated query plan when the current one no longer appears optimal.

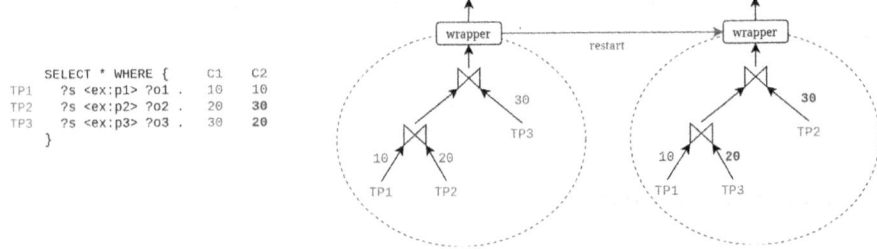

Fig. 1. Once a different plan is produced based on updated cardinalities (TP2, TP3), the wrapper transparently restarts the query plan.

The query plan wrapper operates under bag semantics, under the assumption that a plan, when restarted, produces its full output again from the beginning. The wrapper internally keeps track of all output produced by the plan it encapsulates. Upon restarting the plan, the wrapper uses this record to discard previously produced output, avoiding any spurious duplicates. This record is maintained fully in memory, although practical solutions should consider flushing it to disk as with adjoin [1].

Alongside restarting the query plan, the wrapper operator is also responsible for evaluating the optimality of the chosen plan, by comparing it against a hypothetical plan that would be chosen by the query engine at the time of the evaluation, given the triple pattern cardinalities available at that moment. If the two plans differ, the wrapper performs the join plan restart, but if they remain identical, then it continues the current execution. The wrapper can be configured to perform its join plan evaluation using two different approaches:

1. *Timeout-based*: When the join plan is initially started, the wrapper sets a timeout. After this timeout, the join plan evaluation is carried out once.
2. *Change-based*: Every time the cardinality estimate of a triple pattern is updated, the join plan evaluation is carried out.

The join plan evaluation relies on cardinality information on triple patterns being updated as new information becomes available. If the cardinality information does not change, the evaluation will produce the same plan every time, and the experiments would be identical. Ideally, any new cardinality estimate would be closer to the true cardinality value known only at the end of the processing. Within this work, we have chosen to employ the following three cardinality estimation techniques:

1. A *variable counting-based approach*, that estimates the relative selectivities of triple patterns and creates a join plan based on these. The initial plan is always created using this approach.
2. A *VoID-based approach*, that uses the VoID dataset descriptions of the Solid pods to estimate the cardinality of that triple pattern using the formulae from Hagedorn et al. [9].
3. A *simplified VoID-based approach*, that functions like approach 2, but assumes the cardinality of a triple pattern to equal the predicate occurrence count.

5 Experiment Setup

The approaches discussed in Sect. 4 were implemented in Comunica [17], a modular SPARQL query engine framework that provides a baseline link traversal implementation, also previously used to benchmark the relative impact of query plans compared to network overhead in related work [18]. Our implementation is available as open source[1]. Through changes in the query engine configuration, we set up the following test cases to measure the impact of our approaches:

- *Baseline*, as the default configuration of the engine without any of our implementation, doing link traversal with zero-knowledge query planning.
- *Overhead*, with VoID description parsing and cardinality estimation logic in place, but no query plan evaluation or restarts. This measures the overhead introduced by our implementation.
- *Timeout*, identical to the overhead test, but with query plan evaluation taking place once after a set timeout value.
- *Cardinality*, identical to the overhead test, but with query plan evaluation and potential restart taking place every time the cardinality estimate is updated.

---
[1] https://github.com/surilindur/comunica-components.

The dataset and queries were generated using SolidBench[2], a benchmark to simulate a distributed social network use case across Solid pods using the LDBC SNB social network dataset [8]. To support the cardinality estimation, VoID descriptions were generated for each pod.

The experiments were all executed on the same virtual machine, with the server and query engine client running locally, using the $jbr.js$[3] [18] benchmark runner tool. Query timeout was set to 120 s following the example set by prior work [18], causing all queries from the complex templates to time out, likewise aligning with such prior work, leaving a total of 75 queries to execute for each configuration. The experiments and our results are available online[4] for reproducibility and validation.

6 Results and Discussion

Beyond query execution time, there was significant variance in the result arrival rates. To capture these differences, we employ the *diefficiency metrics* [2], namely *dief@k*. The *dief@k* value is the integral of result arrivals recorded as a function of time, from the time of 0 results to the time of having produced k results. For our comparison, we have chosen to set k to the *total number of results* for each query, producing the diefficiency value at 100% result completeness. Lower diefficiency values are considered better for the same query with the same results.

From Table 1, one can observe how even the baseline was unable to successfully execute all queries within the allocated timeframe. Thus, we omit these timed-out queries from further analysis. Furthermore, with 63% of queries producing all their results under 5 s, and 82% producing them under 20 s, the 20-s restart timeout configurations do almost nothing to most of the queries. Additionally, the overhead of the implementation itself appears negligible, and the formulae from Hagedorn et al. perform overall best for cardinality estimation.

The timeout-based approach produced the last result 9–84% slower, but exhibited 64% better diefficiency for queries performing better than baseline. This leads us to accept Hypothesis 2, with a uniform timeout clearly not working for all queries. Evaluating join plans upon cardinality estimate updates produced anywhere between 63% better and 245× worse diefficiency, or 36% lower and 73% higher query execution time. The last result was likewise produced anywhere between 37% faster and 78% slower than the baseline. For the queries performing better than baseline, diefficiency improvements of 40–63% could be observed. Thus, we reject Hypothesis 3 due to update-based restarts not being universally beneficial, but accept Hypothesis 1 due to tangible improvements attainable.

---

[2] https://github.com/SolidBench/SolidBench.js.
[3] https://github.com/rubensworks/jbr.js.
[4] https://github.com/surilindur/comunica-experiments.

Table 1. Overview of the benchmark results for different configurations: average time taken to produce the first and last result (s), average total query duration (s), average *dief@k* when *k* is the total number of results, the share of finished queries for which *dief@k* was below or above the baseline, the average decrease or increase of that metric relative to baseline for those queries respectively, as well as the he number of queries finished successfully and the average number of join restarts per query execution.

# Configuration	First result	Last result	Query duration	Below baseline	Above baseline	Average dief@k	dief@k decrease	dief@k increase	Queries finished	Average restarts
1 baseline	7.4	9.5	10.5	0%	0%	23.9	0%	0%	51/75	0.0
2 overhead	8.5	9.9	11.2	43%	54%	22.7	33%	156%	46/75	0.0
3 overhead simple	8.3	9.1	10.5	38%	60%	24.5	41%	123%	42/75	0.0
4 cardinality once	9.4	10.8	11.9	57%	41%	17.2	47%	3,253%	49/75	0.8
5 cardinality once void	4.6	6.4	7.3	39%	59%	19.4	40%	1,878%	44/75	0.9
6 cardinality once void simple	13.0	17.0	18.2	93%	5%	37.9	44%	22,744%	43/75	0.8
7 cardinality unlimited	8.2	9.3	10.5	71%	27%	18.2	63%	2,660%	48/75	2.2
8 cardinality unlimited void	4.6	6.0	6.8	50%	48%	15.2	52%	808%	42/75	1.3
9 cardinality unlimited void simple	7.7	9.7	11.1	93%	5%	22.9	52%	24,555%	41/75	1.3
10 timeout 100	6.8	10.7	13.4	89%	11%	110.2	37%	189%	36/75	1.1
11 timeout 100 void	5.6	10.5	13.8	72%	28%	173.6	40%	196%	32/75	1.0
12 timeout 100 void simple	9.8	17.3	21.1	35%	65%	183.4	49%	403%	31/75	0.9
13 timeout 1,000	9.7	14.5	17.6	17%	83%	144.1	64%	231%	29/75	0.7
14 timeout 1,000 void	5.9	10.6	13.2	61%	39%	138.4	47%	212%	33/75	0.9
15 timeout 1,000 void simple	10.5	17.5	20.6	71%	29%	163.9	62%	503%	34/75	0.8
16 timeout 2,000	9.3	13.4	15.8	71%	26%	77.2	49%	190%	34/75	0.6
17 timeout 2,000 void	7.4	13.9	16.3	22%	75%	112.3	48%	392%	36/75	0.8
18 timeout 2,000 void simple	8.1	15.1	18.3	26%	74%	167.6	50%	326%	35/75	0.7
19 timeout 5,000	10.6	16.2	18.5	17%	80%	140.3	50%	465%	35/75	0.5
20 timeout 5,000 void	8.4	14.3	17.1	73%	24%	140.1	44%	317%	37/75	0.6
21 timeout 5,000 void simple	8.5	15.4	17.9	65%	35%	181.9	53%	347%	37/75	0.4
22 timeout 10,000	8.7	12.7	14.9	18%	77%	119.1	40%	9,850%	44/75	0.4
23 timeout 10,000 void	9.4	13.5	17.5	18%	78%	91.7	40%	3,442%	45/75	0.4
24 timeout 10,000 void simple	9.7	15.1	17.8	22%	78%	149.2	41%	325%	37/75	0.4
25 timeout 20,000	7.0	10.4	14.6	69%	25%	94.3	24%	12,381%	51/75	0.2
26 timeout 20,000 void	9.1	13.4	17.8	0%	0%	124.1	37%	13,497%	49/75	0.3
27 timeout 20,000 void simple	10.3	16.2	20.0	24%	74%	141.8	32%	386%	38/75	0.3

7 Conclusions

In related work [18], the *theoretical* impact of better query planning was shown. In our work, we proved this theory using a restart-based query planning approach, and achieved average reductions of up to 36% in query execution time. Our results show that client-side approaches are instrumental in achieving the levels of query performance needed for real-world interactive applications over decentralised environments such as Solid. This brings us a step closer towards addressing the challenges around privacy and data management at scale, and to lower the barriers of entry to the data-driven market.

Acknowledgements. The described research activities were supported by SolidLab Vlaanderen (Flemish Government, EWI and RRF project VV023/10). Ruben Taelman is a postdoctoral fellow of the Research Foundation – Flanders (FWO) (1202124N).

References

1. Acosta, M., Vidal, M.E., Lampo, T., Castillo, J., Ruckhaus, E.: ANAPSID: an adaptive query processing engine for SPARQL endpoints. In: International Semantic Web Conference, pp. 18–34 (2011)
2. Acosta, M., Vidal, M.E., Sure-Vetter, Y.: Diefficiency metrics: measuring the continuous efficiency of query processing approaches. In: International Semantic Web Conference, pp. 3–19 (2017)
3. Capadisli, S., Berners-Lee, T., Verborgh, R., Kjernsmo, K.: Solid protocol 0.10.0. W3C community group technical report, W3C (2022). https://solidproject.org/TR/2022/protocol-20221231
4. Cole, R.L., Graefe, G.: Optimization of dynamic query evaluation plans. In: ACM SIGMOD International Conference on Management of Data, pp. 150–160 (1994)
5. Cyganiak, R., Alexander, K., Zhao, J., Hausenblas, M.: Describing linked datasets with the VoID vocabulary. W3C note, W3C (2011). https://www.w3.org/TR/2011/NOTE-void-20110303/
6. Deshpande, A., Hellerstein, J.M.: Lifting the burden of history from adaptive query processing. In: International Conference on Very Large Databases, pp. 948–959 (2004)
7. Deshpande, A., Ives, Z., Raman, V., et al.: Adaptive query processing. Found. Trends Databases **1**(1), 1–140 (2007)
8. Erling, O., et al.: The LDBC social network benchmark: interactive workload. In: PACM SIGMOD International Conference on Management of Data, pp. 619–630 (2015)
9. Hagedorn, S., Hose, K., Sattler, K.U., Umbrich, J.: Resource planning for SPARQL query execution on data sharing platforms. In: 5th International Conference on Consuming Linked Data, pp. 49–60 (2014)
10. Hartig, O.: Zero-knowledge query planning for an iterator implementation of link traversal based query execution. In: Extended Semantic Web Conference, pp. 154–169 (2011)
11. Hartig, O., Bizer, C., Freytag, J.C.: Executing SPARQL queries over the web of linked data. In: International Semantic Web Conference, pp. 293–309 (2009)
12. Hartig, O., Langegger, A.: A database perspective on consuming linked data on the web. Datenbank-Spektrum **10**, 57–66 (2010)
13. Hartig, O., Özsu, M.T.: Walking without a map: optimizing response times of traversal-based linked data queries (extended version). arXiv preprint arXiv:1607.01046 (2016)
14. Neumann, T., Moerkotte, G.: Characteristic sets: accurate cardinality estimation for RDF queries with multiple joins. In: 2011 IEEE 27th International Conference on Data Engineering, pp. 984–994 (2011)
15. Stocker, M., Seaborne, A., Bernstein, A., Kiefer, C., Reynolds, D.: SPARQL basic graph pattern optimization using selectivity estimation. In: 17th International Conference on World Wide Web, pp. 595–604 (2008)
16. Taelman, R.: Towards applications on the decentralized web using hypermedia-driven query engines. ACM SIGWEB Newslett. (2024)
17. Taelman, R., Van Herwegen, J., Vander Sande, M., Verborgh, R.: Comunica: a modular SPARQL query engine for the web. In: International Semantic Web Conference, pp. 239–255 (2018)

18. Taelman, R., Verborgh, R.: Link traversal query processing over decentralized environments with structural assumptions. In: International Semantic Web Conference, pp. 3–22 (2023)
19. Verborgh, R.: Re-decentralizing the web, for good this time. In: Linking the World's Information: Essays on Tim Berners-Lee's Invention of the World Wide Web, pp. 215–230 (2023)

Interoperable Cyber-Physical Multi-Agent Systems Through Web of Things

Roman Binkert[1](✉)[iD], Fady Salama[1][iD], Ege Korkan[2][iD], Sebastian Käbisch[2][iD], and Sebastian Steinhorst[1][iD]

[1] TUM School of Computation, Information and Technology, Technical University of Munich, Munich, Germany
{roman.binkert,fady.salama,sebastian.steinhorst}@tum.de
[2] Siemens AG, Garching, Germany
{ege.korkan,sebastian.kabisch}@siemens.com

Abstract. With the rise of Internet of Things (IoT) systems, new paradigms are introduced to overcome their increasing complexity. One such paradigm is the Multi-Agent System (MAS), which consists of highly autonomous, reactive, and self-organizing agents. Many MAS frameworks exist but suffer from fragmentation and limit agents' interoperability, which remains a highly-discussed problem. Additionally, integrating Cyber-Physical Systems (CPSs) into MASs remains complex, limiting their physical applicability.

In this paper, we present Web of Multi-Agent Things (WoMAT), a novel concept to directly include the W3C Web of Things (WoT) standard into agent-to-agent communication. Our method leverages the standardized interoperability of WoT to seamlessly integrate heterogeneous MASs with each other and into CPSs while preserving their autonomy, decentralized coordination, and the expressive reasoning capabilities provided by AgentSpeak programming. We propose a systematic mapping between WoT Interaction Affordances (IAs) and AgentSpeak performatives, enabling agents to interact directly with diverse CPSs and exchange knowledge with other agents independent of the underlying communication protocols. Furthermore, our approach enables semantic interoperability between heterogeneous agents and CPSs by utilizing the descriptive powers of ontology-enriched WoT Thing Descriptions.

We provide an open-source implementation of our methodology, integrated with the JaCoMo framework for agent programming. Using multiple scenarios, we demonstrate and evaluate our approach and show that our method leverages MASs to be a more viable solution on the cyber-physical edge.

Keywords: Interoperability · Web of Things · Multi-Agent Systems · Cyber-Physical-Systems · Internet of Things

1 Introduction

The Internet of Things (IoT) is a significant driver for Industry 4.0. Via IoT, Cyber-Physical Systems (CPSs) are interconnected with each other, which leads to higher automation and intelligence and, therefore, maximizes the efficiency in manufacturing and production. However, its exponential growth has led to multiple IoT platforms, manufacturers, and protocols, which has caused fragmentation. To tackle this interoperability challenge, the W3C proposes the WoT, which provides a standardized description of IoT device interactions. This allows us to interact with many different devices. However, a central organizer must orchestrate these different devices to work towards a common goal.

A well-studied approach for more autonomous and self-organizing systems are Multi-Agent Systems (MASs) with the Beliefs-Desires-Intentions (BDI) architecture. In MAS, multiple autonomous agents work together to find the best solution. The field of MASs is a long-studied field, and currently, multiple different agent development frameworks follow similar guidelines. However, the concrete implementation often varies, and especially when agents communicate over the web, a uniform interaction interface between the agents is not given, which hinders the collaboration of heterogeneous agents. To solve this issue, a uniform interaction interface between agents has been of interest to many research approaches [8]. Additionally, we have found that MASs often lack integration with the physical world since the integration and control of real devices often remain complex, which limits the applicability of MASs in CPS environments.

1.1 Problem Statement

The combination of WoT, for interoperability, and MASs, for autonomy and self-organization, has become of more interest in recent years, and it was shown that the combination can benefit both sides [11]. Recent approaches integrate the WoT into MAS by allowing agents to discover and communicate with new entities using the WoT Resource Description Framework (RDF) graphs [4,7,15]. However, these approaches require the agent programmer to directly include the WoT programming into the agent code and, therefore, require advanced knowledge of the WoT standards. Additionally, while allowing agents to communicate with Things, these approaches do not increase the interoperability between heterogeneous agents. Therefore, interoperability in heterogeneous agent environments is still a challenge.

1.2 Approach and Contributions

In this paper, we present our framework and its open-source implementation, Web of Multi-Agent Things (WoMAT), which utilizes the powers of WoT for diverse, protocol-independent multi-agent communication applications. As shown in Fig. 1, our approach allows agents to interact with diverse IoT devices in a uniform, agent communication-like style. Furthermore, this communication approach can be used not only for agent-device communication but also for agent-to-agent communication. This increases the interoperability of heterogeneous agents by leveraging the descriptive and interoperability powers of WoT for MAS communication. Lastly, we show how the descriptive powers of WoT and suiting ontologies can be used not only for communication and description

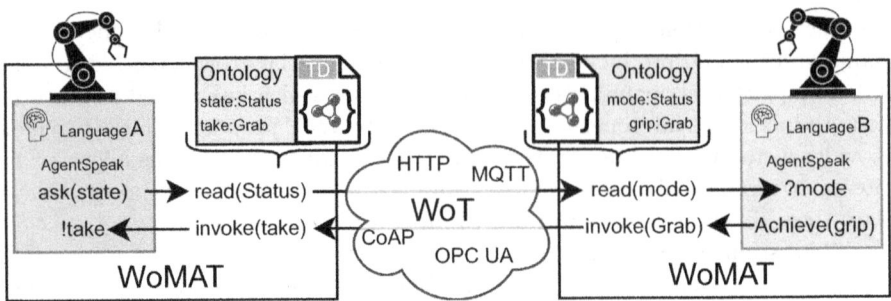

Fig. 1: The figure shows two agents (A_A, A_B), each running an instance of our framework, WoMAT. A_A and A_B use different internal namings for the same concept (e.g. state, mode for Status). Based on the ontology-enhanced TD of A_A, our framework in A_A maps the ask(state) request to the WoT IA readProperty representing Status, and finds and invokes the according property in A_B's TD. Our framework in A_B then translates this request to the naming of A_B (mode) and creates a source-annotated test goal in the belief base of A_B, which can then take action to respond.

of the agent but also to exchange knowledge and plans between heterogeneous agents. In particular, we perform the following contributions:

- We propose a mapping schema between AgentSpeak performatives and WoT Interaction Affordances (IAs) for protocol agnostic agent-device and agent-agent communication in Sect. 4.2.
- We show how our approach leverages the descriptive powers of Thing Descriptions (TDs) to semantically abstract from different internal namings of heterogeneous agents to automatically exchange knowledge and especially plans in Sect. 4.3.
- We evaluate our approach and open-source implementation with example use cases in Sect. 5.

The rest of the paper is structured as follows: We provide a short overview of the WoT features needed for this implementation, especially IAs and the TD, with its ability to integrate semantic tags in Sect. 2.1. An overview of the MAS concepts, especially for the JaCoMo agent development framework, is given in Sect. 2.2. We discuss related work in Sect. 3, present our approach in Sect. 4, evaluate in Sect. 5, and finally conclude in Sect. 6.

2 Background

Our framework is built upon two system designs, the WoT and MASs. This section will introduce both concepts.

2.1 WoT and TD

The WoT [13] is an amalgamation of multiple web standards aimed at providing a standardized interface in the heterogeneous landscape of IoT. At the core of

WoT is the TD [14], a document that describes the interface of the underlying Thing. It is a JSON for Linked Data (JSON-LD) document and, therefore, is highly human- and machine-readable.

The three kinds of IAs define three ways of communicating or interacting with a Thing [13]. These IAs are defined as follows:

- **Property Affordance**: A property exposes the state or settings of a Thing. This state can be read and/or written. Additionally, it can be observable, informing observers of a change in this state. It can be used for, e.g., the value of a sensor (then read-only), the current status of a lamp (on, off), or to set the measurement interval of a sensor.
- **Action Affordance**: An action affects the state of the Thing or triggers a process on the Thing. This can be toggling a lamp or dimming a lamp over time.
- **Event Affordance**: The emission of an event leads to an asynchronous update to all subscribers. It is similar to an observable property but has no current state. It can be used, e.g., to inform that the Thing is overheating.

The semantic meaning of the data and IA can be described with so-called semantic annotations by using ontologies. Also, the structure of the input and output data of each IA can be precisely described with schemas and semantically annotated. Lastly, the protocol bindings define how the IA is mapped to the concrete protocol. Besides the IAs, a TD can hold meta information regarding the interaction with a Thing, like security definitions.

2.2 Multi-agent Systems (MASs)

Agent programming generally focuses on creating autonomous, proactive, and reactive entities. In MASs, multiple agents work together and exchange information, and, therefore, it promises more flexible and scaleable solutions for complex tasks [10]. An established way of programming such agents is with the BDI architecture [6]. As shown in Fig. 2, an agent perceives new beliefs about its environment through sensors or by communication from other agents. These beliefs about the environment are then compared to the agent's desires. If there is a difference between the current and desired states, the desire becomes an active goal. The agent will then seek a suitable plan to reach that goal and take action towards it.

Agent programming languages, like e.g. Jason, are commonly referred to as AgentSpeak and distinguish test (?) and achieve (!) goals. As shown in Fig. 3, a plan has a plan trigger (+!process(green)) that defines when the plan is triggered, in this case, when a goal of name !process with input green is added. Once the plan is triggered, the actions of the plan (lines 2–5) will be executed in order. An agent programming language often comes with an agent programming framework, like JaCaMo, which provides further agent programming tools, such as a *mind inspector*, that allows the inspection of an agent's current beliefs (belief base) or intentions.

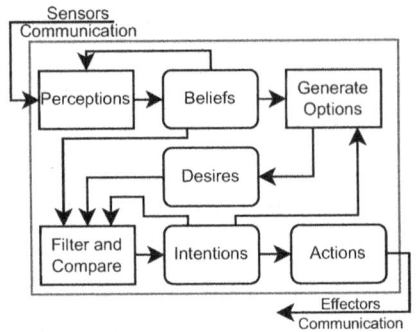

```
1  +!process(green) <-
2     .print("Processing green");
3     !moveTo(0.2, - 0.35, 0.3);
4     !dropObject;
5     !goHome.
```

Fig. 2: Basic reasoning cycle of a BDI agent. Beliefs are added through perception or communication from other agents. The beliefs are then compared to the desires. If there is a difference, the agent will intend to change this, resulting in an action. Figure adapted from [5].

Fig. 3: An agent plan programmed in Jason. If a new achievement goal to process(green) is added, the agent will follow this plan. It consists of four steps. First, it prints some information to the terminal, and then it adds three achievement goals, each needing to be fulfilled before moving to the next goal. With the first goal, it wants to move to some position, then drop the object, and finally go home.

Agent Communication. In MASs, multiple of the above-presented agents are present that can communicate with each other and exchange information. So-called Agent Communication Languages (ACLs) are used to define the information exchange between agents, An ACL unifies the message format and adds an ontology for all agents to communicate and interpret received messages. [10].

One central aspect of an ACL are the so-called *performatives.* A performative describes what an agent wants to express or reach with its message [1]. The Foundation for Intelligent Physical Agents (FIPA) defines several performatives like *inform, request, agree, and subscribe* [2]. However, the actual performatives vary between different agent-development frameworks, which also hinders the interoperability between agents.

For our implementation, we use the agent development framework JaCoMo with the following performatives:

- **Tell**: Agent A wants to share a belief with Agent B.
- **Ask**: Agent A wants to know whether Agent B knows something.
- **Achieve**: Agent A wants Agent B to achieve a goal.
- **AskHow**: Agent A wants to know if Agent B has a plan for a specified event.

3 Related Work

Integrating agents and MASs with real devices to enable them for manufacturing, the main potential application of MASs, or other cyber-physical applications is a long-studied problem [8].

Some approaches strive to directly integrate agents into Embedded Systems by allowing agents to control them via a serial port communication [16] and show that connecting via an IoT network can be a viable solution for, e.g., the management of crisis events [12]. However, we see agent programming as best applicable on a higher level of abstraction, like the WoT provides, especially if the target system is already IoT-enabled.

While WoT has not yet been used for agent-to-agent communication as we propose, several approaches integrate WoT for agent-to-device communication and see WoT as the first-class abstraction for IoT devices in MASs [9]. It has been demonstrated that with WoT-enabled MASs, agents can manage manufacturing systems, and based on the RDF representation of the TD, agents can interact with IoT devices and even refactor manufacturing systems on the fly. [9]. By Hypermedia, which can be described as RDF, relations among WoT devices can be shown. The framework *Yggdrasil* uses this to discover TD-described WoT devices and ways to interact with them at runtime. By the use of ontologies, knowledge about the devices can be represented in a standardized way and understood by the agents [8]. However, the representation of interacting with devices in AgentSpeak remains complex, limiting its descriptive powers. Hypermedia has been proven useful for agents, especially for planning with WoT devices. Different approaches provide artifacts that can discover things, how to interact with them, and comprehensively plan with them by using Knowledge Graphs [15] or through Linked Data navigation [7]. Therefore, the integration of WoT into MAS is an acknowledged approach that enables agents to interact with IoT devices in a standardized way. All these approaches focus on how agents can control devices and, mainly at runtime, find plans that include these devices. By introducing agent-to-agent communication through WoT, our contribution enables these works' discovery and planning mechanisms to be extended to heterogeneous agents in MASs.

The FIPA provides several standards for more interoperable MASs [17]. However, the standards focus on agent organization or message structure rather than the actual semantic interoperability of heterogeneous agents. Only a few approaches towards semantic interoperability of MASs have been made. But they introduce additional agents with the sole purpose of translating between different internal namings [3] instead of leveraging a standardized description of the agent's understanding.

4 Approach

In our approach, we combine MAS with WoT via a systematic mapping to easily connect heterogeneous agents and diverse CPSs. The capabilities of each agent are uniformly described as IA via the agent's TD, which allows to communicate with agnostic programmed agents via various protocols. On the other hand, CPSs and other heterogeneous agents described with a TD can be uniformly interacted with from agent plans in conventional AgentSpeak. In this section, we will elaborate on our fundamental mapping schema and how it leverages protocol-agnostic communication of WoT for uniform communication between agents and

WoT-enabled devices. Additionally, we show how our approach utilizes semantic annotations in TDs to enable knowledge and plan exchange between semantically heterogeneous agents.

In WoT, a Thing that exposes its IAs through a TD is called exposing Thing, and a Thing interacting with that Thing is called consuming Thing. Following this naming convention, we use the terms *exposed agent* and *consuming agent*.

4.1 Framework Architecture

To enable MAS communication through WoT, our framework consists of two independent components that handle the mapping and semantic abstraction between internal v to WoT communication. The first component maps the AgentSpeak intent (performative) of the *consuming agent* to one of the WoT IA according to our mapping schema presented in Sect. 4.2 and shown in Fig. 4. The second component semantically abstracts the concrete intent and data to a general ontology both agents understand, as presented in Sect. 4.3 and shown in Fig. 5. Based on the abstracted intent and the annotated TD of the *exposed agent*, the *consuming agent* finds the according IA of the *exposed agent* and invokes it with the abstracted data. In the *consuming agent*, the same happens backward to translate everything from semantically abstracted, WoT IA to the internally used AgentSpeak of it. Notably, an agent can simultaneously act as an *exposed agent* in one information exchange while being the *consuming agent* in another.

4.2 Mapping Schema

To enable not only agent-to-device but also agent-to-agent communication through WoT while using the expressive AgentSpeak, we map AgentSpeak to WoT IAs in the *consuming agent* and also back from IAs to AgentSpeak in the *exposed agent*. Both parts will be described in the following.

Mapping from AgentSpeak to WoT IAs. As shown on the left side of Fig. 4, most performatives can be mapped directly to IAs and are, therefore, universally applicable for all WoT devices. For some other performatives, we propose a dedicated action.

In AgentSpeak, the *ask* performative is used when an agent wants to request some information about a certain entity from another agent. In WoT, properties and events can be used to request information about something. Therefore, we map the *ask* performative to reading or observing a property or subscribing to an event, depending on how the information is exposed. If not indicated otherwise, the property is observed such that the agent gets updates repeatedly.

The *achieve* performative is used when the *consuming agent* wants to delegate a goal to the *exposed agent* and, therefore, asks the *exposed agent* to do something. In the WoT, the action IA triggers a process on the exposed Thing. Therefore, we map the *achieve* performative to invoking an action.

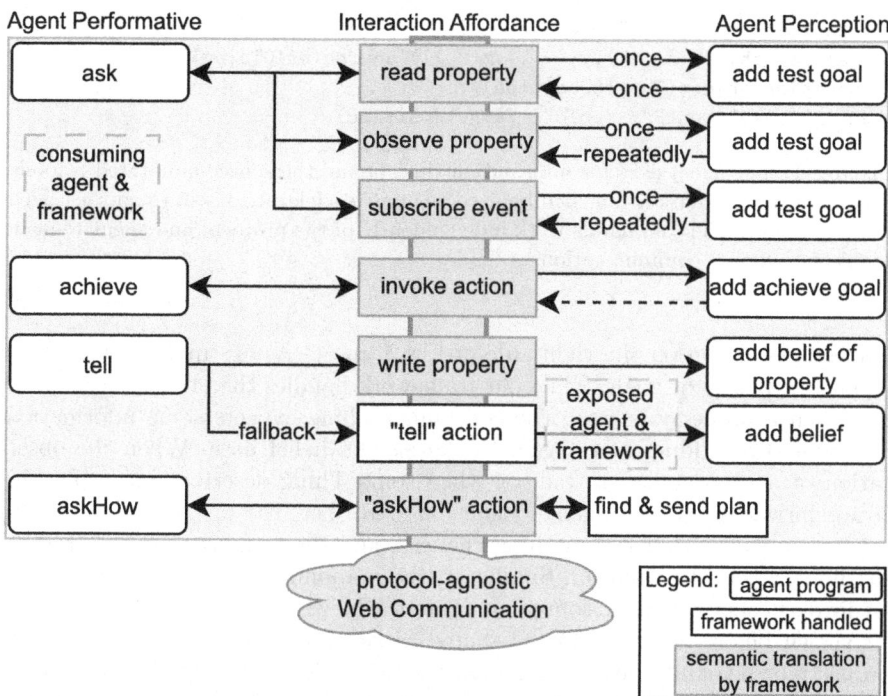

Fig. 4: The mapping schema from AgentSpeak to WoT IA and vice versa. The AgentSpeak in the *consuming agent* is first mapped to IAs, then sent through the WoT stack to the *exposed agent*, and there again mapped to AgentSpeak. Therefore, this approach also works if one side is not an agent. The framework handles semantic translation, particularly of plans and distribution of responses to the right *consuming agent* as described in Sect. 4.3. Most requests are forwarded to the *exposed agent* as translated, source-annotated beliefs or goals.

Both asking and delegating goals can or should lead to a response from the other agent or device. The response is represented in the agent's belief base as a source-annotated belief. In MASs, agents can also share information proactively. We map this to writing the according property of the *exposed agent*. If no semantically matching property is exposed, the information is communicated through a dedicated *tell* action. Finally, agents can exchange plans for achieving something, which is mapped to a dedicated *askHow* action. How a plan can be exchanged between semantically different agents will be elaborated in Sect. 4.3.

With the above-presented mapping, the desire of the *consuming agent* can be translated from AgentSpeak to invoking WoT IAs on other agents or conventional WoT devices. In the following, we will continue with the mapping from IAs back to AgentSpeak for the *exposed agent*.

Mapping from WoT IA to AgentSpeak. If an IA gets invoked on an agent's TD, this must be represented and forwarded to the agent so that it can react to this

```
1 wotAskOne("ur10Thing", "position").
2 position(object(x(155),y(-205),z(80)))[source(ur10Thing)]
3 ?position(object(TargetPosition));
4 wotAchieve("agentB", "goTo", TargetPosition).
```

Listing 1: The agent asks for information (line 1) and the source-annotated response (line 2). The information can then be used as input to delegate a goal to another agent (lines 3 and 4). The commands work independently of the protocol and agent-to-agent or agent-to-device communication.

request. As shown on the right side of Fig. 4, most IAs are mapped to source-annotated beliefs or goals, while our framework handles the other requests.

When a property is read, the consuming Thing expects some information, represented as adding a test goal to the agent's belief base. When the observation of a property is started, or when some Thing describes an event, this is not forwarded to the agent's belief base. Rather, the agent is expected to send updates by itself if something changes, and the framework keeps track of the information distribution. Similar to the mapping in the *consuming agent*, an invoked action adds a source-annotated achieve goal to the *exposed agent*. As shown before, a belief can be shared proactively by writing the according property or invoking the *tell* action with the belief as input. Both result in the addition of a source-annotated belief in the agent's belief base. If an IA has input data, this gets annotated as part of the belief or goal. Output data can be matched to the corresponding request via a generated message ID. Finally, the agent-specific *askHow* action triggers the plan exchange. This request, however, is not forwarded to the agent itself but handled by our framework. We will elaborate on this in detail in Sect. 4.3.

4.3 Semantic Abstraction

With the above-presented mapping schema, we can translate from AgentSpeak performatives to WoT IAs and vice versa. This allows agents to interact with other agents and WoT devices by using AgentSpeak. Based on this, we use the WoT semantic annotation functionality to enhance the interoperability between agents with heterogeneous naming conventions. In the following section, we show how this is done and how it can be used to translate heterogeneous plans.

We have N agents that use a different internal naming convention I_n for concepts C^{I_n}. By using the WoT as the communication layer as proposed above, agents are syntactically interoperable. With a mapping $M_{I_{n1}-I_{n2}}$ between the different namings I_{n1} and I_{n2}, we can make these agents semantically interoperable. But for N agents, we need $\#M = \frac{N(N-1)}{2}$ mappings M.

As shown in Sect. 2.1, a TD can be enhanced with so-called semantic annotations, which again can be used to include an ontology in the TD. We use the semantic-annotated TDs to generate a mapping $M_{I_{n1}TD-O}$ between the internal naming I_{n1} and a shared ontology O. We reduce the required mappings to

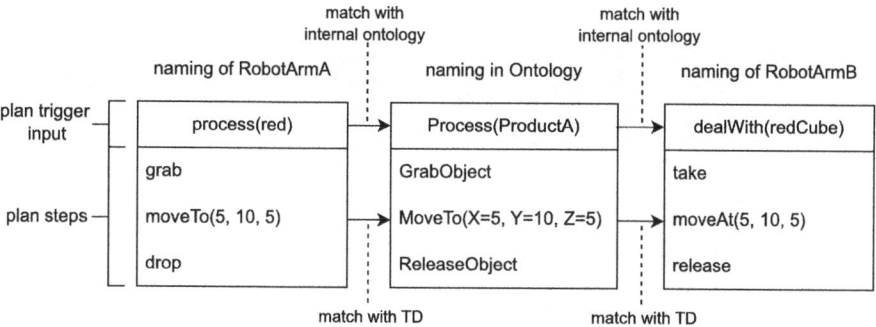

Fig. 5: The process of plan translation. Plan steps and inputs are mapped with the TD. Plan trigger and input are translated with a user-defined mapping.

$\#M = N$ by this. Not all necessary concepts C might be represented in the TD of an agent, and, therefore, the generated mapping $M_{I_{n1TD}-O}$ might be incomplete. We allow a user-defined mapping $M_{I_{n1UD}-O}$ either in each function call or as a dictionary in the beginning for these concepts. For that, we have to map $M_{I_{n1}-O} = M_{I_{n1TD}-O} + M_{I_{n1UD}-O}$, which can map all concepts of the internal naming C_{n1}^I to the ontology.

If a *consuming agent* CA wants to get information for a concept C, it can send a request with the internal name of that concept $C^{I_{CA}}$. Our framework on the *consuming agent* side will then use the mapping $M_{I_{CA}-O}$ to translate the concept to the ontology C^O. Our framework will then crawl the TD of the *exposed agent* EA to find the according IA and invoke it. This will result in adding a source-annotated belief or goal of the concept in the internal naming of the *exposed agent* $C^{I_{EA}}$ to its belief base.

With these two mechanisms, the *exposed agent* and the *consuming agent* can work with their own internal naming conventions. Since the translation is done on the *consuming agent*'s side, it also works if the exposed Thing is a conventional WoT device. This works similarly for all performatives; only the translation of plans needs some extra steps, which we will elaborate on in the following.

Plan Translation. A plan consists of a plan trigger T_P, representing the higher level goal, with optional input J_P and one or several steps S_P, which all can have input J_{SP}. All of these can have a different internal name C^P. Therefore, contrary to beliefs and goals, plans are more complex to translate between different internal namings I.

In theory, the steps S_P could be anything. However, we state that only plans consisting of steps both agents can perform would make sense to translate. Therefore, we limit the translateable plans to only include goals exposed as IA in the TD or goals referring to third devices' IAs. Especially for steps S_P with inputs J_{SP}, the TD provides a structured way to annotate and find a mapping that would otherwise be hard to describe.

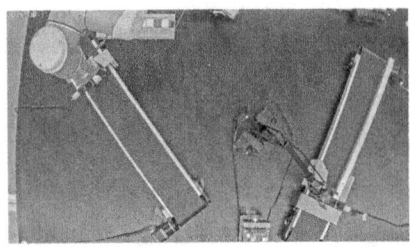
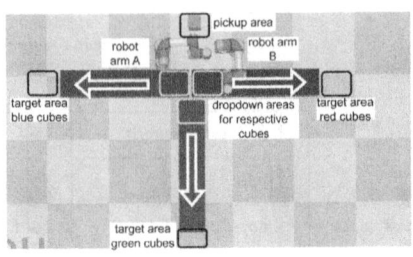

Fig. 6: The real manufacturing lane setup contains two robot arms (uarm and ur10) that should transport cubes between the two conveyor belts.

Fig. 7: The simulated robot arm setup contains three colored conveyor belts to which the two agent-controlled robot arms shall move the equally colored cubes.

As shown in Fig. 5, with the mapping of the TD M_{TD-O}, the plan steps can be translated similarly to beliefs and goals by our framework. Only for the plan trigger T_P and plan input J_P the user-defined mapping M_{UD-O} is necessary. Together with the above-presented translation for beliefs and goals, as well as the mapping schema from AgentSpeak to WoT IAs and back, we allow heterogeneous agents to communicate with each other as if they would have the same concrete naming.

5 Evaluation

In the previous section, we have shown how our approach enables agents to communicate over the WoT using conventional AgentSpeak, even if the agents use different internal namings. In this section, we evaluate our approach regarding interoperability between heterogeneous agents and WoT-enabled CPSs and performance.

We have implemented the approach with a CArtAgO artifact for the JaCoMo[1] agent-development framework for the agent side. For the WoT-side, we use the reference implementation of the WoT Scripting API node-wot[2].

5.1 Experimental Setups

To demonstrate and evaluate the contributions of our approach, we conduct experiments in the following setups. The implementation of our approach, the code for the experiments, and videos showing the experiments are publicly available[3].

S_1: *Real Cyber-Physcial MAS Setup:* The first setup contains a real manufacturing setup with two robot arms and two conveyor belts, as shown in Fig. 6. The task of the robot arms is to transport a cube from one conveyor belt to

---

[1] https://jacamo-lang.github.io/.
[2] https://github.com/eclipse-thingweb/node-wot.
[3] https://github.com/tum-esi/WoMAT.

```
1  {"@type": "thing",
2  "title": "robot agent",
3  "@context": [{"e0": "exampleOntology"}],
4  "properties": { "state": { "@type": "e0:State" }},
5  "actions": {
6    "goHome": { "@type": "e0:GoHome"},
7    "moveTo": { "@type": "e0:MoveToPosition",
8      "input": { "properties": {
9        "x": { "@type": "e0:PositionX"},
10       "y": { "@type": "e0:PositionY"},
11       "z": { "@type": "e0:PositionZ"} }}},
12   "gripObject": { "@type": "e0:GrabObject" },
13   "dropObject": { "@type": "e0:ReleaseObject"},
14   "askHow": {},
15   "tell": {} }}
```

Listing 2: An example of an agent's TD. It contains our proposed agent-specific IAs "askHow" (Line 15) and "tell" (Line 16). The non-agent-specific IAs are annotated with an ontology. The rest of the TD is omitted for brevity.

the other. A dedicated agent controls each device. While robot arms only consist of one Thing, the conveyor belts consist of a sensor for object detection and the conveyor belt with the motor. The agents communicate with the WoT representation of their corresponding device, and the robot arms communicate with the conveyor belt to know when a new cube is ready to pick up. The video demonstrating this use case can be found under the name *Real CPS Demo* in our above-linked GitHub repo.

S_2: *Simulated Manufacturing Setup:* The second setup contains two robot arms and three colored conveyor belts. The robot arms are controlled by agents $A_{R1,R2}$ with different internal namings $I_{R1,R2}$. A WoT-enabled sensor can detect a new cube and its color in the pickup area and has to be contacted by the agents $A_{R1,R2}$. The robot arms should pick up the colored cubes from the pickup area and drop them on the dedicated conveyor belt, as shown in Fig. 7. However, only A_{R1} has plans for blue and green cubes $P_{B,G}$. The example TD A_{R1} exposes its capabilities with I_{R1} as shown in Listing 2. The video demonstrating this use case can be found under the name *Simulated Manufacturing Demo* in our above-linked GitHub repo.

S_3: *Protocol Agnostic Agents:* This setup consists of four agents $A_{1,2,3,4}$. A_2 only supports HTTP, A_3 only supports CoAP, while A_1 supports both protocols. All of $A_{1,2,3}$ use different internal namings I. A_1 should communicate with both, A_2 and A_3, through our framework. A_4 is a standard JaCoMo agent with same naming as A_1 to which A_1 shall communicate for comparison.

5.2 Interoperability Evaluation

Using the above-presented setups, we evaluate our approach regarding protocol and semantic interoperability between heterogeneous agents and WoT devices.

Real CPS Integration: In S_1 and S_2, agents control their corresponding devices. In total, we controlled six different TD-described devices. All interactions with these devices, reading properties, invoking actions, and listening to events, could be done with a universal command for each interaction type, as shown in Listing 1.

Protocol Agnostic Agent Communication: In S_3, A_2 and A_3 use different protocols. However, A_1 can communicate with A_2 and A_3 using the same command, which does not include the protocol (similar to Listing 1). This proves that agents can communicate equally with agents and devices independent of the protocol.

Semantic Agnostic Agent Communication: In S_2, A_{R2} does not know how to process red and green cubes. Therefore, A_{R2} asks A_{R1} for the according plans. In the experiment A_{R1} and A_{R2} use different I. However, the plans in A_{R1} can be translated from I_{R1} to $IR2$ by our framework and then executed by A_{R2}. This shows that with our framework, knowledge and plans can be exchanged and used between heterogeneous agents.

5.3 Performance Evaluation

We evaluate the influence of our approach on the performance of the agent communication regarding the processing time and the necessary lines of code.

Processing Time Evaluation: To evaluate the processing time, we measure the translating times for plans with different amounts of steps and compare it to the total execution time, including the search in the agents plan library and the communication between AgentThing and CArtAgO artifact. As shown in Fig. 9, the plan translation time grows linear with the number of steps but is marginal compared to the total execution time. The processing time performance evaluation was done using a laptop with an 11th Gen Intel Core i7-11800H processor containing 8 cores and running at 2.30 GHz frequency, 16 GB of DDR4 RAM, and NVIDIA GeForce RTX 3060 Laptop GPU.

```
1  // Jason
2  .send(agentB, askOne, status).   // A asks
3  // answer by agent B
4  +?status[source(Source)]: status(Status) <-
5      .send(Source, tell, status(Status)).
6  // WoMAT
7  wotAskOne(agentB, status).   // A asks
8  // answer by agent B
9  +?status(MsgID): status(Current) <-
10     wotSendTestResponse(Current, MsgID).
11
12 // define TD address for agentB
13 {"agentB": "http://localhost:8080/agentB"}
```

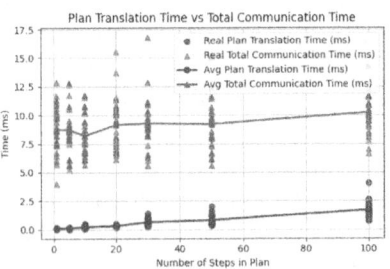

Fig. 8: The code lines needed for agent communication in plain Jason and with our framework. The *consuming agent* only needs the TD address of agentB additonally. The *exposed agent* needs a TD as shown in listing 2. Therefore, the AgentSpeak overhead is minimal.

Fig. 9: The time needed for just the plan translation grows linear with the number of steps the plan has. It is marginal compared to the total communication time, which shows that the overhead for the semantic translation is small.

Code Line Evaluation: Our approach provides protocol and semantic agnostic communication between agents. When the agents use the same internal naming, they can still communicate protocol agnostic through the web with our framework. As shown in Fig. 8, a similar AgentSpeak is used. Only the TD address and the agent's own TD must be defined once. When the agents use different internal naming, the same is still needed, but the TD needs to be enhanced with ontology tags and mappings that are not defined there need to be defined additionally. However, in the agent programming, the necessary code stays the same. This shows that for homogeneous agents, our approach provides a protocol-agnostic web communication with minimal overhead, and especially for heterogeneous agent programming, the added overhead stays minimal.

6 Conclusion

This paper presents WoMAT, our novel approach that enables heterogeneous agent-to-agent communication through WoT. Our method uniquely enables agents to interact with WoT devices with the expressive powers of AgentSpeak.

We demonstrate how our approach maps WoT IAs to AgentSpeak performatives, leveraging the descriptive powers of the TD to provide uniform and ontology-enriched agent descriptions. This enables semantically heterogeneous agents to exchange knowledge and plans while keeping their internal naming conventions. Additionally, the mapping enables agents to utilize AgentSpeak's expressive reasoning to interact with other agents and conventional WoT-enabled devices, independent of the underlying protocols and semantics.

We provide an open-source implementation of our approach with the JaCoMo agent framework and the node-wot scripting API. Our evaluation across multiple scenarios demonstrates that WoMAT effectively integrates CPSs into MASs and enables the exchange of knowledge and plans between heterogeneous agents. In the future, our approach could be combined with other frameworks, such as [7], to extend their agent-to-device planning and discovery capabilities to agent-to-agent interactions.

Disclosure of Interests. The authors have no competing interests to declare that are relevant to the content of this article.

References

1. FIPA ACL Message Structure Specification. http://www.fipa.org/specs/fipa00061/SC00061G.html#_Toc26669706. Accessed 02 Apr 2024
2. FIPA Communicative Act Library Specification. http://www.fipa.org/specs/fipa00037/PC00037E.html#_Toc505673625. Accessed 02 Apr 2024
3. Amrani, N.E.A., Snineh, S.M., Youssfi, M., Abra, O.E.K., Bouattane, O.: Interoperability model between heterogeneous MAS platforms based on mobile agent and reinforcement learning. In: ICDS (2021). https://doi.org/10.1109/ICDS53782.2021.9626723

4. Bienz, S., Ciortea, A., Mayer, S., Gandon, F., Corby, O.: Escaping the streetlight effect: semantic hypermedia search enhances autonomous behavior in the web of things. In: IoT '19 (2019). https://doi.org/10.1145/3365871.3365901
5. Boissier, O., Bordini, R.H., Hübner, J.F., Ricci, A.: Multi-agent oriented programming - the jacamo platform (2016). https://www.emse.fr/~boissier/enseignement/maop16/pdf/aop.pdf
6. Bordini, R.H., Hübner, J.F.: BDI agent programming in agentspeak using jason (2006). https://doi.org/10.1007/11750734_9
7. Charpenay, V., Zimmermann, A., Lefrançois, M., Boissier, O.: Hypermedea: a framework for web (of things) agents. In: WWW 2022 (2022). https://doi.org/10.1145/3487553.3524243
8. Ciortea, A., Boissier, O., Ricci, A.: Engineering world-wide multi-agent systems with hypermedia. In: EMAS (2019). https://doi.org/10.1007/978-3-030-25693-7_15
9. Ciortea, A., Mayer, S., Michahelles, F.: Repurposing manufacturing lines on the fly with multi-agent systems for the web of things. EMAS (2018)
10. Dorri, A., Kanhere, S., Jurdak, R.: Multi-agent systems: a survey. IEEE Access **6** (2018). https://doi.org/10.1109/ACCESS.2018.2831228
11. Kampik, T., et al.: Governance of autonomous agents on the web: challenges and opportunities. ACM Trans. Internet Technol. (2022). https://doi.org/10.1145/3507910
12. Lazarin, N.M., Alexandre, T., Moreira de Paiva, M., Pantoja, C.E., Viterbo, J., Bernardini, F.: A decentralized agent-based model for crisis events using embedded systems. In: PAAMS (2025). https://doi.org/10.1007/978-3-031-70415-4_14
13. Matsukura, R., McCool, M., Toumura, K., Lagally, M.: Wot architecture 1.1. Recommendation, W3C (2023). https://www.w3.org/TR/2023/REC-wot-architecture11-20231205/
14. McCool, M., Korkan, E., Käbisch, S.: Wot thing description 1.1. Recommendation, W3C (2023). https://www.w3.org/TR/2023/REC-wot-thing-description11-20231205/
15. Noura, M., Siegert, V., Gaedke, M.: Wat: autonomous hypermedia-driven web agents for web of things devices. In: CEUR Workshop Proceedings (2021). https://ceur-ws.org/Vol-3111/short6.pdf
16. Pantoja, C.E., Souza de Jesus, V., Lazarin, N.M., Viterbo, J.: a spin-off version of jason for iot and embedded multi-agent systems. In: Intelligent Systems (2023). https://doi.org/10.1007/978-3-031-45368-7_25
17. Poslad, S., Charlton, P.: Standardizing agent interoperability: the fipa approach (2001). https://doi.org/10.1007/3-540-47745-4_5

Distributed Detection of Complex Events on Streams of Linked Data

Daniel Schraudner[1]( ) , Sebastian Schmid[1] , and Andreas Harth[1,2]

[1] Friedrich-Alexander-Universität Erlangen-Nürnberg, Nuremberg, Germany
{daniel.schraudner,sebastian.schmid,andreas.harth}@fau.de
[2] Fraunhofer Institute for Integrated Circuits IIS, Nuremberg, Germany

Abstract. The Internet of Things has created the need for scalable, distributed detection of complex events across organizational boundaries. We present a RESTful architecture that enables distributed detection of complex events on streams of Linked Data. Our approach transforms declarative event patterns expressed in a DatalogMTL-based temporal logic formalism into a network of stream containers and reasoning agents that can operate across organizational boundaries. Key contributions include: (1) A modular architecture based on the Linked Data Platform for federated stream processing, (2) A method for transforming declarative patterns into executable components, (3) A formal model using Colored Stochastic Petri Nets to validate correctness and analyze performance, and (4) an implementation and experimental validation of our approach. Experimental results demonstrate that our system achieves high throughput through parallel processing while maintaining a predictable latency that scales linearly with program depth.

Keywords: Complex Event Processing · RDF Stream Processing · Linked Data Platform · DatalogMTL

1 Introduction

The rise of the Internet of Things (IoT) has led to a ubiquity of connected sensors that produce vast amounts of data [7]. As the Web of Things (WoT) is gaining traction as a unified application layer for the IoT, it is becoming easier than ever to access all of this data.

In an environment with a lot of volatile data, the data is typically processed in a streaming fashion. This means that it is processed in (near) real time as it is generated. One of the most common tasks in stream processing is to identify patterns in a stream of data that represent a particular event. Events can be simple (e.g., an accelerometer reading of 1 g) or complex, involving temporal sequences of sensor readings (e.g., detecting a fall based on smartwatch accelerometer data).

This work is partially funded by the German Federal Ministry of Education and Research via the MANDAT project (FKZ 16DTM107A).

© The Author(s), under exclusive license to Springer Nature Switzerland AG 2026
H. Verma et al. (Eds.): ICWE 2025, LNCS 15749, pp. 327–341, 2026.
https://doi.org/10.1007/978-3-031-97207-2_25

However, only by embedding complex event detection into the architecture of the (semantic) Web can the real power of the IoT/WoT can be unleashed: A web of interoperable stream processing systems with a clear RESTful Read-Write Linked Data interface allows one to seamlessly share data (i.e., sensor readings, detected complex events, and intermediate results) and distribute computation arbitrarily across organizational boundaries.

Distributing the computation of complex event detection becomes necessary for a stream processing system to scale well. A RESTful architecture for a stream processing system may seem unusual for streaming data. However, using a RESTful architecture allows a system to scale massively using techniques such as caching, clustering, and load balancing that are built into REST [14].

When we say that a stream processing system scales well, we mean that we can improve the throughput of the system by distributing its computations across multiple nodes. The throughput of the system refers to the number of events the system can detect and the amount of data it can process per unit of time. In contrast, low-latency stream processing systems can provide output much faster after receiving input than a high-latency system. RESTful architectures are typically not optimized for low latency and are therefore not well suited for (hard) real-time applications. While throughput and latency are important characteristics, the main challenge in distributing computations for complex event detection is in ensuring that the system's data processing remains correct and complete.

The flexibility of RESTful architectures allows instances of client and server components to be created and adapted ad hoc based on the events to be detected. Therefore, a domain-independent and declarative formalism is needed to specify complex event patterns. A declarative formalism provides a more modular and reusable approach to composing events, making it better suited to parallelizing evaluation [11]. By restricting recursion in the formalism, the data flow within the system is limited to a directed acyclic graph, simplifying the overall system architecture. However, not allowing recursion does not remove too much expressiveness since complex event patterns usually do not consist of smaller events of the same pattern nested arbitrarily deep. Finally, a method is needed to transform a set of event patterns in the declarative formalism into a set of components that can be deployed across the Web to perform event detection.

To address the above challenges, we propose a RESTful architecture for scalable, declarative complex event detection on streams of Linked Data. Specifically, our contributions include (1) a modular architecture comprising client and server components for detecting complex events on streams of Linked Data, (2) a transformation method for declarative event patterns into executable components, (3) a formal model to validate the system's soundness, completeness, and scalability, and (4) an implementation and experimental validation of our approach.

2 Running Example

Schneider et al. [16] created a traffic scenario with multiple different sensors and different events that can be detected based on sensor data. We will use a condensed version of this scenario as a running example throughout the paper. It comprises a road with multiple cars and a traffic light. Each car has a sensor that measures the current speed of the car, and the traffic light has a sensor that records the current color of the traffic light. In Fig. 1, we can see the speed of $car1$ measured by a sensor. We can use DatalogMTL formulas to make claims about the speed of cars. Figure 2 shows four different DatalogMTL formulas and whether they hold at each point in time or not. $speed(car1, 10)$ and $speed(car1, 15)$ hold at exactly those points in time where the sensor readings detect a speed of 10 (or 15, respectively). The Minus-Diamond operator takes the interval that is between one and three time units in the past and checks whether the speed of $car1$ is equal to 10 on *at least one* of the discrete time points in the interval. The Minus-Box operator, on the other hand, checks whether the speed of $car1$ equals 10 on *all* of the discrete time points in the interval.

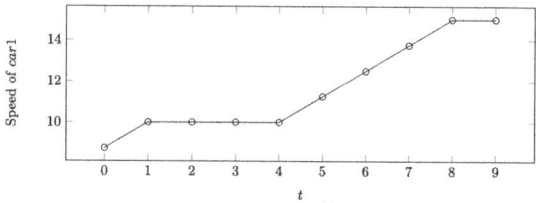

Fig. 1. Speed of $car1$ over time t. Each circle represents a reading of the speed sensor.

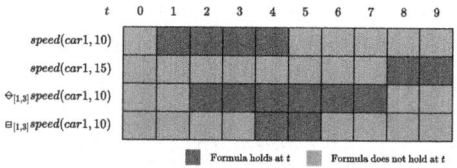

Fig. 2. Different DatalogMTL formulas and whether they hold at different t.

In our scenario, e.g. a traffic surveillance authority could be interested in detecting the following complex events: (1) A car stopped because the traffic light turned red, (2) the speed of a car has been above 50 km/h for the last five seconds, and (3) a car is involved in a traffic jam.

3 Approach

To specify complex event patterns for our system, we need a domain-independent declarative formalism. We choose to use a fragment of the logic-based DatalogMTL because it can be easily mapped to the Resource Description Framework (RDF) (see Sect. 3.2) and the temporal aspect of DatalogMTL maps well to the windowing mechanism of stream containers (see Sect. 3.3).

DatalogMTL has first been proposed by Brandt et al. [4]. We will use the forward-propagating fragment of DatalogMTL, which Wałęga et al. [19] showed to be the most suitable for stream reasoning. Furthermore, we only use the non-recursive fragment of DatalogMTL limiting the event patterns we can express. In practice, however, most event patterns do not require recursion, as complex event patterns usually do not consist of smaller events of the same pattern nested arbitrarily deep. We will refer to the non-recursive, forward-propagating fragment of DatalogMLT as $\text{Datalog}_{nr}\text{MTL}^{\text{FP}}$ from now on.

3.1 $\text{Datalog}_{nr}\text{MTL}^{\text{FP}}$

Definition 1. Let p be a predicate, s_i with $0 \leq i \leq n$ each a constant or a variable, and $I \subseteq \mathbb{N}$ a time interval. We call $p(s_0, ..., s_n)$ an atom. When all s_i in an atom are constants, the atom is grounded. A grounded atom together with a time interval $p(s_0, ..., s_n)@I$ is called a fact. A set of facts D is called a dataset.

Example 1. $speed(car1, 10)@[1, 4]$ is a valid fact from our running example.

Definition 2. Let A and B be formulas according to the following grammar:

$$A := p(s_1, ..., s_n) \mid \boxminus_I A \mid \diamondminus_I A \qquad B := p(s_1, ..., s_n) \mid \boxplus_I B$$

A rule is of the form $B \leftarrow A_1, \wedge ... \wedge A_n$ for $n \geq 1$. A set of rules Π is called a program. We assume that rules are safe, i.e. every variable that is mentioned in the head of a rule is also mentioned in the body.

Example 2. The complex event patterns of our running example (see Sect. 2) can be expressed using the following $\text{Datalog}_{nr}\text{MTL}^{\text{FP}}$ rules:

- $stop\_red\_light(?car) \leftarrow \diamondminus_{[0,5]} speed(?car, 0) \wedge traffic\_light(red)$
- $speed\_gt50(?car) \leftarrow \diamondminus_{[0,5]} speed(?car, ?speed)) \wedge gt(?speed, 50)$
- $jam(?car) \leftarrow \boxminus_{[0,60]} \diamondminus_{[0,5]} speed(?car, 0)$

Definition 3. Be $\Delta \neq \emptyset$ a domain and $\mathfrak{M}$ an interpretation based on Δ. Then $\mathfrak{M}$ determines for each ground atom whether it holds at a certain point in time or not, i.e. whether $p(s_1, ..., s_n) \in \mathfrak{M}(t)$.

Be V a countably infinite set of variables, and $\nu : V + \Delta \mapsto \Delta$ a variable assignment that maps variables into Δ and constants back to themselves, i.e. $\nu(c) = c$ for every constant $c \in \Delta$.

The satisfaction relation between a model $\mathfrak{M}$ and a time point t on the one side and a formula on the other side is then defined inductively:

$$\mathfrak{M}, t \models^\nu p(s_1, ..., s_n) \text{ iff } p(\nu(s_1), ..., \nu(s_n)) \in \mathfrak{M}(t)$$
$$\mathfrak{M}, t \models^\nu \boxminus_{[u,v]} \psi \text{ iff } \forall t - u \geq p \geq t - v. \mathfrak{M}, p \models^\nu \psi$$
$$\mathfrak{M}, t \models^\nu \diamondminus_{[u,v]} \psi \text{ iff } \exists t - u \geq p \geq t - v. \mathfrak{M}, p \models^\nu \psi$$
$$\mathfrak{M}, t \models^\nu \boxplus_{[u,v]} \psi \text{ iff } \forall t + u \leq p \leq t + v. \mathfrak{M}, p \models^\nu \psi$$

An interpretation $\mathfrak{M}$ satisfies a rule if for every ν, $\mathfrak{M}, t \models^\nu A_i$ with $1 \leq i \leq n$ then $\nu, \mathfrak{M}, t \models^\nu B$. An interpretation is a model of a Datalog$_{nr}$MTL^{FP} program Π if it satisfies every rule in it. An interpretation $\mathfrak{M}$ satisfies a fact $p(s_1, ..., s_n)@I$ iff $\forall t \in I.p(s_1, ..., s_n) \in \mathfrak{M}(t)$. An interpretation is a model of a data set D if it satisfies each fact in it.

3.2 Mapping Between RDF Graphs and DatalogMTL Datasets

In order to be able to detect events of a specific Datatlog$_{nr}$MTL^{FP} pattern in RDF data, a mapping between the two formalisms is required.

We assume that stream data always follow a set of patterns. For example, a sensor producing RDF data will always output a graph adhering to a certain format. This format can be expressed using a Basic Graph Pattern (BGP) [10].

In Fig. 3 we can see on the left-hand side an RDF graph that contains more than one triple. On the right hand side we see the BGP to which the data points in the stream adhere[1]. This BGP can now be mapped to a Datalog$_{nr}$MTL^{FP} atom, such as ?$property$(?$result$). The resulting DatalogMTL fact for the example will then be $speed(car1, 12.5)$[2].

```
<#obs>  a              sosa:Observation ;           []  a              sosa:Observation ;
    sosa:hasFeatureOfInterest  car:1 ;                  sosa:hasFeatureOfInterest   ?car  ;
    sosa:hasSimpleResult       12.5 ;                   sosa:hasSimpleResult        ?result ;
    sosa:observedProperty      voc:speed ;              sosa:observedProperty       ?property .
    sosa:resultTime            6 .
```

Fig. 3. Left: a stream data point having more than one triple. Right: the BGP to which the data points in the stream adhere.

3.3 Stream Containers

For the RESTful read-write interface of our server components for storing the streams, we built on our previous work of stream containers [17]. Stream containers extend the Linked Data Platform (LDP) W3C Recommendation [18] by introducing a new type of container that represents an RDF stream. Each container contains a set of resources, each representing a data point within the stream. For our task of distributed complex event detection, stream containers are particularly well suited because the temporal operators of DatalogMTL can be directly mapped to the windowed interface of stream containers.

Figure 4 illustrates the functionality of a stream container. Any agent capable of sending HTTP requests, e.g. sensors, can add new data points to the stream

---

[1] Note, that sosa:resultTime is not part of the BGP as this is the special timestamp predicate handled by the Stream Container (see Sect. 3.3).

[2] Note, that for conciseness we will abbreviate URIs in the DatalogMTL notation, e.g. http://vocab.ex.org/speed becomes *speed*.

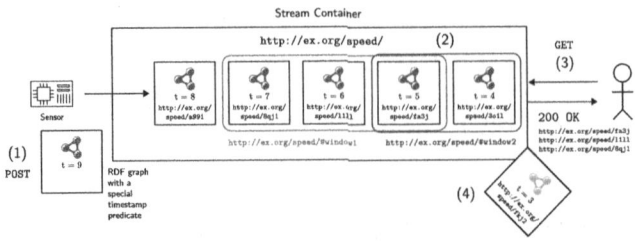

Fig. 4. Schematic functionality of a Stream Container

by sending an HTTP POST request with an RDF graph to the Stream Container (1). Among the triples of the graph must be one with a special timestamp predicate[3]. The object of the triple determines the position of the data point in the stream. The data point (e.g. a sensor reading) can be accessed by its (assigned) URI from now on.

Windows may be declared by modifying the RDF of the Stream Container; they are defined by their start and end in relation to the current point in time and can be used to precisely retrieve those data points that fall within the specified time window, e.g. data from the last three seconds (2), by sending a GET request to the URI of the window (3). From the membership triples in the response, one can deduce the URIs of the data points currently in the window and use GET requests to obtain the actual RDF graphs of the data points in question. As the Stream Container continuously receives new data points, any data points that are no longer required are discarded (4).

3.4 System Architecture

To detect complex event patterns, we have to evaluate a given $\text{Datalog}_{nr}\text{MTL}^{FP}$ program over the data in the stream containers. The evaluation is carried out by two distinct components: stream containers for storing and accessing the stream data and reasoning agents. Reasoning agents utilize HTTP requests to GET data points from Stream Container windows and transform them in accordance with their internal rules. The resulting data points are then POSTed to another Stream Container for further processing.

The topology of the stream containers and reasoning agents (connected by HTTP requests) directly reflects the $\text{Datalog}_{nr}\text{MTL}^{FP}$ program (the set of rules). To ensure an efficient data flow through our system, we first have to transform the program into its normal form.

Definition 4. A $\text{Datalog}_{nr}\text{MTL}^{FP}$ program Π is in a normal form if it only contains rules of the following form:

$$p_0(s_1, ..., s_n) \leftarrow \diamondsuit_I p_1(s_1, ..., s_n) \qquad p_0(s_1, ..., s_n) \leftarrow \boxminus_I p_1(s_1, ..., s_n)$$

---

[3] It can be determined by the Stream Container which predicate is the special one, similar to `ldp:insertedContentRelation` for Indirect Containers.

$$p_0(s_1,...,s_n) \leftarrow p_1(s_1,...,s_n) \wedge \cdots \wedge p_n(s_1,...,s_n)$$

Example 3. The normal form of the three rules for *stop_red_light*, *avg_speed_5*, and *jam* from our example in Sect. 2 is:

$$diamond\_speed\_0\_5(?car, ?speed) \leftarrow \Diamond_{[0,5]} speed(?car, ?speed)$$

$$stop\_red\_light(?car) \leftarrow diamond\_speed\_0\_5(?car, 0) \wedge traffic\_light(red)$$

$$speed\_gt50(?car) \leftarrow diamond\_speed\_0\_5(?car, ?speed) \wedge gt(?speed, 50)$$

$$jam(?car) \leftarrow \boxminus_{[0,60]} diamond\_speed\_0\_5(?car, 0)$$

Here we can see that transforming a program to its normal form can introduce new auxiliary predicates that were not needed before (*diamond_speed_0_5*).

Figure 5 shows the plan generated from the normal form, where the rectangles represent the stream containers with their respective windows, and the circles represent the reasoning agents. The arrows represent the direction of the data flow using HTTP requests.

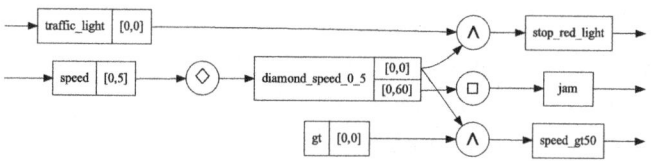

Fig. 5. Plan generated from the $Datalog_{nr}MTL^{FP}$ program normal form from Example 3 (Note: As *gt* just compares numbers and does not depend on any sensor input it could be implemented as a built in predicate on the reasoning agents instead of creating an own stream container for it.)

In general, the topology of a complex event detection system for arbitrary complex event patterns is constructed by creating a stream container for every distinct predicate occurring in the normal form of the program. The windows are constructed by creating one window for every atom in the normal form. If the atom is prefixed by a Minus-Box or Minus-Diamond operator, then the operator interval defines the start and end of the window; otherwise, start and end are both zero. Furthermore, an edge is added from the stream container to every window that belongs to the predicate of the atom. Reasoning agents are constructed by creating one agent for every rule in the normal form. The operator in the rule determines the type of reasoning agent (Box, Diamond, or Conjunction). For every atom in the rule body, an edge from the atom's window to the reasoning agent is added. In addition, an edge from the agent to the stream container is created that corresponds to the predicate in the rule head.

3.5 Synchronization Using Watermarks

To ensure the completeness of reasoning in our system, we need a synchronization mechanism for the reasoning agents to know if they have processed all data points for a given point in time or if there are still some missing data points.

We assume that we can always decide whether the input to our overall system is complete for a given time point, i.e. all sensors know whether they have already sent out all measurements for that time point or not. We thus can assume that all sensors annotate the data points they send with a flag that indicates whether it was the last data point for that time point or not. We propagate this annotation through the different stream containers and reasoning agents in the plan; this mechanism is a variant of the *Watermark* [3] synchronization.

We a special predicate in the data point's RDF graph (similar to the timestamp predicate) for watermarking; we call the triple with this predicate the watermark flag. A stream container is at watermark t if it contains a data point of timestamp t with the watermark flag set. A window is at watermark t if all data points in the window on the Stream Container are at least at watermark t. Reasoning agents set the watermark flag for the data points of the timestamp t they POST to their stream container once all the windows from which they GET data points are at least at the watermark t.

4 Results and Discussion

4.1 Soundness and Completeness

In DatalogMTL, the soundness can be shown by proving that every fact computed follows logically from the rules and the data in the stream. In our system, each reasoning agent is responsible for processing exactly one rule of the program normal form, i.e. each reasoning agent implements exactly one rule. Since the agents only derive new facts according to their rule and no rules are transformed or new rules are added, the correctness of the reasoning follows trivially.

In order to evaluate the completeness of our system, we construct an abstract model of the behavior of the system using colored stochastic Petri nets (CSPN).

Definition 5. Be P a set of *places*, T a set of *transitions*, A a set of *arcs*, Σ a set of *color sets*, $C : P \to \Sigma$ a color function, $N : A \to (P \times T) \cup (T \times P)$ a node function, $E : A \to L_\Sigma$ an arc expression function, $I : P \to L_\Sigma$ an initialization function, $\Lambda : T \to \mathbb{R}$ the firing rate function, and $O : T \to \mathbb{N}_0$ a priority function where L_Σ is the set of all expressions over Σ. Then a tuple $N = (P, T, A, \Sigma, C, N, E, I, \Lambda, O)$ is called a Colored Stochastic Petri Net.

A CSPN for our reasoning system is constructed by mapping all stream containers and all reasoning agents to a particular CSPN pattern. In Fig. 6 we can see on the left the CSPN pattern for stream containers and on the right the CSPN pattern for reasoning agents. The stream container is represented by a place where each token (of type integer) represents a point in time for which

Fig. 6. Left: CSPN for a stream container. Right: CSPN for a reasoning agent.

the watermark flag has already arrived in the stream container. The *discard* transition is responsible for discarding old data points (see Sect. 3.3).

On the right is the CSPN pattern for reasoning agents. The *operator* transition firing corresponds to the next missing watermark being processed by the reasoning agent. This increases the agent's internal counter, which is modeled by the *counter* place. Since reasoning agents cannot perceive a new watermark in a stream container at any time but instead execute GET requests against that stream container at fixed time intervals, the firing of each *operator* transition is controlled by a *clock*.

Each reasoning agent's *operator* transition has an arc to the *stream container* place if there is an edge from agent to stream container in the plan. *Stream container* places have arcs to *operator* transitions if there is an edge from a window of that stream container to the agent in the plan. The number of arcs is determined by the size of the window (one for every time point in the window).

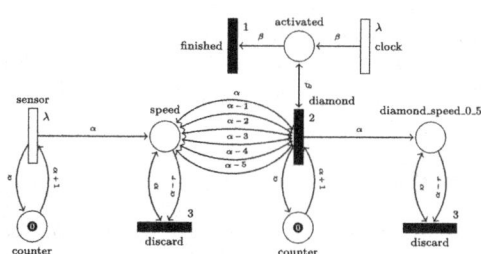

Fig. 7. CSPN for a part of the running example

In Fig. 7 a part of the CSPN for our running example can be seen. To ensure completeness of our reasoning, we need to make sure that no tokens (representing the watermarks) are lost. Therefore, we need to check that the *discard* transitions only remove tokens that have been passed on by the *operator* transition before.

We can analyze the probability of an early removal using a continuous-time Markov chain (CTMC). Each state in the reachability graph of our CSPN can be mapped to a state in the CTMC. The rates between the states can be derived from the rates in the CSPN. We map all states in the reachability graph where a token has been discarded too early into one state in the CTMC (we call it the error state) and all other states into CTMC states representing the number of tokens still unprocessed in the *stream container* place. We can then use numeric methods to calculate the expected time to failure (i.e. removing a token before it has been passed on) for the system.

In Fig. 9 we see the CTMC for the system in Fig. 7 where the parameter r (the retention policy) has been fixed to 39. As new tokens enter the stream container at the rate λ, the number of unprocessed timestamps increases until it is in the state 36. From now on, the number of unprocessed timestamps can increase or be set back to 35.

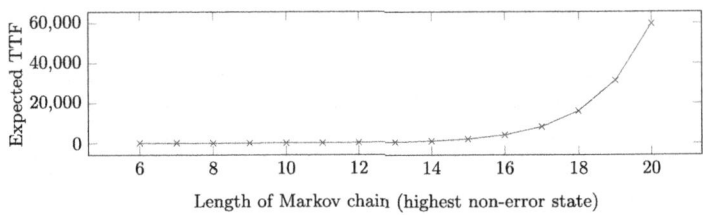

Fig. 8. Expected time until an error state occurs for CTMCs of different length

We used the PRISM model checker [13] to analyze CTMCs of different length, i.e. different retention policies r for our system. The result is shown in Fig. 8. The expected time until failure increases exponentially with the length of the CTMC and thus with r. This means that we can adjust the probability of a failure in our system to be small enough to never occur in practice by slightly increasing the value of r. Thus, we can ensure the completeness of the reasoning of our system simply by choosing r high enough.

4.2 Throughput and Latency

As we are building a distributed pipelined system, the throughput and latency of our system are the two most interesting performance measures. For a pipelined system, the focus lies on achieving high throughput (through massive parallelism). Once the system is running, the latency does not matter so much for many complex event detection use cases.

Looking at the CSPN, we can easily see that the throughput of the system is λ if the CSPN is not in a livelock situation: New tokens come into the net only at the *sensor* transition[4] and are removed only at the *discard* transition. In the previous section, we showed how to ensure that the *discard* transitions only remove tokens that have been passed on by the *operator* transition before. Thus, every token that came into the net must eventually arrive at the next stream container with the same average rate as they entered the system.

---

[4] We are neglecting the *activated* token which is not important here.

The latency of our system depends on the size of the dependency graph of the program. If the dependency graph has a low depth[5] but a high breadth[6] but the resulting CSPN will also have a low depth and thus evidently a low latency. If, on the other hand, the breadth of the dependency graph is low and the depth is high, the resulting latency will be higher (as the token has to pass through many more transitions).

This means that, assuming the CSPN runs to infinity, the throughput is the sum of all tokens reaching an output place in a time step, and the latency is the average time all tokens that enter the CSPN at an input place take to reach an output place.

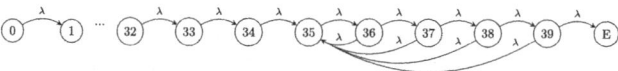

Fig. 9. CTMC for the number of time points in a Stream Container that have not been processed by the following agent yet.

4.3 Experiments

We use our implementation[7] to test the theoretical results of Sect. 4.1 with different program sizes. We created simple programs with given depth and breadth. We then inject new data points with a rate of $1/s$ into every sensor and measure the number of data points that arrive in the output stream containers. We let the system run for 10 min and then take the average number of tokens arriving per second over the time to calculate the throughput.

In Table 1 we can see the different depths and breadths and the resulting number of rules in the program. We can also see that the input load on the system increases with the breadth. That is because the broader the system is, the more input sensors it can have. When we compare the throughput with the input load, we can see that the throughput increases with increasing input load, as we would expect from our theoretical results. The (increasing) small discrepancy between the two can be explained by numerous factors: Firstly, in larger systems, more tokens are still in the pipeline, i.e. they have been counted as input but not yet as output. Also, fluctuations such as those occurring in network latencies and scheduling effects tend to be on the larger side for larger systems. As we tested our system only on one machine for practicability instead of multiples distributed machines, the limited CPU resources also begin to play a role here when it comes to the larger programs.

---

[5] We define the depth of a dependency graph as the number of nodes on the longest path from a root node to any other node in the graph.

[6] We define the breadth of a dependency graph as the number of nodes in the DAG divided by its depth.

[7] The source code is available on GitHub under an open-source license: https://github.com/wintechis/distributed-event-detection/.

Table 1. Throughput for programs with different depths and breadths

Depth	Breadth	Number of rules	Data points in	Input load	Data points out	Throughput
2	2	2	1,198	1.99/s	1,188	1.98/s
3	3	6	1,800	3.00/s	1,747	2.91/s
4	4	12	2,412	4.02/s	2,312	3.85/s
5	5	20	3,040	5.07/s	2,876	4.79/s
6	6	30	3,717	6.20/s	3,394	5.65/s
7	7	42	4,480	7.47/s	3,889	6.48/s

In Table 2 we can see the latency of our system for programs of different depth on the left and breadth on the right. To measure latency, we injected 100 data points into our system and measured how much time each of them would take to reach an output stream container. As expected, we can see that the latency is increasing linearly with the depth (the factor of approx. $3s$ is due to the window size of $3s$) of the program and is roughly constant over increasing program breadths.

Table 2. Latency for programs with different depths and breadths

Depth	Breadth	Average Latency
2	2	03.496 s
3	2	06.438 s
4	2	10.519 s
5	2	13.435 s
6	2	16.972 s
7	2	20.314 s

Depth	Breadth	Average Latency
2	2	3.215 s
2	3	3.725 s
2	4	3.422 s
2	5	3.308 s
2	6	3.374 s
2	7	3.372 s

All experiments were carried out on an HPE ProLiant DL380 Gen10 equipped with two Intel Xeon Gold 6130 CPU (2.1 GHz and 16 cores each) and 768 GB of RAM.

5 Related Work

General-Purpose Stream Processing Frameworks. These frameworks utilize general-purpose programming languages, such as Java, and are capable of processing streams of any data type. Their main focus is on scalability, fault tolerance, and low-latency distributed processing. There are several general-purpose stream processing frameworks available, such as Apache Kafka [12], Apache Flink [6], and Apache Spark [21].

Contrary to our system, these systems are not designed to facilitate the sharing of data between organizational boundaries. The stream processing computations are typically programmed into the system using a product-specific API for an iterative programming language, rather than a declarative formalism like ours.

Complex Event Processing. CEP frameworks such as CQL [1] and SASE [9] offer languages and engines to specify and detect complex event patterns in data streams. CQL enables users to define continuous queries over data streams, including complex event patterns and conditions. SASE is designed for pattern matching and signal extraction over data streams.

Unlike general-purpose stream processing frameworks, CEP frameworks share the declarative formalism for expressing complex events with our approach. But just like general purpose frameworks, CEP frameworks suffer from the missing ability to reach across organizational boundaries.

RDF Stream Processing. C-SPARQL [2] is a continuous query engine for RDF data streams that enables the formulation and evaluation of continuous SPARQL queries over RDF streams. $SPARQL_{Stream}$ [5] extends SPARQL with temporal operators to handle continuous querying over RDF streams. CQELS [15] is a continuous query engine for Linked Data streams that supports temporal queries over RDF data streams. RSP-QL [8] is a framework for RDF stream processing, that aims to unify various previous approaches and languages for RDF stream processing.

RDF stream processing can be seen as a direct extension of CEP for RDF. Consequently, these frameworks share the same advantages and disadvantages with CEP frameworks as compared to our approach.

DatalogMTL Reasoning. DatalogMTL is an extension of Datalog with Metric Temporal Logic which is well suited to expressing complex temporal sequences of data and thus complex event patterns. Although DatalogMTL has already been successfully applied for stream reasoning by Walega et al. [19], DatalogMTL reasoners are designed for batch processing and operate on a static data set. To our knowledge, the only existing DatalogMTL reasoner so far is MeTeor [20].

Compared to Walega et al. [19] our approach, however, works in a distributed manner.

6 Conclusion

We showed how complex event patterns, expressed using the $Datalog_{nr}MTL^{FP}$ formalism, can be detected in a distributed and streaming way. To do this, we transform $Datalog_{nr}MTL^{FP}$ programs trough their normal form into a working system comprising Stream Containers, windows, and reasoning agents. We also provide an abstract model for the behavior of our system over time in the form of a CSPN net. We use our model to show that our system is a distributed, pipelined system that scales well with respect to the program size. We also provide an implementation of our system and performed experiments to support our theoretical findings.

References

1. Arasu, A., Babu, S., Widom, J.: The CQL continuous query language: semantic foundations and query execution. VLDB J. **15**(2), 121–142 (2006). https://doi.org/10.1007/S00778-004-0147-Z
2. Barbieri, D.F., Braga, D., Ceri, S., Valle, E.D., Grossniklaus, M.: C-SPARQL: a continuous query language for RDF data streams. Int. J. Semantic Comput. **4**(1), 3–25 (2010). https://doi.org/10.1142/S1793351X10000936
3. Begoli, E., et al.: Watermarks in stream processing systems: semantics and comparative analysis of apache Flink and google cloud dataflow. Proc. VLDB Endow. **14**(12), 3135–3147 (2021). https://doi.org/10.14778/3476311.3476389. http://www.vldb.org/pvldb/vol14/p3135-begoli.pdf
4. Brandt, S., Kalayci, E.G., Kontchakov, R., Ryzhikov, V., Xiao, G., Zakharyaschev, M.: Ontology-based data access with a horn fragment of metric temporal logic. In: Singh, S., Markovitch, S. (eds.) Proceedings of the Thirty-First AAAI Conference on Artificial Intelligence, 4–9 February 2017, San Francisco, California, USA, pp. 1070–1076. AAAI Press (2017). http://aaai.org/ocs/index.php/AAAI/AAAI17/paper/view/14881
5. Calbimonte, J.-P., Corcho, O., Gray, A.: Enabling ontology-based access to streaming data sources. In: Patel-Schneider, P.F., et al. (eds.) ISWC 2010. LNCS, vol. 6496, pp. 96–111. Springer, Heidelberg (2010). https://doi.org/10.1007/978-3-642-17746-0_7
6. Carbone, P., Katsifodimos, A., Ewen, S., Markl, V., Haridi, S., Tzoumas, K.: Apache Flink^{TM}: stream and batch processing in a single engine. IEEE Data Eng. Bull. **38**(4), 28–38 (2015). http://sites.computer.org/debull/A15dec/p28.pdf
7. Chen, Y.K.: Challenges and opportunities of internet of things. In: 17th Asia and South Pacific Design Automation Conference, pp. 383–388 (2012). https://doi.org/10.1109/ASPDAC.2012.6164978
8. Dell'Aglio, D., Valle, E.D., Calbimonte, J., Corcho, Ó.: RSP-QL semantics: a unifying query model to explain heterogeneity of rdf stream processing systems. Int. J. Semant. Web Inf. Syst. **10**(4), 17–44 (2014). https://doi.org/10.4018/IJSWIS.2014100102
9. Gyllstrom, D., Wu, E., Chae, H., Diao, Y., Stahlberg, P., Anderson, G.: SASE: complex event processing over streams. CoRR abs/cs/0612128 (2006). http://arxiv.org/abs/cs/0612128
10. Harris, S., Seaborne, A., Prud'hommeaux, E.: SPARQL 1.1 query language. W3C Recommendation **21**(10), 778 (2013)
11. Hellerstein, J.M.: The declarative imperative: experiences and conjectures in distributed logic. SIGMOD Rec. **39**(1), 5–19 (2010). https://doi.org/10.1145/1860702.1860704
12. Kreps, J., Narkhede, N., Rao, J., et al.: Kafka: a distributed messaging system for log processing. In: Proceedings of the NetDB, Athens, Greece, vol. 11, pp. 1–7 (2011)
13. Kwiatkowska, M., Norman, G., Parker, D.: PRISM 4.0: verification of probabilistic real-time systems. In: Gopalakrishnan, G., Qadeer, S. (eds.) CAV 2011. LNCS, vol. 6806, pp. 585–591. Springer, Heidelberg (2011). https://doi.org/10.1007/978-3-642-22110-1_47
14. Pautasso, C., Zimmermann, O., Leymann, F.: RESTful web services vs. "Big" web services: making the right architectural decision. In: Huai, J., et al. (eds.) Proceedings of the 17th International Conference on World Wide Web, WWW 2008,

Beijing, China, 21–25 April 2008, pp. 805–814. ACM (2008). https://doi.org/10.1145/1367497.1367606
15. Le-Phuoc, D., Dao-Tran, M., Xavier Parreira, J., Hauswirth, M.: A native and adaptive approach for unified processing of linked streams and linked data. In: Aroyo, L., et al. (eds.) ISWC 2011. LNCS, vol. 7031, pp. 370–388. Springer, Heidelberg (2011). https://doi.org/10.1007/978-3-642-25073-6_24
16. Schneider, P., Alvarez-Coello, D., Le-Tuan, A., Duc, M.N., Phuoc, D.L.: Stream reasoning playground. In: Groth, P., et al. (eds.) The Semantic Web - 19th International Conference, ESWC 2022. LNCS, vol. 13261, pp. 406–424. Springer (2022). https://doi.org/10.1007/978-3-031-06981-9_24
17. Schraudner, D., Harth, A.: Stream containers for resource-oriented RDF stream processing. In: Stream Reasoning Workshop 2021 (2021). https://arxiv.org/abs/2202.13630
18. Speicher, S., Arwe, J., Malhotra, A.: Linked data platform 1.0. W3C Recommendation **26** (2015)
19. Walega, P.A., Kaminski, M., Grau, B.C.: Reasoning over streaming data in metric temporal Datalog. In: The Thirty-Third AAAI Conference on Artificial Intelligence, AAAI 2019, pp. 3092–3099. AAAI Press (2019). https://doi.org/10.1609/aaai.v33i01.33013092
20. Wang, D., Hu, P., Walega, P.A., Grau, B.C.: MeTeoR: practical reasoning in datalog with metric temporal operators. In: Thirty-Sixth AAAI Conference on Artificial Intelligence, AAAI 2022, pp. 5906–5913. AAAI Press (2022). https://ojs.aaai.org/index.php/AAAI/article/view/20535
21. Zaharia, M., et al.: Apache spark: a unified engine for big data process. Commun. ACM **59**(11), 56–65 (2016). https://doi.org/10.1145/2934664

LLM-MaGe: A Generative Mashup Planner for the Web of Things

Fady Salama[1]()✉, Franz J. Ennemoser[1], Roman Binkert[1],
Ege Korkan[2], Sebastian Käbisch[2], and Sebastian Steinhorst[1]

[1] TUM School of Computation, Information and Technology, Technical University of Munich, Munich, Germany
fady.salama@tum.de
[2] Siemens AG, Munich, Germany

Abstract. The rapid expansion of the Internet of Things (IoT) has led to various standards and protocols from multiple manufacturers, creating interoperability challenges. The Web of Things (WoT) is a specification proposed by the World Wide Web Consortium (W3C) to integrate IoT devices in a standard way, primarily using the concept of Thing Descriptions (TD). This paper proposes a novel system for automating the generation and execution of IoT mashups using a Large Language Model (LLM) to transform high-level system descriptions into Planning Domain Definition Language (PDDL) models. Users need only provide natural language descriptions of their desired system behavior and the TDs of the available devices, which are used to create a goal using an LLM. Then it utilizes a PDDL planner to generate a solution for the problem to align the current system state with the desired one. Simpler mashups can often achieve 100% accuracy on the first try, requiring no additional refinement steps from the user. Not only does this reduce the effort to integrate IoT devices, it simplifies the process for people with lower technical skills. Therefore, it makes the IoT and the WoT framework accessible to a wider range of users.

Keywords: Internet of Things · Web of Things · PDDL · Mashup

1 Introduction

The world is increasingly utilizing a growing network of Internet-enabled devices, easily surpassing the human population with recent estimates of around 20 to 30 billion devices [4]. This network is collectively known as the Internet of Things (IoT) and can be found in applications from smart homes to industrial automation. It often presents significant opportunities for enhancing efficiency and other benefits. This exponential growth of the IoT has spawned many devices developed with their own specifications, communication protocols, and operational standards. As these devices are often required to work together in a combined system, market fragmentation creates a significant challenge for interoperability between devices of different manufacturers [1].

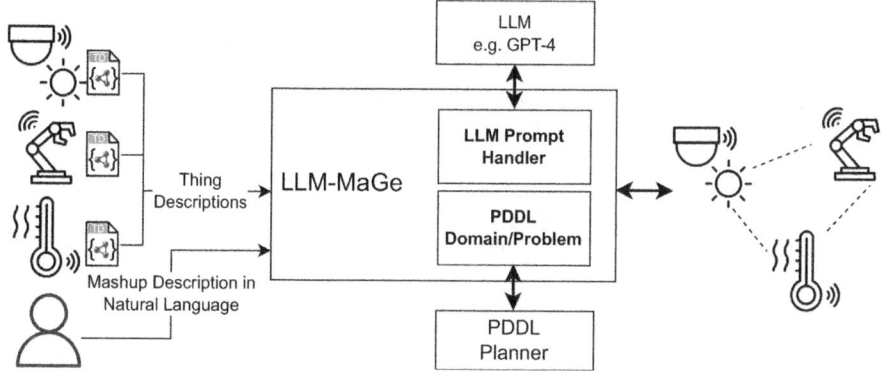

Fig. 1. We propose LLM-MaGe as a methodology that takes a natural language description of a desired IoT Mashup alongside a set of Thing Descriptions (TDs) as an input and outputs a Planning Domain Description Language (PDDL) problem that can be solved to realize the desired mashup.

To address these challenges, the World Wide Web Consortium introduced the Web of Things (WoT) architecture, which standardizes how IoT devices are described and how they interact with each other on the network. A crucial component of the WoT framework is the Thing Description (TD). This standardized JSON-LD document documents all network-accessible device capabilities, making it easier for different devices to communicate and work together. Despite introducing TDs, the challenge of creating these so-called mashups is still present, especially when creating complex functionalities that require multiple devices to work together.

1.1 Problem Statement

Designing mashups of IoT devices remains a manual and labor-intensive process. It requires the developer to have a deep understanding of each device's capabilities and details of the interactions. It also involves writing custom code to handle the communication between devices, which is not only time-consuming but also prone to errors. As a result, the development of IoT mashups is often restricted to individuals with significant technical expertise, which limits broader adoption and innovation in the IoT space [15].

A way to address this would be a system that automatically generates IoT mashups based on high-level, natural language descriptions provided by end-users. It should be capable of interpreting the TDs of available devices, understanding the user's intent, and dynamically creating a plan that coordinates the devices to achieve the desired functionality. Such a system would significantly reduce the time and technical knowledge required to develop IoT mashups, making the process accessible to a broader range of users.

```
1  {"title": "SmartAC", "@type": "saref:Device",
2    "properties": {
3      "isOn": {
4        "title": "Power Status", "@type": "saref:Property",
5        "type": "boolean"}},
6    "actions": {
7      "turnOn": {
8        "title": "Turn On", "@type": "saref:OnCommand",
9        "affects": {"id": "/properties/isOn"}},
10     "turnOff": {
11       "title": "Turn Off", "@type": "saref:OffCommand",
12       "affects": {"id": "/properties/isOn"}}}}
```

Listing 1: A minimal Thing Description (TD) example for a Smart Air Conditioner.

1.2 Contributions

In this paper, we introduce **LLM-MaGe**, a methodology and an open-source software pipeline that allows end users to build, improve, and execute a mashup of IoT devices only by inputting a list of TDs and a natural language description of the desired system functionality. To be specific, we make the following contributions:

- We introduce a methodology that takes TDs and natural language descriptions as input and outputs real-time instructions for the IoT devices to keep the current system state aligned with the desired state in Sect. 3.1, Sect. 3.2, and Sect. 3.3.
- We develop a fully open-source tool with a user-friendly interface outlined in Sect. 3.4 and Sect. 3.5. An overview of the resulting system is shown in Sect. 1.
- We evaluate our approach using multiple predefined scenarios regarding its accuracy in generating correct mashups and the overall performance of our approach in Sect. 4.

The rest of the paper is structured as follows: Sect. 2 discusses both the WoT and PDDL, the cornerstones of our approach. Section 5 discusses related work and Sect. 6 proposes possible future work. Section 7 concludes.

2 Background

2.1 The Web of Things (WoT) & Thing Description (TD)

The W3C Web of Things (WoT) is a set of building blocks that aims to enhance the interoperability and usability of Internet of Things (IoT) devices in an increasingly heterogeneous ecosystem [2].

One of the key components of the WoT is the Thing Description (TD) [9]. The TD is a standardized JSON-LD format that models the capabilities, interfaces,

```
1   (define (domain hello_world)
2     (:predicates
3        (at ?loc)
4        (connected ?loc1 ?loc2)
5     )
6     (:action move
7        :parameters (?from ?to)
8        :precondition
9          (and
10             (at ?from)
11             (connected ?from ?to)
12         )
13      :effect
14      (and
15             (at ?to)
16             (not (at ?from))
17     )))
18
```

(a) PDDL domain example

```
1   (define (problem h_w_problem)
2     (:domain hello_world)
3     (:objects
4        loc1 loc2
5     )
6     (:init
7        (at loc1)
8        (connected loc1 loc2)
9     )
10    (:goal
11       (at loc2)
12  ))
```

(b) PDDL problem example

```
1   (move loc1 loc2)
```

(c) Solution for the domain and problem given in Listing 2a and Listing 2b

Listing 2: An example of a PDDL domain (a), problem (b), and a corresponding solution (c).

and data models of IoT devices. It serves as a blueprint for how a device can be interacted with, detailing interaction affordances [8]. It is human- and machine-readable and allows developers to programmatically discover and interact with devices consistently, reducing the complexity of integrating multiple devices from different manufacturers. A typical TD includes the device's name, description, properties, interaction possibilities, and data schema.

The TD models the interface of an IoT device using three types of interaction affordances: properties, actions, and events:

Properties. Properties in a TD can be compared to variables that hold data reflecting the current state or configuration of the device. A property affordance typically includes details like the data type (such as "boolean", "string" etc.), a short human-readable description, and possible operations (see Listing 1 Lines 2–7). A property can either be read or written.

Actions. Actions in a TD describe the operations can be invoked to change the state of the device or to trigger some behavior (see Listing 1 Lines 2–7).

Please note that the "affects" (Listing 1 Lines 12,18) keyword is not part of the standard and will be discussed in Sect. 3.2.

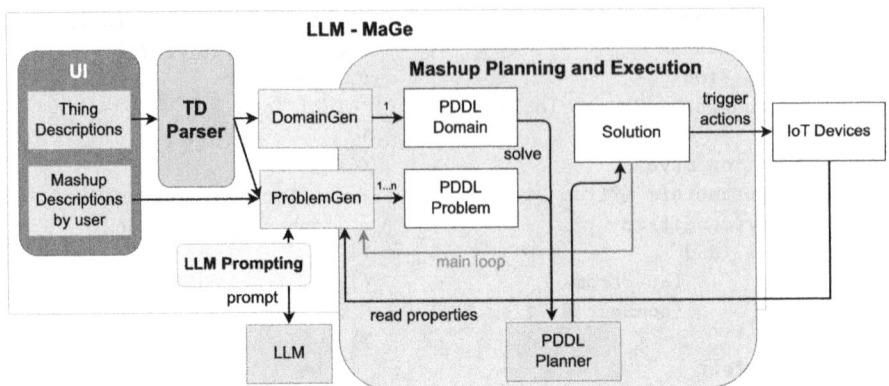

Fig. 2. Data flow overview of LLM-MaGe. The TDs and user mashup description are fed using the UI. The TD Parser extracts needed information from TDs and passes them to the PDDL domain and problem generators. The problem generator prompts the LLM to translate user descriptions to logical goals. PDDL domain and goal are fed into a planner to determine a mashup solution which is used to trigger the actions on IoT devices. The state of the current IoT devices are read to start another round of planning.

Events. Events in a TD represent any notification-style interactions that a Thing provides. They can be subscribed to or unsubscribed from. We omit them in Listing 1 for brevity.

2.2 Planning Domain Definition Language (PDDL)

The Planning Domain Definition Language (PDDL) is a formal language for defining planning and scheduling problems [6]. It specifies the initial world state, the goal state, and the actions that transition between them. PDDL is applied in domains such as robotics, logistics, game AI, and space research [5].

A PDDL problem typically consists of two files: the domain file and the problem file. The domain file outlines the planning domain—defining object types, predicates, and actions (with their preconditions and effects). For example, a simple domain (Listing 2a) might include predicates like **at** (to indicate an agent's location) and **connected** (to show connectivity between locations), alongside an action **move** that changes the agent's location.

The problem file details the initial state and goal state (e.g., an agent starting at location 1 and needing to reach location 2), specifying object instances, initial conditions, and the desired end state.

PDDL files are structured around types and objects (defining entities and instances), predicates (describing properties and relationships), actions (with preconditions and effects), the initial state, and the goal state. Over time, several versions of PDDL have emerged; our approach uses PDDL 2.0.

3 System Overview

3.1 High-Level Architecture

Intending to reduce IoT mashup challenges, we propose LLM-MaGe, a software pipeline that both generates and executes mashups for end users. Acting as an intermediary between users and IoT devices, LLM-MaGe uses a Large Language Model (LLM) to convert a natural language description into a Planning Domain Definition Language (PDDL) model. This model is continuously planned to output coordinated actions that keep the system aligned with the user's description in real time, enabling seamless IoT management without advanced technical expertise.

The method requires a list of TDs and a natural language description of the desired functionality, which are transformed through multiple steps into PDDL domain and problem files representing the system's current state, available actions, and desired state.

Mashup execution involves continuously polling property values, updating the initial state, and using an external PDDL planner to generate the necessary actions to realign the system.

For further details, we divide LLM-MaGe into four components: TD Parser, LLM Prompter, UI Design, and Mashup Execution, each discussed in the following sections. A visualization of the overall architecture, components and data flow can be viewed in Fig. 2.

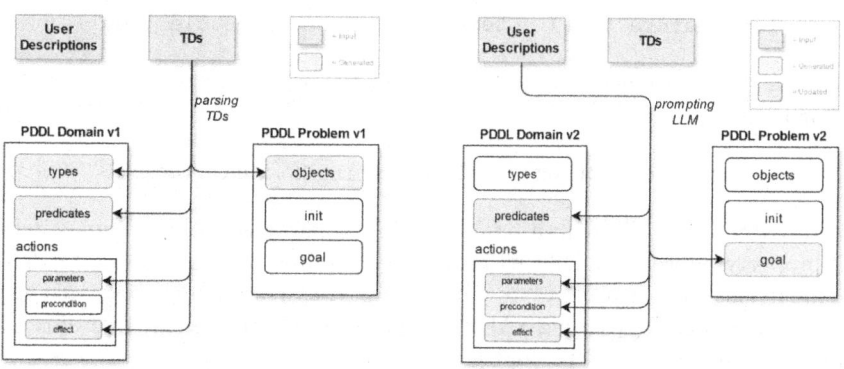

(a) The flow of data in the TD parsing component

(b) The flow of data in the LLM prompting component

Fig. 3. Figures (a) and (a) show the effect of the deterministic TD parsing and the non-deterministic LLM prompting respectively.

3.2 TD Parsing

The TD Parser is the first step in our pipeline. It extracts meta-information (e.g., titles and descriptions) and specific parameters for properties and actions

```
[{"name": "SmartAC-isOn-isTrue",
  "type": "boolean",
  "comparison_value": true},
 {"name": "TempS-status-strMatched",
  "type": "string",
  "enum": ["On", "Off"]},
 {"name": "TempS-temp-aboveThreshold",
  "type": "number",
  "comparison_value": [26, "inf"]}]
```

Listing 3. Comparison table for a temperature-controlled air conditioner.

```
(define (domain iot-mashup)
(:requirements :typing)
(:types ac)

(:predicates
  (SmartAC-isOn-isTrue ?a - ac))

(:action SmartAC-turnOn
  :parameters (?a - ac)
  :precondition ()
  :effect (SmartAC-isOn-isTrue ?a)))
```

Listing 4. PDDL Domain after parsing the TD from Listing 1.

to form the basis of the PDDL domain and problem files. The extracted data is converted into LLM-MaGe's internal format and used to generate a basic domain structure, as highlighted in Fig. 3a (with some components updated later).

A major function of the TD Parser is converting properties into boolean predicates. We support booleans, integers, numbers, and strings. Since PDDL predicates are inherently boolean, non-boolean properties must be converted first. In our implementation, numeric properties are compared to a threshold (extracted from user descriptions) to yield an over/under boolean:

$$\texttt{temperature (int)} \mapsto \texttt{temperatureAboveThreshold (bool)}$$

Similarly, string properties are compared against a predefined list (provided via an "enum") to produce:

$$\texttt{status (string)} \mapsto \texttt{statusStringMatched (bool)}$$

We extend the TD definition by adding a parameter that couples action and property affordances [13], which is essential for generating accurate PDDL action effects. Furthermore, we require the "@type" parameter to tag each affordance with an ontology (using SAREF), offering semantic context that aids both manual parsing and LLM prompt generation.

All required TD parameters are validated by the software, and an error is thrown if any are missing. A minimal parseable TD example is provided in Listing 1. After parsing, LLM-MaGe prints the domain by filling the barebones domain file with the newly acquired data (see Listing 4). The requirements—akin to import statements in programming languages—are hard-coded based on the PDDL planner's needs (e.g., enforcing typing derived from the mandatory ontology).

The resulting PDDL domain, now descriptive of the device capabilities, serves as the foundation for subsequent LLM-MaGe components. The problem file exists as well but is omitted here due to its limited mashup-specific content.

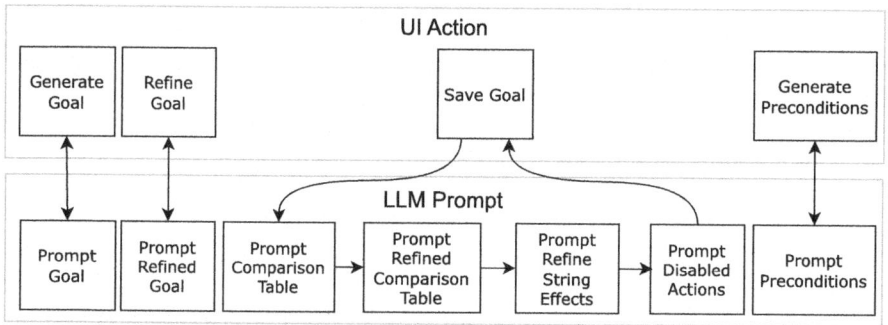

Fig. 4. This image shows all the UI actions that the user can perform and which LLM prompt they correspond to. The actions are meant to be performed in order from right to left; e.g. **Refine Goal** cannot be performed **Generate Goal**. A detailed list with each prompt is available in our repository.

3.3 LLM Prompting

Integrating a Large Language Model (LLM) into the mashup generation pipeline bridges user descriptions with the PDDL models needed for automated planning. The LLM interprets natural language inputs to enhance the PDDL model created by the TD parser. The prompt handler fills pre-defined prompts with mashup-specific data and sends them to the selected LLM API. Responses are checked for proper structure and, if they deviate, additional context is provided until the expected output is achieved or a retry limit is met.

LLM prompting is divided into seven prompts that have some dependencies regarding the sequence in which they can be triggered. For instance, prompts can only be triggered after the TDs have been parsed and the basic domain and problem files have been created. A detailed list with each prompt is available in our repository.

- **Goal Prompt:** Serves as the core prompt, outlining the method's objectives and providing essential background. Subsequent prompts are appended as chat messages to maintain context; however, a new goal prompt starts a fresh chain to avoid confusion. A **Refine Goal Prompt** is available for users to adjust the goal if it does not yield the desired mashup output.
- **Comparison Table Prompt:** Transforms non-boolean properties into predicates using a provided JSON list, with the LLM filling in the comparison values to ensure a parseable output. A **Comparison Refinement Prompt** addresses any missing predicate values (see Listing 3).
- **String Effect Refinement Prompt:** Updates the effects of actions that affect string properties based on the defined comparison values. For example, in a ConveyorBelt TD with three actions affecting the *status* property, only *startBeltForward* should set the predicate for "MovingForward," as determined by the comparison table.

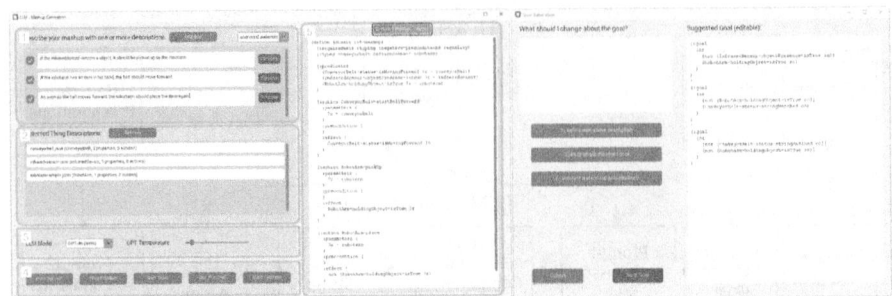

(a) The main screen of the user interface. The full image can be viewed here.

(b) The goal generation screen. The full image can be viewed here.

Fig. 5. The user interface, described in detail in Sect. 3.4. Note the panel numbering in Fig. 5a.

- **Disable Actions Prompt:** Cleans up the PDDL model by disabling irrelevant actions and removing unnecessary predicates, which improves readability and reduces execution errors.
- **Generate Preconditions Prompt:** The last prompt introduces preconditions for actions based on the user description and device states.

Maintaining a low temperature setting for the LLM is crucial to prevent deviations from the expected output format—minor errors in PDDL syntax can render outputs unprocessable. To mitigate this, prompts enforce a strict format with directives such as *Do not explain*, although some error handling and additional parsing remain necessary to consistently obtain a parseable goal.

3.4 User Interface

The user interface of the LLM-MaGe pipeline is built with CustomTkinter, which provides an easy way to create a simple but modern-looking UI that integrates well into Python.

Main Screen. The UI (Fig. 5a) places all input options on the left and outputs on the right.

In Subpanel (1) users describe system functionality via one or more text boxes, which can be toggled to experiment with different description combinations. A dropdown is also provided to select a standard test scenario (see Sect. 4.1).

Subpanel (2) displays all TDs from the `input_tds` folder, showing each device's meta information (name, type, capabilities) and highlighting errors (e.g., missing parameters) in red.

Subpanel (3) lists supported LLM options, allowing users to select a model and adjust the temperature setting to control response randomness, facilitating configuration experiments and performance comparisons.

Subpanel (4) contains the primary control buttons, such as triggering a prompt or starting the mashup execution.

The side pane (5) shows operation results in text boxes with a tab view (highlighted in blue) for switching between the generated domain file, problem file, and mashup loop output log. The first 4 buttons correspond to the UI actions in Fig. 4.

Goal Generation Screen. Figure 5b displays the dedicated window for generating and refining goals, with inputs on the left and outputs on the right.

For simple mashups, the initial recommended goals are usually accurate. In complex cases, refinement is essential. Refinement is done by resubmitting previous prompts to the LLM with an additional change request entered in the top-left text box. Once satisfied, users click "Save Goal" to return to the main screen. The saved goal text is then parsed into n different editable goals.

3.5 Mashup Planning and Execution

After completing all previously mentioned pipeline components, LLM-MaGe has a single domain file and multiple problem files - one for each goal generated by the earlier processes. This approach is meant to conquer complex goals by dividing them into multiple smaller independent goals.

These goals are prompted together to ensure the LLM maintains context but are planned separately. This approach allows us to handle side effects more effectively, as each smaller goal can be managed independently, reducing the likelihood of conflicting actions being triggered simultaneously. The separate plan results of each goal are then combined to form a cohesive system output for the mashup. This is illustrated in the red zone of Fig. 2.

This modification does come with a slight trade-off. The maximum output frequency of our system is reduced due to the increased computational overhead of managing multiple planning processes, but the support for more complex goals is significantly enhanced. By breaking down the system's objectives into manageable parts, we can better handle the dependencies and interactions between sensors and actuators.

As a PDDL planner, we have selected the ENHSP-20 planner [14], which implements heuristics to solve PDDL 2.1 plans.

Table 1. This table showcases all scenarios used for testing our approach.

Scenario	Descriptions	Devices
(1) Automate a smart lamp to turn on when someone enters a room.	"I want the smart lamp to turn on when someone is present in the room."	• Presence Sensor • Smart Lamp
(2) Maintain a comfortable room temperature by controlling an air conditioner	"I want the air conditioner to turn on if the temperature exceeds 26 degrees Celsius. Turn it off if the temp is below 26 degrees."	• Temperature Sensor • Air Conditioner
(3) Automate a conveyor belt and robotic arm in an industrial setting.	• "If the infrared sensor detects an object, it should be picked up by the robot arm." • "If the robot arm has an item in its hand, the belt should move forward." • "As soon as the belt moves forward, the robot arm should place the item again."	• Infrared sensor • Robot arm • Conveyor belt
(4) Maintain optimal conditions for plant growth by controlling multiple systems in a greenhouse.	• "Monitor and adjust the greenhouse environment by turning on the AC if the temperature rises above 25°C." • "Also turn on the AC if the humidity rises above 70" • "Water the plants if the soil moisture is below 20" • "Additionally, ensure the ventilation system is on if AC is not running and the watering system is not active."	• Temperature sensor • Humidity sensor • Soil moisture sensor • Air Conditioner • Ventilation System • Watering System

4 Evaluation and Analysis

4.1 Experimental Setup

For the verification and testing of LLM-MaGe[1] we are conducting tests in two main categories: Accuracy and Performance. Since the integration of LLMs into this pipeline introduces a non-deterministic behavior, we have to take the limitations this comes with into account while testing. For testing, we, therefore, define a set of scenarios where the input is predetermined, which allows us to compare the expected output with the actual one easily. As these scenarios differ in complexity, we can also use them to test the limitations in performance in various categories[2].

Test Scenarios. To evaluate the performance and functionality of our mashup generation system, we designed a series of test scenarios that incorporate all the different supported features. These scenarios range from simple to more complex configurations, enabling us to systematically test various aspects of the system, including the handling of boolean and non-boolean values, goal generation, and the overall performance of the pipeline. Each scenario is defined via a list of descriptions and TDs used.

4.2 Evaluation Metrics

We evaluated our system using key metrics focused on mashup accuracy and control loop performance. Accuracy was measured as the percentage of expected actions—aligned with the user's intended functionality, including cases where "no action needed" was appropriate—and by the number of refinements per goal.

Control loop performance was assessed by measuring the maximum frequency at which the system updated the mashup with new actions, as well as the stability of this frequency over time. We also analyzed how the number and complexity (number of predicates) of goals affected system speed and stability.

4.3 Results

Accuracy. We evaluated accuracy using predefined scenarios to ensure mashup functionality matched descriptions. In each scenario, four to six simulated sensor data points were fed into the system, and expected outputs were defined based on intended behavior. Accuracy was quantified as the percentage of correct actions over total expected actions, and tests were repeated ten times per scenario.

For simpler scenarios (1–3), GPT-4o achieved perfect accuracy with zero refinements, confirming our approach's effectiveness. In the more challenging agricultural scenario 4, a random sample of five tests never reached 100% accuracy on the first attempt; however, four out of five cases achieved full accuracy

---

[1] The open-source tool and verification data are available in our repository.
[2] All tests were performed on a computer running on a 11th Gen Intel(R) Core(TM) i7-11700KF @ 3.60 GHz CPU, 32 GB DDR4-3600 MHz RAM and Windows 11 Home.

after a maximum of five refinements. Notably, while no incorrect actions were taken, some expected actions were consistently missing. Two recurring issues were observed: an inverted predicate causing the system to water when soil moisture exceeded 20% instead of below, and a failure to activate ventilation due to an erroneous simultaneous test of the air conditioner and watering system states.

Despite these challenges, system performance remained resilient, with overall accuracy stable in subsequent trials. One test, however, did not reach 100% accuracy even after five refinements, which was our predefined limit.

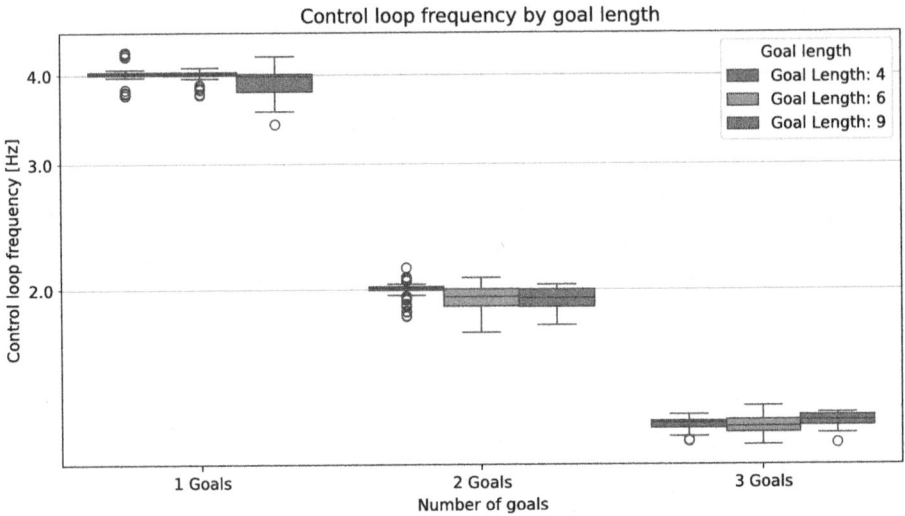

Fig. 6. Control loop frequency by goal length. Each test was performed 100 times.

Performance. We analyzed overall mashup performance to determine if the maximum update rate meets user needs. As shown in Fig. 6, the highest control loop frequency was 4 Hz (250 ms delay), which decreases with additional goals due to extra planning time. This impact might be reduced by introducing parallelization since the goals are independent and known from the starts. The control loop frequency had a low standard deviation (n=10), attributed to short solutions and the planner's overhead.

We also examined the effect of goal complexity by varying goal length (i.e. the number of words used in the goal prompt) while keeping the number of goals constant. Scenario 4 was omitted due to its complexity making it difficult to vary the length of the goal and still get meaningful results. Our findings (see Fig. 6) indicate that goal length does not significantly affect frequency; rather, the number of goals is the primary factor. This insight suggests that improved prompts and LLM models could handle more complex goals, reducing the need for goal splitting and enhancing performance for real-time IoT scenarios.

5 Related Work

The increasing diversity of IoT devices has driven interest in mashup generation, as end users need tools to create IoT applications with minimal technical expertise. [11] presents a visual, flow-based approach using Node-Red to lower the entry barrier, yet it still requires manual development. Our approach aims to further reduce the need for technical know-how.

In contrast, [7] generates atomic mashups from TDs, which must then be combined to form more complex solutions. While A-MaGe relies on predefined templates, user-configurable rules, semantic filtering, and NLP to select among atomic mashups, LLM-MaGe directly produces a single, full mashup.

Similarly, [10] leverages ontologies and PDDL to automate robotic system configurations in industrial settings, providing a semantic foundation for flexibility and scalability. Inspired by this, we extend the use of PDDL to general IoT systems.

Additionally, there has been recent research on integrating LLM in IoT pipelines. [3] introduces AutoIoT, which harnesses LLMs and formal verification to extract device information from screenshots or photos, generate trigger-action rules, and automatically synthesize code that detects and resolves four classes of conflicts before deployment, but it remains tied to specific smart-home platforms and separates rule generation from verification rather than unifying them in a single declarative model. [12] presents SAGE, which employs autonomous LLM agents with dynamic prompt trees—augmented by vision-based device disambiguation, API-driven control, code-generated persistent automations, and personalization memory—to flexibly plan and execute smart-home commands (76 % success over 50 tasks) without device-specific code, yet it is confined to home scenarios, relies on custom agent pipelines, and lacks direct support for standardized WoT descriptions.

LLM-MaGe dramatically outperforms prior work: it delivers 100 % first-try accuracy on routine mashups and full compliance in complex mashup scenarios after only minimal refinements, versus SAGE's 76 % success rate on its 50-task benchmark and AutoIoT's qualitative evaluations; it sustains a 4 Hz real-time planning loop, a capability neither one-shot rule deployments nor fixed agent pipelines provide; and by directly ingesting W3C Thing Descriptions, it scales seamlessly across any IoT domains without bespoke image/manual parsing or platform-specific code.

6 Future Work

There are several areas for future improvement of LLM-MaGe to simplify user interaction and support more complex mashups. Currently, our approach does not support event affordances, which are common in IoT systems, nor does it handle property writes and input-based action invocations—modeling these in PDDL remains an open research question.

Enhancing the TD parsing component to support a broader range of TDs (including advanced types like "objects" or "arrays") would increase the system's applicability across domains. Integrating standard Web of Things ontologies could further improve interoperability and streamline mashup generation.

There are numerous areas where LLM-MaGe could also improve in the future, which would make it either easier for the user or increase support for more complex mashups.

7 Conclusion

In this paper, we propose LLM-MaGe, a novel approach to simplifying the creation of mashups for the Web of Things (WoT). Our method bridges the gap between the user and the mashup generation process, allowing non-technical users to create IoT mashups simply by explaining them in natural language and providing the TDs for all available devices.

Our system converts the supplied TDs into PDDL domain and problem files and uses modern LLMs like GPT-4o to parse the natural language descriptions into additional information like preconditions and goals. For the execution of the mashup, we continuously read all relevant properties and event triggers of the devices, plan the PDDL problem, and trigger the resulting actions to keep the system true to the user description. This pipeline significantly reduces the technical expertise needed for configuring mashups in the IoT ecosystem.

Our evaluation demonstrates the system's effectiveness in generating accurate and functional mashups and therefore validates the feasibility of using PDDL in this context. For simpler scenarios we were also able to achieve 100% accuracy without any refinements through the user, surpassing current state of the art approaches. We also show the maximum control loop frequency the current implementation is able to reach and most importantly what parameters impact it the most. Furthermore, we evaluate how different iterations of AI models compare in performance and accuracy when used in LLM-MaGe.

References

1. Aly, M., Khomh, F., Guéhéneuc, Y.G., Washizaki, H., Yacout, S.: Is fragmentation a threat to the success of the internet of things? IEEE Internet Things J. **6**, 472–487 (2018). https://doi.org/10.1109/JIOT.2018.2863180
2. Charpenay, V., Käbisch, S., Kosch, H.: Introducing the web of things: interoperability for thing descriptionss. In: Proceedings of the 7th International Conference on the Internet of Things. ACM (2017). https://ceur-ws.org/Vol-1783/paper-06.pdf
3. Cheng, Y., Xu, M., Zhang, Y., Li, K., Wang, R., Yang, L.: Autoiot: Automated iot platform using large language models. IEEE Internet Things J., (2024). https://doi.org/10.1109/JIOT.2024.3523907
4. Cisco: Cisco annual internet report (2018–2023) (2023). https://www.cisco.com/c/en/us/solutions/executive-perspectives/annual-internet-report/index.html. Accessed 07 July 2024

5. Fox, M., Long, D.: PDDL2.1: an extension to PDDL for expressing temporal planning domains. J. Artif. Intell. Res. (2003). https://www.jair.org/index.php/jair/article/view/10237
6. Ghallab, M., et al.: Pddl - the planning domain definition language. Technical report, Yale Center for Computational Vision and Control (1998)
7. Korkan, E., Salama, F., Steinhorst, S.: A-mage: atomic mashup generator for the web of things. J. Internet Serv. Appl. (2021). https://doi.org/10.1007/978-3-030-74296-6_24
8. Käbisch, S.: Web of things (wot) architecture (2023). https://www.w3.org/TR/wot-architecture/. Accessed 29 June 2024
9. Käbisch, S., McCool, M., Korkan, E.: Web of Things (WoT) Thing Description 1.1 (2023). https://www.w3.org/TR/wot-thing-description11/
10. Merdan, M., Hoebert, T., Lepuschitz, W., Vincze, M., Merdan, M.: Knowledge-driven framework for industrial robotic systems. J. Intell. Manuf. (2021). https://doi.org/10.1007/s10845-021-01826-8
11. Papadopoulos, V., Tzavaras, A., Petrakis, E.G.M.: Moon: flow-based programming with openapi in the web of things. Springer, Heidelberg (2023). https://doi.org/10.1007/978-3-031-29056-5_44
12. Rivkin, D., et al.: Aiot smart home via autonomous llm agents. IEEE Internet Things J. **12**(3), 2458–2472 (2025). https://doi.org/10.1109/JIOT.2024.3471904
13. Salama, F., Korkan, E., Käbisch, S., Steinhorst, S.: Towards a behavioral description of cyber-physical systems using the thing description. In: DAI-SNAC '21. Association for Computing Machinery (2021). https://doi.org/10.1145/3488661.3494030
14. Scala, E.: The enhsp planning system (2023). https://sites.google.com/view/enhsp/. Accessed 07 July 2024
15. Taivalsaari, A., Mikkonen, T.: On the development of iot systems. In: 2018 Third International Conference on Fog and Mobile Edge Computing (FMEC) (2018). https://doi.org/10.1109/FMEC.2018.8364039

Demos and Posters

The Efficiency of Rust and WebAssembly Compared to Plain JavaScript

Kasper Jan Seweryn[✉][iD]

Faculty of Computer Science, Bialystok University of Technology, Wiejska 45A, 15-351 Bialystok, Poland
kasper.seweryn@pb.edu.pl

Abstract. This study investigates the performance differences between Rust compiled to WebAssembly and plain JavaScript, focusing on their efficiency in client-side web applications. By conducting a series of tests across various computational tasks, this research aims at providing insights into the potential advantages of using Rust and WebAssembly. The study evaluates metrics such as execution time, serialization overhead, and the impact of SIMD operations. I evaluated selected algorithms implemented in each technology on different input data sizes with varying numbers of repetitions. The results reveal that Rust implementations can achieve significant speedups, particularly when serialization overhead is minimized. The study also highlights the impact of JIT compilation on JavaScript's performance, which improves with increased repetitions, while Rust's performance remains stable. The findings suggest that for applications requiring consistent performance, WebAssembly and Rust should be the preferred choice. However, the study also notes the challenges of DOM API interactions, which require data to be passed back to JavaScript, potentially impacting performance.

Keywords: WebAssembly · Rust · efficiency · JavaScript

1 Introduction

The purpose of this study is to evaluate the performance differences between Rust compiled to WebAssembly and plain JavaScript. Understanding these differences is crucial, as client-side web applications often demand high performance and efficiency, especially for computationally intensive tasks. By conducting a series of tests across various computational tasks, this research aims at obtaining insights into the efficiency and potential advantages of using Rust and WebAssembly in web development. The study focuses on metrics such as execution time, serialization overhead, and the impact of SIMD operations, offering a comparison to guide developers in choosing the most suitable technology for their applications.

2 Related Work

In their study, Tushar and Mohan [1] concluded that WebAssembly outperforms JavaScript in tasks involving large computations, while Nilsson and Trattner [2] found that Rust compiled to WebAssembly outperforms JavaScript when the serialization overhead is minimal. This study expands on their works and covers additional algorithms and DOM manipulation as well as examines the impact of SIMD operations, JIT compilation, and various Rust compiler optimization levels, on the performance and stability of WebAssembly compared to JavaScript.

3 Method

I have implemented selected algorithms such as Base64 encoding, k-th Fibonacci number, 4×4 matrix multiplication, CRC-32, CRC-64, and creation, update and deletion of DOM elements in both technologies and evaluated them on different input data sizes and varying numbers of repetitions, and varying Rust compiler optimization levels resulting in a total of 327 test instances. The source code for all tests can be accessed in the GitHub repository [3].

To understand the performance differences between both technologies, I have focused on measuring their execution times. For JavaScript, I have measured only algorithm execution time $T_{A_{JS}}$. However, in case of Rust, a serialization of data passed to WebAssembly's memory is often needed. Hence, I have measured deserialization time $T_{D_{RS}}$, algorithm execution time $T_{A_{RS}}$, and serialization time $T_{S_{RS}}$.[1] Then, I have derived the total execution times for both JavaScript and Rust functions as in Eq. (1).

$$T_{T_{RS}} = T_{D_{RS}} + T_{A_{RS}} + T_{S_{RS}} \qquad T_{T_{JS}} = T_{A_{JS}} \qquad (1)$$

To compare and assess relative efficiency of both technologies, I have calculated the total speedup S_T and algorithm speedup S_A in relation to JavaScript implementation as in Eq. (2).

$$S_T = \frac{\overline{T}_{T_{JS}}}{\overline{T}_{T_{RS}}} \qquad S_A = \frac{\overline{T}_{A_{JS}}}{\overline{T}_{A_{RS}}} \qquad (2)$$

Each test consisted of zero or more JS functions and one or more Rust functions. Measurements were averaged over n runs on multiple variably sized input data which was randomly generated before each test. I tested the algorithms sequentially, and before benchmarking each function the browser tab was automatically refreshed to clean up the environment and JIT optimizations.

I have conducted all tests on Google Chrome (version 136.0.7103.93) on an M1 MacBook Air, equipped with 16 GB RAM and running macOS Sequoia 15.3.2. The Rust code was compiled into a single release binary using rustc 1.78.0 and wasm-pack 0.12.1 with *lto=true* and *opt_level* flag set to "*3*", "*s*" and "*z*".

---

[1] Note that $T_{D_{RS}}$ refers to the total time of serialization in the JS context and deserialization in the WASM context. Similarly, the $T_{S_{RS}}$ refers to time taken for serialization in WASM context and deserialization in JS context.

4 Results

Algorithms that do not require serialization demonstrated improved performance in Rust implementations. Calculating 40th Fibonacci number recursively was 5.87 times faster. Depending on the input data size, non-LUT CRC-32 exhibited speedups of 1.77 to 3.33 times, non-LUT CRC-64 exhibited speedups of 20.48 to 38.42, while LUT CRC-64 exhibited speedups of 4.42 up to 12.49

For algorithms requiring serialization step, Rust implementations showed varying performance improvements, depending on the size and shape of the data. With minimal data, Base64 encoding was 1.74 times slower than identical JavaScript implementation but for larger data it has shown 4.5 times performance increase. When comparing algorithm execution time only, the Rust implementation was 1.3 and 8.4 times faster respectively. 4×4 matrix multiplication was 3.46 times slower than JavaScript implementation, as the data was passed as a nested array, which required serialization. However, with serialization overhead omitted, the algorithm execution time was 1.22 times faster.

Among all SIMD algorithms, only the 4×4 matrix multiplication demonstrated a performance decrease when compared to manual scalar implementations. This was a direct result of the time spent on the serialization of nested arrays. Pure algorithm performance, however, demonstrated up to 1.35 times speedup. Base64 encoding demonstrated an 8.21 times increase in performance and was up to 49.4 times faster when serialization time was excluded, while CRC-64 (LUT) exhibited the most significant results, achieving a total speedup of 92.93 and an algorithmic speedup of 98.83.

At the time of testing, there was no direct way of interacting with DOM API through the WebAssembly. All API calls needed to be passed down to JavaScript context resulting in overall poor performance and around 2.5 times slowdown.

5 Conclusions

The comparative analysis of Rust compiled to WebAssembly and plain JavaScript reveals significant implications for the performance of client-side web applications. In scenarios where data is minimal, the serialization overhead results in Rust implementations exhibiting up to a 3.46 decrease in total execution speed, despite achieving algorithmic speeds up to 1.3 times as fast. Further testing demonstrated that with sufficiently large data, the serialization impact becomes negligible, resulting in Rust implementations being up to 4.51 times faster overall and up to 8.4 times faster in terms of pure algorithm execution time. However, when data can be transferred to a WASM context directly, Rust-implemented algorithms outperformed their JavaScript counterparts by factors of 1.77 to 38.42.

The unexpectedly high difference of speedups between non-LUT versions of CRC-64 and CRC-32, might be the result of inefficient BigInt type as JavaScript does not support 64-bit bitwise operands for the Number type [4].

The disproportion between total speedup and algorithm speedup sheds light at the issue of serialization overhead. When selecting Rust as the implementation language, one should carefully consider the structure of the data. In case of 4×4 matrix multiplication, the matrix was passed as a nested array resulting in slowdowns. This could have been omitted if it was represented as a flat array.

As the number of test repetitions n increased, JavaScript execution times improved due to JIT compiler, whereas Rust's execution times remained stable. This suggests that for applications requiring consistent performance, WebAssembly and Rust should be the preferred implementation choice. However, for 4×4 matrix multiplication and CRC-32 tests, when n was rising, the time spent on serialization was going down. This indicates that serialization depends on JavaScript APIs and may lead to performance instability, particularly when the WASM function is executed a limited number of times.

When the application requires stability and performance, one could consider developing it entirely in Rust with WebAssembly. Better algorithm performance and ability to utilize SIMD operations can significantly enhance the efficiency and speed of computational tasks. However, naive DOM API calls require passing data back and forth between the contexts which may impact the performance negatively. Hence, using optimized Rust frontend frameworks like Leptos or Sycamore might be a better option.

Acknowledgments. This paper summarizes the findings presented in my M.Sc. thesis (written in Polish), which is accessible in the GitHub repository containing the source code for the tests conducted [3]. The participation in the ICWE 2025 conference was sponsored by the NAWA PROM program. I would like to thank Marek Tabedzki for supervising the experimentation process and Marek Druzdzel for editorial help. Thanks to Jacek Pruciak for setting up and sharing his devices for use as a testing environment.

Disclosure of Interests. The author has no competing interests to declare that are relevant to the content of this article.

References

1. Tushar, M.B.R.: Comparative analysis of JavaScript and WebAssembly in the browser environment. In: 2022 IEEE 10th Region 10 Humanitarian Technology Conference (R10-HTC), pp. 232–237. https://doi.org/10.1109/R10-HTC54060.2022.9929829
2. Nilsson, J., Trattner, A.: Analyzing front-end performance using WebAssembly. LU-CS-EX (2022). http://lup.lub.lu.se/student-papers/record/9094683

3. Source code for the conducted tests. https://github.com/wvffle/masters-thesis. Accessed 05 May 2025
4. ECMAScript spec. https://262.ecma-international.org/#sec-numberbitwiseop. Accessed 04 Apr 2025

KuBench: A Kubernetes-Based Environment for Standardized REST API Framework Performance Evaluation

Ondrej Olsak[✉][iD], Matej Sauer[iD], Marta Jaros[iD], and Jiri Jaros[iD]

Faculty of Information Technology, Brno University of Technology,
Brno, Czech Republic
iolsak@fit.vut.cz

Abstract. Selecting the optimal REST API framework is a critical decision that directly impacts application performance, scalability, and development efficiency. KuBench solves this challenge by providing an environment for comparison of multiple REST API frameworks. Unlike existing tools that only test single implementations, our Kubernetes-based solution enables developers to evaluate multiple implementations of identical APIs across different programming languages and libraries under the same conditions. This paper presents our approach for consistent benchmarking using containerization and comprehensive performance metrics that capture response times, throughput, and resource utilization. KuBench empowers development teams to make decisions when selecting REST API frameworks that genuinely meet their performance requirements.

Keywords: REST API · benchmarking · performance testing · resource utilization

1 Introduction

In today's microservices architecture landscape, REST APIs form the critical communication backbone of modern applications. Developers face a daunting choice among dozens of REST API frameworks spanning multiple programming languages, each promising optimal performance and developer experience.

Most developers select frameworks based on language familiarity, community popularity, or documentation quality–not empirical performance data under real-world conditions. This approach can lead to costly performance issues discovered only after significant development investment.

While tools like RestTestGen [3], bBOXRT [2], and EvoMaster [1] focus on testing individual API implementations, none provide the comparative analysis capabilities needed for informed framework selection decisions. Traditional load testing tools like Apache JMeter offer valuable insights but lack the standardized environment required for fair cross-framework comparisons.

KuBench addresses this gap by providing a platform that enables direct side-by-side comparison of multiple REST API implementations across different frameworks and languages, all under identical conditions. This comparative approach is crucial for development teams seeking to make data-driven technology decisions rather than relying on assumptions or incomplete information.

2 The Kubernetes-Based Benchmarking Environment

KuBench allows developers to define custom API endpoints that precisely emulate those in the application they intend to implement. This customization ensures that benchmark results reflect the actual use case rather than generic scenarios. Developers can create endpoint definitions that mirror their specific application requirements, including complex database interactions with PostgreSQL for data persistence and retrieval operations. By testing against these tailored endpoints, teams gain insights into how each framework performs under conditions relevant to their specific application needs. The architecture of the benchmarking system is presented in Fig. 1.

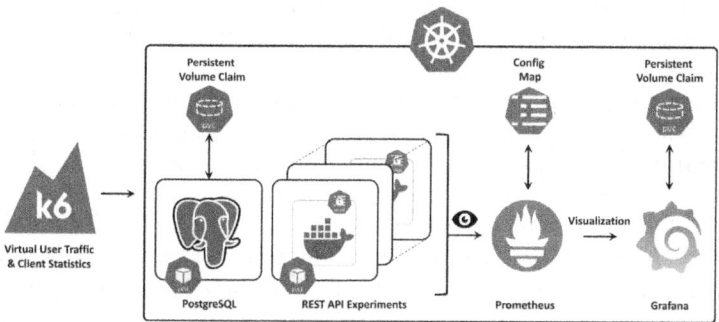

Fig. 1. The KuBench Architecture provides a standardized environment for comparing multiple REST frameworks under identical conditions.

KuBench delivers four key advantages that make it a considerable tool for REST API framework evaluation:

Side-by-Side Comparison: Our Kubernetes-based architecture ensures each API implementation runs with identical resource constraints and environment conditions. This eliminates variables that typically skew benchmark results, allowing for fair comparison across different frameworks within the same language.

Real-World Performance Measurement: KuBench provides comprehensive metrics that matter in production environments. It captures response times and throughput under various load conditions, detailed CPU and memory utilization patterns, and error rates under stress.

Containerized Consistency: By leveraging Kubernetes, we ensure precisely controlled resource allocation across all tested frameworks. Each implementation operates with identical network conditions and consistent database access patterns. This approach guarantees reproducible results whether testing locally with Minikube or in cloud-based clusters.

Extensible Testing Framework: Developers can easily extend KuBench by adding new framework implementations to the comparison pool. The environment supports custom testing scenarios that match specific application requirements, along with configurable workload patterns ranging from hundreds to thousands of virtual users. This flexibility ensures the benchmarking remains relevant to each team's unique needs.

3 Adding Framework to the Benchmark

The benchmarking environment provides a systematic process for integrating new REST API frameworks. The detailed setup process involves several technical steps:

1. **Implement REST API Endpoints** - Create an API implementation using your target framework that implements all required API endpoints. These endpoints should represent typical application REST API usage, and could optionally include database interactions.
2. **Metrics Exposure** - Add Prometheus-compatible metrics and expose them through a dedicated endpoint for monitoring performance characteristics.
3. **Containerize the Implementation** - Create a Docker image that exposes the appropriate ports for API access and metrics collection, ensuring consistent deployment across environments.
4. **Update Kubernetes Manifests** - Add deployment and service manifests for your implementation to the Kubernetes cluster. Existing manifests that are part of the environment can serve as templates.
5. **Configure Prometheus** - Modify the Prometheus configuration to include your new service, specifying the address of your Kubernetes service, path to metrics endpoint, and the name of your experiment.
6. **Prepare Grafana Visualization** - Add panels to existing dashboards or create a new dashboard to visualize the performance metrics of your framework, ensuring metrics are properly scraped by Prometheus. The example dashboard is provided.
7. **Configure Load Testing** - Modify k6 load testing scripts to include your implementation. If your service runs on a standard address similar to other experiments, you can simply add your experiment's port to the ports defined in the bash scripts.

The entire environment is maintained as Infrastructure as Code (IaC), which enables reproducing test results across different environments. The environment can be deployed directly to the target device or cloud infrastructure where the real application will be executed, ensuring that benchmark results accurately reflect production conditions.

4 Conclusions

KuBench has the potential to transform how development teams select REST API frameworks by replacing subjective evaluation with empirical evidence. It offers direct comparisons of multiple implementations under identical conditions, providing comprehensive performance metrics that go well beyond simple response times. The environment ensures reproducible results across different infrastructure setups, giving teams confidence in their technology decisions.

Future enhancements will focus on including concurrent testing capabilities to accelerate the evaluation process, simplified workflow configuration, and expanded support for distributed deployment scenarios that better reflect modern microservice architectures.

By making API framework selection a data-driven decision rather than a subjective choice, KuBench helps development teams build more performant, scalable, and resource-efficient applications from the start. This approach eliminates costly technology pivots and ensures applications are built on frameworks truly suited to their performance requirements.

Appendices

The first version of the KuBench benchmarking environment is published on GitHub under the following link: https://github.com/SC-FIT/KuBench. It includes the environment itself with a predefined example set of REST API implementations, making it easy to try and extend the benchmarking environment as well as the number of test cases, or add new REST API implementations.

Acknowledgments. This work was supported by the Ministry of Education, Youth and Sports of the Czech Republic through the e-INFRA CZ (ID:90254). This project has received funding from the European Union's Horizon Europe research and innovation programme under grant agreement No 101071008. This work was supported by Brno University of Technology under project number FIT-S-23-8141.

References

1. Arcuri, A.: EvoMaster: evolutionary multi-context automated system test generation. In: 2018 IEEE 11th International Conference on Software Testing, Verification and Validation (ICST), pp. 394–397 (2018). https://doi.org/10.1109/ICST.2018.00046
2. Laranjeiro, N., Agnelo, J., Bernardino, J.: A black box tool for robustness testing of rest services. IEEE Access **9**, 24738–24754 (2021). https://doi.org/10.1109/ACCESS.2021.3056505
3. Viglianisi, E., Dallago, M., Ceccato, M.: RESTTESTGEN: automated black-box testing of restful APIs. In: 2020 IEEE 13th International Conference on Software Testing, Validation and Verification (ICST), pp. 142–152 (2020). https://doi.org/10.1109/ICST46399.2020.00024

Leveraging LLMs for Voice-Based form Filling on the Web: The ConWeb Approach

Ludovica Piro[✉], Giulia Di Fede, Emanuele Pucci, Stefano Tolomeo, and Maristella Matera

Dipartimento di Elettronica Informazione e Bioingegneria, Politecnico di Milano, Milan 20133, Italy
{ludovica.piro,giulia.difede,emanuele.pucci,stefano.tolomeo, maristella.matera}@polimi.it

Abstract. Web forms are among the most challenging components for individuals using assistive technologies. Improper coding practices can significantly impede screen readers, preventing them from correctly interpreting or even accessing input fields. Conversational interaction presents an opportunity to increase form accessibility. This demonstration presents ConWeb, a conversational platform with which users can interact with web forms using natural language interaction. Our work aims at introducing an alternative and inclusive paradigm to visual web browsing.

Keywords: Voice interaction · Conversational form filling · Accessibility

1 Introduction

The development of accessible digital services is essential to ensuring inclusion and the right to access information, most importantly to people with disabilities (whether permanent, temporary, or situational). Lately, numerous public services, such as those provided by public administrations, have been digitalized, with many procedures now requiring users to fill out online forms. However, due to poor coding, these forms often remain among the most challenging components for assistive technologies, such as screen readers. Many individuals risk being excluded from fully benefiting from digital services.

Recent advancements in natural language understanding and generation, driven by Large Language Models (LLMs), have facilitated tackling the form filling task with conversational approaches. Cuadra et al. [2], for example, propose a multi-modal interface based on LLMs to fulfill forms for health data targeted at elderly people. Despite these new efforts, there is still a lack of proposals for a full-fledged integration of Conversational AI within Web architectures, and conversational agents (CA) development and deployment are usually detached from Web architectures. Currently, CAs are seen as tools that complement the Web access experience by providing additional content (e.g., FAQs access), not granting access to the website content itself.

With the aim of changing this perspective, we propose *conversational web browsing* as a paradigm for performing web browsing tasks, such as navigation, content reading, and form filling, by using natural-language interaction. Few works in the literature explore this new paradigm (e.g., [1]), and present it as an alternative or an addition to screen reader-based web browsing. Still, form-filling remains a task that has yet to be addressed in this context.

2 Demonstration

This work introduces ConWeb, an LLM-based conversational platform for browsing the web using voice interaction. The demo (https://shorturl.at/Qrnxt), shows the ConWeb approach to conversational form-filling. Attendees can interact with ConWeb through voice interaction and fill out a web form on a desktop browser.

Our approach allows users to fulfill forms in a flexible way, maintaining the context of the interaction and allowing users to complete the form by communicating data in chunks or a different order from the one used on the web page. Users will be able to navigate across form pages, get a summary of each page overall goal, and perform data entry. Furthermore, users can upload files, correct errors, and modify data as they go.

3 ConWeb

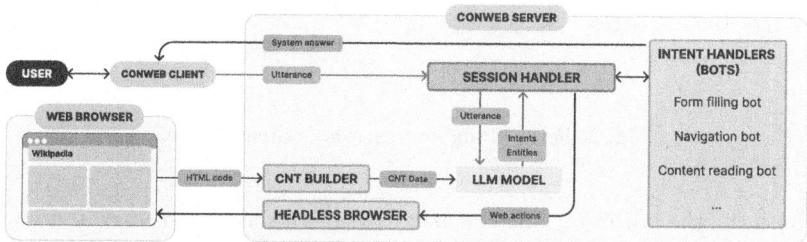

Fig. 1. ConWeb architecture showing the main components.

The dialogical interaction with Web pages is supported by the architecture depicted in Fig. 1, which is articulated into two main components. First, a client, deployed as a *browser extension*, intercepts users' utterances and presents the system's responses to users using Google's Speech-to-Text and Text-to-Speech APIs, respectively. Secondly, a server processes users' utterances and performs actions on webpages according to the user intent. To do so, the server comprises many independent microservices, called *bots* in our architecture, managed by a *session handler* that handles the requests. To actuate actions on the page, the server uses a headless browser. A data structure stored in a JSON file, the *Content Navigation Tree* (CNT), is built by the *CNT Builder* to store the current web page elements, and is accessed by the bots to build the dialog based on the navigation context.

To process users' utterances, we use OpenAI's GPT-4o model, which is accessed through APIs. When the session handler receives a user utterance, GPT-4o is utilized to classify the intents and entities through an appropriate prompt. According to this classification, the session handler calls the correct bot to handle the request. Each bot manages one or more user intents, produces the corresponding actions on the browser, and builds the dialog according to specific *conversational interaction patterns* defined through co-design sessions with blind and visually impaired users [3].

Bots' behaviors are shaped by four classes of patterns: *orientation patterns* refer to strategies to improve the understandability of the navigational context, like providing link previews; *navigation patterns* correspond to navigation actions, such as moving across pages or Q&A requests; *content reading patterns* refer to strategies for accessing content, such as summarization and segmentation; *scaffolding patterns* refer to system commands such as starting and stopping the conversation.

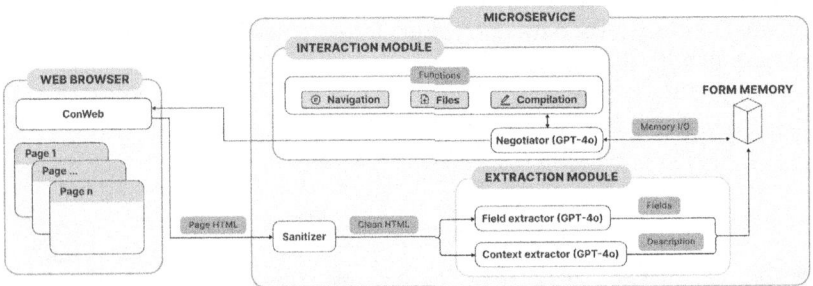

Fig. 2. Form-filling microservice's architecture.

Recently, the bot library has been extended with a *Form-Filling Bot* responsible for interpreting web forms and their completion (Fig. 2). It is the most complex bot in terms of voice interaction and is composed of two main modules: the *Extraction Module* and the *Interaction Module*. After sanitizing the page code to filter relevant elements, the Extraction Module sends the HTML code to GPT-4o APIs to extract the form fields and the page's context. It stores this information in the *Form Memory*, a JSON file following the CNT model, which gets updated as the conversation goes on with the data inputted by the user. The Interaction Module then manages the dialog between the user and the form. We created a prompt to instruct the LLM model to interpret intents specific to form filling: data entry, file upload, and navigation within the module. When the Interaction Module recognizes one of those intents, it calls specific functions that actuate the intent through a corresponding action on the page. Additionally, the prompt contains specific instructions to manage the voice interaction with the form according to the aforementioned interaction patterns:

Orientation: Conversational Context. Users are informed of where they are on the page and what is the status of the system, i.e., whether they have finished filling in the data on the page or if they are still missing some parts.

Content Reading: Summarization and Segmentation. The form is summarized at the beginning to give an overview of what is requested from the user. Then, to limit the cognitive demand, the data are requested in chunks, also allowing the user to communicate multiple data items at once.

Navigation: In-Depth and In-Breath Navigation. Users can skip entire sections of the form or form fields and flexibly move across pages in multi-page forms. Users can also ask clarification questions.

Scaffolding: Data Review and Error Handling. At any point of interaction, users can ask the system to repeat the entered data and the missing information. The system also supports error correction and deletion of previously entered data.

4 Conclusion and Future Work

In this demonstration we present ConWeb, a conversational platform to browse the Web. ConWeb allows users to access various kinds of web content, including web forms. We propose our approach based on co-design sessions with blind and visually impaired people. We apply the identified patterns on form-filling, a challenging accessibility task, to propose a conversational approach to the problem. Future work will focus on further evaluating ConWeb with end-users to assess response accuracy and system usability. Furthermore, we will also evaluate alternative LLMs, such as open-source models like LLama, to improve scalability and cut costs.

Acknowledgments. This was supported by the Italian Ministry of University and Research (MUR) under grant PRIN 2022 "PROTECT project (imPROving ciTizEn inClusivity Through Conversational AI)". CUP: H53D23008150001.

References

1. Cambre, J., et al.: Firefox voice: an open and extensible voice assistant built upon the web. In: Proceedings of the 2021 CHI Conference on Human Factors in Computing Systems, CHI 2021. ACM, New York (2021). https://doi.org/10.1145/3411764.3445409
2. Cuadra, A., et al.: Digital forms for all: a holistic multimodal large language model agent for health data entry. Proc. ACM Interact. Mob. Wearable Ubiquitous Technol. 8(2) (2024). https://doi.org/10.1145/3659624
3. Pucci, E., Possaghi, I., Cutrupi, C.M., Baez, M., Cappiello, C., Matera, M.: Defining patterns for a conversational web. In: Proceedings of the 2023 CHI Conference on Human Factors in Computing Systems, CHI 2023. ACM, New York (2023). https://doi.org/10.1145/3544548.3581145

Troubleshooting Microservices with Heterogeneous Graph Neural Network

Juyoung Yang[✉], EunChan Park, KyeongDeok Baek, and In-Young Ko

School of Computing, Korea Advanced Institute of Science and Technology, Daejeon, Republic of Korea
{didwndud3299,eunchan.park,kyeongdeok.baek,iko}@kaist.ac.kr

Abstract. Microservices architecture (MSA) is becoming the preferred choice for web applications due to its scalability and maintainability. However, troubleshooting microservices remains challenging due to the complex dependencies of microservices. Additionally, recent state-of-the-art methods rely heavily on labeled training data. To address these challenges, we propose HERO, a unified framework for both anomaly detection and root cause localization in MSA applications. HERO effectively captures complex dependencies of microservices by utilizing a heterogeneous graph neural network. Unlike existing machine learning approaches, HERO does not require root cause labeled data for training through a novel explainability technique. In our experiments on a widely used MSA benchmark dataset, HERO outperformed existing methods in both anomaly detection and root cause localization tasks.

Keywords: Microservice · Anomaly detection · Root cause localization

1 Introduction

In recent years, web applications have been transitioning from monolithic architecture to microservices architecture (MSA) for scalability and maintainability [2]. However, anomalies are inevitable in microservices due to their complexity and dynamism. An anomaly in one microservice could propagate to others and magnify its impact, which can lead to poor user experience and incur huge economic losses [6]. Specifically, at the logical level, anomalies can propagate among microservices in the call path, as illustrated in Fig. 1a. At the physical level, microservices deployed on the same virtual machine (VM) can influence each other's performance due to shared resources, as shown in Fig. 1b.

To address the aforementioned challenges, we propose HERO, **HE**terogeneous graph neural network-based t**RO**ubleshooting framework for microservices. The key ideas of HERO are as follows. First, HERO utilizes heterogeneous graph neural network (HGNN) [1], which can have multiple types of edges, to model both logical and physical dependencies among microservices. This enables HERO to effectively capture both logical and physical anomaly propagation scenarios in MSA applications. Second, unlike existing ML-based approaches that require separate ML models for anomaly detection and root cause localization, HERO localizes root causes by applying perturbations to the input graph fed into the anomaly detection ML model, eliminating the need for a separate root cause localization ML model that requires labeled data for training.

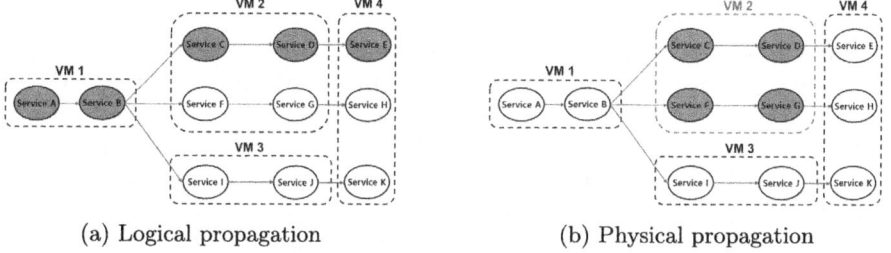

(a) Logical propagation (b) Physical propagation

Fig. 1. Two types of anomaly propagation in MSA applications.

2 Approach: HERO

We present our unified framework for anomaly detection and root cause localization, HERO. Figure 2 displays the overview of HERO:

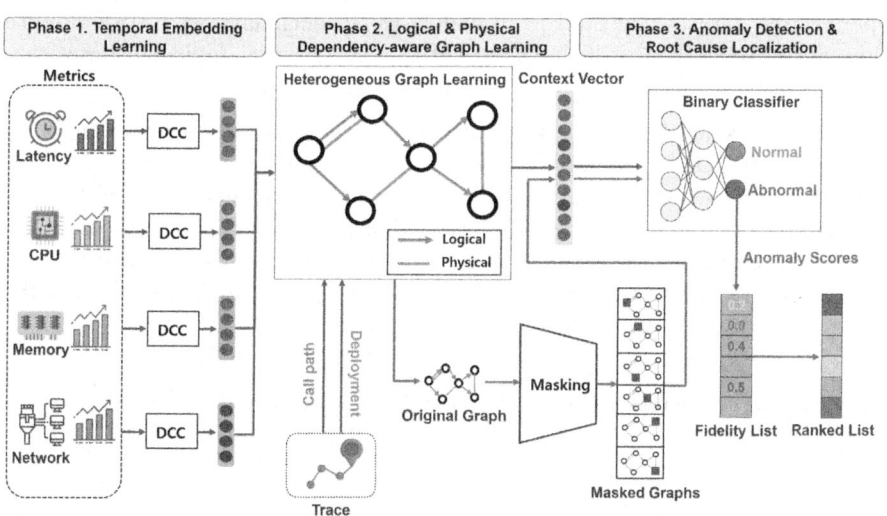

Fig. 2. Overview of HERO and its three phases. (Color figure online)

(1) Temporal Embedding Learning: In this phase, HERO captures the temporal patterns of dynamically changing multi-metric data over time at the microservice level. To obtain temporal vectors, we employ dilated causal convolution (DCC) [5], which is particularly well-suited for capturing correlations in time-series data.

(2) Logical & Physical Dependency-aware Graph Learning: In this phase, HERO models the logical and physical interactions among microservices to obtain a context vector that encapsulates the overall state of the MSA application. To this end, we utilize HGNN, a specialized variant of GNN that supports multiple edge types. Unlike traditional GNNs, HGNN has edge-type-aware neighbor aggregation mechanism [1], which means that the unique characteristics of logical and physical dependencies can be captured.

(3) Anomaly Detection & Root Cause Localization: In this phase, HERO performs anomaly detection by using a deep neural network (DNN)-based binary classifier. If an anomaly is detected, HERO identify the culprit microservices as a ranked list. To localize root causes, HERO applies perturbation-based explainability techniques [4] by masking edges in the input graph. These masks reduce a node s influence in the graph by isolating it from neighbor aggregation in the HGNN model. By comparing anomaly confidence scores before and after masking, HERO computes *fidelity* scores that reflect each node's contribution to the anomaly. Nodes are then ranked by fidelity to identify root causes. The red lines in Fig. 2 illustrate the flow of this root cause localization process.

3 Evaluation and Discussion

In this section, we present our experimental evaluation results of HERO on an open-source dataset collected from widely-used benchmark web MSA application, SocialNetwork [3], which consists of 28 microservices implementing various features of real-world social networking web applications.

Effectiveness in Anomaly Detection. For the anomaly detection task, we compared HERO with a state-of-the-art GNN-based approach, Eadro [6]. For statistical significance, we repeated the experiment five times for each method and averaged the results. In all the evaluation metrics for binary classification, HERO outperformed the baseline method, as illustrated in Table 1. These performance gaps demonstrate that our heterogeneous graph learning enables HERO to detect anomalies more effectively.

Table 1. Average F1-score, Recall and Precision for anomaly detection

Approaches	F1-score	Recall	Precision
Eadro [6]	0.85	0.83	0.88
HERO	**0.92**	**0.91**	**0.92**

Effectiveness in Root Cause Localization. For the root cause localization task, we evaluated HERO against heuristic methods that require no labeled data, using two widely used evaluation metrics, AC@k and Avg@k [6,9]. AC@k represents the probability that the actual root causes are included in the top-k ranked list, and Avg@k calculates the average AC@k from 1 to k. HERO significantly outperformed the baselines, as shown in Table 2. These results demonstrate the effectiveness of HERO in root cause localization without labeled data.

Table 2. AC@k (k = 1 to 5) and Avg@5 for root cause localization

Approaches	AC@1	AC@2	AC@3	AC@4	AC@5	Avg@5
N-Sigma [7]	0.259	0.432	0.573	0.687	0.745	0.539
ϵ-Diagnosis [8]	0.696	0.768	0.783	0.815	0.873	0.787
HERO	**0.730**	**0.908**	**0.934**	**0.952**	**0.963**	**0.898**

4 Conclusion

In this paper, we propose HERO, a unified troubleshooting framework for microservices. HERO captures both logical and physical anomaly propagation scenarios by using HGNN. Furthermore, HERO eliminates the need for a separate ML model and labeled data for root cause localization by leveraging the explainability of our HGNN-based anomaly detection model. Our experimental results demonstrate that HERO outperformed existing methods. For future work, we aim to improve the performance of root cause localization by developing a more advanced masking technique. Our poster is available at: https://drive.google.com/file/d/1_foo_w3WpBrWRZ8dEPVqoB1MxO6nesqO/view?usp=drive_link.

Acknowledgments. This work was supported by the Institute of Information & communications Technology Planning & Evaluation(IITP) grant funded by the Korea government(MSIT) (RS-2024-00406245, 40%), IITP grant funded by MSIT (RS-2025-02218761, 40%), and IITP-ITRC(Information Technology Research Center) grant funded by MSIT (IITP-2025-RS-2020-II201795, 20%).

References

1. Bing, R., et al.: Heterogeneous graph neural networks analysis: a survey of techniques, evaluations and applications. Artif. Intell. Rev. **56**(8), 8003–8042 (2022)
2. Di Francesco, P., et al.: Research on architecting microservices: trends, focus, and potential for industrial adoption. In: ICSA, pp. 21–30 (2017)
3. Gan, Y., et al.: An open-source benchmark suite for microservices and their hardware-software implications for cloud & edge systems. In: ASPLOS, pp. 3–18 (2019)
4. Kakkad, J., et al.: A survey on explainability of graph neural networks (2023)
5. Lea, C., et al.: Temporal convolutional networks: a unified approach to action segmentation. In: ECCV Workshops, pp. 47–54 (2016)

6. Lee, C., et al.: Eadro: an end-to-end troubleshooting framework for microservices on multi-source data. In: ICSE, pp. 1750–1762 (2023)
7. Lin, J., et al.: Microscope: pinpoint performance issues with causal graphs in microservice environments. In: ICSOC, pp. 3–20 (2018)
8. Shan, H., et al.: ?-diagnosis: unsupervised and real-time diagnosis of small-window long-tail latency in large-scale microservice platforms. In: WWW, pp. 3215–3222 (2019)
9. Somashekar, G., et al.: Gamma: graph neural network-based multi-bottleneck localization for microservices applications. In: WWW, pp. 3085–3095 (2024)

Post-hoc LLM-Supported Debugging of Distributed Processes

Dennis Schiese[✉] and Andreas Both

Web and Software Engineering Research Group, Leipzig University of Applied Sciences, Leipzig, Germany
dennis.schiese@htwk-leipzig.de, andreas.both@htwk-leipzig.de

Abstract. In this paper, we address the problem of manual debugging, which nowadays remains resource-intensive and in some parts archaic. This problem is especially evident in increasingly complex and distributed software systems. Therefore, our objective of this work is to introduce an approach that can possibly be applied to any system, at both the macro- and micro-level, to ease this debugging process. This approach utilizes a system's process data, in conjunction with generative AI, to generate natural-language explanations. These explanations are generated from the actual process data, interface information, and documentation to guide the developers more efficiently to understand the behavior and possible errors of a process and its sub-processes. Here, we present a demonstrator that employs this approach on a component-based Java system. However, our approach is language-agnostic. Ideally, the generated explanations will provide a good understanding of the process, even if developers are not familiar with all the details of the considered system. Our demonstrator is provided as an open-source web application that is freely accessible to all users.

Keywords: AI-supported Software Development · Debugging · LLM

1 Introduction

Software development, as with many other areas, is subject to rapidly growing automation, which has a considerable effect on the efficiency with which software is developed. As a result, the volume and complexity of existing software continue to grow. This is particularly evident in the context of distributed systems, where processes utilize multiple software components (e.g., Web services), and in the development of complex software architectures, where intricate dependencies and large codebases add further challenges. However, as software development accelerates, traditional workflows such as conception, implementation, debugging, or testing remain fundamental, even as AI agents begin to adopt them. In the case of debugging, concepts like *automated program repair* (APR) offer many different techniques and tools to tackle this problem [1,7]. Despite their increasing performance, these approaches encounter instances of failure. In such cases, manual debugging becomes a necessary process.

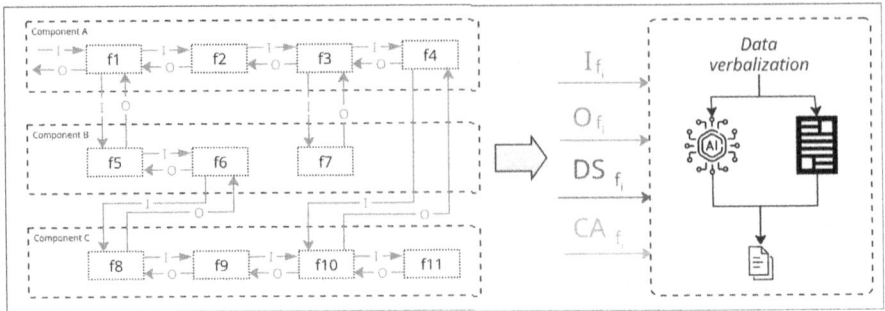

Fig. 1. An abstract process involving three interacting components. Each unit (f) may call another with or without arguments and possibly receive a return value. These calls, along with values like input (I_{f_i}), output (O_{f_i}), docstring (DS_{f_i}), and caller (CA_{f_i}), are logged and used by a *Data verbalizer* to generate explanations for f_i, using templates or generative AI.

In this demonstration, one of the considered processes – consisting of just two components (Web services) – can trigger over 5000 trackable inter- and intra-component method calls (excluding external libraries). The manual debugging of such a process is cumbersome and time-consuming. To address this challenge, we proposed in [4,5] an approach that inspects a system during runtime and verbalizes process' data post-hoc for each method. Here, we extended this approach with a clear focus on component-oriented explanations (see Fig. 1) to ease the debugging process and implemented a corresponding demonstrator. In order to reduce the overhead of having to search through too many explanations, Large Language Models (LLMs) are employed in order to extract the most relevant aspects of the sub-called methods' explanations and to integrate them into the natural-language explanation of the current method. We aim to propagate all relevant aspects of all subprocesses, while less relevant aspects may not be used for parent methods, s.t., developers receive a compact explanation of what actually happened within the specific process. This or analogous approaches, i.e., any work that utilizes process data to generate explanations with the usage of generative AI for manual debugging, are, to the best of our knowledge, not currently known. However, in the field of APR, the utilization of generative AI has been found to be a prevailing trend [3,6]; [2] proposed an approach towards (automated) debugging while aiming for LLM-supported patch generation.

2 LLM-Driven Debugging for Component-Based Systems

In our approach, we are considering any, distributed or not, (component-based) system, e.g., a set of Web services. As our approach is built on top of the concrete process data, we established a triplestore for storing the data persistently. As an exemplary system, we use Qanary[1]. It was chosen as its architecture utilizes Web services, which makes it particularly well-suited for analyzing distributed

---

[1] https://github.com/WDAqua/Qanary

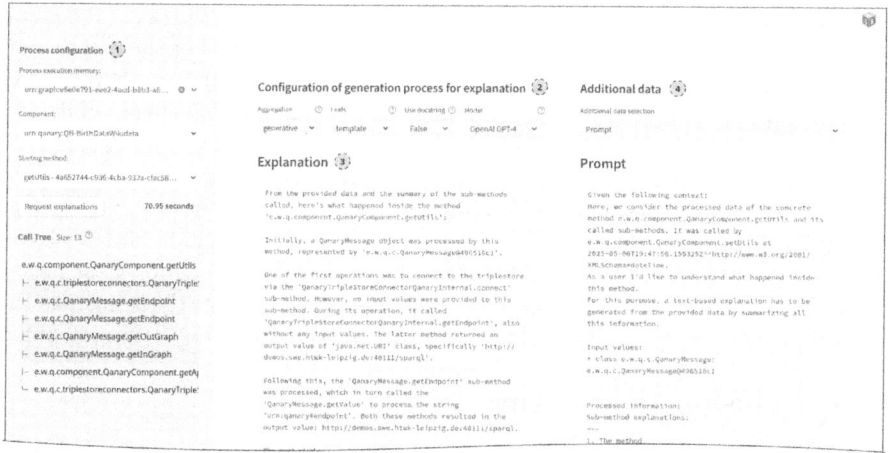

Fig. 2. Screenshot of the demonstrator. It shows an LLM-generated explanation and the corresponding prompt for the selected process, component, and method of the considered (currently debugged) exemplary component-based system.

systems—and a special and challenging case for debugging. After an executed process, the stored data of each method call (in any component) is utilized in a post-hoc manner to generate the explanations using a Java service[2]. We have implemented a template-based generation and one using a user-selected LLM.

As illustrated in Fig. 2, the demonstrator is a frontend that facilitates the explanation of concrete methods for previously executed calls to the considered exemplary (but real-world) component-based system. It is available online on our research group's website[3] and GitHub[4]. A video walkthrough is available[5].

Process configuration – 1 Users select one out of the last (already executed) processes, the component where at least one method creates a log entry, and the start method (i.e., from the entire call tree of a process, the root method of the subtree, which should be explained). Following the vision of providing a complete explanation of the behavior of the application, it is imperative that all subordinate method calls (i.e., those from the subtree) are explained. Moreover, these explanations are utilized when generating hierarchically higher-level method explanations, either by incorporating them within the prompt or the template. Methods from the call sequence (also shown subsequently called methods from any component) can be selected to generate the explanation and show it.

Configuration of generation process for explanations – 2 Users can decide on how to generate the explanation for the selected method from the call tree.

---

[2] https://github.com/WSE-research/qanary-explanation-service.
[3] https://wse-research.org/llm-driven-debugging/.
[4] MIT License licensed source code is available at
https://github.com/WSE-research/frontend_aggregated_explanations.
[5] https://wse-research.org/LLM-supported-debugging-video.

As indicated previously, subordinate calls are also explained on demand. Two scenarios are defined: First, a method that calls no others (leaf of the call tree) is explained using only the method's process data. Second, caller methods aggregate the explanations of their subordinate calls by summarizing them, while also including their own processed data. Explanations – both leaf and aggregate – can be generated using templates or the selected LLMs. The user can also choose whether to include a method's docstring and which LLM to use.

Explanation – 3 The explanation of the selected method is shown. Here, users can test which configuration returns the best explanations for their needs.

Additional data – 4 Users can select and show several other data, such as the prompt for generative-based explanations or the used docstring - if applicable.

3 Conclusions and Future Work

In this paper, we presented an approach for improved and efficient manual debugging of an exemplary software system. The idea of storing actual process data (input and output) during the execution of the application and using this data to explain executed processes appears applicable to systems of any scale. In particular, our approach is language-agnostic and is suited for explaining distributed component systems. The demonstrator shows the usefulness of this data by generating explanations of various methods, processes, and components through LLMs so that an efficient analysis of the software system under consideration is possible. Our primary focus of this demonstrator was to show the feasibility of our approach built on top of process-dependent data such as input arguments and return values. However, by incorporating docstrings, we also took an initial step toward using supporting (static) data, which may lead to further quality improvements. In the future, further additional data, such as the source code or performance information (if available), could further improve quality.

References

1. Anand, A., Gupta, A., Yadav, N., Bajaj, S.: A comprehensive survey of AI-driven advancements and techniques in automated program repair and code generation. CoRR **abs/2411.07586** (2024)
2. Kang, S., Chen, B., Yoo, S., Lou, J.G.: Explainable automated debugging via large language model-driven scientific debugging. Empirical Softw. Eng. **30**(2), 45 (2024)
3. Kwon, S., Lee, S., Kim, T., Ryu, D., Baik, J.: Exploring LLM-based automated repairing of ansible script in edge-cloud infrastructures. J. Web Eng. **22**(6) (2023)
4. Schiese, D., Perevalov, A., Both, A.: Post-hoc insights: natural-language explanations for AI-enhanced/-integrated software systems. In: SEMANTiCS 2024 (2024)
5. Schiese, D., Perevalov, A., Both, A.: Towards LLM-generated explanations for component-based knowledge graph question answering systems. In: 23rd International Conference on WWW/Internet (ICWI). IADIS (2024)
6. Xia, C.S., Wei, Y., Zhang, L.: Automated program repair in the era of large pre-trained language models. In: 2023 IEEE/ACM 45th International Conference on Software Engineering (ICSE), pp. 1482–1494 (2023)
7. Zhang, Q., Fang, C., Ma, Y., Sun, W., Chen, Z.: A survey of learning-based automated program repair. ACM Trans. Softw. Eng. Methodol. **33**(2) (2023)

PhD Symposium

Human-AI Collaborative UAV Visual Object Search via Web Platform

Yatai Ji, Sihang Qiu(✉), Zhengqiu Zhu, and Rusheng Ju

National University of Defense Technology, Changsha, China
jiyatai_1209@nudt.edu, sihangq@acm.org, zhuzhengqiu@nudt.edu.cn,
jrscy@sina.com

Abstract. Utilizing Unmanned Aerial Vehicles (UAVs) for visual object search tasks in indoor or urban environments is a focal issue in the current research of embodied intelligence. However, significant challenges remain, including difficulties for agents in comprehensively understanding the surrounding environment and insufficient levels of intelligence in task planning and execution. This study proposes a Multimodal Large Language Model (MLLM)-driven Human-AI collaborative UAV visual object search framework based on the web platform. Specifically, we develop a web platform for leveraging its ease of interaction, collaboration, and accessibility to enable online access to MLLM-based agents and facilitate real-time human-AI cooperation. Additionally, an online task planning method for MLLM-based agents and a dialogic human-AI collaboration approach based on web crowdsourcing is proposed to enhance the effectiveness of visual object search task execution. This research emphasizes the crucial bridging role of web engineering in the collaboration between LLMs and human-AI systems, contributing to the interdisciplinary integration of artificial intelligence, embodied intelligence, and web engineering.

Keywords: visual object search · web platform · multimodal large language models · human-AI collaborative

1 Introduction

Unmanned Aerial Vehicles (UAVs) are widely employed for object search tasks in indoor and urban environments, with typical applications including last-mile delivery in intelligent logistics systems and emergency rescue operations. However, traditional approaches based on intelligent optimization and decision-making methods face challenges such as limited autonomy, insufficient intelligence, and poor interpretability. In recent years, the rapid development of large language models (LLMs) and embodied intelligence has offered new approaches to solving search problems. Agents powered by the multimodal large language model (MLLM) inherently possess strong multimodal input comprehension and reasoning capabilities, making them well-suited for tasks like indoor visual object search and navigation. This research project aims to integrate technologies of LLMs with embodied intelligence to enhance UAV agents' autonomy and improve their understanding of complex urban environments. Furthermore, we will leverage the user-friendly features of a web platform to foster interaction, collaboration, and accessibility, enabling online access to MLLM-based agents and supporting real-time human-AI cooperation. The primary problems this research seeks to address are as follows.

How to establish a human-AI collaboration web platform for UAV visual object search tasks? To enable online access to MLLM and facilitate real-time human-AI interaction, we will develop a web-based UAV search platform. This platform will support remote UAV control and real-time data transmission, while providing an intuitive interface for human-machine interaction. It will enable UAVs to carry out search tasks and deliver continuous feedback on relevant parameters. Additionally, the platform will support crowdsourced collection of search task datasets through its web interface. Ultimately, this will establish a web-based human-machine collaborative UAV control system tailored for visual object search tasks.

How to utilize MLLM to enhance the environmental understanding and online task planning capabilities of UAV agents? Visual object search tasks require UAVs to search for the location of visual objects in urban environments from a first-person perspective. The information perceived by UAVs consists of first-person RGB images and depth maps. A key focus of this research is how to leverage this visual perceptual information to aid in planning. MLLMs can endow agents with the capability to understand and reason with multimodal inputs, enabling UAV agents to analyze and infer from images captured in urban environments. Investigating how to utilize this capability better to enhance the planning of search tasks remains an open area for further study.

How to design the human-AI collaboration method to improve search task execution processes? This problem focuses on developing human-AI collaborative search methods based on web crowdsourcing. Initially, the MLLM-based agents designed for search problems will be implemented using techniques such as prompt engineering and few-shot learning. Then, a human-AI collaboration method is required to be developed. Through the web platform, human participants will not only contribute search information to the UAVs during the search process but also control the actions of the UAVs. Furthermore, the UAV agents engaged in search tasks in urban spaces will provide reconnaissance information back to the web platform, ultimately facilitating human-machine collaborative decision-making.

2 Related Work

Recently, Large Language Models (LLMs) have been widely applied in the object search methods [2]. L3MVN [11] leveraged LLMs to impart commonsense for searching objects and help to more efficient semantic exploration. Zhou et al. [12] presented the Commonsense constraints (ESC) method to transfer commonsense knowledge in pre-trained models to open-world object navigation. VoroNav [10] is a novel semantic exploration framework that enables LLM to ascertain waypoints for navigation by harnessing topological and semantic information. The aforementioned methods utilize the common sense of LLMs to assist in object navigation. However, more research is needed to integrate the reasoning capabilities of LLMs with object navigation tasks.

A crowdsourcing system enlists a crowd of users to explicitly collaborate to build a long-lasting artifact that is beneficial to the whole community [1]. Well-known examples include Wikipedia and Linux. Doan et al. [1] introduced the transition of crowdsourcing from practical applications to web-based applications. Web crowdsourcing enables participants to engage in tasks via the internet and has been widely applied in fields such as emotion recognition [9] and sound classification [4].

Research on human-AI collaboration has garnered significant attention in recent years [3]. The integration of human intelligence and AI can facilitate the emergence of Artificial Superintelligence [6]. One crucial challenge of human-AI collaboration is that many AI algorithms operate in a black-box manner. The emergence of Large Language Models (LLMs) has transformed this landscape. LLMs-based agents possess the ability to engage in dialogue with humans, enhancing the interpretability of human-machine collaboration during interactions [8]. The method proposed in this study establishes a bridge for interaction and collaboration between humans and large models based on a web platform, promoting the development of human-AI collaboration.

3 The Research Methodology

This research aims to enhance the autonomy and intelligence of UAVs in visual object search tasks by integrating artificial intelligence, web engineering, embodied intelligence, and human-machine collaboration technologies. This will be accomplished through the establishment of a human-AI collaboration web platform specifically designed for UAV visual object search. Additionally, MLLM will be incorporated into these tasks, fostering innovative online planning methods. By implementing web-crowdsourcing-based human-AI collaborative search techniques, the project aims to broaden the paradigm of collaborative decision-making between humans and agents.

3.1 The Human-AI Collaborative Web Platform for UAV Visual Object Search

The interface of the web-based human-machine collaboration UAV control platform is depicted in the figure. Utilizing this platform, multiple human participants can apply for the control of several UAVs to perform visual object search tasks in urban spaces through an SDK, while also adjusting the parameters of the UAVs. Only invited participants can receive the SDK. The platform provides real-time feedback of the first-person perspective images of the urban environment captured by the UAVs (Fig. 1).

Fig. 1. A diagram of the human-machine collaboration platform.

The environment used in the experiment and datasets is the EmbodiedCity proposed by Li et al. [5]. It contains high-fidelity urban streets, buildings, trees, vehicles, and pedestrians, which are hosted by Unreal Engine 5.3. By integrating AirSim [7], the environment provides a realistic platform for testing the performance of autonomous UAVs in urban settings. The technical approach for the web-based human-machine interaction platform involves using FFmpeg for video streaming, with Caddy serving as the webserver to stream the environmental data to the web interface. Users can control the UAVs within the virtual environment through the web interface, enabling web-based human-machine collaboration.

3.2 Online Search Task Planning Methods Based on Multimodal Large Models

The overview of the online search task planning method for UAVs based on multimodal large models is illustrated in Fig. 2. UAVs equipped with visual sensors collect images and videos while performing search tasks in urban environments. The research will first focus on performing semantic segmentation and spatial coordinate matching on the visual signals from the UAVs to generate a semantic map of the urban environment. Subsequently, multimodal large models will be employed to infer the correlation between the semantic map and the target, resulting in the creation of a cognitive map. This cognitive map, combined with an uncertainty map, will together form an estimation of the search object. Finally, strategies for UAV actions and path planning will be designed, balancing exploration and exploitation.

3.3 The Web Crowd-Sourcing Based Human-AI Collaborative Method

By adopting techniques such as prompt engineering, chain-of-thought reasoning, and fine-tuning, MLLM-based UAV agents will possess a certain level of

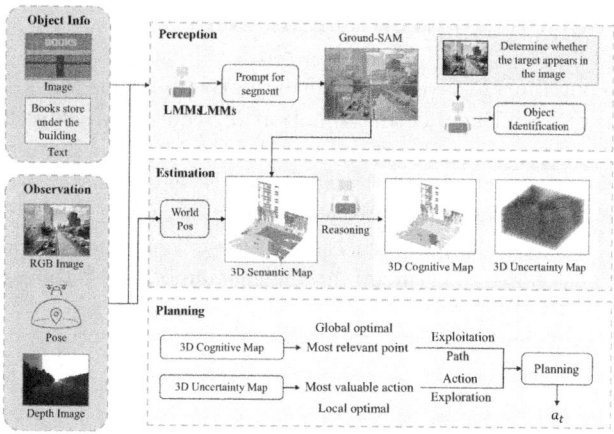

Fig. 2. An overview of the online search task planning methods based on multimodal large models.

understanding and execution capability for search tasks. Using a web platform centered on human-machine interaction and collaboration, we establish an interactive dialogue channel between MLLM-based agents and human participants. When all human participants and MLLM-based agents jointly perform the same task, a central controller uniformly assigns the tasks. However, during the execution of subtasks, AI agents report task status to human participants and can modify their own subtask plans through the dialogue. Through dialogue-based collaboration between agents and human participants, the search task solution is co-planned. This approach not only leverages MLLM-based agents to reduce the workload of human participants but also enhances the agents' search task planning abilities by incorporating human intelligence. This integrated method aims to combine human and machine intelligence to optimize search task solutions through iterative interactions with large model agents.

4 Current State and Roadmap

This research forms the basis of a doctoral study and is also a sub-project within a key laboratory initiative focused on the object search task in urban environments. The project spans four years, and we are currently in the early stages of the second year. We have developed the human-AI collaboration platform that enables remote real-time control of UAVs and facilitates human-machine interaction via the web. Presently, we are training an agent for visual object search using a foundational MLLM and designing online task planning methods, with an expected completion date of December this year. The web crowdsourcing-based human-AI collaboration method is set to be finalized by June next year. We anticipate spending an additional six months to a year to complete the integration of the entire web platform and related experimental work.

5 Contributions to Web Engineering

Our research contributes to web engineering in the following ways. This research highlights the essential connecting function of web engineering in facilitating collaboration between large language models (LLMs) and human-AI systems. This integration demonstrates how large models can enhance user experience and operational efficiency in web-based applications while facilitating real-time human input into UAV decision processes. It plays a significant role in the interdisciplinary convergence of artificial intelligence, embodied intelligence, and web engineering.

References

1. Doan, A., Ramakrishnan, R., Halevy, A.Y.: Crowdsourcing systems on the worldwide web. Commun. ACM **54**(4), 86–96 (2011)
2. Dorbala, V.S., Mullen, J.F., Manocha, D.: Can an embodied agent find your "Cat-shaped mug"? LLM-based zero-shot object navigation. IEEE Robot. Autom. Lett. **9**(5), 4083–4090 (2023)
3. Fragiadakis, G., Diou, C., Kousiouris, G., Nikolaidou, M.: Evaluating human-AI collaboration: a review and methodological framework. arXiv preprint arXiv:2407.19098 (2024)
4. Frasier, K.E.: A machine learning pipeline for classification of cetacean echolocation clicks in large underwater acoustic datasets. PLoS Comput. Biol. **17**(12), e1009613 (2021)
5. Gao, C., et al.: EmbodiedCity: a benchmark platform for embodied agent in real-world city environment. arXiv preprint arXiv:2410.09604 (2024)
6. Kim, H., et al.: The road to artificial superintelligence: a comprehensive survey of superalignment. arXiv preprint arXiv:2412.16468 (2024)
7. Shah, S., Dey, D., Lovett, C., Kapoor, A.: AirSim: high-fidelity visual and physical simulation for autonomous vehicles. In: Field and Service Robotics: Results of the 11th International Conference, pp. 621–635. Springer (2018)
8. Sidji, M., Smith, W., Rogerson, M.J.: Human-AI collaboration in cooperative games: a study of playing codenames with an LLM assistant. Proc. ACM Hum.-Comput. Interact. **8**(CHI PLAY), 1–25 (2024)
9. Vryzas, N., Vrysis, L., Kotsakis, R., Dimoulas, C.: A web crowdsourcing framework for transfer learning and personalized speech emotion recognition. Mach. Learn. Appl. **6**, 100132 (2021)
10. Wu, P., et al.: VoroNav: Voronoi-based zero-shot object navigation with large language model. arXiv preprint arXiv:2401.02695 (2024)
11. Yu, B., Kasaei, H., Cao, M.: L3MVN: leveraging large language models for visual target navigation. In: 2023 IEEE/RSJ International Conference on Intelligent Robots and Systems (IROS), pp. 3554–3560. IEEE (2023)
12. Zhou, K., et al.: ESC: exploration with soft commonsense constraints for zero-shot object navigation. In: International Conference on Machine Learning, pp. 42829–42842. PMLR (2023)

Methodological Framework and Digital Environment to Optimize the Treatment of Genetic Markers, Based on Data Science and Artificial Intelligence

Ramon Canelo-Gil(✉), Nicolas Sánchez-Gómez, Julian Alberto García-García, and Maria Jose Escalona

University of Seville, Seville, Spain
ramcangil@alum.us.es

Abstract. Cancer is the second leading cause of death globally and is expected to affect 1 in 2 men and 1 in 3 women by 2030. Despite advances in surgery and pharmacology, the lack of implementation of personalized medicine protocols means that patients with very different genetic profiles are treated the same way. Minimal Residual Disease (MRD) has emerged as a crucial prognostic factor, allowing precision medicine to evaluate treatment responses and predict relapses. MRD tests identify tumor cells that survive therapy and cause relapses. Massive sequencing has provided a useful tool for detecting tumor DNA with high sensitivity. However, challenges remain in detecting real tumor signals amidst noise and artifacts, clinical implementation faces hurdles due to lack of standardization and automation, sensitivity and specificity values are not 100%, and costs are high. This research thesis proposes a methodology and digital framework, based on Model Driven Engineering (MDE), to optimize MRD detection and monitoring using data science and artificial intelligence.

Keywords: Next Generation Sequencing (NGS) · Minimal Residual Disease (MRD) · Circulating tumor DNA · Model Driven Engineering (MDE)

1 Problem Statement

Cancer is the second leading cause of death globally and is expected to affect 1 in 2 men and 1 in 3 women by 2030, according to the World Health Organization (WHO). The prevalence of cancer has increased significantly, driven by an aging population, environmental factors, and lifestyles. In 2020, cancer caused nearly 10 million deaths, accounting for one in six globally. The latest clinical trials presented at international oncology congresses indicate that about 40% of cancer patients do not receive the best therapeutic treatment. Despite the great advances in surgery and pharmacological developments, the lack of implementation of personalized medicine protocols means that patients with very different genetic profiles and levels of disease are being treated in the same way.

One of the most important problems that an oncologist faces after diagnosing and treating a patient is that he or she does not know precisely which patient has been cured and which one will relapse; therefore, patients who have all the conventional negative tests after finishing treatment can progress in a few months and die. This occurs because current cancer detection and monitoring techniques do not allow the identification of minority cells that survive therapy and cause these relapses (Minimal Residual Disease, MRD). Minimal Residual Disease (MRD) has emerged as a crucial prognostic factor, describing the presence of post-treatment cancer cells undetectable by conventional methods. These high-risk patients need additional treatment and much more intensive follow-up. On the other hand, some patients receive preventive treatments for years for fear of the existence of a residual tumor, even if all the tests are negative. These treatments, which are extremely toxic, cause adverse side effects that can even lead to the death of the patient. MRD tests are making it possible to identify these patients who are not going to relapse and who are not going to benefit from toxic and expensive treatments because they do not have a tumor, avoiding unnecessary side effects and improving their survival and quality of life.

In addition, massive sequencing and liquid biopsy emerges as a promising alternative, allowing the detection of tumor DNA in blood using ultra-sensitive techniques such as Next Generation Sequencing (NGS). This innovation promises to improve patients' quality of life, increase survival and reduce healthcare costs.

However, one of the greatest challenges of NGS to study tumor DNA with such depth and sensitivity is the detection of real tumor signal against artifacts or noise, either due to PCR errors, sequencing or the genetic basis of each patient. For this reason, the analysis of each patient's sample is currently compared with samples from healthy donors. This makes it possible to accurately quantify the presence or not of this signal and to establish the basal noise of each marker, thus differentiating it from the real tumor signal in patients. Predicting noise and digitizing this experimental phase will make it possible to choose the most sensitive markers from the beginning and reduce the cost of their determination, increasing sensitivity and specificity. This is especially important in patients undergoing surgery or curative treatments with minimal levels of disease in the blood.

This thesis aims to research and start developing a comprehensive framework, methodology and a digital solution for the detection and monitoring of MRD in cancer patients, addressing almost all technical requirements of diagnostic tests, which will allow progress in the process of implementing this test in the clinical routine. In addition, it will alleviate the workload of data management and will shorten the response time of the test, speeding up decision-making in the clinical field and reducing the wait and uncertainty of cancer patients.

2 Related Work

Next-generation sequencing or NGS is an advanced technology that allows genetic studies to be carried out on a massive, fast and cost-effective basis. Since its inception approximately 15 years ago, NGS has revolutionized the study of complex genetic diseases, such as cancer. It allows detecting alterations in the DNA sequence that are useful to explain the origin of the disease, stratifying patients into risk groups, guiding treatment using drugs aimed at specific genetic targets, etc. More recently, NGS is also being applied to monitor tumor cells that resist minimal residual disease (MRD) therapy. These cells are responsible for the relapse and eventual death of patients, so detecting their presence after therapy is becoming the most relevant prognostic factor. Conventional tests are unable to detect such minimum levels and, therefore, do not allow patients to be adequately prognostic or to detect relapse early enough to extend their survival. In this field, there were developed technology to study MRD in any cancer patient by NGS from a simple blood sample and with unprecedented sensitivity. However, the technology must be enhanced and optimized with computer systems using computational techniques and AI to achieve an eventual commercialization of the test and its definitive introduction into the clinical routine. This technology has been clinically validated in several hematological tumors where the results were published in high-impact scientific journals. In all these articles [1, 2], it is shown that the result of the test at the end of treatment allowed to identify with high sensitivity and specificity those patients with a high risk of relapse. However, the sensitivity and specificity values are not 100% and the cost is still high for mass use, so it is vitally important to design digital tools that allow laboratory data and NGS data to be properly managed and stored, improve bioinformatic analysis, increase the predictive capacity of the test to identify patients with a high risk of relapse and differentiate them from those who are potentially cured for relapse.

Due to errors in PCR and in sequencing or the genetic basis of each patient, arise the need to accurately quantify and establish the basal noise of each marker, thus differentiating it from the real tumor signal in patients. Predicting noise and digitizing this experimental phase will make it possible to choose the most sensitive markers from the beginning and reduce the cost of their determination, increasing sensitivity and specificity. This is especially important in patients undergoing surgery or curative treatments with minimal levels of disease in the blood. In this area, a series of techniques and methodologies were developed, and most of these methods establish a model for the expected frequency of errors and then assess the mutational signal using a statistical test. Examples of general somatic variant callers applicable for most NGS data include Mutect2 [6], Strelka2 [7], and Shearwater [8]. Other methods, such as MRDetect [9] and INVAR [10], are specifically tailored to detect circulating tumor DNA (ctDNA) [3, 4, 5] in NGS data. Another approach, iDES [11], identifies mutations in paired reads by combining a specialized stranded barcoding scheme with a polisher that filters out erroneous mutational signals based on various criteria, including an error model. Finally, a new recent model DREAMS [12] based on neural network model.

3 Proposed Research

The main objective of this research thesis is to design and develop a comprehensive methodology and a digital framework solution to optimize the detection and monitoring of MRD in cancer patients using Data Science and AI. In addition, by aiming to achieve a reduction in response time and improved sensitivity and specificity, clinical decision-making will be streamlined and uncertainty for cancer patients will be reduced.

The research thesis will focus on optimizing the analysis and detection of MRD through the modelling and development of a framework based on Model Driven Engineering (MDE) to provide a digital solution based on Data Science and advanced computational artificial intelligence techniques based on deep learning. These techniques will allow the optimization, automation and standardization of diagnostic tests that use NGS for the analysis of MRD in cancer patients.

The research thesis arises from the following needs:

- To develop a methodology and a framework that allows the integration of analysis software to obtain MRD test results in less time and facilitate therapeutic decision-making in real time and ensure the traceability of biological samples and all pre-analytical, analytical and post-analytical data, Digitalization will increase the efficiency of the analysis process, reduce turnaround time and facilitate scalability, allowing MRD tests to finally be introduced into clinical practice.
- Propose a solution to the problem of intrinsic noise of NGS. Predicting noise and digitizing this experimental phase will make it possible to choose the most sensitive markers from the beginning and reduce the cost of their determination, increasing sensitivity and specificity.
- Improve the predictive capacity of the test by including more variables. The level of precision required for personalized medicine is forcing the generation and consideration of huge volumes of clinical, demographic, genetic and imaging data to correctly monitor the level of disease and prescribe the best treatment.

Therefore, and based on the initial needs, the general objectives of this research thesis are the following:

- [Goal-01] Develop a robust and flexible framework, based on Model Driven Engineering (MDE), that allows provisioning of a and a technological stack for digitization of the entire MRD evaluation process. In addition, the design of the data model is a challenge, since it requires in-depth knowledge of both cancer biology, and the computer tools used in the development of these tests. In Fig. 1, the initial technology stack is shown because of the implementation of the final solution based on the application of the proposed MDE framework.
- [Goal-02] Characterize the noise in the genome, supported by the proposed framework, and using artificial intelligence models to optimize the predictive capacity of the test. These models will focus on distinguishing the noise present in healthy individuals from the real tumor signal, improving the sensitivity and specificity of detection, as well as reducing the costs of experimental determination.
- [Goal-03] Integrate more types of data and improve the predictive capacity of the test. Develop deep learning models that integrate the genetic data obtained by NGS with other clinical, demographic, biochemical and genetic variables, improving the test's ability to predict the risk of relapse, optimizing the therapeutic strategy and providing more complete and accurate information for decision-making.
- [Goal-04] Validate the predictive algorithms developed and test them in real cohorts of patients with tumors. It will begin by testing with data on breast, lung, bladder and head and neck cancer.

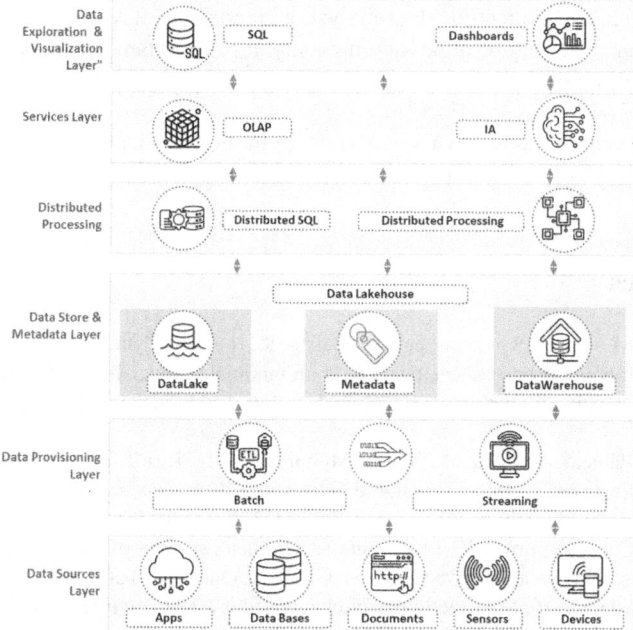

Fig. 1. Conceptual Model of the Proposed Initial Technology Stack

4 Research Methodology

The proposed methodology for this thesis incorporates several methodologies such as Systematic Reviews, Research and Validation Methodology. Systematic Review is a process where related works are examined. For this study, we propose using the method proposed by Kitchenham, which is a method for conducting systematic reviews in the field of software engineering. The method proposed by Kitchenham for conducting systematic reviews in the field of software engineering consists of three phases: planning, execution and presentation of results. Our research method is based on McTaggart Action research method which will lead the accomplishment of this thesis. This method combines theory and practice and has a set of common features that has been reckoned particularly in Software Engineering. This method is focused on particular issues and has a model of process with systematic steps and iterations. The action research method combines theory and practice and focuses on particular issues. In addition, it has a process model with systematic and iterative steps that allows an early evaluation of the actions and feedback to adjust the actions of the next cycle. On the other hand, regarding validation, two classical techniques will be used: experimentation, based on the Juristo and Moreno approach, which proposes a life cycle that includes the definition of objectives, design and execution of experimentation and analysis of results; and the case study. To guide our case studies, we will follow a set of guidelines proposed by Runeson and Höst, which consist of five phases: design of the case study, preparation of data collection, data collection, data analysis and reporting of results. Although data collection and analysis can be done incrementally, it is important to set specific objectives from the beginning of the case study.

Acknowledgments. This research was supported by the EQUAVEL project PID2022-137646OB-C31, funded by MICIU/AEI/10.13039/501100011033 and by ERDF, EU.

References

1. Martinez-Lopez, J., Sanchez-Vega, B., Barrio, S., et al.: Analytical and clinical validation of a novel in-house deep-sequencing method for minimal residual disease monitoring in a phase II trial for multiple myeloma. Leukemia **31**, 1446–1449 (2017). https://doi.org/10.1038/leu.2017.58
2. Jiménez-Ubieto, A., Poza, M., Martin-Muñoz, A., et al.: Real-life disease monitoring in follicular lymphoma patients using liquid biopsy ultra-deep sequencing and PET/CT. Leukemia **37**, 659–669 (2023). https://doi.org/10.1038/s41375-022-01803-x
3. Hu, Z., Chen, H., Long, Y., Li, P., Gu, Y.: The main sources of circulating cell-free DNA: apoptosis, necrosis and active secretion. Crit. Rev. Oncol. Hematol. **157**, 103166 (2021)
4. Bettegowda, C., et al.: Detection of circulating tumor DNA in early- and late-stage human malignancies. Sci. Transl. Med. **6**, 224ra224 (2014)
5. Phallen, J., et al.: Direct detection of early-stage cancers using circulating tumor DNA. Sci. Transl. Med. **9**, eaan2415 (2017)
6. Kim, S., et al.: Strelka2: fast and accurate calling of germline and somatic variants. Nat. Methods **15**, 591–594 (2018)
7. Gerstung, M., Papaemmanuil, E., Campbell, P.J.: Subclonal variant calling with multiple samples and prior knowledge. Bioinformatics **30**, 1198–1204 (2014)
8. Zviran, A., et al.: Genome-wide cell-free DNA mutational integration enables ultra-sensitive cancer monitoring. Nat. Med. **26**, 1114–1124 (2020)
9. Wan, J.C.M., et al.: ctDNA monitoring using patient-specific sequencing and integration of variant reads. Sci. Transl. Med. **12**, eaaz8084 (2020)
10. Newman, A.M., et al.: Integrated digital error suppression for improved detection of circulating tumor DNA. Nat. Biotechnol. **34**, 547–555 (2016)
11. Christensen, M.H., Drue, S.O., Rasmussen, M.H., et al.: DREAMS: deep read-level error model for sequencing data applied to low-frequency variant calling and circulating tumor DNA detection. Genome Biol. **24**, 99 (2023). https://doi.org/10.1186/s13059-023-02920-1

ResearchFlow: An End-User Development Approach to Research Data Management Workflow Composition

Jan Ingo Haas(✉), Martin Gaedke, Sheeba Samuel, and Jeffrey Kelling

Chemnitz University of Technology, Chemnitz, Germany
{jan-ingo.haas,martin.gaedke,sheeba.samuel}@informatik.tu-chemnitz.de,
jeffrey.kelling@physik.tu-chemnitz.de

Abstract. Research Data Management (RDM) is a crucial aspect of scientific work, yet many researchers still struggle to adopt best data management practices, despite significant developments in critical infrastructure supporting RDM processes. In this PhD proposal, we highlight three main problems that the current RDM infrastructure landscape faces: the misalignment of theoretical RDM models with actual research practices, the fragmented nature of related services, and the high resource investment needed to manage research data effectively. To address these issues, we sketch out a End-User oriented approach to RDM, where scientists - the End-Users - can visually compose individual research data workflows based on a set of pre-defined workflow components. The resulting workflows comprise a combination of manual tasks, automated processes, and AI-assisted operations through the Model Context Protocol, adaptable to researchers' specific needs. We additionally provide an overview of our research plan and of potential contributions to the field of Web Engineering.

Keywords: Research Data Management · Research Data Lifecycle · End-User Development · Workflow Composition · Workflow Automation · Microfrontends · Model Context Protocol

1 Introduction and Research Objectives

As data plays a fundamental role in scientific inquiries, proper Research Data Management (RDM) becomes crucial for research success, particularly in data-driven fields where experimentation, observation, and simulation generate significant datasets. Despite the development of numerous software solutions to address domain-specific data management challenges, and despite extensive efforts to raise awareness through workshops and infrastructure development, only a subset of scientists actually follow RDM best practices such as data sharing, repository utilization, or compliance with metadata standards [9].

1.1 Problem Statement

Three main problems can be observed that hinder progress in this aspect.

Insufficient Alignment of Research Data Management Theory and Practice. Scientific efforts have established theoretical frameworks to guide Research Data Management practices. The FAIR principles [10] outline fundamental requirements for data to be Findable, Accessible, Interoperable, and Reusable. These principles are operationalized through the Research Data Lifecycle (RDL) model, which conceptualizes data flowing through sequential stages from planning to reuse by other researchers.

In practice, however, research activities rarely conform to the RDL model's rigid, sequential stages. [5] note that these lifecycle models oversimplify the complexity of actual research workflows. [2] argue that RDM discourse employs an oversimplified binary view contrasting open science benefits against implementation barriers, failing to address the interactions between researchers managing daily challenges, funding agencies establishing policies, and information professionals developing infrastructure.

This fundamental disconnect between theory and practice manifests throughout the research ecosystem. RDM planning tools like RDMO produce Data Management Plans (DMPs) that reflect static and idealized rather than actual research processes. Data management processes must be outlined before projects begin, resulting in static, waterfall-like plans poorly aligned with actual research. Furthermore, the lifecycle model's stages are treated as separate entities, with tools designed for each stage operating in isolation. This creates fragmented infrastructure without effective methods for orchestrating these tools into cohesive systems tailored to researchers' specific workflows, hindering adaptation to FAIR principles.

Fragmented Data Infrastructure: Barrier for Data Sharing and Collaboration. The current RDM landscape features numerous data repositories with incompatible metadata schemas. [7] highlight data heterogeneity in repositories like DSpace, Invenio, and Dataverse, which use varied vocabularies that complicate data sharing. This fragmentation extends across the RDL's stages. For data management planning, tools like RDMO and Argos remain incompatible despite efforts to standardize exchange formats [3]. During analysis, chemistry and physics researchers must choose from 44 different Electronic Laboratory Notebook (ELN) options (according to the ELN finder). For data publishing, on-premise repositories like CKAN or DSpace, compete with cloud-based solutions like Zenodo.

This technological fragmentation diverts time from actual research activities. Even with infrastructure in place, interoperability barriers persist both within and across RDL stages. Within stages, sharing experimental data between ELNs is hindered by incompatible exchange formats despite their similar purpose. Between stages, publishing ELN data to repositories like Zenodo requires redundant manual metadata annotation, as existing metadata remains trapped in incompatible formats. This challenge is increased by low metadata standard adoption, with [1] reporting that 60.1% of researchers do not follow standards.

While governance policies exist, they "do not necessarily support implementation or reflect the researchers' needs," [1] further hindering FAIR principles adoption.

Costly Resource Investment in Research Data Management. The fragmented RDM landscape creates significant resource burdens at both institutional and individual levels. Organizations frequently invest in redundant tools - such as multiple similar ELNs across departments - increasing costs and complicating maintenance. Individual researchers, meanwhile, must allocate substantial time and funding to manage data effectively, without clear evidence of how this investment benefits their scientific work. This creates frustration, particularly when funding organizations enforce practices like submission of Data Management Plans without considering researchers' actual needs. Both challenges - institutional redundancy and researcher burden - ultimately undermine efforts to realize the FAIR principles, as limited resources are diverted to navigating fragmented infrastructure rather than improving actual data management practices.

Research Objectives. We aim to address the presented problems and advance the state of the art through three key objectives:

OBJ 1: Aligning RDM theory with actual research practices. This objective seeks to bridge the gap between theoretical models of RDM and researchers' everyday workflows. It aims to enable data management processes that adapt to the diverse requirements of different disciplines and evolve alongside research projects, respecting individual researchers' practices rather than imposing rigid, predefined stages.

OBJ 2: Integrating existing RDM systems into a shared ecosystem. This objective focuses on connecting the currently isolated RDM services to enable seamless data sharing both across different lifecycle stages and between tools serving the same purpose, facilitating better collaboration among researchers.

OBJ 3: Reducing resource investment required for effective RDM. This objective addresses the need to decrease both the institutional overhead and individual researcher effort associated with data management. It aims to make RDM more accessible to researchers regardless of their technical expertise while maintaining compliance with FAIR principles.

2 Related Work

The authors of [6] address DMP implementation challenges by reframing RDM through their "ROMPi" framework, which integrates project management methodologies to organize research into work packages and their outputs. While ROMPi offers a conceptual approach without technical implementation, our PhD work aims to build upon its process orientation but employs executable workflows rather than predefined work packages, enabling automation of RDM tasks while maintaining FAIR compliance through integration with existing infrastructure.

Recent advances in devising machine-actionable Data Management Plans (maDMPs) offer promising foundations for our work. [8] leverages maDMPs

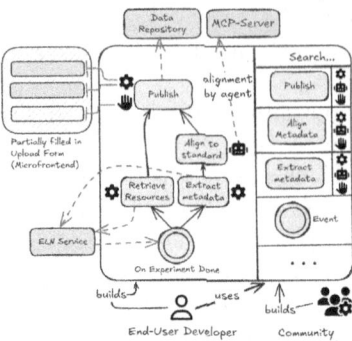

Fig. 1. Visual representation of the ResearchFlow approach.

to partially automate DMP creation and curation, conceptualizing RDM as a dynamically evolving process where DMPs become living documents that adapt to changes. Building on this concept, [11] proposes a service architecture to facilitate interoperability between different RDM services, automatically keeping DMPs synchronized with evolving research needs. Our work extends these machine-actionability and interoperability concepts, but focuses on web-based composition of reusable workflow tasks rather than fixed workflows, empowering researchers to orchestrate their own data management processes.

We also draw inspiration from the OMELETTE approach [4], which introduced an interactive, user-centric environment for visually composing mashups from reusable widget components. Particularly relevant is its support for dynamic inter-widget communication, allowing End-Users to easily orchestrate interactions between different widgets without in-depth programming skills. Adopting this idea, our proposed method facilitates similar visual orchestration of research data management tasks, simplifying construction of complex workflows for researchers.

3 Research Methodology

We plan to validate our approach by developing a prototype system for the chemistry domain, integrating with the **HYP*MOL** research project on spin polarization and hyperpolarization in molecular systems. We'll evaluate this prototype through user studies with chemistry researchers to assess its effectiveness in addressing the identified problems.

Our proposed framework - visualized in Fig. 1 - enables researchers to visually compose research data workflows by arranging and connecting workflow components on a canvas. These components represent either manual tasks, AI-assisted tasks or automated operations executed by the workflow engine. By allowing researchers to model their research data practices using a visual workflow language, the system seeks to bridge theoretical RDM models with actual research practices (**OBJ 1**).

Task Registry and Service Integration. The system will include a centralized task registry (see right side in 1) where researchers can select from a growing collection of pre-defined activities that connect to external web-services like ELNs and data repositories. These components serve as **basic building blocks** that are inherently reusable across different research workflows, enabling flexible composition of custom data management processes in a low-code/no-code fashion. Community contributions to this registry will facilitate integration of existing and future RDM systems (**OBJ 2**) while distributing development efforts across the research community (**OBJ 3**).

End-User Interface Components. When pre-defined components for certain tasks are not fully automated, researchers must provide manual input. To avoid forcing end-users to interact with raw data formats or perform complex technical operations, we'll employ reusable microfrontends implemented as Web Components (see top-left in Fig. 1) These interfaces are automatically generated based on specific schemas - for example, creating intuitive metadata input forms based on a repository's requirements when metadata cannot be automatically extracted from source datasets. This approach aligns with our End-User Development philosophy by reducing technical barriers (**OBJ 2**) while minimizing time investment (**OBJ 3**). These components serve as reusable building blocks that researchers can seamlessly integrate with automated components in the same canvas.

Integration of Agentic AI. We'll integrate agentic AI through the Model Context Protocol (MCP) by developing custom MCP servers for both our workflow engine and selected existing RDM infrastructure services. This development effort will enable: (1) natural language interfaces for workflow creation and modification, (2) intelligent transformation of data between incompatible formats for systems lacking native integration (as visualized in Fig. 1), similar to approaches already employed, and (3) partial automation of previously manual data management tasks. These AI capabilities will advance both the integration of isolated RDM services (**OBJ 2**) and the reduction of resource investment (**OBJ 3**). Due to the significant implementation work, we limit the initial MCP integration to only a subset of services, focusing on those most relevant to the HYP*MOL project.

4 Research Plan and Contributions

Our five-semester research plan progresses from requirement analysis (S1), through technology selection and initial development (S2), to building the task registry and integrating with chemistry-related RDM services (S3), refining AI features (S4), and finally comprehensive evaluation (S5). Currently in S2, we've completed the elicitation phase and are selecting technologies. Throughout the project (S2 - S5), we'll conduct usability studies with the End-Users - chemistry researchers - to validate our approach and gather feedback for iterative improvements.

Potential contributions to Web Engineering include: **(a)** A web-based visual modeling framework that enables orchestration of research data workflows, addressing UI composition challenges in domain-specific web applications, as well as, **(b)** integration techniques for connecting heterogeneous web services into a cohesive ecosystem, including exploration of AI-assisted data transformation between incompatible APIs. **(c)** Design patterns for community-driven component registries that enhance web application extensibility through distributed development efforts, and **(d)** advancements in microfrontend architectures using Web Components for dynamically generated interfaces that adapt to end-user needs without requiring programming expertise. We will continuously prove the feasibility of our research through publications, demonstrating incremental progress in addressing the outlined objectives.

Acknowledgements. funded by German Research Foundation (DFG), TRR-386, TP INF, project number 514664767.

Disclosure of Interests. The authors have no competing interests to declare that are relevant to the content of this article.

References

1. Birkbeck, G., Nagle, T., D.S.: Challenges in research data management practices: a literature analysis. J. Decis. Syst. **31**(sup1), 153–167 (2022). https://doi.org/10.1080/12460125.2022.2074653
2. Bishop, B., et al.: Data curation profiling to assess data management training needs and practices to inform a toolkit. Data Sci. J. **19**(1) (2020). https://doi.org/10.5334/dsj-2020-004
3. Cardoso, J., et al.: DCSO: towards an ontology for machine-actionable data management plans. J. Biomedi. Semant. **13**(1), 21 (2022). https://doi.org/10.1186/s13326-022-00274-4
4. Chudnovskyy, O., et al.: End-user-oriented telco mashups: the omelette approach. In: Proceedings of the 21st International Conference on World Wide Web, pp. 235–238 (2012)
5. Cox, A.M., Tam, W.: A critical analysis of lifecycle models of the research process and research data management. Aslib J. Inf. Manag. **70**(2), 142–157 (2018). https://doi.org/10.1108/AJIM-11-2017-0251
6. Della Chiesa, S., Sikder, S.K.: Rethinking data management planning: introducing research output management planning (rompi) approach. Data Sci. J. **23**(1) (2024)
7. Efeoglu, S., et al.: Converter: enhancing interoperability in research data management. In: The Semantic Web: ESWC 2024 Satellite Events, pp. 202–206. Springer, Cham (2025). https://doi.org/10.1007/978-3-031-78952-6_27
8. Miksa, T., Oblasser, S., Rauber, A.: Automating research data management using machine-actionable data management plans. ACM Trans. Manag. Inf. Syst. **13**(2), 1–22 (2022). https://doi.org/10.1145/3490396
9. Tenopir, C., et al.: Data sharing, management, use, and reuse: practices and perceptions of scientists worldwide. PLoS ONE **15**(3), 1–26 (2020). https://doi.org/10.1371/journal.pone.0229003

10. Wilkinson, M.D., et al.: The FAIR guiding principles for scientific data management and stewardship. Sci. Data **3**(1), 160018 (2016). https://doi.org/10.1038/sdata.2016.18
11. Zoubek, F., Miksa, T., Rauber, A.: Conceptual service architecture to synchronise research data management services using machine-actionable data management plans. ACM Trans. Manage. Inf. Syst. (2025). https://doi.org/10.1145/3712014

You Are What You Click: Web Interaction Analysis for User Profile Detection

Leonardo Germán Loza Bonora[1,2(✉)], Julián Grigera[1,2,3], and Alejandra Garrido[1,2]

[1] LIFIA, Facultad de Informatica, Universidad Nacional de La Plata, La Plata, Argentina
{lloza,juliang,garrido}@lifia.info.unlp.edu.ar
[2] CONICET, Buenos Aires, Argentina
[3] CICPBA, Buenos Aires, Argentina

Abstract. Evaluation of web user interaction serves various purposes like analysis and evolution of UX, but it requires significant resources. To reduce the time and cost associated with such assessments, several automated solutions have been developed to analyze interactions by capturing logs. However, many of these approaches assume that all users interact similarly, disregarding individual characteristics such as mouse and keyboard movement speeds. Additionally, they often overlook the time required for analysis. We propose that identifying a user's interaction profile can enhance the quality of automated log analysis. To achieve this, in this proposal interactive user profiles on the web will be studied and defined. Through experimentation, we will analyze real user behavior and its relationship with these profiles. Finally, the detection of user profiles and interactive characteristics will be automated, considering key variables such as detection speed and prediction accuracy.

Keywords: Web Interaction · User profiling · Log analysis

1 Introduction

The evaluation of user interaction on the web is used for many purposes, such as discovering usability or accessibility problems. By simply observing how users use different standard input devices, such as the mouse and keyboard, diagnostics can be obtained to help improve interaction. This type of evaluations, however, usually require a considerable number of resources. The most commonly used technique for evaluating interaction aspects is user testing, which requires the recruitment of volunteers and specialized professionals to analyze their behavior. To reduce the time and cost that these types of assessments entail, several solutions have emerged that propose to automate interaction analysis by capturing interaction logs in different areas such as usability [1] or accessibility [2].

Many of the works that propose to capture and analyze the interaction in an automated way do not take into account the characteristics of the users that generate the logs, assuming that they all interact in a similar way. This leads to a uniform interpretation of the behavior of users with very different characteristics, such as mouse or keyboard movement speeds, or waiting times between actions. In addition, in many cases, logs are captured anonymously, which adds the challenge of not knowing the user beforehand [3,4]. However, users show different behaviors in aspects like clicking, scrolling speed or pause durations. These differences, moreover, cannot always be explained solely on the basis of demographics such as age or computer experience.

Most of the studies on user interaction with interfaces have been conducted in the context of desktop applications. These works highlight the importance of low-level event capture and analysis [5]. They also indicate that the metrics used to classify user behavior vary according to the context studied [6,7].

Furthermore, there are studies that analyze user interaction in web applications, but they are far from our idea of recognizing and evaluating user profiles. In general, these studies focus on analyzing the importance of captured events [8] or on predicting future actions, such as abandoning a web page [9].

In general, studies in these areas also do not consider the time required to perform this analysis. In some scenarios, user profile classification needs to be done quickly without compromising quality or efficiency. This is the case with adaptive interfaces, which must rapidly recognize user interactions to adjust the interface to their needs [10]. Delaying customization can result in users becoming accustomed to a less efficient or less suitable UI, reducing their satisfaction.

We hypothesize that knowing the user's interaction profile helps improve the quality of automated log analysis. For example, if a person usually moves the mouse cursor slowly, a sudden and fast movement could indicate the presence of a problem [11]. Moreover, having a deeper knowledge on user interaction behavior would serve various purposes, like helping designers adapt the UIs to different interaction styles for improved usability and accessibility. Our focus is in desktop web applications.

2 Related Work

Several authors have worked on the characterization of users based on interaction logs, especially in the area of desktop applications. However, these studies tend to focus on user ability in specific task-oriented programs, leaving aside general interaction. For example, Ghazarian et al. [5] presented methods and experiments to build automatic skill classifiers, in order to adapt interfaces to the user's needs according to their level of proficiency. Importantly, they note the lack of studies that lead to modeling user skill level from low-level events on the interface, such as mouse movement.

Along the same lines, Grossman et al. [12] explored the viability of software applications, such as AutoCAD, automatically inferring user experience levels based on their in-situ usage patterns. Their results show us that the approaches in other studies of human-computer interaction apply not only to low-level and short-term competence, but also to high-level software competence. It also shows that metrics captured from in-situ data, without knowledge of the user's environment or task, can be correlated with software proficiency.

Moreover, in the context of web applications, Duran et al. [13] introduced methods to detect collaborative behavior patterns automatically using "Web Usage Mining" techniques to generate collaborative student profiles. These techniques attempt to discover knowledge from data obtained from user interaction with the web, such as web logs, browser logs, user profiles, user sessions, bookmarks, folders, and scrolls. However, these approaches do not consider user interaction while using a web page, as proposed in this plan. They also provide insight into the profiles that are interesting to analyze and various techniques to perform analysis, preprocessing and predictive modeling.

Finally, in the area of web interaction capture and analysis, several studies have investigated user behavior characteristics and patterns. Huang et al. [14] analyzed mouse cursor behavior on search engine results pages (SERPs), focusing on clicks, movements, and hovers, and demonstrated that analysis of this data is valuable for estimating the relevance of a result and distinguishing types of search abandonment. Similarly, Kirsh [15] conducted a study focused on mouse movement directions and speeds, suggesting that these factors may be more revealing than simple cursor position. These studies are focused on the importance of individual events or analyzing a user's behavior to predict their next action, far from our idea of understanding and predicting the characteristics of their interaction. However, these findings are fundamental to identify which events should be captured and how to do it efficiently to predict the user's actions in the shortest time or with the least amount of data possible.

3 Objectives

This research aims to analyze user interaction to study and define user profiles on the Web. To achieve this, the following objectives are defined:

- Analyze through experimentation the behavior of real users and their relationship with the profiles studied.
- Study and define interactive user profiles on the web, according to specific criteria.
- Automate the detection of user profiles or interactive features, considering different variables such as detection speed and prediction accuracy. The detection is designed to be anonymous, i.e., avoiding user's personal data or the pages the user goes through.
- Validate the found user's profiles with other metrics established in the literature.

To study user interaction to the required level of detail, we will conduct different tests and experiments in which we will capture real users interaction.

We also propose to study our metrics related to user profiling with other established metrics, for example, a statistical analysis to evaluate the relationship between the effort a user must make when using widgets in a user interface [16] and the time it takes to use them.

4 Methodology

Due to the nature of the research topic, which is closely related to HCI, the primary method will consist on user studies. For this reason, several experiments will be conducted that require special preparation for working with volunteers. In some cases, it will be necessary to develop test web applications, and in others, to modify existing applications to record interactions or evaluate changes in the interface, such as when comparing different versions of the same interface. In addition, recruitment and experiment execution processes are required that take into account the multiple biases that can affect human studies. We will use user recruiting platforms due to the high volume of users required.

Interaction captures will be performed using tools that we have developed and continue to improve. These consist of configurable browser extensions, which allow to select the low level events to capture in the most used browsers and define to which server to send the collected data.

We aim to define meaningful profiles that help different scenarios, looking for common characteristics to avoid overfitting.

5 Preliminary Results

We aim to create predictive models for web interactive characteristics, such as cursor speed or interaction styles. For this purpose, we proposed the Composite Interaction Speed (CIS) metric that allows us to find how early we can estimate web users interaction speed. CIS is the equally weighted sum of three key velocities in the literature: mouse, scroll, and intra-keyboard speed. Since these use different units, they were normalized using a relative unit based on the average unit of each user's captured session. This allows the speeds to be compared at different times of a user's total interaction and to choose an optimal speed point, looking for the earliest time where the average speed is close to the final speed and there is little standard deviation.

A preliminary study was conducted analyzing the behavior of users on web interfaces with a high interaction in the context of user testing. We used logs from a previous study [17], which contain captures of users performing tasks on various web pages. The data relevant to the study were extracted from these captures, and the CIS metric was calculated. Early results suggest that the optimal speed point is at 500 events or 50 s [18]. Even if we worked closely with each participant, we applied anonymization techniques on the captured events, since we intend our detection mechanisms to avoid keeping personal data.

A second long-term experiment was carried out, where interaction of several volunteers was captured over a longer time period. To achieve this, a browser extension was built to capture web events in a private way. Using the captured data, the CIS was calculated and the result was that the optimal speed point is at 2000 events or 8.3 min. An alternative criteria result was also proposed that gave us a different optimal speed point at 800 events or 5.7 min.

We are capturing new volunteers interactions to ensure statistical validity. Also, we are studying how to optimize the weights for the CIS metric calculation.

Following the objective of validating the user profiles with other metrics, we performed an experiment to evaluate an interaction complexity metric called 'Big I' [19]. This metric allows to evaluate web interface alternatives by estimating the interaction complexity of each of them by measuring the number of steps to complete a task. We recruited 100 users to completed a task on a fictitious web page, which allowed us to measure interaction times, speed, and relate the complexity of the steps to the time required to complete them [20].

6 Contributions

The expected contributions of this work will be:

- An analysis of low-level interaction behavior on the web, and how different users behave differently in general cases.
- One or more taxonomies of web users depending on their interaction habits
- Experiments that demonstrate the different users profiles, and the captured data for other researchers to use
- Detection mechanisms for predicting user profiles based on the studied taxonomies, considering aspects such as detection speed, efficiency and quality.

Acknowledgment. This study was funded by the Argentinian National Agency for Scientific and Technical Promotion (ANPCyT), grant number PICT-2019-02485

Disclosure of Interests. The authors have no competing interests to declare that are relevant to the content of this article.

References

1. Carta, T., Paternò, F., De Santana, V.F.: Web usability probe: a tool for supporting remote usability evaluation of web sites. In: Human-Computer Interaction–INTERACT 2011: 13th IFIP TC 13 International Conference, Lisbon, Portugal, 5-9 September 2011, Proceedings, Part IV 13, pp. 349–357. Springer (2011)
2. Kacorri, H., Mascetti, S., Gerino, A., Ahmetovic, D., Takagi, H., Asakawa, C.: Supporting orientation of people with visual impairment: analysis of large scale usage data. In: Proceedings of the 18th International ACM SIGACCESS Conference on Computers and Accessibility, pp. 151–159 (2016)
3. Speicher, M., Both, A., Gaedke, M.: Tellmyrelevance! predicting the relevance of web search results from cursor interactions. In: Proceedings of the 22nd ACM International Conference on Information & Knowledge Management, pp. 1281–1290 (2013)

4. Grigera, J., Garrido, A., Rivero, J.M., Rossi, G.: Automatic detection of usability smells in web applications. Int. J. Hum.-Comput. Stud. **97**, 129–148 (2017)
5. Ghazarian, A., Noorhosseini, S.M.: Automatic detection of users' skill levels using high-frequency user interface events. User Model. User-Adapt. Interact. **20**, 109–146 (2010)
6. Hurst, A., Hudson, S.E., Mankoff, J.: Dynamic detection of novice vs. skilled use without a task model. In: Proceedings of the SIGCHI Conference on Human Factors in Computing Systems, pp. 271–280 (2007)
7. Attig, C., Then, E., Krems, J.F.: Show me how you click, and i'll tell you what you can: predicting user competence and performance by mouse interaction parameters. In: Intelligent Human Systems Integration 2019: Proceedings of the 2nd International Conference on Intelligent Human Systems Integration (IHSI 2019): Integrating People and Intelligent Systems, 7–10 February 2019, San Diego, California, USA, pp. 801–806. Springer (2019)
8. Lagun, D., Ageev, M., Guo, Q., Agichtein, E.: Discovering common motifs in cursor movement data for improving web search. In: Proceedings of the 7th ACM International Conference on Web Search and Data Mining, pp. 183–192 (2014)
9. Diriye, A., White, R., Buscher, G., Dumais, S.: Leaving so soon? understanding and predicting web search abandonment rationales. In: Proceedings of the 21st ACM international conference on Information and knowledge management, pp. 1025–1034 (2012)
10. Rathnayake, N., Meedeniya, D., Perera, I., Welivita, A.: A framework for adaptive user interface generation based on user behavioural patterns. In: 2019 Moratuwa Engineering Research Conference (MERCon), pp. 698–703 (2019)
11. Hernandez, J., Paredes, P., Roseway, A., Czerwinski, M.: Under pressure: sensing stress of computer users. In: Proceedings of the SIGCHI Conference on Human Factors in Computing Systems, pp. 51–60 (2014)
12. Grossman, T., Fitzmaurice, G.: An investigation of metrics for the in situ detection of software expertise. Hum.-Comput. Interact. **30**(1), 64–102 (2015)
13. Duran, E.B., Amandi, A.: Web usage mining approach to detect student's collaborative skills. J. Web Eng. 093–112 (2009)
14. Huang, J., White, R.W., Dumais, S.: No clicks, no problem: using cursor movements to understand and improve search. In: Proceedings of the SIGCHI Conference on Human Factors in Computing Systems, pp. 1225–1234 (2011)
15. Kirsh, I.: Directions and speeds of mouse movements on a website and reading patterns: a web usage mining case study. In: Proceedings of the 10th International Conference on Web Intelligence, Mining and Semantics, pp. 129–138 (2020)
16. Gardey, J.C., Grigera, J., Rodríguez, A., Rossi, G., Garrido, A.: Predicting interaction effort in web interface widgets. Int. J. Hum.-Comput. Stud. **168**, 102919 (2022)
17. Grigera, J., Gardey, J.C., Rodriguez, A., Garrido, A., Rossi, G.: One metric for all: calculating interaction effort of individual widgets. In: Extended Abstracts of the 2019 CHI Conference on Human Factors in Computing Systems, pp. 1–6 (2019)
18. Bonora, L.G.L., Grigera, J., Gardey, J.C., Garrido, A.: Web user interaction speed study. In: 2022 41st International Conference of the Chilean Computer Science Society (SCCC), pp. 1–4. IEEE (2022)
19. Degen, H.: Big i notation to estimate the interaction complexity of interaction concepts. Int. J. Hum.-Comput. Interact. **38**(16), 1504–1528 (2022)
20. Germán Loza Bonora, L., Grigera, J., Degen, H.: A study on interaction complexity and time (2025)

Designing Hybrid Quantum-Classical Web Applications Across the Computing Continuum

Álvaro M. Aparicio-Morales[✉][iD], Enrique Moguel[iD], and Jose Garcia-Alonso[iD]

Universidad de Extremadura, Avenida de la Universidad, S/N, 10003 Cáceres, Spain
{amapamor,enrique,jgaralo}@unex.es

Abstract. Modern web applications often rely on complex computational processes that can be time-consuming and resource-intensive. Quantum Computing has emerged as a promising paradigm to accelerate these tasks. However, incorporating quantum computing into current web application architecture poses significant challenges. Also, Quality of Service attributes are crucial for current web applications, these attributes will need to be considered for the deployment of hybrid web applications that leverage quantum and classical computing. This work outlines the general research directions and objectives to be addressed throughout this PhD. thesis. The core objective is to design a workflow for obtaining an optimal deployment configuration that maximizes the Quality of Service attributes. Moreover, a dynamic reconfiguration of the distribution of hybrid web application services in terms of demand fluctuations to ensure performance, resource utilization and responsiveness will be composed. This work lays the foundation for novel tools and methodologies to bridge classical and quantum paradigms in service-oriented computing.

Keywords: Quantum Software Engineering · Quantum Computing · Web Service Applications · Computing Continuum

1 Introduction and Motivation

Modern web applications are increasingly complex systems that require high levels of availability, scalability, security, performance, and usability to ensure a high-quality user experience. However, the Quality of Services (QoS) is often impacted by factors like latency, response time of some processes, and efficient resource management. To address these challenges, a wide range of technologies have emerged, such as the computing continuum spectrum solutions to, among others, reduce latency, DevOps tools for assurance of automation and reliability, and cloud-native architectures for scalability. These advancements help optimize performance, enhance resilience, and improve overall service quality in modern web applications. However, there are existing tasks which require long computation times for current digital computers, like weather simulation, big data analysis, or the learning stage for IA models. For example, real-time rendering in web-based 3D modeling applications and augmented reality platforms relies on complex simulations that process vast amounts of graphical data. In scenarios such as remote surgery, efficient load balancing across Cloud, Fog, and Edge computing within Content Delivery Networks (CDNs) is crucial to ensure ultra-low latency and seamless performance.

In this context, Quantum Computing (QC) is presented as an emerging technology which could further enhance these systems by accelerating real-time data processing, allowing augmented reality-assisted surgeries. Taking that into account, future web applications will incorporate this paradigm to handle complex tasks more efficiently [1]. The coexistence between the two realms, classical and quantum paradigms, forming what is known as a hybrid system, will need the application of software engineering [2]. Following this line, Quantum Services Engineering, tries, from the Service Oriented-Computing (SOC) perspective, to integrate quantum services in services applications with the finality of leveraging the advantages of QC [2]. However, despite the advances in quantum hardware, it is still difficult to develop a quantum service in the same way as in classical programming. Nevertheless, through the approach proposed in the work of Garcia-Alonso et al. [3], it is feasible to integrate a quantum algorithm into an existing classical service. Those services, which encapsulate a quantum algorithm in them, are called *hybrid services*, so hybrid applications will be compounded by classical and hybrid services. The current approach is plausible due to the Software Development Kits (SDK) created by the cloud service providers that offer access, via their platforms, to quantum computers. Despite this, those providers follow the pay-per-use model and, because of quantum technology novelty, the economic cost of its usage, is generally quite high [4].

This thesis focuses on addressing the placement problem for hybrid applications: how to optimally deploy services across classical and quantum resources along the computing continuum. While existing tools support QoS-aware deployment for classical services, they fall short when applied to hybrid systems. This research proposes the design of a methodology and toolset for defining, evaluating, and dynamically reconfiguring hybrid service distributions to meet QoS goals under changing conditions.

2 Related Work

This section is organized around two key areas that form the core of this work. On the one hand, the *placement problem* for classical service applications and, on the other hand, hybrid quantum-classical service applications.

Web Service Placement. Research studies in the service placement problem and application behaviour analysis, essential for optimizing service deployment, have been highlighted. For example, the work by Herrera et al. [5] offers recommendations based on the service application composition and user requirements. Also, the work of Selimi et al. [6], which leverages network state information to support service placement decisions. Another relevant study is the work of C mara et al. [7], where application behaviour under uncertainty is analyzed using probabilistic formal verification.

Quantum Computing. Notable studies in addressing *the placement problem* for quantum computing include Sivarajah et al. [8] and JavadiAbhari et al. [9], and the NISQ Analyzer [10] which focus on selecting quantum computers for specific quantum algorithms. On the other hand, regarding studies focused on the coexistence of classical and quantum services notable works include that of Romero et al. [11] proposed a quantum circuit scheduler for cloud providers, while Alvarado et al. [12] offered a guide for converting quantum circuits to web services. Also, Nguyen et al. [13] introduced quantum function-as-a-service using a serverless model.

These studies lay the foundation for this work, which aims to unify both areas by proposing an innovative tool for hybrid quantum-classical service application placement. To the best of our knowledge, no research has addressed the placement problem for hybrid quantum-classical applications from this perspective.

3 Aims and Objectives

The core objective of this doctoral thesis is to propose the research and development of a methodology for the deployment in the computing continuum of hybrid web applications. The objective is to solve the placement problem for hybrid applications, providing elasticity and liquidity to the web application while meeting the established QoS criteria. To achieve this main goal, the following research questions have been established, which will subsequently lead to the specific objectives:

(**RQ1**): How do existing standards for service definition support the description of hybrid web applications? Modern web applications are composed of services that address the resolution of a task, e.g., finding an item in a list. However, by incorporating QC, this task can be addressed using quantum services, classical services or hybrid services, which will imply a complexity in the composition of my application. Therefore, service definition standards will be studied and modified to incorporate the formal description of web services hybrid applications. For this purpose, we will use as a basis the standard for the description of services defined in OpenAPI and HAIQ Specification [14] for service behaviours.

(**RQ2**): How can we ensure that the obtained hybrid web application deployment will meet the defined QoS? The complex composition of hybrid web applications requires the use of tools and techniques to analyze various deployment configurations and identify the optimal service distribution at a given moment. Verification and formalization tools are essential to ensure that the set of possible distributions complies with the structural constraints of hybrid service applications while also enabling the study of their qualitative properties. To achieve this, an architectural style for hybrid applications will be defined to properly generate different configurations, along with the use of probabilistic model-checking tools to analyze system behaviour in stochastic environments.

(**RQ3**): Which criteria will be defined to determine when the distribution of the hybrid web application will be recalculated? A DevOps process will be proposed with the goal of managing both deployment and monitoring the application's behaviour to enable automated adjustments based on the context. These adjustments may involve allocating new computational resources, modifying the computing layer of services, or even replacing a specific service with a functionally equivalent alternative. For the latter, it is crucial to define a threshold that determines the appropriate moment for service substitution.

4 Research Methodology

In order to achieve the mentioned objectives of this PhD. thesis and given its research nature in IT field, this study will adopt the Design Science methodology [15]. This approach, widely used in IT research, focuses on creating artifacts, which, as defined by Hevner et al. [15], can include models, methods, development processes, or software. By following this methodology, the research aims to provide a more practical approach to the stated objectives. Following the proposed guidelines of this methodology in the Fig. 1 a research plan is presented.

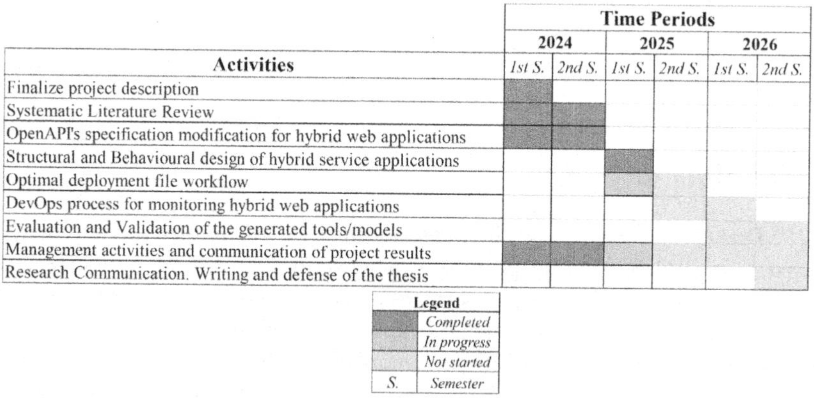

Activities	2024		2025		2026	
	1st S.	2nd S.	1st S.	2nd S.	1st S.	2nd S.
Finalize project description						
Systematic Literature Review						
OpenAPI's specification modification for hybrid web applications						
Structural and Behavioural design of hybrid service applications						
Optimal deployment file workflow						
DevOps process for monitoring hybrid web applications						
Evaluation and Validation of the generated tools/models						
Management activities and communication of project results						
Research Communication. Writing and defense of the thesis						

Legend: Completed / In progress / Not started / S. Semester

Fig. 1. PhD. Thesis Timeline

Figure 2 presents a proposed workflow architecture that outlines the process from web application specification to deployment and monitoring. The specification is divided into a service specification and the intended behaviour of the application (described as an abstract workflow). Based on the specification, suitable classical and quantum machines for each service will be identified. A formalized architectural style of hybrid service application, the suitable machines and the behavioural model will be combined into a unified model, which is evaluated by a probabilistic model-checking tool to check QoS system properties. The results of each possible combination will be ranked by using a utility function of the QoS parameters to determine the optimal deployment. After the deployment of services, a monitor will be in charge of collecting information to provide feedback, allowing recalculation of service distribution based on the current context.

Initial progress in this thesis research has been made, with the thesis itself being nearly 50% complete. This includes a preliminary approach to the main workflow for obtaining a Deployment File.

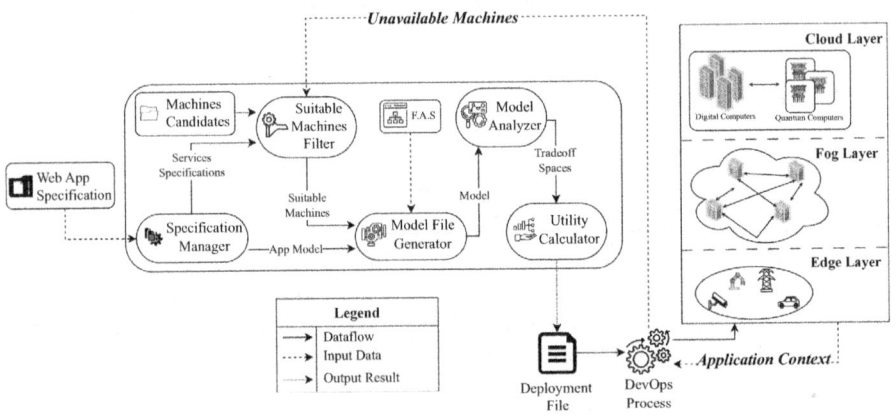

Fig. 2. PhD. Thesis Project

5 Conclusion

This PhD thesis addresses the challenges of integrating quantum computing into modern web applications by proposing a methodology for the optimal deployment of hybrid quantum-classical services across the computing continuum. This approach combines formal service specification, architectural modeling, probabilistic analysis, and DevOps-based dynamic reconfiguration to ensure Quality of Service under varying conditions. This work contributes to the advancement of quantum software engineering by providing practical tools and strategies to support the seamless coexistence of classical and quantum services, paving the way for the next generation of high-performance web applications.

Acknowledgments. The present work has been partially funded by the QSERV project (PID2021-124045O B-C31), supported by the Ministry of Science and Innovation and FEDER and the Regional Ministry of Economy, Science, and Digital Agenda of the Junta de Extremadura (GR21133), and partially funded and supported by the Ibero-American Program for Science and Technology for Development (CYTED), through RIPAISC - Ibero-American Network for the Advancement of Quantum Software Engineering (525RT0174).

References

1. Piattini, M., Pérez-Castillo, R., Murillo, J.M., et al.: The talavera manifesto for quantum software engineering and programming. In: Short Papers Proceedings of the 1st International Workshop on the QuANtum SoftWare Engineering & pRogramming, Talavera de la Reina, Spain, 11–12 February 2020, ser. CEUR Workshop Proceedings, Piattini, M., Peterssen, G., Pérez-Castillo, R. Hevia, J.L., Serrano, M.A. (eds.), vol. 2561. CEUR-WS.org, pp. 1–5 (2020)
2. Murillo, J.M., Garcia-Alonso, J., E. M. et al.: Quantum software engineering: roadmap and challenges ahead. ACM Trans. Softw. Eng. Methodol. January 2025
3. García-Alonso, J., Rojo, J., Valencia, D., Moguel, E., Berrocal, J., Murillo, J.M.: Quantum software as a service through a quantum API gateway. IEEE Internet Comput. **26**(1), 34–41 (2022)
4. Aparicio-Morales, Á.M., Herrera, J.L., et al.: Minimizing deployment cost of hybrid applications. In: Cour, B.L., Yeh, L., Osinski, M., (eds.) IEEE International Conference on Quantum Computing and Engineering, QCE 2023, Bellevue, WA, USA, 17–22 September 2023, pp. 191–194. IEEE (2023)
5. Herrera, J.L., Galan-Jimenez, J., Garcia-Alonso, J., Berrocal, J., Murillo, J.M.: Joint optimization of response time and deployment cost in next-gen IoT applications. IEEE Internet Things J. **10**, 3968–3981 (2023)
6. Selimi, M., Cerda-Alabern, L., Sanchez-Artigas, M., Freitag, F., Veiga, L.: Practical service placement approach for microservices architecture. In: Proceedings IEEE/ACM International Symposium on CCGRID, pp. 401–410, July 2017
7. Cámara, J., Garlan, D., Schmerl, B.: Synthesizing tradeoff spaces with quantitative guarantees for families of software systems. J. Syst. Softw. **152**, 33–49 (2019)
8. Sivarajah, S., Dilkes, S., Cowtan, A., Simmons, W., Edgington, A., Duncan, R.: t— ket¿: a retargetable compiler for nisq devices. Quantum Sci. Technol. **6**(1), 014003 (2020)
9. JavadiAbhari, A., et al.: Scaffcc: a framework for compilation and analysis of quantum computing programs. In: ACM Conference on Computing Frontiers, pp. 1–10 (2014)
10. Salm, M., et al.: The nisq analyzer: automating the selection of quantum computers for quantum algorithms. In: Symposium and Summer School on Service-Oriented Computing, pp. 66–85. Springer (2020)
11. Romero-Álvarez, J., et al.: Using open api for the development of hybrid classical-quantum services. In: International Conference on Service-Oriented Computing, pp. 364–368. Springer (2022)
12. Alvarado-Valiente, J., Romero-Álvarez, J., Garcia-Alonso, J., Murillo, J.M.: A guide for quantum web services deployment. In: International Conference on Web Engineering, pp. 493–496. Springer (2022)
13. Nguyen, H.T., Usman, M., Buyya, R.: Qfaas: a serverless function-as-a-service framework for quantum computing. Futur. Gener. Comput. Syst. **154**, 281–300 (2024)
14. Cámara, J.: Haiq: synthesis of software design spaces with structural and probabilistic guarantees. In: Proceedings of the 8th International Conference on Formal Methods in Software Engineering, pp. 22–33 (2020)
15. Hevner, A.R., March, S.T., Park, J., Ram, S.: Design science in information systems research. MIS Quart. 75–105 (2004)

Tutorials

A Tutorial on Social Media Data Analytics for Disaster Management

Sanjay Madria[✉]

Department of Computer Science, Missouri University of Science and Technology, Rolla, USA
madrias@mst.edu

Abstract. A disaster can refer to an effect and result of natural hazards like the hurricane, flood, earthquake, tornado, heatwave, etc. Every activity of a disaster management such as taking precautions, managing evacuation, running rescue missions demands accurate and up-to-date information to allow a quick, easy and cost-effective process and hence reduce the loss of lives and properties. Social media has emerged as a valuable supplementary tool in this context, providing real-time data that can assist authorities in developing prompt and effective response strategies. However, despite its potential, utilizing social media data for disaster management presents several challenges. It needs a multi-faceted approach that leverages deep learning and natural language processing (NLP) techniques tackling the complexities of contextual information and the relevance of social media content. The tutorial will offer actionable insights that significantly enhance situational awareness information, decision-making, and resource allocation during disasters. The tutorial will focus on i) How can we detect, classify, and analyze hate and offensive emotions during large-scale events based on the social media data such as tweets? ii) How can deep learning models improve sentiment analysis by identifying low-level emotions in major events? iii) How can fine-grained data enhance crisis communication classification and decision-making in disaster response? iv) How can we assess information relevance and urgency to prioritize emergency responses? v) How can we identify and classify first responders during emergencies? vi) How can we develop an automated fact-checking system to verify disaster claims and combat misinformation? vii) How can unsupervised learning be used to extract key phrases and detect critical sub-events from unstructured disaster data?

Keywords: Social Media · Disaster · NLP

1 Introduction

Effective and efficient communication during disasters or crises is essential, as it helps ensure a fast and organized response, reduces injuries and deaths, and uses resources wisely. When emergency responders, government agencies, and aid organizations have precise, timely, and accurate information, they can understand how serious the situation is, focus on the most affected areas, and provide help quickly. Communication channels allow for real-time updates, which help authorities coordinate rescue efforts, manage evacuations, and address urgent medical needs. Additionally, strong communication prevents misinformation, which can cause panic, misallocate resources, and slow down response times. Using social networks, machine learning, and artificial intelligence (AI) technology can improve how information is shared, ensuring that essential and accurate information reaches both decision-makers and those in need as quickly as possible. Effective communication strategies, by enhancing awareness and coordination, significantly empower us in how we prepare for, respond to, and recover from disasters. Today, social media platforms like Twitter, Facebook, Instagram, and TikTok and others serve as crucial tools for disaster management. They enable affected individuals to share live updates, photos, videos, and requests for help, making social media a valuable source of real-time information during emergencies. ML emerges as a powerful tool in disaster response [1–11]. It aids in the analysis and understanding of large volumes of data from social media, facilitating quicker decisions and more effective disaster management. Machine learning offers a promising way to tackle these issues by using artificial intelligence algorithms to:

- Detect disasters as they happen by looking at patterns by analyzing social media.
- Spot areas that need urgent attention by analyzing geotagged posts.
- Filter and confirm information to reduce misinformation.
- Improve how resources are allocated for emergency help.

Machine learning plays a pivotal role in enhancing disaster response. Automatically analyzing large amounts of data from social media, sensors, and satellite images provides real-time information and supports better decision-making. Here are some of its key benefits:

- Speed and Efficiency: AI-driven models can quickly process vast amounts of unstructured data from the Web like text, images, and videos much faster than people can. This allows for quick understanding and response to the situation.
- Scalability: Machine learning algorithms can instantly analyze millions of social media posts, geotagged images, and emergency reports. This makes them very effective for monitoring and managing large-scale disasters.
- Accuracy: AI models trained on past disaster data can improve how well they detect, classify, and predict events. This helps responders identify high-risk areas, plan for resource needs, and check the credibility of reports on social media.
- Resource Optimization: Predictive analytics help efficiently allocate emergency workers, medical supplies, and rescue teams. They do this by forecasting demand and pinpointing critical areas needing help based on real-time data.
- Misinformation Filtering: Machine learning tools like natural language processing models can identify and remove misleading or false information during crises. This ensures that emergency responders have access to trustworthy and verified data.
- Cross-Modal Data Integration: Machine learning combines data from different sources, including satellite images, seismic sensors, weather reports, and social media. This integration helps create a complete framework for responding to disasters.

Topics to be covered:

1. Event/Sub-Event Classification for Disaster Response
2. Context-aware Relevance and Urgency Determination for Effective Disaster Management
3. Learning Models for First Responder Classification System for Disaster Management
4. Learning Models for Extracting Minimal Key Phrases for Subevents in Disaster Situations
5. Learning Models for Domain-Specific Automatic Fact-Checking for Disaster Claims

Target Audience and its Assumed Background: This tutorial is designed for academicians and researchers working in the area social media data analysis. It is to help data analytics professionals and business analysts, such as big data processing project and technical managers, people involved in planning, designing, developing, implementing analytics applications using social media data. It is also for students of computer and information science who are pursuing or planning to pursue a higher research degree in data analytics.

Speaker Biography: Sanjay K Madria (www.mst.edu/~cswebdb) is a Curators' Distinguished Professor in the Department of Computer Science at the Missouri University of Science and Technology (formerly, University of Missouri-Rolla, USA). He has published over 300 Journal and conference papers in the areas of mobile and sensor computing, big data and cloud computing, data analytics and cybersecurity. He won five IEEE best papers awards in conferences such as IEEE MDM and IEEE SRDS. He is a co-author of a book (published with his two PhD graduates) on Secure Sensor Cloud published by Morgan and Claypool in Dec. 2018. He has graduated 21 PhDs and 34 MS thesis students, with 12 current PhDs. NSF, NIST, ARL, ARO, AFRL, DOE, Boeing, CDC NIOSH, ORNL, Honeywell, and others have funded his research projects of over $25M. He has been awarded JSPS (Japanese Society for Promotion of Science) invitational visiting scientist fellowship, and ASEE (American Society of Engineering Education) fellowship. In 2012 and in 2019, he was awarded NRC Fellowship by National Academies, US. He is ACM Distinguished Scientist and served as an ACM and IEEE Distinguished Speaker He is an IEEE Senior Member and IEEE Golden Core Awardee.

Acknowledgments. The author is thankful to Dr. Ademola Adesokan for help in the preparation of this manuscript. The author is also thankful to NSF for providing funding for this research.

References

1. Adesokan, A., Madria, S., Nguyen, L.: DisTGranD: granular event/sub-event classification for disaster response. Online Soc. Netw. Media (2025)
2. Adesokan, A., Madria, S., Nguyen, H.L.: FReCS: a first responder classification system. In: 16th International Conference on Advances in Social Networks Analysis and Mining -ASONAM-2024 (2024, to appear)

3. Adesokan, A., Madria, S.: CURD: context-aware relevance and urgency determination. In: 36th International Conference on Scientific and Statistical Database Management (SSDBM), France (2024)
4. Adesokan, A., Madria, S.: KeyMinES: extracting minimal keyphrases for sub-events in disaster situations. In: IEEE BigData (2024)
5. Adesokan, A., Madria, S.: DisFact: fact-checking disaster claims. In: International Web Information Systems Engineering Conference, Doha, Qatar, December 2024. Accessed 25
6. Alam, F., Sajjad, H., Imran, M., Ofli, F.: CrisisBench: benchmarking crisis-related social media datasets for humanitarian information processing. In: Proceedings of the International AAAI Conference on Web and Social Media, vol. 15 (2021). https://doi.org/10.1609/icwsm.v15i1.18115
7. Guo, Z., Schlichtkrull, M., Vlachos, A.: A survey on automated fact-checking. In: Transactions of the ACL, vol. 10, pp. 178–206 (2022)
8. Koshy, R., Elango, S.: Utilizing social media for emergency response: a tweet classification system using attention-based BiLSTM and CNN for resource management. Multimed. Tools Appl. (2023). https://doi.org/10.1007/s11042-023-16766-z
9. Li, H., Caragea, D., Caragea, C.: Combining self-training with deep learning for disaster tweet classification. In: Proceedings of the International ISCRAM Conference, vol. 2021, May 2021. ISSN: 24113387
10. Mittal, V., Jahanian, M., Ramakrishnan, K.K.: Online delivery of social media posts to appropriate first responders for disaster response. In: ACM International Conference Proceedings Series (2021). https://doi.org/10.1145/3427477.3429272
11. Zou, L., et al.: Social media for emergency rescue: an analysis of rescue requests on Twitter during hurricane Harvey. Int. J. Disaster Risk Red. **85** (2023). https://doi.org/10.1016/j.ijdrr.2022.103513

Enhancing Reproducibility and Replicability in Information Retrieval: A Path Towards Scientific Integrity and Effective Research

Antonio Ferrara[1], Claudio Pomo[1(✉)], and Nicola Tonellotto[2]

[1] Politecnico di Bari, Bari, Italy
{antonio.ferrara,claudio.pomo}@poliba.it
[2] University of Pisa, Pisa, Italy
nicola.tonellotto@unipi.it

Abstract. While Information Retrieval (IR) and Recommender Systems (RecSys) have made significant strides, reproducibility and replicability remain elusive due to methodological inconsistencies and pressures for high-impact results. Despite reproducibility tracks, guidelines, and frameworks, inconsistent application and limited motivation for rigorous reproducibility hinder progress. This tutorial introduces tools and methodologies for reproducibility in IR and RecSys research. It focuses on foundational concepts like selecting appropriate baselines and designing replicable experimental pipelines, and practical case studies demonstrating the impact of minor experimental variations. This session equips researchers with actionable strategies for producing robust, transparent studies, fostering scientific integrity within the IR and RecSys communities and supporting more reliable and impactful research advancements.

Keywords: Reproducibility · Replicability · Information Retrieval · Recommender Systems · Scientific Integrity

1 Motivations and Scope of the Tutorial

Reproducibility is crucial in scientific inquiry for validating experiments and building trust. In Information Retrieval and Recommender Systems, it is vital. Innovations rely on empirical results for academic and practical advancements. Achieving reproducibility involves more than detailed methods and results; it needs standardized procedures for consistent verification by researchers.

Reproducibility and replicability are crucial for science, enabling rigorous testing and questioning of findings. They help confirm generalizability, challenge conclusions, and uncover limitations. Reproducibility also guards against bias, especially where pressure for impactful results may affect integrity. This validation and critique cycle is vital for refining our understanding and ensuring scientific and technological progress.

Reproducibility is a significant issue in IR and RecSys, with studies like Dacrema et al. [4] and Armstrong et al. [2] highlighting gaps and inflated performance claims due to poor baselines. Lin [11] points to "neural hype", where weak baselines falsely inflate incremental improvements, undermining rigor and progress. The community is addressing these concerns [8] by promoting reproducibility through initiatives like the ACM RecSys Challenge and developing frameworks [1,17] and platforms (e.g., Pyserini [12], PyTerrier [13,14], TIREx [9]). These efforts are seen as advancements from previous frameworks [5,10] and lead to more reliable, impactful research [3,18].

This three-hour tutorial covers the essentials of reproducibility and replicability in RecSys and IR research. Participants will gain a clear understanding of required principles and practices, building on core scientific methodologies, including hypothesis formulation, experimental design, data collection, and result analysis. The tutorial aims to instill a culture of scientific rigor and transparency, empowering researchers to create trustworthy and robust studies.

2 Tutorial Outline

Our proposed lecture will consist of three main sections, featuring two session types, both **theoretical** and **practical** ones. We estimate the total lecture duration to be *180 min*.

[**Theoretical part**] The Role of Reproducibility and Replicability in Recommendation Research and Information Retrieval → *50 min*

- Importance of Reproducibility in Scientific Research
- Reproducibility challenges in RecSys and IR

[**Theoretical part**] Reproducibility Tools and Frameworks → *60 min*

- Overview of the reproducibility Tools and Frameworks for RecSys and IR
- Best practices to achieve reproducibility in RecSys and IR research
- Avoiding common pitfalls in experimental replicability

[**Practical part**] Hands-On Session: Implementing Reproducible Experiments Using Open-Source Frameworks → *60 min*

- Guided setup of a reproducible experiment using selected frameworks for RecSys and IR scenario
- Case Studies: Examples of (Non-)Reproducible Research

Closing remarks and Q&A → *10 min*

3 Additional Information

Intended Learning Outcomes. The tutorial equips participants with tools and methods for reproducible research, covering observation, hypothesis formulation, data collection, experimentation, and results analysis. Attendees will gain practical experience and guidelines to implement best practices, critically assess their findings, and avoid pitfalls like selective reporting and "virtual progress".

Intended Audience. This tutorial is for those interested in reproducibility and replicability in IR and recommendation research. It builds on existing knowledge and covers introductory to intermediate topics in the scientific method, reproducibility and replicability principles, framework development, and their applications in these fields.

Supporting Material. Several support materials will be provided: i) a GitHub repository containing an overview of the program with further details about the tutorial; ii) tutorial slides with references to all the relevant works; iii) notebooks to test reproducibility, replicability, and frameworks in RecSys and IR.

4 Related Lectures and Tutorials

Many top-tier conferences in computational science now have mandatory reproducibility guidelines or specific tracks, but dedicated tutorials on reproducibility and replicability are rare. The "The AI4Europe Reproducibility Initiative" tutorial at ECAI 2023 emphasised the importance of reproducibility in scientific discoveries and research impact. Our tutorial covers topics that receive limited attention in broader evaluation in recommender systems or database-related sessions. Said and Bellogín [16] at RecSys, Fisher et al. [7] and Mauerer et al. [15] at pVLDB and ICDM, are relevant examples.

This tutorial provides a comprehensive approach to reproducibility and replicability in computational research, especially for RecSys and IR. Unlike general evaluation sessions, it focuses on unique methodological issues, common pitfalls, and practical steps for ensuring reproducibility and validation. We aim to contribute to the growing push for transparent and reliable scientific practices, which are crucial for the field's progress and credibility. Versions of this tutorial have been presented at ECIR 2025 [6] and the RecSys Summer School 2024[1].

5 Tutorial Presenters

Antonio Ferrara is an assistant professor at the Polytechnic University of Bari, affiliated with the Information Systems Laboratory (SisInfLab). His research focuses on differential privacy, federated learning, and their applications in privacy-oriented recommender systems and knowledge-aware user decision modeling. He is a contributor to Elliot and has published in journals like TORS, with papers, demos, and tutorials at SAC, ECIR, SIGIR, and RecSys. He has served as a PC member and co-chaired LBR&Demos at RecSys 2024 and other venues.

Claudio Pomo is an assistant professor at the Polytechnic University of Bari, affiliated with SisInfLab. His work centers on responsible AI for personalization, emphasizing reproducibility and multi-objective evaluation. His contributions appear in top conferences (SIGIR, RecSys, ECIR, UMAP) and journals (Information Science, IPM). He co-hosted tutorials at RecSys 2021 and LoG 2023 on privacy in recommender systems and graph neural networks for recommendation.

---

[1] https://acmrecsys.github.io/rsss2024/.

Nicola Tonellotto is an associate professor at the Department of Information Engineering, University of Pisa. Previously, he was a researcher at ISTI-CNR (2002–2019). His expertise spans cloud computing, web search, and information retrieval, focusing on efficient data processing and neural retrieval. With over 100 peer-reviewed publications, he has been an honorary research fellow at the University of Glasgow since 2020 and an ACM distinguished member since 2023.

References

1. Anelli, V.W., et al.: Elliot: a comprehensive and rigorous framework for reproducible recommender systems evaluation. In: SIGIR, pp. 2405–2414. ACM (2021)
2. Armstrong, T.G., Moffat, A., Webber, W., Zobel, J.: Improvements that don't add up: ad-hoc retrieval results since 1998. In: CIKM, pp. 601–610. ACM (2009)
3. Bellogín, A., Said, A.: Improving accountability in recommender systems research through reproducibility. User Model. User Adapt. Interact. **31**(5), 941–977 (2021)
4. Dacrema, M.F., Boglio, S., Cremonesi, P., Jannach, D.: A troubling analysis of reproducibility and progress in recommender systems research. ACM Trans. Inf. Syst. **39**(2), 20:1–20:49 (2021)
5. Ekstrand, M.D., Ludwig, M., Kolb, J., Riedl, J.: Lenskit: a modular recommender framework. In: RecSys, pp. 349–350. ACM (2011)
6. Ferrara, A., Pomo, C., Tonellotto, N.: Enhancing reproducibility and replicability in information retrieval: a path towards scientific integrity and effective research. In: ECIR (5), LNCS, vol. 15576, pp. 266–272. Springer (2025)
7. Fischer, T., Hirn, D., Kul, G.: A reproducible tutorial on reproducibility in database systems research. Proc. VLDB Endow. **17**(12), 4221–4224 (2024)
8. Freire, J., Bonnet, P., Shasha, D.E.: Computational reproducibility: state-of-the-art, challenges, and database research opportunities. In: SIGMOD Conference, pp. 593–596. ACM (2012)
9. Fröbe, M., et al.: The information retrieval experiment platform. In: SIGIR, pp. 2826–2836. ACM (2023)
10. Gantner, Z., Rendle, S., Freudenthaler, C., Schmidt-Thieme, L.: Mymedialite: a free recommender system library. In: RecSys, pp. 305–308. ACM (2011)
11. Lin, J.: The neural hype and comparisons against weak baselines. SIGIR Forum **52**(2), 40–51 (2018). https://doi.org/10.1145/3308774.3308781
12. Lin, J., Ma, X., Lin, S., Yang, J., Pradeep, R., Nogueira, R.: Pyserini: a python toolkit for reproducible information retrieval research with sparse and dense representations. In: SIGIR, pp. 2356–2362. ACM (2021)
13. Macdonald, C., Tonellotto, N.: Declarative experimentation in information retrieval using pyterrier. In: ICTIR, pp. 161–168. ACM (2020)
14. Macdonald, C., Tonellotto, N., MacAvaney, S., Ounis, I.: Pyterrier: declarative experimentation in python from BM25 to dense retrieval. In: CIKM, pp. 4526–4533. ACM (2021)
15. Mauerer, W., Scherzinger, S.: Nullius in verba: reproducibility for database systems research, revisited. In: ICDE, pp. 2377–2380. IEEE (2021)
16. Said, A., Bellogín, A.: Replicable evaluation of recommender systems. In: RecSys, pp. 363–364. ACM (2015)
17. Sun, Z., et al.: Are we evaluating rigorously? benchmarking recommendation for reproducible evaluation and fair comparison. In: RecSys, pp. 23–32. ACM (2020)
18. Zangerle, E., Bauer, C.: Evaluating recommender systems: survey and framework. ACM Comput. Surv. **55**(8), 170:1–170:38 (2023)

Creating Accessible Digital Content and Applications

Ombretta Gaggi[(✉)]

Department of Mathematics, University of Padua, via Trieste 63, Padua, Italy
ombretta.gaggi@unipd.it

Abstract. Access to digital content and to web pages is a fundamental right for all citizens and is crucial for people with disabilities to participate fully in society and the workforce. Unfortunately, imposing accessibility by law is insufficient, considering many websites still present relevant accessibility issues. Moreover, there is a lack of culture about accessibility, even among designers and developers. This tutorial teaches some basic concepts to create accessible digital content like web pages, papers, and presentations. It also introduces some innovative solutions for the accessibility of mathematical function graphs. Finally, an initial comparison of support for accessibility of mobile applications by frameworks for cross-platform mobile development will be discussed.

Keywords: Web Accessibility · Digital Content

1 Introduction

Are modern websites and technologies inclusive? Unfortunately, the answer is often no, and many devices and services represent a significant digital barrier for users with disabilities. The same question holds for science: many research papers are not accessible to people with visual impairments, as are other materials used during research work. Many presentations are not accessible by design due to issues with the slides or how the speaker conducts the talk.

According to the last report on the top one million pages by WebAIM [1], the number of pages that failed during *Web Content Accessibility Guidelines (WCAG)* [2] tests stood at 96.8%, an enormous number, even if it is a little better than the previous year. In this context, one of the main problems is the lack of knowledge about accessibility among web designers and developers: they are often not aware of either international guidelines about accessibility or national regulations. Thus, they cannot consider accessibility during the development and compile a complete list of tests the website must pass. Moreover, a tool that automatically tests all accessibility issues does not exist [7], and developers often do not know how to test each feature. Even the use of Large Language Models (LLMs) does not completely solve the problem [8].

Many websites use CAPTCHAs, Completely Automated Public Turing-test-to-tell Computers and Humans Apart, i.e., tests developed to prevent robotic access to websites and services for thwarting spam and automated extraction of data. They have always been a problem from the point of view of accessibility [6], because they often base their tests on the use of sight, since the ability to see an image or a text and recognize or understand its content is a way to make out a human being from a bot. But visually impaired users are unable to see; nevertheless, they are human beings, and CAPTCHAs are a barrier for them. The result is that CAPTCHAs are often better at preventing access to users with visual impairment than to bots.

Creating accessible content, i.e., web pages, web applications, papers, books, didactic materials, etc., is a critical issue in providing access to all users to education, services, research, knowledge, etc. Although the European laws impose accessibility for new products and the definition of an updated version of WCAG by W3C, this goal is often not reached due, not only to technological limitations, but also to the lack of knowledge among developers and researchers.

2 Tutorial Overview

This tutorial allows researchers and PhD students to experience the difficulties encountered by people with disabilities when using a digital device through a set of exercises and describes how to create accessible content and presentations. It will start with a set of experiences to guide users who can see in the world of users who cannot see.

Moreover, this tutorial can interest many researchers since it will present the state of the art of research in areas of web accessibility and some development results.

2.1 Intended Audience

This tutorial is intended for PhD students, researchers, and practitioners. Creating accessible content is an important topic to remove barriers from research. Besides websites, many papers and didactic materials are not accessible to blind people, and the same holds for other materials used during research work. This means that culture, education, and research are often off limits for people with disabilities. Many presentations are not accessible, either for issues in the slides or in the way the speaker conducts the talk. This tutorial aims to contribute to fill this gap.

This tutorial provides basic knowledge about creating accessible digital content and how to conduct an accessible talk. Some knowledge about HTML could help, but it is not strictly required. During the tutorial, a laptop is needed.

2.2 Tutorial Structure

The tutorial will start with an exercise that allows attendees to experience digital barriers encountered by people with visual impairments. Then, the tutorial will show digital barriers for other kinds of impairment (e.g., cognitive impairments) and an overview of both American and European laws and regulations.

The tutorial will provide a set of instructions to create digital content, including papers and presentations. Moreover, it will describe some hints to deliver an accessible speech and show some useful tools to check the accessibility of web pages and presentations.

Some useful tools will be presented to simulate the navigation of people with impairment. An example is Silktyde, an extension for the Chrome browser that helps you test web pages for common accessibility failures, e.g., color contrast, alternative text for images, keyboard navigation, simulation of different impairments, etc.

The second part of the tutorial discusses the state of the art in web accessibility and a tool to help people with visual impairments learn mathematical functions through the extensive use of sounds and touch [4,5]. STEM subjects like mathematics are difficult for this kind of user, since concepts like lines or curves heavily depend on visual content to convey essential information. Grafici-Accessibili [4] is a mobile app that allows users to draw lines and parabolas in the Cartesian plane incorporating sound and haptic feedback to make them perceivable by all users. Mathematical functions are sonified, enabling users to discern the position of their points on the quarters of the Cartesian plane through sound cues. Furthermore, the application assists users in exploring the Cartesian plane through touch, giving haptic feedback for curves and axes. In this way, the user can mentally visualize the graphical representation of the function.

Finally, we will discuss the impact of frameworks for cross-platform mobile development on the accessibility of mobile applications [3], presenting an initial analysis of *Flutter* by Google and *React Native* by Meta.

References

1. WebAIM Million: The 2022 report on the accessibility of the top 1,000,000 home pages (2022). https://webaim.org/projects/million/
2. Web Accessibility Initiative Group: Web Content Accessibility Guidelines (WCAG) 2.2 (2021). https://www.w3.org/TR/WCAG22/
3. Perinello, L., Gaggi, O.: Accessibility of mobile user interfaces using flutter and react native. In: 2024 IEEE 21st Consumer Communications & Networking Conference (CCNC), Las Vegas, NV, USA, pp. 1–6 (2024). https://doi.org/10.1109/CCNC51664.2024.10454681
4. Gatto, S., Gaggi, O., Grosset, L., Fovino, L.G.N.: Accessible Mathematics: representation of functions through sound and touch. IEEE Access **12**, 121552–121569 (2024). https://doi.org/10.1109/ACCESS.2024.3448509
5. Gaggi, O., Grosset, L., Pante, G.: A virtual reality application to make mathematical functions accessible. In: Proceedings of the 2023 ACM Conference on Information Technology for Social Good (GoodIT 2023) (2023). https://doi.org/10.1145/3582515.3609542
6. Gaggi, O.: A study on accessibility of google ReCAPTCHA systems. In: Proceedings of the 2022 Workshop on Open Challenges in Online Social Networks (OASIS 2022) (2022). https://doi.org/10.1145/3524010.3539498

7. Gaggi, O., Perinello, L.: Improving accessibility of web accessibility rules. In: Conference on Information Technology for Social Good (GoodIT 2022). Limassol, Cyprus (2022). https://doi.org/10.1145/3524458.3547267
8. Bassi, B., et al.: Supporting accessibility auditing and HTML validation using large language models. In: Proceedings of the 40th ACM/SIGAPP Symposium on Applied Computing (SAC 2025), pp. 27–31. Catania, Italy (2025)

Author Index

A
Abbate, Andrea 145
Agha, Milad 89
Amalfitano, Domenico 145
Aparicio-Morales, Álvaro M. 410
Auer, Sören 11, 56, 217

B
Baek, KyeongDeok 374
Banchs, Rafael 160
Binkert, Roman 312, 342
Both, Andreas 177, 379
Brambilla, Marco 41

C
Cabot, Jordi 253
Campi, Riccardo 41
Canelo-Gil, Ramon 391
Casaburi, Julián 287
Cellier, Peggy 193
Ceolin, Davide 119, 128

D
Di Fede, Giulia 370
Distante, Damiano 145

E
Eltsova, Maria 177
Ennemoser, Franz J. 342
Escalona, Maria Jose 391

F
Farfar, Kheir Eddine 217
Ferrara, Antonio 423
Ferré, Sébastien 193
Firmenich, Sergio 287
Frasincar, Flavius 89, 104
Fraternali, Piero 41

G
Gaedke, Martin 136, 209, 269, 397
Gaggi, Ombretta 427
Garcia-Alonso, Jose 410
García-Fernández, Alejandro 245
García-García, Julian Alberto 391
Garrido, Alejandra 404
Gashkov, Aleksandr 177
Giudici, Mathyas 41
Göpfert, Christoph 209
Gottschalk, Philipp 104
Goudar, Abhishek Divakar 226
Grigera, Julián 404
Gutierrez, Juan Guajardo 226

H
Haas, Jan Ingo 397
Han, Sooji 160
Hanski, Jonni 303
Harth, Andreas 327
Heil, Sebastian 136, 269
Herstad, Eyo 104
Huang, Jiaheng 71

J
Jaradeh, Mohamad Yaser 11
Jaros, Jiri 366
Jaros, Marta 366
Ji, Yatai 71, 385
Jin, Virginia 226
John, Lena 217
Ju, Rusheng 71, 385

K
Käbisch, Sebastian 312, 342
Karras, Oliver 56, 217
Kelling, Jeffrey 397
Ko, In-Young 374
Koch, Rebekka 3
Korkan, Ege 312, 342

L
Lamercerie, Aurélien 193
Li, Chengkai 226
Liusnando, Calvin 269
Loza Bonora, Leonardo Germán 404

M
Madria, Sanjay 419
Manto, Vincenzo 26
Martinez Pandiani, Delfina S. 119, 128
Matera, Maristella 26, 370
Moguel, Enrique 410
Münch, Tobias 136

N
Nandini, Durgesh 3
Nirumand, Atefeh 253

O
Oelen, Allard 11, 56
Olsak, Ondrej 366

P
Parejo, José Antonio 245
Park, EunChan 374
Perevalov, Aleksandr 177
Pinciroli Vago, Nicolò Oreste 41
Piro, Ludovica 370
Pomo, Claudio 423
Propst, Timothy 226
Pucci, Emanuele 26, 370

Q
Qiu, Sihang 71, 385

R
Rinaldi, Antonio M. 145
Robal, Tarmo 89
Roberts, Dan 226
Rodriguez-Guisado, Pablo Barrachina 41
Ruiz-Cortés, Antonio 245
Russo, Cristiano 145

S
Salama, Fady 312, 342
Samuel, Sheeba 209, 397
Sánchez-Gómez, Nicolas 391
Sang, Erik Tjong Kim 119
Sauer, Matej 366
Schiese, Dennis 379
Schmid, Sebastian 327
Schmidt, Andreas 136
Schönfeld, Mirco 3
Schraudner, Daniel 327
Seweryn, Kasper Jan 361
Shirvani-Mahdavi, Nasim 226
Steinhorst, Sebastian 312, 342
Stewart, Catherine 226
Stütz, Jan-David 56
Su, Jianzhong 226

T
Taelman, Ruben 303
Tjong Kim Sang, Erik 128
Tolomeo, Stefano 370
Tommasino, Cristian 145
Tonellotto, Nicola 423
Tran, Mai 226

U
Urbieta, Mario Matías 287

V
Van Braeckel, Simon 303
Verborgh, Ruben 303

W
Wingfield, Devin 226
Woodward-Greene, Jennifer 226

Y
Yang, Juyoung 374
Yang, Yung-Ching 160

Z
Zhang, Haiqi 226
Zhang, Zeyu 226
Zhao, Yong 71
Zhu, Beilly 89
Zhu, Zhengqiu 71, 385
Zhu, Zhengyuan 226
Ziegler Felix, Luca Mario 56

Made in the USA
Monee, IL
03 May 2026